2006 CASE SUPPLEMENT AND STATUTORY APPENDIX

CASES AND MATERIALS

TRADEMARK AND UNFAIR COMPETITION LAW

THIRD EDITION

by

JANE C. GINSBURG
Morton L. Janklow Professor of
Literary and Artistic Property Law
Columbia University School of Law

JESSICA LITMAN
Professor of Law
University of Michigan

MARY L. KEVLIN
Cowan, Liebowitz and Latman, P.C.
Adjunct Professor, New York University School of Law

FOUNDATION PRESS
2006

395 Hudson Street
New York, NY 10014
Phone Toll Free 1–877–888–1330
Fax (212) 367–6799
foundation–press.com
Printed in the United States of America

ISBN–13: 978–1–59941–047–0
ISBN–10: 1–59941–047–8

TABLE OF CONTENTS

TABLE OF CASES

Principal cases are in bold type. Non-principal cases are in roman type. References are to Pages.

2006 CASE SUPPLEMENT AND STATUTORY APPENDIX

CASES AND MATERIALS

TRADEMARK AND UNFAIR COMPETITION LAW

*

CHAPTER 1

Concepts of Trademarks and Unfair Competition

A. Competition

Page 43. Add new Question 4 (renumber previous 4 as 5):

4. Is it a "false designation of origin" to list as a work's author a person who did not in fact write the book? For example, for an unknown writer of thrillers to present her work as Stephen King's? Or to publish Stephen King's work under the unknown writer's name? Does it matter whether or not Stephen King's work is still protected by copyright? See *Dastar v. Twentieth Century Fox* (U.S. 2003), *infra* this Supplement, Chapter 9.

B. Trademarks

Page 65. Insert after *Stork Restaurant v. Sahati*:

QUESTION

1. How important was it to the court's analysis that there was "no need" for the defendant to "appropriate" plaintiff's "fanciful" or "arbitrary" STORK name? If the mark at issue instead had been a common surname, such as BRENNAN'S for the well-known restaurant in New Orleans, would the court have enjoined such a geographically remote user? *Cf. Brennan's, Inc. v. Brennan's Restaurant, L.L.C.*, 360 F.3d 125 (2d Cir.2004) (affirmed denial of preliminary injunction against New York City restaurant Terrance Brennan's Seafood & Chop House named after its owner and chef).

CHAPTER 2

WHAT IS A TRADEMARK?

A. SUBJECT MATTER OF TRADEMARK PROTECTION

1. WORD MARKS

Pages 92. Delete the note on the Right to Use One's Own Name in Business and Substitute the following decision:

Peaceable Planet v. Ty, Inc.

362 F.3d 986 (7th Cir. 2004).

■ POSNER, J.

. . .

Like the defendant, the much larger and better known Ty Inc. ..., Peaceable Planet makes plush toys in the shape of animals, filled with bean-like materials to give the toys a soft and floppy feel. Ty's plush toys are, of course, the famous "Beanie Babies."

In the spring of 1999, Peaceable Planet began selling a camel that it named "Niles." The name was chosen to evoke Egypt, which is largely desert except for the ribbon of land bracketing the Nile. The camel is a desert animal, and photos juxtaposing a camel with an Egyptian pyramid are common. The price tag fastened to Niles's ear contains information both about camels and about Egypt, and the Egyptian flag is stamped on the animal.

A small company, Peaceable Planet sold only a few thousand of its camels in 1999. In March of the following year, Ty began selling a camel also named "Niles." It sold a huge number of its "Niles" camels—almost two million in one year—precipitating this suit. The district court ruled that "Niles," being a personal name, is a descriptive mark that the law does not protect unless and until it has acquired secondary meaning, that is, until there is proof that consumers associate the name with the plaintiff's brand. Peaceable Planet did not prove that consumers associate the name "Niles" with its camel....

The reluctance to allow personal names to be used as trademarks reflects valid concerns.... One of the concerns is a reluctance to forbid a person to use his own name in his own business. [Citations omitted.] Supposing a man named Brooks opened a clothing store under his name, should this prevent a second Brooks from opening a clothing store under his own (identical) name even though consumers did not yet associate the name with the first Brooks's store? It should not. [Citations omitted.]

Another and closely related concern behind the personal-name rule is that some names are so common—such as "Smith," "Jones," "Schwartz," "Wood," and "Jackson"—that consumers will not assume that two products having the same name therefore have the same source, and so they will not be confused by their bearing the same name. [Citations omitted.] If there are two bars in a city that are named "Steve's," people will not infer that they are owned by the same Steve.

The third concern, which is again related but brings us closest to the rule regarding descriptive marks, is that preventing a person from using his name to denote his business may deprive consumers of useful information. Maybe "Steve" is a well-known neighborhood figure. If he can't call his bar "Steve's" because there is an existing bar of that name, he is prevented from communicating useful information to the consuming public. [Citations omitted.] . . .

The personal-name "rule," it is worth noting, is a common law rather than statutory doctrine. All that the Lanham Act says about personal names is that a mark that is "primarily merely a surname" is not registrable in the absence of secondary meaning. 15 U.S.C. §§ 1052(e)(4), (f). There is no reference to first names. The reason for the surname provision is illustrated by the Brooks example. The extension of the rule to first names is a judicial innovation and so needn't be pressed further than its rationale, as might have to be done if the rule were codified in inflexible statutory language. Notice too the limitation implicit in the statutory term "primarily."

In thinking about the applicability of the rationale of the personal-name rule to the present case, we should notice first of all that camels, whether real or toy, do not go into business. Peaceable Planet's appropriation of the name "Niles" for its camel is not preventing some hapless camel in the Sahara Desert who happens to be named "Niles" from going into the water-carrier business under its own name. The second thing to notice is that "Niles" is not a very common name; in fact it is downright rare. And the third thing to notice is that if it were a common name, still there would be no danger that precluding our hypothetical Saharan water carrier from using its birth name "Niles" would deprive that camel's customers of valuable information. In short, the rationale of the personal-name rule is wholly inapplicable to this case.

What is more, if one wants to tie the rule in some fashion to the principle that descriptive marks are not protectable without proof of second meaning, then one must note that "Niles," at least when affixed to a toy camel, is a suggestive mark, like "Microsoft" or "*Business Week*," or—coming closer to this case—like "Eor" used as the name of a donkey, or the proper names in *Circuit City Stores, Inc. v. CarMax, Inc., supra*, 165 F.3d at 1054, rather than being a descriptive mark. Suggestive marks are protected by trademark law without proof of secondary meaning. [Citations omitted.] Secondary meaning is not required because there are plenty of alternatives to any given suggestive mark. There are many more ways of suggesting than of describing. Suggestive names for camels include "Lawrence [of Arabia]" (one of Ty's other Beanie Babies *is* a camel named "Lawrence"); "Desert Taxi," "Sopwith" (the Sopwith Camel was Snoopy's World War I fighter plane), "Camelia," "Traveling Oasis," "Kamelsutra," "Cameleon," and "Humpy–Dumpy."

If "Niles" cannot be a protected trademark, it must be because to give it legal protection would run afoul of one of the purposes of the common law rule that we have identified rather than because it is a descriptive term, which it is not. But we have seen that it does not run afoul of any of those purposes. "Niles" is not the name of the defendant—it's not as if Peaceable Planet had named its camel "Ty Inc." or "H. Ty Warner." It also is not a common name, like "Smith" or "Jackson." And making Ty use a different name for its camel would not deprive the consumer of valuable information about Ty or its camel....

3. OTHER IDENTIFYING INDICIA

Page 107. After paragraph on *In re Clarke*, add:

Can a food product's flavor constitute nonfunctional trade dress? *See Perk Scientific, Inc. v. Ever Scientific, Inc.*, 2005 WL 851078 (E.D. Pa. 2005) (lack of carbonation and flavor selection held functional for glucose tolerant beverage products).

B. DISTINCTIVENESS

1. ARBITRARY, FANCIFUL, SUGGESTIVE AND DESCRIPTIVE TERMS

Page 116. Add before Questions:

In re Oppedahl & Larson, 373 F.3d 1171 (Fed. Cir. 2004). In affirming the refusal to register "patents.com" for software that tracks patent records, the court rejected the contention that the addition of the ".com" suffix made the composite term inherently distinctive.

> The PTO ... argue[s] that ".com" possesses no source-identifying characteristics just as "Co." and "Corp." did not affect registrability in *Goodyear['s Rubber Manufacturing Co. v. Goodyear Rubber Co.*, 128 U.S. 598, 602, 32 L. Ed. 535, 9 S. Ct. 166, 1889 Dec. Comm'r Pat. 257 (1888)] ... which held that adding terms such as "Corp.," "Inc.," and "Co." to a generic term does not add any trademark significance to an otherwise unregistrable mark.... Although not a perfect analogy, the comparison of TLDs (i.e., ".com," ".org," etc.) to entity designations such as "Corp." and "Inc." has merit. The commercial impression created by ".com" is similar to the impression created by "Corp." and "Co.," that is, the association of a commercial entity with the mark.

TLDs, however, can convey more than simply the organizational structure of the entity that uses the mark. For example, TLDs immediately suggest a relationship to the Internet. Thus, the per se rule in *Goodyear* that "Corp.," etc. never possess source-indicating significance does not operate as a per se rule, but more as a general rule, with respect to TLDs.

. . .

Appellant offers [a] hypothetical, Amazon.com, to argue that the addition of ".com" will generally, if not always, add source-identifying significance. According to appellant, saying the word "Amazon" to a person on the street may conjure images of a river or a fierce female warrior. In the hypothetical, however, the entire mark Amazon.com changes the impression to invoke an online retailer. This hypothetical, however, has a serious flaw in the context of this case. The Board must, of course, determine the commercial impression of a mark in the proper context of the goods or services associated with that mark. *See* 15 U.S.C. § 1052(e)(1) (2000). In its proper context, appellant's proposed hypothetical yields a different result. In context, appellant's hypothetical would state, "I bought this book from Amazon," and "I bought this book from Amazon.com." In that setting, the addition of ".com" adds no source-identifying significance, which is likely to be the case in all but the most exceptional case.

The "Amazon" hypothetical also illustrates another principle that the Board properly recognized, namely that TLD marks may obtain registration upon a showing of distinctiveness. Thus Amazon.com may well denote the source of services of an on-line retailer (rather than a used car dealer or some other association) because the mark has acquired that secondary meaning. The Board properly left that door open for this patents.com mark as well.

In this case, the Board concluded that ".com" conveys to the public that the mark is owned or used by a commercial entity or business. To support that conclusion, the Board cites various dictionary definitions indicating that ".com" is an abbreviation for "company" used in Internet addresses. Appellant argues that domain name registries no longer enforce the use of particular TLDs based on the type of entity seeking to register the domain name, i.e., ".com" for companies and ".org" for non-profit organizations. Regardless of the current state of Internet governance, the Board is correct that the overall impression of ".com" conveys to consumers the impression of a company or commercial entity on the Internet. "Any competent source suffices to show the relevant purchasing public's understanding of a contested term, including . . . dictionary definitions." *Dial–A–Mattress*, 240 F.3d at 1345. Accordingly, substantial evidence supports the Board's conclusion that ".com" indicates a commercial entity. Moreover, under *Goodyear*, as qualified above, that impression bears no trademark significance. The dictionary definitions in the record also establish that ".com" conveys the use of the Internet in association with the mark.

Appellant's identification of goods includes the use of the Internet. Accordingly, ".com" is descriptive of this feature of the goods listed in the application.

Substantial record evidence also supports the Board's finding that "patents" is descriptive of a feature of the appellant's goods. Appellant's website shows that it offers software to track, inter alia, patent applications and issued patents using the Internet. Tracking patents falls within the scope of the goods identified in the application, i.e., "tracking records." Thus, the term "patents" describes a feature of the goods offered.

The Board also concluded that the combination of "patents" and ".com" does not render the mark as a whole distinctive and registrable. The Board reached this conclusion based on its application of the *Goodyear* analysis, i.e., finding that ".com" holds no source-indicating significance just as "Corp." An analysis of the commercial impression of the mark as a whole as required under the analysis stated above still yields the same result on this record.

Appellant asserts that domain names are inherently distinctive because they can only be associated with one entity or source at a time. The simple fact that domain names can only be owned by one entity does not of itself make them distinctive or source identifying. Telephone numbers and street addresses are also unique, but they do not by themselves convey to the public the source of specific goods or services. Thus, this court declines to adopt a per se rule that would extend trademark protection to all Internet domain names regardless of their use. Trademark law requires evaluation of a proposed mark to ascertain the commercial impression conveyed in light of the goods or services associated with the mark, not a simple check for ownership of an Internet address.

Appellant's goods include patent tracking software by means of the Internet. The term patents.com merely describes patent-related goods in connection with the Internet. The two terms combined do not create a different impression. Rather, the addition of ".com" to the term "patents" only strengthens the descriptiveness of the mark in light of the designation of goods in the application. "Patents" alone describes one feature of the goods—that of tracking patent applications and issued patents. Adding ".com" to the mark adds a further description of the Internet feature of the identified goods. Thus, appellant's argument to consider the mark as a whole only strengthens the descriptiveness finding.

III.

When examining domain name marks, the PTO must evaluate the commercial impression of the mark as a whole, including the TLD indicator. The addition of a TLD such as ".com" or ".org" to an otherwise unregistrable mark will typically not add any source-identifying significance, similar to the analysis of "Corp." and "Inc." in

Goodyear. This, however, is not a bright-line, per se rule. In exceptional circumstances, a TLD may render an otherwise descriptive term sufficiently distinctive for trademark registration. In this case, the mark patents.com, as a whole, is merely descriptive of appellant's goods.

Page 117. Add to list of marks in Question 3:

l. "Lawoffices" for a database of attorneys—descriptive. *See DeGidio v. West Group Corp.*, 355 F.3d 506 (6th Cir. 2004).

m. "Better–N–Butter" for oil-based butter substitute—suggestive. *See Blendco v. Conagra*, 132 Fed.Appx. 520 (5th Cir. 2005)

n. "Tumblebus" for a "mobile gym on wheels" (school buses retrofitted with gymnastics equipment)—suggestive. *See Tumblebus v. Cranmer*, 399 F.3d 754 (6th Cir. 2005).

o. "Instant messenger" for computer services providing multiple user access to networks—descriptive. *See In re America Online*, 77 U.S.P.Q.2d 1618 (TTAB 2006).

p. "Steelbuilding.com" for computerized on-line retail sales of pre-engineered metal buildings—descriptive. *See In re Steelbuilding.com*, 75 U.S.P.Q.2d 1420 (Fed. Cir. 2005).

q. "Perfect pitch" for ear training course.

Page 117. Add new Question 4:

4. Georgi brand vodka has introduced a new orange-flavored product; the label features a large "O" rendered as a vertical oval, with the outline of the "O" slightly wider along the sides (about one quarter inch thick) and narrowing at the top and bottom (about one eighth inch thick); the outline of the "O" is colored orange and decorated with two thin gold lines, one bordering the inside and one bordering the outside of the outline. Bacardi, a second-comer in the orange-flavored spirit market, also sports an outsize "O" on the "Bacardi O" label. Georgi's sales have not been sufficiently numerous to build secondary meaning in its "O" design, but Georgi's suit against Bacardi claims the design is inherently distinctive. Is Georgi's "O" design inherently distinctive, or rather merely descriptive? *See Star Indus. v. Bacardi*, 412 F.3d 373 (2d Cir. 2005).

CHAPTER 3

Acquisition of Trademark Rights

A. Adoption and Use

Page 151. Insert following Case and Note after *Larry Harmon Pictures Corp.*:

DaimlerChrysler AG v. Bloom

315 F.3d 932 (8th Cir. 2003).

■ Hansen, Circuit Judge

DaimlerChrysler and Mercedes–Benz U.S.A. appeal an adverse grant of summary judgment in this trademark action. For the reasons stated below, we affirm the judgment of the district court.

DaimlerChrysler is the registered owner of the trademarks and service marks MERCEDES and MERCEDES–BENZ (collectively, hereinafter "Marks"). Mercedes–Benz U.S.A. is the exclusive licensee of the Marks in the United States. We refer to both of them collectively as "Mercedes."

In 1984, Donald Bloom (hereinafter "Bloom") became part owner of a Mercedes–Benz dealership in Owatonna, Minnesota. In the mid–1980s, Bloom acquired the toll-free telephone number 1–800–637–2333, one possible alphanumeric translation of which is 1–800–MERCEDES. Bloom advertised the vanity phone number in conjunction with his dealership, and he believes that the use of the phone number was a key component in reviving what had otherwise been a moribund dealership. In 1989, Mercedes granted Bloom a second dealership in St. Paul.

Between 1988 and 1992, Mercedes made several attempts to acquire the 1–800–637–2333 phone number from Bloom. The parties entered into negotiations, but the negotiations never came to fruition, and Bloom retained the rights to the phone number. On October 22, 1992, Mercedes sent Bloom a cease and desist letter stating that he could no longer use the 1–800 phone number because such use violated his Dealer Agreement. In the same letter, Mercedes informed Bloom that his continued possession and use of the 1–800 phone number interfered with Mercedes' plan to use that number for its Client Assistance Center (hereinafter "CAC"). The CAC provides Mercedes customers with 24–hour, 365–days per year customer service. Because Bloom refused to relinquish his right to use the toll free number, Mercedes was forced to acquire and use a different telephone number, 1–800–367–6372 (1–800–FORMERCEDES), for the CAC.

In 1994, Bloom formed MBZ Communications (hereinafter "MBZ"). MBZ is located in Owatonna and is an independent telecommunications company that specializes in the use of vanity phone numbers. Bloom formed MBZ to manage the shared use of the 1–800–MERCEDES phone number with other Mercedes dealers throughout the country. MBZ licensed the number to six Mercedes dealers throughout the country. MBZ granted the dealers "exclusive use ... of the telephone number 1–800–637–2333 and/or its mnemonic translation within an area" defined geographically by area code and provided call pattern analysis and other marketing services to the licensee dealers in exchange for payment of an initial set up fee and additional monthly fees. The licensees then marketed the phone number in the agreed to areas. Through the use of call routing technology, any call made to 1–800–MERCEDES originating in a contracted for area code is automatically rerouted to the appropriate dealership. Any call originating from an area code not covered by a licensing agreement terminates at the MBZ office and is processed by MBZ personnel.

The following description is a concrete example of how MBZ's licensing system works. The House of Imports, Inc. (hereinafter "House"), a Los Angeles based Mercedes dealer, entered into a licensing agreement with MBZ for the exclusive use of the number 1–800–637–2333 in the territory falling within area codes 213, 310, 619, 714, 805, 818, and 909, which encompasses the Los Angeles and San Diego metropolitan areas. House paid MBZ an initial fee of $39,200 and agreed to make additional monthly payments of $3150 for the continued right to use the number within the agreed to area codes. House used various marketing devices to promote the vanity phone number 1–800–MERCEDES. Per the licensing agreement, any call made to 1–800–MERCEDES from the aforementioned area codes is automatically routed to House. House then services the call.

As mentioned above, a call originating from an area code not covered by a licensing agreement terminates at the MBZ office and is processed by MBZ personnel. MBZ receives approximately 100 calls per day from Mercedes customers who intend to reach the CAC but reach MBZ instead. Mercedes contends that the mere fact that people reach MBZ instead of the CAC is detrimental to Mercedes because the CAC is open 24 hours per day whereas MBZ is open only weekdays from 8 a.m. to 6 p.m. Therefore, Mercedes argues, its customers become frustrated when no one answers the phone after hours and on weekends and holidays.

In 1997, Mercedes terminated its Dealer Agreements with Bloom. In February 2000, Mercedes filed this action against Bloom and MBZ, asserting that the MBZ licensing plan violated the Lanham Act, the Federal Trademark Dilution Act, and state trademark and unfair competition laws. The parties filed cross motions for summary judgment. The district court denied Mercedes' motion and granted MBZ's motion on the ground that

MBZ did not "use" the Marks within the meaning of the acts. Mercedes appeals.

* * *

[Mercedes asserts violations of the Lanham Act's provisions on infringement and dilution of trademarks.] Each provision requires, as a prerequisite to finding liability, that the defendant "use in commerce" the protected mark or a colorable imitation thereof. [citations omitted] The district court concluded that the mere licensing of a telephone number, without the active promotion or advertising of the Marks, did not constitute a "use" of Mercedes' marks. We review the district court's grant of summary judgment de novo.

There is no dispute that MBZ only licensed the phone number but did not advertise or promote Mercedes' protected marks. Mercedes argues that MBZ can be liable even though MBZ did not promote the Marks because . . . the advertising and promotion performed by MBZ's licensees is a "use" that can be imputed to MBZ and, independently, that the "use" requirement can be met here because MBZ intended to exploit the marks. We reject these arguments . . .

Mercedes' argument that the licensee dealers' promotion of the vanity number should be imputed to MBZ is . . . without merit. Besides the facts that the licensee dealers are entitled to use the Marks under their Dealer Agreements, and that if Mercedes was truly concerned about dilution and/or infringement, it could itself prevent its dealers from wrongfully using the Marks, the cases and statutory provision on which Mercedes relies have no application to the case at hand. [Those cases] and 15 U.S.C. § 1055 only answer the question of when the use of a mark by a related company can inure to the benefit of the registrant of the mark. A related company is one whose use of the mark is controlled by the registrant of the mark. It is undisputed that MBZ's licensees are not related companies for the purposes of the statute. . . .

Finally, Mercedes argues that the district court erroneously looked only at advertising and promotion as indicators of use. Mercedes relies on a series of internet domain name cases, the most prominent of which is *Panavision Int'l L.P. v. Toeppen*, 141 F.3d 1316 (9th Cir. 1998), for the propositions that "use" is a broad term and that the intent to exploit a mark can be a "use" within the meaning of the Lanham Act. In *Panavision,* Panavision attempted to register the domain name Panavision.com, but could not because Toeppen had already registered that domain name. Toeppen was a cybersquatter whose "business" involved registering trademarks as domain names and then selling the domain names back to the mark owners. The court concluded that Toeppen's intent to arbitrage domain names and his attempt to sell the mark was a commercial use within the meaning of the statute. MBZ concedes that the only value it derives from the toll-free number stems from the fact that one of its possible translations is 1–800–MERCEDES. Even so, we conclude that *Panavision* is distinguishable and that applying *Panavision* to the facts of this case would stretch the outer limits of the Lanham Act. . . .

Unlike the defendant in *Panavision*, MBZ has not registered the mark, advertised the mark, or incorporated the mark into a web page. Furthermore, while the defendant in Panavision attempted to sell a domain name which directly and explicitly incorporated the protected mark, MBZ merely licenses a telephone number, one alphanumeric translation of which can spell 1–800–MERCEDES. Unlike the similarity between the Panavision mark and the domain name www.panavision.com, the number 1–800–637–2333 is neither phonetically nor visually similar enough to the Marks such that it could be considered a reproduction or a colorable imitation thereof. *See Holiday Inns*, 86 F.3d at 623 (stating that the defendants used "the phone number, 1–800–405–4329—that is, a number which is neither phonetically nor visually similar to Holiday Inn's trademark"). Mercedes argues, rather arrogantly we believe, that this phone number is the same as a domain name because everyone knows that 1–800–6372333 really means 1–800–MERCEDES. We doubt this proposition is as self-evident as Mercedes believes. It is more probable that callers would not associate 1–800–6372333 with Mercedes in the same way that computer users would associate www.panavision.com with the Panavision company and Panavision's protected marks. *See Brookfield Communs., Inc. v. West Coast Entm't Corp.*, 174 F.3d 1036, 1055 (9th Cir. 1999) (explaining that web users are likely to associate a web address containing a protected mark plus "dot com" with the protected mark and the mark holder).

Although Mercedes attempts to distinguish them, we conclude that the cases actually involving vanity phone numbers are more on point than the internet domain name cases and that they demonstrate that MBZ did not actually "use" Mercedes' marks. *Holiday Inns* is the leading case. In that case, Holiday Inns promoted its vanity phone number, 1–800–HOLIDAY. The defendants operated an independent travel agency and hoped to capture Holiday Inns' customers. The defendants obtained the complementary phone number 1–800–H[zero]LIDAY for the sole purpose of intercepting misdialed calls from customers attempting to reach Holiday Inns. The defendants did not advertise the vanity phone number, but conceded that they reaped benefits in direct proportion to Holiday Inns' advertising expenditures. The district court granted summary judgment in favor of Holiday Inns, permanently enjoining defendants from using the complementary phone number. The Sixth Circuit reversed, concluding that the defendants did not "use" Holiday Inns' mark within the meaning of the Lanham Act. The court reasoned that Holiday Inns had trademark rights in its marks only and did not have rights to enjoin the operation of phone numbers whose potential translations were similar to Holiday Inns' mark. The court concluded that because the defendants never advertised or otherwise promoted the protected marks, then the defendants did not "use" the marks within the meaning of the act. *Holiday Inns* is virtually indistinguishable from the present case, and we find it persuasive. The fact that MBZ is contacted by individuals who correctly dial a telephone number that they mistakenly believe belongs to Mercedes as opposed to individuals who misdial their intended number makes no difference in the outcome of this case.

Review of the vanity phone number cases reveals that the mark holder is generally not entitled to relief unless the defendant advertises or otherwise promotes the alphanumeric translation of the phone number thereby causing the public to see the protected mark and associate the infringer's goods or services with those of the mark holder. *Cf. U–Haul*, 943 F. Supp. at 810–12 (denying relief to U–Haul, where competitor used three complementary phone numbers but did not advertise or promote the numbers, on the ground that receiving calls on complementary numbers intended for U–Haul is not a "use" of the mark within the meaning of the Lanham Act); *Miss Dig System*, 944 F. Supp. at 604 (denying relief where plaintiff excavation company possessed the local phone number MISS–DIG and the defendant excavation company possessed the toll free number 1–800–MISS–DIG because the defendants never advertised their services using an alphanumeric translation of the telephone number, much less one incorporating and displaying the plaintiff's trademark), *with Am. Airlines, Inc. v. 1–800–Am. Corp.*, 622 F. Supp. 673, 686–87 (N.D. Ill. 1985)(granting preliminary injunctive relief to plaintiff against defendant travel agency where defendant advertised its vanity phone 1–800–AMERICAN in yellow pages under "Airline Companies" even though it offered no air service and specifically noting that "but for such intentionally misleading listing, [the defendant] would be free to use its name and telephone number for all legitimate purposes").

We thus conclude that the licensing of a toll-free telephone number, without more, is not a "use" within the meaning of the Lanham Act, even where one possible alphanumeric translation of such number might spell-out a protected mark. This conclusion is bolstered by those cases granting injunctive relief in favor of mark holders and against those who possess vanity phone numbers corresponding to protected marks. In those cases, the courts have fashioned limited remedies, enjoining only the advertisement of the alphanumeric translation of the number which incorporates the protected mark but not the use of the number generally. [citations omitted] In accord with these cases, we conclude that the district court did not err in granting summary judgment in favor of MBZ.

The judgment of the district court is affirmed.

QUESTION

If MBZ promotes its service to DaimlerBenz dealers, makes money licensing 1–800–MERCEDES to them, why is this not a "use"?

NOTE: "POP–UP ADVERTISEMENTS," "KEYING" AND OTHER TRIGGERING TECHNIQUES

Several recent cases have addressed techniques employed by Internet search engines and advertisers to key or trigger the appearance of a paid advertisement or listing when an Internet user enters a trademark as a search term. The search engine sells what one might call "trigger rights," allowing, for example, a rival business' advertisement to appear when a user enters the name of a business as a search query. The entrepreneurs whose trademarks "key" the appearance of competitors' advertisements have alleged violations of the Lanham Act and related state law claims. The search engines and advertisers have responded that sale or use of trademarks to call up other entrepreneurs' advertisements or webpage listings is not a "use in commerce" in the trademark sense, and that, in any event, the technique is not likely to confuse web users as to the origin or sponsorship of the link.

The results have so far been mixed. For analyses of likelihood of confusion, see *infra* this Supplement, Chapter 6A. Regarding "use," the first wave of litigations involving pop up ads challenged the internet advertising companies' Gator and WhenU's distribution of "adware" that keyed clients' pop-up advertisements to the URLs (usually of the advertisers' competitors) entered by users. In *Wells Fargo & Co. v. WhenU.com*, 293 F.Supp.2d 734 (E.D.Mich.2003) and *U–Haul Int'l. v. WhenU.com*, 279 F.Supp.2d 723 (E.D.Va.2003), the courts held that WhenU and its clients had not "used" the plaintiff's marks. In *1–800 Contacts, Inc. v. WhenU.com*, 309 F.Supp.2d 467 (S.D.N.Y.2003), the district court found "use," but the Second Circuit reversed, holding, as a matter of law, that "WhenU does not 'use' 1–800's trademarks within the meaning of the Lanham Act when it (1) includes 1–800's website address, which is almost identical to 1–800's trademark, in an unpublished directory of terms that trigger delivery of WhenU's contextually relevant advertising to C[omputer]-users; or (2) causes separate, branded pop-up ads to appear on a C-user's computer screen either above, below, or along the bottom edge of the 1–800 website window."

By contrast, in *Playboy v. Netscape*, 354 F.3d 1020 (9th Cir. 2004), the Ninth Circuit reversed the District Court's entry of summary judgment for defendant Netscape. The appellate court appears to have assumed that Netscape's conduct, in keying its customers' banner ads to the search terms "Playboy" and "Playmate," constituted "use in commerce." The court's only discussion of "use" occurred in the context of Playboy's dilution claim, in which the court held that Playboy had demonstrated Netscape's "commercial use in commerce." (The *Playboy v. Netscape* court's analysis of likelihood of confusion is excerpted, *infra*, this Supplement, Chapter 6A.) In *Google v. American Blind & Wallpaper Factory*, 74 U.S.P.Q.2d 1385 (N.D.Cal. 2005), the district court, following the Ninth Circuit's *Playboy v. Netscape* decision, declined to rule, as a matter of summary judgment, that Google's keyword-triggered "AdWord" advertising program, which included unlicensed trademarks among the keywords, did not constitute "use" within the meaning of the Lanham Act. Finally, in GEICO v. Google, 330 F.Supp.2d 700 (E.D. Va. 2004), the court held that the search engine "used" the trademarks it sold as links to the advertisers' sites.

Excerpts from the *GEICO* and *1–800 Contacts* decisions follow; consider which (if either) decision you find persuasive and why or why not.

GEICO v. Google, 330 F.Supp.2d 700 (E.D. Va. 2004).

[D]efendants argue that the complaint fails to alleges facts supporting a claim that defendants use the marks "in commerce" and "in connection with the sale, offering for sale, distribution, or advertising of goods and services'' (hereinafter ''trademark use''), because the complaint does not allege that defendants used plaintiff's trademarks in a way that identifies the user as the source of a product or indicates the endorsement of the mark owner. Defendants further argue that because they only use the trademarks in their internal computer algorithms to determine which advertisements to show, this use of the trademarks never appears to the user. Therefore, the user cannot be confused as to the origin of goods.

Defendants support their argument as to the legal meaning of trademark use with cases that have found the use of trademarks by software companies to generate pop-up Internet advertisements not to constitute ''trademark use'' of those marks under the Lanham Act. Those cases are based on a finding that the marks were not used by the company making the pop-up software to identify the source of its goods or services. *See U–Haul Int'l, Inc. v. WhenU.com, Inc.*, 279 F.Supp.2d 723, 727 (E.D.Va.2003); *Wells Fargo & Co. v. WhenU.com, Inc.*, 293 F.Supp.2d 734, 762 (E.D.Mich.2003). In *U–Haul*, the court held that WhenU, the pop-up software company, did not place the U–Haul trademarks in commerce, it merely used them for a ''pure machine-linking function.'' . . .

Plaintiff focuses on cases which have reached the opposite conclusion. In *1–800 Contacts, Inc. v. WhenU.com*, 309 F.Supp.2d 467 (S.D.N.Y.2003), on facts identical to those found in the U–Haul and Wells Fargo cases, the court found that WhenU was making ''trademark use'' of the plaintiff's trademark in two ways-by using plaintiff's mark in the advertising of competitor's Websites, and by including plaintiff's mark in the directory of terms that triggers pop-up advertisements. Similarly, on facts nearly identical to the facts pled by GEICO, the Ninth Circuit held that the use of plaintiff's trademarks as advertising keywords by the Netscape and Excite search engines potentially created the likelihood of confusion, and the court found no dispute that the defendants used the marks in commerce. *Playboy Enterprises, Inc. v. Netscape Comm. Corp.*, 354 F.3d 1020, 1024 (9th Cir.2004). In the Fourth Circuit's *PETA* decision, it specifically rejected the argument that the defendant's use of the PETA trademark in a domain name was not in connection with goods and services: ''[the defendant] need only have prevented users from obtaining or using PETA's goods or services, or need only have connected the website to other's goods or services.'' 263 F.3d at 365. Similarly, courts have found that the use of trademarks in ''metatags,'' which are invisible text within Websites that are used by search engines for indexing, constitute a use in commerce under the Lanham Act. *See Bihari v. Gross*, 119 F.Supp.2d 309 (S.D.N.Y.2000); *Playboy Enterprises, Inc. v. Asiafocus Int'l, Inc.*, 1998 WL 724000 (E.D.Va. April 10, 1998).

Of the two lines of cases cited by the parties, the Court finds that plaintiff's authorities are better reasoned. Under those cases, as well as an unstrained reading of the complaint, the Court finds that plaintiff has pled sufficient facts which, taken as true for purposes of this motion, allege "trademark use." Contrary to defendants' argument, the complaint is addressed to more than the defendants' use of the trademarks in their internal computer coding. The complaint clearly alleges that defendants use plaintiff's trademarks to sell advertising, and then link that advertising to results of searches. Those links appear to the user as "sponsored links." Thus, a fair reading of the complaint reveals that plaintiff alleges that defendants have unlawfully used its trademarks by allowing advertisers to bid on the trademarks and pay defendants to be linked to the trademarks.

Under the analysis in *PETA*, defendants' offer of plaintiff's trademarks for use in advertising could falsely identify a business relationship or licensing agreement between defendants and the trademark holder. In other words, when defendants sell the rights to link advertising to plaintiff's trademarks, defendants are using the trademarks in commerce in a way that may imply that defendants have permission from the trademark holder to do so. This is a critical distinction from the U–Haul case, because in that case the only "trademark use" alleged was the use of the trademark in the pop-up software-the internal computer coding. WhenU allowed advertisers to bid on broad categories of terms that included the trademarks, but did not market the protected marks themselves as keywords to which advertisers could directly purchase rights.

Plaintiff further alleges that under theories of contributory and vicarious liability, defendants are liable when the advertisers themselves make "trademark use" of the GEICO marks by incorporating them into the advertisements, which are likely to deceive customers into believing that the advertisers provide accurate information about GEICO products or are somehow related to GEICO. Plaintiff also alleges that defendants exercise significant control over the content of advertisements that appear on their search results pages, and accordingly defendants are liable for Lanham Act violations by the advertisers. Accepting as true the facts alleged by plaintiff regarding the inclusion of the marks in advertisements and defendants' overall control of their advertising program, we find that plaintiffs have alleged facts sufficient to support their claims that advertisers make a "trademark use" of GEICO's marks, and that defendants may be liable for such "trademark use."

[*Editors' Note*: In a subsequent stage of the case the court found that Google's use of the marks was not likely to cause confusion as to the sponsorship by GEICO of Google's service or of the rival advertisers. *See, GEICO v. Google*, 77 U.S.P.Q.2d 1841 (E.D. Va. 2005).]

1–800 Contacts, Inc. v. WhenU.com, 414 F.3d 400 (2d Cir. 2005).

The primary issue to be resolved by this appeal is whether the placement of pop-up ads on a C-user's screen contemporaneously with either the 1–800 website or a list of search results obtained by the C-user's input of the 1–800 website address constitutes "use" under the Lanham Act. The district court reasoned that WhenU, by "causing pop-up advertisements for Defendant Vision Direct to appear when SaveNow users have specifically attempted to access [1–800]'s website, ... [is] displaying [1–800]'s mark in the ... advertising of ... Vision Direct's services." *1–800 Contacts*, 309 F.Supp.2d at 489.

The fatal flaw with this holding is that WhenU's pop-up ads do not display the 1–800 trademark. The district court's holding, however, appears to have been based on the court's acceptance of 1–800's claim that WhenU's pop-up ads appear "on" and affect 1–800's website. *See, e.g., id.* at 479 (stating that WhenU has "no relationship with the companies on whose websites the pop-up advertisements appear") (emphasis omitted) (emphasis added). [But] the WhenU pop-up ads appear in a separate window that is prominently branded with the WhenU mark; they have has absolutely no tangible effect on the appearance or functionality of the 1–800 website.

More important, the appearance of WhenU's pop-up ad is not contingent upon or related to 1–800's trademark, the trademark's appearance on 1–800's website, or the mark's similarity to 1–800's website address. Rather, the contemporaneous display of the ads and trademarks is the result of the happenstance that 1–800 chose to use a mark similar to its trademark as the address to its web page and to place its trademark on its website. The pop-up ad, which is triggered by the C-user's input of 1–800's website address, would appear even if 1–800's trademarks were not displayed on its website. A pop-up ad could also appear if the C-user typed the 1–800 website address, not as an address, but as a search term in the browser's search engine, and then accessed 1–800's website by using the hyperlink that appeared in the list of search results.

In addition, 1–800's website address is not the only term in the SaveNow directory that could trigger a Vision Direct ad to "pop up" on 1–800's website. For example, an ad could be triggered by a C-user's search for "contacts" or "eye care," both terms contained in the directory, and then clicked on the listed hyperlink to 1–800's website.

Exemplifying the conceptual difficulty that inheres in this issue, the district court's decision suggests that the crux of WhenU's wrongdoing—and the primary basis for the district court's finding of "use"—is WhenU's alleged effort to capitalize on a C-user's specific attempt to access the 1–800 website. As the court explained it,

> WhenU.com is doing far more than merely "displaying" Plaintiff's mark. WhenU's advertisements are delivered to a SaveNow user when the user directly accesses Plaintiff's website—thus allowing Defendant Vision Direct to profit from the goodwill and reputation in Plaintiff's website that led the user to access Plaintiff's website in the first place.

1–800 Contacts, 309 F.Supp.2d at 490. Absent improper use of 1–800's trademark, however, such conduct does not violate the Lanham Act. *See*

TrafFix Devices, Inc. v. Marketing Displays, Inc., 532 U.S. 23, 29, 149 L.Ed.2d 164 (2001); *Kellogg Co. v. National Biscuit Co.*, 305 U.S. 111, 122, 83 L.Ed. 73 (1938) (holding that Kellogg's sharing in the goodwill of the unprotected "Shredded Wheat" market was "not unfair"); *see also* William P. Kratzke, *Normative Economic Analysis of Trademark Law*, 21 Memphis St. U. L. Rev. 199, 223 (1991) (criticizing importation into trademark law of "unjust enrichment" and "free riding" theories based on a trademark holder's goodwill). Indeed, it is routine for vendors to seek specific "product placement" in retail stores precisely to capitalize on their competitors' name recognition. For example, a drug store typically places its own store-brand generic products next to the trademarked products they emulate in order to induce a customer who has specifically sought out the trademarked product to consider the store's less-expensive alternative. WhenU employs this same marketing strategy by informing C-users who have sought out a specific trademarked product about available coupons, discounts, or alternative products that may be of interest to them.

1–800 disputes this analogy by arguing that unlike a drugstore, only the 1–800 website is displayed when the pop-up ad appears. This response, however, ignores the fact that a C-user who has installed the SaveNow software receives WhenU pop-up ads in a myriad of contexts, the vast majority of which are unlikely to have anything to do with 1–800 or the C-user's input of the 1–800 website address.

The cases relied on by 1–800 do not alter our analysis. As explained in detail by the court in *U-Haul*, they are all readily distinguishable because WhenU's conduct does not involve any of the activities those courts found to constitute "use." *U-Haul*, 279 F.Supp. at 728–29 (collecting cases). Significantly, WhenU's activities do not alter or affect 1–800's website in any way. Nor do they divert or misdirect C-users away from 1–800's website, or alter in any way the results a C-user will obtain when searching with the 1–800 trademark or website address. *Compare Playboy Enters., Inc. v. Netscape Communications Corp.*, 354 F.3d 1020, 1024 (9th Cir. 2004) (holding that infringement could be based on defendant's insertion of unidentified banner ads on C-user's search-results page); *Brookfield Communications v. West Coast Entm't Corp.*, 174 F.3d 1036 (9th Cir. 1999) (holding that defendant's use of trademarks in "metatags," invisible text within websites that search engines use for ranking results, constituted a "use in commerce" under the Lanham Act); *see generally Bihari v. Gross*, 119 F.Supp.2d 309 (S.D.N.Y. 2000) (discussing *Brookfield* and similar cases).

In addition, unlike several other internet advertising companies, WhenU does not "sell" keyword trademarks to its customers or otherwise manipulate which category-related advertisement will pop up in response to any particular terms on the internal directory. *See, e.g., GEICO*, 330 F.Supp.2d at 703–04 (finding that Google's sale to advertisers of right to use specific trademarks as "keywords" to trigger their ads constituted "use in commerce"). In other words, WhenU does not link trademarks to any particular competitor's ads, and a customer cannot pay to have its pop-up ad appear on any specific website or in connection with any particular trademark. *See id.* at 704 (distinguishing WhenU's conduct on this basis). Instead, the SaveNow directory terms trigger categorical associations (e.g., www. 1800Contacts.com might trigger the category of "eye care"), at which point, the software will randomly select one of the pop-up ads contained in the eye-care category to send to the C-user's desktop.

Perhaps because ultimately 1–800 is unable to explain precisely how WhenU "uses" its trademark, it resorts to bootstrapping a finding of "use" by alleging other elements of a trademark claim. For example, 1–800 invariably refers to WhenU's pop-up ads as "unauthorized" in an effort, it would seem, to establish by sheer force of repetition the element of unauthorized use of a trademark. Not surprisingly, 1–800 cites no legal authority for the proposition that advertisements, software applications, or any other visual image that can appear on a C-user's computer screen must be authorized by the owner of any website that will appear contemporaneously with that image. The fact is that WhenU does not need 1–800's authorization to display a separate window containing an ad any more than Corel would need authorization from Microsoft to display its WordPerfect word-processor in a window contemporaneously with a Word word-processing window. Moreover, contrary to 1–800's repeated admonitions, WhenU's pop-up ads are authorized—if unwittingly—by the C-user who has downloaded the SaveNow software.

1–800 also argues that WhenU's conduct is "use" because it is likely to confuse C-users as to the source of the ad. It buttresses this claim with a survey it submitted to the district court that purportedly demonstrates, inter alia, that (1) a majority of C-users believe that pop-up ads that appear on websites are sponsored by those websites, and (2) numerous C-users are unaware that they have downloaded the SaveNow software. 1–800 also relies on several cases in which the court seemingly based a finding of trademark "use" on the confusion such "use" was likely to cause. *See, e.g., Bihari*, 119 F.Supp.2d at 318 (holding that defendant's use of trademarks in metatags constituted a "use in commerce" under the Lanham Act in part because the hyperlinks "effectively act[ed] as a conduit, steering potential customers away from Bihari Interiors and toward its competitors"); *GEICO*, 330 F.Supp.2d at 703–04 (finding that Google's sale to advertisers of right to have specific trademarks trigger their ads was "use in commerce" because it created likelihood of confusion that Google had the trademark holder's authority to do so). Again, this rationale puts the cart before the horse. Not only are "use," "in commerce," and "likelihood of confusion" three distinct elements of a trademark infringement claim, but "use" must be decided as a threshold matter because, while any number of activities may be "in commerce" or create a likelihood of confusion, no such activity is actionable under the Lanham Act absent the "use" of a trademark. Because 1–800 has failed to establish such "use," its trademark infringement claims fail.

QUESTION

Do you understand the differences in how the *Google* and *WhenU* ad programs work? Are these sufficient to explain the different outcomes?

Page 155. Insert following case after *Buti v. Impressa Perosa*:

International Bancorp, LLC v. Société des Bains de Mer et du Cercle des Etrangers à Monaco

329 F.3d 359 (4th Cir. 2003).

■ LUTTIG, CIRCUIT JUDGE:

Plaintiff companies appeal from the district court's summary judgment that their registration and use of forty-three domain addresses infringe a foreign corporation's rights under the Lanham Act and violate the Anticybersquatting Act, where the foreign corporation advertised its trademark domestically, but only rendered services under it abroad. . . .

I.

Appellee, Societe des Bains de Mer et du Cercle des Etrangers a Monaco ("SBM"), owns and operates historic properties in Monte Carlo, Monaco, including resort and casino facilities. One of its properties, a casino, has operated under the "Casino de Monte Carlo" trademark since 1863. The mark is registered in Monaco, but not in the United States. SBM promotes this casino, along with its other properties, around the world. For 18 years, SBM has promoted its properties from a New York office staffed with four employees. SBM's promotions within the United States, funded with $1 million annually, include trade show participation, advertising campaigns, charity partnerships, direct mail solicitation, telephone marketing, and solicitation of media coverage.

Appellants, the plaintiff companies, are five companies formed and controlled by a French national, which operate more than 150 web sites devoted to online gambling. Included in this roster are 53 web sites whose domain addresses incorporate some portion of the term "Casino de Monte Carlo."[1] These web sites, along with the gambling software they employ, also exhibit pictures of *the* Casino de Monte Carlo's exterior and interior, contain renderings that are strikingly similar to the Casino de Monte Carlo's interior, and make allusion to the geographic location of Monte Carlo, implying that they offer online gambling as an alternative to *their* Monaco-based casino, though they operate no such facility.

* * *

1. *E.g.*, casinodemontecarlo.com, casinodemontecarlo.net, casinomontecarlo.com, casinomontecarlo.net, casinomontecarlo.org, and casino-montecarlo.net.

III.

The plaintiff companies first challenge the district court's determination that their use of 43 domain addresses violated 15 U.S.C. § 1125(a) of the Lanham Act, infringing on SBM's trademark. Central to their challenge is the claim that SBM did not have a protectible interest in the "Casino de Monte Carlo" mark, a prerequisite to SBM's ability to claim against the plaintiff companies under the Act....

A.

Both parties have agreed, in their briefs and at oral argument, that the critical question in assessing whether SBM "used its mark in commerce" is whether the *services* SBM provided under the "Casino de Monte Carlo" mark were *rendered in commerce*. As shown below, the Lanham Act's plain language makes this conclusion unavoidable and the parties' agreement unsurprising.

We must first contend with a threshold matter, however. This circuit has never directly addressed the scope of the term "commerce" within the Lanham Act. Because of the clarity of the Act's own definition of the term, *see* 15 U.S.C. § 1127 (defining "commerce" as "all commerce which may lawfully be regulated by Congress"), we now hold that "commerce" under the Act is coterminous with that commerce that Congress may regulate under the Commerce Clause of the United States Constitution....

Understanding commerce under the Act to be coterminous with that commerce Congress may regulate under the Commerce Clause, we turn next to the determination of what constitutes "*use in* commerce" under the Act. Again we rely on section 1127, which provides, of particular relevance here, a specific definition of that term as it relates to servicemarks, which the "Casino de Monte Carlo" mark unquestionably is....

Consistent with this definition of the statutory "use in commerce" requirement, the Supreme Court has said that "there is no such thing as property in a trade-mark except as a right appurtenant to an established business or trade in connection with which the mark is employed. ... The right to a particular mark grows out of its use, not its mere adoption;" *United Drug Co.* v. *Theodore Rectanus, Co.*, 248 U.S. 90, 97, 63 L. Ed. 141, 39 S.Ct. 48, 1918 Dec. Comm'r Pat. 369 (1918). Because a mark is used in commerce only if it accompanies services rendered in commerce, *i.e.*, it is employed appurtenant to an established business or trade that is in commerce, "mere advertising" of that mark does not establish its protectibility, though advertising is itself commerce that Congress may regulate.

With these principles in clear view, we proceed to address whether the "Casino de Monte Carlo" mark was used in commerce. In their briefs and before the court below, the parties debate principally whether the activities of SBM's New York office conducted under the "Casino de Monte Carlo" mark constitute services rendered in interstate commerce. SBM, for its part, contends that the office's booking of reservations is a rendered service, and that its maintenance of the office, its advertising in this country, and its promotional web page attach the "Casino de Monte Carlo" mark for sales and advertising purposes to this interstate service, thereby satisfying the "use in commerce" requirement. The plaintiff companies argue, to the contrary, that there is no evidence in the record that the New York office books reservations to the casino, and that, as a result, the office engages in no activity beyond "mere advertising." They argue further that the casino gambling services are the only established business to which the trademark applies, and that *that* service, being rendered in Monaco, is not rendered in commerce that Congress may regulate. . . .

Because SBM presented no record evidence that the New York office did anything other than advertise the "Casino de Monte Carlo" mark, if its case rested on this alone, the plaintiff companies would have the better of the argument. When they appeared before the court, however, we asked the parties to address themselves to the question of whether the casino services at issue were rendered in foreign trade, and the plaintiff companies conceded that the record contained evidence that United States citizens went to and gambled at the casino. This concession, when taken together with the undisputed fact that the Casino de Monte Carlo is a subject of a foreign nation, makes unavoidable the legal conclusion that foreign trade was present here, and that as such, so also was "commerce" under the Lanham Act.

Since the nineteenth century, it has been well established that the Commerce Clause reaches to foreign trade. And, for the same length of time, the Supreme Court has defined foreign trade as trade between subjects of the United States and subjects of a foreign nation. *See In re: Trade-Mark Cases*, 100 U.S. 82, 96, 25 L. Ed. 550, 1879 Dec. Comm'r Pat. 619 (1879) ("commerce with foreign nations means commerce between citizens of the United States and citizens and subjects of foreign nations"); . . . And, of course, commerce does not solely apply "to traffic, to buying and selling, or the interchange of commodities . . . Commerce, undoubtedly, is traffic, but it is something more: it is [commercial] intercourse." *Gibbons* v. *Ogden*, 22 U.S. 1, 189, 6 L. Ed. 23 (1824) (C.J. Marshall). Service transactions are clearly commercial intercourse, and by extension can clearly constitute foreign trade. . . . Thus, while SBM's promotions within the United States do not on their own constitute a use in commerce of the "Casino de Monte Carlo" mark, the mark is nonetheless used in commerce because United States citizens purchase casino services sold by a subject of a foreign nation, which purchases constitute trade with a foreign nation that Congress may regulate under the Commerce Clause. And SBM's promotions "use[ ] or display[ ] [the mark] in the sale or advertising of [these] services ... rendered in commerce." ...

The plaintiff companies' first argument fails because the *locality* in which foreign commercial intercourse occurs is of no concern to Congress' power under the Constitution to regulate such commerce. In *United States* v. *Holliday*, when examining the extent of Congress' authority over Indian commerce, the Supreme Court noted that under *Gibbons* v. *Ogden* the foreign commerce power "must be exercised wherever the *subject* exists. ... The *locality* of the traffic can have nothing to do with the power." *Holliday*, 70 U.S. at 417–18 (emphasis added). The subject of foreign trade, as the Supreme Court noted in *In re: Trademark Cases*, *Henderson*, and *Holliday*, is defined not by where the trade occurs, but by the characteristics of the parties who engage in the trade, just as the *Holliday* Court concluded that the subject of Indian commerce is defined not by whether the commerce occurs on Indian territory, but rather by whether the trade brings United States citizens and tribal Indians together as transacting partners. *See also United States* v. *Mazurie*, 419 U.S. 544, 554, 42 L. Ed. 2d 706, 95 S. Ct. 710 (1975) ("This Court has repeatedly held that [the Indian commerce clause] affords Congress the power to prohibit or regulate the sale of alcoholic beverages to tribal Indians, *wherever situated* ..." (emphasis added))....

Nor, in modern times, has the Supreme Court ever suggested that Congress' authority over foreign trade is limited in the manner that the plaintiff companies suggest. To the contrary, when it has considered the scope of Congress' authority over foreign trade, the Court has emphasized the expansive nature of that authority. *See, e.g., Pfizer, Inc.* v. *India*, 434 U.S. 308, 313 n.11, 54 L. Ed. 2d 563, 98 S. Ct. 584 (1978) ("The Chief Justice's dissent seems to contend that the Sherman Act's reference to commerce with foreign nations was intended only to reach conspiracies affecting goods imported into this county. But the scope of congressional power over foreign commerce has never been so limited ..." (citations omitted))....

The plaintiff companies' second argument, that the purchase of gambling services by United States citizens at the Casino de Monte Carlo is not commerce because it does not have a substantial effect on the foreign commerce of the United States, also fails. The substantial effects test is not implicated here at all.

The Supreme Court has articulated the substantial effects test to ensure that Congress does not exceed its constitutional authority to regulate interstate commerce by enacting legislation that, rather than regulating interstate commerce, trammels on the rights of states to regulate purely intra-state activity for themselves pursuant to their police power. But while "Congress' power to regulate interstate commerce may be restricted by considerations of federalism and state sovereignty[,] it has never been suggested that Congress' power to regulate foreign commerce could be so limited." *Japan Line Ltd.* v. *Los Angeles County*, 441 U.S. 434,

448 n.13, 60 L. Ed. 2d 336, 99 S. Ct. 1813 (1979). . . . The rationale that underlies application of the substantial effects test in the analysis of congressional legislation purporting to regulate interstate commerce is therefore absent from analysis of congressional legislation purporting to regulate foreign commerce. . . .

The plaintiff companies, seeking to avoid the full import of this foreign trade analysis, ask us to be wary in addressing whether United States trademark protection can extend to services rendered abroad and suggest that other courts have decided this question in the negative with reasoning that should persuade us not to extend trademark protection in this instance. In particular, the plaintiff companies point to the Second Circuit's opinion in *Buti* v. *Perosa, S.R.L.*, 139 F.3d 98 (2nd Cir. 1998). In *Buti*, the Second Circuit decided that the *ad hoc* distribution in the United States of an Italian restaurant's t-shirts, key chains, and cards, by the owner of the restaurant who was also the owner of a modeling agency, to his colleagues in the modeling industry, did not establish that the mark was used in commerce.

Buti is not persuasive authority to us for several reasons, however. First, the *Buti* court did not analyze the application of the Lanham Act to foreign trade because, as it noted, the plaintiff, in a "pivotal concession[], . . . conceded at oral argument that . . . the food and drink services [it sells] form no part of the trade between Italy and the United States." *Id.* at 103. And in fact, even though the *Buti* court did not analyze trademark rights created via foreign trade, it did acknowledge the basis for such. *See id.* (noting that a key inquiry is "whether [the plaintiff] has conducted the affairs of its Milan Fashion Cafe in such a way as to 'substantially affect' United States interstate or *foreign commerce*, and thereby fall within Congress' authority under the Commerce Clause"). Secondly, even had the *Buti* plaintiff not explicitly conceded that his business was not foreign trade, it is not clear that the facts before the *Buti* court would have established that the plaintiff used the mark in that putative foreign trade. As the Second Circuit carefully noted, the restaurant undertook no "formal advertising or public relations campaign [aimed at United States citizens]." *Id.* at 100.

Here, SBM does *not* concede that its services do not constitute foreign trade when United States citizens purchase them. Instead, the plaintiff companies concede the very elements we conclude constitute foreign trade. And quite clearly SBM has used the mark in its foreign trade, formally, and at great cost, advertising its services intentionally to United States citizens under the "Casino de Monte Carlo" mark. Because SBM used its mark in the sale and advertising of its gambling services to United States citizens; because its rendering of gambling services to United States citizens constitutes foreign trade; because foreign trade is commerce Congress may lawfully regulate; and because commerce under the Lanham Act comprises all commerce that Congress may lawfully regulate, the services SBM renders under the "Casino de Monte Carlo" mark to citizens of the United States are services rendered in commerce, and the "use in commerce" requirement that the Lanham Act sets forth for the mark's protectibility is satisfied.

B.

* * *

CONCLUSION

For the reasons provided herein, the judgment of the district court is affirmed.

AFFIRMED

■ DIANA GRIBBON MOTZ, CIRCUIT JUDGE, dissenting:

The majority reaches the unprecedented conclusion that an entity's use of its foreign trademark solely to sell services in a foreign country entitles it to trademark protection under United States law, even though the foreign mark holder has never used or registered its mark in the United States. In my view, the majority errs in holding that the protection of United States trademark law extends to a mark used exclusively in Monaco by a company incorporated there. For this reason and others set forth within, I respectfully dissent.

I.

Under United States law, the holder of an unregistered mark must demonstrate "use in commerce" of that mark in order to be eligible for trademark protection. The Lanham Act provides that "[a] mark shall be deemed to be in use in commerce ... on services when it is used or displayed in the sale or advertising of services and the services are rendered in commerce." 15 U.S.C.A. § 1127 (West Supp. 2003). Thus, there are two essential elements that must be present to constitute "use in commerce" for Lanham Act purposes: (1) advertising that employs the mark and (2) the rendering of services to which the mark attaches. Neither alone is sufficient. This two-pronged statutory meaning of "use in commerce" is what I refer to when I say that SBM did not "use" its mark in commerce because it did not "use" the mark in the United States.

Prior to today's holding, all existing authority, employing precisely this same two-pronged understanding of use, has similarly concluded that use in the United States is necessary to meet the Lanham Act's use in commerce requirement. None of this authority has ever suggested that if one element of the use in commerce requirement—advertising—takes place in the United States while the other—the rendering of services—occurs outside the United States, there has been use in the United States. Both elements must occur in the United States in order to satisfy the use in commerce requirement.

Indisputably, SBM has satisfied the first element of the use in commerce requirement, for no one questions that SBM employed the Casino de Monte Carlo mark in the United States to advertise and promote the gambling services that it provides exclusively at its casino in Monaco. This is not and has never been a case about advertising. Rather, the question here is whether the second element of the use in commerce requirement has been satisfied, *i.e.* have the services that give rise to the Casino de Monte Carlo mark been rendered in commerce of the United States....

A.

In this case, some United States citizens purchased "casino services" in Monaco from the Société des Bains de Mer et du Cercle des Etrangers à Monaco (SBM), a "subject of a foreign nation." The majority determines that those services "constitute trade with a foreign nation that Congress may regulate under the Commerce Clause." Based on this determination, the majority accords SBM, the holder of the foreign mark, "Casino de Monte Carlo," eligibility for trademark protection under the Lanham Act for that mark even though SBM has *never* used the mark in the United States.

SBM has not argued, and the district court did not hold, that the mark was entitled to protection under the Lanham Act simply because SBM used it to sell gambling services in Monaco to United States citizens. Nor did SBM argue, or the trial court hold, that these sales of gambling services in Monaco to United States citizens constitute foreign trade that has been regulated by Congress under the Lanham Act. Indeed, prior to today, no court, administrative agency, or treatise has ever espoused or adopted this theory.

Rather, it has long been recognized that use of a foreign mark in a foreign country creates no trademark rights under United States law. As the foremost trademark authority has explained, "for purposes of trademark rights in the United States, 'use' means use in the United States, not use in other nations." 2 J. Thomas McCarthy, McCarthy on Trademarks and Unfair Competition § 17.9 (4th ed. 2000) ("McCarthy") [other citation omitted].[3]

Until today, every court to address this issue has held that use of a *foreign trademark* in connection with goods and services sold *only* in a foreign country by a foreign entity does not constitute "use of the mark" in United States commerce sufficient to merit protection under the Lanham Act. As the Federal Circuit explained in rejecting the contention that a Japanese mark holder's use of a trademark solely in Japan in connection with goods sold to a United States citizen constituted use of the mark in commerce for Lanham Act purposes:

Such foreign use has no effect on U.S. commerce and can not form the basis for a holding that appellant has priority here. The concept of

3. This principle, that use in the United States provides the foundation for U.S. trademark rights, is a corollary of the well-established principle that trademark rights exist in each country solely as determined by that country's law. *See Ingenohl v. Olsen & Co., Inc.*, 273 U.S. 541, 544, 71 L. Ed. 762, 47 S. Ct. 451 (1927) ("A trade-mark started elsewhere would depend for its protection in Honkong upon the law prevailing in Honkong and would confer no rights except by the consent of that law.")....

territoriality is basic to trademark law; trademark rights exist in each country solely according to that country's statutory scheme.

Person's Co., Ltd. v. Christman, 900 F.2d 1565, 1568–69 (Fed. Cir. 1990); [other citations omitted]; *see also La Societe Anonyme des Parfums Le Galion v. Jean Patou*, 495 F.2d 1265, 1270 n.4 (2d Cir. 1974) ("It is well settled that foreign use [of a trademark] is ineffectual to create trademark rights in the United States.").... *cf. Buti v. Perosa*, 139 F.3d 98, 103 (2d Cir. 1998) (noting that plaintiff conceded that "Congress has no constitutional authority to regulate the operation of the Fashion Cafe in Milan" perhaps in "recognition of the fact that ... registration and use of the Fashion Cafe name in Italy has not, given the territorial nature of trademark rights, secured it any rights under the Lanham Act").

Aside from its singularly unpersuasive attempt to distinguish *Buti*, the majority ignores all of this authority. The majority also ignores the fact that courts have uniformly rejected its precise argument, *i.e.*, use of a foreign mark in a foreign country somehow grants the foreign holder of the mark *priority* over one who uses the mark first in the United States. [citations omitted] ...[5]

Nor is the rule any different when, as here, the mark is used in a foreign country in connection with services or goods *sold to United States citizens. See, e.g., Person's*, 900 F.2d at 1567–69 (rejecting argument that use of trademark on goods sold in Japan by Japanese company to a U.S. citizen could establish priority rights against person using mark first in the United States)....

Before concluding, I must note the potential consequences of adoption of the majority's rule. The rule announced by the majority today would mean that any entity that uses a foreign mark to advertise and sell its goods or services to United States citizens in a foreign country would be eligible for trademark protection under United States law. Such a rule threatens to wreak havoc over this country's trademark law and would have a stifling effect on United States commercial interests generally. Before investing in a mark, firms and individuals would be forced to scour the globe to determine when and where American citizens had purchased goods or services from foreign subjects to determine whether there were trademarks involved that might be used against them in a priority contest or in an infringement action in the United States. On the other hand, SBM and companies like it would, under the majority's rule, suddenly acquire a windfall of potential United States trademark rights for all of the goods and services advertised to and purchased by United States citizens while traveling in their countries. Like some sort of foreign influenza, these new entitlements would accompany American travelers on their return home,

5. Even if the plaintiff companies knew of SBM's use of its foreign mark in connection with services rendered in Monaco, this does not render the plaintiff companies bad-faith users of the mark in the United States or preclude them from using the mark in the United States. *See Person's*, 900 F.2d at 1570 ("Knowledge of a foreign use does not preclude good faith adoption and use in the United States."); *accord Buti*, 139 F.3d at 106; Callman § 19.24 and cases cited therein ("Even an intentional imitator may acquire domestic trademark rights if the mark he imitates is used in a foreign country.").

creating a vast array of new duties for individuals in the United States seeking to use the same or similar marks on goods or services sold in the United States.

Of course, if the law required us to permit this sort of reverse imperialism, whereby foreign subjects would be allowed to colonize American markets with their foreign trademarks based on sales conducted exclusively abroad, we would have no choice but to allow it. But the law does not compel this. Rather, the majority's new theory is contrary to all extant authority. Applying this authority here leads to only one conclusion: SBM's use in Monaco of its "Casino de Monte Carlo" mark does not constitute "use in commerce" of the United States sufficient to gain protection under the Lanham Act. Therefore, the grant of summary judgment to SBM should be reversed. On this ground, the plaintiff companies were entitled to judgment as a matter of law.

QUESTIONS

1. Look at the sec. 27 definition of "use in commerce" in connection with *goods*. Suppose a brand of French clothing and accessories is sold only in France (often to American tourists), but the brand is advertised in U.S. travel magazines. Is that trademark "used in commerce?" If not, is there a reason the outcome should be so different for service marks?

2. What is the difference between SBM's U.S.-related exploitation of the mark and the Milan Fashion Café's?

3. If SBM had a website, accessible in the U.S., that allowed U.S. residents to book tables at the Monaco casino's restaurant, would this be a "use in commerce?" If the website allowed U.S. residents to gamble online, would this be a "use" in commerce?

B. Ownership

Page 162. Add to end of Question following *Robi v. Reed*:

See, e.g., Brother Records, Inc. v. Jardine, 318 F.3d 900 (9th Cir. 2003) (use of "Beach Boys" name in band formed by former member of the Beach Boys).

C. Priority and Concurrent Use

1. Priority

Page 168–69. Delete *Lucent Information Management v. Lucent Technologies, Inc.*

Page 174. Insert before *Maryland Stadium*:

What difference does it make to the analysis of priority if the senior user has been using the mark in another country? Normally, the principle of territoriality would make non U.S. use irrelevant (but see *Société des Bains de Mer*, *supra* this Supplement). But the "famous mark" exception may confer rights in the U.S. when the mark is well-known and the U.S. junior user has adopted the mark after it became famous in this country. Tourism, crossborder advertising and immigration may make a foreign mark, particularly one widely used in a neighboring country, well-known in this one. In **Grupo Gigante SA v. Dallo & Co.,** 391 F.3d 1088 (9th Cir. 2004), plaintiff proprietor of over 100 "Gigante" grocery stores in Mexico, including in California-adjacent Tijuana, alleged that two family-owned "Gigante Markets" in Southern California infringed the Mexican group's rights in the mark. The California grocers adopted their mark well after the Mexican group, but the Mexican group had not opened stores in California.

The exception for famous and well-known foreign marks

A fundamental principle of trademark law is first in time equals first in right. But things get more complicated when to time we add considerations of place, as when one user is first in time in one place while another is first in time in a different place. The complexity swells when the two places are two different countries, as in the case at bar.

Under the principle of first in time equals first in right, priority ordinarily comes with earlier *use* of a mark in commerce. It is "not enough to have invented the mark first or even to have registered it first." If the first-in-time principle were all that mattered, this case would end there. It is undisputed that Grupo Gigante used the mark in commerce for decades before the Dallos did. But the facts of this case implicate another well-established principle of trademark law, the "territoriality principle." The territoriality principle, as stated in a treatise, says that "priority of trademark rights in the United States depends solely upon priority of use in the United States, not on priority of use anywhere in the world." Earlier use in another country usually just does not count. Although we have not had occasion to address this principle, it has been described by our sister circuits as "basic to trademark law," in large part because "trademark rights exist in each country solely according to that country's statutory scheme." While Grupo Gigante used the mark for decades before the Dallos used it, Grupo Gigante's use was in Mexico, not in the United States. Within the San Diego area, on the northern side of the border, the Dallos were the first users of the "Gigante" mark. Thus, according to the territoriality principle, the Dallos' rights to use the mark would trump Grupo Gigante's.

Grupo Gigante does not contest the existence of the territoriality principle. But like the first-in-time, first-in-right principle, it is not absolute. The exception, as Grupo Gigante presents it, is that when foreign use of a mark achieves a certain level of fame for that mark within the United States, the territoriality principle no longer serves to deny priority to the earlier foreign user. The Dallos concede that there is such an exception, but dispute what it takes for a mark to qualify for it. Grupo Gigante would interpret the exception broadly, while the Dallos would interpret it narrowly.

. . .

There is no circuit-court authority—from this or any other circuit—applying a famous-mark exception to the territoriality principle. At least one circuit judge has, in a dissent, called into question whether there actually is any meaningful famous-mark exception. We hold, however, that there is a famous mark exception to the territoriality principle. While the territoriality principle is a long-standing and important doctrine within trademark law, it cannot be absolute. An absolute territoriality rule without a famous-mark exception would promote consumer confusion and fraud. Commerce crosses borders. In this nation of immigrants, so do people. Trademark is, at its core, about protecting against consumer confusion and "palming off." There can be no justification for using trademark law to fool immigrants into thinking that they are buying from the store they liked back home.

It might not matter if someone visiting Fairbanks, Alaska from Wellington, New Zealand saw a cute hair-salon name—"Hair Today, Gone Tomorrow," "Mane Place," "Hair on Earth," "Mary's Hair'em," or "Shear Heaven"—and decided to use the name on her own salon back home in New Zealand. The ladies in New Zealand would not likely think they were going to a branch of a Fairbanks hair salon. But if someone opened a high-end salon with a red door in Wellington and called it Elizabeth Arden's, women might very well go there because they thought they were going to an affiliate of the Elizabeth Arden chain, even if there had not been any other Elizabeth Ardens in New Zealand prior to the salon's opening. If it was not an affiliate, just a local store with no connection, customers would be fooled. The real Elizabeth Arden chain might lose business if word spread that the Wellington salon was nothing special.

The most cited case for the famous-mark exception is *Vaudable v. Montmartre, Inc.*, a 1959 trial court decision from New York. A New York restaurant had opened under the name "Maxim's," the same name as the well-known Parisian restaurant in operation since 1893, and still in operation today. The New York Maxim's used similar typography for its sign, as well as other features likely to evoke the Paris Maxim's—particularly among what the court called "the class of people residing in the cosmopolitan city of New York who dine out" (by which it apparently meant the sort of people who spend for dinner what some people spend for a month's rent). The court enjoined the New York use, even though the Paris restaurant did not operate in New York, or in the United States, because the Maxim's mark was "famous."

While *Vaudable* stands for the principle that even those who use marks in other countries can sometimes—when their marks are famous enough—gain exclusive rights to the marks in this country, the case itself tells us little about just how famous or well-known the foreign mark must be. The opinion states in rather conclusory terms that the Paris Maxim's "is, of course, well known in this country," and that "there is *no doubt* as to its unique and eminent position as a restaurant of international fame and prestige." This language suggests that Maxim's had achieved quite a high degree of fame here, and certainly enough to qualify for the exception to the territoriality principle, but it suggests nothing about just how much fame was necessary. It does not suggest where the line is between "Shear Heaven" and Maxim's.

The Patent and Trademark Office's Trademark Trial and Appeal Board, whose expertise we respect and whose decisions create expectations, has recognized the validity of the famous-mark exception. But as with *Vaudable*, none of these cases helps us to establish a clear threshold for just how famous a mark must be to qualify for the exception.

Grupo Gigante urges us to adopt the approach the district court took. The district court held that the correct inquiry was to determine whether the mark had attained secondary meaning in the San Diego area. Secondary meaning refers to a mark's actual ability to trigger in consumers' minds a link between a product or service and the source of that product or service. That is, a mark has secondary meaning "when, in the minds of the public, the primary significance of a mark is to identify the source of the product rather than the product itself." Determining whether a mark has secondary meaning requires taking into account at least seven considerations, which the district court did in this case.

Applying its interpretation of the famous-mark exception, the district court concluded that Grupo Gigante's use of the mark had achieved secondary meaning in the San Diego area by the time the Dallos opened their first store, and thus the court held that Grupo Gigante's use was eligible for the exception to the territoriality principle. Grupo Gigante asserts that we, too, should adopt secondary meaning as the definition of the exception. We decline to go quite this far, however, because following the district court's lead would effectively cause the exception to eclipse the territoriality rule entirely.

... [S]econdary meaning defines the geographic area in which a user has priority, regardless of who uses the mark first. Under what has become known as the *Tea Rose-Rectanus* doctrine, priority of use in one geographic area within the United States does not necessarily suffice to establish priority in another area. Thus, the first user of a mark will not necessarily be able to stop a subsequent user, where the subsequent user is in an area of the country "remote" from the first user's area. The practical effect is that one user may have priority in one area, while another user has priority over the very same mark in a different area. The point of this doctrine is that in the remote area, where no one is likely to know of the earlier user, it is unlikely that consumers would be confused by the second user's use of the mark. Secondary meaning comes into play in determining just how far each user's priority extends. Courts ask whether the first, geographically limited use of the mark is well-known enough that it has gained secondary meaning not just within the area where it has been used, but also within the remote area, which is usually the area where a subsequent user is claiming the right to use the mark.

Assume, for example, that Grupo Gigante had been using the mark in Arizona as well as in various parts of Mexico, and that it had met all the other requirements of having a protectable interest in the mark, including having established secondary meaning throughout Arizona. If the Dallos later began using the same mark in San Diego without knowledge of Grupo Gigante's earlier "remote" use in Arizona, whether Grupo Gigante could stop them would depend on what the mark meant to consumers in San Diego. Under the *Tea-Rose-Rectanus* doctrine, Grupo Gigante would have priority in San Diego, and thus be able to stop the Dallos' use of the mark, only if the secondary meaning from Grupo Gigante's use of the mark in Arizona extended to San Diego as well. If, on the other hand, the secondary meaning from Grupo Gigante's use were limited to Arizona, then the Dallos might be free to continue using the mark in San Diego.

Thus, if the dispute before us were between a Mexican and Arizonan Grupo Gigante on the one hand, and the Dallos on the other, we would analyze, under the *Tea Rose-Rectanus* doctrine, whether Grupo Gigante's use of the mark had achieved secondary meaning in San Diego. This is how the district court analyzed the actual dispute, as a result of having defined the exception to the territoriality principle in terms of secondary meaning. In other words, the district court treated Grupo Gigante's use of the mark exactly as it would have had Grupo Gigante used the mark not only in Mexico, but also in another part of the United States. Under the district court's interpretation of the exception to the territoriality principle, the fact that Grupo Gigante's earlier use of the mark was entirely outside of the United States becomes irrelevant.

The problem with this is that treating international use differently is what the territoriality principle does. This interpretation of the exception would effectively eliminate the territoriality principle by eliminating any effect of international borders on protectability. We would end up treating foreign uses of the mark just as we treat domestic uses under the *Tea Rose-Rectanus* doctrine, asking in both cases whether the use elsewhere resulted in secondary meaning in the local market.

We would go too far if we did away with the territoriality principle altogether by expanding the famous-mark exception this much. The territoriality principle has a long history in the common law, and at least two circuits have described it as "basic to trademark law." That status reflects the lack of a uniform trademark regime across international borders. What one must do to acquire trademark rights in one country will not always be the same as what one must do in another. And once acquired, trademark rights gained in other countries are governed by each country's own set of laws.... Thus, we reject Grupo Gigante's argument that we should define the well-known mark exception as merely an inquiry into whether the mark has achieved secondary meaning in the area where the foreign user wishes to assert protection.

To determine whether the famous-mark exception to the territoriality rule applies, the district court must determine whether the mark satisfies the secondary meaning test. The district court determined that it did in this case, and we agree with its persuasive analysis. But secondary meaning is not enough.

In addition, where the mark has not before been used in the American market, the court must be satisfied, by a preponderance of the evidence, that a *substantial* percentage of consumers in the relevant American market is familiar with the foreign mark. The relevant American market is the geographic area where the defendant uses the alleged infringing mark. In making this determination, the court should consider such factors as the intentional copying of the mark by the defendant, and whether customers of the American firm are likely to think they are patronizing the same firm that uses the mark in another country. While these factors are not necessarily determinative, they are particularly relevant because they bear heavily on the risks of consumer confusion and fraud, which are the reasons for having a famous-mark exception.

Almacenes Exito v. El Gallo Meat Market, 381 F.Supp.2d 324 (S.D.N.Y. 2005).

Plaintiff (whose mark means "success stores") is the self-styled "Wal–Mart of Colombia," and has used the mark extensively in Colombia and Venezuela since 1949, but does not have stores in the U.S. The EXITO mark has come to be known and recognized as a designation of source throughout Latin America and by a high percentage of the Hispanic population in New York City. Defendants operate several small EXITO grocery stores in Upper Manhattan and the Bronx, neighborhoods with substantial Colombian immigrant populations. Defendants' stores offer groceries and fresh foods with a particular emphasis on Latin American produce. Each store features an exact replica of plaintiff's EXITO mark. The court found that defendants adopted the EXITO mark with intent to cause consumer confusion and to capitalize on plaintiff's good will. Defendants asserted that the plaintiff's lack of a U.S. trademark registration or of use of the mark in the U.S. doomed its infringement claim. Plaintiff rejoined that the "famous mark doctrine" would nonetheless afford it protection in the U.S.

To the extent the doctrine is a creature of common law it may support state causes of action, see *infra,* but it has no place in federal law where Congress has enacted a statute, the Lanham Act, that carefully prescribes the bases for federal trademark claims. The Lanham Act nowhere specifies the well-known or famous marks doctrine.

Plaintiff, however, argues that it is there by implication because Article 6bis of the Paris Convention of 1883, an international treaty to which both the United States and Columbia are parties, specifies that

> the signatory nations undertake, ex officio if their legislation so permits, or at the request of an interested party, to refuse or to cancel the registration, and to prohibit the use, of a trademark which constitutes a reproduction, an imitation, or a translation, liable to create confusion, of a mark considered by the competent authority of the country of registration or use to be well known in that country as being already the mark of a person entitled to the benefits of this Convention and used for identical or similar goods. These provisions shall also apply when the essential part of the mark constitutes a reproduction of any such well-known mark or an imitation liable to create confusion therewith.

Paris Convention, Art. 6bis (1). Similarly, Article 8 of the Paris Convention, on which plaintiff also relies, provides:

> A trade name shall be protected in all the countries of the Union without the obligation of filing or registration, whether or not it forms part of a trademark.

Paris Convention, Art. 8.

In turn, Section 44(b) of the Lanham Act provides that

> [a]ny person whose country of origin is a party to any convention or treaty relating to trademarks ... to which the United States is also a party ... shall be entitled to the benefits of this section under the conditions expressed herein to the extent necessary to give effect to any provision of such convention, treaty or reciprocal law, in addition to the rights to which any owner of a mark is otherwise entitled by this Act.

15 U.S.C. § 1126(b) (emphasis added). So, plaintiff's argument goes, the Lanham Act provides a foreign plaintiff with additional substantive rights created by the Paris Convention.

So far as the Second Circuit is concerned, however, any argument along these lines has effectively been rejected by that Court's recent decision in *Empresa Cubana*, [399 F.3d 642 (2d Cir. 2005)]. For there, although not reaching the precise question here presented, the Second Circuit, in rejecting a similar argument relating to unfair competition, expressly adopted the view of the Eleventh Circuit in Int'l Cafe, *S.A.L. v. Hard Rock Cafe Int'l Inc.*, 252 F.3d 1274, 1277–78 (11th Cir.2001) as follows:

> We agree that Section 44 of the Lanham Act incorporated to some degree the Paris Convention. But we disagree that the Paris Convention creates substantive rights beyond those independently provided in the Lanham Act. As other courts of appeals have

> noted, the rights articulated in the Paris Convention do not exceed the rights conferred by the Lanham Act. Instead, we conclude that the Paris Convention, as incorporated by the Lanham Act, only requires "national treatment."

Int'l Cafe, 252 F.3d at 1277–78, quoted in *Empresa Cubana*, 399 F.3d at 484–85. See also *Empresa Cubana*, 399 F.3d at 484 ("The Paris Convention requires that 'foreign nationals be given the same treatment in each of the member countries as that country makes available to its own citizens,' " *quoting Vanity Fair Mills v. T. Eaton Co.*, 234 F.2d 633, 640 (2d Cir.1956), cert. denied, 352 U.S. 871). Since it is conceded that a United States citizen who claimed to own the EXITO mark could not bring a Lanham Act claim for infringement or the like against the defendants here if he had neither registered the mark in the United States nor made prior use of it in the United States, it follows from the above-quoted language that the Second Circuit has effectively concluded that a foreign owner of an EXITO mark could not bring such an action either.

It is true that the Ninth Circuit in *Grupo Gigante*, as well as at least two district courts in this district, see De Beers, 2005 WL 1164073, at *7, 2005 U.S. Dist. LEXIS 9307 at *19–20; *Empresa Cubana del Tabaca v. Culbro Corp.*, 2004 WL 602295, at *29–39, 2004 U.S. Dist. LEXIS 4935 at *87–116 (S.D.N.Y. March 29, 2004) *rev'd on other grounds*, 399 F.3d at 465 (2d Cir.2005), have recognized, on "policy" grounds, a limited exception to the territoriality principle for a famous marks doctrine (albeit an exception that they each define differently). It is also true, as noted, that the Second Circuit in *Empresa Cubana* expressly left open this possibility as well. However, such a radical change in basic federal trademark law may, in this Court's view, only be made by Congress, not the courts. Accordingly, since it is conceded that plaintiff has not satisfied the territorial principle, plaintiff's three Lanham Act claims must be dismissed.

The same, however, is not true of plaintiff's state law claims, for the territoriality principle is part of federal law, not New York state law, and New York has fully adopted the well-known or famous marks doctrine as part of its common law. Indeed, it was a New York case that first introduced the doctrine to modern law. *Maison Prunier v. Prunier's Restaurant & Cafe, Inc.*, 159 Misc. 551, 288 N.Y.S. 529 (1936) (interpreting the Paris Convention as applied to New York common law).

The *Maison Prunier* court's reliance on the Paris Convention is not foreclosed by the Eleventh Circuit's ruling adopted by the Second Circuit in *Empresa Cubana*. For, as quoted above, the ruling was that the Paris Convention did not provide substantive rights "beyond those independently provided in the Lanham Act." *Empresa Cubana*, 399 F.3d at 485. Neither the Eleventh Circuit in *Int'l Cafe* nor the Second Circuit in *Empresa Cubana* said anything as to the Paris Convention's interplay with state common law. Moreover, the Lanham Act has never been read to be preemptive of state trademark and unfair competition law.

QUESTION

Does it make sense to entertain the "famous marks" doctrine only as a matter of state law? Is it clear, in ensuring that foreign mark holders receive "national treatment" in the U.S., that the Lanham Act forecloses according foreigners *better* treatment if that treatment is also required by the international treaty? Does the Paris Convention require adoption of the "famous marks" doctrine?

2. Concurrent Use

Page 188. Add after Eds. Note:

In *Thrift Cars*, the good faith junior user was permitted to continue to advertise its business in the local area in which it had been operating before the senior user's registration issued. Under the court's order, the local advertising was in the print media and was geographically pinpointed to the East Taunton area. Broadcast advertising risks greater spillover, and therefore may require even more careful line drawing. Attempts geographically to constrain broadcast advertising may present a different set of problems, notably for the user whose federal registration entitles it to nationwide rights, but those rights are subject to the senior use or good faith junior use rights of local operators. The registrant's obligation to leave those markets clear for local operators may in fact undermine its ability to advertise to the rest of the U.S. On the other hand, to permit the registrant's nationwide advertising would override the senior user's geographic claims.

In **V&V Food Products v. Cacique Cheese,** 2003 WL 255235, 66 U.S.P.Q.2d (BNA) 1170 (N.D. Ill. 2003), the court endeavored to reconcile these kinds of conflicting rights. Cacique, the federal registrant of the mark RANCHERO for *queso fresco* Mexican-style cheese, sought a modification of an injunction issued 15 years earlier that barred it from advertising in a four-State area in the Midwest in which V & V was the senior common law user of the mark RANCHERITO for the same goods. Cacique argued that the injunction prevented it from advertising on national Spanish-language television networks, and thereby placed it at a competitive disadvantage in the 46 States in which it had federal rights. V & V objected that national television advertising would enter the four States in which it had superior rights, and was not necessary to Cacique's business, because Cacique could continue to advertise in local media in the other 46 States. The court agreed with Cacique's contentions that "the dispersion of the Latino population into new, unexpected geographical markets; the advent of national, Spanish-language network media; and the targeting of Latino consumers by general-market cheese manufacturers such as Kraft" all made national advertising "necessary both to reach the newly dispersed Latino market and to compete with its new competitors who exploit this medium to reach Cacique's core customer base." Moreover, "[w]ith the advent of Spanish-language national media, such companies [as Cacique] are able to reach Latino consumers regardless of where they are located. And, as the evidence has established, they are dispersed throughout the country to a degree that was unexpected in 1988 [when the injunction originally issued]. Yet Cacique is enjoined from exploiting this same medium and is therefore at a competitive disadvantage in the forty-six states where the injunction was never intended to hamper its activities and in which it has superior trademark rights. It is not possible for Cacique to accomplish the same advertising coverage by placing local commercials because many affiliate stations and cable providers do not have the capacity to provide local ad insertions. Even if full coverage through spot advertising were possible, the cost likely would be prohibitive."

In a later motion, 2003 WL 1145425, 66 U.S.P.Q.2d (BNA) 1179, Cacique also sought to advertise on Spanish-language nationwide network radio, and in English-language national media. The court rejected this further enlargement:

> [W]hereas Cacique convincingly established that it could not mount a national advertising campaign on Spanish-language television while excluding the four-state area, it has presented no such evidence in the case of Spanish-language radio. Far from establishing that local spot insertions are not possible in the four-state area, [Cacique's senior vice-president for Sales] testified that he did not know whether Radio Unica affiliates are able to perform insertions. Similarly, Cacique did not establish that it cannot structure a network radio campaign that avoids the four-state area ... [Similarly] a modification permitting Cacique to advertise Ranchero products on national, English-language media is not suitably tailored to the changed circumstances Cacique has previously established. The three changed factual conditions upon which Cacique relied in moving for modification all related to Cacique's need to advertise in Spanish.... Gilbert de Cardenas, Jr., president of Cacique Distributors, U.S., even testified that Cacique did not consider advertising a certain Cacique-brand campaign on English-language networks because "we target Hispanic consumers that are predominantly Spanish-speaking. Those networks do not cater to that group." All the evidence Cacique presented with respect to its need to reach the Latino population was similarly focused on Spanish-language media, sometimes to the exclusion of English-language media....
>
> Moreover, Cacique has made no effort to demonstrate the impossibility, or even difficulty, of exploiting English-language media while avoiding the four-state area.... To the contrary, the record contains a suggestion that the limitations that exist on Spanish-language television networks may not apply in the English-media context: Cacique's expert witness Kathy Gregory, a specialist in Spanish-language media consulting; submits that, unlike Spanish-language networks, "ABC, NBC, and CBS now have established regional advertising programs (in which an advertisement is run only on the network's affiliates in one of

five defined geographic regions)." Thus there is at least some evidence that regional campaigns are possible and no evidence to suggest that the four states cannot be avoided. Because Cacique has submitted no evidence that it cannot exploit English-language media without violating the injunction, Cacique's potential need to conduct English-language network advertising at some time in the future does not warrant modification.

Can the "limited area exception" apply if the contending trademark users are doing business on the Internet? What is a junior Internet user's "limited area"? *See Pure Imagination, Inc. v. Pure Imagination Studios, Inc.*, 2004 WL 2222269 (N.D. Ill. 2004).

Page 188. Add the following highlighted words to the last sentence of the second paragraph of the *Dawn Donut* excerpt:

Defendant adopted the mark "Dawn" **subsequent to plaintiff's registration but** without **actual** knowledge of plaintiff's use . . .

Page 189. Add after *Dawn Donut*:

For a more recent expression of this principle, see *Emergency One v. American Eagle Fire Apparatus*, 332 F.3d 264 (4th Cir. 2003):

> Although federal registration of a mark does not itself confer ownership rights, registration constitutes "prima facie evidence of the validity of the registered mark . . ., of the registrant's ownership of the mark, and of the registrant's exclusive right to use the registered mark. . . ." 15 U.S.C.A. § 1057(b) (West 1997). Moreover, the presumption of priority enjoyed by the registrant of a mark is "nationwide in effect." 15 U.S.C.A. § 1057(c). Thus, registration of a trademark under the Lanham Act "creates a presumption that the registrant is entitled to use the registered mark throughout the nation." *Draeger Oil Co. v. Uno–Ven Co.*, 314 F.3d 299, 302 (7th Cir. 2002). By contrast, a user claiming ownership of a mark under common-law principles does not enjoy the benefit of the presumptions conferred by registration and must "establish his right to exclusive use"; in effect, registration "shifts the burden of proof from the plaintiff . . . to the defendant, who must introduce sufficient evidence to rebut the presumption of plaintiff's right to such [exclusive] use." *Pizzeria Uno Corp. v. Temple*, 747 F.2d 1522, 1529 (4th Cir. 1984) (internal quotation marks omitted). Accordingly, a plaintiff asserting a claim of infringement against common-law trademark ownership rights bears the burden of establishing its exclusive right to use the mark by actual use in a given territory.
>
> The nature of common-law trademark rights in large measure determines the appropriate scope of any injunctive relief. Thus, the owner of common-law trademark rights in an unregistered mark is not entitled to injunctive relief in those localities where it has failed to establish actual use of the mark. *See Spartan Food*, 813 F.2d at 1282–84. By limiting injunctive relief to the territory where the mark is being used, courts ensure that a trademark does not precede its owner

into "markets that [the owner's] trade has never reached." *Hanover Milling*, 240 U.S. at 416. For this reason, even the owner of a federally registered mark—who enjoys the presumption of nationwide priority—is not "entitled to injunctive relief except in the area actually penetrated" through use of the mark. *Lone Star Steakhouse & Saloon, Inc. v. Alpha of Virginia, Inc.*, 43 F.3d 922, 932 (4th Cir. 1995) (internal quotation marks omitted).[3] Accordingly, even though the senior user of an unregistered mark has established priority over a junior user through prior appropriation, injunctive relief is appropriate only in those areas where the senior user can show sufficient actual use. *See Spartan Food*, 813 F.2d at 1283–84 (reversing the award of injunctive relief to the extent that it covered territory beyond the area in which the senior user established actual use); *cf. Armand's Subway*, 604 F.2d at 849–50 (explaining that even though the owner of a registered trademark has an exclusive right of use that enjoys nationwide protection, "the protection is only potential in areas where the registrant in fact does not do business" and "[a] competing user could use the mark there until the registrant extended its business to the area").

D. INTENT TO USE

Page 197. After Questions (before Problems), add:

Medinol Ltd. v. Neuro Vasx, 67 U.S.P.Q.2d 1205 (T.T.A.B. 2003). Neuro Vasx filed an intent-to-use based application reciting its intended goods as "medical devices, namely, neurological stents and catheters." At the time it filed its statement of use (and at all times since), it used the mark on catheters but not on stents. Its statement of use, however, Neuro Vasx stated that it was using the mark on both. Faced with Medinol's cancellation petition alleging fraud on the Trademark Office, Neuro Vasx admitted an error, and agreed that the registration should be cancelled as to stents, but should be maintained with respect to the medical equipment on which it had in fact been using the mark. The Board rejected Neuro Vasx's contention that fraud required a showing of specific intent to deceive:

> Respondent's explanation for the misstatement (which we accept as true)—that the inclusion of stents in the notice of allowance was "apparently overlooked"—does nothing to undercut the conclusion that respondent knew or should have known that its statement of use was materially incorrect. Respondent's knowledge that its mark was not in use on stents—or its reckless disregard for the truth—is all that is required to establish intent to commit fraud in the procurement of a registration. While it is clear that not all incorrect statements consti-

3. The owner of a registered mark "has a nationwide *right*, but the injunctive *remedy* does not ripen until the registrant shows a likelihood of entry into the disputed territory.... [The junior user's] use of the mark can continue only so long as the federal registrant remains outside the market area." *Lone Star*, 43 F.3d at 932 (internal quotation marks omitted).

tute fraud, the relevant facts in this record allow no other conclusion. We find that respondent's material misrepresentations made in connection with its statement of use were fraudulent.

Standard Knitting v. Toyota, 77 U.S.P.Q.2d 1917 (T.T.A.B. 2006). Standard Knitting opposed issuance of a registration for TUNDRA for automobiles, on the ground that opposer had used the TUNDRA and TUNDRA SPORT marks for clothing. Toyota rejoined by seeking cancellation of opposer's registrations on the ground that the marks had not been used on the claimed clothing, and that opposer's Chief Executive Officer knew this when he signed the applications and the declarations of use. Opposer's Chief Operating Officer

> indicate[d] that he did not make any effort to confirm that the marks TUNDRA and TUNDRA SPORT were in fact then being used on each of the goods listed in the applications when the applications were filed, and that he made no effort to verify what goods were in fact then being sold, and sold in the United States, although he admitted that there were sources of documentary information that could have been consulted (possibly invoices, if not destroyed and if they could be located), or price lists and cost sheets, for at least some of the goods.
>
> As support for his claim of current use on all of the identified goods, Mr. Groumoutis [the COO] states that he "had personal knowledge or knowledge of looking at past brochures that they, in fact, had done those in the past" [the meaning of "done" in this context being unclear], and he indicates that some brochures would have been current, and some three or more years old. At various points in his deposition, he states that he may have discussed the goods to be included in the applications . . ., and would have asked "have we ever sold these goods" or have we made, or did we make these goods or that he "may have spoken" . . . to find out if the list was correct but "it may have been just general, are we using these, yes, we are, and that would have been the end of it." However, when asked by applicant's counsel, "did you make any . . ." [then proceeding to list items of children's clothing], Mr. Groumoutis answered "not sure" as to children's sweaters, and "no" as to hats, jackets, coats, t-shirts, vests, shorts and shirts for children.

The Company's CEO, who signed the registration application was no more assiduous:

> Mr. Wang [the CEO] states that Mr. Groumoutis,
>
> > Told me that this was an application to register, I think it was to register our trademark. I asked him, if he has read it. And he said yes. I asked him if it was accurate. And he said yes. And I signed it.
>
> Mr. Wang indicated that he did not look at any other documents in connection with the applications at that time and that the process took five minutes.

Finding it clear from the record that the marks were not in fact in use on most of the goods claimed, the Board addressed whether opposer's officers' statements were fraudulent.

> Mr. Wang, who signed the underlying applications for these registrations, did not personally know, at the time of signing, whether or not certain of the identified goods, specifically, hats and coats, were being sold under the TUNDRA mark in the United States. He also stated that to his personal knowledge hats, jackets, coats and shorts were not being sold under the TUNDRA SPORT mark in the United States. Mr. Wang relied on Mr. Groumoutis's representation that the applications were accurate. However, that representation turned out to be false.
>
> It is opposer's contention that the false statement was the result of an honest mistake, and not due to any fraudulent intent; that opposer was making and selling a variety of clothing items; that the evidence, including invoices and spec sheets, shows that all of the listed products were actually made and/or sold by Standard Knitting, and substantiates the first use dates for each of its challenged registrations; that opposer did not know or understand the legal meaning of "use in commerce" and that its understanding of use was that the item was made or was sold; and that opposer had a reasonable belief, after making inquiries, that the marks were being used with the listed goods. As to the statement of use, opposer argues that it was filed on the basis of a mistaken belief that use was being made . . . and that the mark was in use with at least some goods as of the statement of use date.
>
> Mr. Groumoutis's asserted mistake, assuming it truly was a mistake, was not a reasonable one. The language in the application that the mark "is now in use in commerce" is clear, and its meaning is unambiguous. It was not reasonable for Mr. Groumoutis to believe that if the items of clothing were ever made or sold, even if the last sale took place 20 years ago, it would support a claim that the mark "is" in use on the goods. . . .
>
> Mr. Groumoutis clearly understood, prior to filing the applications, that "use" of a mark meant use in the United States. Given that none of Standard Knitting's clothing was made in the United States, Mr. Groumoutis could not have honestly believed that "use" simply meant that the goods were "made." This is not a situation where opposer misunderstood the significance of the statements it signed. Rather, opposer disregarded the significance.
>
> Considering that Mr. Groumoutis did not personally know whether the marks were in use on children's clothing in the United States, he was obligated to inquire and to the extent he did inquire, by looking at prior registrations, relying on his attorney's representations, and asking [company employees] whether the goods were ever made or sold, those inquiries were grossly insufficient. See *Medinol* ("Statements made with such degree of solemnity clearly are—or should be—investi-

gated thoroughly prior to signature and submission to the USPTO.")…. Opposer is charged with knowing what it is signing and by failing to make any appropriate inquiry, [opposer's officer] signed the statement of use with a "reckless disregard for the truth."

QUESTION

Were opposer's officers uncommonly ignorant, or is the TTAB requiring that a company's top officers know more about daily operations than they normally would or should?

Page 198. Add new Problem 6:

6. SureStream Inc. operates websites offering website design services under the domain names surestream.com and surestream.net. The domain names were registered on July 14, 1998; the websites were up and running by July 24, 1998. On August 3, 1998, RealNetworks filed an ITU application for SURE STREAM for streaming music services, and began use in September 1998. SureStream's websites and domain name registration had not appeared on the trademark search report commissioned by RealNetworks, but RealNetworks learned of SureStream's sites shortly after filing its ITU applications. RealNetworks requested that SureStream include on its websites a disclaimer of affiliation with RealNetworks, but SureStream refused, and, after converting the Surestream.com site to offer music streaming services, ultimately initiated a trademark infringement action against RealNetworks. SureStream's websites have generated no income, and received no visitors when they first went up. SureStream has been unable to attract traffic to the websites though well-placed links on the major search engines because RealNetworks had already obtained those placements for its websites. Who has prior use of the SureStream mark? *See Burns v. Realnetworks*, 359 F.Supp.2d 1187 (W.D. Okla. 2004).

Page 209–11. Delete from *Shalom Children's Wear* through Questions.

Page 213. Add new Review Problem 4:

4. Charles Shaw Wineries produces California table wine at a very low price for sale in supermarkets. An employee at one of Shaw's biggest distributors, the Trader Joe's chain, coined the name "Two–Buck Chuck," and posted eponymous display signs at the point of sale of Shaw's wines. The name stuck, and Trader Joes' customers began to ask for the Shaw wines by the "Two Buck Chuck" name. Articles about inexpensive quality California wines and Trader Joe's "Two Buck Chuck" bottles also appeared in the popular press.

Will's Swill is a chain of discount wine and liquor stores. It buys wine in bulk from Argentine producers and bottles it and sells it under its own "Two Buck Chuck" label. Charles Shaw has threatened to sue Will's Swill, claiming that "Two Buck Chuck" is his wine. Assess the likely outcome of his claim.

CHAPTER 4

REGISTRATION OF TRADEMARKS

A. THE PROCESS

Page 225. Insert the following Note after the "Maintenance and Renewal of Registration" Note:

U.S. ADHERENCE TO THE MADRID PROTOCOL

The Madrid Protocol is an international trademark filing treaty among over 50 countries to which the United States recently acceded. On October 17, 2002, the United States Senate gave its advice and consent to the treaty which allows non-U.S. applicants in member countries to extend their international registrations to the United States and allows domestic mark owners to obtain international registrations extending to member countries based upon the owner's U.S. applications or registrations. On November 2, 2002, President Bush signed the implementing legislation that adds sections 60 through 74 to the Lanham Act (see sections 60 through 74 of the Lanham Act in the Statutory Appendix A). The international registration system is administered by the World Intellectual Property Organization ("WIPO") located in Geneva, the same organization that administers a number of international agreements pertaining to intellectual property. The mark owner can select the member countries to which the international registration will extend, and those countries then have the ability to accept or refuse the extension. The international registration offers several benefits, such as the ability to renew registrations and to record assignments in one place for a single registration that covers many countries. There are a number of changes to the procedure for obtaining and maintaining an extension of an international registration in the United States to those discussed in the Chapter 4.A of the casebook.

A non-U.S. mark owner can extend the international registration it obtains from WIPO to the United States based on the international registration holder's "basic application" or "basic registration" in a Protocol country (other than the U.S.) in which it is a national, is domiciled or has a real and effective industrial or commercial establishment. The extension of the registration to the United States is submitted to the USPTO by WIPO and must be accompanied by a verified declaration that the international registration holder has a bona fide intent to use the mark in commerce. The date of the international registration (if the request for extension is filed in the international application) or the date the request for extension is recorded by WIPO (if the request is made after the international registration issued) is treated as the constructive first use date under section 7(c) of the Lanham Act. The USPTO examines the application as it normally does, and if it is approved, the application is published for opposition. In the event that no oppositions are filed or are overcome, the USPTO will issue a certificate of extension that will have the same effect as a registration on the Principal Register. If the application is not approved by the USPTO or an opposition is filed, the USPTO will issue a notice of refusal within 18 months from the date on which WIPO transmits the request for extension to the USPTO, stating the grounds. In addition, the USPTO will issue a notice of the possibility of refusal within 18 months if an opposition is possible.

A unique feature of an international registration under the Protocol is that if the basic application or registration upon which the international registration is based is restricted, abandoned or cancelled with respect to some of all of the covered goods or services within 5 years of the international registration or more than 5 years if the change resulted from an action within the 5 years, then the extensions, including to the United States, will be similarly restricted, abandoned or cancelled. If the international registration is cancelled in whole or in part, the international registration holder has the option to transform its extension to the U.S. to a U.S. application under section 70(c) by filing an application in the U.S. for the same mark and goods or services covered by the cancelled registration within 3 months of the cancellation of the international registration. This application can be made under either section 1 or section 44 of the Lanham Act and will be accorded the same filing date as that of the international registration or recordal of the extension.

Once an extension of protection has issued, the international registration holder is not required to renew it at the USPTO under section 9 of the Lanham Act since renewal of the international registration takes place centrally through WIPO. However, the international registration holder will nevertheless be required to submit declarations of use (or of excusable nonuse) under section 71 of the Lanham Act within 5 to 6 years after the certificate of extension to the U.S. has been issued and within the 6 month period prior to (or a 3-month grace period after) successive 10 year intervals after the certificate of extension issued. Compare the time periods specified in section 8 of the Lanham Act for registrations issued under section 1 or 44 of the Lanham Act. Are they the same?

C. BARS TO REGISTRATION

1. SECTION 2(a) OF THE LANHAM ACT: IMMORAL, DECEPTIVE, SCANDALOUS OR DISPARAGING MATTER

Page 229. Insert the following after Section 2(a) language:

Todd Anton, Self–Disparaging Trademarks and Social Change

106 COLUMBIA L. REV. 388 (2006).

. . .

B. *Section 2(a) and the Doctrine of Disparagement*

Section 2(a) of the Lanham Act bars the registration of, inter alia, "immoral ... or scandalous matter; or matter which may disparage ... persons, living or dead, institutions, beliefs, or national symbols, or bring them into contempt, or disrepute." Though Congress did not lay out an explicit justification for section 2(a), many scholars have concluded that the driving rationales behind this provision are that "the government should not waste its resources on protecting unseemly marks" and should not "provide its imprimatur to unseemly marks." A third possible rationale, uniquely relevant to disparagement law, is that the federal registration of a disparaging mark "is essentially a violation of one's right of privacy—the right to be 'let alone' from contempt or ridicule."[97] Despite, or perhaps because of, the many possible justifications for enacting section 2(a), the application of disparagement doctrine by examining attorneys has been murky at best.

. . .

1. *Defining "Disparaging."*—Though section 2(a) forbids the registration of disparaging marks, the Lanham Act neglects to define the term "disparage."[98] The TTAB and courts initially solved this problem by ignoring it, appearing to apply a "we know it when we see it" standard. For example, a 1951 court held that the mark DOUGH–BOY "obviously" disparaged American soldiers when placed on anti-venereal medication for condoms alongside a picture of a soldier, because " 'Doughboy' is the name given to the American soldier in the first World War."[100] In 1969, the

97. Greyhound Corp. v. Both Worlds Inc., 6 U.S.P.Q.2d (BNA) 1635, 1639 (T.T.A.B. 1988).

98. See In re Old Glory Condom Corp., 26 U.S.P.Q.2d (BNA) 1216, 1221 n.4 (T.T.A.B. 1993) (noting existence of "little precedent on the meaning of 'disparage' in Section 2(a)").

100. Doughboy Indus., Inc. v. Reese Chem. Co., 88 U.S.P.Q. (BNA) 227, 228 (P.T.O. 1951).

TTAB similarly declared, without citing support, that "there can be no question" that a mark depicting a large red "X" superimposed upon a hammer and sickle disparaged the Communist Party.[101] It was not until 1999 that the TTAB finally solidified a formal definition of "disparage" based on the "ordinary and common" definition of the word in 1946, the year Congress adopted the Lanham Act.[102] Looking to definitions in contemporaneous dictionaries, the TTAB concluded that a mark "may disparage"[103] a person, belief, institution, or national symbol when it "may dishonor by comparison with what is inferior, slight, deprecate, degrade, or affect or injure by unjust comparison."[104]

2. *Determining Whether a Mark Is Disparaging.*—. . . In *Harjo v. Pro-Football Inc.*, seven Native Americans sought to cancel the registration of the marks REDSKINS, REDSKINETTES, and THE WASHINGTON REDSKINS as applied to football entertainment services on the basis that "the word 'redskin(s)' 'was and is a pejorative, derogatory, denigrating, offensive, scandalous, contemptuous, disreputable, disparaging and racist designation for a Native American person.' "[106]

. . .

With *Harjo*, the TTAB provided the most complete procedural account to date of how to evaluate allegedly disparaging marks. Distinguishing the analysis of disparaging marks from that for scandalous marks, the TTAB held that "in deciding whether the matter may be disparaging, we look, not to American society as a whole but to the views of the referenced group."[107]

101. In re Anti-Communist World Freedom Cong., Inc., 161 U.S.P.Q. (BNA) 304, 305 (T.T.A.B. 1969).

102. Harjo v. Pro-Football Inc., 50 U.S.P.Q.2d (BNA) 1705, 1738 (T.T.A.B. 1999), rev'd on other grounds, 284 F. Supp. 2d 96, 121–22 (D.D.C. 2003) (adopting TTAB's definition as correct).

103. The TTAB reasoned that the word "may" was included "to avoid an interpretation of this statutory provision that would require a showing of intent to disparage. Such a showing would be extremely difficult in all except the most egregious cases." Id.

104. Id. An earlier case also defined the term "disparage" by looking to dictionaries, but did not look to 1946 definitions. See In re Hines, 31 U.S.P.Q.2d (BNA) 1685, 1688 (T.T.A.B. 1994) (presenting definitions of "disparage," including "to lower in esteem or reputation; diminish the respect for; to speak slightingly of: run down: depreciate" and "to speak of or treat slightingly; depreciate; belittle; to bring reproach or discredit upon; lower the estimation of" (internal quotation marks and citations omitted)), rev'd on other grounds, 32 U.S.P.Q.2d (BNA) 1376 (T.T.A.B. 1994).

106. 50 U.S.P.Q.2d (BNA) at 1708.

107. Id. at 1739 (citing In re Hines, 31 U.S.P.Q.2d (BNA) at 1688) ("In determining whether or not a mark is disparaging, the perceptions of the general public are irrelevant. Rather, because the portion of Section 2(a) proscribing disparaging marks targets certain persons, institutions or beliefs, only the perceptions of those ... implicated in some recognizable manner ... are relevant to this determination." (citation omitted)).

A separate test exists for circumstances when a mark "may disparage" an individual or a corporation. See Order Sons of Italy in Am. v. Memphis Mafia Inc., 52 U.S.P.Q.2d (BNA) 1364, 1368 n.13 (T.T.A.B. 1999) ("There are different tests for disparagement depending upon whether the party alleging disparagement is an individual or commercial corporate entity, or a non-commercial group, such as a religious or racial group." (citations omitted)). The steps for determining whether a mark may

Based upon this explicit adoption of a policy where a mark's disparaging nature is gauged through the eyes of its alleged targets, the TTAB laid out a two-step test for determining whether a mark is disparaging: (1) Would the mark be understood, in its context, as referring to an identifiable group of people?; and (2) May that reference be perceived as disparaging to a "substantial composite"[108] of that group?

Determining whether a mark implicates an identifiable group[110] is inherently a case-specific[111] and context-specific[112] inquiry. In addition to the obvious step of looking to the dictionary definition of the allegedly disparaging term, examiners also consider (1) the relationship between the disparaging term and other elements of the mark; (2) the type of product upon which the mark appears; and (3) how the mark will appear in the marketplace.

. . .

For self-disparaging marks, the first prong is usually a nonissue; such marks will clearly refer to an identifiable group of people because successful reappropriation of a slur depends on viewers connecting the word to the group.

3. *Evidentiary Grounds That a Mark Is Disparaging.*—Once it has been established that the mark at issue refers to an identifiable group of people, the examining attorney must evaluate whether a substantial composite of people in that referenced group would view the use of the mark, in the context presented, as disparaging. In making this assessment, the PTO has a strong preference for erring on the side of publication. The TTAB

disparage an individual or corporate entity are "(1) that the communication reasonably would be understood as referring to the plaintiff; and (2) that the communication is disparaging, that is, would be considered offensive or objectionable by a reasonable person of ordinary sensibilities." Greyhound Corp. v. Both Worlds Inc., 6 U.S.P.Q.2d (BNA) 1635, 1639 (T.T.A.B. 1988).

108. Harjo, 50 U.S.P.Q.2d (BNA) at 1739 ("The views of the referenced group are reasonably determined by the views of a substantial composite thereof."). Though a "substantial composite" does not rise to the level of "majority," courts have not yet arrived at a fixed percentage that constitutes a "substantial composite." See, e.g., Pro-Football, Inc. v. Harjo, 284 F. Supp. 2d 96, 133 n.32 (D.D.C. 2003) (finding that 36.6% of Native Americans did not constitute "substantial composite"); cf. In re McGinley, 660 F.2d 481, 485 (C.C.P.A. 1981) (stating that "a substantial composite" is "not necessarily a majority").

110. Targets of disparagement are not limited only to certain preselected groups; rather, any mark that disparages "certain persons, institutions or beliefs" violates section 2(a). As the TTAB explained in Harjo:

> If the alleged disparagement is of a religious group or its iconography, the relevant group may be the members and clergy of that religion; if the alleged disparagement is of an academic institution, the relevant group may be the students, faculty, administration, and alumni; if the alleged disparagement is of a national symbol, the relevant group may be citizens of that country.

50 U.S.P.Q.2d (BNA) at 1739.

111. Id. ("Who comprises the targeted, or relevant, group must be determined on the basis of the facts in each case.")

112. Id. at 1738 ("The question of disparagement must be considered in relation to the goods or services identified by the mark in the context of the marketplace.").

first explained this policy in 1990 when it rejected an examiner's assertion that the mark MOONIES as applied to a doll that exposes its buttocks was not registrable because it may disparage religious followers of the Unification Church:

> Because the guidelines [for determining whether a mark is disparaging] are somewhat vague and because the determination is so highly subjective, we are inclined to resolve doubts on the issue of whether a mark is . . . disparaging in favor of [the] applicant and pass the mark for publication with the knowledge that if a group does find the mark to be . . . disparaging, an opposition proceeding can be brought and a more complete record can be established.[120]

The PTO suggests that examiners look to "dictionary definitions, newspaper articles and magazine articles." Supporting materials an applicant provides in response to an initial rejection, such as affidavits from members of the disparaged group,[125] public opinion surveys, and historical accounts,[126] may also be persuasive.

4. *The Difference Between "Disparaging" Marks and "Scandalous" Marks.*—Section 2(a) prohibits the registration of not only disparaging marks, but also marks containing "immoral . . . or scandalous matter."[136] While the Lanham Act does not define the term "scandalous,"[137] courts interpret it to mean "giving offense to the conscience or moral feelings" and "shocking to the sense of truth, decency, or propriety; disgraceful,

120. In re In Over Our Heads Inc., 16 U.S.P.Q.2d (BNA) 1653, 1654–55 (T.T.A.B. 1990). The Federal Circuit recently supported such action in a case involving a scandalous mark, stating:

> We have commended the practice of resolving the issue of whether a mark comprises scandalous matter by first permitting the mark to pass for publication, and then allowing interested members of a composite of the general public who consider the mark to be scandalous to bring opposition proceedings. By so doing, the PTO avoids the risk of prejudging public attitudes toward a proposed registration based on ad hoc responses by government officials, while at the same time affording the affected public an opportunity to effectively participate in the question of whether the registration is proper.

Ritchie v. Simpson, 170 F.3d 1092, 1094 (Fed. Cir. 1999) (citations omitted).

125. See, e.g., Serial No. 78/281,746, Paper Correspondence Incoming at 4–7, Aug. 23, 2004 (DYKES ON BIKES) (responding to examining attorney's initial rejection of application by supplying statements from lesbians attesting to word's reappropriated usage in lesbian community).

126. Cf. Order Sons of Italy in Am. v. Memphis Mafia Inc., 52 U.S.P.Q.2d (BNA) 1364, 1366–67 (T.T.A.B. 1999) (noting that opposers submitted dictionary definitions, information on historical use of "mafia," and one public opinion survey). While Order Sons of Italy involved a third-party opposition, the TTAB suggests that applicants may supply such evidence when supplementing their applications. See id.

136. 15 U.S.C. § 1052(a) (2000). Case law treats "immoral" and "scandalous" as synonymous. See In re McGinley, 660 F.2d 481, 484 n.6 (C.C.P.A. 1981) ("We note the dearth of reported trademark decisions in which the term 'immoral' has been directly applied."); T.M.E.P., supra note 67, 1203.01 ("Although the words 'immoral' and 'scandalous' may have somewhat different connotations, case law has included immoral matter in the same category as scandalous matter.").

137. See In re McGinley, 660 F.2d at 485 (noting difficulty in defining "scandalous" due to "paucity of legislative history").

offensive.''[138] Expletives,[139] sexual references,[140] crude images,[141] and offensive phrases[142] have all been denied federal registration based on their scandalous natures.

Though scandalous and disparaging marks share similarities, such as their joint presence in section 2(a), they are also separated by important differences. The primary distinction is that scandalous marks are shocking to the general public, while disparaging marks offensively target an identifiable subgroup.[143]

. . .

Examiners often claim that a mark is scandalous because it disparages a particular group of people, failing to clarify exactly who the mark offends.[147] Such findings confuse matters because determining whether lesbians find the word ''dyke'' to be offensive, for example, is a different task than determining whether the general public finds ''dyke'' to be vulgar, shocking, and disgraceful.[148] As one commentator notes, when an examiner ''sloppily'' treats scandalous and disparaging marks as being synonymous, ''This does a disservice to the statutory language, leads to

138. Id. at 485–86 (internal quotation marks omitted) (quoting various dictionaries); see also In re Wilcher Corp., 40 U.S.P.Q.2d (BNA) 1929, 1930 (T.T.A.B. 1996) (discussing various definitions of ''scandalous'' used in earlier cases).

139. See, e.g., In re Tinseltown, Inc., 212 U.S.P.Q. (BNA) 863, 865 (T.T.A.B. 1981) (rejecting mark BULLSHIT as scandalous); Serial No. 78/491,710, Office Action Outgoing at 1, May 2, 2005 (FUCK YOU YOU FUCKIN' FUCK) (rejecting mark because it is ''slang obscenity'').

140. See, e.g., In re McGinley, 660 F.2d at 482, 487 (rejecting ''a photograph of a nude man and woman kissing and embracing in a manner appearing to expose the male genitalia'' as scandalous); Serial No. 78/509,841, Office Action Outgoing at 2, June 29, 2005 (DICK'S HALFWAY IN PULL OUT BY 2 COME ON INN) (rejecting mark as scandalous ''because it refers to a penis being half way [sic] inside something, and it also refers to pulling the penis out at a certain specific moment'').

141. See, e.g., Greyhound Corp. v. Both Worlds Inc., 6 U.S.P.Q.2d (BNA) 1635, 1639 (T.T.A.B. 1988) (rejecting mark containing image of defecating dog as scandalous).

142. See, e.g., Serial No. 78/368,298, Office Action Outgoing at 2, Dec. 23, 2004 (WHITE PRIDE COUNTRY WIDE) (rejecting mark ''because the proposed mark consists of or comprises immoral or scandalous matter''); Serial No. 78/322,569, Office Action Outgoing at 2, May 17, 2004 (STUPID BITCHES) (rejecting mark ''because the proposed mark consists of or comprises immoral or scandalous matter'').

143. See Harjo v. Pro–Football Inc., 50 U.S.P.Q.2d (BNA) 1705, 1738 (T.T.A.B. 1999) ('' 'Scandalous' [analysis] looks at the reaction of American society as a whole ... to establish whether such matter violates the mores of 'American society'.... 'Disparage' has an entirely different focus, as disparagement has an identifiable object....''), rev'd on other grounds, 284 F. Supp. 2d 96 (D.D.C. 2003).

147. See, e.g., Serial No. 76/623,949, Office Action Outgoing at 1, July 24, 2005 (NIGGA) (rejecting mark because ''NIGGA means nigger and is thus scandalous because it disparages African–Americans''); Serial No. 78/164,481, Office Action Outgoing at 1, Mar. 14, 2003 (FAG) (rejecting mark as scandalous on basis that ''fag'' is a '' 'derogatory,' 'offensive' or 'derisive' word referring to a male homosexual'').

148. One of the unexpected results noted by the district court in Harjo was that the general public found the word ''redskin'' to be more offensive than did Native Americans as a subgroup. Pro–Football, Inc. v. Harjo, 284 F. Supp. 2d 96, 128 (D.D.C. 2003).

injustice in the individual case without gains in the predictability of outcomes, and makes for bad public policy."

. . .

QUESTIONS

1. The author of the above piece suggests that Examiners should not refuse to register self-disparaging terms when filed by a member of the disparaged group, such as DYKES ON BIKES by a lesbian group, or NIGGA by an African American. The author reasons that the membership of an applicant in the supposedly disparaged group suggests that the term may not be disparaging to that group and that the ability of other members of the group to oppose the application is a sufficient check. Do you agree?

2. Are the differences in standards for determining whether a mark is disparaging to a group (which requires reference only to the group being disparaged) and for determining whether a mark is scandalous (which requires reference to the general public) convincing? How persuasive is the distinction in standards made by the Board for marks disparaging to a group (which references the reactions of the group) with those disparaging to a commercial entity or individual (which looks to the reaction of "a reasonable person of ordinary sensibilities")?

Page 231. Delete the T.T.A.B.'s *Harjo* decision and substitute the D.C. Circuit's decision below:

Pro–Football, Inc. v. Harjo

415 F.3d 44 (D.C. Cir. 2005).

■ Per Curiam

I.

. . .

Not all marks ... can be registered. Under 15 U.S.C. § 1052, the PTO must deny registration to certain types of marks, including those which, in subsection (a)'s language, "may disparage or falsely suggest a connection with persons, living or dead, institutions, beliefs, or national symbols, or bring them into contempt, or disrepute."

Another section, 15 U.S.C. § 1064(3), provides that if a mark is registered in violation of section 1052(a), "any person who believes that he is or will be damaged by the registration" may file a petition "at any time" with the PTO to cancel the registration. This triggers a proceeding before the TTAB, *see* 15 U.S.C. § 1067, which takes evidence and determines whether to cancel the mark. Yet another provision, 15 U.S.C. § 1069, states that "in all ... proceedings equitable principles of laches, estoppel, and acquiescence, where applicable may be considered and applied."

This case concerns the registrations of six trademarks owned by Pro–Football, the corporate owner of the Washington Redskins football team, that include the word "Redskin." The first—"The Redskins" written in a stylized script—was registered in 1967, three more in 1974, another in 1978, and the sixth—the word "Redskinettes"—in 1990. Pro–Football uses all these marks in connection with goods and services related to its football team, including merchandise and entertainment services.

In 1992, seven Native Americans petitioned for cancellation of the registrations, claiming that the marks had disparaged Native Americans at the times of registration and had thus been registered in violation of section 1052(a). Pro–Football defended its marks, arguing among other things that laches barred the Native Americans' claim. Rejecting this argument, the TTAB found laches inapplicable due to the "broader interest—an interest beyond the personal interest being asserted by the present petitioners—in preventing a party from receiving the benefits of registration where a trial might show that respondent's marks hold a substantial segment of the population up to public ridicule." *Harjo v. Pro–Football Inc.*, 1994 TTAB LEXIS 9, 30 U.S.P.Q.2d 1828, 1831 (TTAB 1994).

On the merits, the parties presented the TTAB with a variety of evidence, including (1) dictionary entries for "redskin," some of which contained usage labels identifying the term as offensive and others of which did not; (2) book and media excerpts from the late nineteenth century through the 1940s that used the term "redskin" and portrayed Native Americans in a pejorative manner; (3) a study that found derogatory use of the term in Western-genre films from before 1980; (4) petitioners' testimony about their views of the term; (5) results from a 1996 survey of the general population and Native Americans that asked whether various terms, including "redskin," were offensive; (6) newspaper articles and game program guides from the 1940s onward using Native American imagery in connection with Washington's football team; and (7) testimony and documents relating to Native American protests, including one in 1972, aimed specifically at the team. In a lengthy opinion, the TTAB concluded that a preponderance of the evidence showed the term "redskin" as used by Washington's football team had disparaged Native Americans from at least 1967 onward. The TTAB cancelled the registrations. Cancellation did not require Pro–Football to stop using the marks, but it did limit the team's ability to go after infringers under the Lanham Act.

Pursuant to 15 U.S.C. § 1071(b), Pro–Football filed suit in the U.S. District Court for the District of Columbia, seeking reinstatement of its registrations on the grounds that: (1) laches barred the Native Americans' petition; (2) the TTAB's finding of disparagement was unsupported by substantial evidence; and (3) section 1052(a) violates the First and Fifth Amendments to the U.S. Constitution both facially and as applied by the TTAB. Although in suits challenging TTAB decisions parties may introduce new evidence in the district court, *see Material Supply Int'l, Inc. v. Sunmatch Indus. Co.*, 331 U.S. App. D.C. 42, 146 F.3d 983, 989–90 (D.C. Cir. 1998), in this case the only such evidence of note related to laches.

After discovery, the parties cross-moved for summary judgment. Without reaching the constitutional issues, the district court granted summary judgment to Pro–Football on the alternate grounds that laches barred the Native Americans' petition and that the TTAB's conclusion of disparagement was unsupported by substantial evidence. *Pro-Football, Inc. v. Harjo*, 284 F. Supp. 2d 96 (D.D.C. 2003). This appeal followed.

II.

. . .

The Native Americans also offer several reasons why, in their view, the district court erred in its assessment of laches in this case. At this point, we need only consider one: their claim that the district court mistakenly started the clock for assessing laches in 1967—the time of the first mark's registration—for *all* seven Native Americans, even though one, Mateo Romero, was at that time only one year old.

We agree with the Native Americans that this approach runs counter to the well-established principle of equity that laches runs only from the time a party has reached his majority. . . .

III.

While retaining jurisdiction over the case, we remand the record to the district court for the purpose of evaluating whether laches bars Mateo Romero's claim.

So ordered.

Page 249. Delete Questions 2, 3 and 4 and substitute the following Questions:

2. Pro–Football appealed the decision of the Trademark Trial and Appeal Board to the district court rather than to the Federal Circuit. The district court, unlike the Federal Circuit, can consider the matter *de novo* and can hear new evidence. Why do you think that Pro–Football chose the district court? Do you think that the fact that the Board dismissed Pro–Football's First Amendment defense on the ground that it lacked jurisdiction to decide constitutional issues influenced the choice of appeal venues? Would there ever be any reasons for a losing party to appeal to the Federal Circuit rather than to seek a *de novo* review by a district court?

3. Should disparagement be assessed at the time of a mark's adoption, e.g. 1967 in the case of REDSKINS, or at the time of challenge to the mark? Why or why not?

4. Does the Circuit Court's decision in *Harjo* mean that a mark can always be challenged on grounds of disparagement as long as the challenger is a member of the allegedly disparaged group who was not born at the time of the registration? Does this make sense?

Page 254. Add Question 6:

6. TITANIUM for recreational vehicles. *See Glendale Int'l Corp. v. U.S.P.T.O.*, 374 F.Supp.2d 479, 75 U.S.P.Q.2d 1139 (E.D. Va. 2005).

3. SECTION 2(d) OF THE LANHAM ACT: CONFUSION

Page 260. Add Question 3 below Questions 1 and 2:

3. In determining likelihood of confusion, the Board gives a broader scope of protection to famous marks. Should the test of fame in this context be the same as the test of fame for dilution under section 43(c)(1)? *See Palm Bay Imports, Inc. v. Veuve Clicquot Ponsardin Maison Fondee En 1772*, 396 F.3d 1369 (Fed. Cir. 2005) ("While dilution fame is an either/or proposition—fame either does or does not exist—likelihood of confusion fame varies along a spectrum from very strong to very weak' ").

* * *

Page 269. Insert the following before the last sentence of the *Editor's Note*:

Examine the language in Section 13, 15 U.S.C. §§ 1063, which states that "any person who believes that he would be damaged by the registration of a mark . . . , including as a result of dilution under Section 43(c)" may file an opposition. Could an opposer rely upon dilution under state law as a ground to oppose an application? *See Enterprise Rent-A-Car Co. v. Advantage Rent-A-Car, Inc., 330 F.3d 1333 (Fed. Cir.2003)* (state dilution not a ground for opposition).

4. SECTION 2(e) OF THE LANHAM ACT: GEOGRAPHIC TERMS

Page 277. Delete *In re Bacardi* and the Questions following it and substitute the case and Questions below:

In re California Innovations, Inc.

329 F.2d 1334 (Fed. Cir. 2003).

■ RADER, CIRCUIT JUDGE

California Innovations, Inc. (CA Innovations), a Canadian-based corporation, appeals the Trademark Trial and Appeal Board's refusal to register its mark—CALIFORNIA INNOVATIONS. Citing section 2(e)(3) of the Lanham Act, 15 U.S.C. § 1052(e)(3) (2000), the Board concluded that the mark was primarily geographically deceptively misdescriptive. Because the Board applied an outdated standard in its analysis under § 1052(e)(3), this court vacates the Board's decision and remands.

I.

CA Innovations filed an intent-to-use trademark application, Serial No. 74/650,703, on March 23, 1995, for the composite mark CALIFORNIA INNOVATIONS and Design. The application sought registration for the following goods:

> automobile visor organizers, namely, holders for personal effects, and automobile trunk organizers for automotive accessories in International Class 12; backpacks in International Class 18; thermal insulated bags for food and beverages, thermal insulated tote bags for food or beverages, and thermal insulated wraps for cans to keep the containers cold or hot in International Class 21; and nylon, vinyl, polyester and/or leather bags for storage and storage pouches in International Class 22.

. . .

The PTO ... refused registration under § 1052(e)(3), concluding that the mark was primarily geographically deceptively misdescriptive.

II.

The Lanham Act addresses geographical marks in three categories. The first category, § 1052(a), identifies geographically deceptive marks:

> No trademark by which the goods of the applicant may be distinguished from the goods of others shall be refused registration on the principal register on account of its nature unless it—(a) Consists of or comprises ... deceptive ... matter; ...

15 U.S.C. § 1052(a) (2000) (emphasis added). Although not expressly addressing geographical marks, § 1052(a) has traditionally been used to reject geographic marks that materially deceive the public. A mark found to be deceptive under § 1052(a) cannot receive protection under the Lanham Act. To deny a geographic mark protection under § 1052(a), the PTO must establish that (1) the mark misrepresents or misdescribes the goods, (2) the public would likely believe the misrepresentation, and (3) the misrepresentation would materially affect the public's decision to purchase the goods. *See In re Budge Mfg. Co.*, 857 F.2d 773, 775, 8 U.S.P.Q.2d 1259, 1260 (Fed. Cir. 1988). This test's central point of analysis is materiality because that finding shows that the misdescription deceived the consumer. *See In re House of Windsor*, 221 U.S.P.Q. 53, 56–57 (TTAB 1983).

The other two categories of geographic marks are (1) "primarily geographically descriptive" marks and (2) "primarily geographically deceptively misdescriptive" marks under § 1052(e). The North American Free

Trade Agreement, *see* North American Free Trade Agreement, Dec. 17, 1992, art. 1712, 32 I.L.M. 605, 698 [hereinafter NAFTA], as implemented by the NAFTA Implementation Act in 1993, *see* NAFTA Implementation Act, Pub. L. No. 103–182, 107 Stat. 2057 (1993), has recently changed these two categories. Before the NAFTA changes, ... [t]he law treated these two categories of geographic marks identically....

. . .

NAFTA and its implementing legislation obliterated the distinction between geographically deceptive marks and primarily geographically deceptively misdescriptive marks. Article 1712 of NAFTA provides:

> 1. Each party [United States, Mexico, Canada] shall provide, in respect of geographical indications, the legal means for interested persons to prevent:
>
> (a) the use of any means in the designation or presentation of a good that indicates or suggests that the good in question originates in a territory, region or locality other than the true place of origin, in a manner that misleads the public as to the geographical origin of the good....

See NAFTA, Dec. 17, 1992, art. 1712, 32 I.L.M. 605, 698. This treaty shifts the emphasis for geographically descriptive marks to prevention of any public deception. Accordingly, the NAFTA Act amended § 1052(e) to read:

> No trademark by which the goods of the applicant may be distinguished from the goods of others shall be refused registration on the principal register on account of its nature unless it—
>
> (e) Consists of a mark which (1) when used on or in connection with the goods of the applicant is merely descriptive or deceptively misdescriptive of them, (2) when used on or in connection with the goods of the applicant is primarily geographically descriptive of them, except as indications of regional origin may be registrable under section 4 [15 U.S.C.S. § 1054], (3) when used on or in connection with the goods of the applicant is primarily geographically deceptively misdescriptive of them, ...
>
> (f) Except as expressly excluded in subsections (a), (b), (c), (d), (e)(3), and (e)(5) of this section, nothing herein shall prevent the registration of a mark used by the applicant which has become distinctive of the applicant's goods in commerce.

15 U.S.C. § 1052(e)–(f) (2000).

Recognizing the new emphasis on prevention of public deception, the NAFTA amendments split the categories of geographically descriptive and geographically deceptively misdescriptive into two subsections (subsections (e)(2) and (e)(3) respectively). Under the amended Lanham Act, subsection (e)(3)—geographically deceptive misdescription—could no longer acquire distinctiveness under subsection (f). Accordingly, marks determined to be primarily geographically deceptively misdescriptive are permanently denied registration, as are deceptive marks under § 1052(a).

Thus, § 1052 no longer treats geographically deceptively misdescriptive marks differently from geographically deceptive marks. Like geographically deceptive marks, the analysis for primarily geographically deceptively misdescriptive marks under § 1052(e)(3) focuses on deception of, or fraud on, the consumer. The classifications under the new § 1052 clarify that these two deceptive categories both receive permanent rejection. Accordingly, the test for rejecting a deceptively misdescriptive mark is no longer simple lack of distinctiveness, but the higher showing of deceptiveness.

. . .

Before NAFTA, the PTO identified and denied registration to a primarily geographically deceptively misdescriptive mark with a showing that (1) the primary significance of the mark was a generally known geographic location, and (2) "the public was likely to believe the mark identified the place from which the goods originate and that the goods did not come from there." *In re Loew's [Theatres, Inc.]*, 769 F.2d [764,] at 768 [Fed. Cir. 1985]. The second prong of the test represents the "goods-place association" between the mark and the goods at issue. This test raised an inference of deception based on the likelihood of a goods-place association that did not reflect the actual origin of the goods. A mere inference, however, is not enough to establish the deceptiveness that brings the harsh consequence of non-registrability under the amended Lanham Act. As noted, NAFTA and the amended Lanham Act place an emphasis on actual misleading of the public.

Therefore, the relatively easy burden of showing a naked goods-place association without proof that the association is material to the consumer's decision is no longer justified, because marks rejected under § 1052(e)(3) can no longer obtain registration through acquired distinctiveness under § 1052(f). To ensure a showing of deceptiveness and misleading before imposing the penalty of non-registrability, the PTO may not deny registration without a showing that the goods-place association made by the consumer is material to the consumer's decision to purchase those goods. This addition of a materiality inquiry equates this test with the elevated standard applied under § 1052(a). [Citation omitted] This also properly reflects the presence of the deceptiveness criterion often overlooked in the "primarily geographically deceptively misdescriptive" provision of the statute. . . .

Since the NAFTA amendments, this court has dealt with two cases involving § 1052(e)(3). *Wada*, 194 F.3d 1297; *In re Save Venice New York, Inc.*, 259 F.3d 1346, 59 U.S.P.Q.2d 1778 (Fed. Cir. 2001). Although neither of those cases explores the effect of the NAFTA Act on the test for determining geographically deceptive misdescription, both cases satisfy the new NAFTA standard. "If there is evidence that goods like applicant's or goods related to applicant's are a principal product of the geographical area named by the mark, then the deception will most likely be found material and the mark, therefore, deceptive." *House of Windsor*, 221 U.S.P.Q. at 57. "If the place is noted for the particular goods, a mark for such goods which do not originate there is likely to be deceptive under § 2(a) and not registrable under any circumstances." *Loew's Theatres*, 769 F.2d at 768, n.6.

In *Save Venice*, this court affirmed the Board's refusal to register applicant's marks "THE VENICE COLLECTION" and "SAVE VENICE, INC." because of the "substantial evidence available showing that Venice, Italy is known for glass, lace, art objects, jewelry, cotton and silk textiles, printing and publishing." 259 F.3d at 1354 (emphasis added). Although the court in *Save Venice* did not expressly address the materiality issue, because it was not officially recognized in this context, the court emphasized that "all of the applicant's goods are associated with traditional Venetian products." *Id.* at 1350 (emphasis added). The court in *Save Venice* concluded that the public would mistakenly believe they were purchasing "traditional Venetian products" because the applicant's products were "indistinguishable" from the products traditionally originating in Venice. *Id.* at 1350–54. Thus, the record in *Save Venice* satisfies the test for deception.

Similarly, in *Wada*, this court affirmed the Board's refusal to register applicant's mark "NEW YORK WAYS GALLERY" because there was "evidence that showed ... New York is well-known as a place where leather goods and handbags are designed and manufactured." *Wada*, 194 F.3d at 1299–1300 (emphasis added). Again, the court in *Wada* did not expressly make a finding that the goods-place association would materially influence the consumer. However, this court noted that the public, "upon encountering goods bearing the mark NEW YORK WAYS GALLERY, would believe that the goods" originate in New York, "a world-renown fashion center ... well-known as a place where goods of this kind are designed, manufactured, or sold." *Id.* This showing that the place was not only well-known, but renowned for the products at issue supports a finding of materiality. *See House of Windsor*, 221 U.S.P.Q. at 57.

Thus, due to the NAFTA changes in the Lanham Act, the PTO must deny registration under § 1052(e)(3) if (1) the primary significance of the mark is a generally known geographic location, (2) the consuming public is likely to believe the place identified by the mark indicates the origin of the goods bearing the mark, when in fact the goods do not come from that place, and (3) the misrepresentation was a material factor in the consumer's decision.

As a result of the NAFTA changes to the Lanham Act, geographic deception is specifically dealt with in subsection (e)(3), while deception in general continues to be addressed under subsection (a). Consequently, this court anticipates that the PTO will usually address geographically deceptive marks under subsection (e)(3) of the amended Lanham Act rather than subsection (a). While there are identical legal standards for deception in each section, subsection (e)(3) specifically involves deception involving geographic marks.

III.

CA Innovations unequivocally states in its opening brief that its "petition seeks review only of that portion of the [Board's] decision that pertains to 'thermal insulated bags for food and beverages and thermal insulated wraps for cans' " as identified in International Class 21 in the application. Therefore, because of applicant's decision not to challenge the Board's judgment with respect to all goods other than those identified in class 21, that part of the Board's decision is not affected by this opinion.

The parties agree that CA Innovations' goods do not originate in California.

Under the first prong of the test—whether the mark's primary significance is a generally known geographic location—a composite mark such as the applicant's proposed mark must be evaluated as a whole.... It is not erroneous, however, for the examiner to consider the significance of each element within the composite mark in the course of evaluating the mark as a whole. *Save Venice*, 259 F.3d at 1352 (citations omitted).

The Board found that "the word CALIFORNIA is a prominent part of applicant's mark and is not overshadowed by either the word INNOVATIONS or the design element." Although the mark may also convey the idea of a creative, laid-back lifestyle or mindset, the Board properly recognized that such an association does not contradict the primary geographic significance of the mark. Even if the public may associate California with a particular life-style, the record supports the Board's finding that the primary meaning remains focused on the state of California. Nonetheless, this court declines to review at this stage the Board's finding that CA Innovations' composite mark CALIFORNIA INNOVATIONS and Design is primarily geographic in nature. Rather the PTO may apply the entire new test on remand.

The second prong of the test requires proof that the public is likely to believe the applicant's goods originate in California. The Board stated that the examining attorney submitted excerpts from the Internet and the NEXIS database showing "some manufacturers and distributors of backpacks, tote bags, luggage, computer cases, and sport bags ... headquartered in California." The Board also acknowledged articles "which make reference to companies headquartered in California which manufacture automobile accessories such as auto organizers," as well as the "very serious apparel and sewn products industry" in California.

A great deal of the evidence cited in this case relates to the fashion industry, which is highly prevalent in California due to Hollywood's influence on this industry. However, clothing and fashion have nothing to do with the products in question. At best, the record in this case shows some general connection between the state of California and backpacks and automobile organizers. However, because CA Innovations has limited its appeal to insulated bags and wraps, the above referenced evidence is immaterial. Therefore, this opinion has no bearing on whether the evidence of record supports a rejection of the application with regard to any goods other than those identified in CA Innovations' application under International Class 21, namely insulated bags and wraps.

CA Innovations argues that the examining attorney provided no evidence at all concerning insulated bags for food and wraps for cans in California. The Government contends that the evidence shows some examples of a lunch bag, presumed to be insulated, and insulated backpacks. According to the government, the evidence supports a finding of a goods-place association between California and insulated bags and wraps. This court has reviewed the publications and listings supplied by the examining attorney. At best, the evidence of a connection between California and insulated bags and wraps is tenuous. Even if the evidence supported a finding of a goods-place association, the PTO has yet to apply the materiality test in this case. This court declines to address that issue and apply the new standard in the first instance. Accordingly, this court vacates the finding of the Board that CA Innovations' mark is primarily geographically deceptively misdescriptive, and remands the case for further proceedings. On remand, the Board shall apply the new three-prong standard.

VACATED and REMANDED.

QUESTIONS

1. Applying the new test articulated in *In re California Innovations*, how should the Board rule on remand? Is the Board free to determine that the primary significance of CALIFORNIA INNOVATIONS is not a known place name but rather a phrase suggestive of a laid-back life style? What evidence would be required to determine that a mistaken belief that applicant's goods come from California would be material to purchasers?

2. Is "Japan Telecom" as a trade name for a California company in the business of selling and installing telephone and computer networking equipment primarily geographically deceptively misdescriptive? Does it influence the outcome if the company services mainly the Japanese–American community in California? *See Japan Telecom, Inc. v. Japan Telecom America Inc.*, 287 F.3d 866 (9th Cir. 2002).

3. Does the fact that services, rather than goods, are identified by a mark make any difference in applying the three-prong test for finding a mark primarily geographically deceptively misdescriptive? For example, how should the Trademark Office analyze the mark LE MARAIS, the name of a Jewish neighborhood in Paris, for a restaurant located in New York City? Would it be sufficient for the Examiner to show that the Parisian neighborhood was well-known for restaurants to find that the term is primarily geographically deceptively misdescriptive? *See In re Les Halles De Paris J.V.*, 334 F.3d 1371 (Fed. Cir. 2003).

5. SECTION 2(e) OF THE LANHAM ACT: SURNAMES AND OTHER ISSUES

Page 285. Renumber Question as 1 and add Question 2 below:

2. Fiore, which has over 5,000 telephone listings as a surname, means "flower" in Italian. Should Isabella Fiore be able to register FIORE for bags, luggage and other goods or should the application be refused as being primarily merely a surname? *See In re Fiore*, 75 U.S.P.Q.2d 1564 (2005).

6. SECTION 2(e)(5) OF THE LANHAM ACT: FUNCTIONALITY

Page 294. Delete *In re Babies Beat* and substitute the following case:

Talking Rain Beverage Co. v. South Beach Beverage Co., 349 F.3d 601 (9th Cir. 2003). Talking Rain, owner of a trademark registration for the shape of its bottle, sued the producer of SoBe beverages for trademark infringement. SoBe counterclaimed for cancellation of Talking Rain's trademark registration. The Court of Appeals concluded that the bottle design was functional:

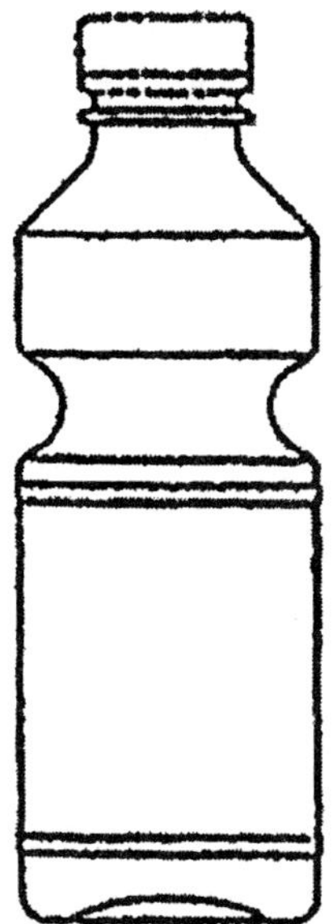

Talking Rain's trademarked design and SoBe's bottle both resemble a typical "bike bottle." . . . Specifically, the bottles have smooth sides and a recessed, grip area approximately two-thirds of the way up from the bottoms of the bottles. SoBe contends that it modeled its bottle after a traditional bike bottle. Talking Rain refers to its bottle as the "Grip Bottle" and has promoted the bottle under the slogan "Get a Grip!" Talking Rain acknowledges that its trademarked design, which it spent millions of dollars developing and promoting, also resembles a bike bottle. Both bottles fit easily into the bottle holders that are often used on bicycles. According to both parties, the recessed "grip" area also offers structural support, which helps a bottle retain its shape.

. . .

The evidence in this case, even when viewed in the light most favorable to Talking Rain, establishes that Talking Rain's trademark is functional. First, Talking Rain's advertising touts its bottle's utilitarian features. Talking Rain, which refers to its bottle as the "Grip Bottle," argues that its "Get a Grip!" slogan involves a double-meaning because the slogan is a slang expression meaning "get in control." No matter the plausibility of Talking Rain's "double-entendre" argument, at least one meaning of its advertising is that the bottle is easy to grip. We are not required to ignore advertising that touts functional features just because those ads may include messages—subtle or otherwise—aimed at nonfunctional features.

Second, Talking Rain has acknowledged that manufacturing considerations explain why its bottle looks the way it does. In particular, the grip feature, aside from making the bottle easier to hold, offers structural support. Talking Rain misunderstands the functionality inquiry in contending that manufacturing considerations cut against a finding of functionality because the bottle was costly to design. Through its investment, Talking Rain learned that by adding a recessed/grip area, it could manufacture a plastic bottle with curved sides that would not collapse. Talking Rain's initiative is commendable, but to the extent its product design is functional, trademark law does not prohibit SoBe from also using this efficient manufacturing process. . . .

Third, the bike bottle design yields a utilitarian advantage. SoBe contends that the bottle fits easily into a bicycle bottle holder and that the grip area helps the bottle to retain its shape for reuse. SoBe also contends that the grip area makes the bottle easier to grip, particularly for bicyclists and others who might use the bottle while exercising. . . .

Here, Talking Rain's advertising emphasizes functionality, the bottle's shape is motivated by manufacturing efficiencies and the bottle itself offers utilitarian advantages that non-bike bottles do not possess. Moreover, that recessed/grip areas appear to be common in the beverage industry tends to corroborate SoBe's assertion that the grip area is indeed functional and not arbitrary. Talking Rain points to no distinctive feature shared by Talking Rain's and SoBe's bottles, beyond the functional grip area. . . . In short, the functional grip area *is* the essence of Talking Rain's claimed distinctiveness.

CHAPTER 5

LOSS OF TRADEMARK RIGHTS

A. GENERICISM

3. GENERICISM AND CONFUSION

Pages 349–53. Delete discussions of *Hoffman-La Roche v. Medisca* and *Stocker v. General Conference Corp. of Seventh-Day Adventists*.

Page 353. Insert before "Dial 1-800-[G-E-N-E-R-I-C]":

TE-TA-MA Truth Foundation v. World Church of the Creator, 297 F.3d 662 (7th Cir. 2002), *cert. denied*, 537 U.S. 1111 (2003).

> The "Church of the Creator" and the "World Church of the Creator" have irreconcilable creeds. The Church of the Creator (the operating name of TE-TA-MA Truth Foundation—Family of URI, Inc.) [hereinafter Foundation] believes in universal love and respect. World Church of the Creator [hereinafter World Church], by contrast, does not worship God but instead depicts the "white race" as the "Creator" and calls for the elimination of Jews, blacks, and what it labels "mud races." Its slogan is: "Dedicated to the Survival, Expansion, and Advancement of the White Race".... Foundation charged World Church with trademark infringement, and World Church asserted the genericism of "Church of the Creator" in defense.

Reversing the district court, the Seventh Circuit, per Judge Easterbrook, found "Church of the Creator" to be descriptive rather than generic.

> Both sides moved for summary judgment, so each was required to introduce evidence to show that a material issue of disputed fact remained for decision. Confronted with the Foundation's motion, the World Church produced—nothing but a dictionary. It did not offer any evidence about how religious adherents use or understand the phrase as a unit. It offered only lexicographers' definitions of the individual words. That won't cut the mustard, because dictionaries reveal a range of historical meanings rather than how people use a particular phrase in contemporary culture. (Similarly, looking up the words "cut" and "mustard" would not reveal the meaning of the phrase we just used.)
>
> Contemporary usage does not treat "Church of the Creator" as the name for monotheistic religion—or any other genus of religion. If it were, then the World Church itself would be misusing the phrase, for it is not theistic in any traditional sense and has nothing in common with Judaism, Christianity, or Islam. The World Church's web site, and

much of its literature, feature one international negation symbol (a circle with a diagonal bar) superimposed over a Star of David and another superimposed over a cross. It condemns the Bible as a hoax.

A mark is "generic" when it has become the name of a product (e.g., "sandwich") for meat between slices of bread or class of products (thus "church" is generic). But "Church of the Creator" is descriptive, like "lite beer." It does not name the class of monotheistic religions. In the contemporary United States, variations on "Church of [Deity]" are used to differentiate individual denominations, not to denote the class of all religions. The list is considerable: Church of God; Church of God (Anderson, Indiana); First Church of God; Worldwide Church of God (see *Worldwide Church of God v. Philadelphia Church of God, Inc.*, 227 F.3d 1110 (9th Cir. 2000)); Church of God in Christ; Assembly of God; Korean Assembly of God; Church of the Nazarene; Church of Christ; United Church of Christ; Disciples of Christ; Church of Christ, Scientist; Church of Jesus Christ of Latter Day Saints. There is room for extension with Church of Our Savior, Church of the Holy Spirit, Church of the Holy Trinity, Church of Jehovah, and so on. Yet all of these are recognizable as denominational names, not as the designation of the religion to which the denominations belong. No Jewish, Islamic, Baha'i, or Unitarian group would say that it belongs to a "Church of the Creator"; and a Christian congregation would classify itself first into its denomination (e.g., Baptist, Lutheran, Russian Orthodox, Society of Friends), then into one of the major groupings (Roman Catholic, Orthodox, and Protestant), and finally into Christianity, but never into a "Church of the Creator." No one called or emailed a *Baptist* church to complain about its complicity in the hate-mongering of the World Church of the Creator; people recognized the name as denominational, and that's why protests ended up in the Church of the Creator's in box.

What is more, as these lists show, using "Church of the Creator" as a denominational name leaves ample options for other sects to distinguish themselves and achieve separate identities. It is not remotely like one firm appropriating the word "sandwich" and thus disabling its rivals from explaining to consumers what's to eat. When the line between generic and descriptive terms is indistinct—as it is, for example, with a phrase such as "liquid controls," see *Liquid Controls Corp. v. Liquid Control Corp.*, 802 F.2d 934 (7th Cir. 1986)—it is helpful to ask whether one firm's exclusive use of the phrase will prevent a rival from naming itself and describing its product. (As far as the Lanham Act is concerned, a denomination is a producer and religious services and publications are products. Neither side has questioned the application of trademark laws to religion.) Because there are so many ways to describe religious denominations, there is no risk that exclusive use of "Church of the Creator" will appropriate a theology or exclude essential means of differentiating one set of beliefs from another.

B. ABANDONMENT

1. NON USE

Page 363. Insert after *Silverman*, but before Note:

ITC Limited v. Punchgini, 373 F.Supp.2d 275 (S.D.N.Y. 2005). The plaintiff ITC Hotels and Restaurants owns a chain of Indian restaurants under the name Bukhara. "The restaurant's look is pure Flintstones: walls of boulders, solid-wood tables and menus printed on laminated sections of tree." ITC licensed the Bukhara trademark, for which it had obtained a U.S. registration, and trade dress to several franchisees, including one in New York City. The New York branch opened in 1986 and closed in 1991. In 1999, the defendants, former employees of the New York restaurant, opened a Bukhara Grill in New York. In addition to the name, defendants also allegedly emulated aspects of the prior restaurant's trade dress, including the rustic decor, heavy wooden menus, use of checkered bibs in lieu of napkins, and logo font. In 2000, ITC sent a cease and desist letter; the New York restaurant replied that the mark had been abandoned, and thus was legitimately taken up by the New York entrepreneurs. ITC ultimately sued in 2003. In response to defendants' motion for summary judgment, ITC conceded that it had not used the mark for over three years before defendants' appropriation, but it claimed a genuine issue of material fact as to its intent to resume use, sufficient to rebut the statutory presumption at trial and precluding summary judgment.

> ITC's evidence may be grouped into two categories. First, ITC has produced internal documents (and one news report) purportedly showing a commitment by ITC to increase the international recognition of the "Bukhara" mark. These internal memoranda show that periodic reorganizations took place within ITC for the purpose of heightening and renewing efforts to expand the "Bukhara" brand internationally. The last of these reorganizations, however, occurred in 1998, tolling the statutory presumption until 2001 at the latest. In any event, these reorganizations do not appear to have been directed in any specific manner toward expansion in the United States. Similarly, a July 22, 2002, news report in the Times of India cited by ITC describes ITC's plans to "cash in on its popular Bukhara and Dum Pukht restaurants," but makes no mention of specific investment opportunities or plans in the United States....
>
> Second, ITC attempts to establish that concrete franchise opportunities in the United States have been pursued by providing the Court with standard franchise agreements "representative of agreements that ITC has been implementing for years with franchisees throughout the world" and by including correspondence with potential franchisees over the years. The executed franchise agreements provided, however,

are for franchises in Bangladesh, Bahrain, and the United Arab Emirates and none of the potential franchisees to whom information, including "concept note[s]" and "salient features of franchise agreement[s]" was provided to initiate negotiations were located in the United States. Although communication with one potential franchisee, located in Canada, referenced possible development in the United States, this communication took place in 1993, long before ITC ceased using the mark in the United States, and thus cannot serve to rebut the inference of abandonment.

ITC claims to have entered franchise negotiations for "Bukhara" restaurants with five parties in the United States since the 1997 closure of their Chicago restaurant, but, as a careful exploration of the evidence adduced in connection with each of these putative negotiations reveals, ITC has provided no real evidence of its own efforts, and thus, intent, to resume restaurant services. . . . These putative negotiations, no more than a handful in the seven years since 1997, amount to little more than a series of unsolicited proposals, which ITC neither initiated nor pursued, and, in the case of Starwood, vague, unsubstantiated plans for resuming use in unspecified non-Indian locations. While ITC is free to pick and choose among proposals received for use of its mark according to its own business judgment, and executed franchise agreements are not necessary to show intent to resume use, ITC has provided no evidence whatever of any actions on its part during the relevant time frame to develop restaurant services utilizing the "Bukhara" mark in the United States.

To explain the absence of any real activity to resume use of the mark in the United States, ITC asserts that it is simply waiting for the "right partner" to come along. For the abandonment doctrine to have any teeth at all, however, more is required than simply the owner's inchoate wish to keep the mark for some vague, unspecified future use; this would constitute precisely the impermissible "warehousing" of the mark against which the doctrine guards. On this record, while reasonable people could differ about whether ITC had a purely subjective desire to retain rights to the "Bukhara" mark in the United States and an inchoate willingness to consider using it again here if the right opportunity came along, no reasonable fact finder could conclude that ITC had taken any action—or even conceived any concrete plan—evidencing an intent to resume use in the reasonably foreseeable future. The statutory presumption of abandonment accordingly stands unrebutted.

ITC's remaining arguments do nothing to disturb this conclusion. ITC claims that it has maintained the goodwill of the "Bukhara" mark in the United States through continued marketing efforts in the United States, consisting primarily of use of the "Bukhara" mark to promote a line of packaged goods, including one product named "Dal Bukhara" and marketed as identical to the signature lentil dish of that name served at their "Bukhara" restaurants. . . . "Dal Bukhara" made appearances at the International Fancy Foods Festival in New York in 2003 and 2004, and at least two shipments of "Dal Bukhara" were sold in the United States in May 2003. ITC has also applied for trademark registrations for the "Bukhara" mark in connection with pre-packaged food items, and Sekhar avers that "discussions for marketing its packaged food products including Bukhara products in [the] USA are in advanced stage of discussions with a leading distributor of food products in [the] USA."

Although promotional materials distributed for "Dal Bukhara" in connection with its trade show appearances reference ITC's New Delhi "Bukhara" restaurant, appearance at two trade shows, sale of two shipments of the product in the United States, and an unsubstantiated, yet-to-be concluded distribution agreement postdating the commencement of litigation are nothing more than "minor activities" insufficient to "rekindle the public's identification of the mark with the proprietor" several years after the cessation of restaurant services in the United States. Aside from conclusory assertions in its briefing, ITC has provided nothing to suggest that the sale of packaged foods under the "Bukhara" mark was somehow intended to herald a return to the restaurant services market in United States. Therefore, ITC's use of the mark in connection with its packaged foods establishes neither continued goodwill of the mark in the United States, nor ITC's intent to resume use of its "Bukhara" mark or dress for restaurant services.

QUESTIONS

1. Suppose that ITC had not licensed new Bukhara restaurants in the U.S. after closing the U.S. operations in 1991, but that in the interim it licensed numerous Bukhara restaurants and food products in many foreign countries, including Mexico and Canada, as well as in countries whose nationals emigrate in large numbers to the U.S. Should that make a difference to the court's analysis of abandonment? *Cf. Grupo Gigante, supra*, this Supplement.

2. Nicole Bédé authors a successful French comic book series, *Les triplés*. In 1998, Nicole obtained a U.S. trademark registration on the basis of her French registration and her declaration of an intent to use the triplés mark in the U.S. (regarding U.S. registrations of foreign trademarks, see *infra*, Chapter 14A). Although Nicole has sought and continues to seek U.S. licensees for an English-language version of her comic books, or for other merchandizing properties, she has so far been unsuccessful. Color Comics seeks to register the mark Triplets for a series of its own. Denied registration on the ground that Color's mark is likely to cause confusion with Nicole's, Color brings a cancellation action. How should the Board rule? *See Cromosoma S.A. v. Nicole Lambert*, 2005 WL 548068 (T.T.A.B. 2005).

3. Vincent George sold his eponymous family wiget manufacturing business to Barton Robert, and returned home to Albania, his health shattered by long years of work. Fully recovered, George later returned to the U.S. and resumed manufacturing wigets under the same name. George's Wigets,

Inc. brings a trademark infringement action, and George defends on the ground that he cannot "abandon" his own name. How should the court rule? *See Vais Arms, Inc. v. Vais*, 383 F.3d 287 (5th Cir. 2004).

2. ASSIGNMENT IN GROSS, NAKED LICENSING AND FAILURE TO POLICE

Page 371. Renumber Question after *Clark & Freeman* as "1" and add a new Question 2:

2. Is transfer of a domain name, without the business formerly conducted under the domain name, an assignment in gross? *See interState Net Bank v. NetB@nk*, 348 F.Supp.2d 340 (D.N.J. 2004) (despite increase in value of domain names, they may not constitute a "tangible asset" necessary to accompany the transfer of a trademark; in any event, the acquiror of the domain name did not offer a service "substantially similar" to the services offered by the previous domain name holder).

Page 374. Insert after *Yocum v. Covington*:

Barcamerica International USA Trust v. Tyfield Importers, Inc.

289 F.3d 589 (9th Cir. 2002).

■ O'SCANNLAIN, CIRCUIT JUDGE:

We must decide whether a company engaged in "naked licensing" of its trademark, thus resulting in abandonment of the mark and ultimately its cancellation.

I

This case involves a dispute over who may use the "Leonardo Da Vinci" trademark for wines.

A

Barcamerica International USA Trust ("Barcamerica") traces its rights in the Leonardo Da Vinci mark to a February 14, 1984 registration granted by the United States Patent and Trademark Office ("PTO"), on an application filed in 1982. On August 7, 1989, the PTO acknowledged the mark's "incontestability." *See* 15 U.S.C. § 1115(b). Barcamerica asserts that it has used the mark continuously since the early 1980s. In the district court, it produced invoices evidencing two sales per year for the years 1980 through 1993: one to a former employee and the other to a barter exchange company. Barcamerica further produced invoices evidencing between three and seven sales per year for the years 1994 through 1998. These include sales to the same former employee, two barter exchange companies, and various sales for "cash." The sales volume reflected in the invoices for the years 1980 through 1988 range from 160 to 410 cases of wine per year.

Barcamerica also produced sales summaries for the years 1980 through 1996 which reflect significantly higher sales volumes; these summaries do not indicate, however, to whom the wine was sold.

In 1988, Barcamerica entered into a licensing agreement with Renaissance Vineyards ("Renaissance"). Under the agreement, Barcamerica granted Renaissance the nonexclusive right to use the "Da Vinci" mark for five years or 4,000 cases, "whichever comes first," in exchange for $2,500. The agreement contained no quality control provision. In 1989, Barcamerica and Renaissance entered into a second agreement in place of the 1988 agreement. The 1989 agreement granted Renaissance an exclusive license to use the "Da Vinci" mark in the United States for wine products or alcoholic beverages. The 1989 agreement was drafted by Barcamerica's counsel and, like the 1988 agreement, it did not contain a quality control provision.[2] In fact, the only evidence in the record of any efforts by Barcamerica to exercise "quality control" over Renaissance's wines comprised (1) Barcamerica principal George Gino Barca's testimony that he occasionally, informally tasted of the wine, and (2) Barca's testimony that he relied on the reputation of a "world-famous winemaker" employed by Renaissance at the time the agreements were signed.[3] (That winemaker is now deceased, although the record does not indicate when he died.) Nonetheless, Barcamerica contends that Renaissance's use of the mark inures to Barcamerica's benefit. *See* 15 U.S.C. § 1055.

B

Cantine Leonardo Da Vinci Soc. Coop. a.r.l. ("Cantine"), an entity of Italy, is a wine producer located in Vinci, Italy. Cantine has sold wine products bearing the "Leonardo Da Vinci" tradename since 1972; it selected this name and mark based on the name of its home city, Vinci. Cantine began selling its "Leonardo Da Vinci" wine to importers in the United States in 1979. Since 1996, however, Tyfield Importers, Inc. ("Tyfield") has

2. In fact, the 1989 Agreement specifically states that Renaissance "shall be solely responsible for any and all claims or causes of action for negligence, breach of contract, breach of warranty, or products liability arising from the sale or distribution of Products using the Licensed Mark."

3. After the commencement of this litigation, Barcamerica proposed a new agreement to Renaissance. The proposed agreement included a quality control provision, and the letter from Barcamerica's attorney proposing this new agreement acknowledged that the agreement "addresses requirements of trademark law that the licensor maintain some control over the licensed product." Renaissance never accepted Barcamerica's invitation to enter into this new agreement. In 1999, Barcamerica again acknowledged it had an obligation to perform quality control for the licensed product and requested that Renaissance execute a declaration stating, *inter alia*, that Barcamerica had been involved in the quality control of the licensed product. Renaissance refused to execute this declaration, because it was "neither truthful nor accurate." Indeed, in a letter to Barcamerica, Renaissance's counsel stated:

> Never at any time, to [Renaissance's] knowledge, has Mr. Barca ever had any involvement of any kind whatsoever regarding quality, quality control, the use of the *Da Vinci* label, or the marketing of the *Da Vinci* label wines, nor has he ever "examined" Renaissance's wine, "sampled" it, or had any involvement whatsoever regarding the quality of the wine and maintaining it at any level.

been the exclusive United States importer and distributor of Cantine wine products bearing the "Leonardo Da Vinci" mark. During the first eighteen months after Tyfield became Cantine's exclusive importer, Cantine sold approximately 55,000 cases of wine products bearing the "Leonardo Da Vinci" mark to Tyfield. During this same period, Tyfield spent between $250,000 and $300,000 advertising and promoting Cantine's products, advertising in *USA Today*, and such specialty magazines as *The Wine Spectator*, *Wine and Spirits*, and *Southern Beverage Journal*.

Cantine learned of Barcamerica's registration of the "Leonardo Da Vinci" mark in or about 1996, in the course of prosecuting its first trademark application in the United States. Cantine investigated Barcamerica's use of the mark and concluded that Barcamerica was no longer selling any wine products bearing the "Leonardo Da Vinci" mark and had long since abandoned the mark. As a result, in May 1997, Cantine commenced a proceeding in the PTO seeking cancellation of Barcamerica's registration for the mark based on abandonment. Barcamerica responded by filing the instant action on January 30, 1998, and thereafter moved to suspend the proceeding in the PTO. The PTO granted Barcamerica's motion and suspended the cancellation proceeding. . . .

Thereafter, Tyfield and Cantine moved for summary judgment on various grounds. The district court granted the motion, concluding that Barcamerica abandoned the mark through naked licensing. . . . This timely appeal followed.

* * *

III

We now turn to the merits of the appeal. Barcamerica first challenges the district court's conclusion that Barcamerica abandoned its trademark by engaging in naked licensing. It is well-established that "[a] trademark owner may grant a license and remain protected provided quality control of the goods and services sold under the trademark by the licensee is maintained." *Moore Bus. Forms, Inc. v. Ryu*, 960 F.2d 486, 489 (5th Cir. 1992). But "uncontrolled or 'naked' licensing may result in the trademark ceasing to function as a symbol of quality and controlled source." *McCarthy on Trademarks and Unfair Competition* § 18:48, at 18–79 (4th ed. 2001). Consequently, where the licensor fails to exercise adequate quality control over the licensee, "a court may find that the trademark owner has abandoned the trademark, in which case the owner would be estopped from asserting rights to the trademark." *Moore*, 960 F.2d at 489. Such abandonment "is purely an 'involuntary' forfeiture of trademark rights," for it need not be shown that the trademark owner had any subjective intent to abandon the mark. *McCarthy* § 18:48, at 18–79. Accordingly, the proponent of a naked license theory "faces a stringent standard" of proof. *Moore*, 960 F.2d at 489.

A

Judge Damrell's analysis of this issue in his memorandum opinion and order is correct and well-stated, and we adopt it as our own. As that court explained,

In 1988, [Barcamerica] entered into an agreement with Renaissance in which [Barcamerica] granted Renaissance the non-exclusive right to use the "Da Vinci" mark for five years or 4,000 cases, "whichever comes first." There is no quality control provision in that agreement. In 1989, [Barcamerica] and Renaissance entered into a second agreement in place of the 1998 agreement. The 1989 agreement grants Renaissance an exclusive license to use the "Da Vinci" mark in the United States for wine products or alcoholic beverages. The 1989 agreement was to "continue in effect in perpetuity," unless terminated in accordance with the provisions thereof. The 1989 agreement does not contain any controls or restrictions with respect to the quality of goods bearing the "Da Vinci" mark. Rather, the agreement provides that Renaissance is "solely responsible for any and all claims or causes of action for negligence, breach of contract, breach of warranty, or products liability arising from the sale or distribution of Products using the Licensed Mark" and that Renaissance shall defend and indemnify plaintiff against such claims.

The lack of an express contract right to inspect and supervise a licensee's operations is not conclusive evidence of lack of control. "There need not be formal quality control where 'the particular circumstances of the licensing arrangement [indicate] that the public will not be deceived.' " [citations omitted]. Indeed, "courts have upheld licensing agreements where the licensor is familiar with and relies upon the licensee's own efforts to control quality." [citations omitted]

Here, there is no evidence that [Barcamerica] is familiar with or relied upon Renaissance's efforts to control quality. Mr. Barca represents that Renaissance's use of the mark is "controlled by" plaintiff "with respect to the nature and quality of the wine sold under the license," and that "the nature and quality of Renaissance wine sold under the trademark is good." [Barcamerica]'s sole evidence of any such control is Mr. Barca's own apparently random tastings and his reliance on Renaissance's reputation. According to Mr. Barca, the quality of Renaissance's wine is "good" and at the time plaintiff began licensing the mark to Renaissance, Renaissance's winemaker was Karl Werner, a "world famous" winemaker.

Mr. Barca's conclusory statements as to the existence of quality controls is insufficient to create a triable issue of fact on the issue of naked licensing. While Mr. Barca's tastings perhaps demonstrate a minimal effort to monitor quality, Mr. Barca fails to state when, how often, and under what circumstances he tastes the wine. Mr. Barca's reliance on the reputation of the winemaker is no longer justified as he is deceased. Mr. Barca has not provided any information concerning the successor winemaker(s). While Renaissance's attorney, Mr. Goldman, testified that Renaissance "strives extremely hard to have the highest possible standards," he has no knowledge of the quality control procedures utilized by Renaissance with regard to testing wine. Moreover, according to Renaissance, Mr. Barca never "had any involvement whatsoever regarding the quality of the wine and maintaining it at any level." [Barcamerica] has failed to demonstrate any knowledge of or reliance on the actual quality controls used by Renaissance, nor has it demonstrated any ongoing effort to monitor quality.

[Barcamerica] and Renaissance did not and do not have the type of close working relationship required to establish adequate quality control in the absence of a formal agreement. *See, e.g., Taco Cabana Int'l, Inc.*, 932 F.2d at 1121 (licensor and licensee enjoyed close working relationship for eight years); *Transgo*, 768 F.2d at 1017–18 (licensor manufactured 90% of components sold by licensee, licensor informed licensee that if he chose to use his own parts "[licensee] wanted to know about it," licensor had ten year association with licensee and was familiar with his ability and expertise); *Taffy Original Designs, Inc. v. Taffy's Inc.*, 1966 U.S. Dist. LEXIS 7237, 161 U.S.P.Q. 707, 713 (N.D. Ill. 1966) (licensor and licensee were sisters in business together for seventeen years, licensee's business was a continuation of the licensor's and licensee's prior business, licensor visited licensee's store from time to time and was satisfied with the quality of the merchandise offered); *Arner v. Sharper Image Corp.*, 1995 U.S. Dist. LEXIS 21156, 39 U.S.P.Q.2d 1282 (C.D. Cal. 1995) (licensor engaged in a close working relationship with licensee's employees and license agreement provided that license would terminate if certain employees ceased to be affiliated with licensee). No such familiarity or close working relationship ever existed between [Barcamerica] and Renaissance. Both the terms of the licensing agreements and the manner in which they were carried out show that [Barcamerica] engaged in naked licensing of the "Leonardo Da Vinci" mark. Accordingly, [Barcamerica] is estopped from asserting any rights in the mark.

Barcamerica, No. CV–98–00206–FCD, at 9–13 (E.D. Cal. filed Apr. 13, 2000) (record citations and footnote omitted).

B

On appeal, Barcamerica does not seriously contest any of the foregoing. Instead, it argues essentially that because Renaissance makes good wine, the public is not deceived by Renaissance's use of the "Da Vinci" mark, and thus, that the license was legally acceptable. This novel rationale, however, is faulty. Whether Renaissance's wine was objectively "good" or "bad" is simply irrelevant. What matters is that Barcamerica played no meaningful role in holding the wine to a standard of quality—good, bad, or otherwise. As McCarthy explains,

> It is important to keep in mind that "quality control" does not necessarily mean that the licensed goods or services must be of "high" quality, but merely of equal quality, whether that quality is high, low or middle. *The point is that customers are entitled to assume that the nature and quality of goods and services sold under the mark at all licensed outlets will be consistent and predictable.*

McCarthy § 18:55, at 18–94 (emphasis added) (footnotes omitted). And "it is well established that where a trademark owner engages in naked licensing, without any control over the quality of goods produced by the licensee, such a practice is *inherently deceptive* and constitutes abandonment of any rights to the trademark by the licensor." *First Interstate Bancorp v. Stenquist*, 1990 U.S. Dist. LEXIS 19426, 16 U.S.P.Q. 2d 1704, 1706 (N.D. Cal. 1990).

Certainly, "it is difficult, if not impossible to define in the abstract exactly how much control and inspection is needed to satisfy the requirement of quality control over trademark licensees." *McCarthy*, § 18:55, at 18–94. And we recognize that "the standard of quality control and the degree of necessary inspection and policing by the licensor will vary with the wide range of licensing situations in use in the modern marketplace." *Id.*, at 18–95. But in this case we deal with a relatively simple product: wine. Wine, of course, is bottled by season. Thus, at the very least, one might have expected Barca to sample (or to have some designated wine connoisseur sample) on an annual basis, in some organized way, some adequate number of bottles of the Renaissance wines which were to bear Barcamerica's mark to ensure that they were of sufficient quality to be called "Da Vinci." But Barca did not make even this minimal effort.

C

We therefore agree with Judge Damrell, and hold that Barcamerica engaged in naked licensing of its "Leonardo Da Vinci" mark—and that by so doing, Barcamerica forfeited its rights in the mark. We also agree that cancellation of Barcamerica's registration of the mark was appropriate. *See McCarthy* § 18:48, at 18–82 (explaining that " 'naked' licensing can result in such a loss of significance of a trademark that its federal registration should be cancelled"). * * *

AFFIRMED.

Page 377. Add new Question 4:

4. Licensor offers internet services. A two-page trademark licensing agreement specifies the following; does it establish quality control sufficient to ward off charges of "naked licensing?" The license does not include a right to inspect or supervise the services rendered under the mark.

> Licensee shall employ reasonable commercial efforts to maintain the positive business value of the mark; it will limit mark use to that substantially as shown in the pending applications and with services substantially as recited; and, it shall cooperate with licensor to mitigate the confusion or likelihood of confusion between the parties' respective marks.

See Halo Mgmt. v. Interland, 76 U.S.P.Q.2d 1199 (N.D. Cal. 2004).

CHAPTER 6

INFRINGEMENT

A. LIKELIHOOD OF CONFUSION

1. THE "POLAROID" FACTORS

Page 393. Insert new case before *Nabisco v. Warner–Lambert*:

Borinquen Biscuit Co. v. MV Trading Co., 443 F.3d 112 (1st Cir. 2006). Plaintiff Borinquen produces "RICA" "galletas" (cookies, but the term also can mean crackers). The packaging has always borne a logo that consists of a red circle encompassing the white-lettered phrase "Galletas RICA Sunland." Borinquen registered both the mark "RICA" and the product's logo with the Puerto Rico Department of State in 2000. It currently sells the product in predominantly red-and-white packaging, with the circular logo centered against a background consisting of rows of the galletas. Borinquen's "RICA" is the only cookie, cracker, or biscuit registered under that name in the United States. Borinquen was the only company to use the word "rica" in connection with the marketing or distribution of galletas in Puerto Rico.

Defendant MV subsequently sold in Puerto Rico a round, yellowish, salty galleta bearing the name "Nestle Ricas." The product logo consists of a white oval with the name "Ricas" centered in red letters and with a red square in the upper right-hand corner of the oval bearing the white-lettered brand name "Nestle." M.V.'s packaging is mostly red and white, albeit with some yellow and blue design. The logo is centered in the upper half of the box against a background of scattered galletas.

> The court below applied the eight-factor screen and concluded that, on the whole, the evidence preponderated in favor of a finding that M.V.'s use of its mark in Puerto Rico was likely to result in consumer confusion. This conclusion was predicated on a measured view of the evidence. On the one hand, the court noted that the parties' goods were dissimilar, that no actual confusion had been shown, and that no evidence existed that M.V. intended to mislead consumers. On the other hand, the court found that the remaining factors all tended to favor a likelihood of confusion. The court then performed the necessary balancing and determined that the latter points outweighed the former.
>
> M.V. assails this determination, arguing that the court misapplied the eight-factor test in two principal ways: by underestimating the significance of Borinquen's failure to present a consumer survey de-

signed to show actual confusion and by deeming "RICA" a strong mark. After careful perscrutation of the record, we reject both arguments.

To begin, a trademark holder's burden is to show likelihood of confusion, not actual confusion. While evidence of actual confusion is "often deemed the best evidence of possible future confusion," Attrezzi, LLC v. Maytag Corp., 436 F.3d 32, 40 (1st Cir.2006), proof of actual confusion is not essential to finding likelihood of confusion. . . .

Historically, we have attached substantial weight to a trademark holder's failure to prove actual confusion only in instances in which the relevant products have coexisted on the market for a long period of time. This is not such a case: M.V.'s product was introduced to the Puerto Rican market in April of 2003, and M.V.'s own evidence suggests that sales did not proliferate until the summer of 2004. This corresponds to the time frame in which Borinquen discovered the presence of Nestle Ricas and took action to protect its mark. Since the preliminary injunction issued just over a year later, there was no protracted period of product coexistence. Nor is there any other compelling reason why, in this case, survey evidence should be required at the preliminary injunction stage. We hold, therefore, that while survey evidence would have been helpful, it was not indispensable to a finding of likelihood of confusion.

In much the same vein, the court did not clearly err in determining that "RICA" is a relatively strong mark. Various factors are relevant in ascertaining the strength of a trademark, including the length of time the mark has been used, the trademark holder's renown in the industry, the potency of the mark in the product field (as measured by the number of similar registered marks), and the trademark holder's efforts to promote and protect the mark. See Boston Athletic Ass'n, 867 F.2d at 32; see also Keds, 888 F.2d at 222. In assessing the strength of Borinquen's mark, the district court found that the mark had been registered for more than three decades; that Borinquen's "RICA" was the only cookie, cracker, or biscuit trademarked under that name in the United States; and that Borinquen's efforts in promoting and protecting its mark were in conformance with industry standards. These three findings, all of which are supported by substantial evidence in the record, furnish ample grounding for the court's conclusion that "RICA" should be considered a strong mark.

Page 393. Delete *Nabisco v. Warner–Lambert*. This decision has now been affirmed on grounds other than those excerpted in the casebook. *See* 220 F.3d 43 (2d Cir. 2000).

Page 416. Insert after *Kendall–Jackson*, before Questions:

Sutter Home v. Madrona Vinyards, 2005 WL 701599 (N.D. Cal. 2005). Plaintiff Sutter Home is a large California winery, whose wines include the "Ménage à Trois" series of wines, sold under the "Folie à Deux" label. The wines sell at about $12 per bottle, and over 80,000 cases have been sold since 1997. Defendant Madrona Vinyards is a small California winery, whose, Rhone-style "Mélange de Trois" wines sell for $16 a bottle; since 2001, Madrona has produced 1711 cases of "Mélange de Trois," of which it has sold 1388. The court considered how the use by both wines of a foreign language affected the analysis of the similarity of the marks:

> Here, the court's attempt to evaluate the similarity of the relevant marks from the perspective of the average American wine purchaser is complicated by the fact that both marks are comprised of French words. Literally translated, plaintiff's "Ménage à Trois" mark refers to a household ("ménage") of three ("trois"), although it commonly connotes a sexual relationship involving three persons. By way of comparison, defendant's "Mélange de Trois" means a "blend of three," a name that is intended both to reflect the fact that the wine is a blend of three grape varietals and to evoke the French origin of the Rhone varietals from which the wine is made. These definitions are distinctly different and would be perceived as such by anyone with even a passing familiarity with the French language.
>
> The inquiry into the similarity of the two marks does not end there, however. As plaintiff points out, the sound and appearance of the two marks differ only in the substitution of two consonants in "Mélange" vis-a-vis "Ménage" and in the replacement of the preposition "de" with the word "a" as the second word of the marks. Plaintiff argues that these phonetic and orthographic parallels are sufficient to induce confusion in the average American consumer, who, being stubbornly monolingual, is unlikely to perceive the marks as anything more than "French-sounding" words.
>
> In addressing the merits of plaintiff's argument, the court is guided by the so-called "doctrine of foreign equivalents." Under the doctrine, foreign words from common languages are translated into English before undertaking the confusing similarity analysis. However, the doctrine does not apply to every foreign word that appears in a trade-or service mark. Indeed, the Federal Circuit has characterized the doctrine as a "guideline" rather than an "absolute rule," observing that "it should be applied only when it is likely that the ordinary American purchaser would stop and translate the [foreign] word-into its English equivalent."
>
> The Ninth Circuit has yet to opine on the applicability of the doctrine of foreign equivalents. However, the doctrine is well-established in trademark registration proceedings. In addition, a number of courts, including the Second, Fourth, and Fifth Circuits, have applied the doctrine in the context of trademark infringement actions. This court sees no reason to depart from the weight of precedent and thus follows the rules that these courts have developed in applying the doctrine.
>
> That said, there is no authoritative guidance on the question of whether the doctrine of foreign equivalents applies where, as here, both of the relevant marks are of foreign origin. The typical doctrine of foreign equivalents case involves the comparison of one foreign-word

mark to a mark written in English, and there is some authority to suggest that the doctrine is operative only under those circumstances. However, another view would hold the doctrine to apply with equal force to the instant action despite the fact that the likelihood of confusion inquiry here entails the comparison of two foreign-word marks. As the Trademark Trial and Appeal Board observed in *In re Lar Mor International, Inc.*, 221 U.S.P.Q. 180 (T.T.A.B. 1983), "the fact that both marks may be comprised of foreign words should not mean that [a court] can disregard their meanings." *Id.* at 181. The court went onto compare the English-language equivalent of the mark "Très Jolie"—roughly speaking, "exceptionally beautiful"—with that of the mark "Bien Jolie," which the court translated as "quite pretty," and concluded that the two marks were not confusingly similar. In reaching this conclusion, the court relied on the fact that "many members of the American public, even those who have only a rudimentary acquaintance with the French language, are likely to understand the significance of the respective terms." Again, the question is whether the consumer is likely to translate the foreign words. "When it is unlikely that an American buyer will translate the foreign mark and will take it as is, then the doctrine of foreign equivalents will not be applied."

The court finds this analysis to be conceptually sound. Indeed, as the above-cited passage demonstrates, La Mor's reliance on the doctrine of foreign equivalents to compare two foreign-word marks is merely an application of the general rule that two marks are confusingly similar only when their use "would cause confusion of any appreciable number of ordinary prudent purchasers as to source of the goods." This inquiry in turn depends on whether an "appreciable number of purchasers in the United States," who courts presume to speak English as well as the pertinent foreign language, will understand the meaning of the foreign-word mark at issue and translate that mark into its English equivalent. The court finds this standard applicable to the instant action and thus must consider whether an appreciable number of United States consumers of the parties' products would understand the meaning of the phrases "Ménage à trois" and "Mélange de trois."

As noted above, plaintiff argues that this precondition to applying the doctrine of foreign equivalents is not met here, asserting that the typical wine purchaser perceives the parties' marks as little more than "French-sounding" words. However, plaintiff's "Ménage à Trois" mark is so commonly used and understood that it could just as aptly be characterized as part of the lexicon of American English as it could be considered a foreign-language expression. The French words that comprise defendant's mark are almost as widely understood, particularly if one focuses on likely purchasers of the parties' wines. As defendant points out, the word "Mélange" is commonly used to describe wines such as defendant's "Mélange de Trois" that are comprised of a blend of more than one grape varietal. And of course, anyone with even a

> passing familiarity with the French language would understand the meaning of "de trois." Thus, the English-language definitions of the parties' marks are both familiar to an appreciable number of likely purchasers of the parties' products. The court therefore concludes that the dissimilar meaning of the parties' marks reduces the likelihood that consumers will be confused by defendant's use of the phrase "Mélange de Trois" in connection with the sale of wine.
>
> Against these clearly different meanings, the court must weigh considerations of sound and appearance. *See Horn's, Inc. v. Sanofi Beaute Inc.*, 963 F.Supp. 318, 323 (S.D.N.Y. 1997) (*quoting* 3 J. Thomas McCarthy, Trademarks and Unfair Competition § 23:37, at 23–84 (4th ed. 1996)) (observing that even where the English translation of a foreign mark is used to determine similarity of meaning, "the foreign mark is used when examining similarity in sight and sound"). Plaintiff notes that the marks are each four syllables long and are consonant in significant respects. It is true that the confusion caused by these similarities in sound and appearance might in certain circumstance be mitigated by the information provided by the parties' trade dress and the use of other trademarks in association with the marks at issue here (e.g., "Madrona Vineyards"or "Folie à Deux"). However, while the "[u]se of differing names or distinctive logos in connection with similar marks can reduce the likelihood of confusion," it does not always do so. Plaintiff correctly points out that differences in trade dress and, to a lesser extent, differences in brand, cannot be relied on to distinguish the parties' products in an "on premises" setting, where consumers may order a glass of wine at a bar or make their purchasing decisions based on a restaurant wine list. Thus, it is certainly possible that some consumers, upon viewing or hearing the two marks, would be confused by their phonetic and orthographic similarity, although it is worth noting that wine lists, even by the glass, usually include the source of the wine.
>
> In short, the court finds that a comparison of the definitions of the parties' marks weighs against a conclusion that consumer confusion is likely, whereas considerations of orthography and phonetics favor plaintiff's claim that the marks are confusingly similar. Balancing these disparate findings, the court concludes that the similarity of the parties' marks does not strongly favor either party. However, in the absence of any evidence in the record as it now stands that would quantify these conflicting inferences, the court finds that on balance this factor tips slightly in defendant's favor.

The court next found that the strength of the mark factor favored plaintiff, and that the products, as premium wines sold at similar prices, were closely proximate. By contrast the "marketing channels used" differed markedly: plaintiff sells to wholesalers and retailers; defendant sells from its on-site tasting room and through wine clubs. The court did not find the parties' common use of websites to market their wines probative of similarity of marketing channels, given "the broad use of the Internet today." The court also found no intent to confuse consumers in defendant's selection of its "Mélange de trois" mark, pointing out that defendant's wine is indeed a blend of three grape varietals. The court held that Sutter Home had not established a likelihood of success on the merits of its infringement claim.

Page 416. Add new Question 4:

4. Does "size matter"? Where defendant is a small producer, and particularly if its goods are high quality or addressed to an elite audience, is a court less likely to find confusion? *See Starbucks Corp. v. BlackBear Micro Roastery*, 2004 WL 2158120 (S.D.N.Y. 2004) (summary judgment for Starbucks denied in action against boutique producer of "Charbucks" dark-roasted coffee beans).

Page 420. Delete *New York Stock Exchange, Inc. v. New York, New York Hotel, LLC.* This decision has now been affirmed in part and reversed in part, on grounds other than those excerpted in the casebook. *See* 293 F.3d 550 (2d Cir. 2002).

Page 420–23. Delete Note on "What Are Infringing Uses?" and *Playboy v. Netscape.* Substitute the following:

WHEN DOES A COMPETITOR "CAUSE" CONFUSION?

Holiday Inns Inc. v. 800 Reservations Inc., 86 F.3d 619 (6th Cir. 1996). Holiday Inns' 1–800 "vanity" number for hotel reservations was 1–800–HOLIDAY [465–4329]. A significant number of phone users misdial the number zero in place of the letter "O." Frequently misdialed "vanity" numbers of this kind are known as "complementary" numbers. In order to retrieve misdialing customers, many 1–800 "vanity" number holders also subscribe to the "complementary" number. Holiday Inns, however, did not.

800 Reservations Inc. is an independent hotel room booking service. It makes reservations for its phone-in customers at a variety of hotels, including Holiday Inns. 800 Reservations is not sponsored by or affiliated with Holiday Inns. 800 Reservations uses as its phone number 1–800–H0LIDAY, 0 being the Number zero rather than the letter "O." 800 Reservations responds to each call with the following message: "Hello. You have misdialed and have not reached Holiday Inns or any of its affiliates. You've called 800 Reservations, America's fastest growing independent computerized hotel reservation service . . ."

Holiday Inns charged that 800 Reservations' adoption of the "complementary" 800 number was likely to cause confusion with Holiday Inns' reservation service, in violation of § 43(a). The Sixth Circuit agreed with the district court that 800 Reservations "did not create the consumers' confusion, but . . . merely took advantage of confusion already in existence." But where the district court had found Reservations' conduct "a clear violation of the spirit, if not the letter, of the Lanham Act," the appellate court held Reservations' conduct not only less objectionable, but also distinguishable from other 1–800 number controversies. In the other cases, e.g., *Dial–A–Mattress Franchise Corp. v. Page*, 880 F.2d 675 (2d Cir.

1989), the defendants had not merely adopted a confusingly similar telephone number, but "intentionally promoted [the] vanity number and caused confusion." Here, by contrast, asserted the court, Reservations did not "use" the complementary number because it did not publicize the number: Reservations may have been reaping the benefits of preexisting confusion, but it did not "create" that confusion, and thus cannot be held to have violated the Lanham Act.

Page 424. Add after Note on House Marks:

Bumble Bee Seafoods, L.L.C. v. UFS Industries, Inc., 2004 WL 1637017 (S.D.N.Y. 2004). Sally Sherman Foods uses Bumble Bee brand tuna to make tuna salads, which it sells in five-pound tubs. A label on the lid of the tub truthfully states that the salad "made with Bumble Bee tuna." Bumble Bee claimed that the label would confuse consumers into believing that Bumble Bee had authorized or sponsored the Sally Sherman salads, and therefore sued to enjoin mention of its tuna brand on the lids of the salad containers.

> Should the makers of tuna salad be preliminarily enjoined from stating on its label that it is "Made with Bumble Bee Tuna" when the trademark to "Bumble Bee Tuna" is owned by another entity? The answer, in the context of the facts of this action, is "no." . . .
>
> Bumble Bee is a leading provider of tuna in the United States and owns several well-established and widely recognized trademarks under which it has marketed its products since 1910. Bumble Bee has created a Quality Assurance Program by which it authorizes tuna salad processing companies to manufacture and market tuna salad using its products and bearing its marks.
>
> At the end of 2002, Bumble Bee and Sally Sherman discussed the possibility that Sally Sherman would become a participant in the Quality Assurance Program, thereby allowing Sally Sherman to use the Bumble Bee mark on its tuna salad. As part of that application process, Sally Sherman completed and passed a Quality Assurance Survey designed to screen potential participants in the Quality Assurance Program. As the next step in the application process, Bumble Bee then scheduled an onsite inspection at Sally Sherman's facilities, but Sally Sherman withdrew its application one week later.
>
> Sally Sherman purchased a "substantial" amount of Bumble Bee tuna in 2003 "for use in making its tuna salad." In February 2004, Bumble Bee discovered that Sally Sherman distributed to delicatessens and supermarkets its five pound tubs of tuna salad, the lid of which stated: Sally Sherman Tuna Salad (with the Sally Sherman logo); Made with 100% Hellmann's Real Mayonnaise (with Hellmann's logo); Made with Bumble Bee Tuna (without the Bumble Bee logo). Bumble Bee had never authorized Sally Sherman to state "Made with Bumble Bee Tuna" on its lids. . . . Extensive correspondence between Bumble Bee and Sally Sherman ensued; defendant insisted it was making fair use of Bumble Bee's name, triggering this litigation. . . .

There is No Trademark Violation Because There Is No Deception

On the one hand, Bumble Bee concedes that Sally Sherman is entitled to list in small type within the ingredients on its tuna salad lids the words "made with Bumble Bee tuna a registered trademark of Bumble Bee Seafoods, LLC not affiliated." On the other hand, Sally Sherman concedes that it cannot simply label its tuna salad with "Bumble Bee" as the brand identifier. The lid at issue presents a use of Bumble Bee's trademark that lies somewhere between those examples. "Made with Bumble Bee Tuna" is not written along with the other ingredients; nor does the label falsely state that it is Bumble Bee Tuna Salad. This Court's analysis focuses upon whether the lids are deceptive—in other words, do they lead the consumer to believe that Bumble Bee is the source of Sally Sherman's tuna *salad* or endorses this tuna salad?

To understand whether these lids are deceptive, this Court's analysis begins with the specific audience that will read the label's contentious phrase: "Sally Sherman Tuna Salad: Made with Bumble Bee Tuna." These labels are affixed solely on five pound tubs of tuna salad and are sold exclusively to delicatessens and supermarkets for further sale out of the deli counter. The counterman will use the Sally Sherman product to sell to the retail customer a certain weight of tuna salad or it can be used to make sandwiches for the retail customer. The lidded tubs themselves do not find their way to the ultimate consumer of the tuna salad; the tubs are sold to commercial entities whose employees remove the tuna salad from the tubs to sell it in smaller quantities to the ultimate consumer.

There is nothing in the record of this action to support the proposition that a buyer for delicatessens and supermarkets lacks the commercial familiarity and sophistication to understand that Sally Sherman makes the tuna salad, and one component of that salad is Bumble Bee Tuna. Moreover, a deli buyer must affirmatively place an order with Sally Sherman—not Bumble Bee—for this tuna salad. The law permits the use of a component owner's trademark for descriptive use provided that use is not deceptive.... No reasonable deli buyer would be deceived after ordering tuna salad from Sally Sherman to think that instead he received Bumble Bee tuna salad....

Page 430. Add to end of Question 3 (re WINGS):

Cf. Sullivan v. CBS, 385 F.3d 772 (7th Cir. 2004) ("Survivor" for rock band v. "Survivor" for TV show).

Pages 431–38. Delete *TNN v. CBS*.

Page 438. After *TNN v. CBS*, add the following Editors' Note and case:

Editors' Note: TNN has recently announced a change in the character of its transmissions, and has selected a new name to complement the content. Calling itself "the first network for men," and "unapologetically male,"

TNN has selected the name "Spike TV." This has prompted film director Spike Lee to sue TNN for violation of his right of publicity. For accounts of the controversy, *see, e.g.*, Julie Hilden, *Spike Lee v. Spike TV: Testing the Limits of Trademark and Right of Publicity Claims*, http://writ.news.findlaw.com/hilden/20030609.html. On the right of publicity, *see infra* Chapter 9B.

Page 438. Replace squib of district court opinion in *Playboy v. Netscape* with the following:

Playboy Enterprises, Inc. v. Netscape Communications Corporation

354 F.3d 1020 (9th Cir. 2004).

■ T.G. NELSON, CIRCUIT JUDGE:

Playboy Enterprises International, Inc. (PEI) appeals from the district court's grant of summary judgment in favor of Netscape Communications Corporation and Excite, Inc. PEI sued defendants for trademark infringement and dilution. We have jurisdiction pursuant to 28 U.S.C. § 1291. Because we conclude that genuine issues of material fact preclude summary judgment on both the trademark infringement and dilution claims, we reverse and remand.

I. FACTS

This case involves a practice called "keying" that defendants use on their Internet search engines. Keying allows advertisers to target individuals with certain interests by linking advertisements to pre-identified terms. To take an innocuous example, a person who searches for a term related to gardening may be a likely customer for a company selling seeds. Thus, a seed company might pay to have its advertisement displayed when searchers enter terms related to gardening. After paying a fee to defendants, that company could have its advertisements appear on the page listing the search results for gardening-related terms: the ad would be "keyed" to gardening-related terms. Advertisements appearing on search result pages are called "banner ads" because they run along the top or side of a page much like a banner.

Defendants have various lists of terms to which they key advertisers' banner ads. Those lists include the one at issue in this case, a list containing terms related to sex and adult-oriented entertainment. Among the over–400 terms in this list are two for which PEI holds trademarks: "playboy" and "playmate." Defendants *require* adult-oriented companies to link their ads to this set of words. Thus, when a user types in "playboy," "playmate," or one of the other listed terms, those companies' banner ads appear on the search results page.

PEI introduced evidence that the adult-oriented banner ads displayed on defendants' search results pages are often graphic in nature and are confusingly labeled or not labeled at all. In addition, the parties do not dispute that buttons on the banner ads say "click here." When a searcher complies, the search results page disappears, and the searcher finds him or herself at the advertiser's website. PEI presented uncontroverted evidence that defendants monitor "click rates," the ratio between the number of times searchers click on banner ads and the number of times the ads are shown. Defendants use click rate statistics to convince advertisers to renew their keyword contracts. The higher the click rate, the more successful they deem a banner ad.

* * *

III. DISCUSSION

* * *

2. PEI's case for trademark infringement.

The "core element of trademark infringement," the likelihood of confusion, lies at the center of this case. No dispute exists regarding the other requirements set forth by the statute: PEI clearly holds the marks in question and defendants used the marks in commerce without PEI's permission.

PEI's strongest argument for a likelihood of confusion is for a certain kind of confusion: initial interest confusion. Initial interest confusion is customer confusion that creates initial interest in a competitor's product. Although dispelled before an actual sale occurs, initial interest confusion impermissibly capitalizes on the goodwill associated with a mark and is therefore actionable trademark infringement.

PEI asserts that, by keying adult-oriented advertisements to PEI's trademarks, defendants actively create initial interest confusion in the following manner. Because banner advertisements appear immediately after users type in PEI's marks, PEI asserts that users are likely to be confused regarding the sponsorship of unlabeled banner advertisements. In addition, many of the advertisements instruct users to "click here." Because of their confusion, users may follow the instruction, believing they will be connected to a PEI cite. Even if they realize "immediately upon accessing" the competitor's site that they have reached a site "wholly unrelated to" PEI's, the damage has been done: Through initial consumer confusion, the competitor "will still have gained a customer by appropriating the goodwill that [PEI] has developed in its [ ] mark."

PEI's theory strongly resembles the theory adopted by this court in *Brookfield Communications, Inc. v. West Coast Entertainment Corporation.* In *Brookfield,* a video rental company, West Coast Entertainment Corporation, planned on using "moviebuff.com" as a domain name for its website and using a similar term in the metatags for the site. Brookfield had trademarked the term "MovieBuff," however, and sued West Coast for trademark infringement. The court ruled in favor of Brookfield. It reasoned that Internet users entering Brookfield's mark (plus ".com") or searching for Brookfield's mark on search engines using metatags, would find themselves at West Coast's website. Although they might "realize, immediately upon accessing 'moviebuff.com,' that they have reached a site operated by West Coast and wholly unrelated to Brookfield," some customers who were originally seeking Brookfield's website "may be perfectly content with West Coast's database (especially as it is offered free of charge)." Because those customers would have found West Coast's site due to West Coast's "misappropriation of Brookfield's goodwill" in its mark, the court concluded that Brookfield withstood summary judgment.

In this case, PEI claims that defendants, in conjunction with advertisers, have misappropriated the goodwill of PEI's marks by leading Internet users to competitors' websites just as West Coast video misappropriated the goodwill of Brookfield's mark. Some consumers, initially seeking PEI's sites, may initially believe that unlabeled banner advertisements are links to PEI's sites or to sites affiliated with PEI. Once they follow the instructions to "click here," and they access the site, they may well realize that they are not at a PEI-sponsored site. However, they may be perfectly happy to remain on the competitor's site, just as the *Brookfield* court surmised that some searchers initially seeking Brookfield's site would happily remain on West Coast's site. The Internet user will have reached the site because of defendants' use of PEI's mark. Such use is actionable.

Although analogies to *Brookfield* suggest that PEI will be able to show a likelihood of confusion sufficient to defeat summary judgment, we must test PEI's theory using this circuit's well-established eight-factor test for the likelihood of confusion to be certain. Accordingly, we turn to that test now.

The Ninth Circuit employs an eight-factor test, originally set forth in *AMF Inc. v. Sleekcraft Boats*, to determine the likelihood of confusion....

In the Internet context, courts must be flexible in applying the factors, as some may not apply. Moreover, some factors are more important than others. For example, a showing of actual confusion among significant numbers of consumers provides strong support for the likelihood of confusion. For that reason, we turn first to an examination of factor four: evidence of actual confusion.

a. *Factor 4: Evidence of Actual Confusion.*

The expert study PEI introduced establishes a strong likelihood of initial interest confusion among consumers. Thus, factor four alone probably suffices to reverse the grant of summary judgment.

PEI's expert, Dr. Ford, concluded that a statistically significant number of Internet users searching for the terms "playboy" and "playmate" would think that PEI, or an affiliate, sponsored banner ads containing adult content that appear on the search results page. When study participants were shown search results for the term "playboy," 51% believed that PEI sponsored or was otherwise associated with the adult-content banner ad displayed. When shown results for the term "playmate," 31% held the same belief. Using control groups, Dr. Ford also concluded that for 29% of those participants viewing "playboy" searches and 22% of those viewing "playmate" searches, the confusion stemmed from the targeting of the banner advertisements. The individuals were not confused by random, untargeted advertisements.

Defendants criticize Dr. Ford's procedures and conclusions. They offer their own interpretations of his data, with significantly lower rates of confusion. Defendants cite cases identifying probabilities of confusion of 7.6% and less as *de minimis* and then argue that Dr. Ford's results showed *de minimis* confusion as well. Their critique of Dr. Ford's methods and interpretations formed the basis of a motion to exclude his expert testimony and report before the district court. The district court denied that motion, however, and allowed the introduction of the evidence.

Defendants may have valid criticism of Dr. Ford's methods and conclusions, and their critique may justify reducing the weight eventually afforded Dr. Ford's expert report. The district court's evidentiary ruling is not before us on appeal, however, and weighing admissible evidence at this stage is improper. Defendants' arguments prove the point that a genuine issue of material fact exists regarding actual confusion. The presence of Dr. Ford's criticized (but uncontradicted) report, with its strong conclusions that a high likelihood of initial interest confusion exists among consumers, thus generates a genuine issue of material fact on the actual confusion issue.

Because actual confusion is at the heart of the likelihood of confusion analysis, Dr. Ford's report alone probably precludes summary judgment. In the interest of being thorough, however, we will examine the other seven *Sleekcraft* factors. On balance, they also support PEI.

b. *Factor One: Strength of the Mark.*

PEI has established that strong secondary meanings for its descriptive marks exist, and that a genuine issue of material fact exists as to whether it created the secondary meanings. Thus, the first *Sleekcraft* factor favors PEI.

At this point, defendants concede that they use the marks for their secondary meanings.[32] Thus, they concede that the marks have secondary meanings. They offer only a weak argument regarding the strength of the meanings. Given that defendants themselves use the terms precisely because they believe that Internet searchers associate the terms with their secondary meanings, disputing the strength of the secondary meanings is somewhat farfetched. The only meaningful dispute is whether PEI created the strong secondary meanings associated with the mark.

PEI offered evidence, in the form of expert reports, tending to show that PEI did create the secondary meanings of "playboy" and "playmate." PEI's expert evidence countered the defendants' expert evidence to the

32. Indeed, to argue that they use the marks for their primary meaning, as defendants did below, is absurd. Defendants obviously do not use the term "playmate," for example, for its dictionary definition: "a companion, especially of a child, in games and play." WEBSTER'S NEW WORLD DICTIONARY, 3d coll. ed. (1988).

contrary, and suffices to generate a genuine issue of material fact on this issue.

c. *Factor Two: Proximity of the Goods.*

From an Internet searcher's perspective, the relevant "goods" are the links to the websites being sought and the goods or services available at those sites. The proximity between PEI's and its competitor's goods provides the reason Netscape keys PEI's marks to competitor's banner advertisements in the first place. Accordingly, this factor favors PEI as well.

d. *Factor Three: Similarity of the Marks.*

No doubt exists regarding this factor. Aside from their lack of capitalization, their font, and the fact that defendants use the plural form of "playmate," the terms defendants use are identical to PEI's marks. Thus, they are certainly similar.

e. *Factor Five: Marketing Channels Used.*

This factor is equivocal. PEI and the advertisers use identical marketing channels: the Internet. More specifically, each of their sites appears on defendants' search results pages. Given the broad use of the Internet today, the same could be said for countless companies. Thus, this factor merits little weight.

f. *Factor Six: Type of Goods and Degree of Consumer Care Expected.*

This factor favors PEI. Consumer care for inexpensive products is expected to be quite low. Low consumer care, in turn, increases the likelihood of confusion.

In addition to price, the content in question may affect consumer care as well. We presume that the average searcher seeking adult-oriented materials on the Internet is easily diverted from a specific product he or she is seeking if other options, particularly graphic ones, appear more quickly. Thus, the adult-oriented and graphic nature of the materials weighs in PEI's favor as well.

g. *Factor Seven: Defendants' Intent in Selecting the Mark.*

This factor favors PEI somewhat. A defendant's intent to confuse constitutes probative evidence of likely confusion: Courts assume that the defendant's intentions were carried out successfully. In this case, the evidence does not definitively establish defendants' intent. At a minimum, however, it does suggest that defendants do nothing to prevent click-throughs that result from confusion. Moreover, they profit from such click-throughs.

Defendants monitor "click-through" rates on the advertisements they display. That is, they monitor the number of times consumers are diverted to their advertisers' sites. They use the click-through rates as a way to gauge the success of the advertisements and to keep advertisers coming back to their services. Although some click-throughs may be the result of legitimate consumer interest, not confusion, some may be expected to result from confusion. Defendants will profit from both kinds of click-throughs. And they do nothing to ensure that only click-throughs based on legitimate interest, as opposed to confusion, occur.

PEI introduced evidence suggesting that labeling the advertisements would reduce click-through rates. It would also reduce confusion. However, although defendants control the content of advertisements in other contexts, defendants do not require that advertisers identify themselves on their banner ads. Moreover, they do not label the advertisements themselves. Perhaps even more telling, defendants refuse to remove the highly-rated terms "playboy" and "playmate" from their lists of keywords, even when advertisers request that they do so.

The above evidence suggests, at a minimum, that defendants do nothing to alleviate confusion, even when asked to do so by their advertisers, and that they profit from confusion. Although not definitive, this factor provides some evidence of an intent to confuse on the part of defendants. This factor thus favors PEI.

h. *Factor Eight: Likelihood of Expansion of Product Lines.*

Because the advertisers' goods and PEI's are already related, as discussed within factor two, this factor is irrelevant.

Having examined all of the *Sleekcraft* factors, we conclude that the majority favor PEI. Accordingly, we conclude that a genuine issue of material fact exists as to the substantial likelihood of confusion.

* * *

■ BERZON, CIRCUIT JUDGE, concurring:

I concur in Judge Nelson's careful opinion in this case, as it is fully consistent with the applicable precedents. I write separately, however, to express concern that one of those precedents was wrongly decided and may one day, if not now, need to be reconsidered *en banc*.

I am struck by how analytically similar keyed advertisements are to the metatags found infringing in *Brookfield Communications v. West Coast Entertainment Corp.*, 174 F.3d 1036 (9th Cir. 1999). In *Brookfield*, the court held that the defendant could not use the trademarked term "moviebuff" as one of its metatags. Metatags are part of the HTML code of a web page, and therefore are invisible to internet users. Search engines use these metatags to pull out websites applicable to search terms. *See also Promatek Indus., Ltd. v. Equitrac Corp.*, 300 F.3d 808, 812–13 (7th Cir. 2002) (adopting the *Brookfield* holding).

Specifically, *Brookfield* held that the use of the trademarked terms in metatags violated the Lanham Act because it caused "initial interest confusion." *Brookfield*, 174 F.3d at 1062–66. The court explained that even though "there is no source confusion in the sense that consumers know [who] they are patronizing, ... there is nevertheless initial interest confusion in the sense that, by using 'moviebuff.com' or 'MovieBuff' to divert people looking for 'MovieBuff' to its website, [the defendant] improperly benefits from the goodwill that [the plaintiff] developed in its mark." *Id.* at 1062.

As applied to this case, *Brookfield* might suggest that there could be a Lanham Act violation *even if* the banner advertisements were clearly labeled, either by the advertiser or by the search engine. I do not believe that to be so. So read, the metatag holding in *Brookfield* would expand the reach of initial interest confusion from situations in which a party is initially confused to situations in which a party is never confused. I do not think it is reasonable to find initial interest confusion when a consumer is never confused as to source or affiliation, but instead knows, or should know, from the outset that a product or web link is not related to that of the trademark holder because the list produced by the search engine so informs him.

There is a big difference between hijacking a customer to another website by making the customer think he or she is visiting the trademark holder's website (even if only briefly), which is what may be happening in this case when the banner advertisements are not labeled, and just distracting a potential customer with another *choice*, when it is clear that it is a choice. True, when the search engine list generated by the search for the trademark ensconced in a metatag comes up, an internet user might *choose* to visit westcoastvideo.com, the defendant's website in *Brookfield*, instead of the plaintiff's moviebuff.com website, but such choices do not constitute trademark infringement off the internet, and I cannot understand why they should on the internet.

For example, consider the following scenario: I walk into Macy's and ask for the Calvin Klein section and am directed upstairs to the second floor. Once I get to the second floor, on my way to the Calvin Klein section, I notice a more prominently displayed line of Charter Club clothes, Macy's own brand, designed to appeal to the same people attracted by the style of Calvin Klein's latest line of clothes. Let's say I get diverted from my goal of reaching the Calvin Klein section, the Charter Club stuff looks good enough to me, and I purchase some Charter Club shirts instead. Has Charter Club or Macy's infringed Calvin Klein's trademark, simply by having another product more prominently displayed before one reaches the Klein line? Certainly not. . . .

Similarly, suppose a customer walks into a bookstore and asks for Playboy magazine and is then directed to the adult magazine section, where he or she sees Penthouse or Hustler up front on the rack while Playboy is buried in back. One would not say that Penthouse or Hustler had violated Playboy's trademark. This conclusion holds true even if Hustler paid the store owner to put its magazines in front of Playboy's.

One can test these analogies with an on-line example: If I went to Macy's website and did a search for a Calvin Klein shirt, would Macy's violate Calvin Klein's trademark if it responded (as does Amazon.com, for example) with the requested shirt and pictures of other shirts I might like to consider as well? I very much doubt it.

Accordingly, I simply cannot understand the broad principle set forth in *Brookfield*. Even the main analogy given in *Brookfield* belies its conclusion. The Court gives an example of Blockbuster misdirecting customers from a competing video store, West Coast Video, by putting up a highway billboard sign giving directions to Blockbuster but telling customers that a West Coast Video store is located there. *Brookfield*, 174 F.3d at 1064. Even though customers who arrive at the Blockbuster realize that it is not West Coast Video, they were initially misled and confused. *Id.*

But there was no similar misdirection in *Brookfield*, nor would there be similar misdirection in this case were the banner ads labeled or otherwise identified. The *Brookfield* defendant's website was described by the court as being accurately listed as westcoastvideo.com in the applicable search results. Consumers were free to choose the official moviebuff.com website and were not hijacked or misdirected elsewhere. I note that the billboard analogy has been widely criticized as inapplicable to the internet situation, given both the fact that customers were not misdirected and the minimal inconvenience in directing one's web browser back to the original list of search results....

Pages 439–40. Delete *Playboy v. Universal Teletalk*.

3. Reverse Confusion

Page 454. Add new Question 3:

3. Surfvivor is a coined word, and a trademark registered for Hawaiian beach-themed products, and has been in use in Hawaii for some years before the inauguration of the reality-television show, *Survivor*. The show's producers have licensed "Survivor" for a variety of consumer merchandise, including beachwear. The producers were aware of the Surfvivor mark when they adopted Survivor for the television show. There has been no evidence of actual confusion of the marks. How should the court rule on Surfvivor's reverse confusion claim? *See Surfvivor Media v. Survivor Productions*, 406 F.3d 625 (9th Cir. 2005).

Nissan Motor Co. v. Nissan Computer Corp., 378 F.3d 1002 (9th Cir. 2004), in which the Ninth Circuit further refined its *Brookfield* analysis of initial interest confusion, suggests a further distinction based on the nature of the business to which the consumer's initial interest is diverted. In *Nissan*, the defendant, Uzi Nissan, registered "Nissan.com" in 1994 as a domain name for a website promoting Nissan Computer Corp., a store he had operated in North Carolina since 1991. In 1999, Uzi Nissan also used the domain name and website for various advertising ventures, including advertisements for automobile-related products and services. The Ninth Circuit agreed with the district court that the "automobile-related advertising constituted trademark infringement on the basis of initial interest confusion, but that non-automobile-related advertising did not."

> Nissan Computer argues that it did not infringe the NISSAN mark because it did nothing to draw potential Nissan Motor customers to its website or to divert customers who were looking for Nissan vehicles, and that there is at least a factual dispute whether Nissan Computer "captured" the initial interest of internet users looking for Nissan

Motor products. Nissan Computer reasons that it did not offer automobiles or automobile-related services, rather it posted advertisements on its website much as a newspaper does. . . .

As we hypothesized initial interest confusion in *Brookfield*, it would occur if Blockbuster Video put up a billboard that advertised West Coast Video at Exit 7, when in actuality West Coast was located at Exit 8, but Blockbuster was at Exit 7. Customers looking for West Coast would leave the freeway at Exit 7, but after not finding it, rent from Blockbuster rather than reentering the freeway in search of West Coast. Customers are not confused that they are renting from Blockbuster instead of West Coast, but Blockbuster misappropriates West Coast's acquired goodwill through the initial consumer confusion. *See Brookfield*, 174 F.3d at 1064. . . .

Nissan Computer's use of nissan.com to sell non-automobile-related goods does not infringe because Nissan is a last name, a month in the Hebrew and Arabic calendars, a name used by many companies, and "the goods offered by these two companies differ significantly." However, Nissan Computer traded on the goodwill of Nissan Motor by offering links to automobile-related websites. Although Nissan Computer was not directly selling automobiles, it was offering information about automobiles and this capitalized on consumers' initial interest. An internet user interested in purchasing, or gaining information about Nissan automobiles would be likely to enter nissan.com. When the item on that website was computers, the auto-seeking consumer "would realize in one hot second that she was in the wrong place and either guess again or resort to a search engine to locate" Nissan Motor's site. A consumer might initially be incorrect about the website, but Nissan Computer would not capitalize on the misdirected consumer. However, once nissan.com offered links to auto-related websites, then the auto-seeking consumer might logically be expected to follow those links to obtain information about automobiles. Nissan Computer financially benefitted because it received money for every click. Although nissan.com itself did not provide the information about automobiles, it provided direct links to such information. Due to the ease of clicking on a link, the required extra click does not rebut the conclusion that Nissan Computer traded on the goodwill of Nissan Motor's mark.

If the car-searching consumer remains on and makes a purchase from Nissan Computer's site, or goes to another non automobile-related site to which Nissan Computer's site links, and for which click-through Nissan Computer receives a commission, can it be said that Nissan has not "capitalized on the misdirected consumer" or at least made money from her mistake? Even if Nissan Computer does benefit from the mistake, are there nonetheless good reasons to decline to find trademark infringement? Does the analysis change if Nissan Motors also alleges dilution? See *infra* this Supplement, Chapter 10.

B. Contributory Infringement

Page 474. Add the following:

In the *WhenU* cases, and *GEICO v. Google*, *supra* Chapter 3A, this Supplement, and in *Playboy v. Netscape*, *supra* Chapter 6A, this Supplement, the defendants were keying their customers' banner ads or pop up ads to others' trademarks. As part of the keying, defendants entered the trademarks into their directories; this conduct allegedly directly infringed plaintiffs' trademarks. Defendants' ad placement mechanism also enabled their customers to attract (or divert) trade from the trademark owners; this conduct, the trademark owners claimed, made the defendants derivatively liable for the confusion their customers' advertisements allegedly caused. How does this claim fare under *Ives*? Under *Lockheed-Martin*?

C. Statutory Defenses/Incontestability

2. Defenses to Incontestably Registered Marks

Page 486. Add the following citation at the end of the first paragraph:

See also Daesang Corp. v. Rhee Bros., Inc., 2005 WL 1163142 (D.Md. 2005)(failure of registrant to inform PTO that transliteration of mark meant Soon Chang, a place in Korea well known for sauces of the type covered by the application, and that registrant's customers would be aware of this association constituted fraud on the PTO).

3. Fair Use

Page 496. Replace citation at the end of Question 2 with the subsequent appellate decision citation:

EMI Catalogue Partnership v. Hill, Holliday, Connors, Cosmopulos, Inc., 228 F.3d 56 (2d Cir. 2000).

Page 496. After Question 2, add the following Question:

3. International Stamp Art, Inc. designs and produces note cards and greeting cards bearing reproductions of postage stamp art. For certain of these products, ISA used a perforation design to serve as a border for the card's design or illustration. ISA has obtained a trademark registration for the perforated border design. The U.S. Postal Service also issues greeting cards incorporating the designs of postage stamps, and which display a perforated border. In response to ISA's infringement action, the Postal Service contends that the perforated border is being used as an integral aspect of the image of a postage stamp. Is the Postal Service making a descriptive use "other than as a mark" that would qualify it for the § 33(b)(4) exception? See *International Stamp Art v. U.S. Postal Service*, 78 U.S.P.Q.2d 1116 (N.D. Ga. 2005).

Page 496. After Questions following *Car Freshner*, add the following decisions and Question:

KP Permanent Make–Up, Inc. v. Lasting Impression I, Inc.

543 U.S. 111 (2004).

■ JUSTICE SOUTER.

The question here is whether a party raising the statutory affirmative defense of fair use to a claim of trademark infringement, 15 U.S.C. § 1115(b)(4), has a burden to negate any likelihood that the practice complained of will confuse consumers about the origin of the goods or services affected. We hold it does not.

I

Each party to this case sells permanent makeup, a mixture of pigment and liquid for injection under the skin to camouflage injuries and modify nature's dispensations, and each has used some version of the term "micro color" (as one word or two, singular or plural) in marketing and selling its product. Petitioner KP Permanent Make-Up, Inc., claims to have used the single-word version since 1990 or 1991 on advertising flyers and since 1991 on pigment bottles. Respondents Lasting Impression I, Inc., and its licensee, MCN International, Inc. (Lasting, for simplicity), deny that KP began using the term that early, but we accept KP's allegation as true for present purposes; the District and Appeals Courts took it to be so, and the disputed facts do not matter to our resolution of the issue. In 1992, Lasting applied to the United States Patent and Trademark Office (PTO) under 15 U.S.C. § 1051 for registration of a trademark consisting of the words "Micro Colors" in white letters separated by a green bar within a black square. The PTO registered the mark to Lasting in 1993, and in 1999 the registration became incontestable. § 1065.

It was also in 1999 that KP produced a 10-page advertising brochure using "microcolor" in a large, stylized typeface, provoking Lasting to demand that KP stop using the term. Instead, KP sued Lasting in the Central District of California, seeking, on more than one ground, a declaratory judgment that its language infringed no such exclusive right as Lasting claimed. Lasting counterclaimed, alleging, among other things, that KP had infringed Lasting's "Micro Colors" trademark.

KP sought summary judgment on the infringement counterclaim, based on the statutory affirmative defense of fair use, 15 U.S.C. § 1115(b)(4). After finding that Lasting had conceded that KP used the term only to describe its goods and not as a mark, the District Court held that KP was acting fairly and in good faith because undisputed facts showed that KP had employed the term "microcolor" continuously from a time before Lasting adopted the two-word, plural variant as a mark. Without enquiring whether the practice was likely to cause confusion, the court concluded that KP had made out its affirmative defense under § 1115(b)(4) and entered summary judgment for KP on Lasting's infringement claim.

On appeal, 328 F.3d 1061 (2003), the Court of Appeals for the Ninth Circuit thought it was error for the District Court to have addressed the fair use defense without delving into the matter of possible confusion on the part of consumers about the origin of KP's goods. The reviewing court took the view that no use could be recognized as fair where any consumer confusion was probable, and although the court did not pointedly address the burden of proof, it appears to have placed it on KP to show absence of consumer confusion. *Id.*, at 1072 ("Therefore, KP can only benefit from the fair use defense if there is no likelihood of confusion between KP's use of the term 'micro color' and Lasting's mark"). Since it found there were disputed material facts relevant under the Circuit's eight-factor test for assessing the likelihood of confusion, it reversed the summary judgment and remanded the case.

We granted KP's petition for certiorari, 540 U.S. 1099, 540 U.S. 1099, 157 L. Ed. 2d 811, 124 S. Ct. 981 (2004), to address a disagreement among the Courts of Appeals on the significance of likely confusion for a fair use defense to a trademark infringement claim, and the obligation of a party defending on that ground to show that its use is unlikely to cause consumer confusion. *Compare* 328 F.3d at 1072 (likelihood of confusion bars the fair use defense); *PACCAR Inc. v. TeleScan Technologies, L. L. C.,* 319 F.3d 243, 256 (CA6 2003) ("[A] finding of a likelihood of confusion forecloses a fair use defense"); and *Zatarains, Inc. v. Oak Grove Smokehouse,* 698 F.2d 786, 796 (CA5 1983) (alleged infringers were free to use words contained in a trademark "in their ordinary, descriptive sense, so long as such use [did] not tend to confuse customers as to the source of the goods"), *with Cosmetically Sealed Industries, Inc. v. Chesebrough–Pond's USA Co.,* 125 F.3d 28, 30–31 (CA2 1997) (the fair use defense may succeed even if there is likelihood of confusion); *Shakespeare Co. v. Silstar Corp. of Am.,* 110 F.3d 234, 243 (CA4 1997) ("[A] determination of likely confusion [does not] preclud[e] considering the fairness of use"); *Sunmark, Inc. v. Ocean Spray Cranberries, Inc.,* 64 F.3d 1055, 1059 (CA7 1995) (finding that likelihood of confusion did not preclude the fair use defense). We now vacate the judgment of the Court of Appeals.

II

A

The holder of a registered mark (incontestable or not) has a civil action against anyone employing an imitation of it in commerce when "such use is likely to cause confusion, or to cause mistake, or to deceive." § 1114(1). Although an incontestable registration is "conclusive evidence ... of the registrant's exclusive right to use the ... mark in commerce," § 1115(b), the plaintiff's success is still subject to "proof of infringement as defined in section 1114," § 1115(b). And that, as just noted, requires a showing that the defendant's actual practice is likely to produce confusion in the minds of consumers about the origin of the goods or services in question. (Citations omitted) This plaintiff's burden has to be kept in mind when reading the relevant portion of the further provision for an affirmative defense of fair use, available to a party whose

> "use of the name, term, or device charged to be an infringement is a use, otherwise than as a mark, ... of a term or device which is descriptive of and used fairly and in good faith only to describe the goods or services of such party, or their geographic origin...." § 1115(b)(4).

Two points are evident. Section 1115(b) places a burden of proving likelihood of confusion (that is, infringement) on the party charging infringement even when relying on an incontestable registration. And Congress said nothing about likelihood of confusion in setting out the elements of the fair use defense in § 1115(b)(4).

Starting from these textual fixed points, it takes a long stretch to claim that a defense of fair use entails any burden to negate confusion. It is just not plausible that Congress would have used the descriptive phrase "likely to cause confusion, or to cause mistake, or to deceive" in § 1114 to describe the requirement that a markholder show likelihood of consumer confusion, but would have relied on the phrase "used fairly" in § 1115(b)(4) in a fit of terse drafting meant to place a defendant under a burden to negate confusion. "[W]here Congress includes particular language in one section of a statute but omits it in another section of the same Act, it is generally presumed that Congress acts intentionally and purposely in the disparate inclusion or exclusion." *Russello v. United States,* 464 U.S. 16, 23, 78 L. Ed. 2d 17, 104 S. Ct. 296 (1983) (quoting *United States v. Wong Kim Bo,* 472 F.2d 720, 722 (CA5 1972)) (alteration in original).[4]

Nor do we find much force in Lasting's suggestion that "used fairly" in § 1115(b)(4) is an oblique incorporation of a likelihood-of-confusion test developed in the common law of unfair competition. Lasting is certainly correct that some unfair competition cases would stress that use of a term by another in conducting its trade went too far in sowing confusion, and would either enjoin the use or order the defendant to include a disclaimer. (Citations omitted). But the common law of unfair competition also tolerated some degree of confusion from a descriptive use of words contained in another person's trademark. (Citations omitted). While these cases are

4. Not only that, but the failure to say anything about a defendant's burden on this point was almost certainly not an oversight, not after the House Subcommittee on Trademarks declined to forward a proposal to provide expressly as an element of the defense that a descriptive use be " '[un]likely to deceive the public.' " Hearings on H. R. 102 et al. before the Subcommittee on Trade-Marks of the House Committee on Patents, 77th Cong., 1st Sess., 167–168 (1941) (hereinafter "Hearings") (testimony of Prof. Milton Handler).

consistent with taking account of the likelihood of consumer confusion as one consideration in deciding whether a use is fair, *see* Part II–B, *infra*, they do not stand for the proposition that an assessment of confusion alone may be dispositive. Certainly one cannot get out of them any defense burden to negate it entirely.

Finally, a look at the typical course of litigation in an infringement action points up the incoherence of placing a burden to show nonconfusion on a defendant. If a plaintiff succeeds in making out a prima facie case of trademark infringement, including the element of likelihood of consumer confusion, the defendant may offer rebutting evidence to undercut the force of the plaintiff's evidence on this (or any) element, or raise an affirmative defense to bar relief even if the prima facie case is sound, or do both. But it would make no sense to give the defendant a defense of showing affirmatively that the plaintiff cannot succeed in proving some element (like confusion); all the defendant needs to do is to leave the factfinder unpersuaded that the plaintiff has carried its own burden on that point. A defendant has no need of a court's true belief when agnosticism will do. Put another way, it is only when a plaintiff has shown likely confusion by a preponderance of the evidence that a defendant could have any need of an affirmative defense, but under Lasting's theory the defense would be foreclosed in such a case. "[I]t defies logic to argue that a defense may not be asserted in the only situation where it even becomes relevant." *Shakespeare Co. v. Silstar Corp.,* 110 F.3d at 243. Nor would it make sense to provide an affirmative defense of no confusion plus good faith, when merely rebutting the plaintiff's case on confusion would entitle the defendant to judgment, good faith or not.

Lasting tries to extenuate the anomaly of this conception of the affirmative defense by arguing that the oddity reflects the "vestigial" character of the fair use defense as a historical matter. Tr. of Oral Arg. 39. Lasting argues that, because it was only in 1988 that Congress added the express provision that an incontestable markholder's right to exclude is "subject to proof of infringement," Trademark Law Revision Act of 1988, § 128(b)(1), 102 Stat. 3944, there was no requirement prior to 1988 that a markholder prove likelihood of confusion. Before 1988, the argument goes, it was sensible to get at the issue of likely confusion by requiring a defendant to prove its absence when defending on the ground of fair use. When the 1988 Act saddled the markholder with the obligation to prove confusion likely, § 1115(b), the revision simply failed to relieve the fair use defendant of the suddenly strange burden to prove absence of the very confusion that a plaintiff had a new burden to show in the first place.

But the explanation does not work. It is not merely that it would be highly suspect in leaving the claimed element of § 1115(b)(4) redundant and pointless. (Citation omitted) The main problem of the argument is its false premise: Lasting's assumption that holders of incontestable marks had no need to prove likelihood of confusion prior to 1988 is wrong. *See, e.g., Beer Nuts, Inc. v. Clover Club Foods Co.,* 805 F.2d 920, 924–925 (CA10 1986) (requiring proof of likelihood of confusion in action by holder of incontestable mark); *United States Jaycees v. Philadelphia Jaycees,* 639 F.2d 134, 137, n. 3 (CA3 1981) ("[I]ncontestability [does not] mak[e] unnecessary a showing of likelihood of confusion . . ."); 5 J. McCarthy, Trademarks and Unfair Competition § 32:154, p 32–247 (4th ed. 2004) ("Before the 1988 Trademark Law Revision Act, the majority of courts held that while incontestability grants a conclusive presumption of the 'exclusive right to use' the registered mark, this did not relieve the registrant of proving likelihood of confusion").

B

Since the burden of proving likelihood of confusion rests with the plaintiff, and the fair use defendant has no free-standing need to show confusion unlikely, it follows (contrary to the Court of Appeals's view) that some possibility of consumer confusion must be compatible with fair use, and so it is. The common law's tolerance of a certain degree of confusion on the part of consumers followed from the very fact that in cases like this one an originally descriptive term was selected to be used as a mark, not to mention the undesirability of allowing anyone to obtain a complete monopoly on use of a descriptive term simply by grabbing it first. (Citation omitted). The Lanham Act adopts a similar leniency, there being no indication that the statute was meant to deprive commercial speakers of the ordinary utility of descriptive words. "If any confusion results, that is a risk the plaintiff accepted when it decided to identify its product with a mark that uses a well known descriptive phrase." *Cosmetically Sealed Industries, Inc. v. Chesebrough-Pond's USA Co.,* 125 F.3d at 30. *See also Park 'N Fly, Inc. v. Dollar Park & Fly, Inc.,* 469 U.S. 189, 201, 83 L. Ed. 2d 582, 105 S. Ct. 658 (1985) (noting safeguards in Lanham Act to prevent commercial monopolization of language); *Car-Freshner Corp. v. S. C. Johnson & Son, Inc.,* 70 F.3d 267, 269 (CA2 1995) (noting importance of "protect[ing] the right of society at large to use words or images in their primary descriptive sense"). This right to describe is the reason that descriptive terms qualify for registration as trademarks only after taking on secondary meaning as "distinctive of the applicant's goods," *15 U.S.C. § 1052(f),* with the registrant getting an exclusive right not in the original, descriptive sense, but only in the secondary one associated with the markholder's goods, 2 McCarthy, *supra,* § 11:45 ("The only aspect of the mark which is given legal protection is that penumbra or fringe of secondary meaning which surrounds the old descriptive word").

While we thus recognize that mere risk of confusion will not rule out fair use, we think it would be improvident to go further in this case, for deciding anything more would take us beyond the Ninth Circuit's consideration of the subject. It suffices to realize that our holding that fair use can occur along with some degree of confusion does not foreclose the relevance of the extent of any likely consumer confusion in assessing whether a defendant's use is objectively fair. Two Courts of Appeals have found it relevant to consider such scope, and commentators and *amici* here have urged us to say that the degree of likely consumer confusion bears not only on the fairness of using a term, but even on the further question whether an originally descriptive term has become so identified as a mark that a defendant's use of it cannot realistically be called descriptive. *See Shakespeare Co. v. Silstar Corp., supra,* at 243 ("[T]o the degree that confusion is likely, a use is less likely to be found fair ..." (emphasis omitted)); *Sunmark, Inc. v. Ocean Spray Cranberries, Inc.*, 64 F.3d at 1059; Restatement (Third) of Unfair Competition.

Since we do not rule out the pertinence of the degree of consumer confusion under the fair use defense, we likewise do not pass upon the position of the United States, as *amicus*, that the "used fairly" requirement in § 1115(b)(4) demands only that the descriptive term describe the goods accurately. Tr. of Oral Arg. 17. Accuracy of course has to be a consideration in assessing fair use, but the proceedings in this case so far raise no occasion to evaluate some other concerns that courts might pick as relevant, quite apart from attention to confusion. The Restatement raises possibilities like commercial justification and the strength of the plaintiff's mark. Restatement § 28. As to them, it is enough to say here that the door is not closed.

III

In sum, a plaintiff claiming infringement of an incontestable mark must show likelihood of consumer confusion as part of the prima facie case, 15 U.S.C. § 1115(b), while the defendant has no independent burden to negate the likelihood of any confusion in raising the affirmative defense that a term is used descriptively, not as a mark, fairly, and in good faith, § 1115(b)(4).

Because we read the Court of Appeals as requiring KP to shoulder a burden on the issue of confusion, we vacate the judgment and remand the case for further proceedings consistent with this opinion.

KP Permanent Make–Up, Inc. v. Lasting Impression I, Inc., 408 F. 3d 596 (9th Cir. 2005). On remand, the Ninth Circuit interpreted the Supreme Court's statement that its holding did "not foreclose the relevance of the extent of any likely consumer confusion in assessing whether a defendant's use is objectively fair" and reversed summary judgment for the declaratory judgment plaintiff because there were genuine issues of fact as to likelihood of confusion:

> The fair use defense only comes into play once the party alleging infringement has shown by a preponderance of the evidence that confusion is likely. *See KP II*, 125 S. Ct. at 549. We hold in accordance with *Shakespeare Co.*, 110 F.3d at 243, that the degree of customer confusion remains a factor in evaluating fair use.
>
> Summary judgment on the defense of fair use is also improper. There are genuine issues of fact that are appropriate for the fact finder to determine in order to find that the defense of fair use has been established. Among the relevant factors for consideration by the jury in determining the fairness of the use are the degree of likely confusion, the strength of the trademark, the descriptive nature of the term for

the product or service being offered by KP and the availability of alternate descriptive terms, the extent of the use of the term prior to registration of the trademark, and any differences among the times and contexts in which KP has used the term.

QUESTION

Is the Ninth Circuit's multifactor test for determining fair use a good one? Is it consistent with *Park & Fly*?

CHAPTER 7

FALSE DESIGNATION OF ORIGIN

B. TRADE DRESS

Page 525. Delete Question 2, and the four illustrations on pages 526–27, and replace it with new Question 2:

2. How should courts distinguish between trade dress and product design? In *In re Slokevage,* 441 F.3d 957 (Fed. Cir. 2006), the manufacturer of Flash Dare brand sportswear sought to register a mark consisting of the phrase "Flash Dare" flanked by two peek-a-boo holes in the rear hip area. The applicant argued that the mark was trade dress; the court concluded that it was product design:

> Slokevage urges that her trade dress is not product design because it does not alter the entire product but is more akin to a label being placed on a garment. We do not agree. The holes and flaps portion are part of the design of the clothing—the cut-out area is not merely a design placed on top of a garment, but is a design incorporated into the garment itself. Moreover, while Slokevage urges that product design trade dress must implicate the entire product, we do not find support for that proposition. Just as the product design in Wal–Mart consisted of certain design features featured on clothing, Slokevage's trade dress similarly consists of design features, holes and flaps, featured in clothing, revealing the similarity between the two types of design.
>
> In addition, the reasoning behind the Supreme Court's determination that product design cannot be inherently distinctive is also instructive to our case. The Court reasoned that, unlike a trademark whose "predominant function" remains source identification, product design often serves other functions, such as rendering the "product itself more useful or more appealing." *Wal–Mart*, 529 U.S. at 212, 213. The design at issue here can serve such utilitarian and aesthetic functions. For example, consumers may purchase Slokevage's clothing for the utilitarian purpose of wearing a garment or because they find the appearance of the garment particularly desirable. Consistent with the Supreme Court's analysis in *Wal–Mart*, in such cases when the purchase implicates a utilitarian or aesthetic purpose, rather than a source-identifying function, it is appropriate to require proof of acquired distinctiveness.
>
> Finally, the Court in *Wal–Mart* provided guidance on how to address trade dress cases that may be difficult to classify: "To the extent that there are close cases, we believe that courts should err on

the side of caution and classify ambiguous trade dress as product design, thereby requiring secondary meaning." 529 U.S. at 215. Even if this were a close case, therefore, we must follow that precedent and classify the trade dress as product design. We thus agree with the Board that Slokevage's trade dress is product design and therefore that she must prove acquired distinctiveness in order for her trade dress mark to be registered.

2. Functionality Revisited

Page 534. Insert the following two cases after *Leatherman Tool Group v. Cooper Industries*:

Tie Tech, Inc. v. Kinedyne Corp., 296 F.3d 778 (9th Cir. 2002). Tie Tech sued Kinedyne for marketing a device that was "virtually indistinguishable" from Tie Tech's Safecut™ web cutter.

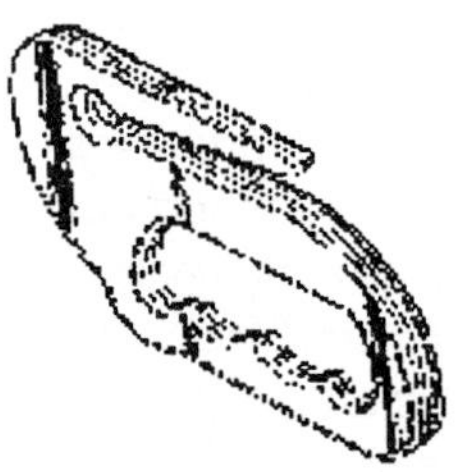

Safecut had succeeded in registering the overall design of the device as a trademark on the principal register in 1998. Kinedyne argued that the product configuration was functional and therefore unprotectable. The 9th Circuit agreed:

> To begin, there is nothing inherently wrong with Kinedyne's interest in copying the SAFECUT's configuration: "The requirement of nonfunctionality is based 'on the judicial theory that *there exists a fundamental right to compete through imitation of a competitor's product*, which right can only be *temporarily* denied by the patent or copyright laws.' " *Clamp[Mfg. Co. v. Enco Mfg. Co.,*], 870 F.2d at 516 (quoting *Morton–Norwich*, 671 F.2d at 1336 (emphasis added)). Consequently, as early as *Vuitton[et Fils S.A. v. J. Young Enters., Inc.*, 644 F.2d 769, 775 (9th Cir. 1981)], we characterized the distinction between "features which constitute the actual benefit that the consumer wishes to purchase," which do not engender trademark protection, "as distinguished from an assurance that a particular entity made, sponsored, or endorsed a product," which, if incorporated into the product's design by virtue of arbitrary embellishment, does have trademark significance. 644 F.2d at 774 (internal quotations and citations omitted); *see also Qualitex Co. v. Jacobson Prods. Co.*, 514 U.S. 159, 164, 115 S.Ct. 1300, 131 L.Ed.2d 248 (1995) ("The functionality doctrine prevents trademark law, which seeks to promote competition by pro-

tecting a firm's reputation, from instead inhibiting legitimate competition by allowing a producer to control a useful product feature.'').

Unfortunately for Tie Tech, it has not pointed to any evidence of distinctiveness of the SAFECUT design other than those elements essential to its effective use. Instead, Tie Tech suggests something different when it claims that it ''is not asking that Kinedyne be barred from having a webcutter with an enclosed blade, a slot and prong to guide the webbing into the blade, or even an opening through which the user can put their [sic] hand,'' but instead that Kinedyne should ''be barred from arranging those elements into a shape that mimics that of the SAFECUT tm.'' In other words, Tie Tech argues that the overall appearance of its cutter, and not its separate functional parts, is what deserves protection as a non-functional aspect of its configuration. This cannot be the case. Where the plaintiff only offers evidence that ''the whole is nothing other than the assemblage of functional parts,'' our court has already foreclosed this argument, holding that ''it is semantic trickery to say that there is still some sort of separate 'overall appearance' which is non-functional.'' *Leatherman*, 199 F.3d at 1013.

Likewise, Tie Tech's evidence of alternative designs fails to raise a material factual issue under *Leatherman*. As was the case with the pocket tool at issue in *Leatherman*, Tie Tech has presented evidence that there are other webcutters with a variety of appearances and features that effectively cut webbing. In particular, Tie Tech cites to a trade journal which evaluated several webcutters including the SAFECUT and another, the Ortho, which is strikingly similar to Kinedyne's original cutter and is described in the article as ''the simplest design—a rectangle with rounded corners [that] several testers found . . . cut the webbing faster than any of the other products.'' As for the SAFECUT, its shape was ''lauded immediately''; one tester was quoted as saying ''I like the grip. . . . It seems like a natural shape.'' Narrowing their preferences down to the Ortho and the SAFECUT, the article's testers

> split on their ultimate preference in web cutters. But all present agreed that either of the two finalists—Ortho's Web Cutter or Tie Tech's Safecut—admirably did the job. They both ripped through the test webbing in a single motion. *It simply came down to personal preference*. (Emphasis added).

This evidence certainly supports Tie Tech's contention that adequate alternative designs exist which ''admirably'' do the job, but to Tie Tech's detriment, it goes further. Because the product review not only demonstrates that a design such as the Ortho may be ''highly functional and useful,'' it also undisputedly shows that the Ortho does not ''offer *exactly* the same features as [the SAFECUT],'' in particular the secured-grip handle, and thus fails as matter of law to support Tie Tech's interest in precluding competition by means of trademark protection. *Id.* at 1013–14 (emphasis in original).

In *Leatherman* we held that a product's manufacturer "does not have rights under trade dress law to compel its competitors to resort to alternative designs which have a different set of advantages and disadvantages. Such is the realm of patent law." *Id.* at 1014 n.7. Here, Tie Tech does not dispute that some customers may prefer a specific functional aspect of the SAFECUT, namely its closed-grip handle, even though other functional designs may ultimately get the job done just as well. As *Leatherman* reminds us, though, a customer's preference for a particular functional aspect of a product is wholly distinct from a customer's desire to be assured "that a particular entity made, sponsored, or endorsed a product." *Id.* at 1012 (quoting *Vuitton*, 644 F.2d at 774). Whereas the latter concern encompasses the realm of trademark protection, the former does not. We therefore conclude on this record that the district court appropriately granted summary judgment in favor of Kinedyne.

Eco Manufacturing LLC v. Honeywell International Inc., 357 F.3d 649 (7th Cir. 2003).

Eco Manufacturing proposes to make a thermostat similar in appearance to Honeywell's well-known circular, convex model with a round dial. . . .

. . . This appeal is from the district court's order declining to issue a preliminary injunction that would block Eco from bringing its product to market. . . . [T]he district court concluded that the shape of Honeywell's thermostat is functional—or, to be precise, that the likelihood of such a finding after a trial on the merits is sufficiently high, and damages are sufficiently easy to calculate if Honeywell turns out to win in the end, that Eco should be allowed to sell its competing product while the litigation proceeds. . . .

Honeywell's lead argument in this court is that it does not matter whether, or to what extent, the thermostat's shape is functional. That is so, Honeywell submits, because the trademark registration became incontestable in 1996, before Eco brought a competing product to market. Once a mark has been used for five years following registration, it becomes "incontestable". 15 U.S.C. § 1065. Incontestability is "conclusive evidence of the validity of the registered mark and ... the registrant's exclusive right" to use the mark in commerce. 15 U.S.C. § 1115(b). See Park'N Fly, Inc. v. Dollar Park and Fly, Inc., 469 U.S. 189, 105 S.Ct. 658, 83 L.Ed.2d 582 (1985).

The words "incontestable" and "exclusive" sound more impressive than the legal rights that the Lanham Act actually conveys, however. Section 1065 says that even "incontestable" marks must yield to prior users, and that the protection dissipates if the mark becomes generic. Moreover, and more to the point, § 1065 says that a claim based on an incontestable mark may be defeated "on a ground for which application to cancel may be filed at any time under paragraphs (3) and (5) of section 1064 of this title". Section 1064(3) provides that a mark may be cancelled if it is, or becomes, functional. Thus incontestability does not avoid the question whether the thermostat's round shape is functional.

. . .

It is not hard to think of three ways in which a round thermostat could be functional, at least in principle. First, rectangular objects may clash with other architectural or decorative choices. Just as a building designed by Ludwig Mies van der Rohe demands controls made from regular or semi-regular polyhedra, so a building designed by Frank Gehry could not tolerate boxy controls. Second, round thermostats (and other controls) may reduce injuries, especially to children, caused by running into protruding sharp corners. Third, people with arthritis or other disabilities may find it easier to set the temperature by turning a large dial (or the entire outer casing of the device) than by moving a slider or pushing buttons on boxes. The record does not contain much along any of these lines, but they are sufficiently plausible to disable Honeywell from prevailing at this preliminary stage, given the burden it bears as a result of the expired patents. Although the three possibilities we have mentioned do not show that roundness is "essential" to a thermostat, that's not required. *TrafFix* rejected an equation of functionality with necessity; it is enough that the design be useful. The Justices told us that a feature is functional if it is essential to the design *or* it affects the article's price or quality. 532 U.S. at 33.

Thus the district court did not abuse its discretion in holding that Eco may go forward with a round thermostat—at its own risk, of course, should the decision come out otherwise on the merits. Although we have not endorsed all of the district court's legal analysis, it would be pointless to remand for another hearing on interlocutory relief. The case should proceed expeditiously to final decision; another "preliminary" round would waste everyone's time. It would be especially inappropriate to direct the district judge to issue a preliminary injunction when issues other than functionality remain to be addressed. Eco contends, for example, that Honeywell bamboozled the Patent and Trademark Office when seeking registration during the 1980s, and material deceit would scotch this enforcement action whether or not the trade dress is functional. We do not express any view on that issue, or any ultimate view about functionality; it is enough to say that the record compiled to date adequately supports the district judge's interlocutory decision.

Page 538. Renumber Question as 1 and insert the following Question 2 and case:

2. Cartier sells expensive luxury watches. It promotes its watches through extensive advertising campaigns. Globe Jewelry makes watches that resemble Cartier watches in outward appearance, but retail for significantly lower prices. Globe's watches are almost indistinguishable from Cartier watches in design and shape, but do not bear the Cartier mark. Cartier sues Globe for trade dress infringement, claiming that Globe has infringed the trade dress of these Cartier watches:

Globe contends that the designs of the watches are functional, and therefore cannot be protected as trade dress. How should the court rule? *See Cartier, Inc. v. Four Star Jewelry Creations, Inc.*, 348 F.Supp.2d 217 (S.D.N.Y. 2004).

Gateway, Inc. v. Companion Products, Inc., 384 F.3d 503 (8th Cir. 2004).

Gateway is a corporation, founded in 1985, based in North Sioux City, South Dakota, that sells computers, computer products, computer peripherals, and computer accessories throughout the world. By 1988, Gateway began its first national advertising campaign using black-and-white cows and black-and-white cow spots. By 1991, black-and-white cows and spots became Gateway's company symbol. Gateway used "Welcome to Gateway Country" and "Gateway Country" as its theme and in association with its stores. In 1992, Gateway registered a black-and-white cow-spots design in association with computers and computer peripherals as its trademark.

CPI, a Colorado company, sells stuffed animals trademarked as "Stretch Pets." Stretch Pets have an animal's head and an elastic body that can wrap around the edges of computer monitors, computer cases, or televisions. CPI produces sixteen Stretch Pets using a variety of animals, including a polar bear, moose, cow, several dogs, and a penguin. Each Stretch Pet has a tag hanging from its ear and a tag sewn into its seam that contains the trademark "Stretch Pets" and the name "Companion Products."[2]

2. CPI advertises and sells its Stretch Pets through flyers, catalogs, the Internet, magazines, independent sales representatives, and phone calls to various retailers. CPI has used the phrase "Welcome to Stretch Pet Country" in some of its advertisements. In retail stores, "Stretch Pets" and "Companion Products" are prominently displayed on each box.

One of CPI's top-selling products is a black-and-white cow that CPI identifies as "Cody Cow." CPI began selling Cody Cow in 1999. CPI has sold approximately 45,000 Stretch Pets and approximately 7,000 of those are Cody Cow. Cody Cow's design and marketing is the catalyst for this case.

. . .

CPI urges that the district court erred in finding Gateway's mark to be nonfunctional, and thus protected as trade dress. Specifically, CPI contends that Gateway's trademark is a functional or ornamental feature of their computer products, and thus Gateway's product is unable to be protected as a trade dress or a trademark.

. . .

Gateway's trade dress clearly reflects characteristics that are non-functional. Black-and-white cow spots are an arbitrary embellishment that serve only to distinguish Gateway computers from computers produced by other manufacturers. The purely decorative nature of the design plays no part whatsoever in the performance of Gateway's computers. Surely, no consumer believes that the presence of this design affects the operation of electronic components and peripherals associated with Gateway. Gateway's competitors in the field of computers and their peripherals are not hindered in the least from producing comparable or superior products dressed in some other manner than black-and-white cow spots.

Gateway's trade dress does not prevent CPI from using other colors and designs for their computer-decorative products. They are not placed at a disadvantage to other makers of such products because those companies may not use Gateway's protected trade dress either. CPI produced testimony that collectors of cows prefer cows that have black-and-white spots and that Cody Cow was manufactured for sale to cow collectors. However, the district court made credibility findings regarding Byer's true motives for the production and sale of Cody Cow. Specifically, the court discredited Byer's testimony and found that the product was actually created with Gateway in mind. In sum, CPI may make and sell a collectible cow but it may not sell one like Cody Cow that is specifically identified with Gateway's trademark.

3. Trade Dress Infringement

Page 538. Insert the following case before *Best Cellars v. Grape Finds*:

Gibson Guitar Corp. v. Paul Reed Smith Guitars

423 F.3d 539 (6th Cir. 2005).

[Gibson Guitar Corporation has manufactured the Les Paul solid body guitar since 1952. Gibson registered the shape of the Les Paul guitar on the principal register in 1987. The mark is incontestable. Paul Reed Smith Guitars(PRS) introduced the Singlecut, a similarly shaped solid-body guitar, in 2000. Gibson sued PRS for trademark infringement. The district court granted Gibson's summary judgment motion on its trademark claim, and PRS appealed. Gibson conceded before the district court and on appeal that there was no point-of-sale confusion between its Les Paul guitars and PRS's SingleCut guitars. It nonetheless argued that the similarity in guitar shapes was likely to cause actionable confusion before and after the point of sale.]

■ Karen Nelson Moore, Circuit Judge.

1. Gibson's Theories of Purchaser Confusion

Gibson argues that despite the lack of actual confusion at the point of sale, the district court's decision can be affirmed under a theory of either initial-interest confusion (the theory relied on by the district court), post-sale confusion, or some combination of the two. Initial-interest confusion takes place when a manufacturer improperly uses a trademark to create initial customer interest in a product, even if the customer realizes, prior to purchase, that the product was not actually manufactured by the trademark-holder. [Citations] Post-sale confusion occurs when use of a trademark leads individuals (other than the purchaser) mistakenly to believe that a product was manufactured by the trademark-holder [Citation]. We conclude that neither initial-interest confusion, nor post-sale confusion, nor any combination of two, is applicable in this case.

Gibson Les Paul Guitar

PRS Singlecut Guitar

a. Initial–Interest Confusion

. . . .

Gibson essentially argues that the shape of the PRS guitar leads consumers standing on the far side of the room in a guitar store to believe they see Gibson guitars and walk over to examine what they soon realize are PRS guitars. We decline to adopt such a broad reading of the initial-interest-confusion doctrine. Many, if not most, consumer products will tend to appear like their competitors at a sufficient distance. Where product shapes themselves are trademarked, such a theory would prevent competitors from producing even *dissimilar* products which might appear, from the far end of an aisle in a warehouse store, somewhat similar to a trademarked shape. Accordingly, we hold that initial-interest confusion cannot substitute for point-of-sale confusion on the facts of this case.

b. Post–Sale Confusion

The one published case where we have applied post-sale confusion is also clearly distinguishable from the present case. *Esercizio [v. Roberts*, 944 F.2d 1235 (6th Cir. 1991), *cert. denied*, 505 U.S. 1219 (1992)], a trade-dress case, involved Ferrari sports cars which were manufactured in deliberately limited quantities "in order to create an image of exclusivity." *Esercizio*,

944 F.2d at 1237. The alleged infringer built fiberglass kits intended to be "bolted onto the undercarriage of another automobile such as a Chevrolet Corvette or a Pontiac Fiero" in order to make the "donor car" look like a far-more-expensive Ferrari. *Id.* at 1238. Our concern in *Esercizio* was that "Ferrari's reputation in the field could be damaged by the marketing of Roberts' [clearly inferior] replicas." *Id.* at 1245. Such a concern is not present here, where Gibson concedes that PRS guitars are not clearly inferior to Gibson guitars. Accordingly, post-sale confusion cannot serve as a substitute for point-of-sale confusion in this case.

c. Gibson's Smoky–Bar Theory of Confusion

Finally, Gibson argues that, taken together, the initial-interest-confusion and post-sale-confusion doctrines should be extended to include something that we can only describe as a "smoky-bar theory of confusion." Initial-interest-confusion doctrine, which we have already rejected on the facts of this case, applies when allegedly improper use of a trademark attracts potential purchasers to consider products or services provided by the infringer. Post-sale-confusion doctrine, which we have also rejected on the facts of this case, applies when allegedly improper use of protected trade dress on a lower-quality product diminishes the reputation of the holder of the rights to that trade dress. In the smoky-bar context, however, Gibson does not suggest that consumer confusion as to the manufacturer of a PRS guitar would lead a potential purchaser to consider purchasing a PRS, rather than a Gibson, or that Gibson's reputation is harmed by poor-quality PRS guitars. Rather, Gibson argues that this confusion occurs when potential purchasers see a musician playing a PRS guitar and believe it to be a Gibson guitar:

> In the context of guitar sales, initial interest confusion is of real consequence. Guitar manufacturers know that they can make sales by placing their guitars in the hands of famous musicians. On a distant stage, a smoky bar, wannabe musicians see their heroes playing a guitar they then want.

Gibson Br. at 20–21. As Gibson concedes that PRS produces high-quality guitars, we do not believe such an occurrence could result in confusion harmful to Gibson. If a budding musician sees an individual he or she admires playing a PRS guitar, but believes it to be a Gibson guitar, the logical result would be that the budding musician would go out and purchase a Gibson guitar. Gibson is helped, rather than harmed, by any such confusion.

2. The Summary Judgment Motions

We have determined as a matter of law that initial-interest confusion, post-sale confusion, and Gibson's "smoky-bar theory of confusion" cannot be used to demonstrate infringement of the trademark at issue in this case. Gibson has conceded that point-of-sale confusion does not occur between these high-priced guitars, and our review of the record does not suggest otherwise. Accordingly, there is simply no basis on which Gibson can show confusion that would demonstrate trademark infringement in violation of the Lanham Act. *See KP Permanent Make–Up, Inc. v. Lasting Impression I, Inc.*, 543 U.S. 111 (2004) (noting that a claim of trademark infringement under the Lanham Act "requires a showing that the defendant's actual practice is likely to produce confusion in the minds of consumers about the origin of the goods or services in question"). Accordingly, PRS, rather than Gibson, must be granted summary judgment on Gibson's trademark-infringement claim.

. . . .

■ KENNEDY, CIRCUIT JUDGE, concurring in part and dissenting in part.

I agree that the district court erred in granting summary judgment in favor of Gibson and I also agree that Gibson cannot maintain its trademark infringement claim either on a theory of likelihood of confusion at the point-of-sale (for it has disclaimed that a consumer could be confused at the point-of-sale) or on a theory of post-sale confusion. However, because I believe that a product shape trademark holder should be able to present evidence to maintain a trademark infringement claim on the theory of initial-interest confusion, I dissent with respect to this issue.

. . . .

The majority's reason for rejecting the application of initial interest confusion to product shapes is based upon the concern that since many product shapes within the same category will appear similar when viewed from a sufficient distance, if the initial-interest confusion doctrine were applied to product shapes, a product shape trademark holder could prevent competitors from producing even dissimilar products that appeared from a sufficient distance to be somewhat similar to a trademarked shape. This concern, however, is misplaced. Evidence that a competitor's product shape is similar to a trademark holder's product shape when viewed from afar is irrelevant unless the product shape trademark holder maintains that its product shape identifies its source when viewed from afar. For if a product shape trademark holder does not assert that its product shape identifies its source when viewed from a certain distance, then any alleged confusion between the trademark holder's product shape and a competitor's product shape would not support the trademark holder's claim for infringement. If a product shape trademark holder does assert that its product shape serves to identify the product's source when viewed from a distance where many competitor products appear substantially the same, then this will be evidence that the trademark holder's product shape does not identify its source. If most product shapes in the same product category have similar shapes, a product shape trademark holder will have a difficult time establishing that its trademark identifies the source of its product when viewed from afar, for the further one is away from a product, the more similar products in the same category will look to each other and, thus, the less likely a product shape will identify the source of the product (i.e. serve as a trademark) from that vantage point. In other words, a product shape trademark holder will not be able to present probative evidence of initial interest confusion unless it first shows that its product shape identifies its source when viewed from the vantage point where the confusion is alleged to have occurred.

Page 553. Insert the following material after *Best Cellars v. Grape Finds*:

What are the elements of Best Cellars' protected trade dress? The colors, names and images designating its eight taste categories? The light wood and stainless steel décor? The color-coded wall signs? The layout and arrangement of wine bottles? On page 548, Judge Sweet lists 14 elements that plaintiff claimed as elements of its protected trade dress. How many of these elements does Judge Sweet determine are entitled to protection? How many of these elements did Grape Finds copy?

Best Cellars v. Wine Made Simple, 320 F.Supp.2d 60 (S.D.N.Y. 2003). Best Cellars brought a trade dress infringement suit against a second purveyor of wines by taste categories. Like Grape Finds, defendant Wines Made Simple operated a wine store that sold moderately priced wines sorted into eight taste categories. Judge Gerard Lynch agreed with Best Cellars that the trade dress of its stores was inherently distinctive, but found it more difficult to determine whether Wines Made Simple infringed it:

> Plaintiff Best Cellars owns and operates four wine stores, including its flagship store on the Upper East Side of Manhattan, which pursue the novel marketing strategy of organizing wines by taste category rather than by grape type or country of origin. The flagship store has a clean, crisp, modern decor that demonstrates that the owners invested energy and capital in the design of the store as well as in the development of the marketing theme. Best Cellars opened its flagship store in November 1996. . . . The interior design included wine racks built into a wall, which consist of tubes to hold bottles of wine horizontally, creating the appearance of a grid of steel rimmed holes in a light wood-paneled wall. The graphic design elements include computer-generated icons and brightly colored signs associated with each taste category.
>
> . . .
>
> Like Best Cellars, Bacchus aims to sell wine to novice wine consumers by organizing the store's inventory by taste category, and by retailing modestly-priced wines in an imaginatively-decorated store. The Bacchus stores have a Mediterranean-themed decor consisting of white stucco and dark wood beams, and display wine bottles horizontally in racks which are constructed to resemble a grid of holes in a white stucco wall.
>
> . . .
>
> In this case, it is undisputed that there are a number of similarities between the interior designs of plaintiff's and defendants' stores. Both stores have racks of wine arranged around the perimeter of the store. The wine racks store the wine bottles horizontally in what

appears to be a grid of holes in a wall. Both stores have one display bottle of wine presented vertically above a column of that identical wine stored horizontally in holes. Both stores have a method of illuminating the wine racks from behind the wine bottles. Both stores separate wine into eight taste categories, in addition to one to two other non-taste-based categories. Each taste category is identified by single words describing a taste property. Both stores have a farm table for display. Both stores have signs above the wine racks indicating the category stored in that area. Both stores use index card identifiers posted at eye-level on the wine racks describing individual wines. Both stores use different individual colors on signs and index cards to identify the categories of wine. Both stores sell books about wine as well as wineglasses and other items related to wine drinking. Both stores stock approximately 100 different varieties of wine that retail for less than 20 dollars a bottle.

On the other hand, it is also undisputed that there are a number of dissimilar elements between the store designs. Plaintiff's dominant building materials are blonde wood paneling and stainless steel detail, while defendants use primarily white stucco and dark-brown stained wood beams. Plaintiff's store prominently features large color-coded signs containing unique computer-generated graphics that serve as iconic identifiers for the different categories of wine. In fact, plaintiff has won numerous awards for its computer-generated graphics and has sought and received trademark protection for those graphic designs. Defendants utilize no such icon-coding system, and rely instead on tarnished-looking metal signs with no pictorial image to identify the different categories of wine. The lettering of defendants' category signs appears to be roughly cut out of the sheet of metal that comprises each sign. While each sign is of the same colored metal, the lettering of each sign is in the unique color associated with the category of wine. Plaintiff's and defendants' stores use different colors and different names to delineate categories of wine. Plaintiff has sought and received trademark protection for the specific words used to identify six of its eight taste categories. Plaintiff does not allege that defendants infringed any trademarked element of plaintiff's trade dress such as the icon identifiers or the specific category names. The only graphic image associated with defendants' store is a classically-styled painted "fresco" of Bacchus, the Roman god of wine for whom the store is named. In contrast, plaintiff's trade dress does not associate its store with any personality, either human or divine, and plaintiff's store features modern computer graphic images, not faux-classical painted images. The names of the stores too are not similar. To state the obvious, the name "Best Cellars" is a play on words, punning between a "best seller" as a popular consumer item, and a "best cellar" in the sense of a superior wine collection. The name "Bacchus" straightforwardly references a mythological enjoyer of wine. It is undisputed that the store names figure prominently in both defendants' and plaintiff's respective trade dress.

Overall Visual Image

What *is* disputed is the overall effect of the interior decor of the wine stores on consumer perception of those stores. Courts are instructed to proceed very carefully with respect to the similarity of the overall impression of trade dress, because issues of consumer confusion are normally factual in nature and thus rarely appropriate for summary judgment. [Citation] A judge can look at photographs of the respective stores and form his or her own opinion of how similar they appear. Undoubtedly, there will be cases where the similarity is so patent, or the divergence so dramatic, that reasonable jurors necessarily must agree that the appearances are either closely similar or distinctly different. But in most cases, the subjectivity of perception counsels judges not to assume that their assessment of overall similarity will necessarily be shared by all reasonable jurors. In this case, as is apparent from the listing of similar and different features of the stores' trade dress, the question is really whether the similar features or the divergent ones dominate the viewer's response to the overall "look" of the stores. This is a matter about which reasonable people can easily differ.

In this case, moreover, the interaction of marketing theme with trade dress presents an additional complication. " 'An idea, a concept, or a generalized type of appearance' cannot be protected under trade dress law, although 'the concrete expression of an idea in a trade dress has received protection.' " *Grape Finds*, 90 F.Supp.2d at 451, quoting *Jeffrey Milstein*, 58 F.3d at 32–33 (internal citations omitted). The idea of marketing wine by taste, however innovative it may be, is not protected by trade dress law, and Best Cellars cannot invoke the Lanham Act to preserve a monopoly on operating retail stores that categorize wines by taste. "Uniqueness of an idea and not the trade dress itself is not a proper basis upon which a court can base a finding that a trade dress is capable of being a source identifier. The connection must be between the trade dress and the product, not the idea and the product." *Sports Traveler [Inc. v. Advance Magazine Publishers, Inc.*, 25 F.Supp.2d 154, 163 (S.D.N.Y. 1998)], 25 F.Supp.2d at 163.

In this case, plaintiff claims, in effect, that its (formerly) unique marketing style is part of its trade dress. Uniqueness of marketing style is not a factor in the *Polaroid* test, and this Court will discount marketing theme in its analysis of the similarity of the trade dresses because that alone is not the focus of the legal inquiry. When the analytic focus is trained on trade dress, that is, on the general appearance of the interior decor of the stores which includes a marketing concept, rather than on marketing ideas alone, then the stores appear similar in some key respects, and dissimilar on others. Plaintiff's store is characterized by light wood-paneled walls, stainless steel finishings and brightly colored computer-generated icons. Defendants' store, by contrast, presents an atmosphere distinguished by white stucco walls with dark wood beams, rusted metal signs, and a classically-styled painting of the Roman god of wine. Rather than slavishly imitating plaintiff's decor, defendants have deviated from it in very significant ways. The similarity of the wine rack system is apparent, but is merely one element in the general appearance of the stores. The similarity of the categories of wine is also apparent, but the stores use different names for the categories and different colors associated with the categories as well as very different signs. Reasonable viewers could well disagree about whether the similarities outweigh the differences, or vice versa, in determining the overall similarity or differences of the decor.

Conclusion

Because in this case the similarity of the marks element is at the heart of the consumer confusion prong of the trade dress infringement test, and because reasonable minds could disagree as to the degree of similarity, this question is not suited for summary judgment. For this reason, and because there are material issues of fact as to virtually all of the Polaroid factors in this case, plaintiff's and defendants' cross-motions for summary judgment on the Lanham Act 43(a) claim for injunctive relief are denied.

QUESTION

1. Philip Morris, makers of Marlboro cigarettes, sued Cowboy Cigarettes for trade dress infringement. Cowboy markets its Cowboys Cigarettes in a red package showing the silhouette of a cowboy on a horse. The Cowboys package design does not resemble the design of the Marlboros package, but Philip Morris argues that its long use of cowboy imagery to promote Marlboros is itself trade dress, and Cowboy's use of cowboy imagery and the Cowboys name constitutes trade dress infringement. How should the court rule? *See Philip Morris USA v. Cowboy Cigarette*, 70 U.S.P.Q. 2d 1092 (S.D.N.Y. 2003).

2. J.K. Rowling's Harry Potter books have been wildly successful. The books follow Harry, a talented young wizard, through his years as a student at Hogwarts School of Witchcraft and Wizardry. Rowling has so far published six books in what she projects to be a seven book series. The U.S. book publishing, motion picture and merchandising rights are owned by Scholastic Books and Warner Brothers Pictures. Warner Brothers has made four Harry Potter movies, and is currently planning the fifth. Warner Brothers has registered the marks HARRY POTTER and HOGWARTS for motion pictures, toys, calendars, figurines, candy, clothing, and art.

The Fox Creek School is a non-profit private school. Although Fox Creek's tuition is substantial, it is not able to meet its budget on tuition alone. It relies on outside foundation support and a variety of fundraising activities for additional funds. The most important of its fundraising activities is a summer day camp program, which it views both as a chance to recruit new potential students and an opportunity to raise significant funds to offset the substantial deficit incurred during the school year. The summer camp program offers one-week sessions to children from age 5 to age 13, focusing on a variety of subjects. Recent summer sessions have featured Spanish, astronomy, Arabic, filmmaking, computer programming, gardening, Japanese, chemistry, and tournament chess.

By far the most popular and successful summer camp program at Fox Creek is one that it calls "A Very Special Week at Hogwarts." Fox Creek introduced the Hogwarts camp four years ago. The camp was full within a week of its announcement. The following year, Fox Creek offered two one-week sessions of Hogwarts camp, but was unable to fulfill demand. Last year, Fox Creek ran three one-week sessions; this coming year, it is planning on at least four. The camp is inspired by and based on J.K. Rowling's Harry Potter books and the Warner Brothers movies derived from those books.

Fox Creek advertises its camp on its website, in flyers it distributes to its students, and in ads placed in local newspapers. The ads, which do not mention either Scholastic Books or Warner Brothers, explain that

> *A Very Special Week at Hogwarts* is our overwhelmingly popular Harry Potter camp. For three consecutive weeks, Fox Creek is transformed into Hogwarts School, where the summer campers learn sorcery and spells, play Quidditch, and encounter many of the characters from the Harry Potter books. Summer fun at its best!

Fox Creek has not sought permission from Rowling, Warner Brothers, or Scholastic Books to operate its camp. Do you see a likelihood of confusion?

Page 566. Replace the material on pages 566–568 with the following new section:

Dastar Corporation v. Twentieth Century Fox Film Corporation

539 U.S. 23 (2003).

■ Justice Scalia delivered the opinion of the Court.

In this case, we are asked to decide whether § 43(a) of the Lanham Act, 15 U.S.C. § 1125(a), prevents the unaccredited copying of a work. . . .

I

In 1948, three and a half years after the German surrender at Reims, General Dwight D. Eisenhower completed *Crusade in Europe*, his written account of the allied campaign in Europe during World War II. Doubleday published the book, registered it with the Copyright Office in 1948, and granted exclusive television rights to an affiliate of respondent Twentieth Century Fox Film Corporation (Fox). Fox, in turn, arranged for Time, Inc., to produce a television series, also called *Crusade in Europe*, based on the book, and Time assigned its copyright in the series to Fox. The television series, consisting of 26 episodes, was first broadcast in 1949. It combined a soundtrack based on a narration of the book with film footage from the United States Army, Navy, and Coast Guard, the British Ministry of Information and War Office, the National Film Board of Canada, and unidentified "Newsreel Pool Cameramen." In 1975, Doubleday renewed the copyright on the book.... Fox, however, did not renew the copyright on the *Crusade* television series, which expired in 1977, leaving the television series in the public domain.

In 1988, Fox reacquired the television rights in General Eisenhower's book, including the exclusive right to distribute the *Crusade* television series on video and to sub-license others to do so. Respondents SFM Entertainment and New Line Home Video, Inc., in turn, acquired from Fox the exclusive rights to distribute *Crusade* on video. SFM obtained the negatives of the original television series, restored them, and repackaged the series on videotape; New Line distributed the videotapes.

Enter petitioner Dastar. In 1995, Dastar decided to expand its product line from music compact discs to videos. Anticipating renewed interest in World War II on the 50th anniversary of the war's end, Dastar released a video set entitled *World War II Campaigns in Europe*. To make *Campaigns*, Dastar purchased eight beta cam tapes of the *original* version of the *Crusade* television series, which is in the public domain, copied them, and then edited the series. Dastar's *Campaigns* series is slightly more than half as long as the original *Crusade* television series. Dastar substituted a new opening sequence, credit page, and final closing for those of the *Crusade* television series; inserted new chapter-title sequences and narrated chapter introductions; moved the "recap" in the *Crusade* television series to the beginning and retitled it as a "preview"; and removed references to and images of the book. Dastar created new packaging for its *Campaigns* series and (as already noted) a new title.

Dastar manufactured and sold the *Campaigns* video set as its own product. The advertising states: "Produced and Distributed by: *Entertainment Distributing*" (which is owned by Dastar), and makes no reference to the *Crusade* television series. Similarly, the screen credits state "DASTAR CORP presents" and "an ENTERTAINMENT DISTRIBUTING Production," and list as executive producer, producer, and associate producer, employees of Dastar. The *Campaigns* videos themselves also make no reference to the *Crusade* television series, New Line's *Crusade* videotapes, or the book. Dastar sells its *Campaigns* videos to Sam's Club, Costco, Best Buy, and other retailers and mail-order companies for $25 per set, substantially less than New Line's video set.

In 1998, respondents Fox, SFM, and New Line brought this action alleging that Dastar's sale of its *Campaigns* video set infringes Doubleday's copyright in General Eisenhower's book and, thus, their exclusive television rights in the book. Respondents later amended their complaint to add claims that Dastar's sale of *Campaigns* "without proper credit" to the *Crusade* television series constitutes "reverse passing off"[1] in violation of § 43(a) of the Lanham Act, 15 U.S.C. § 1125(a)....

1. Passing off (or palming off, as it is sometimes called) occurs when a producer misrepresents his own goods or services as someone else's. See, *e.g., O. & W. Thum Co.*

The Court of Appeals for the Ninth Circuit affirmed the judgment for respondents on the Lanham Act claim, but reversed as to the copyright claim and remanded. With respect to the Lanham Act claim, the Court of Appeals reasoned that "Dastar copied substantially the entire *Crusade in Europe* series created by Twentieth Century Fox, labeled the resulting product with a different name and marketed it without attribution to Fox [,and] therefore committed a 'bodily appropriation' of Fox's series." *Id.*, at 314. It concluded that "Dastar's 'bodily appropriation' of Fox's original [television] series is sufficient to establish the reverse passing off."

II

The Lanham Act was intended to make "actionable the deceptive and misleading use of marks," and "to protect persons engaged in ... commerce against unfair competition." 15 U.S.C. § 1127. While much of the Lanham Act addresses the registration, use, and infringement of trademarks and related marks, § 43(a), 15 U.S.C. § 1125(a) is one of the few provisions that goes beyond trademark protection. As originally enacted, § 43(a) created a federal remedy against a person who used in commerce either "a false designation of origin, or any false description or representation" in connection with "any goods or services." 60 Stat 441. As the Second Circuit accurately observed with regard to the original enactment, however—and as remains true after the 1988 revision—§ 43(a) "does not have boundless application as a remedy for unfair trade practices," *Alfred Dunhill, Ltd.* v. *Interstate Cigar Co.*, 499 F.2d 232, 237 (1974). "Because of its inherently limited wording, § 43(a) can never be a federal 'codification' of the overall law of 'unfair competition,'" 4 J. McCarthy Trademarks and Unfair Competition § 27:7, p. 27–14 (4th ed. 2002) (McCarthy), but can apply only to certain unfair trade practices prohibited by its text.

Although a case can be made that a proper reading of § 43(a), as originally enacted, would treat the word "origin" as referring only "to the geographic location in which the goods originated," *Two Pesos, Inc.* v. *Taco Cabana, Inc.*, 505 U.S. 763, 777, 120 L. Ed. 2d 615, 112 S. Ct. 2753 (1992) (Stevens, J., concurring in judgment), the Courts of Appeals considering the issue, beginning with the Sixth Circuit, unanimously concluded that it "does not merely refer to geographical origin, but also to origin of source or manufacture," *Federal–Mogul–Bower Bearings, Inc.* v. *Azoff*, 313 F.2d 405, 408 (1963), thereby creating a federal cause of action for traditional trademark infringement of unregistered marks. See 4 McCarthy § 27:14; *Two Pesos, supra*, at 768, 120 L. Ed. 2d 615, 112 S Ct 2753. Moreover, every Circuit to consider the issue found § 43(a) broad enough to encompass reverse passing off. [Citations] The Trademark Law Revision Act of 1988 made clear that § 43(a) covers origin of production as well as geographic origin. Its language is amply inclusive, moreover, of reverse

v. *Dickinson*, 245 F. 609, 621 (CA6 1917). See, *e.g.*, Reverse passing off, as its name implies, is the opposite: The producer misrepresents someone else's goods or services as his own. *Williams* v. *Curtiss-Wright Corp.*, 691 F.2d 168, 172 (CA3 1982).

passing off—if indeed it does not implicitly adopt the unanimous court-of-appeals jurisprudence on that subject. [Citations]

Thus, as it comes to us, the gravamen of respondents' claim is that, in marketing and selling *Campaigns* as its own product without acknowledging its nearly wholesale reliance on the *Crusade* television series, Dastar has made a "false designation of origin, false or misleading description of fact, or false or misleading representation of fact, which ... is likely to cause confusion ... as to the origin ... of his or her goods." That claim would undoubtedly be sustained if Dastar had bought some of New Line's *Crusade* videotapes and merely repackaged them as its own. Dastar's alleged wrongdoing, however, is vastly different: it took a creative work in the public domain—the *Crusade* television series—copied it, made modifications (arguably minor), and produced its very own series of videotapes. If "origin" refers only to the manufacturer or producer of the physical "goods" that are made available to the public (in this case the videotapes), Dastar was the origin. If, however, "origin" includes the creator of the underlying work that Dastar copied, then someone else (perhaps Fox) was the origin of Dastar's product. At bottom, we must decide what § 43(a)(1)(A) of the Lanham Act means by the "origin" of "goods."

III

The dictionary definition of "origin" is "the fact or process of coming into being from a source," and "that from which anything primarily proceeds; source." Webster's New International Dictionary 1720–1721 (2d ed. 1949). And the dictionary definition of "goods" (as relevant here) is "[w]ares; merchandise." *Id.*, at 1079. We think the most natural understanding of the "origin" of "goods"—the source of wares—is the producer of the tangible product sold in the marketplace, in this case the physical *Campaigns* videotape sold by Dastar. The concept might be stretched (as it was under the original version of § 43(a)) to include not only the actual producer, but also the trademark owner who commissioned or assumed responsibility for ("stood behind") production of the physical product. But as used in the Lanham Act, the phrase "origin of goods" is in our view incapable of connoting the person or entity that originated the ideas or communications that "goods" embody or contain. Such an extension would not only stretch the text, but it would be out of accord with the history and purpose of the Lanham Act and inconsistent with precedent.

Section 43(a) of the Lanham Act prohibits actions like trademark infringement that deceive consumers and impair a producer's goodwill. It forbids, for example, the Coca–Cola Company's passing off its product as Pepsi–Cola or reverse passing off Pepsi–Cola as its product. But the brand-loyal consumer who prefers the drink that the Coca–Cola Company or PepsiCo sells, while he believes that that company produced (or at least stands behind the production of) that product, surely does not necessarily believe that that company was the "origin" of the drink in the sense that it was the very first to devise the formula. The consumer who buys a branded product does not automatically assume that the brand-name company is the same entity that came up with the idea for the product, or designed the product—and typically does not care whether it is. The words of the Lanham Act should not be stretched to cover matters that are typically of no consequence to purchasers.

It could be argued, perhaps, that the reality of purchaser concern is different for what might be called a communicative product—one that is valued not primarily for its physical qualities, such as a hammer, but for the intellectual content that it conveys, such as a book or, as here, a video. The purchaser of a novel is interested not merely, if at all, in the identity of the producer of the physical tome (the publisher), but also, and indeed primarily, in the identity of the creator of the story it conveys (the author). And the author, of course, has at least as much interest in avoiding passing-off (or reverse passing-off) of his creation as does the publisher. For such a communicative product (the argument goes) "origin of goods" in § 43(a) must be deemed to include not merely the producer of the physical item (the publishing house Farrar, Straus and Giroux, or the video producer Dastar) but also the creator of the content that the physical item conveys (the author Tom Wolfe, or—assertedly—respondents).

The problem with this argument according special treatment to communicative products is that it causes the Lanham Act to conflict with the law of copyright, which addresses that subject specifically. The right to copy, and to copy without attribution, once a copyright has expired, like "the right to make [an article whose patent has expired]—including the right to make it in precisely the shape it carried when patented—passes to the public." *Sears, Roebuck & Co.* v. *Stiffel Co.*, 376 U.S. 225, 230 (1964); see also *Kellogg Co.* v. *National Biscuit Co.*, 305 U.S. 111, 121–122 (1938). "In general, unless an intellectual property right such as a patent or copyright protects an item, it will be subject to copying." *TrafFix Devices, Inc.* v. *Marketing Displays, Inc.*, 532 U.S. 23, 29 (2001). The rights of a patentee or copyright holder are part of a "carefully crafted bargain," *Bonito Boats, Inc.* v. *Thunder Craft Boats, Inc.*, 489 U.S. 141, 150–151 (1989), under which, once the patent or copyright monopoly has expired, the public may use the invention or work at will and without attribution. Thus, in construing the Lanham Act, we have been "careful to caution against misuse or over-extension" of trademark and related protections into areas traditionally occupied by patent or copyright. *TrafFix*, 532 U.S., at 29. "The Lanham Act," we have said, "does not exist to reward manufacturers for their innovation in creating a particular device; that is the purpose of the patent law and its period of exclusivity." *Id.*, at 34. Federal trademark law "has no necessary relation to invention or discovery," *Trade-Mark Cases,* 100 U.S. 82, 94 (1879), but rather, by preventing competitors from copying "a source-identifying mark," "reduces the customer's costs of shopping and making purchasing decisions," and "helps assure a producer that it (and not an imitating competitor) will reap the financial, reputation-related rewards associated with a desirable product," *Qualitex Co.* v. *Jacobson Products Co.*, 514 U.S. 159, 163–164 (1995) (internal quotation marks and citation omitted). Assuming for the sake of argument that Dastar's representation of itself as the "Producer" of its videos amounted to a representation that it originated the creative work conveyed by the videos, allowing a cause of action under § 43(a) for that representation would create a species of mutant copyright law that limits the public's "federal right to 'copy and to use,' " expired copyrights, *Bonito Boats*, *supra*, at 165.

. . . .

Reading "origin" in § 43(a) to require attribution of uncopyrighted materials would pose serious practical problems. Without a copyrighted work as the basepoint, the word "origin" has no discernable limits. A video of the MGM film *Carmen Jones*, after its copyright has expired, would presumably require attribution not just to MGM, but to Oscar Hammerstein II (who wrote the musical on which the film was based), to Georges Bizet (who wrote the opera on which the musical was based), and to Prosper Merimee (who wrote the novel on which the opera was based). In many cases, figuring out who is in the line of "origin" would be no simple task. Indeed, in the present case it is far from clear that respondents have that status. Neither SFM nor New Line had anything to do with the production of the *Crusade* television series—they merely were licensed to distribute the video version. While Fox might have a claim to being in the line of origin, its involvement with the creation of the television series was limited at best. Time, Inc., was the principal if not the exclusive creator, albeit under arrangement with Fox. And of course it was neither Fox nor Time, Inc., that shot the film used in the *Crusade* television series. Rather, that footage came from the United States Army, Navy, and Coast Guard, the British Ministry of Information and War Office, the National Film Board of Canada, and unidentified "Newsreel Pool Cameramen." If anyone has a claim to being the *original* creator of the material used in both the *Crusade* television series and the *Campaigns* videotapes, it would be those groups, rather than Fox. We do not think the Lanham Act requires this search for the source of the Nile and all its tributaries.

Another practical difficulty of adopting a special definition of "origin" for communicative products is that it places the manufacturers of those products in a difficult position. On the one hand, they would face Lanham Act liability for *failing* to credit the creator of a work on which their lawful copies are based; and on the other hand they could face Lanham Act liability for *crediting* the creator if that should be regarded as implying the creator's "sponsorship or approval" of the copy, 15 U.S.C. § 1125(a)(1)(A). In this case, for example, if Dastar had simply "copied [the television series] as *Crusade in Europe* and sold it as *Crusade in Europe*," without changing the title or packaging (including the original credits to Fox), it is hard to have confidence in respondents' assurance that they "would not be here on a Lanham Act cause of action," Tr. of Oral Arg. 35.

Finally, reading § 43(a) of the Lanham Act as creating a cause of action for, in effect, plagiarism—the use of otherwise unprotected works and inventions without attribution—would be hard to reconcile with our previous decisions. For example, in *Wal-Mart Stores, Inc.* v. *Samara Brothers, Inc.*, 529 U.S. 205 (2000), we considered whether product-design trade dress can ever be inherently distinctive. Wal–Mart produced "knockoffs" of children's clothes designed and manufactured by Samara Brothers, containing only "minor modifications" of the original designs. *Id.*, at 208. We concluded that the designs could not be protected under § 43(a) without a showing that they had acquired "secondary meaning," *id.*, at 214, so that they " 'identify the source of the product rather than the product itself,' " *id.*, at 211, (quoting *Inwood Laboratories, Inc.* v. *Ives Laboratories, Inc.*, 456 U.S. 844, 851, n. 11 (1982)). This carefully considered limitation would be entirely pointless if the "original" producer could turn around and pursue a reverse-passing-off claim under exactly the same provision of the Lanham Act. Samara would merely have had to argue that it was the "origin" of the designs that Wal–Mart was selling as its own line. It was not, because "origin of goods" in the Lanham Act referred to the producer of the clothes, and not the producer of the (potentially) copyrightable or patentable designs that the clothes embodied.

. . . .

In sum, reading the phrase "origin of goods" in the Lanham Act in accordance with the Act's common-law foundations (which were *not* designed to protect originality or creativity), and in light of the copyright and patent laws (which *were*), we conclude that the phrase refers to the producer of the tangible goods that are offered for sale, and not to the author of any idea, concept, or communication embodied in those goods. Cf. 17 U.S.C. § 202 [17 U.S.C.S. § 202] (distinguishing between a copyrighted work and "any material object in which the work is embodied"). To hold otherwise would be akin to finding that § 43(a) created a species of perpetual patent and copyright, which Congress may not do.

Bretford Manufacturing, Inc. v. Smith System Manufacturing Corporation

419 F.3d 576 (7th Cir. 2005).

■ EASTERBROOK, CIRCUIT JUDGE.

Bretford makes a line of computer tables that it sells under the name Connection™. Since 1990 many of these tables have featured one rather than two legs on each end. The leg supports a sleeve attached to a V-shaped brace, making it easy to change the table's height while keeping the work surface stable. Although the sleeve and brace together look like a Y, Bretford calls it the V–Design table, and we employ the same usage.

This illustration, from Bretford's web site, shows the idea:

Between 1990 and 1997 Bretford was the only seller of computer tables with a V-shaped height-adjustment system. It sold about 200,000 V–Design tables during that period. Smith System, one of Bretford's competitors, decided to copy the sleeve and brace for its own line of computer tables. Smith System made its initial sales of the knockoff product to the Dallas school system in 1997, and this trademark litigation quickly followed.

Invoking § 43(a) of the Lanham Act, 15 U.S.C. § 1125(a), Bretford contends that the V-shaped design is its product's trade dress, which Smith System has infringed. It also contends that Smith System engaged in "reverse passing off" when it incorporated some Bretford hardware into a sample table that it showed purchasing officials in Dallas. The parties waived their right to a jury trial, and the district court held evidentiary hearings and issued opinions over a number of years. Although at one point the judge found Smith System liable and awarded damages in Bretford's favor, he reversed course in light of *Wal–Mart Stores, Inc. v. Samara Brothers, Inc.*, 529 U.S. 205 (2000), and *Dastar Corp. v. Twentieth Century Fox Film Corp.*, 539 U.S. 23 (2003). The appeal presents two principal questions: whether Smith System is entitled to copy Bretford's design, and, if yes, whether it was nonetheless wrongful for Smith System to use Bretford components in a sample table shown to the Dallas buyers.

. . . .

The district court found that V-shaped legs do not signal Bretford as a source. The record supports this conclusion; indeed, Bretford has *no* evidence that the leg design prompts "Bretford" in buyers' minds. There are no surveys and no evidence of actual confusion. Both Bretford and Smith System sell through distributors and field representatives to sophisticated buyers who know exactly where their goods are coming from.

Many buyers ask for tables with V-shaped legs, and Bretford insists that this shows that they want its Connections™ furniture; quite the contrary, this form of specification does more to imply that the leg design is functional than to show that anyone cares who makes the table. In the end, all Bretford has to go on is the fact that it was the only maker of such tables for eight years and spent more than $4 million to promote sales. If that were enough to permit judgment in its favor, new entry would be curtailed unduly by the risk and expense of trademark litigation, for *every* introducer of a new design could make the same sort of claim. "Consumers should not be deprived of the benefits of competition with regard to the utilitarian and esthetic purposes that product design ordinarily serves by a rule of law that facilitates plausible threats of suit against new entrants based on alleged inherent distinctiveness." *Wal-Mart*, 529 U.S. at 213.

. . . .

When Smith System decided to copy Bretford's table, it subcontracted the leg assemblies to a specialized metal fabricator, whose initial efforts were unsatisfactory. This left Smith System in a bind when the Dallas school system asked to see a table. Smith System cobbled a sample together by attaching the leg assembly from a Bretford table (which Smith System had repainted) to a top that Smith System had manufactured itself. (Who supplied other components, such as the cable guides and grommets, is disputed but irrelevant.) Dallas was satisfied and placed an order. All of the tables delivered to Dallas included legs manufactured by Smith System's subcontractor. Nonetheless, Bretford contends, by using its leg assemblies on even the one sample, Smith System engaged in reverse passing off and must pay damages.

Passing off or palming off occurs when a firm puts someone else's trademark on its own (usually inferior) goods; reverse passing off or misappropriation is selling someone else's goods under your own mark. See *Roho, Inc. v. Marquis*, 902 F.2d 356, 359 (5th Cir. 1990). It is not clear what's wrong with reselling someone else's goods, if you first buy them at retail. If every automobile sold by DeLorean includes the chassis and engine of a Peugeot, with DeLorean supplying only the body shell, Peugeot has received its asking price for each car sold and does not suffer any harm. Still, the Supreme Court said in *Dastar* that "reverse passing off" can violate the Lanham Act if a misdescription of goods' origin causes commercial injury. . . .

Dastar added that the injury must be a *trademark* loss—which is to say, it must come from a misrepresentation of the goods' origin. Dastar thus had the right (so far as the Lanham Act is concerned) to incorporate into its videos footage taken and edited by others, provided that it manufactured the finished product and did not mislead anyone about who should be held responsible for shortcomings. No one makes a product from scratch, with trees and iron ore entering one end of the plant and a finished consumer product emerging at the other. Ford's cars include Fram oil filters, Goodyear tires, Owens–Corning glass, Bose radios, Pennzoil lubricants, and many other constituents; buyers can see some of the other producers' marks (those on the radio and tires for example) but not others, such as the oil and transmission fluid. Smith System builds tables using wood from one supplier, grommets (including Teflon from du Pont) from another, and vinyl molding and paint and bolts from any of a hundred more sources—the list is extensive even for a simple product such as a table. If Smith System does not tell du Pont how the Teflon is used, and does not inform its consumers which firm supplied the wood, has it violated the Lanham Act? Surely not; the statute does not condemn the way in which all products are made.

Legs are a larger fraction of a table's total value than grommets and screws, but nothing in the statute establishes one rule for "major" components and another for less costly inputs. The right question, *Dastar* holds, is whether the consumer knows who has produced the finished product. In the *Dastar* case that was Dastar itself, even though most of the product's economic value came from elsewhere; just so when Smith System includes components manufactured by others but stands behind the finished product. The portion of § 43(a) that addresses reverse passing off is the one that condemns false designations of origin. "Origin" means, *Dastar* holds, "the producer of the tangible product sold in the marketplace". 539 U.S. at 31. As far as Dallas was concerned, the table's "origin" was Smith System, no matter who made any component or subassembly.

Much of Bretford's argument takes the form that it is just "unfair" for Smith System to proceed as it did, making a sale before its subcontractor could turn out acceptable leg assemblies. Businesses often think competition unfair, but federal law encourages wholesale copying, the better to drive down prices. Consumers rather than producers are the objects of the law's solicitude. . . .

. . . .

AFFIRMED.

QUESTIONS

1. What is the difference between "false designation of origin" and ordinary trademark infringement? One obvious answer is that section 43(a) permits suits even when no registered trademark is involved. Putting to one side the fact that false designation of origin claims vindicate trademark-like interests in trademark-like symbols, is there any difference between the sort of conduct that is actionable as trademark infringement under section 32 and the conduct reached by section 43(a)?

2. In *Bretford*, Judge Easterbrook questions the policy justification for reading the Lanham Act to permit recovery for reverse passing off: "It's not clear what's wrong with reselling someone else's goods, if you first buy them at retail." If the trademark owner has already made a profit on a retail sale, why might it object to some other seller's reselling the product under a different trademark? Are those objections persuasive?

3. If Smith wants to use Bretford's V-shaped leg assemblies as components of its tables, may it advertise that it does so? *Cf. Bumble Bee Seafoods v. UFS Industries, supra* this supplement Chapter 6A.

4. America Online files a 43(a) lawsuit against defendants who send mass emailings of unsolicited commercial email ("spam") to AOL subscribers. AOL claims that defendants forged AOL subscriber return addresses in the "from" line of the email and and that the forged return addresses were false designations of origin within the meaning of the statute. Defendant insists that however unwelcome its commercial email may be, it has done nothing to violate the Lanham Act. How should the court rule? *See America Online v. LCGM*, 46 F.Supp.2d 444 (E.D. Va. 1998); *America Online v. IMS*, 24 F.Supp.2d 548 (E.D. Va. 1998).

CHAPTER 8

ADVERTISING

B. FALSE REPRESENTATIONS

Page 590. Insert the following case after *United Industries v. Clorox*:

Schick Manufacturing, Inc. v. The Gillette Company, 372 F.Supp.2d 273 (D. Conn. 2005). Schick sued Gillette, claiming that Gillette's advertising for its M3 Power Razor System violated section 43(a)(1)(B):

> Gillette's original advertising for the M3 Power centered on the claim that "micro-pulses raise hair up and away from skin," thus allowing a consumer to achieve a closer shave. This "hair-raising" or hair extension claim was advertised in various media, including the internet, television, print media, point of sale materials, and product packaging. For example, Gillette's website asserted that, in order to combat the problem of "facial hair growing in different directions," the M3 Power's "micro-pulses raise hair up and away from skin ..." Of Gillette's expenditures on advertising, 85% is spent on television advertising. At the time of the launch, the television advertising stated, "turn on the first micro-power shaving system from Gillette and turn on the amazing new power-glide blades. Micro-pulses raise the hair, so you shave closer in one power stroke." The advertisement also included a 1.8 second-long animated dramatization of hairs growing. In the animated cartoon, the oscillation produced by the M3 Power is shown as green waves moving over hairs. In response, the hairs shown extended in length in the direction of growth and changed angle towards a more vertical position.
>
> ...
>
> Gillette conceded during the hearing that the M3 Power's oscillations do not cause hair to change angle on the face. Its original advertisements depicting such an angle change are both unsubstantiated and inaccurate. Gillette also concedes that the animated portion of its television advertisement is not physiologically exact insofar as the hairs and skin do not appear as they would at such a level of magnification and the hair extension effect is "somewhat exaggerated." The court finds that the hair "extension" in the commercial is greatly exaggerated. Gillette does contend, however, that the M3 Power's oscillations cause beard hairs to be raised out of the skin. Gillette contends that the animated product demonstration showing hair extension in its revised commercials is predicated on its testing showing that oscillations cause "trapped" facial hairs to lengthen from

the follicle so that more of these hairs' length is exposed. Gillette propounds two alternative physiological bases for its "hair extension" theory. First, Gillette hypothesizes that a facial hair becomes "bound" within the follicle due to an accumulation of sebum and corneocytes (dead skin cells). Gillette contends that the oscillations could free such a "bound" hair. Second, Gillette hypothesizes that hairs may deviate from their normal paths in the follicle and become "trapped" outside the path until vibrations from the M3 Power restore them to their proper path.

. . .

The challenged advertising consists of two basic components: an animated representation of the effect of the M3 Power razor on hair and skin and a voice-over that describes that effect. The animation, which lasts approximately 1.8 seconds, shows many hairs growing at a significant rate, many by as much as four times the original length. During the animation, the voice-over states the following: "Turn it on and micropulses raise the hair so the blades can shave closer." Schick asserts that this M3 Power advertising is false in three ways: first, it asserts the razor changes the angle of beard hairs; second, it portrays a false amount of extension; and third, it asserts that the razor raises or extends the beard hair.

With regard to the first claim of falsity, if the voiceover means that the razor changes the angle of hairs on the face, the claim is false. Although Gillette removed the "angle changing" claim from its television advertisements, it is unclear whether it has completely removed all material asserting this angle-change claim. The court concludes that the current advertising claim of "raising" hair does not unambiguously mean to changes angles.[8] See *Novartis Consumer Health, Inc. v. Johnson & Johnson-Merck Consumer Pharms. Co.*, 290 F.3d 578, 587 (3d Cir. 2002) ("only an unambiguous message can be literally false"). Thus, the revised advertising is not literally false on this basis.

With regard to the second asserted basis of falsity, the animation, Gillette concedes that the animation exaggerates the effect that the razor's vibration has on hair. Its own tests show hairs extending approximately 10% on average, when the animation shows a significantly greater extension. The animation is not even a "reasonable approximation," which Gillette claims is the legal standard for non-falsity. Here, Schick can point to Gillette's own studies to prove that the animation is false. *See McNeil–P.C.C., Inc.*, 938 F.2d at 1549.

Gillette argues that such exaggeration does not constitute falsity. However, case law in this circuit indicates that a defendant cannot argue that a television advertisement is "approximately" correct or, alternatively, simply a representation in order to excuse a television ad

8. It is the words "up and away" when combined with "raises" that suggest both extension and angle change.

or segment thereof that is literally false. *S.C. Johnson & Son, Inc.*, 241 F.3d at 239–40 (finding that depiction of leaking plastic bag was false where rate at which bag leaked in advertisement was faster than rate tests indicated); *Coca-Cola Co.*, 690 F.2d at 318 (finding that advertisement that displaced fresh-squeezed orange juice being poured into a Tropicana carton was false). Indeed, "[the Court of Appeals has] explicitly looked to the visual images in a commercial to assess whether it is literally false." *S.C. Johnson*, 241 F.3d at 238.[9]

Gillette's argument that the animated portion of its advertisement need not be exact is wrong as a matter of law. Clearly, a cartoon will not exactly depict a real-life situation, here, e.g., the actual uneven surface of a hair or the details of a hair plug. However, a party may not distort an inherent quality of its product in either graphics or animation. Gillette acknowledges that the magnitude of beard hair extension in the animation is false. The court finds, therefore, that any claims with respect to changes in angle and the animated portion of Gillette's current advertisement are literally false.

Page 599. Insert the following Question and cases after *Clorox Puerto Rico v. Proctor & Gamble:*

QUESTION

Mueller's is a regional brand of pasta available only in the North Eastern United States. The company labels packages of its pasta "America's favorite pasta." The best selling brand of pasta in the U.S. is not Mueller's, but Barilla, which is available throughout the United States. The manufacturer of Barilla claims that the "America's Favorite Pasta" label is a false and misleading representation of fact. Mueller insists that the phrase is mere puffing, and therefore not actionable. How should the court rule? *See American Italian Pasta Co. v. New World Pasta,* 371 F.3d 387 (8th Cir. 2004).

Johnson & Johnson Vision Case, Inc. v. Ciba Vision Corp., 348 F.Supp.2d 165 (S.D.N.Y. 2004). Johnson & Johnson, the maker of ACUVUE contact lenses, sued Ciba Vision, alleging that ads promoting CIBA's O_2OPTIX contact lenses were literally false. O_2OPTIX lenses have greater oxygen permeability than ACUVUE lenses, a feature that CIBA claimed made the lenses both more comfortable and better for the health of the wearer's cornea. CIBA's O_2OPTIX ads, directed at eye care professionals, asserted that in a clinical study, "75% of lens wearers preferred O_2OPTIX to ACUVUE ADVANCE. The #1 reason was comfort." Johnson & Johnson argued that CIBA's clinical trial supported neither claim. In the trial, 20 contact lens wearers wore a Johnson & Johnson ACUVUE ADVANCE lens in one eye and a CIBA O_2OPTIX lens in the other eye for four weeks. At several points during the study participants were asked which lens they

9. At least one other circuit has held that picture depictions can constitute false advertising. *Scotts Co. v. United Indus. Corp.*, 315 F.3d 264 (4th Cir. 2002) (finding that while ambiguous graphic on packaging did not constitute literally false advertising, an unambiguous graphic could do so).

preferred, and were asked to choose a reason for that preference. At the end of the study, five participants indicated a preference for ACUVUE ADVANCE, and 15 (or 75%) indicated a preference for O_2OPTIX. When asked the reason for their preference, however, two of the participants who chose ACUVUE and five of the participants who chose O_2OPTIX said that they had made a random choice between the two lenses. Eight of the participants who chose O_2OPTIX (and none of the participants who chose ACCUVUE) identified "Comfort" as the reason for their preference.

Evaluating the data, the court concluded that participants who claimed to have made a random choice did not prefer one lens to the other. Thus, of the 20 participants, 10 preferred O_2OPTIX, three preferred ACCUVUE, and 7 had no preference. The court agreed with Johnson & Johnson that CIBA's claim that "75% of lens wearers preferred O_2OPTIX to ACUVUE ADVANCE" was literally false. The court, however, held that the study supported CIBA's claim that comfort was the #1 reason: "comfort was clearly selected as the primary reason more often than any of the other reasons mentioned in the study, and all 8 of the persons who chose comfort as the primary reason made O_2OPTIX their overall preference choice."

Solvay Pharmaceuticals, Inc. v. Ethex Corporation, 2004 WL 742033 (D. Minn. 2004). Solvay, the producer of Creon brand enzyme supplement, brought a § 43(a) claim against its competitor, alleging that marketing representing that the competing product, Pangestyne, was equivalent or comparable to Creon was false and misleading. The defendant argued that the dispute required a determination whether Creon and Pangestyne were in fact comparable and that the matter was therefore exclusively within the jurisdiction of the FDA. The court disagreed:

> The Court is thus satisfied that Solvay could, based on the allegations in the complaint, prove that Pangestyme and Creon are not substitutable, alternatives, equivalent, or comparable, and that any advertisement to the contrary is literally false. Such a claim does not require the Court to determine anything within the particular jurisdiction of the FDA and is within the purview of the Lanham Act. Plaintiff's claims will therefore not be dismissed on this basis.

Page 601. Delete *Proctor & Gamble v. Haugen*, and substitute the following case:

Sanderson v. Culligan International Co., 415 F.3d 620 (7th Cir. 2005). Magnatech sells "magnetic water conditioners," which, the company claims, reduce lime scale deposits on pipes by exposing water to magnetic fields. Magnatech's competitor, Culligan, manufactures chemical water purification systems. The owner of Magnatech sued Culligan under section 43(a), claiming that Culligan's employees and franchisees assertions that magnetic systems don't work constituted actionable false representations. The district court granted summary judgment to Culligan and plaintiff appealed. Judge Easterbrook found plaintiff's arguments unpersuasive:

> Because the case ended without a trial, we must assume that magnetic systems can reduce lime scale deposits in pipes, the only

benefit that Magnatech and its Superior Manufacturing Division claim for their products. (They do not contend that magnetic treatment removes minerals or biological agents from water.) On a motion to dismiss under Fed. R. Civ. P. 12(b)(6), even highly unlikely propositions must be taken as given. See, e.g., *Miles v. Augusta City Council*, 710 F.2d 1542 (11th Cir. 1983) (assuming, as the complaint alleged, that cats can talk). . . .

Lime deposits in plumbing are calcium carbonate ($CaCO_3$), which is non-magnetic. Sanderson's lawyer could not explain why magnets affect nonferrous materials, and the unpublished study to which his brief refers at length does not do so either. This study finds that non-chemical devices can reduce the hardness of calcium carbonate build-up in industrial air-conditioning systems, but *only* when the water moves faster that 2.3 meters per second—and even so the paper offers Sanderson little support, for it lumps together a variety of non-chemical approaches and does not report separately on the sort of magnetic systems that Magnatech sells. . . . Nonetheless, we shall indulge the assumption that adverse statements about Magnatech's products are calumnies.

. . . .

Section 43(a) covers only "commercial advertising or promotion". The district court concluded that Sanderson had just three examples of supposedly false statements within the period of limitations, and that all three were person-to-person communications at trade shows. We held in *First Health Group Corp. v. BCE Emergis Corp.*, 269 F.3d 800, 804 (7th Cir. 2001), that § 43(a) addresses "promotional material disseminated to anonymous recipients". This leaves to state law the evaluation of oral statements and brochures at trade shows. Sanderson does not contend that the statements of which he complains are "commercial advertising or promotion" as *First Health Group* understood that phrase. Indeed, he does not mention that opinion, though it was the mainstay of the district court's decision.

For that matter, Sanderson does not contend that any of the statements within the period of limitations was uttered by Culligan. He attributes these oral statements and handouts to its franchisees or distributors and says that Culligan must be vicariously liable because it insists that they live up to high standards of business ethics. That Culligan tries to *prevent* its distributors from committing business torts, and reserves the right to stop selling to anyone who does, hardly makes any of the distributors its agent for the purpose of defaming rivals. Unsuccessful efforts at prevention do not imply agency or an assumption of liability. If Culligan told its distributors to avoid reckless driving and to obey all state laws, this would not make it vicariously liable for their auto accidents or oblige it to pay if a distributor shot his neighbor's dog for barking late at night.

Page 614. Insert the following case after *Coors Brewing Co. v. Anheuser–Busch Co.*:

McNeil–PPC, Inc. v. Pfizer Inc.

351 F.Supp.2d 226 (S.D.N.Y. 2005).

■ CHIN, D.J.

In June 2004, defendant Pfizer Inc. ("Pfizer") launched a consumer advertising campaign for its mouthwash, Listerine Antiseptic Mouthrinse. Print ads and hang tags featured an image of a Listerine bottle balanced on a scale against a white container of dental floss, as shown above.

The campaign also featured a television commercial called the "Big Bang." In its third version, which is still running, the commercial announces that "Listerine's as effective as floss at fighting plaque and gingivitis. Clinical studies prove it." Although the commercial cautions that "there's no replacement for flossing," the commercial repeats two more times the message that Listerine is "as effective as flossing against plaque and gingivitis." The commercial also shows a narrow stream of blue liquid flowing out of a Cool Mint Listerine bottle, then tracking a piece of dental floss being pulled from a white floss container, and then swirling around and between teeth—bringing to mind an image of liquid floss.

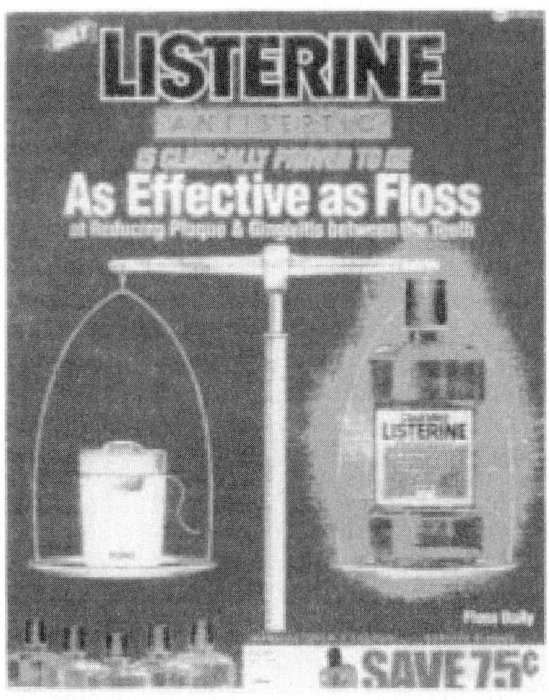

In this case, plaintiff McNeil–PPC, Inc. ("PPC"), the market leader in sales of string dental floss and other interdental cleaning products, alleges that Pfizer has engaged in false advertising in violation of § 43(a) of the

Lanham Act, 15 U.S.C. § 1125(a), and unfair competition in violation of state law. PPC contends that Pfizer's advertisements are false and misleading in two respects. First, PPC contends that Pfizer's literal (or explicit) claim that "clinical studies prove" that Listerine is "as effective as floss against plaque and gingivitis" is false. Second, PPC contends that Pfizer's advertisements also implicitly are claiming that Listerine is a replacement for floss—that all the benefits of flossing may be obtained by rinsing with Listerine—and that this implied message is false and misleading as well.

Before the Court is PPC's motion for a preliminary injunction enjoining Pfizer from continuing to make these claims in its advertisements. For the reasons set forth below, I conclude that Pfizer's advertisements are false and misleading. PPC's motion is granted and a preliminary injunction will be issued. My findings of fact and conclusions of law follow.

STATEMENT OF THE CASE

A. The Facts

1. The Parties and Their Products

PPC, a wholly-owned subsidiary of Johnson & Johnson ("J & J"), manufactures and markets consumer oral health products. PPC is the market leader in the sales of interdental cleaning products, including dental floss—waxed or unwaxed string used to mechanically remove food and debris from between the teeth and underneath the gumline. ...

J & J invented floss nearly 100 years ago. PPC's products include the Reach Access Daily Flosser (the "RADF"), a toothbrush-like device with a snap-on head (to be replaced after each use) containing a piece of string floss. The RADF was launched in August 2003. PPC also sells a battery-powered version of the RADF, called the Reach Access Power Flosser.

Pfizer manufactures and markets consumer and pharmaceutical products, including Listerine, an essential oil-containing antimicrobial mouthrinse. According to its label, Listerine:

> Kills germs that cause Bad Breath, Plaque & the gum disease Gingivitis.

Listerine has been "accepted" by the American Dental Association (the "ADA") and bears the ADA seal of acceptance on its label. The label instructs users to rinse with Listerine full strength for 30 seconds, each morning and night. Listerine also comes in several flavors, including Cool Mint, Fresh Burst, and Natural Citrus.

2. Oral Hygiene and Oral Diseases

Plaque is a biofilm comprised of a thin layer of bacteria that forms on teeth and other surfaces of the mouth. Food debris caught between teeth provides a source of nutrition for this bacteria and will help the bacteria multiply, grow, and persist. Plaque build-up may cause gingivitis, an inflammation of the superficial gum tissues surrounding the tooth. Gingivitis is common, affecting some two-thirds of the U.S. population. Its symptoms include red, inflamed, swollen, puffy, or bleeding gums. Periodontitis is inflammation that develops in deeper tissues, and involves the bone and connection to the tooth (the periodontal ligament). Periodontitis is less common, affecting some 10–15% (more or less) of the population, although it becomes more prevalent with age. It is a major cause of tooth loss.

. . .

The removal of plaque and the prevention of plaque build-up are critical to addressing both gingivitis and periodontitis. In addition, although it is less clear, controlling plaque also helps prevent or reduce "caries"—cavities or dental decay. The ADA recognizes that "plaque is responsible for both tooth decay and gum disease."

The most common method of mechanically removing plaque is brushing, and today the use of toothbrushes and fluoridated toothpastes is "almost universal." Brushing, however, does not adequately remove plaque. In part, this is because many people do not brush properly or they brush less than the recommended two minutes twice a day. In part, it is also because for most people "toothbrushing alone cannot effectively control interproximal plaque," i.e., the plaque in the hard-to-reach places between the teeth. As a consequence, removal of plaque from the interproximal areas by additional methods is particularly important, for it is in these areas between the teeth that plaque deposits appear early and become more prevalent. The direct interproximal area is the area where there is "the most stagnation" and where "periodontal disease usually starts."

Traditionally, the "most widely recommended" mechanical device for removing interproximal plaque is dental floss. ... Flossing provides a number of benefits. It removes food debris and plaque interdentally and it also removes plaque subgingivally. As part of a regular oral hygiene program, flossing helps reduce and prevent not only gingivitis but also periodontitis and caries.

Some 87% of consumers, however, floss either infrequently or not at all. Although dentists and dental hygienists regularly tell their patients to floss, many consumers do not floss or rarely floss because it is a difficult and time-consuming process.

As a consequence, a large consumer market exists to be tapped. If the 87% of consumers who never or rarely floss can be persuaded to floss more regularly, sales of floss would increase dramatically. PPC has endeavored, with products such as the RADF and the Power Flosser, to reach these consumers by trying to make flossing easier.

At the same time, Pfizer has recognized that there is enormous potential here for greater sales of Listerine as well. Pfizer has come to realize that if it could convince consumers who were reluctant flossers that they could obtain the benefits of flossing by rinsing with Listerine, it would be in a position to see its sales of Listerine increase dramatically.

In the context of this case, therefore, Pfizer and PPC are competitors.

3. The Listerine Studies

Pfizer sponsored two clinical studies involving Listerine and floss: the "Sharma Study" and the "Bauroth Study." These studies purported to compare the efficacy of Listerine against dental floss in controlling plaque and gingivitis in subjects with mild to moderate gingivitis.

[Both studies divided subjects with mild to moderate gingivitis into three groups. One group received instruction in flossing and a supply of dental floss, and was directed to brush twice and floss once every day for six months. The second group was given a supply of Listerine and asked to brush twice and rinse twice every day for six months. The final group was given a supply of a placebo rinse and told to brush and rinse twice daily. The subjects returned to the clinic every month for a dental exam and new supplies. After three months, the Listerine and flossing groups had fewer symptoms of gingivitis than the control group. After six months, the Listerine results were better than the flossing results. The authors of both studies suggested that the most probable reason was that the subjects failed to floss consistently in the later months of the study.]

Neither the Bauroth Study nor the Sharma Study purported to examine whether Listerine could replace floss, and neither study examined the efficacy of Listerine with respect to severe gingivitis or periodontitis or tooth decay or the removal of food debris. In addition, neither study considered the adjunctive effects of Listerine when used in addition to brushing and flossing.

. . .

7. The Consumer Advertising Campaign

The consumer advertising campaign was launched in June 2004. . . .

In the third version of the Big Bang, which continues to run, the commercial announces that "Listerine's as effective as floss at fighting plaque and gingivitis. Clinical studies prove it." The commercial cautions that "there's no replacement for flossing," but states that "if you don't floss like you should, you can get its plaque-fighting benefits by rinsing." The commercial goes on to repeat two more times the message that Listerine is "as effective as flossing against plaque and gingivitis."

The commercial also shows a narrow stream of blue liquid flowing out of a Cool Mint Listerine bottle, then tracking a piece of dental floss being pulled from a white floss container, and then swirling around and between teeth—bringing to mind an image of liquid floss. In a superscript that appears briefly on-screen, the commercial also tells viewers to "ask your dental professional."

Pfizer also published print ads, including a freestanding circular with a manufacturer's discount coupon featuring a bottle of Cool Mint Listerine balanced equally on a scale opposite a floss container (similar to the image used in the professional campaign). The ad proclaims that Listerine "Is Clinically Proven To Be As Effective as Floss at Reducing Plaque & Gingivitis between the Teeth." In small print near the bottom of the page, the ad states: "Floss Daily." There is no instruction telling consumers to consult their dentists.

Pfizer also used a hang tag and shoulder labels on its bottles of Listerine. The hang tag features the scale image and is similar to the print ad just described. The shoulder label has gone through three versions. The first version (which was red) stated: "Now Clinically Proven As Effective As Floss," with the words in much smaller print "Against Plaque and Gingivitis Between the Teeth." (PXs 98, 162). The second version (which is blue) reads the same as the first, with the addition in small print of the words: "Ask Your Dentist. Floss Daily." A third version (which is gold and red) is being or is about to be distributed and reads: "As Effective As Floss Against Plaque & Gingivitis Between Teeth," with the following words in smaller print: "Ask Your Dentist. Not a Replacement for Floss."

Pfizer has also featured the "as effective as flossing" claim on its website for Listerine. The first page of the website shows the Cool Mint Listerine bottle shaking, with the stream of blue liquid flowing out (as in the Big Bang commercial), and forming the words "Listerine Antiseptic is as effective as flossing," with a footnote to the words: "Against plaque and gingivitis between teeth. Use as directed. Ask your dentist. Not a replacement for floss." The first page also states:

> It's clinically proven.
>
> A quick easy rinse with Listerine Antiseptic, twice a day, is actually as effective as floss. Because Listerine Antiseptic gets between teeth to kill the germs that cause plaque and gingivitis. Ask your dentist. You'll find out that Listerine Antiseptic truly is the easy way to a healthy mouth.

The website has an entire section entitled "Effective As Floss," spanning many pages. In a question-and-answer section, the website addresses frequently asked questions, including the following:

> Question 3 Most people don't like to floss/don't make the time to floss. Isn't this new data telling people that they don't have to floss?
>
> Answer—No, flossing is essential in preventing gum disease because it helps remove food particles and plaque from between the teeth, areas where the toothbrush can't reach. However, optimal plaque control through brushing and flossing alone can sometimes be difficult to achieve. We believe that the results [of the two studies] suggest the importance of adding an antiseptic mouthwash to patients' daily oral healthcare. . . .

. . .

8. The Surveys

In September and October 2004, at PPC's request, a consumer research firm, Bruno and Ridgway Research Associates, conducted three consumer surveys in connection with this case, in malls and shopping centers in ten different locations throughout the United States. The first was intended to determine the message that consumers took away from the Big Bang commercial. The second sought to determine the message that consumers took away from the first of the three shoulder labels. The third sought to measure the pre-existing beliefs of consumers regarding the use of Listerine and floss.

In the first survey, consumers were shown the third version of Big Bang twice and then asked a series of questions about the ideas that were communicated to them by the commercial. The survey found that 50% of the respondents took away the message that "you can replace floss with Listerine." . . .

In the second survey, eligible consumers were shown a Listerine bottle with the first (or red) version of the shoulder label. They were asked essentially the same questions as were asked in the first survey. Some 45% of the consumers took away the message that Listerine could be used instead of floss. . . .

In the third survey, a control survey, consumers were asked their "pre-existing beliefs" regarding Listerine and floss; the intent was to determine the number of people who did not recall seeing the commercials but who still believed that Listerine could be used instead of floss. A minority of those surveyed did not recall seeing Big Bang, and of those 19% stated the opinion that Listerine could be used in place of floss. . . .

The surveyors then took the three surveys together, subtracted the 19% figure from the 50% and 45% figures, respectively, and concluded that 31% of those who saw the commercial and 26% of those who viewed the shoulder label took away a replacement message.

. . .

DISCUSSION

. . .

I conclude that PPC has demonstrated a likelihood of success on both its literal falsity claim and on its implied falsity claim. I address each claim in turn.

a. Literal Falsity

Pfizer's advertisements make the explicit claim that "clinical studies prove that Listerine is as effective as floss against plaque and gingivitis." As Pfizer purports to rely on "clinical studies," this is an "establishment claim" and PPC need only prove that "the [studies] referred to . . . were not sufficiently reliable to permit one to conclude with reasonable certainty that they established the proposition for which they were cited." *Castrol [Inc. v. Quaker State Corp.*, 977 F.2d 57 (2d Cir. 1992)] at 62–63. Two questions are presented: first, whether the Sharma and Bauroth Studies stand for the proposition that "Listerine is as effective as floss against plaque and gingivitis"; and second, assuming they do, whether the studies are sufficiently reliable to permit one to draw that conclusion with "reasonable certainty."

First, even putting aside the issue of their reliability, the two studies do not stand for the proposition that "Listerine is as effective as floss against plaque and gingivitis." The two studies included in their samples only individuals with mild to moderate gingivitis. They excluded individuals with severe gingivitis or with any degree of periodontitis, and they did not purport to draw any conclusions with respect to these individuals. Hence, the literal claim in Pfizer's advertisements is overly broad, for the studies did not purport to prove that Listerine is as effective as floss "against plaque and gingivitis," but only against plaque and gingivitis in individuals with mild to moderate gingivitis. The advertisements do not specify that the "as effective as floss" claim is limited to individuals with mild to moderate gingivitis. Consequently, consumers who suffer from severe gingivitis or periodontitis (including mild periodontitis) may be misled by the ads into believing that Listerine is just as effective as floss in helping them fight plaque and gingivitis, when the studies simply do not stand for that proposition.

Second, the two studies were not sufficiently reliable to permit one to conclude with reasonable certainty that Listerine is as effective as floss in fighting plaque and gingivitis, even in individuals with mild to moderate gingivitis. What the two studies showed was that Listerine is as effective as floss when flossing is not done properly. The authors of both studies recognized that the plaque reductions in the flossing groups were lower than would be expected and hypothesized that "behavioral or technical causes" were the reason. . . .

Hence, the studies did not "prove" that Listerine is "as effective as floss." Rather, they proved only that Listerine is "as effective as improperly-used floss." The studies showed only that Listerine is as effective as floss when the flossing is not performed properly. . . .

Pfizer and its experts argue that the two studies are reliable, notwithstanding the indications that the participants in the flossing group did not floss properly, because these conditions reflect "real-world settings." But the ads do not say that "in the real world," where most people floss rarely or not at all and even those who do floss have difficulty flossing properly, Listerine is "as effective as floss." Rather, the ads make the blanket assertion that Listerine works just as well as floss, an assertion the two studies simply do not prove. Although it is important to determine how a product works in the real world, it is probably more important to first determine how a product will work when it is used properly.

. . .

Accordingly, I hold that PPC is likely to succeed on its claim of literal false advertisement.

b. Implied Falsity

In considering the claim of implied falsity, in accordance with Second Circuit law, I determine first the message that consumers take away from the advertisements and second whether that message is false.

(i) The Implicit Message

Pfizer argues that its advertisements do not implicitly send the message that Listerine is a replacement for floss. I disagree. Rather, I find that Pfizer's advertisements do send the message, implicitly, that Listerine is a replacement for floss—that the benefits of flossing may be obtained by rinsing with Listerine, and that, in particular, those consumers who do not have the time or desire to floss can switch to Listerine instead.

First, the words and images used in the advertisements confirm that this is the message being sent. The words ("as effective as floss") and images (a stream of blue liquid tracking floss as it is removed from a floss container and then swirling between and around teeth; a bottle of Listerine balanced equally on a scale against a container of floss) convey the impression that Listerine is the equal to floss.

Second, the Ridgway survey is convincing and was conducted in a generally objective and fair manner. ... The Ridgway surveys show that 31% and 26% of the consumers who saw Big Bang and the shoulder label, respectively, took away the message that "you can replace floss with Listerine." Hence, a substantial percentage of the consumers who saw the advertisements took away a replacement message.

. . .

Accordingly, I conclude that the Pfizer ads send an implicit message that Listerine is a replacement for floss.

(ii) Falsity

The final inquiry, then, is whether the implicit message sent by the Pfizer ads is false. Pfizer argues that even assuming the advertisements do send a replacement message, the message is true: Listerine provides all the benefits of flossing.

Pfizer's position is based on two premises. First, Pfizer contends, the Sharma and Bauroth Studies prove that Listerine is as effective as floss in fighting plaque and gingivitis. Second, Pfizer contends, no clinical proof exists to show that flossing provides any benefit other than fighting plaque and gingivitis—there is no clinical proof that flossing reduces tooth decay or periodontitis. Indeed, Pfizer asserts, this notion is a "myth," and goes so far as to argue that there is no proof that reducing plaque will reduce caries or periodontitis. Hence, Pfizer continues, because Listerine does everything that floss can do, Listerine therefore provides all the benefits of floss—and consumers can "toss the floss" and replace it with Listerine.

These arguments are rejected. I conclude that the implicit message sent by Pfizer's advertisements is false, for Listerine is not a replacement for floss.

First, as discussed above, Pfizer's initial premise is wrong. The Sharma and Bauroth Studies do not prove that Listerine is just as effective as floss in fighting plaque and gingivitis. They prove only that Listerine is just as effective in fighting plaque and gingivitis as improperly-used floss. One simply cannot conclude from the two studies that Listerine is just as effective as flossing when the flossing is performed properly.

Second, Pfizer's second premise is wrong as well: there is substantial, convincing clinical, medical, and other proof to show that flossing does fight tooth decay and periodontitis and that Listerine is not a replacement for flossing.

Flossing provides certain benefits that Listerine does not. Floss penetrates subgingivally to remove plaque and biofilm below the gumline. Flossing, as part of a regular oral prevention program, also can reduce periodontitis. Flossing also reduces tooth decay and has an anti-caries effect. Finally, flossing removes food debris interdentally, including pieces of food trapped between the teeth that rinsing cannot dislodge. Numerous articles confirm that tooth decay and periodontitis can be reduced or prevented through interdental plaque control methods, including flossing. . . .

Other substantial evidence also demonstrates, overwhelmingly, that flossing is important in reducing tooth decay and periodontitis and that it cannot be replaced by rinsing with a mouthwash. . . .

Finally, of course, dentists and hygienists have been telling their patients for decades to floss daily. They have been doing so for good reason. The benefits of flossing are real—they are not a "myth." Pfizer's implicit message that Listerine can replace floss is false and misleading.

CONCLUSION

In sum, I find that PPC has demonstrated that it will suffer irreparable harm if a preliminary injunction is not issued, and I find further that PPC has demonstrated a likelihood of success on both its literal falsity claim and on its implied falsity claim. . . . In addition, I find that Pfizer's false and misleading advertising also poses a public health risk, as the advertisements present a danger of undermining the efforts of dental professionals—and the ADA—to convince consumers to floss on a daily basis.

Page 614. Insert the following additional Questions before STANDING TO ASSERT A § 43(a) CLAIM:

2. The Federal Hazardous Substances Act, 15 U.S.C. §§ 1261–1278 (2002), requires manufacturers of flammable products to label their products in conformance with regulations of the Consumer Product Safety Commission. Firebug Auto Products sells "Tirefix," an emergency canned tire inflator. Tirefix is flammable, but the label of the Firebug Tirefix can does not so indicate. Tire inflators containing flammable formulations are dangerous because they are commonly used in circumstances likely to create sparks. Wet Blanket Auto Products sells a competing canned tire inflator with a similar formula, which is labeled "Flammable" in conformance with the Federal Hazardous Substances Act. Wet Blanket believes that Firebug's violation of the law gives it an unfair competitive advantage because consumers may choose "Tirefix" over Wet Blanket's product because they believe, erroneously, that "Tirefix" is not flammable. Is Firebug's label actionable under § 43(a)(1)(B)? *See IQ Products Company v. Pennzoil Products Company*, 305 F.3d 368 (5th Cir. 2002), *cert. denied*, 538 U.S. 944 (2003).

3. Lazar Khidekel was a Russian painter who died in 1986, leaving his unsold paintings to his son, Mark. Rene and Claude Boule are French art collectors who specialize in Russian art, and own paintings attributed to Lazar Khidekel. In the late 1980s, Rene and Claude met Mark. He examined their collection and, at their request (and in return for $8000), executed a certificate of authenticity attesting that sixteen of their paintings were authentic Lazar Khidekel works. In 1992, Rene and Claude loaned those paintings to the Musee d'art de Joliette in Canada for a special exhibit.

Several years later, Mark moved to New York City and sought to sell his late father's paintings. He arranged for the exhibition of his father's work at a gallery, and advertised the show as the "first ever North American exhibition" of Khidekel's work. He sent a letter to 25 important art galleries in which he claimed that the paintings shown in the 1992 exhibit at the Musee d'art de Jolliette were not authentic Khidekels. He later arranged to be interviewed by ARTnews magazine. In the interview as it appeared in the magazine, Mark complained that unscrupulous and dishonest art dealers had misrepresented thousands of fraudulent artworks as his father's paintings. He identified Rene and Claude's collection as a fraudulent one, and maintained that he had viewed their collection, and immediately advised them that none of the paintings they owned had been painted by his father.

The Boules are furious. They consult you to find out whether Mark's letter or the interview published in ARTnews might be actionable. Can they recover under § 43(a)? Why or why not? *See Boule v. Hutton*, 328 F.3d 84 (2d Cir. 2003).

4. Digital Widgets has secured several patents but not yet exploited them. To get the capital to take its inventions to market, Digital Widgets borrowed substantial sums of money from a venture capital firm, and assigned its patents as collateral for the loan. Unfortunately, in today's sluggish economy, Digital Widgets was unable to find the right marketing partner. It failed to market its inventions and defaulted on its loan payments. The venture capital firm informed it that it would therefore foreclose on the loan and take sole control of the collateral. In a desperate maneuver to stave off bankruptcy, Digital Widgets issued a press release and bought a full-page advertisement in *Investors Weekly* seeking additional funding. Both the press release and the advertisement claimed that Digital Widgets presented a unique and worthwhile investment opportunity because of the unrealized value of the patents that it owned. The venture capital firm sues for false advertising, claiming that it is the true owner of the patents, and Digital Widget's representations to the contrary are therefore false representations under 43(a)(1)(b). Digital Widgets concedes that it misrepresented the ownership of the patents, but argues that its only false representation was in connection with patents, not products, and it was therefore not actionable under section 43(a). How should the court rule? *See Digigan v. Invalidate,* 52 UCC Rep.Serv.2d 1022 (S.D.N.Y. 2004).

Page 617. Insert the following material after *Ortho Pharmaceutical Corp. v. Cosprophar, Inc.*:

Ford v. NYLCare Health Plans, 301 F.3d 329 (5th Cir. 2002), *cert. denied,* 538 U.S. 923 (2003). Ford, an orthopedic surgeon, sued five HMOs for deceptive advertising. He claimed that the HMOs' advertising claimed falsely that their health management techniques improved the quality of the health care they supplied to their subscribers. In fact, Ford alleged, the HMOs' cost-containment policies significantly undercut the quality of health care services, and requiring the "rationing" of health care against the will of both doctors and patients. Ford claimed that the deceptive advertising both misled current subscribers and attracted new customers to the HMOs' health plans. The result of the ads were a reduction in the incomes of physicians, like Ford, who cared for patients subscribing to the HMOs.

A divided 5th Circuit held, *sua sponte,* that Ford lacked *constitutional* standing to bring a false advertising claim because the causal connection between the allegedly deceptive ads and the reduction in HMO payments to physicians was too tenuous to support standing under Article III:

> Ford claims that his injury consists of a reduction in his income from his medical practice caused by the defendants' restrictive cost-containment policies, which allegedly have the effect of reducing payments to contract specialists. He contends that the HMO's have been able to lower their payments to contract physicians as a result of increased market power gained by attracting patients through deceptive advertising. This argument fails to satisfy the causation prong of standing.
>
> To meet the causation requirement, Ford would have to present evidence affirmatively proving that the reduction in his income was a consequence of the HMO's' restrictive policies and that those policies in turn were established or at least made more onerous as a result of increased market power created by the acquisition of new customers through the defendants' allegedly deceptive ads. Nothing in the record establishes the validity of either of the two links in this causal chain, and Ford must provide evidence of both if he is to establish the causation necessary for Article III standing. Otherwise, he cannot show that his injury is "fairly traceable to the challenged action of the defendant."

Judge Benavides concurred in the result, but would have held that Ford lacked prudential standing under § 43(a).

PRUDENTIAL STANDING

In *Neyvas v. Morgan,* 309 F.Supp.2d 673 (E.D.Pa. 2004), a patient dissatisfied with the results of his Lasik surgery created an Internet website at www.lasiksucks4u.com expressing his anger at "the doctors who damaged my eyes.'' His former eye surgeons brought a false advertising suit, claiming that the site made false representations about their services. The court agreed that the complaint satisfied the standing requirements under Article III, but dismissed the suit because the surgeons had failed to establish prudential standing:

> [N]owhere in the complaint is it alleged nor is there any evidence whatsoever that the defendants, a disenchanted former patient and the attorney who represented him in a medical malpractice action, are commercial competitors with the plaintiffs. Indeed, there is nothing in the complaint to suggest that, in creating the website and in disseminating the purportedly defamatory statements over it, the defendants sought to divert the plaintiffs' business to themselves or to personally reap any financial benefit from their actions. As was the case in *Conte Bros.*, despite the fact that the plaintiffs may have suffered an injury to their commercial interests, they have not sustained competitive harm. We thus conclude that the plaintiffs here cannot satisfy the prudential requirements to maintain standing to sue under the Lanham Act.

Similarly, in *MCW, Inc. v. Badbusinessbureau.com*, 2004–1 Trade Cases P 74,391 (N.D. Tex. 2004), *supra* this supplement, the court dismissed false advertising claims on the merits but, as an alternative ground, held that plaintiffs lacked prudential standing to bring suit under § 43(a) against a consumer gripe site.

CHAPTER 9

AUTHORS' AND PERFORMERS' RIGHTS

A. AUTHORS' AND PERFORMERS' RIGHTS OF ATTRIBUTION

Pages 622–35. Delete last two lines on page 622 through text on page 635 up to (but not including) *King v. Innovation Books*.

Page 622. Add to end of penultimate paragraph:

Thus, in *Smith v. Montoro*, 648 F.2d 602 (9th Cir. 1981) the court held that the substitution of a fictitious actor's name on a film's credits in place of the actual performer's constituted "reverse passing off" in violation of § 43(a). The same court reached a similar result in *Lamothe v. Atlantic Recording*, 847 F.2d 1403 (9th Cir. 1988), when the credits on a record jacket and the sheet music acknowledged only one of three alleged co-authors of the musical composition. It should be noted, nonetheless, that these cases allowed suits against *mis*attribution of an author's or performer's name; they did not support an affirmative right to compel attribution when no recognition had been conferred at all.

In any event, § 43(a) may no longer afford even the limited scope of attribution rights that this caselaw cobbled together. The Supreme Court's decision in *Dastar Corp. v. Twentieth Century Fox Film Corp., supra* Chapter 7, this Supplement, may significantly undercut the availability of the Lanham Act as a route to implement moral rights in the U.S. The Court's determination that § 43(a)'s reference to the "origin" of goods concerns only the material, not the intellectual, origin of works of authorship appears to disqualify authors' and performers' claims unless the creator physically produced the copies made available to the public. This might leave room for some fine artists, but the Court's emphasis on avoiding trademark-copyright overlap appears to make the Visual Artists' Right Act (VARA) the sole source of attribution and integrity claims, whether or not VARA would in fact cover the creator in question.

> When Congress has wished to create such an addition to the law of copyright, it has done so with much more specificity than the Lanham Act's ambiguous use of "origin." The Visual Artists Rights Act of 1990, § 603(a), 104 Stat. 5128, provides that the author of an artistic work "shall have the right ... to claim authorship of that work." 17 U.S.C. § 106A(a)(1)(A). That express right of attribution is carefully limited and focused: It attaches only to specified "work[s] of visual art," § 101, is personal to the artist, §§ 106A(b) and (e), and endures only for "the

> life of the author," at § 106A(d)(1). Recognizing in § 43(a) a cause of action for misrepresentation of authorship of noncopyrighted works (visual or otherwise) would render these limitations superfluous. A statutory interpretation that renders another statute superfluous is of course to be avoided.

This assertion is troublesome because the interpretation leaves most authors with fewer attribution rights post-VARA than under the pre-*Dastar* § 43(a) caselaw. VARA did grant limited attribution rights, see 17 U.S.C. § 106A(a)(1)(A), but only with respect to an extremely narrow class of works. The class of "work[s] of visual art" is confined to the original work or up to two hundred signed and numbered copies of a painting, drawing, print, sculpture, or a photographic image "produced for exhibition purposes only," so long as the work is not "made for hire." VARA affords artists whose works fall within its restrictive definition a kind of private "Landmarks" law to preserve their works against mutilation or destruction. Attribution rights, albeit included, are not the focus of the Act. Indeed, VARA's restriction to physical originals makes that statute a very feeble measure for enforcing artists' attribution rights: a "work of visual arts" excludes mass market multiples, and VARA attribution (as well as integrity) rights apply only to "works of visual art." Thus, there is no VARA right to compel attribution for one's artwork if the artist's name has been left off anything more than the original or a signed and numbered limited edition of two hundred. And because VARA is limited to visual artists, it affords no moral rights to creators of literary, musical, or most other works or to performers.

The Court's application of the anti-redundancy canon of statutory interpretation is misplaced for another reason: even with respect to the narrow class of authors covered both by VARA and the rejected interpretation of § 43(a), VARA affords a significant right that § 43(a) did not: an affirmative right to claim authorship, not merely a right to object to misrepresentations of authorship that confuse consumers as to the work's "origin."

Decisions subsequent to *Dastar* tend to bear out some of the more ominous predictions about that ruling's impact. In **Williams v. UMG, 281 F.Supp.2d 1177 (C.D.Cal.2003)**, Williams, a film writer and director, contended that his name was left off the credits of a documentary on which he collaborated, and asserted that this "reverse passing off" violated § 43(a). The court acknowledged that Ninth Circuit precedent had recognized such claims in similar contexts, but that *Dastar* now "precludes plaintiff's Lanham Act claim."

> Defendants argue that *Dastar* invalidates Plaintiff's Lanham Act claim. This Court agrees with Defendants. As narrowed in the July Order, Plaintiff's Lanham Act claim is based on the misattribution of credits for "story/screenplay" and "editing" on the Baller Blockin' film. Plaintiff alleges that he should be given credit for "the authoring of the 'Narration Script' . . ., editing film sequences and re-scoring the music." Under Dastar, however, the Supreme Court specifically held

that the phrase "origin of goods" "refers to the producer of tangible goods that are offered for sale, and **not** to the author of any idea, concept, or communication embodied in those goods." 123 S. Ct. at 2050 (emphasis added). As such, Plaintiff would have a claim if Defendants purchased copies of Plaintiff's goods (i.e. the film) and repackaged them as their own. By contrast, Plaintiff does not have a claim for his authorship and direction embodied in that film. His claim, therefore, is barred as a matter of law.

In his Opposition, Plaintiff argues that *Dastar* is not a broad sweeping dismissal of reverse passing off claims but rather is limited to defining "origin of goods," not the origin of services. He claims that the Supreme Court's sole focus was on the term "origin of goods," and that it did not address the origin of services, which is at issue here. This Court disagrees with Plaintiff. As Defendants assert, the Supreme Court in *Dastar* was concerned with a claim materially identical to Plaintiff's claim here. The claim was that Dastar had made false or misleading representations on its own goods (Dastar's Campaigns videotapes)—just as Plaintiff here claims that Defendants made false or misleading representations on Defendants' own goods (the Baller Blockin' video and DVD). The "goods" are the defendants', not the plaintiff's. *Dastar* makes clear that a claim that a defendant's failure to credit the plaintiff on the defendant's goods is actionable only where the defendant literally repackages the plaintiff's goods and sells them as the defendant's own—not where, as here, Defendants are accused only of failing to identify someone who contributed not goods, but ideas or communications (or, for that matter, "services") to Defendants' product. See 123 S. Ct. at 2047 ("As used in the Lanham Act, the phrase 'origin of goods' is in our view incapable of connoting the person or entity that originated the ideas or communications that 'goods' embody or contain.").[10]

Plaintiff contends that his claim survives *Dastar* because he provided "services" as opposed to "goods." However, to the contrary, his claim fails for this reason. All he allegedly provided was "services," rather than goods which Defendants repackaged and resold as their own. See 123 S. Ct. at 2046 (Plaintiff's claim "would undoubtedly be sustained if Dastar had bought some of New Line's Crusade videotapes and merely repackaged them as its own."). Indeed, in *Dastar*, the defendant did exactly what Plaintiff accuses Defendants of doing here—attributing to itself and its employees various "services" that the plaintiffs claimed they, in fact, provided on the defendant's videotapes.... The Supreme Court held that the plaintiffs' claim that these credits were misleading because the plaintiffs really provided those services was non-actionable. As Defendants state, Plaintiff's attempt to

10. Contrary to Plaintiff's argument, based on the *Dastar* Court's holding, the Ninth Circuit cases cited by Plaintiff would be overruled to the extent they find a reverse passing off claim based on the failure to credit the author of any idea, concept or communication embodied in the tangible goods.

> differentiate the "services" of an "executive producer" or "producer" at issue in *Dastar* from his alleged "services" as an "editor" and "writer" is a distinction without a difference.
>
> Plaintiff then asserts that "if defendants [sic] argument were accepted, a talented director who directs a Summer blockbuster for example can be deprived of the immense value of such a credit in the entertainment industry, simply because the producer decides to name himself as the director.... A reading that the Lanham Act does not protect those people who provide services on films permits a form of anarchy in the entertainment industry, where anybody could be credited for anyone else's work and have their credit obliterated." However, the Supreme Court directly addressed Plaintiff's assertion. "The problem with this argument according special treatment to communicative products is that it causes the Lanham Act to conflict with the law of copyright, which addresses that subject specifically." 123 S. Ct. at 2048. In Plaintiff's hypothetical, the director has options to protect his interest—obtaining a contractual right to a credit, relying on the regulation of credits in union collective bargaining agreements (e.g., the Directors Guild) or maintaining the copyright in the film. In light of *Dastar*, this hypothetical director cannot bring a claim under the Lanham Act.
>
> Finally, Plaintiff attempts to distinguish *Dastar* by claiming that "the Court focused its analysis of the case on the concept that the involved works were uncopyrighted and the difficulties associated with the origin of the product." To the contrary, the Supreme Court's holding did not depend on whether the works were copyrighted or not. While the film footage at issue in *Dastar* was not copyrighted at the time of distribution by *Dastar*, the Court's holding is in no way limited to uncopyrighted material. Rather, in being careful not to extend trademark protections, the Court noted that protection for communicative products was available through copyright claims. In fact, this protection would only be available if a valid copyright existed....

See also Chivalry Film Prods. v. NBC Universal, Inc., 2006 WL 89944 (S.D.N.Y. 2006) (screenwriter claimed producer of "Meet the Parents" copied his script and misattributed screenplay to third parties; court held *Dastar* required dismissal of misattribution claim); *A Slice of Pie Prods. v. Wayans Bros. Entm't,* 392 F.Supp.2d 297 (D. Conn. 2005) (same re film "White Chicks"); *Keane v. Fox,* 297 F.Supp.2d 921 (S.D. Tex. 2004), where the court dismissed plaintiff's claim that, as the originator of the idea of the "American Idol" television series, and developer of the "American Idol" mark, he should have been recognized and paid. The court held that Keane had not developed trademark rights in the term "American Idol." The court also ruled against any claim in the concept of the television series, citing *Dastar*: "the Lanham Act does not create a cause of action for 'plagiarism,' that is, 'the use of otherwise unprotected works and inventions without attribution.'"; *Hustlers v. Thomasson,* 73 U.S.P.Q.2d 1923 (N.D. Ga. 2004) (holding that *Dastar*'s limitation of false designation of origin claims to the producer of physical copies bars not only claims by authors, but also by publishers; the court also follows *Williams v. UMG Recordings* in holding *Dastar* not limited to works in the public domain); *Mays & Assoc. v. Euler*, 370 F.Supp.2d 362 (D. Md. 2005) (after *Dastar*, no Lanham Act claim for non-attribution of authorship of web design portfolio); *JB Oxford & Co. v. First Tenn. Bank Nat'l Ass'n.*, 427 F.Supp.2d 784 (M.D. Tenn. 2006) (no § 43(a) claim against advertiser who allegedly copied plaintiff's advertisement and substituted its name for plaintiff's). For critiques of *Dastar* and its implications for authors and the public, see, e.g., F. Gregory Lastowka, *The Trademarks Function of Authorship*, 85 B.U. L. Rev. 1171 (2005); Jane C. Ginsburg, *The Right to Claim Authorship in United States Trademark and Copyright Law*, 41 U. HOUS. L. REV. 263 (2004).

QUESTIONS

1. Octavian, Antony, and Lepidus have co-authored several editions of a Trademarks Law casebook. The book is a best-seller in a limited market. For the most recent edition, however, the authors have had a falling-out, and Lepidus has not participated in the latest revision. If Lepidus' name nonetheless remains on the book cover and inside title pages, would he have any Lanham Act claim to compel its removal? If his name is omitted from the cover and title pages, would he have any Lanham Act claim to compel its reinstatement?

2. Has the Supreme Court removed the Lanham Act as a source of integrity rights for authors? If *Gilliam v. ABC* were to arise after *Dastar*, how should it be decided? Does it matter that ABC retained the title "*Monty Python's* Flying Circus" (emphasis added)? Would broadcasting an altered version thus be a "false designation of origin"? Would it be a "false or misleading description of fact ... which is likely to cause ... mistake or to deceive as to [Monty Python's] approval" of the ABC broadcast?

3. Would using Monty Python's name for ABC's truncated broadcast be a "misrepresent[ation of] the nature" of the program? In the latter case, would that misrepresentation have occurred "in commercial advertising or promotion," as required by sec. 43(a)(1)(B)?

4. *Dastar* declares that reading section 43(a) to create a claim against plagiarism would be inconsistent with the Supreme Court's opinions in *Wal–Mart v. Samara Brothers* and *TrafFix* (both *supra* Chapter 7), and *Bonito Boats* (*supra* Chapter 1). Can you distinguish those cases?

5. *Dastar* addressed a claim of "reverse passing off." Would it make a difference if the claim were for traditional passing off? Suppose the discovery of an obscure anonymous 16th-century English play, falsely published as a newly-unearthed work of Shakespeare. Has the publisher violated § 43(a)(1)(A)? Has it violated any other provision of the Lanham Act?

Page 641. Add before Questions:

In **Flynn v. Peters,** 377 F.3d 13 (1st Cir. 2004), the court, observing that none of the parties had briefed or argued the impact of *Dastar* on the plaintiff author's false attribution claim, nonetheless affirmed the grant of summary judgment for defendants. The author had withdrawn from the revision of a textbook on Mobile Robots when she became dissatisfied with the contributions of one of the revisers. Her name, however, continued to appear on the book, without her consent. She sued, alleging violations of the Lanham Act.

> Flynn claims that AK Peters violated the Lanham Act by listing her as an author of the second edition of Mobile Robots without her consent. More specifically, she alleged in the district court that "the misleading use of her name is likely to cause confusion by consumers as well as plaintiff's academic peers in that it will be assumed that she contributed to the revisions and approved of the changes." Concluding that Flynn failed to demonstrate that her name "is so associated with robotics that within the robotic community it has an independent value or meaning," the district court granted summary judgment to AK Peters on her Lanham Act claim. Flynn claims that this "independent value test" has no basis in First Circuit precedent and that she properly opposed AK Peters' summary judgment motion by citing her experience in the robotics field and by alleging that she is famous within the robotics community.
>
> . . . [B]efore we can consider whether AK Peters infringed upon Flynn's purported use of her name as a trademark, we must evaluate whether Flynn's name has acquired secondary meaning within the relevant class of consumers. . . .
>
> Flynn submitted for the summary judgment record a copy of her curriculum vitae and an affidavit in which she stated that she has worked in the robotics field since 1985, has given seventy invited talks and written twenty-nine papers in the field, and has founded a company that designs micro robots. Viewed in the proper light, she claims that this evidence demonstrates that "she has an esteemed reputation and a well-recognized name." This claim ignores the stringent requirements for secondary meaning evidence. "Such 'opinion' testimony by a [party] is considered self-serving and of little probative value." It would be more important to know, for example, how likely it would be for the average consumer of books like Mobile Robots to be aware of the papers Flynn cites. It is the mindset of these likely consumers and not simply the strength of her publication record in the abstract that matters in determining whether secondary meaning has attached. Moreover, Flynn declared that the authors intended to market the book to "a wide audience" from "high school age to Ph.D. level researchers"; therefore, it is this broad class of consumers and not a select subset of academic "insiders" that matters for secondary meaning purposes. Flynn failed to produce any evidence demonstrating that this extended group of consumers is aware of her academic achievements.
>
> Flynn also says in her affidavit that a handful of strangers have told her that they recognized her from a talk or that they had read her book, and her nephew says in his affidavit that a robotics graduate student that he met said that Flynn was "famous." However, such

limited anecdotal evidence does little to establish that her name has acquired secondary meaning within the class of consumers who would be likely to purchase a book on robotics, and that these consumers would be more likely to purchase books because her name was on the cover.

Flynn's reliance on *Donoghue* [*v. IBC/USA (Publications), Inc.*, 886 F.Supp. 947, 952 (D. Mass. 1995)] highlights the weakness of her case. In that case, the court enjoined a mailing company from using the plaintiff's name and face in an advertisement after the plaintiff, a financial expert, introduced evidence demonstrating that

> [He] is a nationally known investment advisor, with expertise in the subject of money market and mutual fund investing. He has been in the business of providing investment advisory services to the general investing public for approximately twenty-two years. The plaintiff has written ten books on the subject of investment advice and is a nationally syndicated financial columnist. Over the past decade, he has appeared frequently on network, cable and syndicated television shows dealing with financial markets, financial advice, and investments, and, over the past twenty-two years, he has participated in hundreds of seminars and conferences regarding investment strategies.

He also produced a monthly audio cassette investment advisory service and an electronic mutual fund tracking and analysis service and published a print newsletter, which had 17,000 subscribers and was "well-known among consumers and in the financial advisory services industry for its analyses of market trends and its mutual fund recommendations." Given this circumstantial evidence, the court concluded that the plaintiff "has become widely known, due to his efforts during the past twenty-two years, as [a financial] expert" and that his name "through numerous publications and determined self-promotion, has become associated in the public mind with expertise in strategic investment advice." Accordingly, the court did not have difficulty concluding that "the plaintiff's surname has acquired a secondary meaning vesting it with protected trademark status."

Flynn's summary judgment offerings do not remotely approach the evidence of secondary meaning presented in *Donoghue*. If Flynn's evidence demonstrated anything, it is that she has expertise in the robotics field and that a handful of individuals in the field have recognized her name and face. That evidence did not demonstrate that the relevant consumers have associated her name with a product. She did not demonstrate that a reasonable factfinder could conclude that her name serves anything more than its primary function to identify her as an individual. Given this failure to demonstrate that her name has acquired secondary meaning, we must agree with the district court that the Lanham Act does not apply to her claim.

B. RIGHT OF PUBLICITY AND RELATED CLAIMS

Pages 655–57. Delete *Oliveira v. Frito–Lay.*

Pages 676–78. Delete *Cairns v. Franklin Mint.*

Page 678. Insert after Question following *Rogers v. Grimaldi*:

Parks v. LaFace Records

329 F.3d 437 (6th Cir. 2003).

■ HOLSCHUH, DISTRICT JUDGE.

This is a dispute over the name of a song. Rosa Parks is a civil rights icon who first gained prominence during the Montgomery, Alabama bus boycott in 1955. She brings suit against LaFace Records, a record producer, and OutKast, a "rap" (or "hip-hop") music duo, as well as several other named affiliates, for using her name as the title of their song, *Rosa Parks*. Parks contends that Defendants' use of her name constitutes false advertising under § 43(a) of the Lanham Act, 15 U.S.C. § 1125(a), and intrudes on her common law right of publicity under Michigan state law. Defendants argue that they are entitled to summary judgment because Parks has failed to show any violation of the Lanham Act or her right of publicity. Defendants further argue that, even if she has shown such a violation, their First Amendment freedom of artistic expression should be a defense as a matter of law to each of these claims....

For the reasons hereafter set forth, we believe that, with respect to Rosa Parks' claims under the Lanham Act and under the common law right of publicity, "the evidence is such that a reasonable jury could return a verdict for the nonmoving party." We therefore conclude that the district court erred in granting Defendants' motion for summary judgment on those claims....

I. BACKGROUND

A. Facts

Rosa Parks is an historical figure who first gained prominence as a symbol of the civil rights movement in the United States during the 1950s and 1960s. In 1955, while riding in the front of a segregated bus in Montgomery, Alabama, she refused to yield her seat to a white passenger and move to the back of the bus as blacks were required to do by the then-existing laws requiring segregation of the races. A 381–day bus boycott in Montgomery flowed from that one event, which eventually became a catalyst for organized boycotts, sit-ins, and demonstrations all across the South. Her single act of defiance has garnered her numerous public accolades and awards, and she has used that celebrity status to promote various civil and human rights causes as well as television programs and books inspired by her life story. She has also approved a collection of gospel recordings by various artists entitled *Verity Records Presents: A Tribute to Mrs. Rosa Parks* (the "*Tribute*" album), released in 1995.

Defendants are OutKast, comprised of recording artists Andre "Dre" Benjamin and Antwan "Big Boi" Patton; their record producers, LaFace, founded by and named after Antonio "L.A." Reid and Kenny "Babyface" Edmonds; and LaFace's record distributors, Arista Records and BMG Entertainment (collectively "Defendants"). In September 1998, Defendants released the album *Aquemini*. The album's first single release was a song titled *Rosa Parks,* described as a "hit single" by a sticker on the album. The same sticker that contained the name *Rosa Parks* also contained a Parental Advisory warning of "explicit content." Because, as later discussed, the critical issue in this case is a determination of the artistic relevance of the title, *Rosa Parks*, to the content of the song, the lyrics obviously must be considered in their entirety. They are as follows:

(Hook)
Ah ha, hush that fuss
Everybody move to the back of the bus
Do you wanna bump and slump with us
We the type of people make the club get crunk

Verse 1: (Big Boi)

Many a day has passed, the night has gone by
But still I find the time to put that bump off in your eye
Total chaos, for these playas, thought we was absent
We takin another route to represent the Dungeon Family
Like Great Day, me and my nigga decide to take the back way
We stabbing every city then we headed to that bat cave
A-T-L, Georgia, what we do for ya
Bull doggin hoes like them Georgetown Hoyas
Boy you sounding silly, thank my Brougham aint sittin pretty
Doing doughnuts round you suckas like then circles around titties
Damn we the committee gone burn it down
But us gone bust you in the mouth with the chorus now

(Hook)

Verse 2: (Andre)

I met a gypsy and she hipped me to some life game
To stimulate then activate the left and right brain
Said baby boy you only funky as your last cut
You focus on the past your ass'll be a has what
Thats one to live by or either that one to die to
I try to just throw it at you determine your own adventure
Andre, got to her station here's my destination
She got off the bus, the conversation lingered in my head for hours
Took a shower kinda sour cause my favorite group ain't comin with it
But I'm witcha you cause you probably goin through it anyway

But anyhow when in doubt went on out and bought it
Cause I thought it would be jammin but examine all the flawsky-wawsky
Awfully, it's sad and it's costly, but that's all she wrote
And I hope I never have to float in that boat
Up shit creek it's weak is the last quote
That I want to hear when I'm goin down when all's said and done
And we got a new joe in town
When the record player get to skippin and slowin down
All yawl can say is them niggas earned that crown but until then . . .

(Hook)

(Harmonica Solo)

(Hook til fade)

B. Procedural History

Parks sued Defendants in the Wayne County Circuit Court of Michigan alleging, *inter alia*, that Defendants' unauthorized use of her name infringes on her right to publicity, defames her character, and interferes with an ongoing business relationship. Defendants removed this case to the District Court for the Eastern District of Michigan. Parks thereafter filed an amended complaint that reiterated her state law claims and added a false advertising claim under § 43(a) of the Lanham Act.

The parties entered into a stipulation of the facts ("Stipulated Facts") and filed cross-motions for summary judgment. Applying *Rogers v. Grimaldi*, 875 F.2d 994 (2d Cir. 1989), the district court concluded that the First Amendment, as a matter of law, was a defense to Parks' Lanham Act and right of publicity claims. *See Parks v. LaFace Records*, 76 F.Supp.2d 775, 780–84 (E.D. Mich. 1999). Specifically, the court found that (1) an "obvious relationship" between the content of the song and its title *Rosa Parks* renders the right of publicity inapplicable as a matter of law, *id.* at 780; (2) with respect to the Lanham Act, there was no explicit representation that the work was endorsed by Parks, *id.* at 783; (3) the prominent appearance of OutKast's name on their album cured any likelihood of consumer confusion between Plaintiff's and Defendants' albums as a matter of law, *id.* at 784; and (4) even if there were some likelihood of consumer confusion, such risk was outweighed by the First Amendment interests of the Defendants, 76 F. Supp. 2d at 783. . . .

II. DISCUSSION

* * *

[T]he scope of § 43(a) extends beyond disputes between producers of commercial products and their competitors. It also permits celebrities to vindicate property rights in their identities against allegedly misleading commercial use by others. *See Waits v. Frito–Lay, Inc.*, 978 F.2d 1093, 1110 (9th Cir. 1992) (celebrity suit against snack manufacturer for unauthorized use of his distinctive voice in a commercial); *Allen v. Nat'l Video, Inc.*, 610 F. Supp. 612, 624–25 (S.D.N.Y. 1985) (celebrity suit against a video retailer for use of a celebrity look-alike in its advertisements); *Landham v. Lewis Galoob Toys, Inc.*, 227 F.3d 619, 626 (6th Cir. 2000) (actor sued toy company for creating an action figure named after one of his movie characters); *Abdul–Jabbar v. Gen. Motors Corp.*, 85 F.3d 407, 410 (9th Cir. 1996) (professional basketball player sued car manufacturer for using his birth name to sell cars). Celebrities have standing to sue under § 43(a) because they possess an economic interest in their identities akin to that of a traditional trademark holder. *See Waits*, 978 F.2d at 1110. *See also* 4 J. Thomas McCarthy, *McCarthy on Trademarks and Unfair Competition* § 28:15 (4th ed. 2002)(discussing cases).

In order to prevail on a false advertising claim under § 43(a), a celebrity must show that use of his or her name is likely to cause confusion among consumers as to the "affiliation, connection, or association" between the celebrity and the defendant's goods or services or as to the celebrity's participation in the "origin, sponsorship, or approval" of the defendant's goods or services. *See* 15 U.S.C. § 1125(a)(1)(A); *Landham*, 227 F.3d at 626; *Wendt v. Host Int'l, Inc.*, 125 F.3d 806, 812 (9th Cir. 1997); *Cardtoons, L.C. v. Major League Baseball Players Ass'n*, 95 F.3d 959, 966 (10th Cir. 1996); *White v. Samsung Elecs. Am., Inc.*, 971 F.2d 1395, 1399 (9th Cir. 1992). Consumer confusion occurs when "consumers ... believe that the products or services offered by the parties are affiliated in some way," *Homeowners Group, Inc. v. Home Mktg. Specialists, Inc.*, 931 F.2d 1100, 1107 (6th Cir. 1991), or "when consumers make an incorrect mental association between the involved commercial products or their producers," *Cardtoons*, 95 F.3d at 966 (*quoting San Francisco Arts & Athletics, Inc. v. United States Olympic Comm.*, 483 U.S. 522, 564, 97 L. Ed. 2d 427, 107 S. Ct. 2971 (1987) (Brennan, J., dissenting)). A "likelihood" means a "probability" rather than a "possibility" of confusion....

Parks contends that Defendants have violated the Lanham Act because the *Rosa Parks* title misleads consumers into believing that the song is about her or that she is affiliated with the Defendants, or has sponsored or approved the *Rosa Parks* song and the *Aquemini* album. She argues that the risk of confusion is enhanced by the fact that her authorized *Tribute* album is in the marketplace alongside Defendants' album featuring the *Rosa Parks* single. As additional evidence for her claim, Parks points to Defendants' concession that they have used the *Rosa Parks* title to advertise and promote both the song and the *Aquemini* album. She also supplies twenty-one affidavits from consumers affirming that they either believed Defendants' song was about Parks or was connected to the *Tribute* album authorized by her.

Defendants respond that Parks' Lanham Act claim must fail for two reasons. First, they claim that Parks does not possess a trademark right in her name and Defendants have not made a trademark use of her name, as allegedly required for a cause of action under the Lanham Act. Second, they contend that even if use of the title posed some risk of consumer confusion, the risk is outweighed by Defendants' First Amendment right to free expression.

1. Trademark Right In and Trademark Use of Parks' Name

Citing *Rock & Roll Hall of Fame & Museum, Inc. v. Gentile Productions*, 134 F.3d 749, 756 (6th Cir. 1998), Defendants contend that Parks' § 43(a) claim must fail because they have made no trademark use of her name. However, Defendants misconceive the legal basis of a Lanham Act claim. It is not necessary for them to make a "trademark" use of Rosa Parks' name in order for her to have a cause of action for false advertising under § 43(a) of the Lanham Act.

Rosa Parks clearly has a property interest in her name akin to that of a person holding a trademark. It is beyond question that Parks is a celebrity. The parties have stipulated to her international fame and to her prior authorization of television programs and books. We have already established, *supra*, that courts routinely recognize a property right in celebrity identity akin to that of a trademark holder under § 43(a). *See, e.g., Landham*, 227 F.3d at 626; *Waits*, 978 F.2d at 1110; *Allen*, 610 F. Supp. at 624–25. We find Parks' prior commercial activities and international recognition as a symbol of the civil rights movement endow her with a trademark interest in her name the same as if she were a famous actor or musician.

Therefore, even though Rosa Parks' name might not be eligible for registration as a trademark, and even though Defendants were not selling Rosa Parks-brand CD's, a viable cause of action also exists under § 43(a) if consumers falsely believed that Rosa Parks had sponsored or approved the song, or was somehow affiliated with the song or the album. We turn then to Defendants' second argument, that even if Parks could establish some likelihood of confusion, the First Amendment protects Defendants' choice of title.

* * *

The application of *Rogers* ... in cases decided in other circuits, persuades us that *Rogers* is the best test for balancing Defendants' and the public's interest in free expression under the First Amendment against Parks' and the public's interest in enforcement of the Lanham Act. We thus apply the *Rogers* test to the facts before us.

3. Application of the Rogers Test

a. *Artistic Relevance Prong*

The first prong of *Rogers* requires a determination of whether there is any artistic relationship between the title and the underlying work. *Rogers*, 875 F.2d at 999. Parks contends that a cursory review of the *Rosa Parks* title and the lyrics demonstrates that there is no artistic connection between them. Parks also submits two articles in which members of OutKast are purported to have admitted that the song was not about her. As further evidence, she offers a "translation" of the lyrics of the song *Rosa Parks*, derived from various electronic "dictionaries" of the "rap" vernacular to demonstrate that the song truly has nothing to do with Parks herself. The "translation" of the chorus reads as follows:

> "Be quiet and stop the commotion. OutKast is coming back out [with new music] so all other MCs [mic checkers, rappers, Master of Ceremonies] step aside. Do you want to ride and hang out with us? OutKast is the type of group to make the clubs get hyped-up/excited."

Pl. Br. at 5.

Defendants respond that their use of Parks' name is "metaphorical" or "symbolic." They argue that the historical association between Rosa Parks and the phrase "move to the back of the bus" is beyond dispute and that Parks' argument that the song is not "about" her in a biographical sense is simply irrelevant.

The district court was of the opinion that the artistic relationship between the title and the song was "so obvious that the matter is not open to reasonable debate." *Parks*, 76 F.Supp.2d at 782. The court said:

> Rosa Parks is universally known for and commonly associated with her refusal ... to ... "move to the back of the bus." The song at issue makes unmistakable reference to that symbolic act a total of ten times. Admittedly, the song is not about plaintiff in a strictly biographical sense, but it need not be. Rather, defendants' use of plaintiff's name, along with the phrase "move to the back of the bus," is metaphorical and symbolic.

Id. at 780.

Contrary to the opinion of the district court, we believe that the artistic relationship between the title and the content of the song is certainly not obvious and, indeed, is "open to reasonable debate" for the following reasons.

It is true that the phrase "move to the back of the bus" is repeatedly used in the "hook" or chorus of the song. When the phrase is considered *in the context of the lyrics*, however, the phrase has absolutely nothing to do with Rosa Parks. There could be no stronger, no more compelling, evidence of this fact than the admission of "Dre" (Andre "Dre" Benjamin) that, "We (OutKast) never intended for the song to be about Rosa Parks or the civil rights movement. It was just symbolic, meaning that we comin' back out, so all you other MCs move to the back of the bus." J.A. at 333. The composers did *not* intend it to be about Rosa Parks, and the lyrics are *not* about Rosa Parks. The lyrics' sole message is that OutKast's competitors are of lesser quality and, therefore, must "move to the back of the bus," or in other words, "take a back seat." We believe that reasonable persons could conclude that there is no relationship of any kind between Rosa Parks' name and the content of the song—a song that is nothing more and nothing less than a paean announcing the triumph of superior people in the entertainment business over inferior people in that business. *Back of the Bus*, for example, would be a title that is obviously relevant to the content of the song, but it also would not have the marketing power of an icon of the civil rights movement.[6] Choosing Rosa Parks' name as the title to the song unquestionably enhanced the song's potential sale to the consuming public.

The *Rogers* court made an important point which clearly applies in this case. The court said, "poetic license is not without limits. The purchaser of a book, like the purchaser of a can of peas, has a right not to be misled as to the source of the product." *Rogers*, 875 F.2d at 997. The same is also true regarding the content of a song. The purchaser of a song titled *Rosa Parks* has a right not to be misled regarding the content of that song. While the expressive element of titles admittedly requires more protection than the labeling of ordinary commercial products, "[a] misleading title with no artistic relevance cannot be sufficiently justified by a free expression interest," *id.* at 999, and the use of such a title, as in the present case, could be found to constitute a violation of the Lanham Act. Including the phrase "move to the back of the bus" in the lyrics of this song, in our opinion, does not justify, as a matter of law, the appropriation of Rosa Parks' name for the title to the song, and the fact that the phrase is repeated ten times or fifty times does not affect the question of the relevancy of the title to the lyrics....

While Defendants' lyrics contain profanity and a great deal of "explicit" language (together with a parental warning), they contain absolutely nothing that could conceivably, by any stretch of the imagination, be considered, explicitly or implicitly, a reference to courage, to sacrifice, to the civil rights movement or to any other quality with which Rosa Parks is identified. If the requirement of "relevance" is to have any meaning at all, it would not be unreasonable to conclude that the title *Rosa Parks* is *not* relevant to the content of the song in question. The use of this woman's name unquestionably was a good marketing tool—*Rosa Parks* was likely to sell far more recordings than *Back of the Bus*—but its use could be found by a reasonable finder of fact to be a flagrant deception on the public regarding the actual content of this song and the creation of an impression that Rosa Parks, who had approved the use of her name in connection with the *Tribute* album, had also approved or sponsored the use of her name on Defendants' composition.

It is certainly not dispositive that, in response to an interview following the filing of this lawsuit, one of the OutKast members said that using Rosa Parks' name was "symbolic." Where an artist proclaims that a celebrity's name is used merely as a "symbol" for the lyrics of a song, and such use is highly questionable when the lyrics are examined, a legitimate question is presented as to whether the artist's claim is sincere or merely a guise to escape liability. Our task, it seems to us, is not to accept without question whatever purpose Defendants may now claim they had in using Rosa Parks' name. It is, instead, to make a determination as to whether,

6. Suggesting that "Back of the Bus" would have been an appropriate title is not meant to be an application of the "alternative avenues" test discussed *supra*. It simply shows that such a title would clearly be artistically relevant under the first prong of *Rogers*.

applying the law of *Rogers*, there is a genuine issue of material fact regarding the question of whether the title is artistically relevant to the content of the song. As noted above, crying "artist" does not confer *carte blanche* authority to appropriate a celebrity's name. Furthermore, crying "symbol" does not change that proposition and confer authority to use a celebrity's name when none, in fact, may exist.

It appears that the district court's rendition of summary judgment for OutKast was based on the court's conclusion that Defendants' use of Plaintiff's name as the song's title was "metaphorical and symbolic." *Id.* at 780. The obvious question, however, is *symbolic of what*? There is no doubt that Rosa Parks is a symbol. As the parties agree, she is "an international symbol of freedom, humanity, dignity and strength." There is not even a hint, however, of any of these qualities in the song to which Defendants attached her name. In lyrics that are laced with profanity and in a "hook" or chorus that is pure egomania, many reasonable people could find that this is a song that is clearly *antithetical* to the qualities identified with Rosa Parks. Furthermore, the use of Rosa Parks' name in a metaphorical sense is highly questionable. A metaphor is "a figure of speech in which a word or phrase denoting one kind of object or action is used in place of another to suggest a likeness or analogy between them." *Webster's Third New International Dictionary* 1420 (Phillip Babcock Gove, ed. 1976). The use of the phrase "go to the back of the bus" may be metaphorical to the extent that it refers to OutKast's competitors being pushed aside by OutKast's return and being forced to "take a back seat." The song, however, is not titled *Back of the Bus*. It is titled *Rosa Parks*, and it is difficult to equate OutKast's feeling of superiority, metaphorically or in any other manner, to the qualities for which Rosa Parks is known around the world. We believe that reasonable people could find that the use of Rosa Parks' name as the title to this song was not justified as being metaphorical or symbolic of anything for which Rosa Parks is famous. To the contrary, reasonable people could find that the name was appropriated solely because of the vastly increased marketing power of a product bearing the name of a national heroine of the civil rights movement.

We do not mean to imply that Rosa Parks must always be displayed in a flattering manner, or that she should have the ability to prevent any other characterization of her. She is a celebrity and, as such, she cannot prevent being portrayed in a manner that may not be pleasing to her.... The present case, however, does not involve any claim of caricature, parody or satire. It involves, instead, the use of a celebrity's name as the title to a song when it reasonably could be found that the celebrity's name has no artistic relevance to the content of the song. It involves, in short, a reasonable dispute whether the use of Rosa Parks' name was a misrepresentation and false advertising or whether it was a legitimate use of a celebrity's name in some recognized form of artistic expression protected by the First Amendment.

In *Rogers*, the court, in discussing the title to the movie *Ginger and Fred*, observed that "there is no doubt a risk that some people looking at the title 'Ginger and Fred' might think the film was about Rogers and Astaire in a direct, biographical sense. For those gaining that impression, the title is misleading." 875 F.2d at 1001. Likewise, in the present case, some people looking at the title *Rosa Parks* might think the song is about Rosa Parks and for those gaining that impression (as twenty-one consumer affidavits filed in this case indicate happened, J.A. at 342–62), the title is misleading. This, standing alone, may not be sufficient to show a violation of the Lanham Act *if* the title is nevertheless artistically relevant to the content of the underlying work.

There is a clear distinction, however, between the facts in *Rogers* and the facts in the present case. In *Rogers*, the court had no difficulty in finding that the title chosen for the movie *Ginger and Fred* had artistic relevance to the content of the movie. "The central characters in the film are nicknamed 'Ginger' and 'Fred,' and these names are not arbitrarily chosen just to exploit the publicity value of their real life counterparts but instead have genuine relevance to the film's story." 875 F.2d at 1001. The *Rogers* court further pointed out that the title *Ginger and Fred* is "entirely truthful as to its content in referring to the film's fictional protagonists who are known to their Italian audience as 'Ginger and Fred.'" *Id.* In other words, the title in *Rogers* was obviously relevant and truthful as to the film's content, because the film was about the main characters known in the film as Ginger and Fred. In contrast, it cannot be said that the title in the present case, *Rosa Parks*, is clearly truthful as to the content of the song which, as OutKast admits, is not about Rosa Parks at all and was never intended to be about Rosa Parks, and which does not refer to Rosa Parks or to the qualities for which she is known.

* * *

There is a genuine issue of material fact whether the use of Rosa Parks' name as a title to the song and on the cover of the album is artistically related to the content of the song or whether the use of the name Rosa Parks is nothing more than a misleading advertisement for the sale of the song.

b. *Misleading Prong*

In *Rogers*, the court held that if the title of the work is artistically relevant to its content, there is no violation of the Lanham Act *unless* the "title explicitly misleads as to the source or the content of the work." 875 F.2d at 999.

* * *

We considered all the facts presented to us and concluded that, with reference to the first prong of the *Rogers* analysis, the issue of artistic relevance of the title *Rosa Parks* to the lyrics of the song is highly questionable and cannot be resolved as a matter of law. However, if, on remand, a trier of fact, after a full evidentiary hearing, concludes that the title *is* used in some symbolic or metaphorical sense, application of the *Rogers* analysis, under the particular facts of this case, would appear to be complete. In the present case, the title *Rosa Parks* "makes no explicit statement that the work is about that person in any direct sense." In other words, Defendants did not name the song, for example, *The True Life Story of Rosa Parks* or *Rosa Parks' Favorite Rap.*

In short, whether the title *Rosa Parks* has any artistic relevance to the content of the song is an issue that must be resolved by a finder of fact following an evidentiary hearing and not by a judge as a matter of law upon the limited record submitted in support of a motion for summary judgment. If, on remand, the finder of fact determines that OutKast placed the title *Rosa Parks* on a song to which it had no artistic relevance at all, then this would constitute a violation of the Lanham Act and judgment should be entered in favor of Plaintiff. However, if the finder of fact determines that the title is artistically relevant to the song's content, then the inquiry is at an end because the title "is not explicitly misleading as to the content of the work." In that event, judgment should be entered in favor of Defendants.

C. Right of Publicity

* * *

a. *Cognizability of a First Amendment Defense*

Because a plaintiff bears a reduced burden of persuasion to succeed in a right of publicity action, courts and commentators have recognized that publicity rights carry a greater danger of impinging on First Amendment rights than do rights associated with false advertising claims. *See Rogers*, 875 F.2d at 1004; *see also Cardtoons*, 95 F.3d at 967 (noting that publicity rights offer "substantially broader protection" than laws preventing false endorsement); [citation omitted]

We have recognized the importance of a First Amendment defense to right of publicity actions in a recent case. In *Ruffin–Steinback v. dePasse*, friends and family members of the Motown group, the "Temptations," sued the makers of a televised mini-series for the manner in which they and the former group members were portrayed in the film. 82 F.Supp.2d 723, 726–27 (E.D. Mich. 2000), *aff'd,* 267 F.3d 457 (6th Cir. 2001). The plaintiffs alleged that their likenesses were appropriated to endorse a product, the film, without their permission. The court found in that case that the plaintiffs could not overcome the defendant's First Amendment defense, even where the portrayal of the plaintiffs was partly fictionalized, and even where the likenesses of the plaintiffs were used to promote a videocassette version of the mini-series. *Id.* at 730–31; *see also Seale*, 949 F. Supp. at 337 (holding that the film *Panther,* which used the name and likeness of Black Panther founder Bobby Seale, was protected by the First Amendment).

As with the Lanham Act, then, we must conduct another balancing of interests—Parks' property right in her own name versus the freedom of artistic expression....

b. *Application of a First Amendment Defense*

In *Rogers*, the Second Circuit held that movie titles are protected from right of publicity actions unless the title is "wholly unrelated" to the content of the work or was "simply a disguised commercial advertisement for the sale of goods or services." 875 F.2d at 1004. This test is supported in the context of other expressive works by comment c of § 47 of the *Restatement (Third) of Unfair Competition*. It states that "use of another's identity in a novel, play, or motion picture is . . . not ordinarily an infringement [of the right of publicity, unless] the name or likeness is used solely to attract attention to a work that is not related to the identified person." The *Rogers* formulation is also supported by the decision in *dePasse*. In *dePasse,* the court cited *Seale*, 949 F. Supp. at 337, for the proposition that the relationship between a plaintiff's identity and the content of the work is an element of a defense to a right of publicity action. . . .

For the same reasons we have stated earlier and need not repeat, we believe that Parks' right of publicity claim presents a genuine issue of material fact regarding the question of whether the title to the song is or is not "wholly unrelated" to the content of the song. A reasonable finder of fact, in our opinion, upon consideration of all the evidence, could find the title to be a "disguised commercial advertisement" or adopted "solely to attract attention" to the work. *See Rogers*, 875 F.2d at 1004–05.

* * *

III. CONCLUSION

We are not called upon in this case to judge the quality of Defendants' song, and whether we personally regard it as repulsive trash or a work of genius is immaterial to a determination of the legal issues presented to us. . . .

In this case, for the reasons set forth above, the fact that Defendants cry "artist" and "symbol" as reasons for appropriating Rosa Parks' name for a song title does not absolve them from potential liability for, in the words of Shakespeare, filching Rosa Parks' good name.[12] The question of that liability, however, should be determined by the trier of fact after a full evidentiary hearing and not as a matter of law on a motion for summary judgment.

[*Editors' Note*: The case settled without going to trial. *See* D. Shepardson and J. Menard, "Parks Settles Outkast Suit," *Detroit News* (April 15, 2005).]

12. Who steals my purse steals trash; 'tis something, nothing;

'Twas mine, 'tis his, and has been slave to thousands;

But he that filches from me my good name

Robs me of that which not enriches him

And makes me poor indeed.

William Shakespeare, *Othello,* act 3, sc. 3.

O'Grady v. 20th Century Fox, 2003 WL 24174616 (E.D.Tex. 2003). The magistrate judge recommended denial of defendant Fox's motion for summary judgment regarding plaintiff's false advertising claim, but recommended granting summary judgment on the misappropriation claim. Plaintiff, Scott O'Grady, a pilot shot down over Bosnia, had written a best-selling book about his experiences, and also featured in a BBC docudrama. Fox subsequently, without O'Grady's participation, made a movie "loosely based" on the same events. When originally filmed, the docudrama was titled "Missing in Action." The U.S. distributor subsequently re-titled it "Behind Enemy Lines: The Scott O'Grady Story." The Fox film was titled "Behind Enemy Lines." O'Grady alleged that Fox's publicity for its motion picture gave the false and misleading impression that O'Grady endorsed the movie or that it was his story.

The court rejected O'Grady's claim alleging misappropriation of his right of publicity: "the protection of name or likeness under Texas law does not include a person's life story." As to the false advertising claim, however, the magistrate judge ruled that facts necessary to its resolution remained in dispute:

> Plaintiff contends the title *Behind Enemy Lines: The Scott O'Grady Story* used in connection with the Rebroadcast [of the BBC docudrama] to promote the Movie *Behind Enemy Lines* is misleading and gives rise to an actionable claim. In addition, Plaintiff complains that even without the titles, the entire Rebroadcast is false and misleading because of the intermixing of advertisements, promotions, interviews, and other materials [promoting the Fox movie] into the true docudrama, giving viewers the false impression that Plaintiff endorsed the Movie or the Movie was Plaintiff's story.
>
> [Because the claim concerns advertisements for the movie, rather than the movie itself] there is a fact issue whether this is a case about commercial speech, in which case the *Rogers* test may not apply. Even if the Court were to apply the "hybrid speech" test utilized in *Rogers,* there is a genuine issue of material fact whether the title and Defendants' actions in creating the Rebroadcast are artistically related to the expressive elements of the Movie to qualify for First Amendment protection or whether the Rebroadcast is nothing more than a misleading advertisement for the Movie. *See Parks,* 329 F.3d at 458.

QUESTIONS

1. What is the basis of Ms. Parks' Lanham Act claim? If OutKast were to move for reconsideration in light of *Dastar*, how should the court rule?

2. The district court found that Rosa Parks' name had "obvious relevance" to OutKast's song. The court of appeals found it obviously irrelevant. The district court found the song's reference to Ms. Parks to be symbolic and protected by the first amendment. The court of appeals agreed Ms. Parks was a symbol, but not of anything to do with the song. Does *Rogers v. Grimaldi* oblige courts to engage in literary analysis of the references to named celebrities? Does *Parks v. LaFace* suggest courts are particularly competent to do it?

Pages 678–685. Delete *Cardtoons*. Substitute the following decision:

ETW Corp. v. Jireh Publishing, Inc.

332 F.3d 915 (6th Cir. 2003).

■ GRAHAM, DISTRICT JUDGE.

Plaintiff–Appellant ETW Corporation ("ETW") is the licensing agent of Eldrick "Tiger" Woods ("Woods"), one of the world's most famous professional golfers. Woods, chairman of the board of ETW, has assigned to it the exclusive right to exploit his name, image, likeness, and signature, and all other publicity rights. ETW owns a United States trademark registration for the mark "TIGER WOODS" (Registration No. 2,194,381) for use in connection with "art prints, calendars, mounted photographs, notebooks, pencils, pens, posters, trading cards, and unmounted photographs."

Defendant–Appellee Jireh Publishing, Inc. ("Jireh") of Tuscaloosa, Alabama, is the publisher of artwork created by Rick Rush ("Rush"). Rush, who refers to himself as "America's sports artist," has created paintings of famous figures in sports and famous sports events. A few examples include Michael Jordan, Mark McGuire, Coach Paul "Bear" Bryant, the Pebble Beach Golf Tournament, and the America's Cup Yacht Race. Jireh has produced and successfully marketed limited edition art prints made from Rush's paintings.

In 1998, Rush created a painting entitled *The Masters of Augusta*, which commemorates Woods's victory at the Masters Tournament in Augusta, Georgia, in 1997. At that event, Woods became the youngest player ever to win the Masters Tournament, while setting a 72–hole record for the tournament and a record 12–stroke margin of victory. In the foreground of Rush's painting are three views of Woods in different poses. In the center, he is completing the swing of a golf club, and on each side he is crouching, lining up and/or observing the progress of a putt. To the left of Woods is his caddy, Mike "Fluff" Cowan, and to his right is his final round partner's caddy. Behind these figures is the Augusta National Clubhouse. In a blue background behind the clubhouse are likenesses of famous golfers of the past looking down on Woods. These include Arnold Palmer, Sam Snead, Ben Hogan, Walter Hagen, Bobby Jones, and Jack Nicklaus. Behind them is the Masters leader board.

The limited edition prints distributed by Jireh consist of an image of Rush's painting which includes Rush's signature at the bottom right hand corner. Beneath the image of the painting, in block letters, is its title, "The Masters Of Augusta." Beneath the title, in block letters of equal height, is the artist's name, "Rick Rush," and beneath the artist's name, in smaller upper and lower case letters, is the legend "Painting America Through Sports."

As sold by Jireh, the limited edition prints are enclosed in a white envelope, accompanied with literature which includes a large photograph of Rush, a description of his art, and a narrative description of the subject painting. On the front of the envelope, Rush's name appears in block letters inside a rectangle, which includes the legend "Painting America Through Sports." Along the bottom is a large reproduction of Rush's signature two inches high and ten inches long. On the back of the envelope, under the flap, are the words "Masters of Augusta" in letters that are three-eights of an inch high, and "Tiger Woods" in letters that are one-fourth of an inch high. Woods's name also appears in the narrative description of the painting where he is mentioned twice in twenty-eight lines of text. The text also includes references to the six other famous golfers depicted in the background of the painting as well as the two caddies. Jireh published and marketed two hundred and fifty 22 1/2″ x 30″ serigraphs and five thousand 9″ x 11″ lithographs of *The Masters of Augusta* at an issuing price of $700 for the serigraphs and $100 for the lithographs.

ETW filed suit against Jireh on June 26, 1998, in the United States District Court for the Northern District of Ohio, alleging trademark infringement in violation of the Lanham Act, 15 U.S.C. § 1114; . . . and violation of Woods's right of publicity under Ohio common law. Jireh counterclaimed, seeking a declaratory judgment that Rush's art prints are protected by the First Amendment and do not violate the Lanham Act. Both parties moved for summary judgment. The district court granted Jireh's motion for summary judgment and dismissed the case. *See ETW Corp. v. Jireh Pub., Inc.*, 99 F.Supp.2d 829 (N.D. Ohio 2000). ETW timely perfected an appeal to this court.

II. *Trademark Claims Based on the Unauthorized Use of the Registered Trademark "Tiger Woods"*

ETW claims that the prints of Rush's work constitute the unauthorized use of a registered trademark in violation of the Lanham Act, 15 U.S.C. § 1114, . . .

ETW claims that Jireh infringed the registered mark "Tiger Woods" by including these words in marketing materials which accompanied the prints of Rush's painting. The words "Tiger Woods" do not appear on the face of the prints, nor are they included in the title of the painting. The words "Tiger Woods" do appear under the flap of the envelopes which contain the prints, and Woods is mentioned twice in the narrative which accompanies the prints.

The Lanham Act provides a defense to an infringement claim where the use of the mark "is a use, otherwise than as a mark, . . . which is descriptive of and used fairly and in good faith only to describe the goods . . . of such party[.]" 15 U.S.C. § 1115(b)(4); . . . In evaluating a defendant's fair use defense, a court must consider whether defendant has used the mark: (1) in its descriptive sense; and (2) in good faith.

A celebrity's name may be used in the title of an artistic work so long as there is some artistic relevance. *See Rogers v. Grimaldi,* 875 F.2d 994,

997 (2nd Cir. 1989); *New York Racing Ass'n v. Perlmutter Publ'g, Inc.*, No. 95–CV–994, 1996 WL 465298 at *4 (N.D.N.Y. July 19, 1996) (finding the use of a registered mark on the title of a painting protected by the First Amendment). The use of Woods's name on the back of the envelope containing the print and in the narrative description of the print are purely descriptive and there is nothing to indicate that they were used other than in good faith. The prints, the envelopes which contain them, and the narrative materials which accompany them clearly identify Rush as the source of the print. Woods is mentioned only to describe the content of the print.

The district court properly granted summary judgment on ETW's claim for violation of its registered mark, "Tiger Woods," on the grounds that the claim was barred by the fair use defense as a matter of law.

III. *Trademark Claims Under 15 U.S.C. § 1125(a) Based on the Unauthorized Use of the Likeness of Tiger Woods*

. . .

ETW has registered Woods's name as a trademark, but it has not registered any image or likeness of Woods. Nevertheless, ETW claims to have trademark rights in Woods's image and likeness. Section 43 (a) of the Lanham Act provides a federal cause of action for infringement of an unregistered trademark which affords such marks essentially the same protection as those that are registered....

Here, ETW claims protection under the Lanham Act for any and all images of Tiger Woods. This is an untenable claim. ETW asks us, in effect, to constitute Woods himself as a walking, talking trademark. Images and likenesses of Woods are not protectable as a trademark because they do not perform the trademark function of designation. They do not distinguish and identify the source of goods. They cannot function as a trademark because there are undoubtedly thousands of images and likenesses of Woods taken by countless photographers, and drawn, sketched, or painted by numerous artists, which have been published in many forms of media, and sold and distributed throughout the world. No reasonable person could believe that merely because these photographs or paintings contain Woods's likeness or image, they all originated with Woods.

We hold that, as a general rule, a person's image or likeness cannot function as a trademark. Our conclusion is supported by the decisions of other courts which have addressed this issue. In *Pirone v. MacMillan, Inc.*, 894 F.2d 579 (2nd Cir. 1990), the Second Circuit rejected a trademark claim asserted by the daughters of baseball legend Babe Ruth. The plaintiffs objected to the use of Ruth's likeness in three photographs which appeared in a calendar published by the defendant. The court rejected their claim, holding that "a photograph of a human being, unlike a portrait of a fanciful cartoon character, is not inherently 'distinctive' in the trademark sense of tending to indicate origin." *Id.* at 583. The court noted that Ruth "was one of the most photographed men of his generation, a larger than life hero to millions and an historical figure[.]" *Id.* The Second Circuit Court concluded that a consumer could not reasonably believe that Ruth sponsored the calendar:

> An ordinarily prudent purchaser would have no difficulty discerning that these photos are merely the subject matter of the calendar and do not in any way indicate sponsorship. No reasonable jury could find a likelihood of confusion.

Id. at 585. The court observed that "under some circumstances, a photograph of a person may be a valid trademark—if, for example, a particular photograph was consistently used on specific goods." *Id.* at 583. The court rejected plaintiffs' assertion of trademark rights in every photograph of Ruth.

In *Estate of Presley v. Russen*, 513 F. Supp. 1339, 1363–1364 (D.N.J. 1981), the court rejected a claim by the estate of Elvis Presley that his image and likeness was a valid mark. The court did find, however, as suggested by the Second Circuit in *Pirone*, that one particular image of Presley had been consistently used in the advertising and sale of Elvis Presley entertainment services to identify those services and that the image could likely be found to function as a mark.

In *Rock and Roll Hall of Fame*, the plaintiff asserted trademark rights in the design of the building which houses the Rock and Roll Hall of Fame in Cleveland, Ohio, and claimed that defendant's poster featuring a photograph of the museum against a colorful sunset was a violation of its trademark rights. 134 F.3d at 751. This court, with one judge dissenting, reversed the judgment of the district court which granted plaintiff's request for a preliminary injunction. After reviewing the evidence, the majority concluded:

> In reviewing the Museum's disparate uses of several different perspectives of its building design, we cannot conclude that they create a consistent and distinct commercial impression as an indicator of a single source of origin or sponsorship. To be more specific, we cannot conclude on this record that it is likely that the Museum has established a valid trademark in every photograph which, like Gentile's, prominently displays the front of the Museum's building.

Id. at 755. In reaching this conclusion, this court approved and followed *Pirone* and *Estate of Presley*.

Here, ETW does not claim that a particular photograph of Woods has been consistently used on specific goods. Instead, ETW's claim is identical to that of the plaintiffs in *Pirone*, a sweeping claim to trademark rights in every photograph and image of Woods. Woods, like Ruth, is one of the most photographed sports figures of his generation, but this alone does not suffice to create a trademark claim.

The district court properly granted summary judgment on ETW's claim of trademark rights in all images and likenesses of Tiger Woods.

* * *

D. *Right of Publicity Claim*

[The court discussed its own and other circuits' decisions in right of publicity cases.]

In *Comedy III Productions, Inc. v. Gary Saderup, Inc.*, 25 Cal. 4th 387, 106 Cal. Rptr. 2d 126, 21 P.3d 797 (2001), the California Supreme Court adopted a transformative use test in determining whether the artistic use of a celebrity's image is protected by the First Amendment. Saderup, an artist with over twenty-five years experience in making charcoal drawings of celebrities, created a drawing of the famous comedy team, The Three Stooges. The drawings were used to create lithographic and silk screen masters, which were then used to produce lithographic prints and silk screen images on T-shirts. Comedy III, the owner of all rights to the former comedy act, brought suit against Saderup under a California statute, which grants the right of publicity to successors in interest of deceased celebrities.

The California Supreme Court found that Saderup's portraits were entitled to First Amendment protection because they were "expressive works and not an advertisement or endorsement of a product." *Id.* at 396, 21 P.3d at 802. . . .

The court rejected the proposition that Saderup's lithographs and T-shirts lost their First Amendment protection because they were not original single works of art, but were instead part of a commercial enterprise designed to generate profit solely from the sale of multiple reproductions of likenesses of The Three Stooges:

> This position has no basis in logic or authority. No one would claim that a published book, because it is one of many copies, receives less First Amendment protection than the original manuscript ... [A] reproduction of a celebrity image that, as explained above, contains significant creative elements is entitled to as much First Amendment protection as an original work of art.

Id. at 408, 21 P.3d at 810.

Borrowing part of the fair use defense from copyright law, the California court proposed the following test for distinguishing between protected and unprotected expression when the right of publicity conflicts with the First Amendment:

> When artistic expression takes the form of a literal depiction or imitation of a celebrity for commercial gain, directly trespassing on the right of publicity without adding significant expression beyond that trespass, the state law interest in protecting the fruits of artistic labor outweighs the expressive interests of the imitative artist.
>
> On the other hand, when a work contains significant transformative elements, it is not only especially worthy of First Amendment protection, but it is also less likely to interfere with the economic interest protected by the right of publicity. . . .

> Accordingly, First Amendment protection of such works outweighs whatever interest the state may have in enforcing the right of publicity.

Id. at 405, 21 P.3d at 808 (footnote and citations omitted). Later in its opinion, the California court restated the test as follows:

> Another way of stating the inquiry is whether the celebrity likeness is one of the "raw materials" from which an original work is synthesized, or whether the depiction or imitation of the celebrity is the very sum and substance of the work in question.

Id. at 406, 21 P.3d at 809.

Finally, citing the art of Andy Warhol, the court noted that even literal reproductions of celebrity portraits may be protected by the First Amendment.

> Through distortion and the careful manipulation of context, Warhol was able to convey a message that went beyond the commercial exploitation of celebrity images and became a form of ironic social comment on the dehumanization of celebrity itself ... Although the distinction between protected and unprotected expression will sometimes be subtle, it is no more so than other distinctions triers of fact are called on to make in First Amendment jurisprudence.

Id. at 408–409, 106 Cal.Rptr.2d 126, 21 P.3d 797, 21 P.3d at 811 (citations and footnote omitted).

We conclude that in deciding whether the sale of Rush's prints violate Woods's right of publicity, we will look to the Ohio case law and the Restatement (Third) of Unfair Competition. In deciding where the line should be drawn between Woods's intellectual property rights and the First Amendment, we find ourselves in agreement with the dissenting judges in *White*, the Tenth Circuit's decision in *Cardtoons*, and the Ninth Circuit's decision in *Hoffman*, and we will follow them in determining whether Rush's work is protected by the First Amendment. Finally, we believe that the transformative elements test adopted by the Supreme Court of California in *Comedy III Productions*, will assist us in determining where the proper balance lies between the First Amendment and Woods's intellectual property rights. We turn now to a further examination of Rush's work and its subject.

E. *Application of the Law to the Evidence in this Case*

The evidence in the record reveals that Rush's work consists of much more than a mere literal likeness of Woods. It is a panorama of Woods's victory at the 1997 Masters Tournament, with all of the trappings of that tournament in full view, including the Augusta clubhouse, the leader board, images of Woods's caddy, and his final round partner's caddy. These elements in themselves are sufficient to bring Rush's work within the protection of the First Amendment. The Masters Tournament is probably the world's most famous golf tournament and Woods's victory in the 1997 tournament was a historic event in the world of sports. A piece of art that portrays a historic sporting event communicates and celebrates the value our culture attaches to such events. It would be ironic indeed if the presence of the image of the victorious athlete would deny the work First Amendment protection. Furthermore, Rush's work includes not only images of Woods and the two caddies, but also carefully crafted likenesses of six past winners of the Masters Tournament: Arnold Palmer, Sam Snead, Ben Hogan, Walter Hagen, Bobby Jones, and Jack Nicklaus, a veritable pantheon of golf's greats. Rush's work conveys the message that Woods himself will someday join that revered group.

Turning first to ETW's Lanham Act false endorsement claim, we agree with the courts that hold that the Lanham Act should be applied to artistic works only where the public interest in avoiding confusion outweighs the public interest in free expression. The *Rogers* test is helpful in striking that balance in the instant case. We find that the presence of Woods's image in Rush's painting *The Masters Of Augusta* does have artistic relevance to the underlying work and that it does not explicitly mislead as to the source of the work.[18] We believe that the principles followed in *Cardtoons*, *Hoffman* and *Comedy III* are also relevant in determining whether the Lanham Act applies to Rush's work, and we find that it does not....

In regard to the Ohio law right of publicity claim, we conclude that Ohio would construe its right of publicity as suggested in the Restatement (Third) of Unfair Competition, Chapter 4, Section 47, Comment d., which articulates a rule analogous to the rule of fair use in copyright law. Under this rule, the substantiality and market effect of the use of the celebrity's image is analyzed in light of the informational and creative content of the defendant's use. Applying this rule, we conclude that Rush's work has substantial informational and creative content which outweighs any adverse effect on ETW's market and that Rush's work does not violate Woods's right of publicity.

We further find that Rush's work is expression which is entitled to the full protection of the First Amendment and not the more limited protection afforded to commercial speech. When we balance the magnitude of the speech restriction against the interest in protecting Woods's intellectual property right, we encounter precisely the same considerations weighed by the Tenth Circuit in *Cardtoons*. These include consideration of the fact that through their pervasive presence in the media, sports and entertainment celebrities have come to symbolize certain ideas and values in our society and have become a valuable means of expression in our culture. As the Tenth Circuit observed "celebrities ... are an important element of the shared communicative resources of our cultural domain." *Cardtoons*, 95 F.3d at 972.

In balancing these interests against Woods's right of publicity, we note that Woods, like most sports and entertainment celebrities with commercially valuable identities, engages in an activity, professional golf, that in

18. Unlike *Parks*, here there is no genuine issue of material fact about the artistic relevance of the image of Woods in Rush's print....

itself generates a significant amount of income which is unrelated to his right of publicity. Even in the absence of his right of publicity, he would still be able to reap substantial financial rewards from authorized appearances and endorsements. It is not at all clear that the appearance of Woods's likeness in artwork prints which display one of his major achievements will reduce the commercial value of his likeness.

While the right of publicity allows celebrities like Woods to enjoy the fruits of their labors, here Rush has added a significant creative component of his own to Woods's identity. Permitting Woods's right of publicity to trump Rush's right of freedom of expression would extinguish Rush's right to profit from his creative enterprise.

After balancing the societal and personal interests embodied in the First Amendment against Woods's property rights, we conclude that the effect of limiting Woods's right of publicity in this case is negligible and significantly outweighed by society's interest in freedom of artistic expression.

Finally, applying the transformative effects test adopted by the Supreme Court of California in *Comedy III*, we find that Rush's work does contain significant transformative elements which make it especially worthy of First Amendment protection and also less likely to interfere with the economic interest protected by Woods' right of publicity. Unlike the unadorned, nearly photographic reproduction of the faces of The Three Stooges in *Comedy III*, Rush's work does not capitalize solely on a literal depiction of Woods. Rather, Rush's work consists of a collage of images in addition to Woods's image which are combined to describe, in artistic form, a historic event in sports history and to convey a message about the significance of Woods's achievement in that event. Because Rush's work has substantial transformative elements, it is entitled to the full protection of the First Amendment. In this case, we find that Woods's right of publicity must yield to the First Amendment.

. . .

■ CLAY, CIRCUIT JUDGE, dissenting.

. . .

I. Trademark Claims Based on Defendant's Unauthorized Use of the Unregistered Mark—§ 43(a) of the Lanham Act, 15 U.S.C. § 1125(a)

At the outset, it should be noted that the majority's characterization of this claim as the "Unauthorized Use of the Likeness of Tiger Woods" is misleading. Such a characterization bolsters the majority's unfounded position that Plaintiff is seeking protection under the Lanham Act for any and all images of Tiger Woods, but, indeed, such is not the case. Plaintiff's amended complaint squarely sets forth Defendant's conduct to which

Plaintiff takes issue—Defendant's portrayal of Woods in his famous golf swing at the Masters Tournament in Augusta as set forth in Rush's print.

. . .

Simply stated, contrary to the majority's contention, the jurisprudence clearly indicates that a person's image or likeness *can* function as a trademark as long as there is evidence demonstrating that the likeness or image was used as a trademark; which is to say, the image can function as a trademark as long as there is evidence of consumer confusion as to the source of the merchandise upon which the image appears. *See, e.g., Rock & Roll*, 134 F.3d at 753....

Inasmuch as Plaintiff proffered evidence of consumer confusion as to Woods' affiliation with or sponsorship of the poster, Plaintiff proffered evidence that it has used this image of Tiger Woods "as a trademark." ...

With that said, it is difficult to conceive how the majority arrives at its conclusion that Plaintiff "does not claim that a particular photograph of Woods has been consistently used on specific goods" but instead makes "a sweeping claim to trademark rights in every photograph and image of Woods." As indicated in the outset of this discussion, Plaintiff's complaint specifically takes issue with the image of Woods as depicted in Rush's *Masters of Augusta* print and, moreover, Plaintiff has come forward with strong evidence of consumer confusion to support its claim that this image of Woods has been used as a trademark for purposes of supporting its § 43(a) claim. The majority's failure to acknowledge the significance of this evidence constitutes a fatal flaw in its analysis because it is settled that "if the defendant's unauthorized use creates a false suggestion of endorsement or a likelihood of confusion as to source or sponsorship, liability may also be imposed for ... trademark or trade name infringement." Restatement (Third) of Unfair Competition § 46 cmt. b, 537 (1995) (emphasis added); *see also Bird*, 289 F.3d at 877 (noting that "the key question in cases where a plaintiff alleges trademark infringement and unfair competition is whether the defendant's actions create a likelihood of confusion as to the origin of the parties' goods or services").

Finally, as explained in the next section, even by adopting the Second Circuit's balancing approach when considering a Lanham Act claim involving an artistic expression, Plaintiff's likelihood of confusion evidence should, and indeed must, be considered in deciding Plaintiff's claim for infringement of the unregistered mark. As the Second Circuit has also proclaimed, "trademark protection is not lost simply because the alleging infringing use is in connection with an artistic expression." *Cliffs Notes, Inc. v. Bantam Doubleday Dell Publ'g Group, Inc.*, 886 F.2d 490, 493 (2d Cir. 1989) (alteration in *Cliffs Notes*) (quoting *Silverman v. CBS Inc.*, 870 F.2d 40, 49 (2d Cir. 1989)).

. . .

Even under the *Rogers* standard, it is necessary for this case to be remanded on the issue of Plaintiff's false endorsement claim since questions of fact remain as to the degree of consumer confusion associated with Rush's print and Woods' endorsement thereof. To hold otherwise not only runs counter to the approach espoused in *Rogers* and its progeny, but to the express word of Congress: that a plaintiff may prevail on a Lanham Act claim if he can prove that the use in commerce of the trademark "in connection with goods or services" is "*likely to cause confusion, to cause mistake, or to deceive* as to the affiliation, connection, or association of such person with another person, or as to the origin, sponsorship, or approval of his or her goods, services, or commercial activities by another person. . . ." 15 U.S.C. § 1125(a)(1)(A) (emphasis added). This is not to say that the ultimate outcome here would necessarily be a favorable one for Plaintiff; however, a jury should be able to make that decision after hearing all of the evidence presented by Plaintiff, as opposed to the majority's truncated and abbreviated approach which fails to engage in any meaningful consideration of pertinent and relevant evidence of consumer confusion, and fails to engage in any significant balancing of the interests.

. . .

V. Ohio Common Law Right of Publicity Claim

. . .

Despite the various commentary and scholarship assessing the virtues and drawbacks to the right of publicity when compared to First Amendment principles, the fact remains that the right of publicity is an accepted right and striking the balance between an individual's right of publicity against the speaker's First Amendment right is not an easy one. Bearing in mind the principles justifying the two rights, it is clear why Woods' right of publicity does not bow to Defendant's First Amendment rights in this case.

B. Woods' Right of Publicity Claim in this Case

. . .

In the instant case, where we are faced with an expressive work and the question of whether that work is protected under the First Amendment, the reasoning and transformative test set forth in *Comedy III* are in line with the Supreme Court's reasoning in *Zacchini* as well as in harmony with the goals of both the right to publicity and the First Amendment. Applying the test here, it is difficult to discern any appreciable transformative or creative contribution in Defendant's prints so as to entitle them to First Amendment protection. "A literal depiction of a celebrity, even if accomplished with great skill, may still be subject to a right of publicity challenge. The inquiry is in a sense more quantitative than qualitative, asking whether the literal and imitative or the creative elements predominate in the work." *Comedy III*, 21 P.3d at 809 (footnote omitted).

Indeed, the rendition done by Rush is nearly identical to that in the poster distributed by Nike. Although the faces and partial body images of other famous golfers appear in blue sketch blending in the background of Rush's print, the clear focus of the work is Woods in full body image wearing his red shirt and holding his famous swing in the pose which is nearly identical to that depicted in the Nike poster. Rush's print does not depict Woods in the same vein as the other golfers, such that the focus of the print is not the Masters Tournament or the other golfers who have won the prestigious green jacket award, but that of Woods holding his famous golf swing while at that tournament. Thus, although it is apparent that Rush is an adequately skilled artist, after viewing the prints in question it is also apparent that Rush's ability in this regard is "subordinated to the overall goal of creating literal, conventional depictions of [Tiger Woods] so as to exploit his ... fame [such that Rush's] right of free expression is outweighed by [Woods'] right of publicity." *See id.* at 811.

In fact, the narrative that accompanies the prints expressly discusses Woods and his fame:

> But the center of their [other golfers'] gaze is 1997 winner Tiger Woods, here flanked by his caddie, "Fluff", and final round player partner's (Constantino Rocca) caddie on right, displaying that awesome swing that sends a golf ball straighter and truer than should be humanly possible. Only his uncanny putting ability serves to complete his dominating performance that lifts him alongside the Masters of Augusta.

Accordingly, contrary to the majority's conclusion otherwise, it is clear that the prints gain their commercial value by exploiting the fame and celebrity status that Woods has worked to achieve. Under such facts, the right of publicity is not outweighed by the right of free expression. *See Comedy III*, 21 P.3d at 811 (noting that the marketability and economic value of the defendant's work was derived primarily from the fame of the three celebrities that it depicted and was therefore not protected by the First Amendment).

This conclusion regarding Plaintiff's right of publicity claim is in harmony with that regarding Plaintiff's claims brought under the Lanham Act. As the Restatement explains:

> Proof of deception or confusion is not required in order to establish an infringement of the right of publicity. However, if the defendant's unauthorized use creates a false suggestion of endorsement or a likelihood of confusion as to source or sponsorship, liability may also be imposed for deceptive marketing or trademark or trade name infringement.

Restatement, *supra* § 46 cmt. b, 537.

Because Plaintiff has come forward with evidence of consumer confusion as to Woods' sponsorship of the products in question, it is for the jury to decide whether liability should be imposed for Plaintiff's claims brought under the Lanham Act, and this is true whether employing the balancing approach set forth in *Rogers* or simply employing the eight-factor test in the traditional sense. The majority's failure to do so in this case is in complete contravention to the intent of Congress, the principles of trademark law, and the well-established body of jurisprudence in this area....

Consider whether right of publicity claims require first amendment analyses like those undertaken in *ETW v. Jireh*. Where, for example, a state right of publicity statute provides a right of action for nonconsensual use of a person's name or likeness "for purposes of trade," is it clear that "trade" encompasses all for-profit expressive uses? *Tyne v. Time Warner Entertainment,* 901 So.2d 802 (Fla. 2005), concerned a claim brought by the families of the fishermen who died in what became memorialized in a non fiction book and film as "The Perfect Storm." The Florida Supreme Court, ruling on a question certified by the Eleventh Circuit, interpreted the Florida statute, which prohibited a person to "publicly use for purposes of trade or for any commercial or advertising purpose the name, portrait, photograph, or other likeness of any natural person without the express written or oral consent to such use ..." Section 540.08, Florida Statutes (2000). The Florida Supreme Court adopted the reasoning of a lower court in *Loft v. Fuller*, 408 So.2d 619 (Fla. 4th DCA 1981), which had declined to find that the statute covered a claim by the family of an airline pilot who died in a crash against a book and a motion picture containing non fiction accounts of the disaster.

> In our view, section 540.08, by prohibiting the use of one's name or likeness for trade, commercial or advertising purposes, is designed to prevent the unauthorized use of a name to directly promote the product or service of the publisher. Thus, the publication is harmful not simply because it is included in a publication that is sold for a profit, but rather because of the way it associates the individual's name or his personality with something else. Such is not the case here.
>
> While we agree that at least one of the purposes of the author and publisher in releasing the publication in question was to make money through sales of copies of the book and that such a publication is commercial in that sense, this in no way distinguishes this book from almost all other books, magazines or newspapers and simply does not amount to the kind of commercial exploitation prohibited by the statute. We simply do not believe that the term "commercial," as employed by Section 540.08, was meant to be construed to bar the use of people's names in such a sweeping fashion. We also believe that acceptance of appellants' view of the statute would result in substantial confrontation between this statute and the first amendment to the United States Constitution guaranteeing freedom of the press and of speech. Having concluded that the publication as alleged is not barred by Section 540.08, we need not decide if, under the allegations of the

complaint, the book was of current and legitimate public interest, thus removing it entirely from the scope of the statute.

Page 688. Add new Question 6:

6. Major League Baseball publishes statistics of each player's performance. For batters, these include batting average, home runs and RBIs (runs batted in), for pitchers, the win-loss record and the ERA (earned run average). Organizers of baseball "fantasy leagues" assemble imaginary teams based on the players' statistics. The league organizers also use the statistics to calculate the "winning" team at season's end. Some fantasy leagues award cash prizes; the fantasy leagues have become a multi million dollar business. Major League Baseball, asserting the ballplayers' rights of publicity, has demanded that the leagues take a license to use the names and statistics of the ballplayers. The leagues reply that these are unprotectable facts not subject to ownership on any theory. What arguments can you make for the players and MLB? What arguments for the leagues? Who should prevail?

CHAPTER 10

Dilution

B. Dilution Under State Law

Page 714. Add Additional Question below:

4. In Disney's video "George of the Jungle 2," the villains drive bulldozers with recognizable CATERPILLAR trademarks to destroy Ape Mountain, and the narrator refers to the bulldozers as "deleterious dozers" and "maniacal machines." In the comedy film "Dickie Roberts: Former Child Star," the protagonist comically misuses a SLIP 'N SLIDE yellow water slide which results in his injury. This scene appears in advertisements and trailers for the film. Do the owners of the CATERPILLAR or SLIP 'N SLIDE marks have a viable dilution claim? Under what theory? *See Caterpillar Inc. v. Walt Disney Co.*, 287 F.Supp.2d 913 (C.D.Ill.2003) and *Wham–O, Inc. v. Paramount Pictures Corp.*, 286 F.Supp.2d 1254 (N.D.Cal. 2003).

C. Federal Dilution

1. Word Marks

Page 715. Delete *Ringling Bros.-Barnum & Bailey Combined Shows, Inc. v. B.E. Windows:*

Page 724. Delete *Eli Lilly & Co. v. Natural Answers, Inc.* and add the following case:

Moseley v. V Secret Catalogue

537 U.S. 418 (2003).

■ Justice Stevens delivered the opinion of the Court:

In 1995 Congress amended § 43 of the Trademark Act of 1946, 15 U.S.C. § 1125 to provide a remedy for the "dilution of famous marks." 109 Stat. 985–986. That amendment, known as the Federal Trademark Dilution Act (FTDA), describes the factors that determine whether a mark is "distinctive and famous," and defines the term "dilution" as "the lessening of the capacity of a famous mark to identify and distinguish goods or services." The question we granted certiorari to decide is whether objective proof of actual injury to the economic value of a famous mark (as opposed to a presumption of harm arising from a subjective "likelihood of dilution" standard) is a requisite for relief under the FTDA.

Petitioners, Victor and Cathy Moseley, own and operate a retail store named "Victor's Little Secret" in a strip mall in Elizabethtown, Kentucky. They have no employees. Respondents are affiliated corporations that own the VICTORIA's SECRET trademark, and operate over 750 Victoria's Secret stores, two of which are in Louisville, Kentucky, a short drive from Elizabethtown. In 1998 they spent over $55 million advertising "the VICTORIA's SECRET brand—one of moderately priced, high quality, attractively designed lingerie sold in a store setting designed to look like a wom[a]n's bedroom." App. 167, 170. They distribute 400 million copies of the Victoria's Secret catalog each year, including 39,000 in Elizabethtown. In 1998 their sales exceeded $1.5 billion.

In the February 12, 1998 edition of a weekly publication distributed to residents of the military installation at Fort Knox, Kentucky, petitioners advertised the "GRAND OPENING Just in time for Valentine's Day!" of their store "VICTOR's SECRET" in nearby Elizabethtown. The ad featured "Intimate Lingerie *for every woman*;" "Romantic Lighting"; "Lycra Dresses"; "Pagers"; and "Adult Novelties/Gifts." *Id.,* at 209. An army colonel, who saw the ad and was offended by what he perceived to be an attempt to use a reputable company's trademark to promote the sale of "unwholesome, tawdry merchandise," sent a copy to respondents. *Id.,* at 210. Their counsel then wrote to petitioners stating that their choice of the name "Victor's Secret" for a store selling lingerie was likely to cause confusion with the well-known Victoria's Secret mark and, in addition, was likely to "dilute the distinctiveness" of the mark. *Id.,* at 190–191. They requested the immediate discontinuance of the use of the name "and any variations thereof." *Ibid.* In response, petitioners changed the name of their store to "Victor's Little Secret." Because that change did not satisfy respondents, they promptly filed this action in Federal District Court.

The complaint contained four separate claims: (1) for trademark infringement alleging that petitioners' use of their trade name was "likely to cause confusion and/or mistake in violation of 15 U.S.C. § 1114(1)"; (2) for unfair competition alleging misrepresentation in violation of § 1125(a); (3) for "federal dilution" in violation of the FTDA; and (4) for trademark infringement and unfair competition in violation of the common law of Kentucky. *Id.,* at 15, 20–23. In the dilution count, the complaint alleged that petitioners' conduct was "likely to blur and erode the distinctiveness" and "tarnish the reputation" of the VICTORIA's SECRET trademark. *Ibid.*

After discovery the parties filed cross-motions for summary judgment. The record contained uncontradicted affidavits and deposition testimony describing the vast size of respondents' business, the value of the VICTORIA's SECRET name, and descriptions of the items sold in the respective parties' stores. Respondents sell a "complete line of lingerie" and related items, each of which bears a VICTORIA's SECRET label or tag. Petitioners sell a wide variety of items, including adult videos, "adult novelties," and lingerie. Victor Moseley stated in an affidavit that women's lingerie represented only about five per cent of their sales. *Id.,* at 131. In support of their motion for summary judgment, respondents submitted an affidavit by an expert in marketing who explained "the enormous value" of respondents' mark. *Id.,* at 195–205. Neither he, nor any other witness, expressed any opinion concerning the impact, if any, of petitioners' use of the name "Victor's Little Secret" on that value. Finding that the record contained no evidence of actual confusion between the parties' marks, the District Court concluded that "no likelihood of confusion exists as a matter of law" and entered summary judgment for petitioners on the infringement and unfair competition claims. Civ. Action No. 3:98CV–395's (WD Ky., Feb. 9, 2000), App. to Pet. for Cert. 28a, 37a. With respect to the FTDA claim, however, the court ruled for respondents. Noting that petitioners did not challenge Victoria Secret's claim that its mark is "famous," the only question it had to decide was whether petitioners' use of their mark diluted the quality of respondents' mark. Reasoning from the premise that dilution "corrodes" a trademark either by " 'blurring its product identification or by damaging positive associations that have attached to it,' " the court first found the two marks to be sufficiently similar to cause dilution, and then found "that Defendants' mark dilutes Plaintiffs' mark because of its tarnishing effect upon the Victoria's Secret mark." *Id.,* at 38a–39a (quoting *Ameritech, Inc.* v. *American Info. Technologies Corp.*, 811 F.2d 960, 965 (CA6 1987)). It therefore enjoined petitioners "from using the mark 'Victor's Little Secret' on the basis that it causes dilution of the distinctive quality of the Victoria's Secret mark." App. to Pet. for Cert. 38a–39a. The court did not, however, find that any "blurring" had occurred. *Ibid.*

The Court of Appeals for the Sixth Circuit affirmed. 259 F.3d 464 (2001). In a case decided shortly after the entry of the District Court's judgment in this case, the Sixth Circuit had adopted the standards for determining dilution under the FDTA that were enunciated by the Second Circuit in *Nabisco, Inc.* v. *PF Brands, Inc.*, 191 F.3d 208 (1999). *See Kellogg Co.* v. *Exxon Corp.*, 209 F.3d 562 (CA6 2000). In order to apply those standards, it was necessary to discuss two issues that the District Court had not specifically addressed—whether respondents' mark is "distinctive,"[5] and whether relief could be granted before dilution has actually occurred.[6] With respect to the first issue, the court rejected the argument

5. "It is quite clear that the statute intends distinctiveness, in addition to fame, as an essential element. The operative language defining the tort requires that 'the [junior] person's ... use ... caus[e] dilution of the distinctive quality of the [senior] mark.' 15 U.S.C. § 1125(c)(1). There can be no dilution of a mark's distinctive quality unless the mark is distinctive." *Nabisco, Inc.* v. *PF Brands, Inc.*, 191 F.3d 208, 216 (CA2 1999).

6. The Second Circuit explained why it did not believe "actual dilution" need be proved: "Relying on a recent decision by the Fourth Circuit, Nabisco also asserts that proof of dilution under the FTDA requires proof of an 'actual, consummated harm.' " *Ringling Bros.-Barnum & Bailey Combined Shows, Inc. v. Utah Division of Travel Dev.*, 170 F.3d 449, 464 (4th Cir. 1999). We reject the argument because we disagree with the Fourth Circuit's interpretation of the statute. "It is not clear which of two positions the Fourth Circuit adopted by its requirement of proof of 'actual dilution.' *Id.* The narrower position would be that courts may not infer dilution from 'contextual factors (degree of mark and product similarity, etc.),' but must

that Victoria's Secret could not be distinctive because "secret" is an ordinary word used by hundreds of lingerie concerns. The court concluded that the entire mark was "arbitrary and fanciful" and therefore deserving of a high level of trademark protection. 259 F.3d, at 470. On the second issue, the court relied on a distinction suggested by this sentence in the House Report: "Confusion leads to immediate injury, while dilution is an infection, which if allowed to spread, will inevitably destroy the advertising value of the mark." H. R. Rep. No. 104–374, p. 1030 (1995). This statement, coupled with the difficulty of proving actual harm, lent support to the court's ultimate conclusion that the evidence in this case sufficiently established "dilution." 259 F.3d, at 475–477. In sum, the Court of Appeals held: "While no consumer is likely to go to the Moseleys' store expecting to find Victoria's Secret's famed Miracle Bra, consumers who hear the name 'Victor's Little Secret' are likely automatically to think of the more famous store and link it to the Moseleys' adult-toy, gag gift, and lingerie shop. This, then, is a classic instance of dilution by tarnishing (associating the Victoria's Secret name with sex toys and lewd coffee mugs) and by blurring (linking the chain with a single, unauthorized establishment). Given this conclusion, it follows that Victoria's Secret would prevail in a dilution analysis, even without an exhaustive consideration of all ten of the *Nabisco* factors." *Id.*, at 477.

In reaching that conclusion the Court of Appeals expressly rejected the holding of the Fourth Circuit in *Ringling Bros.–Barnum & Bailey Combined Shows, Inc.* v. *Utah Div. of Travel Development*, 170 F.3d 449 (1999). In that case, which involved a claim that Utah's use on its license plates of the phrase "greatest *snow* on earth" was causing dilution of the "greatest *show* on earth," the court had concluded "that to establish dilution of a famous mark under the federal Act requires proof that (1) a defendant has made use of a junior mark sufficiently similar to the famous mark to evoke in a relevant universe of consumers a mental association of the two that (2) has caused (3) actual economic harm to the famous mark's economic value by lessening its former selling power as an advertising agent for its goods or services." *Id.*, at 461 (emphasis added). Because other Circuits have also expressed differing views about the "actual harm" issue, we granted certiorari to resolve the conflict. 535 U.S. 985 (2002).

II

Traditional trademark infringement law is a part of the broader law of unfair competition, *see Hanover Star Milling Co.* v. *Metcalf*, 240 U.S. 403, 413 (1916), that has its sources in English common law, and was largely codified in the Trademark Act of 1946 (Lanham Act). *See* B. Pattishall, D. Hilliard, & J. Welch, Trademarks and Unfair Competition 2 (4th ed. 2000) ("The United States took the [trademark and unfair competition] law of England as its own"). That law broadly prohibits uses of trademarks, trade

instead rely on evidence of 'actual loss of revenues' or the 'skillfully constructed consumer survey.' *Id.* at 457, 464–65. This strikes us as an arbitrary and unwarranted limitation on the methods of proof." *Nabisco*, 191 F.3d, at 223.

names, and trade dress that are likely to cause confusion about the source of a product or service. *See* 15 U.S.C. § 1114 1125(a)(1)(A). Infringement law protects consumers from being misled by the use of infringing marks and also protects producers from unfair practices by an "imitating competitor." *Qualitex Co.* v. *Jacobson Products Co.,* 514 U.S. 159, 163–164 (1995). Because respondents did not appeal the District Court's adverse judgement on counts 1, 2, and 4 of their complaint, we decide the case on the assumption that the Moseleys' use of the name "Victor's Little Secret" neither confused any consumers or potential consumers, nor was likely to do so. Moreover, the disposition of those counts also makes it appropriate to decide the case on the assumption that there was no significant competition between the adversaries in this case. Neither the absence of any likelihood of confusion nor the absence of competition, however, provides a defense to the statutory dilution claim alleged in count 3 of the complaint.

Unlike traditional infringement law, the prohibitions against trademark dilution are not the product of common-law development, and are not motivated by an interest in protecting consumers. The seminal discussion of dilution is found in Frank Schechter's 1927 law review article concluding "that the preservation of the uniqueness of a trademark should constitute the only rational basis for its protection." Rational Basis of Trademark Protection, 40 Harv. L. Rev. 813, 831. Schechter supported his conclusion by referring to a German case protecting the owner of the well-known trademark "Odol" for mouthwash from use on various noncompeting steel products. That case, and indeed the principal focus of the Schechter article, involved an established arbitrary mark that had been "added to rather than withdrawn from the human vocabulary" and an infringement that made use of the identical mark. *Id.,* at 829.[10]

Some 20 years later Massachusetts enacted the first state statute protecting trademarks from dilution. It provided:

10. Schecter discussed this distinction at length: "The rule that arbitrary, coined or fanciful marks or names should be given a much broader degree of protection than symbols, words or phrases in common use would appear to be entirely sound. Such trademarks or tradenames as 'Blue Ribbon,' used, with or without registration, for all kinds of commodities or services, more than sixty times; 'Simplex' more than sixty times; 'Star,' as far back as 1898, nearly four hundred times; 'Anchor,' already registered over one hundred fifty times in 1898; 'Bull Dog,' over one hundred times by 1923; 'Gold Medal,' sixty-five times; '3–in–1' and '2–in–1,' seventy-nine times; 'Nox-all,' fifty times; 'Universal,' over thirty times; 'Lily White' over twenty times;—all these marks and names have, at this late date, very little distinctiveness in the public mind, and in most cases suggest merit, prominence or other qualities of goods or services in general, rather than the fact that the product or service, in connection with which the mark or name is used, emanates from a particular source. On the other hand, 'Rolls–Royce,' 'Aunt Jemima's,' 'Kodak,' 'Mazda,' 'Corona,' 'Nujol,' and 'Blue Goose,' are coined, arbitrary or fanciful words or phrases that have been added to rather than withdrawn from the human vocabulary by their owners, and have, from the very beginning, been associated in the public mind with a particular product, not with a variety of products, and have created in the public consciousness an impression or symbol of the excellence of the particular product in question." *Id.,* at 828–829.

> "Likelihood of injury to business reputation or of dilution of the distinctive quality of a trade name or trade-mark shall be a ground for injunctive relief in cases of trade-mark infringement or unfair competition notwithstanding the absence of competition between the parties or of confusion as to the source of goods or services." 1947 Mass. Acts, p. 300, ch. 307.

Notably, that statute, unlike the "Odol" case, prohibited both the likelihood of "injury to business reputation" and "dilution." It thus expressly applied to both "tarnishment" and "blurring." At least 25 States passed similar laws in the decades before the FTDA was enacted in 1995. See Restatement (Third) of Unfair Competition § 25, Statutory Note (1995).

III

In 1988, when Congress adopted amendments to the Lanham Act, it gave consideration to an antidilution provision. During the hearings on the 1988 amendments, objections to that provision based on a concern that it might have applied to expression protected by the First Amendment were voiced and the provision was deleted from the amendments. H. R. Rep. No. 100–1028 (1988). The bill, H. R. 1295, 104th Cong., 1st Sess., that was introduced in the House in 1995, and ultimately enacted as the FTDA, included two exceptions designed to avoid those concerns: a provision allowing "fair use" of a registered mark in comparative advertising or promotion, and the provision that noncommercial use of a mark shall not constitute dilution. *See* 15 U.S.C. § 1125(c)(4).

On July 19, 1995, the Subcommittee on Courts and Intellectual Property of the House Judiciary Committee held a 1–day hearing on H. R. 1295. No opposition to the bill was voiced at the hearing and, with one minor amendment that extended protection to unregistered as well as registered marks, the subcommittee endorsed the bill and it passed the House unanimously. The committee's report stated that the "purpose of H. R. 1295 is to protect famous trademarks from subsequent uses that blur the distinctiveness of the mark or tarnish or disparage it, even in the absence of a likelihood of confusion." H. R. Rep. No. 104–374, p. 1029 (1995). As examples of dilution, it stated that "the use of DUPONT shoes, BUICK aspirin, and KODAK pianos would be actionable under this legislation." *Id.*, at 1030. In the Senate an identical bill, S. 1513, 104th Cong., 1st Sess., was introduced on December 29, 1995, and passed on the same day by voice vote without any hearings. In his explanation of the bill, Senator Hatch also stated that it was intended "to protect famous trademarks from subsequent uses that blur the distinctiveness of the mark or tarnish or disparage it," and referred to the Dupont Shoes, Buick aspirin, and Kodak piano examples, as well as to the Schechter law review article. 141 Cong. Rec. 38559–38561 (1995).

IV

The Victoria's Secret mark is unquestionably valuable and petitioners have not challenged the conclusion that it qualifies as a "famous mark" within the meaning of the statute. Moreover, as we understand their submission, petitioners do not contend that the statutory protection is confined to identical uses of famous marks, or that the statute should be construed more narrowly in a case such as this. Even if the legislative history might lend some support to such a contention, it surely is not compelled by the statutory text. The District Court's decision in this case rested on the conclusion that the name of petitioners' store "tarnished" the reputation of respondents' mark, and the Court of Appeals relied on both "tarnishment" and "blurring" to support its affirmance. Petitioners have not disputed the relevance of tarnishment, Tr. of Oral Arg. 5–7, presumably because that concept was prominent in litigation brought under state antidilution statutes and because it was mentioned in the legislative history. Whether it is actually embraced by the statutory text, however, is another matter. Indeed, the contrast between the state statutes, which expressly refer to both "injury to business reputation" and to "dilution of the distinctive quality of a trade name or trademark," and the federal statute which refers only to the latter, arguably supports a narrower reading of the FTDA. *See* Klieger, Trademark Dilution: The Whittling Away of the Rational Basis for Trademark Protection, 58 U. Pitt. L. Rev. 789, 812–813, and n. 132 (1997).

The contrast between the state statutes and the federal statute, however, sheds light on the precise question that we must decide. For those state statutes, like several provisions in the federal Lanham Act, repeatedly refer to a "likelihood" of harm, rather than to a completed harm. The relevant text of the FTDA . . . provides that "the owner of a famous mark" is entitled to injunctive relief against another person's commercial use of a mark or trade name if that use "*causes dilution* of the distinctive quality" of the famous mark. 15 U.S.C. § 1125(c)(1) (emphasis added). This text unambiguously requires a showing of actual dilution, rather than a likelihood of dilution.

This conclusion is fortified by the definition of the term "dilution" itself. That definition provides:

> "The term 'dilution' means the lessening of the capacity of a famous mark to identify and distinguish goods or services, regardless of the presence or absence of"
>
> "(1) competition between the owner of the famous mark and other parties, or
>
> "(2) likelihood of confusion, mistake, or deception." § 1127.

The contrast between the initial reference to an actual "lessening of the capacity" of the mark, and the later reference to a "likelihood of confusion, mistake, or deception" in the second caveat confirms the conclusion that actual dilution must be established.

Of course, that does not mean that the consequences of dilution, such as an actual loss of sales or profits, must also be proved. To the extent that language in the Fourth Circuit's opinion in the *Ringling Bros.* case suggests otherwise, *see* 170 F.3d, at 460–465, we disagree. We do agree, however, with that court's conclusion that, at least where the marks at issue are not identical, the mere fact that consumers mentally associate the junior user's mark with a famous mark is not sufficient to establish actionable dilution. As the facts of that case demonstrate, such mental association will not necessarily reduce the capacity of the famous mark to identify the goods of its owner, the statutory requirement for dilution under the FTDA. For even though Utah drivers may be reminded of the circus when they see a license plate referring to the "greatest *snow* on earth," it by no means follows that they will associate "the greatest show on earth" with skiing or snow sports, or associate it less strongly or exclusively with the circus. "Blurring" is not a necessary consequence of mental association. (Nor, for that matter, is "tarnishing.")

The record in this case establishes that an army officer who saw the advertisement of the opening of a store named "Victor's Secret" did make the mental association with "Victoria's Secret," but it also shows that he did not therefore form any different impression of the store that his wife and daughter had patronized. There is a complete absence of evidence of any lessening of the capacity of the Victoria's Secret mark to identify and distinguish goods or services sold in Victoria's Secret stores or advertised in its catalogs. The officer was offended by the ad, but it did not change his conception of Victoria's Secret. His offense was directed entirely at petitioners, not at respondents. Moreover, the expert retained by respondents had nothing to say about the impact of petitioners' name on the strength of respondents' mark.

Noting that consumer surveys and other means of demonstrating actual dilution are expensive and often unreliable, respondents and their *amici* argue that evidence of an actual "lessening of the capacity of a famous mark to identify and distinguish goods or services," § 1127, may be difficult to obtain. It may well be, however, that direct evidence of dilution such as consumer surveys will not be necessary if actual dilution can reliably be proven through circumstantial evidence—the obvious case is one where the junior and senior marks are identical. Whatever difficulties of proof may be entailed, they are not an acceptable reason for dispensing with proof of an essential element of a statutory violation. The evidence in the present record is not sufficient to support the summary judgment on the dilution count. The judgment is therefore reversed, and the case is remanded for further proceedings consistent with this opinion.

It is so ordered.

■ JUSTICE KENNEDY, concurring.

As of this date, few courts have reviewed the statute we are considering, the Federal Trademark Dilution Act, 15 U.S.C. § 1125(c), and I agree with the Court that the evidentiary showing required by the statute can be clarified on remand. The conclusion that the VICTORIA's SECRET mark is a famous mark has not been challenged throughout the litigation, *ante*, at 6, 13, and seems not to be in question. The remaining issue is what factors are to be considered to establish dilution.

For this inquiry, considerable attention should be given, in my view, to the word "capacity" in the statutory phrase that defines dilution as "the lessening of the capacity of a famous mark to identify and distinguish goods or services." 15 U.S.C. § 1127. When a competing mark is first adopted, there will be circumstances when the case can turn on the probable consequences its commercial use will have for the famous mark. In this respect, the word "capacity" imports into the dilution inquiry both the present and the potential power of the famous mark to identify and distinguish goods, and in some cases the fact that this power will be diminished could suffice to show dilution. Capacity is defined as "the power or ability to hold, receive, or accommodate." Webster's Third New International Dictionary 330 (1961); [other citations omitted]. If a mark will erode or lessen the power of the famous mark to give customers the assurance of quality and the full satisfaction they have in knowing they have purchased goods bearing the famous mark, the elements of dilution may be established.

Diminishment of the famous mark's capacity can be shown by the probable consequences flowing from use or adoption of the competing mark. This analysis is confirmed by the statutory authorization to obtain injunctive relief. 15 U.S.C. § 1125(c)(2). The essential role of injunctive relief is to "prevent future wrong, although no right has yet been violated." *Swift & Co.* v. *United States,* 276 U.S. 311, 326 (1928). Equity principles encourage those who are injured to assert their rights promptly. A holder of a famous mark threatened with diminishment of the mark's capacity to serve its purpose should not be forced to wait until the damage is done and the distinctiveness of the mark has been eroded.

In this case, the District Court found that petitioners' trademark had tarnished the VICTORIA's SECRET mark. App. to Pet. for Cert. 38a–39a. The Court of Appeals affirmed this conclusion and also found dilution by blurring. 259 F.3d 464, 477 (CA6 2001). The Court's opinion does not foreclose injunctive relief if respondents on remand present sufficient evidence of either blurring or tarnishment.

With these observations, I join the opinion of the Court.

Page 726. Delete Questions 1–3 and 5 and 6. Renumber Question 4 as Question 1 and add the following material:

2. Justice Kennedy's concurrence in *Moseley* focuses on the word "capacity" as denoting "both the present and potential power of the famous mark to identify and distinguish goods" and concludes that "in some cases the fact that this power *will be* diminished could suffice to show dilution" *(emphasis added).* He also relies on the equitable principle that injunctive relief need not wait for the threatened harm to occur before being granted. Compare this analysis to the Fourth Circuit's in *Ringling–Bros.* in which the court determines that the word "capacity" means "former capacity" and that the prescribed conduct is "another's person's . . . use." Is Justice Kennedy's interpretation at odds with Justice Steven's opinion? Is the Fourth Circuit's analysis congruent with Justice Steven's opinion?

3. What type of evidence would enable the plaintiff to prevail on remand in *Moseley*? Will survey evidence be required? What type of survey would be needed? Would any other type of expert testimony be helpful, for example from a marketing expert?

4. In the case of identical marks, does the *Moseley* decision leave open the possibility that a showing of mental association between the marks at issue would be sufficient for a finding of dilution? Or that dilution can be inferred from the identicality of the marks. If so, what constitutes an identical mark? *See, e.g., Savin Corp. v. Savin Group*, 391 F.3d 439 (2d Cir. 2004) (Savin v. Savin); *CareFirst of Maryland, Inc. v. First Care, P.C., infra* this Supplement (CareFirst v. First Care).

5. Is tarnishment a ground for federal dilution after *Moseley*? *See* Judge Posner's characterization of tarnishment as a sub-species of blurring in *Ty, Inc. v. Perryman, infra* this Supplement Chapter 10.C.2. Is that analysis persuasive? Would tarnishment be a ground for federal dilution under the version of H.R. 683 passed by the Senate, *infra* this Supplement?

6. The lesser requirements for distinctiveness under some state statutes as compared with the more stringent federal dilution requirements have led to different outcomes for federal and state dilution claims in the same case. *See, e.g., New York Stock Exchange, Inc. v. New York, New York Hotel LLC*, 293 F.3d 550 (2d Cir. 2002). Given the distinction drawn by the Supreme Court between some state statutes, which recognize a "likelihood of dilution" standard, and the federal statute, which does not, will state dilution grounds assume even greater significance to potential plaintiffs in the future? *See, e.g., Pfizer, Inc. v. Y2K Shipping & Trading, Inc.*, 70 U.S.P.Q.2d 1592 (E.D.N.Y. 2004) (having withdrawn federal dilution claim after Supreme Court's decision in *Moseley*, owner of VIAGRA mark for a pharmaceutical for erectile dysfunction succeeded on its New York state dilution ground against the mark TRIAGRA for a treatment for the same condition). What is the standard of proving dilution under the version of H.R. 683 passed by the Senate, *infra* this Supplement?

7. Uzi Nissan has used his name in several businesses since 1980. In 1991, he incorporated a computer store under the name Nissan Computer. In 1994, Nissan Computer registered the domain name <nissan.com>. Upset at the registration of the domain name, Nissan Motor Company, the Japanese manufacturer of NISSAN cars, brought a federal dilution claim against Nissan Computer in 1999. Section 43(c)(1) provides for a dilution claim when defendant's "use begins after the mark becomes famous." When did defendant's "use" begin here—in 1980, in 1991 or in 1994? *See Nissan Motor Co. v. Nissan Computer Corp.*, 378 F.3d 1002 (9th Cir. 2004), *cert. denied*, 544 U.S. 974 (2005).

CareFirst of Maryland, Inc. v. First Care, P.C.

434 F.3d 263 (4th Cir. 2006).

■ MOTZ, CIRCUIT COURT JUDGE:

CareFirst of Maryland, Inc., a health maintenance organization associated with Blue Cross Blue Shield, brought this trademark infringement and

Dilution action against First Care, P.C., a small group of family care physicians located in Southeastern Virginia. The district court granted summary judgment to First Care. We affirm.

I.

The CareFirst mark first appeared in 1977, when Metropolitan Baltimore Healthcare began marketing prepaid health care plans under the CareFirst name to approximately 3,000 of its Maryland members. In 1989 the then-owner of the CareFirst mark registered "CAREFIRST" as a trademark, service mark, and collective membership mark with the United States Patent and Trademark Office. Blue Cross and Blue Shield of Maryland acquired the CareFirst mark in 1991. Approximately 250,000 members then held CareFirst plans, but by 1997 that number had declined to 50,000.

In late 1997, Blue Cross and Blue Shield of Maryland agreed with other Blue Cross Blue Shield affiliates to operate jointly and collectively under the CareFirst mark. This umbrella organization has spent millions of dollars advertising its mark; in all of its advertisements, it denominates itself "CareFirst BlueCross BlueShield," often accompanied by the distinctive Blue Cross Blue Shield logo. By the time CareFirst initiated the present action in March 2004, CareFirst had become the largest health maintenance organization in the mid-Atlantic states with 3.2 million members. At least eighty percent of these members reside in CareFirst's direct service area, which consists of Maryland, Delaware, the District of Columbia, and Northern Virginia.

First Care is a Virginia professional corporation of primary care physicians. In late 1994, it registered its corporate name with the state. Since 1995, First Care has operated using the "FIRST CARE" mark. First Care offers traditional family medical services in Portsmouth and Chesapeake, Virginia, which are close to but outside of CareFirst's direct service area. Approximately 2,500 CareFirst members reside in First Care's trade area. First Care currently consists of eleven physicians operating out of seven offices; at its height, it had twelve physicians and nine offices.

First Care's name and a description of its services appeared several times in a series of trademark search reports commissioned by CareFirst from January 1996 through November 2000. CareFirst, however, took no action against First Care until 2004, when First Care submitted a deposition in a separate trademark infringement suit that CareFirst was pursuing against another party.

On February 13, 2004, after determining that at least ninety CareFirst members had received medical services from First Care, CareFirst sent First Care a cease-and-desist letter. When First Care refused to give up use of its mark, CareFirst brought this action, alleging that since 1995 First Care had infringed on and diluted CareFirst's trademark, *see* 15 U.S.C.

§§ 1114(1), 1125(a), 1125(c) (2000), and seeking $28 million in damages. In April 2004, First Care applied for state registration of its mark in Virginia.

After extensive discovery, the parties filed cross-motions for summary judgment. The district court granted summary judgment to First Care. *See CareFirst of Md., Inc. v. First Care, P.C.*, 350 F. Supp. 2d 714, 726 (E.D. Va. 2004). The court found that CareFirst had failed to show that a "likelihood of confusion existed between [the] First Care and CareFirst" marks and so rejected CareFirst's infringement claim. *Id.* Additionally, the court concluded that CareFirst had failed to offer evidence that its mark "was a famous and distinctive mark prior to 1995," when First Care began operations, and for this reason rejected CareFirst's dilution claim. *Id.*

. . .

II.

. . .

A.

CareFirst concedes that the *only* evidence it has proffered of actual confusion is a survey by Dr. Myron Helfgott, which CareFirst commissioned for this litigation. The Helfgott survey interviewed 130 people by telephone, drawn from a list of CareFirst members in or near First Care's place of business. In the unaided portion of the survey, the surveyors asked the respondents whether they had heard of First Care, whether they thought First Care was related to or affiliated with another health organization, and whether they thought First Care needed permission from another health organization to use its name. The surveyors then repeated these unaided questions, focusing on CareFirst on this second pass. In the aided portion of the survey, the surveyors asked the respondents whether they thought First Care and CareFirst were related to or affiliated with each other.

The Helfgott survey does not supply evidence of actual confusion. At best, it shows merely a *de minimis* level of confusion. Only two of the 130 respondents had both heard of First Care and thought that it was related to or affiliated with CareFirst. One additional respondent had not heard of First Care but, judging by its name alone, thought that it might be affiliated with CareFirst. Assuming that all three of these respondents were confused, the survey only shows a confusion rate of 2 percent, hardly a sufficient showing of actual confusion.

CareFirst argues that two other groups of respondents should also be considered actually confused: 28 respondents who stated that First Care was affiliated with Blue Cross Blue Shield; and 16 separate respondents who answered "yes" when asked in the aided portion of the survey whether CareFirst and First Care were related. We do not believe that the responses of either of these groups show actual confusion between CareFirst and First Care. CareFirst offers no evidence besides mere speculation that when the 28 respondents indicated that First Care was affiliated with "Blue Cross Blue Shield," they were actually referring to CareFirst. Indeed, the only evidence on this point suggests the opposite inference: at least two other respondents who indicated First Care's affiliation with "Blue Cross Blue Shield" specified that they were thinking of *Anthem* Blue Cross Blue Shield, and both parties agree that First Care is part of Anthem's network. Similarly, CareFirst offers no evidence that the 16 aided respondents were confused in a way relevant to the likelihood-of-confusion analysis. CareFirst's counsel admitted at oral argument that CareFirst covers the expenses of members who receive medical treatment at First Care clinics, and we know that CareFirst has in fact done so for at least ninety of its members in Southeastern Virginia. The two entities therefore *are* related, and no evidence suggests that the aided respondents' answers reflect anything other than this proper—and not confused—understanding of the relationship between the parties.

. . .

III.

The district court also granted summary judgment to First Care on CareFirst's dilution claim. The Trademark Dilution Act provides that "the owner of a famous mark" can enjoin "another person's commercial use in commerce of a mark or trade name, if such use begins after the mark has become famous and causes dilution of the distinctive quality of the mark." 15 U.S.C. § 1125(c)(1). Dilution means "the lessening of the capacity of a famous mark to identify and distinguish goods or services." *Id.* § 1127. The statutory scheme makes clear that a court may find dilution even if it would not find any likelihood of confusion. *Id.*

The Supreme Court has held that the dilution statute "unambiguously requires a showing of actual dilution, rather than a likelihood of dilution." *Moseley v. V Secret Catalogue, Inc.*, 537 U.S. 418, 433, 123 S. Ct. 1115, 155 L. Ed. 2d 1 (2003). CareFirst offers only two arguments in its attempt to establish that it could prove actual dilution. Neither is persuasive.

First, CareFirst maintains that the similarity of CareFirst's and First Care's marks provides circumstantial evidence of actual dilution. The Supreme Court has suggested that "where the junior and senior marks are *identical,*" there would be "circumstantial evidence" of actual dilution. *Moseley*, 537 U.S. at 434 (emphasis added). "Every federal court to decide the issue has ruled that a high degree of similarity, ranging from 'nearly identical' to 'very similar,' is required" to meet this standard. *Autozone*, 373 F.3d at 806. Thus, "a mere similarity in the marks—even a close similarity—will not suffice to establish per se evidence of actual dilution." *Savin Corp. v. The Savin Grp.*, 391 F.3d 439, 453 (2d Cir. 2004). In addition, "the issue of whether the marks are identical will be context- and/or media-specific and factually intensive in nature." *Id.* Here, the text of the two marks is similar but not identical. Furthermore, as they appear in the marketplace to the average consumer, the two marks are not even "very similar"—company policy requires that CareFirst's mark always appear as "CareFirst BlueCross BlueShield," while the First Care mark appears unadorned. Therefore, the similarity of the marks provides little circumstantial evidence of actual dilution here.

CareFirst's second argument—that the Helfgott survey provides evidence of actual dilution—is no more convincing. As noted above, the Helfgott survey was designed to measure likelihood of confusion, not dilution. *See Avery Dennison Corp. v. Sumpton*, 189 F.3d 868, 875 (9th Cir. 1999) ("In the dilution context, likelihood of confusion is irrelevant."); 4 McCarthy, *supra*, § 24:94.2 (describing surveys that might measure dilution). Thus, the survey at best measured whether consumers believe that First Care is associated with CareFirst, not whether First Care's mark has "reduced the capacity of the [CareFirst] mark to identify the [services] of its owner." *Moseley*, 537 U.S. at 433. The survey's results provide no forecast of actual dilution. *See Ringling Bros.-Barnum & Bailey Combined Shows, Inc. v. Utah Div. of Travel Dev.*, 170 F.3d 449, 462–63 (4th Cir. 1999) (finding that a survey designed only to show "mental association" between competing marks was not evidence of dilution).

Accordingly, the district court did not err in granting First Care summary judgment on CareFirst's dilution claim.

IV.

For the foregoing reasons, the judgment of the district court is

AFFIRMED.

NASDAQ Stock Market Inc. v. Antartica S.r.l., 69 U.S.P.Q.2d 1718 (T.T.A.B. 2003). The Board found a likelihood of confusion under section 2(d) between plaintiff's famous NASDAQ mark for its stock market services and applicant's NASDAQ and Design mark for sports helmets, sport clothing and sports equipment that was based on an Italian application under section 44 of the Lanham Act. With respect to the dilution claim, the Board found that the "actual dilution" standard articulated by the Supreme Court in *Moseley* was not applicable in the opposition context. Instead, the Board reasoned as follows:

> The Supreme Court's recent decision in *Moseley* raises a threshold issue we must address—as the Federal Circuit did not have occasion to address it in *Enterprise [Rent–A–Car Co. v. Advantage Rent–A–Car, Inc.*, 330 F.3d 1333 (Fed. Cir. 2003)], its first FTDA/TAA decision—before we can consider opposer's claim of dilution. In *Moseley*, a case involving a civil action under the FTDA, the Court held that a plaintiff must prove actual dilution, not merely a likelihood of dilution. *Moseley*, 65 U.S.P.Q.2d at 1807. In this opposition, the involved application is based on Section 44 of the Lanham Act and applicant has not used its mark in the United States or in commerce between Italy and the United States. Accordingly, we can only reach opposer's claim of dilution if we first determine that, in Board proceedings, it is sufficient for a plaintiff to establish likelihood of dilution rather than actual dilution.
>
> We find that there is a distinction to be drawn between civil actions and Board proceedings and that, in a Board proceeding, a plaintiff that establishes its ownership of a distinctive and famous

mark may prevail upon showing of likelihood of dilution. We have already held so in an opposition involving an intent to use application, i.e., a situation in which a plaintiff cannot show actual dilution. *See Toro[Co. v. ToroHead, Inc.]*, 61 U.S.P.Q.2d [1164,] at 1174 [T.T.A.B. 2001] ("an application based on an intent to use the mark in commerce satisfies the commerce requirement of the FTDA for proceedings before the Board."). We now extend the holding to this opposition alleging prospective dilution by a mark not yet in use and that is the subject of a Section 44 application. Our determination is supported by the Lanham Act.

Congress, despite the existence and recognition of state dilution statutes that permit relief on a showing of likelihood of dilution, fashioned the FTDA to permit relief for the owner of a famous mark only when it could show the newcomer's mark actually causes dilution. *Moseley*, 65 U.S.P.Q.2d 1807. Moreover, when Congress subsequently passed the TAA, it made no change in the "*causes* dilution" standard applicable in judicial proceedings, yet allowed Board proceedings to be based on a claim that a newcomer's mark "*when* used *would cause* dilution." Compare 15 U.S.C. § 1125(c)(1) and 15 U.S.C. § 1052(f) (emphasis added). Further, the TAA amendment of Section 2(f) of the Lanham Act to allow for dilution claims in Board proceedings specifically refers to Section 13 (oppositions) and Section 14 (cancellations) as the proceedings in which a dilution claim may be raised. Section 13 allows oppositions by any person "who believes that he *would be* damaged ... including as a result of dilution," and Section 14 allows cancellation actions "by any person who believes that he *is* or *will be* damaged, including as a result of dilution..." (emphasis added). The inescapable conclusion is that Congress intended to limit judicial relief under the FTDA to cases where dilution has already occurred but to allow cases involving prospective dilution to be heard by the Board. We see no holding or statement in *Moseley* that runs counter to this conclusion.

QUESTION

Do you agree with the Board's "inescapable conclusion" in *NASDAQ* that Congress intended to distinguish between the standards applied by the courts and by the Board? Why or why not?

Trademark Dilution Revision Act of 2006

CONG. REC. S1921 (Mar. 8, 2006).

On March 8, 2006, the Senate passed an amended version of H.R. 683, which would amend the dilution provisions of the Lanham Act as follows:

Section 43 of the Trademark Act of 1946 (15 U.S.C. § 1125) is amended

(1) by striking subsection (c) and inserting the following:

(c) dilution by Blurring; dilution by Tarnishment.

(1) Injunctive relief. Subject to the principles of equity, the owner of a famous mark that is distinctive, inherently or through acquired distinctiveness, shall be entitled to an injunction against another person who, at any time after the owner's mark has become famous, commences use of a mark or trade name in commerce that is likely to cause dilution by blurring or dilution by tarnishment of the famous mark, regardless of the presence or absence of actual or likely confusion, of competition, or of actual economic injury.

(2) Definitions. (A) For purposes of paragraph (1), a mark is famous if it is widely recognized by the general consuming public of the United States as a designation of source of the goods or services of the mark's owner. In determining whether a mark possesses the requisite degree of recognition, the court may consider all relevant factors, including the following:

(i) The duration, extent, and geographic reach of advertising and publicity of the mark, whether advertised or publicized by the owner or third parties.

(ii) The amount, volume, and geographic extent of sales of goods or services offered under the mark.

(iii) The extent of actual recognition of the mark.

(iv) Whether the mark was registered under the Act of March 3, 1881, or the Act of February 20, 1905, or on the principal register.

(B) For purposes of paragraph (1), "dilution by blurring" is association arising from the similarity between a mark or trade name and a famous mark that impairs the distinctiveness of the famous mark. In determining whether a mark or trade name is likely to cause dilution by blurring, the court may consider all relevant factors, including the following:

(i) The degree of similarity between the mark or trade name and the famous mark.

(ii) The degree of inherent or acquired distinctiveness of the famous mark.

(iii) The extent to which the owner of the famous mark is engaging in substantially exclusive use of the mark.

(iv) The degree of recognition of the famous mark.

(v) Whether the user of the mark or trade name intended to create an association with the famous mark.

(vi) Any actual association between the mark or trade name and the famous mark.

(C) For purposes of paragraph (1), "dilution by tarnishment" is association arising from the similarity between a mark or trade name and a famous mark that harms the reputation of the famous mark.

QUESTIONS

1. If the Senate bill ultimately becomes law, what effect will it have on the actual dilution standard articulated in *Mosley*?

2. How helpful are the factors listed in the bill for determining "dilution by blurring"?

2. DOMAIN NAMES

Page 727. Delete *Panavision v. Toeppen.*

Page 732. Delete *Avery Dennison Corp. v. Sumpton.*

Page 737. Delete *TCPIP Holding Co. v. Haar Communications, Inc.*

Page 739. Insert the following case before Questions:

Ty Inc. v. Perryman

306 F.3d 509 (7th Cir. 2002), *cert. denied*, 538 U.S. 971, 123 S.Ct. 1750 (2003).

■ POSNER, CIRCUIT JUDGE

Ty Inc., the manufacturer of Beanie Babies, the well-known beanbag stuffed animals, brought this suit for trademark infringement against Ruth Perryman. Perryman sells second-hand beanbag stuffed animals, primarily but not exclusively Ty's Beanie Babies, over the Internet. Her Internet address ("domain name"), a particular focus of Ty's concern, is bargainbeanies.com. She has a like-named Web site (http://www. bargainbeanies.com) where she advertises her wares. Ty's suit is based on the federal antidilution statute, 15 U.S.C. § 1125(c), which protects "famous" marks from commercial uses that cause "dilution of the distinctive quality of the mark." *See Nabisco, Inc. v. PF Brands, Inc.*, 191 F.3d 208, 214–16 (2d Cir. 1999). The district court granted summary judgment in favor of Ty and entered an injunction that forbids the defendant to use "BEANIE or BEANIES or any colorable imitation thereof (whether alone or in connection with other terms) within any business name, Internet domain name, or trademark, or in connection with any non-Ty products." Perryman's appeal argues primarily that "beanies" has become a generic term for beanbag stuffed animals and therefore cannot be appropriated as a trademark at all, and that in any event the injunction (which has remained in effect during the appeal) is overbroad.

The fundamental purpose of a trademark is to reduce consumer search costs by providing a concise and unequivocal identifier of the particular source of particular goods. The consumer who knows at a glance whose brand he is being asked to buy knows whom to hold responsible if the brand disappoints and whose product to buy in the future if the brand pleases. This in turn gives producers an incentive to maintain high and uniform quality, since otherwise the investment in their trademark may be lost as customers turn away in disappointment from the brand. A successful brand, however, creates an incentive in unsuccessful competitors to pass off their inferior brand as the successful brand by adopting a confusingly similar trademark, in effect appropriating the goodwill created by the producer of the successful brand. The traditional and still central concern of trademark law is to provide remedies against this practice.

Confusion is not a factor here, however, with a minor exception discussed at the end of the opinion. Perryman is not a competing producer of beanbag stuffed animals, and her Web site clearly disclaims any affiliation with Ty. But that does not get her off the hook. The reason is that state and now federal law also provides a remedy against the "dilution" of a trademark, though as noted at the outset of this opinion the federal statute is limited to the subset of "famous" trademarks and to dilutions of them caused by commercial uses that take place in interstate or foreign commerce. "Beanie Babies," and "Beanies" as the shortened form, are famous trademarks in the ordinary sense of the term: "everybody has heard of them"; they are "truly prominent and renowned," in the words of Professor McCarthy, 4 McCarthy on Trademarks and Unfair Competition § 24: 109, p. 24–234 (2001), as distinguished from having a merely local celebrity. *TCPIP Holding Co. v. Haar Communications Inc.*, 244 F.3d 88, 98–99 (2d Cir. 2001). And while both this court and the Third Circuit have held, in opposition to the Second Circuit's *TCPIP* decision, that "fame," though it cannot be local, may be limited to "niche" markets, *Syndicate Sales, Inc. v. Hampshire Paper Corp.*, 192 F.3d 633, 640–41 (7th Cir. 1999); *Times Mirror Magazines, Inc. v. Las Vegas Sports News, L.L.C.*, 212 F.3d 157, 164 (3d Cir. 2000), this is not a conflict to worry over here; Ty's trademarks are household words. And Perryman's use of these words was commercial in nature and took place in interstate commerce, and doubtless, given the reach of the aptly named World Wide Web, in foreign commerce as well.

But what is "dilution"? There are (at least) three possibilities relevant to this case, each defined by a different underlying concern. First, there is concern that consumer search costs will rise if a trademark becomes associated with a variety of unrelated products. Suppose an upscale restaurant calls itself "Tiffany." There is little danger that the consuming public will think it's dealing with a branch of the Tiffany jewelry store if it patronizes this restaurant. But when consumers next see the name "Tiffany" they may think about both the restaurant and the jewelry store, and if so the efficacy of the name as an identifier of the store will be diminished. Consumers will have to think harder—incur as it were a higher imagination cost—to recognize the name as the name of the store. [citations omitted] So "blurring" is one form of dilution.

Now suppose that the "restaurant" that adopts the name "Tiffany" is actually a striptease joint. Again, and indeed even more certainly than in the previous case, consumers will not think the striptease joint under common ownership with the jewelry store. But because of the inveterate tendency of the human mind to proceed by association, every time they think of the word "Tiffany" their image of the fancy jewelry store will be tarnished by the association of the word with the strip joint. [citations omitted] So "tarnishment" is a second form of dilution. Analytically it is a subset of blurring, since it reduces the distinctness of the trademark as a signifier of the trademarked product or service.

Third, and most far-reaching in its implications for the scope of the concept of dilution, there is a possible concern with situations in which, though there is neither blurring nor tarnishment, someone is still taking a free ride on the investment of the trademark owner in the trademark. Suppose the "Tiffany" restaurant in our first hypothetical example is located in Kuala Lumpur and though the people who patronize it (it is upscale) have heard of the Tiffany jewelry store, none of them is ever going to buy anything there, so that the efficacy of the trademark as an identifier will not be impaired. If appropriation of Tiffany's aura is nevertheless forbidden by an expansive concept of dilution, the benefits of the jewelry store's investment in creating a famous name will be, as economists say, "internalized"—that is, Tiffany will realize the full benefits of the investment rather than sharing those benefits with others—and as a result the amount of investing in creating a prestigious name will rise.

This rationale for antidilution law has not yet been articulated in or even implied by the case law, although a few cases suggest that the concept of dilution is not exhausted by blurring and tarnishment, see *Panavision Int'l,L.P. v. Toeppen*, 141 F.3d 1316, 1326 (9th Cir. 1998); *Intermatic, Inc. v. Toeppen*, 947 F. Supp. 1227, 1238–39 (N.D. Ill. 1996); *Rhee Bros., Inc. v. Han Ah Reum Corp.*, 178 F.Supp.2d 525, 530 (D. Md. 2001), and the common law doctrine of "misappropriation" might conceivably be invoked in support of the rationale that we have sketched. See Rochelle Cooper Dreyfuss & Roberta Rosenthal Kwall, *Intellectual Property: Cases and Materials on Trademark, Copyright and Patent Law* 137–38 (1996). The validity of the rationale may be doubted, however. The number of prestigious names is so vast (and, as important, would be even if there were no antidilution laws) that it is unlikely that the owner of a prestigious trademark could obtain substantial license fees if commercial use of the mark without his consent were forbidden despite the absence of consumer confusion, blurring, or tarnishment. Competition would drive the fee to zero since, if the name is being used in an unrelated market, virtually every prestigious name will be a substitute for every other in that market.

None of the rationales we have canvassed supports Ty's position in this case. Perryman is not producing a product, or a service, such as dining at a restaurant, that is distinct from any specific product; rather, she is selling the very product to which the trademark sought to be defended against her "infringement" is attached. You can't sell a branded product without using its brand name, that is, its trademark. Supposing that Perryman sold only Beanie Babies (a potentially relevant qualification, as we'll see), we would find it impossible to understand how she could be thought to be blurring, tarnishing, or otherwise free riding to any significant extent on Ty's investment in its mark. To say she was would amount to saying that if a used car dealer truthfully advertised that it sold Toyotas, or if a muffler manufacturer truthfully advertised that it specialized in making mufflers for installation in Toyotas, Toyota would have a claim of trademark infringement. Of course there can be no aftermarket without an original market, and in that sense sellers in a trademarked good's aftermarket are free riding on the trademark. But in that attenuated sense of free riding, almost everyone in business is free riding.

Ty's argument is especially strained because of its marketing strategy.... *Ty, Inc. v. GMA Accessories, Inc.*, 132 F.3d 1167, 1173 (7th Cir. 1997), Ty deliberately produces a quantity of each Beanie Baby that fails to clear the market at the very low price that it charges for Beanie Babies. The main goal is to stampede children into nagging their parents to buy the new Baby lest they be the only kid on the block who doesn't have it. A byproduct (or perhaps additional goal) is the creation of a secondary market, like the secondary market in works of art, in which prices on scarce Beanie Babies are bid up to a market-clearing level. Perryman is a middleman in this secondary market, the market, as we said, that came into existence as the result, either intended or foreseen, of a deliberate marketing strategy. That market is unlikely to operate efficiently if sellers who specialize in serving it cannot use "Beanies" to identify their business. Perryman's principal merchandise is Beanie Babies, so that to forbid it to use "Beanies" in its business name and advertising (Web or otherwise) is like forbidding a used car dealer who specializes in selling Chevrolets to mention the name in his advertising.

It is true that Web search engines do not stop with the Web address; if Perryman's Web address were www.perryman.com but her Web page mentioned Beanies, a search for the word "Beanies" would lead to her Web page. Yet we know from the events that led up to the passage in 1999 of the Anticybersquatting Consumer Protection Act, 15 U.S.C. § 1125(d), that many firms value having a domain name or Web address that signals their product. (The "cybersquatters" were individuals or firms that would register domain names for the purpose of selling them to companies that wanted a domain name that would be the name of their company or of their principal product.) After all, many consumers search by typing the name of a company in the Web address space (browser) on their home page rather than by use of a search engine. We do not think that by virtue of trademark law producers own their aftermarkets and can impede sellers in the aftermarket from marketing the trademarked product.

We surmise that what Ty is seeking in this case is an extension of antidilution law to forbid commercial uses that accelerate the transition from trademarks (brand names) to generic names (product names). Words such as "thermos," "yo-yo," "escalator," "cellophane," and "brassiere" started life as trademarks, but eventually lost their significance as source identifiers and became the popular names of the product rather than the name of the trademark owner's brand, and when that happened continued enforcement of the trademark would simply have undermined competition with the brand by making it difficult for competitors to indicate that they were selling the same product—by rendering them in effect speechless. Ty is doubtless cognizant of a similar and quite real danger to "Beanie Babies" and "Beanies." Notice that the illustrations we gave of trademarks that became generic names are all descriptive or at least suggestive of the product, which makes them better candidates for genericness than a fanciful trademark such as "Kodak" or "Exxon." Ty's trademarks likewise are descriptive of the product they denote; its argument that "Beanies" is "inherently distinctive" (like Kodak and Exxon), and therefore protected by trademark law without proof of secondary meaning, is nonsense. A trademark that describes a basic element of the product, as "Beanies" does, is not protected unless the owner can establish that the consuming public accepts the word as the designation of a brand of the product (that it has acquired, as the cases say, secondary meaning). [citations omitted] As the public does with regard to "Beanies"—for now. But because the word is catchier than "beanbag stuffed animals," "beanbag toys," or "plush toys," it may someday "catch on" to the point where the mark becomes generic, and then Ty will have to cast about for a different trademark.

Although there is a social cost when a mark becomes generic—the trademark owner has to invest in a new trademark to identify his brand—there is also a social benefit, namely an addition to ordinary language. A nontrivial number of words in common use began life as trademarks. An interpretation of antidilution law as arming trademark owners to enjoin uses of their mark that, while not confusing, threaten to render the mark generic may therefore not be in the public interest. Moreover, the vistas of litigation that such a theory of dilution opens up are staggering. Ty's counsel at argument refused to disclaim a right to sue the publishers of dictionaries should they include an entry for "beanie," lowercased and defined as a beanbag stuffed animal, thus accelerating the transition from trademark to generic term. He should have disclaimed such a right. *See Illinois High School Ass'n v. GTE Vantage Inc.*, 99 F.3d 244, 246 (7th Cir. 1996); 2 McCarthy on Trademarks and Unfair Competition, *supra*, § 12: 28, pp. 12–79 to 12–81.

We reject the extension of antidilution law that Ty beckons us to adopt, but having done so we must come back to the skipped issue of confusion. For although 80 percent of Perryman's sales are of Ty's products, this means that 20 percent are not, and on her Web page after listing the various Ty products under such names as "Beanie Babies" and "Teenie Beanies" she has the caption "Other Beanies" and under that is a list of products such as "Planet Plush" and "Rothschild Bears" that are not manufactured by Ty. This is plain misdescription, in fact false advertising, and supports the last prohibition in the injunction, the prohibition against using "Beanie" or "Beanies" "in connection with any non-Ty products." That much of the injunction should stand. But Ty has not demonstrated any basis for enjoining Perryman from using the terms in "any business name, Internet domain name, or trademark."

We can imagine an argument that merely deleting "Other Beanies" is not enough; that if the other beanbag stuffed animals look much like Ty's, consumers might assume they are "Beanies," or if not, that they still might associate "Beanies" with these other animals, causing the term to lose its distinctness as the name of Ty's products. But we do not understand Ty to be seeking a broadening of the injunction to require a disclaimer as to the source of the non-Ty products sold by Perryman. This however is a matter that can be pursued further on remand. . . .

Page 739–740. Delete Questions 1–3, 5 & 8 and renumber remaining questions as 1,2, and 3.

Page 740. Change the citation at the end of Question 4 (renumbered as 1) as follows:

Playboy Enterprises, Inc. v. Welles, 279 F.3d 796 (9th Cir. 2002) and in this Supplement *infra* Chapter 12.

Page 740. Add new Questions 4 and 5:

4. Do you agree that use of "Beanies" as part of Perryman's domain and business names does not dilute the distinctiveness of plaintiff's BEANIE BABIES mark? Do uses that tend to genercize a mark dilute its distinctiveness? Should every business in the aftermarket for a product be entitled to use the brand name in its own name or domain name? How should the Supreme Court decide *Ty v. Perryman*?

5. The *Ty* decision recognizes that niche market fame can be sufficient to qualify for federal dilution protection. Is this a correct interpretation of the fame requirement or should a mark be a "household word" in order to qualify? Is recognition of niche market fame acceptable if defendant's product is in the same niche? *See, e.g. Thane Int'l, Inc. v. Trek Bicycle Corp.*, 305 F.3d 894 (9th Cir. 2002) (owner of TREK mark for bicycles could not establish fame for exercise bicycle market occupied by defendant's OrbiTrek mark). Does H.R. 683, as amended by the Senate *supra* this Supplement Chapter 10.C.1, recognize niche fame?

3. Trade Dress

Page 743. Delete *Lund v. Kohler*.

Page 763. Delete Questions 1–4 and renumber Question 5 as Question 1.

Page 764. Add Questions 2 and 3:

2. Do the contextual factors set forth in *Nabisco* have a place in determining dilution after the Supreme Court's decision in *Moseley*? In what situations? How closely do the *Nabisco* factors match the factors in the bill passed by the Senate, *supra*?

3. As product configuration marks cannot be considered inherently distinctive after *Wal–Mart*, is it appropriate to employ a more stringent dilution analysis to such marks? Why or why not? Would *Nabisco* have been decided differently after *Wal–Mart? See TCPIP Holding Co. v. Haar*, 244 F.3d 88 (2d Cir. 2001). Would it be decided any differently under the version of H.R. 683, *supra*?

CHAPTER 11

INTERNET DOMAIN NAMES, SECTION 43(d) AND "CYBERSQUATTING"

A. THE DOMAIN NAME SYSTEM

Page 765. Delete U.S. Department of Commerce Management of Internet Names and Addresses.

B. ANTICYBERSQUATTING CONSUMER PROTECTION ACT

Page 783. Insert the following case and Note following *Morrison & Foerster v. Wick*:

Lucas Nursery and Landscaping, Inc. v. Michelle Grosse

359 F.3d 806 (6th Cir. 2004).

■ R. GUY COLE, JR., CIRCUIT JUDGE.

. . .

I. BACKGROUND

This case arises from a dispute related to landscaping work that was performed by Lucas Nursery at the residence of Michelle Grosse. In March 2000, Grosse hired Lucas Nursery to correct a dip in the soil (known as a swale) that ran horizontally through the center of her front yard. Lucas Nursery's representative, Bob Lucas, Jr., stated that the swale could be corrected by using five large loads of topsoil. Lucas Nursery performed the work on May 16, 2000.

Grosse contends that the work was performed inadequately. After allegedly contacting Lucas Nursery on numerous occasions to express her displeasure with the work and to seek some repair, Grosse filed a complaint with the Better Business Bureau ("the BBB"). After the BBB ended its investigation without making a recommendation, Grosse remained dissatisfied by what she felt had been poor service by Lucas Nursery, and decided to inform others about her experience with the company.

On August 12, 2000, Grosse registered the domain name "lucasnursery.com." She then posted a web page for the sole purpose of relaying her story to the public. The web page was titled, "My Lucas Landscaping Experience." The web page included complaints regarding the poor preparation of the soil prior to Lucas Nursery's laying of the sod, the hasty nature of Lucas Nursery's work, the ineffectiveness of the BBB in addressing her complaint, and the fact that she had to pay an additional $5,400 to a second contractor to repair the work originally performed by Lucas Nursery.

On September 27, 2000, Grosse received a letter from Lucas Nursery's attorney demanding that she cease operating the web site. On October 2, 2000, Grosse removed the web site's content. However, after removing the web site's content, Grosse contacted the Michigan Bureau of Commercial Services Licensing Division and the U.S. Patent & Trademark Office to determine whether there was a registered trademark for Lucas Nursery. After learning that no trademark registration existed, Grosse concluded that Lucas Nursery could not prevent her from retaining the web site. On April 13, 2001, Grosse posted a new narrative on the web site, again describing her experience with Lucas Nursery.

Lucas Nursery filed suit against Grosse on August 17, 2001. Thereafter, each party moved for summary judgment. On April 23, 2002, the district court denied Lucas Nursery's motion for summary judgment and granted Grosse's motion for summary judgment.

II. ANALYSIS

. . .

In order for liability to attach under the ACPA a court must conclude that the defendant's actions constitute "bad faith." ACPA § 3002 (codified at 15 U.S.C. § 1125(d)(1)(A)–(B)). An analysis of whether a defendant's actions constitute bad faith within the meaning of the ACPA usually begins with consideration of several factors, nine of which are listed in the ACPA. *See Sporty's Farm v. Sportsman's Market, Inc.*, 202 F.3d 489, 498 (2d Cir. 2000). The first four factors are those that militate against a finding of bad faith by providing some reasonable basis for why a defendant might have registered the domain name of another mark holder. These factors focus on: whether the defendant has trademark or other rights in the domain name; the extent to which the domain name consists of the defendant's legal name or other common name; any prior use of the domain name for the offering of goods and services; and the bona fide noncommercial use of the site.

Each of the first three factors cuts against Grosse. She does not hold a trademark or other intellectual property rights to the domain name or names included in the registered domain name. The domain name neither consists of her legal name or any name used to refer to her. Grosse has also not used the domain name in connection with any offering of goods or services. The fourth factor cuts in Grosse's favor because the site was used for noncommercial purposes.

Factors five through eight are indicative of the presence of bad faith on the part of the defendant. These factors focus on: whether the defendant seeks to divert consumers from the mark holder's online location either in a way that could harm good will or tarnish or disparage the mark by creating a confusion regarding the sponsorship of the site; whether there has been an offer to transfer or sell the site for financial gain; whether the defendant provided misleading contact information when registering the domain name; and whether the defendant has acquired multiple domain names which may be duplicative of the marks of others.

. . .

None of these factors militates against Grosse. There is no dispute that Lucas Nursery did not have an online location, and hence Grosse's creation of a web site to complain about Lucas Nursery's services could not have been intended "to divert consumers from the mark owners's online location." Nor is there any evidence that Grosse ever sought to mislead consumers with regard to the site's sponsorship. The web site explicitly stated that the site was established by Grosse for the purposes of relaying her experience with Lucas Nursery. Moreover, Grosse never offered to sell the site to Lucas Nursery. She also did not provide misleading contact information when she registered the domain name. Finally, she has not acquired any additional domain names, which would be indicative of either an intent to sell such names to those entities whose trademarks were identical or similar, or exploit them for other uses.

. . .

Lucas Nursery seeks to buttress its argument with *Toronto-Dominion Bank v. Karpachev*, 188 F.Supp.2d 110 (D. Mass. 2002). There, the district court granted Toronto–Dominion's motion for summary judgment against the defendant, concluding that there was sufficient evidence to show that the defendant had acted in bad faith under the ACPA. The defendant, a disgruntled customer, registered sixteen domain names composed of various misspellings of the name tdwaterhouse.com. *Id.* at 111. On the web sites associated with these names, the defendant attacked Toronto–Dominion for "webfacism" and involvement with white collar crime, among other things. *Id.* at 112. The court concluded that the defendant had acted in bad faith, citing four factors: (1) his intention to divert customers from the "tdwaterhouse" web site by creating confusion as to its source or sponsorship; (2) the fact that he had registered sixteen domain names; (3) the fact that he offered no goods or services on the site; and (4) the fact that he had no intellectual property rights in the site. *See id.* at 114.

Although Grosse's actions would arguably satisfy three of the four aforementioned factors, she does not fall within the factor that we consider central to a finding of bad faith. She did not register multiple web sites; she only registered one. Further, it is not clear to this Court that the presence of simply one factor that indicates a bad faith intent to profit, without more, can satisfy an imposition of liability within the meaning of the ACPA. The role of the reviewing court is not simply to add factors and place them in particular categories, without making some sense of what motivates the conduct at issue. The factors are given to courts as a guide, not as a substitute for careful thinking about whether the conduct at issue is motivated by a bad faith intent to profit. Perhaps most important to our conclusion are, Grosse's actions, which seem to have been undertaken in the spirit of informing fellow consumers about the practices of a landscaping company that she believed had performed inferior work on her yard. One of the ACPA's main objectives is the protection of consumers from slick internet peddlers who trade on the names and reputations of established brands. The practice of informing fellow consumers of one's experience with a particular service provider is surely not inconsistent with this ideal.

CONCLUSION

For the foregoing reasons, we AFFIRM the district court's grant of summary judgment in favor of Grosse.

SECTION 43(d) AND "GRIPE" SITES

Recent cases have found the reasoning of *Lucas Nursery* persuasive. In *TMI v. Maxwell*, 368 F.3d 433, 70 U.S.P.Q.2d 1630 (5th Cir. 2004), the Court of Appeals for the 5th Circuit followed *Lucas Nursery* in dismissing both dilution and ACPA claims against a cyber-griper. After an unsatisfactory experience seeking to purchase a home from TrendMarker Homes, Defendant Maxwell had posted a site at <www.trendmakerhome.com> complaining about his experience. TrendMaker sued Maxwell for cybersquatting and dilution. The Fifth Circuit held that "Maxwell's conduct is not the kind of harm the ACPA is designed to prevent." In *Mayflower Transit, LLC v. Prince*, 314 F.Supp.2d 362 (D.N.J. 2004), the court applied the reasoning of *Lucas Nursery* to a cyber-griping case involving the registration of multiple domain names. Brett Prince engaged Lincoln Storage, an intrastate moving company affiliated with Mayflower Van Lines, to move his worldly goods from West Orange, New Jersey to Freehold, New Jersey. Enroute, thieves broke in to the parked moving truck and stole much of Prince's property. Prince sued both the Lincoln and Mayflower, and registered the domain name <mayflowervanlinebeware.com>. He posted a website describing his moving experience under the headline "Beware of Lincoln Storage Warehouse. Beware of Mayflower Van Lines." The website urged consumers contemplating a move to avoid both companies. Prince subsequently registered the domain names <mayflowevanline.com>, <lincolnstoragewarehouse.com>, <newjerseymovingcompany.com>, and posted similar material to those sites. Mayflower sued Prince under the ACPA. The court, relying on *Lucas Nursery*, held that Mayflower had failed to show that Prince had a "bad faith intent to profit," concluding that "genuine cyber-gripers . . . are not covered by the ACPA." Prince's registration and use of multiple domain names did not persuade the court that he acted in bad faith.

In *Coca-Cola Company v. Purdy*, 382 F.3d 774 (8th Cir. 2004), however, the Court of Appeals for the Eighth Circuit distinguished *Lucas Nursery* and upheld a finding of bad faith intent to profit. The case involved the registration and use of domain names for a gripe site that was unrelated to the products or services sold by the owners of trademarks used in the contested domain names. William Purdy set up an anti-abortion web page at <www.abortionismurder.com>, where he posted antiabortion commentary and graphic photos of aborted fetuses. Purdy also posted links to a website offering to sell hats, neckties, and tee shirts adorned with antiabortion messages. Purdy registered the domains <drinkcoke.com>, <mycoca-cola.com>, <my-washingtonpost.com>, <mypepsi.org>, and others, and used those domain names to redirect browsers to <abortionismurder.com>. The trademark owners brought suit under the ACPA. In distinguishing *Lucas Nursery*, the Eighth Circuit emphasized that "[t]he content available at abortionismurder.com contained no references to plaintiffs, their products, or their alleged positions on abortion."

Finally, in *Bosley Medical Institute, Inc. v. Kremer*, 403 F.3d 672 (9th Cir. 2005), the Court of Appeals for the 9th Circuit dismissed a trademark infringement and dilution claim over a gripe cite, but declined to dismiss the ACPA claim. Plaintiff Bosley Medical sued its former hair-transplant patient when he posted a site at <www.BosleyMedical.com> criticizing plaintiff's hair transplant services. The Ninth Circuit concluded that defendant's site did not violate the Lanham Act, because Kremer's actions were not "commercial use in commerce:"

> The dangers that the Lanham Act was designed to address are simply not at issue in this case. The Lanham Act, expressly enacted to be applied in commercial contexts, does not prohibit all unauthorized uses of a trademark. Kremer's use of the Bosley Medical mark simply cannot mislead consumers into buying a competing product—no customer will mistakenly purchase a hair replacement service from Kremer under the belief that the service is being offered by Bosley. Neither is Kremer capitalizing on the good will Bosley has created in its mark. Any harm to Bosley arises not from a competitor's sale of a similar product under Bosley's mark, but from Kremer's criticism of their services. Bosley cannot use the Lanham Act either as a shield from Kremer's criticism, or as a sword to shut Kremer up.

The court remanded the ACPA claim for trial, however, noting that section 43(d) of the Lanham Act does not expressly require commercial use and that other circuits had interpreted it to make non-commercial as well as commercial cybersquatting actionable.

QUESTION

The ACPA limits liability to those domain name registrants who register, use or traffic in a domain name with "a bad faith intent *to profit.*" 15 U.S.C. § 1125(d)(1)(A). How does that differ from simple "bad faith intent?" In what sense was Purdy's activity calculated to yield a "profit?" How does intent to profit differ from commercial use?

Page 785. Substitute the following case for the district court opinion in *Harrods v. Sixty Internet Domain Names*:

Harrods Limited v. Sixty Internet Domain Names

302 F.3d 214 (4th Cir. 2002).

■ MICHAEL, CIRCUIT JUDGE:

This case involves a dispute over Internet domain names between two companies named "Harrods," both with legitimate rights to the "Harrods" name in different parts of the world. The plaintiff, Harrods Limited ("Harrods UK"), is the owner of the well-known Harrods of London department store. The defendants are 60 Internet domain names ("Domain Names" or "Names") registered in Herndon, Virginia, by Harrods (Buenos Aires) Limited ("Harrods BA"). Harrods BA, once affiliated with Harrods UK, is now a completely separate corporate entity that until recently operated a "Harrods" department store in Buenos Aires, Argentina. Harrods UK sued the 60 Domain Names under 15 U.S.C. § 1125(d)(2), the in rem provision of the recently enacted Anticybersquatting Consumer Protection Act (ACPA), Pub. L. No. 106–113, 113 Stat. 1501A–545 (codified in scattered sections of 15 U.S.C.) (1999). Harrods UK alleged that the Domain Names infringed and diluted its American "Harrods" trademark and that Harrods BA registered the Names in bad faith as prohibited by 15 U.S.C. § 1125(d)(1). . . .

I.

Harrods UK and its predecessors have operated a department store named "Harrods" in the Knightsbridge section of London, England, since 1849. In 1912 Harrods UK created a wholly owned subsidiary, Harrods South America Limited, to carry on business in South America. Harrods South America Limited created Harrods BA as an independent company, and in 1914 Harrods BA opened a department store under the name "Harrods" in a new building in downtown Buenos Aires designed to look like Harrods UK's historic London building. Over the following decades Harrods BA registered "Harrods" as a trademark in Argentina, Brazil, Paraguay, Venezuela, and a number of other South American countries. Harrods UK and Harrods BA quickly drifted apart: by the 1920s Harrods BA was operating largely independently of Harrods UK, and the last remaining legal ties between the two companies were severed in 1963.

In the early 1990s Harrods UK and Harrods BA entered into negotiations for Harrods UK to buy Harrods BA's South American trademark rights in the name "Harrods." At one point Harrods UK offered $10 million for the rights, but the parties never reached agreement. . . . Here, we have not been asked to conclusively determine the legitimacy and scope of Harrods BA's rights in the name "Harrods" throughout South America. It appears, however, that Harrods BA has the right to use the name "Harrods" in Argentina and much of South America, and for the limited purposes of this litigation Harrods UK does not attempt to prove otherwise.

Harrods UK, for its part, has exclusive trademark rights in the name "Harrods" in much of the rest of the world, including the United States, where retail catalog and Internet sales generate millions of dollars in revenue each year. Harrods UK's retail business has thrived in recent years, but Harrods BA's business has been in decline since the early 1960s. Over the years, Harrods BA occupied less and less of its large Buenos Aires department store building and leased more and more of the space to other vendors. Some time around 1998 Harrods BA ended its department store operation entirely, and the building now sits vacant. Harrods BA's only current revenue is about $300,000 annually from the continued operation of the building's parking garage.

In February of 1999 Harrods UK launched a website at the domain name harrods.com, and the website became a functioning online retail store in November of 1999. Harrods BA executives testified that sometime in 1999 they also began planning to launch a Harrods store on the Internet. Toward that end, Harrods BA hired a consultant, a Mr. Capuro, to prepare a proposal for an online business. In the fall of 1999, around the same time that Harrods UK was launching its Internet business (and announcing this in the press), Harrods BA began registering the first of what eventually became around 300 Harrods-related domain names. The 60 Domain Names that are defendants in this case were registered with Network Solutions, Inc. (NSI), a domain name registry located in Herndon, Virginia. At that time NSI served as the exclusive worldwide registry for domain names using .com, .net, and .org.

. . .

Harrods BA registered each of its Harrods-related domain names under the .com, .net., and .org top-level domains. For example, Harrods BA registered the second-level domain harrodsbuenosaires as harrodsbuenosaires.com, harrodsbuenosaires.net, and harrodsbuenosaires.org. This case involves 20 distinct second-level domain names, each registered under the three top-level domains .com, .net, and .org, for a total of 60 defendant Domain Names.[1] All told, Harrods BA registered about 300 Harrods-related domain names in the United States. The 20 second-level domain names at issue in this case are harrodsbuenosaires, harrodsargentina, harrodssudamerica, harrodssouthamerica, harrodsbrasil, harrodsbrazil, harrodsamerica, tiendaharrods, cyberharrods, ciberharrods, harrodsbank, harrodsbanking, harrodsfinancial, harrodsservices, harrodsvirtual, harrodsstore, shoppingharrods, harrodsshopping, harrodsbashopping, and harrodsshoppingba.

. . .

On February 16, 2000, Harrods UK sued 60 of the Harrods-related domain names in the United States District Court for the Eastern District of Virginia. Harrods UK sued under 15 U.S.C. § 1125(d)(2), which permits

1. For simplicity's sake we will refer to the names by the second-level domains, such as harrodsbuenosaires, with the understanding that this reference encompasses the three permutations of that second-level domain created by combining it with the three top-level domains, .com, .net, and .org.

the owner of a protected mark to bring an in rem action against domain names that violate "any right of the owner of a mark," subject to certain limitations. For example, the in rem action is available only when the plaintiff cannot find or cannot obtain personal jurisdiction over the domain name registrant. Harrods UK claimed that the Domain Names violated 15 U.S.C. § 1125(d)(1), which prohibits bad faith registration of domain names with intent to profit, and 15 U.S.C. §§ 1114, 1125(a) & (c), which together prohibit trademark infringement and dilution. Harrods BA was easily identified as the registrant of the defendant Domain Names, but the mere act of registering the Domain Names in Virginia was deemed insufficient to provide personal jurisdiction over Harrods BA. *See, e.g., Heathmount A.E. Corp. v. Technodome.com*, 106 F.Supp.2d 860, 866–69 (E.D. Va. 2000). Because Harrods UK could not obtain personal jurisdiction over Harrods BA, the suit was filed in rem against the 60 Domain Names themselves.

. . .

II

. . .

On appeal the Domain Names claim that the district court's exercise of in rem jurisdiction over them violates the Due Process Clause because they lack sufficient minimum contacts with the forum. The Due Process clause of the Fifth Amendment permits a federal court to exercise personal jurisdiction over a defendant only if that defendant has "certain minimum contacts with [the forum] such that the maintenance of the suit does not offend 'traditional notions of fair play and substantial justice.' " *Int'l Shoe Co. v. Washington*, 326 U.S. 310, 316, 90 L. Ed. 95, 66 S. Ct. 154 (1945) (*quoting Milliken v. Meyer*, 311 U.S. 457, 463, 85 L. Ed. 278, 61 S. Ct. 339 (1940)). . . .

In the case of disputes involving property, the presence of the property in the jurisdiction does not always justify the exercise of in rem jurisdiction, but "when claims to the property itself are the source of the underlying controversy between the plaintiff and the defendant, it would be unusual for the State where the property is located not to have jurisdiction." *Shaffer [v. Heitner*, 433 U.S. 186 (1977)], 433 U.S. at 207 (internal footnote omitted). . . . Specifically, the Supreme Court said in *Shaffer* that in rem jurisdiction is appropriate in "suits for injury suffered on the land of an absentee owner, where the defendant's ownership of the property is conceded but the cause of action is otherwise related to rights and duties growing out of that ownership." *Shaffer*, 433 U.S. at 208. The dispute in this case is roughly analogous to such a suit. Harrods UK has allegedly suffered injury by way of property, the Domain Names, owned by Harrods BA, an absentee owner. Harrods BA's initial ownership of the Names is conceded, but the cause of action is related to Harrods BA's rights and duties arising out of that ownership.

Likewise, Virginia's "interests in assuring the marketability of property within its borders and in providing a procedure for peaceful resolution of disputes about the possession of that property" also support the exercise of in rem jurisdiction in this case. *Id.* (internal footnote omitted). Moreover, Virginia's interest in not permitting foreign companies to use rights emanating from, and facilities located in, its territory to infringe U.S. trademarks also supports the exercise of in rem jurisdiction. By registering these Domain Names in Virginia, Harrods BA exposed those Names to the jurisdiction of the courts in Virginia (state or federal) at least for the limited purpose of determining who properly owns the Domain Names themselves. This is not a case where "the only role played by the property is to provide the basis for bringing the defendant into court." *Id.* at 209. Rather, because "claims to the property itself are the source of the underlying controversy," *id.* at 207, and because Virginia has important interests in exercising jurisdiction over that property (the Names), we conclude that courts in Virginia, the state where the Domain Names are registered, may constitutionally exercise in rem jurisdiction over them. Thus, the district court's exercise of in rem jurisdiction over the Domain Names was constitutional.

. . .

Harrods UK argues that § 1125(d)(2) provides for in rem jurisdiction against domain names for traditional infringement and dilution claims under §§ 1114, 1125(a) & (c) as well as for claims of bad faith registration with the intent to profit under § 1125(d)(1). The Domain Names argue that the district court correctly limited the scope of the in rem provision to claims under § 1125(d)(1) for bad faith registration of a domain name with the intent to profit. This argument has not yet been settled by any federal circuit court. . . . While we consider this to be a close question of statutory interpretation, we ultimately conclude that § 1125(d)(2) is not limited to violations of § 1125(d)(1); it also authorizes in rem actions for certain federal infringement and dilution claims.

We begin our analysis with the text of the statute. Section 1125(d)(2)(A) provides that the "owner of a mark" may file an in rem action against a domain name if:

> (i) the domain name violates any right of the owner of a mark registered in the Patent and Trademark Office, or protected under subsection (a) [infringement] or (c) [dilution]; and
>
> (ii) . . . the owner—
>
> > (I) is not able to obtain in personam jurisdiction over a person who would have been a defendant in a civil action under paragraph (1) [§ 1125(d)(1)]; or
> >
> > (II) through due diligence was not able to find a person who would have been a defendant in a civil action under paragraph (1). . . .

15 U.S.C. § 1125(d)(2)(A). We start with the first clause, subsection (d)(2)(A)(i), which provides that an in rem action is available if "(i) the

domain name violates *any right* of the owner of a mark registered in the Patent and Trademark Office, or protected under subsection (a) or (c)." 15 U.S.C. § 1125(d)(2)(A)(i) (emphasis added). The broad language "any right of the owner of a mark" does not look like it is limited to the rights guaranteed by subsection (d)(1), but appears to include any right a trademark owner has with respect to the mark. The language, by itself, would include rights under § 1125(d)(1), and it would also include, for example, rights under § 1125(a) against trademark infringement and rights under § 1125(c) against trademark dilution. If Congress had intended for subsection (d)(2) to provide in rem jurisdiction only for subsection (d)(1) claims, it could easily have said so directly. For example, Congress could have said that an in rem action is available if "the domain name violates subsection (d)(1)." Again, if the first key phrase Congress gave us—"any right of the owner of a mark"—is considered in isolation, it would authorize the in rem pursuit of any of the actions that could be brought in personam under U.S. trademark law, including infringement (subsection (a)), dilution (subsection (c)), and cybersquatting (subsection (d)(1)). . . .

Of course, subsection (d)(2)(A)(i) does not create a claim for the owner of any mark, but rather for the owner of "a mark registered in the Patent and Trademark Office [PTO], or protected under subsection (a) or (c)." Thus, to understand the scope of subsection (d)(2)(A)(i), we must also consider the implications of this additional language. Generally speaking, trademark protection is a common law right that arises from the use of a mark to identify the source of certain goods or services. *Brittingham v. Jenkins*, 914 F.2d 447, 452 (4th Cir. 1990); 3 McCarthy § 19:3. By its terms, subsection (d)(2)(A)(i) does not provide an in rem action for the owner of any type of mark protected under trademark law, but only for the owner of a mark that is either (1) registered in the PTO or (2) protected under §§ 1125(a) or (c).

First, we consider the protection offered a mark registered in the PTO. The owner of a mark may register that mark with the PTO. 15 U.S.C. § 1051. While it is the use of a mark, not its registration, that confers trademark protection, *Brittingham*, 914 F.2d at 452, registration does confer certain benefits on the owner; for example, it serves as prima facie evidence of the mark's validity. Id.; 15 U.S.C. § 1057(b). Subsection (d)(2)(A)(i) provides an additional benefit for registration of a mark: registration now entitles the owner of the mark to proceed on an in rem basis under § 1125(d)(2). The rights of an owner whose mark is registered in the PTO are not limited to rights under § 1125(d)(1), however. They also include, for example, rights against infringement of a registered mark under § 1114.

Second, subsection (d)(2)(A)(i) ends with the provision that even if a mark is not registered, the mark's owner may proceed on an in rem basis under § 1125(d)(2) if the mark is "protected under subsection (a) or (c)." Subsections (a) and (c) are the infringement and dilution provisions of § 1125. Because subsection (d)(2) provides for an in rem action for the violation of "any right . . . of a mark . . . protected under subsection (a) or (c)," it seems to provide in rem jurisdiction over a domain name that infringes a mark under § 1125(a) or dilutes a famous mark under § 1125(c). ... If in rem jurisdiction is only available for subsection (d)(1) bad faith claims, we cannot understand why Congress described the types of marks covered under subsection (d)(2) as those "registered in the [PTO], or protected under subsection (a) or (c)." Subsection (d)(2)(A)(i)'s reference to a mark "registered in the [PTO], or protected under subsection (a) or (c)" reinforces our sense that the phrase "any right" includes more than just subsection (d)(1) rights.

According to the Domain Names, the problem with interpreting subsection (d)(2) as covering more than just bad faith claims under subsection (d)(1) is that subsection (d)(2)(A)(ii) conditions the availability of in rem jurisdiction on proof that the plaintiff is unable to find or obtain personal jurisdiction over the "person who would have been a defendant in a civil action [for bad faith registration] under paragraph (1)," that is, § 1125(d)(1). As the district court explained, "because Congress chose to include in the in rem action the definition of potential defendants used in paragraph (1), we must therefore conclude that Congress intended for the 'bad faith intent to profit' element to be part of any in rem action." *Harrods Ltd. v. Sixty Internet Domain Names*, 110 F.Supp.2d 420, 426 (E.D. Va. 2000). We realize that it is possible to get the impression from reading subsection (d)(2)(A)(ii) that the in rem action is available only for subsection (d)(1) violations. But it is important to distinguish between the language discussing the subject matter covered by the in rem provision and the language discussing the proper defendant in a cybersquatting case. Subsection (d)(2)(A)(i) deals with the former, and subsection (d)(2)(A)(ii) deals with the latter. Subsection (d)(2)(A)(i) identifies the substantive rights actionable under the in rem provision, stating in broad terms that the in rem provision protects "any right of the owner of a mark" that is registered in the PTO or "protected under subsection (a) or (c)." Subsection (d)(2)(A)(ii) deals with the proper defendant to a cybersquatting claim, stating that in rem jurisdiction is available only when personal jurisdiction over the registrant is lacking. It would be odd for Congress to have placed a significant limitation on the scope of the substantive rights identified in subsection (d)(2)(A)(i), which deals with the subject matter of in rem actions, by indirectly tacking something on to subsection (d)(2)(A)(ii), which deals with the proper defendant in cybersquatting actions.

If the only way to understand the phrase "a person who would have been a defendant in a civil action under paragraph (1)" was as a reference to subsection (d)(1)'s bad faith requirement, we would be forced to confront the tension between this language and subsection (d)(2)(A)(i)'s broad language of "any right of the owner of a mark." However, the phrase "a person who would have been a defendant in a civil action under paragraph (1)" can fairly be understood as a shorthand reference to the current registrant of the domain name....

Nonetheless, it is possible to disagree about the meaning of the phrase "a person who would have been a defendant in a civil action under paragraph (1)." As noted above, the district court understood this language not as a shorthand reference to the current domain name registrant, but as limiting in rem jurisdiction to subsection (d)(1) bad faith claims. *Harrods Ltd.*, 110 F.Supp.2d at 426. Because the meaning of this phrase in conjunction with the phrase "any right of the owner of a mark" is not altogether clear, it is appropriate to "look to the legislative history for guidance in interpreting the statute." *United States v. Childress*, 104 F.3d 47, 53 (4th Cir. 1996). The legislative history confirms that the phrase "a person who would have been a defendant in a civil action under paragraph (1)" should be read as a shorthand reference to the domain name registrant, not as requiring a bad faith element in all in rem actions. The House Report says that "in rem jurisdiction is ... appropriate in instances where personal jurisdiction cannot be established over the domain name registrant." H.R. Rep. No. 106–412, at 14 (1999). The registrant is the person who would be the defendant both in a subsection (d)(1) bad faith registration action and in a traditional infringement or dilution action involving the improper use of a domain name.

. . .

On balance, we are left with the following. On its face, subsection (d)(2)(A)(i) provides an in rem action for the violation of "any right" of a trademark owner, not just rights provided by subsection (d)(1). Moreover, subsection (d)(2)(A)(i) authorizes in rem jurisdiction for marks "protected under subsection (a) or (c)," the very subsections underlying two of the claims that were dismissed by the district court as outside the scope of subsection (d)(2). While subsection (d)(2)(A)(ii) provides that the in rem action is available only if the plaintiff is unable to find or obtain personal jurisdiction over the "person who would have been a defendant in a civil action under paragraph (1)," we believe this language is best understood as a shorthand reference to the current registrant of the domain name, who would be the defendant in any trademark action involving a domain name. Finally, the legislative history of the ACPA specifically discussing the in rem provision speaks in terms of domain names that violate "substantive Federal trademark law" or that are "infringing or diluting under the Trademark Act." Sen. Rep. No. 106–140, at 10–11. This reinforces the language of subsection (d)(2)(A)(i), which suggests that the in rem provision is not limited to bad faith claims under subsection (d)(1). Thus, we conclude that the best interpretation of § 1125(d)(2) is that the in rem provision not only covers bad faith claims under § 1125(d)(1), but also covers infringement claims under § 1114 and § 1125(a) and dilution claims under § 1125(c).

QUESTIONS

1. Judge Michael dismisses the Domain Names' due process challenge to § 43(d)(2)'s in rem provisions because of the presence of the disputed property in the state of Virginia. In what sense are the domain names located in Virginia? Is the analogy to "suits for injury suffered on the land of an absentee owner" persuasive?

2. The court concludes that the in rem jurisdiction in section 43(d) allows suits for substantive trademark violations as well as claims for bad faith registration. Do you agree? What are the best arguments supporting a contrary interpretation? What remedies are available in an in rem action for trademark infringement or dilution?

3. The court finds it significant that section 43(d)(2) "does not create a claim for the owner of *any* mark," but only for owners of marks that are registered in the PTO or protected under section 43(a) or 43(c). What trademarks does that exclude?

C. ICANN and the Uniform Trademark Domain Name Dispute Resolution Policy

Page 806. Replace *World Wrestling Federation Entertainment, Inc. v. Michael Bosman* with the following case:

Global Media Resources SA v. Sexplanets

WIPO Arbitration and Mediation Center Case No. D2001–1391 (Jan. 24, 2002).

■ ALAN L. LIMBURY, panelist.

The disputed domain name is <sexplanets.com>.

. . . .

On May 30, 1996, the Complainant registered the domain name <sexplanet.com> and, since June of that year, has used that website as a vehicle for the commercial sale of adult entertainment. . . .

The Complainant claims to be the first site on the Internet to download, live, streaming video. Its site is now claimed to be one of the most popular live show websites available, with between approximately 300,000 and approximately 960,000 hits per month with an average of approximately 700,000. As of November 1, 2001, there were 31,873 members of the website. This site is marketed by affiliate Webmasters with commissions paid for selling memberships to Webmasters who advertise <sexplanet.com>. From 2001 to date, $682,661.21 has been paid in commissions to Webmasters for promoting the site.

[In 2001, Complainant acquired a Canadian trademark registration for the mark sexplanet.com, by assignment from another online adult entertainment business, which had registered it in 2000 on the basis of actual use dating from May, 1996.]

The disputed domain name was registered in the name of SexPlanets as registrant on October 5, 1998. . . .

According to the history page at the Respondent's website (the Respondent invited the Panel to visit), the disputed domain name was registered by two friends in the United Kingdom (Mr. Mark Johnson and Mr. Robert

Brennan) who later moved to Spain. (They were joined in their enterprise by a Mr. Bartal, an investor). The founders had the idea in 1997 of providing a free hosting site to webmasters wishing to establish adult websites. Amongst the Terms and Conditions imposed on webmasters wishing to take advantage of the Respondent's free hosting service are that the webmaster is responsible for all content on its site and that the webmaster is not to manipulate the Respondent's advertising banners (which appear on the pages of the webmasters' sites and which generate income for the Respondent).

The original design of the Respondent's home page (which remained unchanged until some time in 2000) included the name "Sex Planets", followed by "The Only Inter Galactic Online Adult Community" and a series of separate "planets", namely "hardcore planet", "celebrity planet", "teens planet", "toons planet", "anal/oral planet", "bondage/S & M planet", "asian planet", "amateurs planet", "voyeur/spy planet", "fetish planet", "gay planet" and "lesbian planet".

. . .

6. Discussion and Findings

. . .

Substantive issues

To qualify for cancellation or transfer, a Complainant must prove each element of paragraph 4(a) of the Policy, namely that:

(i) the disputed domain name is identical or confusingly similar to a trademark or service mark in which the Complainant has rights; and

(ii) the Respondent has no rights or legitimate interests in respect of the domain name; and

(iii) the disputed domain name has been registered and is being used in bad faith.

Identity or confusing similarity

Essential or virtual identity is sufficient for the purposes of the Policy [Citations].

Respondent concedes that the disputed domain name is identical to Complainant's registered trademark SEXPLANET.COM and the Panel so finds.

The Complainant has established this element.

Illegitimacy

The Complainant is the proprietor of the Canadian registered trade mark SEXPLANET.COM, which was assigned to the Complainant on March 22, 2001. The Complainant has not authorized the Respondent to use that mark nor to register the disputed domain name. However, the disputed domain name was registered on October 5, 1998, before the application to register the trade mark was filed.

Assuming, in the Complainant's favour (although the evidence is by no means satisfactory):

- that the Complainant was using to distinguish its services in Canada the unregistered trade mark SEXPLANET.COM from May 30, 1996 (as well as and as distinct from using the domain name <sexplanet.com> to enable Internauts to connect their computers to that of the Complainant); and
- that the mark had become distinctive of the Complainant's services in Canada by the time of the registration of the disputed domain name in 1998,

there is no evidence that the Respondent was aware of the Complainant nor of the Complainant's use in Canada of the trade mark nor of the Complainant's domain name prior to the Respondent's registration of the disputed domain name.

The Panel does not accept that, as at October 5, 1998, the Complainant's common law Canadian trade mark was so well known that the Respondent, then in the United Kingdom, is likely to have been aware of it.

The Complainant argues that it is likely the Respondent was aware of the Complainant's website before registering the disputed domain name. On all the material before the Panel, the Panel is not prepared to draw such an inference.

The Panel accepts that the Respondent simply chose its desired domain name, enquired whether it was available and, finding that it was, registered it. The combination of the words SEX and PLANETS is not so improbable that, in the context of adult web sites, it could only have come to the Respondent's founders because they were aware of the combination devised by the Complainant of SEX and PLANET. The Panel accepts the Respondent's explanation as to how the name was chosen because the original web page design, long before this dispute arose, accords with that explanation.

Having registered the disputed domain name without knowledge of the Complainant, its mark or its domain name, the Respondent immediately commenced using it to further its business plan of providing bona fide free hosting services to webmasters in exchange for advertising revenue generated from banners displayed on the adult sites hosted. It was almost 2 years later that the Complainant first approached the Respondent. The Panel concludes that the Respondent has demonstrated its rights and legitimate interests in the disputed domain name within paragraph 4(c)(i) of the Policy.

The Complainant has not established this element.

Bad faith registration and use

Some two years after the Respondent registered the disputed domain name, the Complainant approached the Respondent and the Respondent suggested the Complainant might buy out the Respondent. The parties are in heated disagreement as to whether this was an offer to sell the disputed domain name or an offer to sell the Respondent's business.

It is not necessary to resolve this issue because, even if the Respondent was offering in 2000 to sell the disputed domain name, in the absence of a finding that the Respondent was aware of the Complainant, its mark or its domain name at the time of registration in 1998, the conclusion cannot reasonably be drawn that sale at a profit to the Complainant was the primary purpose of the Respondent in registering the disputed domain name.

. . .

Here, the Panel finds the evidence positively establishes good faith registration and accordingly it is unnecessary to determine whether the Respondent has used the disputed domain name in bad faith after having become aware of the Complainant's trade mark and website.

The Complainant has not established this element.

Reverse domain name hijacking

Rule 1 defines reverse domain name hijacking as "using the Policy in bad faith to attempt to deprive a registered domain-name holder of a domain name." See also Rule 15(e). To prevail on such a claim, Respondent must show either that Complainant knew of Respondent's unassailable right or legitimate interest in the disputed domain name or the clear lack of bad faith registration and use, and nevertheless brought the Complaint in bad faith [Citations] or that the Complaint was brought in knowing disregard of the likelihood that the Respondent possessed legitimate interests [Citation].

Here the Respondent informed the Complainant in 2000 of the facts as now found by the Panel. The Complainant waited until it had obtained ownership of the trade mark before commencing this proceeding. Despite this, the Panel does not regard the Complainant as having acted in bad faith in bringing this proceeding, in light of the similarity in content between the Complainant's website and those hosted by the Respondent and the interpretation which the Complainant placed upon the Respondent's offer to sell out to the Complainant.

7. Decision

Pursuant to paragraphs 4(i) of the Policy and 15 of the Rules, the Panel states that this proceeding is outside the scope of the Policy. The Complaint is therefore denied.

Page 812. Delete *CRS Technology v. Condenet, Inc.*

Page 828. Add the following material before *Deutsche Welle v. Diamondware, Ltd.*:

In the five years since ICANN's UDRP took effect, the dispute resolution service provided by the World Intellectual Property Organization, WIPO, has come to dominate UDRP dispute resolution. Recently, the

WIPO Arbitration and Mediation Center posted an informal overview of the weight of WIPO panel authority on UDRP legal issues. The overview is available online at http://arbiter.wipo.int/domains/search/overview/index.html?lang=eng. The overview summarizes WIPO panels' determinations on a number of recurrent legal questions. For example, in connection with questions of confusing similarity under the UDRP, the overview presents this précis:

1.3 Is a domain name consisting of a trademark and a negative term confusingly similar to the complainant's trademark? ("sucks cases")

Majority view: A domain name consisting of a trademark and a negative term is confusingly similar to the complainant's mark. Confusing similarity has been found because the domain name contains a trademark and a dictionary word; or because the disputed domain name is highly similar to the trademark; or because the domain name may not be recognized as negative; or because the domain name may be viewed by non-fluent English language speakers, who may not recognize the negative connotations of the word that is attached to the trademark.

Relevant decisions:

- Wal–Mart Stores, Inc. v. Richard MacLeod d/b/a For Sale D2000–0662 <walmartsucks.com>, Transfer
- A & F Trademark, Inc. and Abercrombie & Fitch Stores, Inc. v. Justin Jorgensen D2001–0900 <abercrombieandfilth.com>, Transfer
- Berlitz Investment Corp. v. Stefan Tinculescu D2003–0465 <berlitzsucks.com>, Transfer
- Wachovia Corporation v. Alton Flanders D2003–0596 <wachoviasucks.com> among others, Transfer

Minority view: A domain name consisting of a trademark and a negative term is not confusingly similar because Internet users are not likely to associate the trademark holder with a domain name consisting of the trademark and a negative term.

Relevant decisions:

- Lockheed Martin Corporation v. Dan Parisi D2000–1015 <lockheedmartinsucks.com>, Denied
- McLane Company, Inc. v. Fred Craig D2000–1455 <mclanenortheastsucks.com>, Denied
- America Online, Inc. v. Johuathan Investments, Inc., and Aollnews.com D2001–0918 <aollnews.com>, <fucknetscape.com> Transfer, Denied in Part

Page 829. Insert the following three cases after *Deutsche Welle v. Diamondware*:

Sallen v. Corinthians Licenciamentos LTDA, 273 F.3d 14 (1st Cir. 2001). The owner of the Brazilian soccer team Corinthiao brought a successful UDRP proceeding against Jay Sallen, the registrant of the domain name <corinthians.com>. Sallen then filed suit under section 43(d)(2)(v) seeking the return of his domain name and a declaration that his registration and use of <corinthians.com> was not unlawful:

> Sallen asserts that (1) this provision of the ACPA creates an explicit cause of action for a declaration that a registrant who has lost a domain name under the UDRP has lawfully registered and used that domain name; (2) this declaration overrides the WIPO panel's decision to the contrary; and (3) federal courts may order the domain name reactivated or transferred back to the aggrieved registrant. Sallen's position is that, despite the terms of his domain name registration agreement, and despite the WIPO panel's interpretation of those terms, he is entitled to retain registration and use of corinthians.com if his registration and use of the domain name is consistent with the ACPA.
>
> This case raises an issue of first impression, requiring us to determine whether a domain name registrant, who has lost in a WIPO-adjudicated UDRP proceeding, may bring an action in federal court under § 1114(2)(D)(v) seeking to override the result of the earlier WIPO proceeding by having his status as a nonviolator of the ACPA declared and by getting an injunction forcing a transfer of the disputed domain name back to him. The answer to this question turns on the relationship between the ACPA, in particular § 1114(2)(D)(v), and decisions of administrative dispute resolution panels contractually empowered to adjudicate domain name disputes under the UDRP.
>
> The district court dismissed Sallen's complaint on the grounds that no actual controversy existed between the parties since CL never claimed that Sallen violated the ACPA. We hold that, although CL represented that it had "no intent to sue [Sallen] under the ACPA for his past activities in connection with corinthians.com," an actual controversy did exist between the parties concerning rights to corinthians.com, and that the district court incorrectly dismissed Sallen's complaint. Section 1114(2)(D)(v) grants domain name registrants who have lost domain names under administrative panel decisions applying the UDRP an affirmative cause of action in federal court for a declaration of nonviolation of the ACPA and for the return of the wrongfully transferred domain names. Accordingly, we reverse and remand to the district court.

Dluhos v. Strasberg, 321 F.3d 365 (3d Cir. 2003). The estate of Lee Strasberg, a famous acting teacher who died in 1982, filed a UDRP proceeding against Dluhos, the registrant of <leestrasberg.com>. Rather than contesting the UDRP proceeding, Dluhos filed an action in federal court challenging the constitutionality of the UDRP. After the UDRP panel ruled that the <leestrasberg.com> should be transferred to the Strasberg estate, Dluhos amended his complaint to add a count seeking the reinstatement of his domain. The district court dismissed Dluhos's constitutional challenge. In reviewing the UDRP decision, the court applied the deferential standard imposed by the Federal Arbitration Act, and upheld the award. On appeal, the Third Circuit held that UDRP decisions are not subject to review under the Federal Arbitration Act, but may be challenged under the ACPA:

> At issue before us then is whether the nonbinding domain name resolution policy (UDRP) proceeding that shifted Appellant's registered domain name to the Strasberg defendants constitutes arbitration under the FAA. If this proceeding qualifies as arbitration under the FAA, then the dispute resolution is subject to extremely limited review. If it does not fall under the FAA umbrella, then the district court lacked jurisdiction to examine—and thus to affirm—the result under the lax FAA review standards.
>
> IV.
>
> We begin our analysis of the FAA's applicability by examining the specific arbitration agreement at issue, a contract-based arrangement for handling disputes between domain name registrants and third parties who challenge the registration and use of their trademarks. In our view, the UDRP's unique contractual arrangement renders the FAA's provisions for judicial review inapplicable.
>
> A.
>
> First, the UDRP obviously contemplates the possibility of judicial intervention, as no provision of the policy prevents a party from filing suit before, after or during the administrative proceedings. See UDRP § 4(k) (stating that domain-name resolution proceedings shall not stop either party from "submitting the dispute to a court of competent jurisdiction for independent resolution"); *Sallen v. Corinthians Licenciamentos Ltda.*, 273 F.3d 14, 26 (1st Cir. 2001) (discussing the likelihood that the "judicial outcome will override the UDRP one"). In that sense, this mechanism would not fall under the FAA because "the dispute will [not necessarily] be settled by this arbitration." *Harrison* [*v. Nissan Motor Corp.*, 111 F.3d 343, 350 (3d Cir. 1997)], at 349.
>
> The UDRP was intended to ensure that the parties could seek independent judicial resolution of domain name disputes, regardless of whether its proceeding reached a conclusion. *See World Intellectual Property Organization, The Management of Internet Names and Addresses: Intellectual Property Issues: Final Reporter of the WIPO Internet Domain Name Process* 139, 150(iv), at http://wipo2.wipo.int/process1/report/finalreport.html (Apr. 30, 1999) (remarking that the parties should be permitted to seek "de novo review" of a UDRP-based dispute resolution); *see also Sallen*, 273 F.3d at 26 (affording independent complete review of a UDRP proceeding rather than addressing it under the FAA); *Weber-Stephen Prods. Co. v. Armitage Hardware & Bldg. Supply, Inc.*, 2000 U.S. Dist LEXIS 6335 (N.D. Ill. May 3, 2000) (concluding that the UDRP takes account of the possibility of parallel litigation in federal court,

and that federal courts are "not bound by the outcome of the administrative proceedings").

Indeed, unlike methods of dispute resolution covered by the FAA, UDRP proceedings were never intended to replace formal litigation. *See Parisi* [*v. Netlearning, Inc.*, 139 F.Supp.2d 745 (E.D. Va. 2001)], at 752 (citing the FAA's requirement that parties to arbitration "agree[ ] that a judgment of the court shall be entered upon the award made pursuant to the arbitration," 9 U.S.C.S. 9, and noting the absence of such an agreement in the UDRP); David E. Sorkin, *Judicial Review of ICANN Domain Name Dispute Decisions*, 18 SANTA CLARA COMPUTER & HIGHTECH L.J. 35, 51–52 (2001) ("Unlike conventional arbitration, the UDRP is not meant to replace litigation, but merely to provide an additional forum for dispute resolution, with an explicit right of appeal to the courts."). Rather, the UDRP contemplates truncated proceedings. It "is fashioned as an 'online' procedure administered via the Internet," *Parisi*, 139 F.Supp.2d at 747, which does not permit discovery, the presentation of live testimony (absent exceptional circumstances), or any remedy other than the transfer or cancellation of the domain name in question. [Citations]

To shove Dluhos' square-peg UDRP proceeding into the round hole of the FAA would be to frustrate this aim, as judicial review of FAA-styled arbitration proceedings could be generously described only as extremely deferential.

B.

Second, because the trademark holder or the trademark holder's representative is not required to avail itself of the dispute resolution policy before moving ahead in the district court, these proceedings do not qualify as the type that would entail a court's compelling party participation prior to independent judicial review—thus removing the proceeding from the warmth of the FAA blanket. Under § 4 of the FAA, a district court may "stay the trial of the action until such arbitration has been had in accordance with the terms of the agreement." 9 U.S.C. § 4. Although "[s]ome courts, relying in part on their inherent equitable powers, have stayed litigation and compelled participation in non-binding procedures so long as there are 'reasonable commercial expectations' that the procedures would 'settle' disputed issues," *Parisi*, 139 F.Supp.2d at 750 n.10 (*quoting AMF*, 621 F.Supp. at 460–461), a UDRP proceeding settles a domain-name dispute only to the extent that a season-finale cliffhanger resolves a sitcom's storyline—that is, it doesn't. It is true that the language of the resolution policy describes the dispute-resolution process as "mandatory," but "the process is not 'mandatory' in the sense that either disputant's legal claims accrue only after a panel's decision." *Parisi*, 139 F.Supp.2d at 751 (*quoting Bankers Ins. Co.*, 245 F.3d at 319). Only the domain-name registrant is contractually obligated to participate in the proceeding if a complaint is filed. Even then, the panel may "decide the dispute based on the complaint" if the registrant declines to participate. UDRP § 5(e). That Dluhos could do precisely that by eschewing the NAF proceeding and filing suit in district court only demonstrates the dispute resolution policy's outcome's relative hollowness. Indeed, it is not the district court litigation that could be stayed pending dispute resolution, but rather the dispute-resolution mechanism itself. *See* UDRP § 18 (giving arbitration panel "the discretion to decide whether to suspend or terminate the administrative proceeding, or to proceed to a decision" while a lawsuit is pending). And that is exactly what the NAF panel did.

C.

The bottom line is that a registrant who loses a domain name to a trademark holder "can effectively suspend [a] panel's decision by filing a lawsuit in the specified jurisdiction and notifying the registrar in accordance with [UDRP § 4(k)]." *Parisi*, 139 F.Supp.2d at 752. From that provision, it is evident that the UDRP provides " 'parity of appeal,' affording a 'clear mechanism' for 'seeking judicial review of a decision of an administrative panel canceling or transferring the domain name.' " *Id.* (*quoting* ICANN, *Staff Report on Implementation Documents for the Uniform Dispute Resolution Policy* (Sept. 29, 1999)).

Accordingly, we hold that UDRP proceedings do not fall under the Federal Arbitration Act.More specifically, judicial review of those decisions is not restricted to a motion to vacate arbitration award under § 10 of the FAA, which applies only to binding proceedings likely to "realistically settle the dispute." The district court erred in reviewing the domain name proceeding under limitations of FAA standards.

V.

Because the UDRP—a private covenant—cannot confer federal jurisdiction where none independently exists, the remaining question is whether the Congress has provided a cause of action to challenge its decisions. In the Anticybersquatting Consumer Protection Act, we hold that it has.

The ACPA, 15 U.S.C. § 1114(2)(D)(v), "provide[s] registrants ... with an affirmative cause of action to recover domain names lost in UDRP proceedings." *Sallen*, 273 F.3d at 27. Under this modern amendment to the Lanham Act, a registrant whose domain name has been "suspended, disabled, or transferred" may sue for a declaration that the registrant is not in violation of the Act, as well as for an injunction returning the domain name. 15 U.S.C. § 1114(2)(D)(v). Congress' authorization of the federal courts to "grant injunctive relief to the domain name registrant, including the reactivation of the domain name or transfer of the domain name to the domain name registrant" gives the registrant an explicit cause of action through which to redress the loss of a domain name under the UDRP. *Id.*

Accordingly, as to the CMG and Strasberg defendants, we will reverse and remand the case for further proceedings consistent with this opinion. This decision in no way reflects an intimation that the NAP panel erred in its judgment, but merely that UDRP resolutions do not fall under the limited judicial review of arbitrators of the FAA.

Barcelona.com, Inc. v. Excelentisimo Ayuntamiento De Barcelona

330 F.3d 617 (4th Cir. 2003).

■ Niemeyer, Circuit Judge:

Barcelona.com, Inc. ("Bcom, Inc."), a Delaware corporation, commenced this action under the Anticybersquatting Consumer Protection Act against Excelentisimo Ayuntamiento de Barcelona (the City Council of Barcelona, Spain) for a declaratory judgment that Bcom, Inc.'s registration and use of the domain name <barcelona.com> is not unlawful under the Lanham Act (Chapter 22 of Title 15 of the United States Code). The district court concluded that Bcom, Inc.'s use of <barcelona.com> was confusingly similar to Spanish trademarks owned by the City Council that include the word "Barcelona." Also finding bad faith on the basis that Bcom, Inc. had attempted to sell the <barcelona.com> domain name to the City Council for a profit, the court ordered the transfer of the domain name to the City Council.

Because the district court applied Spanish law rather than United States law and based its transfer order, in part, on a counterclaim that the City Council never filed, we reverse the judgment of the district court denying Bcom, Inc. relief under the Anticybersquatting Consumer Protection Act, vacate its memorandum opinion and its order to transfer the domain name <barcelona.com> to the City Council, and remand for further proceedings consistent with this opinion.

I

In 1996, Mr. Joan Nogueras Cobo ("Nogueras"), a Spanish citizen, registered the domain name <barcelona.com> in the name of his wife, also a Spanish citizen, with the domain registrar, Network Solutions, Inc., in Herndon, Virginia. In the application for registration of the domain name, Nogueras listed himself as the administrative contact. When Nogueras met Mr. Shahab Hanif, a British citizen, in June 1999, they developed a business plan to turn <barcelona.com> into a tourist portal for the Barcelona, Spain, region. A few months later they formed Bcom, Inc. under Delaware law to own <barcelona.com> and to run the website, and Nogueras, his wife, and Hanif became Bcom, Inc.'s officers. Bcom, Inc. was formed as an American company in part because Nogueras believed that doing so would facilitate obtaining financing for the development of the website. Although Bcom, Inc. maintains a New York mailing address, it has no employees in the United States, does not own or lease office space in the United States, and does not have a telephone listing in the United States. Its computer server is in Spain.

Shortly after Nogueras registered the domain name <barcelona.com> in 1996, he placed some Barcelona-related information on the site. The site offered commercial services such as domain registry and web hosting, but did not offer much due to the lack of financing. Before developing the business plan with Hanif, Nogueras used a web-form on the City Council's official website to e-mail the mayor of Barcelona, Spain, proposing to "negotiate" with the City Council for its acquisition of the domain name <barcelona.com>, but Nogueras received no response. And even after the development of a business plan and after speaking with potential investors, Nogueras was unable to secure financing to develop the website.

In March 2000, about a year after Nogueras had e-mailed the Mayor, the City Council contacted Nogueras to learn more about Bcom, Inc. and its plans for the domain name <barcelona.com>. Nogueras and his marketing director met with City Council representatives, and after the meeting, sent them the business plan that was developed for Bcom, Inc.

On May 3, 2000, a lawyer for the City Council sent a letter to Nogueras demanding that Nogueras transfer the domain name <barcelona.com> to the City Council. The City Council owned about 150 trademarks issued in Spain, the majority of which included the word Barcelona, such as "Teatre Barcelona," "Barcelona Informacio I Grafic," and "Barcelona Informacio 010 El Tlefon Que Ho Contesta Tot." . . .

. . .

Upon Bcom, Inc.'s refusal to transfer <barcelona.com> to the City Council, the City Council invoked the Uniform Domain Name Dispute Resolution Policy ("UDRP") promulgated by the Internet Corporation for Assigned Names and Numbers ("ICANN") to resolve the dispute.

The administrative complaint was resolved by a single WIPO panelist who issued a ruling in favor of the City Council on August 4, 2000. The WIPO panelist concluded that <barcelona.com> was confusingly similar to the City Council's Spanish trademarks, that Bcom, Inc. had no legitimate interest in <barcelona.com>, and that Bcom, Inc.'s registration and use of <barcelona.com> was in bad faith. To support his conclusion that Bcom, Inc. acted in bad faith, the WIPO panelist observed that the only purpose of the business plan was "to commercially exploit information about the City of Barcelona . . . particularly . . . the information prepared and provided by [the City Council] as part of its public service." The WIPO panelist ordered that Bcom, Inc. transfer the domain name <barcelona.com> to the City Council.

In accordance with the UDRP's provision that required a party aggrieved by the dispute resolution process to file any court challenge within ten business days, Bcom, Inc. commenced this action on August 18, 2000 under the provision of the Anticybersquatting Consumer Protection Act (the "ACPA") that authorizes a domain name owner to seek recovery or restoration of its domain name when a trademark owner has overstepped its authority in causing the domain name to be suspended, disabled, or transferred. *See* 15 U.S.C. § 1114(2)(D)(v). Bcom, Inc.'s complaint sought a declaratory judgment that its use of the name <barcelona.com> "does not infringe upon any trademark of defendant or cause confusion as to the origin, sponsorship, or approval of the website <barcelona.com>; . . . [and] that [the City Council] is barred from instituting any action against [Bcom, Inc.] for trademark infringement."

Following a bench trial, the district court entered a memorandum opinion and an order dated February 22, 2002, denying Bcom, Inc.'s request for declaratory judgment and directing Bcom, Inc. to "transfer the domain name <barcelona.com> to the [City Council] forthwith." 189 F.Supp.2d 367, 377 (E.D. Va. 2002). Although the district court concluded that the WIPO panel ruling "should be given no weight and this case must be decided based on the evidence presented before the Court," the court proceeded in essence to apply the WIPO panelist opinion as well as Spanish law. *Id.* at 371. The court explained that even though the City Council did not own a trademark in the name "Barcelona" alone, it owned numerous Spanish trademarks that included the word Barcelona, which could, under Spanish law as understood by the district court, be enforced against an infringing use such as <barcelona.com>. *Id.* Adopting the WIPO panelist's decision, the court stated that "the WIPO decision was correct in its determination that [Bcom, Inc.] took 'advantage of the normal confusion' of an Internet user by using the 'Barcelona route' because an Internet user would 'normally expect to reach some official body . . . for . . . the information.' " *Id.* at 372. Referring to the facts that Bcom, Inc. engaged in little activity and attempted to sell the domain name to the City Council, the court concluded that "these factors clearly demonstrate a bad faith intent on the part of the Plaintiff and its sole shareholders to improperly profit from their registration of the domain name <barcelona.com>." At bottom, the court concluded that Bcom, Inc. failed to demonstrate, as required by 15 U.S.C. § 1114(2)(D)(v), that its use of <barcelona.com> was "not unlawful." *Id.* at 373.

. . .

From the district court's order of February 22, 2002, Bcom, Inc. filed this appeal.

II

. . .

[D]omain names are issued pursuant to contractual arrangements under which the registrant agrees to a dispute resolution process, the UDRP, which is designed to resolve a large number of disputes involving domain names, but this process is not intended to interfere with or modify any "independent resolution" by a court of competent jurisdiction. Moreover, the UDRP makes no effort at unifying the law of trademarks among the nations served by the Internet. Rather, it forms part of a contractual policy developed by ICANN for use by registrars in administering the issuance and transfer of domain names. Indeed, it explicitly anticipates that judicial proceedings will continue under various nations' laws applicable to the parties.

. . .

Moreover, any decision made by a panel under the UDRP is no more than an agreed-upon administration that is *not* given any deference under the ACPA. To the contrary, because a UDRP decision is susceptible of being grounded on principles foreign or hostile to American law, the ACPA authorizes reversing a panel decision if such a result is called for by application of the Lanham Act.

In sum, we conclude that we have jurisdiction over this dispute brought under the ACPA and the Lanham Act. Moreover, we give the decision of the WIPO panelist no deference in deciding this action under § 1114(2)(D)(v). [Citations]. Thus, for our purposes, the WIPO panelist's decision is relevant only to serve as the reason for Bcom, Inc.'s bringing an action under § 1114(2)(D)(v) to reverse the WIPO panelist's decision.

III

Now we turn to the principal issue raised in this appeal. Bcom, Inc. contends that in deciding its claim under § 1114(2)(D)(v), the district court erred in applying the law of Spain rather than the law of the United States. Because the ACPA explicitly requires application of the Lanham Act, not foreign law, we agree.

Section 1114(2)(D)(v), the reverse domain name hijacking provision, states:

> A domain name registrant whose domain name has been suspended, disabled, or transferred under a policy described under clause (ii)(II) may, upon notice to the mark owner, file a civil action to establish that the registration or use of the domain name by such registrant is not unlawful under this chapter. The court may grant injunctive relief to the domain name registrant, including the reactivation of the domain name or transfer of the domain name to the domain name registrant.

15 U.S.C. § 1114(2)(D)(v). Thus, to establish a right to relief against an "overreaching trademark owner" under this reverse hijacking provision, a plaintiff must establish (1) that it is a domain name registrant; (2) that its domain name was suspended, disabled, or transferred under a policy implemented by a registrar as described in 15 U.S.C. § 1114(2)(D)(ii)(II); (3) that the owner of the mark that prompted the domain name to be suspended, disabled, or transferred has notice of the action by service or otherwise; and (4) that the plaintiff's registration or use of the domain name is not unlawful under the Lanham Act, as amended.

. . .

It is the last element that raises the principal issue on appeal. Bcom, Inc. argues that the district court erred in deciding whether Bcom, Inc. satisfied this element by applying Spanish law and then by concluding that Bcom, Inc.'s use of the domain name violated Spanish law.

It appears from the district court's memorandum opinion that it indeed did resolve the last element by applying Spanish law. Although the district court recognized that the City Council did not have a registered trademark in the name "Barcelona" alone, either in Spain or in the United States, it observed that "under Spanish law, when trademarks consisting of two or more words contain one word that stands out in a predominant manner, that dominant word must be given decisive relevance." *Barcelona.com, Inc.*, 189 F.Supp.2d at 371–72. The court noted that "the term 'Barcelona' has been included in many trademarks consisting of two or more words owned by the City Council of Barcelona. In most of these marks, the word 'Barcelona' is clearly the dominant word which characterizes the mark." 189 F.Supp.2d at 372. These observations regarding the substance and effect of Spanish law led the court to conclude that the City Council of Barcelona "owns a legally valid Spanish trademark for the dominant word 'Barcelona.'" *Id.* The district court then proceeded to determine whether Bcom's "use of the Barcelona trademark is not unlawful." *Id.* In this portion of its analysis, the district court determined that there was a "confusing similarity between the <barcelona.com> domain name and the marks held by the Council," *id.*, and that "the circumstances surrounding the incorporation of [Bcom, Inc.] and the actions taken by Nogueras in attempting to sell the domain name evidenced a bad faith intent to profit from the registration of a domain name containing the Council's mark," *id.* Applying Spanish trademark law in this manner, the court resolved that Bcom, Inc.'s registration and use of <barcelona.com> were unlawful.

It requires little discussion to demonstrate that this use of Spanish law by the district court was erroneous under the plain terms of the statute. The text of the ACPA explicitly requires application of the Lanham Act, not foreign law, to resolve an action brought under 15 U.S.C. § 1114(2)(D)(v). Specifically, it authorizes an aggrieved domain name registrant to "file a civil action to establish that the registration or use of the domain name by such registrant is *not unlawful under this chapter*." 15 U.S.C. § 1114(2)(D)(v) (emphasis added). It is thus readily apparent that the cause of action created by Congress in this portion of the ACPA requires the court adjudicating such an action to determine whether the registration or use of the domain name violates the Lanham Act. Because the statutory language has a plain and unambiguous meaning that is consistent with the statutory context and application of this language in accordance with its plain meaning provides a component of a coherent statutory scheme, our statutory analysis need proceed no further. [Citation]

By requiring application of United States trademark law to this action brought in a United States court by a United States corporation involving a domain name administered by a United States registrar, 15 U.S.C. § 1114(2)(D)(v) is consistent with the fundamental doctrine of territoriality upon which our trademark law is presently based. . . .

When we apply the Lanham Act, not Spanish law, in determining whether Bcom, Inc.'s registration and use of <barcelona.com> is unlawful, the ineluctable conclusion follows that Bcom, Inc.'s registration and use of the name "Barcelona" is not unlawful. Under the Lanham Act, and apparently even under Spanish law, the City Council could not obtain a trademark interest in a purely descriptive geographical designation that refers only to the City of Barcelona. *See* 15 U.S.C. § 1052(e)(2); *see also* Spanish Trademark Law of 1988, Art. 11(1)(c) (forbidding registration of marks consisting exclusively of "geographical origin"). Under United States trademark law, a geographic designation can obtain trademark protection if that designation acquires secondary meaning. *See, e.g., Resorts of Pinehurst, Inc. v. Pinehurst Nat'l Corp.*, 148 F.3d 417, 421 (4th Cir. 1998). On the record in this case, however, there was no evidence that the public—in the United States or elsewhere—associates "Barcelona" with anything other than the City itself. Indeed, the Chief Director of the City Council submitted an affidavit stating that "the City does not own and is not using any trademarks in the United States, to identify any goods or services." Therefore, under United States trademark law, "Barcelona" should have been treated as a purely descriptive geographical term entitled to no trademark protection. *See* 15 U.S.C. § 1052(e)(2). It follows then that there was nothing unlawful about Nogueras' registration of <barcelona.com>, nor is there anything unlawful under United States trademark law about Bcom, Inc.'s continued use of that domain name.

For these reasons, we conclude that Bcom, Inc. established entitlement to relief under 15 U.S.C. § 1114(2)(D)(v) with respect to the domain name <barcelona.com>, and accordingly we reverse the district court's ruling in this regard.

QUESTION

Assume the district court was correct in concluding that Bcom's registration and use of <barcelona.com> violated the trademark law of Spain. Indeed, assume that the Barcelona City Council has obtained a Spanish court judgment to that effect. Should Bcom nonetheless be entitled to prevail in an action to recover the domain name on the ground that its registration and use of the domain name does not violate United States law?

Page 829. Add the following paragraph to the Note on NEW GENERIC TLDs:

ICANN has proceeded slowly in permitting the introduction of new top level domains. After significant delays, the seven TLDs listed in the main volume are now up and running. The contracts for all seven domains incorporated mechanisms to allow trademark owners to prevent registration of their marks, and required all seven registries to impose trademark-friendly dispute resolution policies on all domain name registrants. ICANN subsequently approved five new domains with narrow subject matter focus, **.jobs** (help wanted), **.travel** (travel industry), **.mobi** (Internet content optimized for mobile phones), and **.cat** (language and culture of Catalonia, Spain). ICANN is currently considering proposals to establish **.post** (for post offices) and **.tel** (for telephone listings). In 2005, ICANN tentatively approved a **.xxx** domain name for pornographic sites. The United States government expressed objections to the approval of a **.xxx** domain, however, and, in May, 2006, a divided ICANN Board voted to reject the **.xxx** proposal.

CHAPTER 12

TRADEMARKS AS SPEECH

A. REFERENTIAL USE

Page 846. Substitute the following case for *Patmont Motor Werks v. Gateway Marine:*

Dow Jones & Company, Inc. v. International Securities, 451 F.3d 295 (2d Cir. 2006). Dow Jones and McGraw–Hill sued an options trading exchange, which had announced its intention to institute options trading pegged to plaintiffs' stock indices. Plaintiffs argued that defendants' use of the underlying indices misappropriated their intellectual property interests in the indices and infringed and diluted their trademarks. The trail court dismissed both plaintiffs' complaints. The Court of Appeals for the Second Circuit affirmed. Assuming without deciding that plaintiffs did own intellectual property rights in their stock indices, the court held that none of defendant's behavior misappropriated those rights:

> Plaintiffs intentionally disseminate their index values to inform the public. They cannot complain when the defendants do nothing more than draw information from that publication of the index values. The complaints do not specify any use of the indexes likely to be made by the defendants that would constitute misappropriation.

Plaintiff's infringement and dilution claims focused on defendant's use of the trademarks for plaintiffs' indices in promoting its options. The court found that those claims failed as a matter of law:

> While a trademark conveys an exclusive right to the use of a mark in commerce in the area reserved, that right generally does not prevent one who trades a branded product from accurately describing it by its brand name, so long as the trader does not create confusion by implying an affiliation with the owner of the product.

Page 851. Insert the following case after *Kassbaum v. Steppenwolf*:

Playboy Enterprises, Inc. v. Terri Welles

279 F.3d 796 (9th Cir. 2002).

■ T.G. NELSON, CIRCUIT JUDGE:

Playboy Enterprises, Inc. (PEI), appeals the district court's grant of summary judgment as to its claims of trademark infringement, unfair competition, and breach of contract against Terri Welles; Terri Welles, Inc.;

Pippi, Inc.; and Welles' current and former "webmasters," Steven Huntington and Michael Mihalko. We have jurisdiction pursuant to 28 U.S.C. § 1291, and we affirm in part and reverse in part.

. . .

I.

Background

Terri Welles was on the cover of Playboy in 1981 and was chosen to be the Playboy Playmate of the Year for 1981. Her use of the title "Playboy Playmate of the Year 1981," and her use of other trademarked terms on her website are at issue in this suit. During the relevant time period, Welles' website offered information about and free photos of Welles, advertised photos for sale, advertised memberships in her photo club, and promoted her services as a spokesperson. A biographical section described Welles' selection as Playmate of the Year in 1981 and her years modeling for PEI. After the lawsuit began, Welles included discussions of the suit and criticism of PEI on her website and included a note disclaiming any association with PEI.[1]

PEI complains of four different uses of its trademarked terms on Welles' website: (1) the terms "Playboy" and "Playmate" in the metatags of the website;[2] (2) the phrase "Playmate of the Year 1981" on the masthead of the website; (3) the phrases "Playboy Playmate of the Year 1981" and "Playmate of the Year 1981" on various banner ads, which may be transferred to other websites; and (4) the repeated use of the abbreviation "PMOY '81" as the watermark on the pages of the website.[3] PEI claimed that these uses of its marks constituted trademark infringement, dilution, false designation of origin, and unfair competition. The district court granted defendants' motion for summary judgment. PEI appeals the grant of summary judgment on its infringement and dilution claims. We affirm in part and reverse in part.

. . .

III.

Discussion

A. Trademark Infringement

Except for the use of PEI's protected terms in the wallpaper of Welles' website, we conclude that Welles' uses of PEI's trademarks are permissible, nominative uses. They imply no current sponsorship or endorsement by

1. The disclaimer reads as follows: "This site is neither endorsed, nor sponsored, nor affiliated with Playboy Enterprises, Inc. PLAYBOY™ PLAYMATE OF THE YEAR™ AND PLAYMATE OF THE MONTH™ are unregistered trademarks of Playboy Enterprises, Inc."

2. Metatags are hidden code used by some search engines to determine the content of websites in order to direct searchers to relevant sites.

3. PEI claims that "PMOY" is an unregistered trademark of PEI, standing for "Playmate of the Year."

PEI. Instead, they serve to identify Welles as a past PEI "Playmate of the Year."[7]

We articulated the test for a permissible, nominative use in *New Kids On The Block v. New America Publishing, Inc.* The band, New Kids On The Block, claimed trademark infringement arising from the use of their trademarked name by several newspapers. The newspapers had conducted polls asking which member of the band New Kids On The Block was the best and most popular. The papers' use of the trademarked term did not fall within the traditional fair use doctrine. Unlike a traditional fair use scenario, the defendant newspaper was using the trademarked term to describe not its own product, but the plaintiff's. Thus, the factors used to evaluate fair use were inapplicable. The use was nonetheless permissible, we concluded, based on its nominative nature.

We adopted the following test for nominative use:

> First, the product or service in question must be one not readily identifiable without use of the trademark; second, only so much of the mark or marks may be used as is reasonably necessary to identify the product or service; and third, the user must do nothing that would, in conjunction with the mark, suggest sponsorship or endorsement by the trademark holder.[12]

We noted in *New Kids* that a nominative use may also be a commercial one.

In cases in which the defendant raises a nominative use defense, the above three-factor test should be applied instead of the test for likelihood of confusion set forth in [*AMF v.*] *Sleekcraft*.[14] The three-factor test better evaluates the likelihood of confusion in nominative use cases. When a defendant uses a trademark nominally, the trademark will be identical to the plaintiff's mark, at least in terms of the words in question. Thus, application of the *Sleekcraft* test, which focuses on the similarity of the mark used by the plaintiff and the defendant, would lead to the incorrect conclusion that virtually all nominative uses are confusing. The three-factor test—with its requirements that the defendant use marks only when no descriptive substitute exists, use no more of the mark than necessary, and do nothing to suggest sponsorship or endorsement by the mark holder—better addresses concerns regarding the likelihood of confusion in nominative use cases.

We group the uses of PEI's trademarked terms into three for the purpose of applying the test for nominative use. First, we analyze Welles' use of the terms in headlines and banner advertisements. We conclude that

7. *See New Kids on the Block v. New America Publ'g, Inc.*, 971 F.2d 302, 306 (9th Cir. 1992) (describing a nominative use as one that "does not imply sponsorship or endorsement of the product because the mark is used only to describe the thing, rather than to identify its source").

12. *New Kids*, 971 F.2d at 308 (footnote omitted).

14. 599 F.2d at 348–49. [Editors' note: The *Sleekcraft* factors are the 9th Circuit's eight-factor test for likelihood of confusion.]

those uses are clearly nominative. Second, we analyze the use of the terms in the metatags for Welles' website, which we conclude are nominative as well. Finally, we analyze the terms as used in the wallpaper of the website. We conclude that this use is not nominative and remand for a determination of whether it infringes on a PEI trademark.

1. Headlines and banner advertisements.

To satisfy the first part of the test for nominative use, "the product or service in question must be one not readily identifiable without use of the trademark[.]" This situation arises "when a trademark also describes a person, a place or an attribute of a product" and there is no descriptive substitute for the trademark. In such a circumstance, allowing the trademark holder exclusive rights would allow the language to "be depleted in much the same way as if generic words were protectable." In *New Kids*, we gave the example of the trademarked term, "Chicago Bulls." We explained that "one might refer to the 'two-time world champions' or 'the professional basketball team from Chicago,' but it's far simpler (and more likely to be understood) to refer to the Chicago Bulls." Moreover, such a use of the trademark would "not imply sponsorship or endorsement of the product because the mark is used only to describe the thing, rather than to identify its source." Thus, we concluded, such uses must be excepted from trademark infringement law.

The district court properly identified Welles' situation as one which must also be excepted. No descriptive substitute exists for PEI's trademarks in this context. The court explained:

> There is no other way that Ms. Welles can identify or describe herself and her services without venturing into absurd descriptive phrases. To describe herself as the "nude model selected by Mr. Hefner's magazine as its number-one prototypical woman for the year 1981" would be impractical as well as ineffectual in identifying Terri Welles to the public.

We agree. Just as the newspapers in *New Kids* could only identify the band clearly by using its trademarked name, so can Welles only identify herself clearly by using PEI's trademarked title.

The second part of the nominative use test requires that "only so much of the mark or marks may be used as is reasonably necessary to identify the product or service[.]" *New Kids* provided the following examples to explain this element: "[A] soft drink competitor would be entitled to compare its product to Coca–Cola or Coke, but would not be entitled to use Coca–Cola's distinctive lettering." Similarly, in a past case, an auto shop was allowed to use the trademarked term "Volkswagen" on a sign describing the cars it repaired, in part because the shop "did not use Volkswagen's distinctive lettering style or color scheme, nor did he display the encircled 'VW' emblem." Welles' banner advertisements and headlines satisfy this element because they use only the trademarked words, not the font or symbols associated with the trademarks.

The third element requires that the user do "nothing that would, in conjunction with the mark, suggest sponsorship or endorsement by the trademark holder." As to this element, we conclude that aside from the wallpaper, which we address separately, Welles does nothing in conjunction with her use of the marks to suggest sponsorship or endorsement by PEI. The marks are clearly used to describe the title she received from PEI in 1981, a title that helps describe who she is. It would be unreasonable to assume that the Chicago Bulls sponsored a website of Michael Jordan's simply because his name appeared with the appellation "former Chicago Bull." Similarly, in this case, it would be unreasonable to assume that PEI currently sponsors or endorses someone who describes herself as a "Playboy Playmate of the Year in 1981." The designation of the year, in our case, serves the same function as the "former" in our example. It shows that any sponsorship or endorsement occurred in the past.[25]

In addition to doing nothing in conjunction with her use of the marks to suggest sponsorship or endorsement by PEI, Welles affirmatively disavows any sponsorship or endorsement. Her site contains a clear statement disclaiming any connection to PEI. Moreover, the text of the site describes her ongoing legal battles with the company.[26]

For the foregoing reasons, we conclude that Welles' use of PEI's marks in her headlines and banner advertisements is a nominative use excepted from the law of trademark infringement.

Welles includes the terms "playboy" and "playmate" in her metatags. Metatags describe the contents of a website using keywords. Some search engines search metatags to identify websites relevant to a search. Thus, when an internet searcher enters "playboy" or "playmate" into a search engine that uses metatags, the results will include Welles' site.[28] Because Welles' metatags do not repeat the terms extensively, her site will not be at the top of the list of search results. Applying the three-factor test for nominative use, we conclude that the use of the trademarked terms in Welles' metatags is nominative.

As we discussed above with regard to the headlines and banner advertisements, Welles has no practical way of describing herself without using trademarked terms. In the context of metatags, we conclude that she has no practical way of identifying the content of her website without referring to PEI's trademarks.

A large portion of Welles' website discusses her association with Playboy over the years. Thus, the trademarked terms accurately describe the contents of Welles' website, in addition to describing Welles. Forcing Welles and others to use absurd turns of phrase in their metatags, such as

25. We express no opinion regarding whether an individual's use of a current title would suggest sponsorship or endorsement.

26. By noting Welles' affirmative actions, we do not mean to imply that affirmative actions of this type are necessary to establish nominative use. *New Kids* sets forth no such requirement, and we do not impose one here

28. We note that search engines that use their own summaries of websites, or that search the entire text of sites, are also likely to identify Welles' site as relevant to a search for "playboy" or "playmate," given the content of the site.

those necessary to identify Welles, would be particularly damaging in the internet search context. Searchers would have a much more difficult time locating relevant websites if they could do so only by correctly guessing the long phrases necessary to substitute for trademarks. We can hardly expect someone searching for Welles' site to imagine the same phrase proposed by the district court to describe Welles without referring to Playboy—"the nude model selected by Mr. Hefner's organization...." Yet if someone could not remember her name, that is what they would have to do. Similarly, someone searching for critiques of Playboy on the internet would have a difficult time if internet sites could not list the object of their critique in their metatags.

There is simply no descriptive substitute for the trademarks used in Welles' metatags. Precluding their use would have the unwanted effect of hindering the free flow of information on the internet, something which is certainly not a goal of trademark law.[29] Accordingly, the use of trademarked terms in the metatags meets the first part of the test for nominative use.

We conclude that the metatags satisfy the second and third elements of the test as well. The metatags use only so much of the marks as reasonably necessary and nothing is done in conjunction with them to suggest sponsorship or endorsement by the trademark holder. We note that our decision might differ if the metatags listed the trademarked term so repeatedly that Welles' site would regularly appear above PEI's in searches for one of the trademarked terms.

3. *Wallpaper/watermark.*

The background, or wallpaper, of Welles' site consists of the repeated abbreviation "PMOY '81," which stands for "Playmate of the Year 1981."[32] Welles' name or likeness does not appear before or after "PMOY '81." The pattern created by the repeated abbreviation appears as the background of the various pages of the website. Accepting, for the purposes of this appeal, that the abbreviation "PMOY" is indeed entitled to protection, we conclude that the repeated, stylized use of this abbreviation fails the nominative use test.

The repeated depiction of "PMOY '81" is not necessary to describe Welles. "Playboy Playmate of the Year 1981" is quite adequate. Moreover, the term does not even appear to describe Welles—her name or likeness do not appear before or after each "PMOY '81." Because the use of the abbreviation fails the first prong of the nominative use test, we need not apply the next two prongs of the test.

Because the defense of nominative use fails here, and we have already determined that the doctrine of fair use does not apply, we remand to the

29. Admittedly, this hindrance would only occur as to search engines that use metatags to direct their searches.

32. "PMOY" is not itself registered as a trademark. PEI argued before the district court that it is nonetheless protected because it is a well-known abbreviation for the trademarked term "Playmate of the Year." In this court PEI cites one affidavit that supports this argument.

district court. The court must determine whether trademark law protects the abbreviation "PMOY," as used in the wallpaper.

B. Trademark Dilution

The district court granted summary judgment to Welles as to PEI's claim of trademark dilution. We affirm on the ground that all of Welles' uses of PEI's marks, with the exception of the use in the wallpaper which we address separately, are proper, nominative uses. We hold that nominative uses, by definition, do not dilute the trademarks.

Federal law provides protection against trademark dilution:

> The owner of a famous mark shall be entitled, subject to the principles of equity and upon such terms as the court deems reasonable, to an injunction against another person's commercial use in commerce of a mark or trade name, if such use begins after the mark has become famous and causes dilution of the distinctive quality of the mark?

Dilution, which was not defined by the statute, has been described by the courts as "the gradual 'whittling away' of a trademark's value." Traditionally, courts have recognized two forms of dilution: blurring and tarnishment. Blurring occurs when another's use of a mark creates "the possibility that the mark will lose its ability to serve as a unique identifier of the plaintiff's product."[35] Tarnishment, on the other hand, occurs "when a famous mark is improperly associated with an inferior or offensive product or service." As we recognized in Panavision, dilution may occur through uses on the internet as well as elsewhere.

Dilution works its harm not by causing confusion in consumers' minds regarding the source of a good or service, but by creating an association in consumers' minds between a mark and a different good or service. As explained in a First Circuit case, in dilution (as compared to infringement) "an entirely different issue is at stake—not interference with the source signaling function but rather protection from an appropriation of or free riding on the investment [the trademark holder] has made in its [trademark]." Thus, for example, if a cocoa maker began using the "Rolls Royce" mark to identify its hot chocolate, no consumer confusion would be likely to result. Few would assume that the car company had expanded into the cocoa making business. However, the cocoa maker would be capitalizing on the investment the car company had made in its mark. Consumers readily associate the mark with highly priced automobiles of a certain quality. By identifying the cocoa with the Rolls Royce mark, the producer would be capitalizing on consumers' association of the mark with high quality items. Moreover, by labeling a different product "Rolls Royce," the cocoa company would be reducing the ability of the mark to identify the mark holder's product. If someone said, "I'm going to get a Rolls Royce," others could no longer be sure the person was planning on buying an expensive automobile. The person might just be planning on buying a cup of cocoa. Thus, the use

35. *Panavision Int'l, L.P. v. Toeppen,* 141 F.3d 1316, 1326 n. 7 (9th Cir. 1998).

of the mark to identify the hot chocolate, although not causing consumer confusion, would cause harm by diluting the mark.

Uses that do not create an improper association between a mark and a new product but merely identify the trademark holder's products should be excepted from the reach of the anti-dilution statute. Such uses cause no harm. The anti-dilution statute recognizes this principle and specifically excepts users of a trademark who compare their product in "commercial advertising or promotion to identify the competing goods or services of the owner of the famous mark."

For the same reason uses in comparative advertising are excepted from anti-dilution law, we conclude that nominative uses are also excepted. A nominative use, by definition, refers to the trademark holder's product. It does not create an improper association in consumers' minds between a new product and the trademark holder's mark.

When Welles refers to her title, she is in effect referring to a product of PEI's. She does not dilute the title by truthfully identifying herself as its one-time recipient any more than Michael Jordan would dilute the name "Chicago Bulls" by referring to himself as a former member of that team, or the two-time winner of an Academy Award would dilute the award by referring to him or herself as a "two-time Academy Award winner." Awards are not diminished or diluted by the fact that they have been awarded in the past.

Similarly, they are not diminished or diluted when past recipients truthfully identify themselves as such. It is in the nature of honors and awards to be identified with the people who receive them. Of course, the conferrer of such honors and awards is free to limit the honoree's use of the title or references to the award by contract. So long as a use is nominative, however, trademark law is unavailing.

The one exception to the above analysis in this case is Welles' use of the abbreviation "PMOY" on her wallpaper. Because we determined that this use is not nominative, it is not excepted from the anti-dilution provisions. Thus, we reverse as to this issue and remand for further proceedings. We note that if the district court determines that "PMOY" is not entitled to trademark protection, PEI's claim for dilution must fail. The trademarked term, "Playmate of the Year" is not identical or nearly identical to the term "PMOY." Therefore, use of the term "PMOY" cannot, as a matter of law, dilute the trademark "Playmate of the Year."

IV.

Conclusion

For the foregoing reasons, we affirm the district court's grant of summary judgment as to PEI's claims for trademark infringement and trademark dilution, with the sole exception of the use of the abbreviation "PMOY." We reverse as to the abbreviation and remand for consideration of whether it merits protection under either an infringement or a dilution theory.

. . .

QUESTION

Apple Computer Company introduced the iPod MP3 player in October of 2001. It is currently the leading portable MP3 player. Apple filed a trademark application on October 18, 2001 to register "IPOD" as a trademark for portable and handheld electronic devices and associated computer software. Registration issued on April 27, 2004. At the time of Apple's registration, there were several prior registrations for the word "IPOD" for different products, including IPOD Office Furniture, IPOD pulse oximeters, and IPOD financial services. Apple subsequently introduced the iPod Mini, a smaller MP3 player in fruit sherbet colors, and the iPod Photo, a player designed to store and display photos as well as storing and playing music. Apple has not sought registration for "IPOD MINI" or "IPOD PHOTO."

Playboy operates a website at www.playboy.com. In 2004, Playboy introduced a new "iBod" feature, which it made available to the public at www.playboy.com/features/features/ibod. Playboy's iBod site invited members of the public to download 25-image slideshows with pictures of naked women. The site is labeled "**Playboy.com Features iBod—Portable photo technology puts Playboy's sexiest models at your fingertips.**"

The website explains:

> Portable MP3 players and other handheld media toys are this year's must-have geek gadgets. The latest thing is Apple's new-generation iPod—the iPod Photo—which does for pictures what the original iPod did for music. Now you can view individual images or entire slide shows in the palm of your hand at the tap of a button to beautify your dull commute or just to pass the time in the lecture hall.
>
> Playboy has harnessed this latest digital innovation so some of our sexiest girls next door can be added right to your portable player. Simply download this free image gallery to your desktop from Playboy.com and upload it to your iPod Photo handheld device. If iPod Photo is "a feast for the eyes" on its own, it's a veritable ocular orgy now that Playboy.com has dialed up the heat a few notches.

Two slideshows are available at no cost. To download additional slideshows, it is necessary to join the Playboy Cyber Club for $19.95 per month. Is Playboy's "iBod" site actionable under the Lanham Act?

B. PROMOTIONAL GOODS

Page 851. Delete *Boston Professional Hockey Ass'n v. Dallas Cap & Emblem*, *International Order of Job's Daughters v. Lindeburg & Co.*, and questions following, and substitute the following Note:

The widespread use of trademarks on promotional products has posed analytically difficult issues for courts applying the likelihood of confusion standard. In *Boston Professional Hockey Association v. Dallas Cap and Emblem*, 510 F.2d 1004 (5th Cir.), *cert. denied*, 423 U.S. 868 (1975), the Court of Appeals for the Fifth Circuit enjoined the unlicensed duplication of sports logos on embroidered emblems, but found it difficult to articulate precisely what consumers might be likely to be confused about:

> The confusion question here is conceptually difficult. It can be said that the public buyer knew that the emblems portrayed the teams' symbols. Thus, it can be argued, the buyer is not confused or deceived. This argument misplaces the purpose of the confusion requirement. The confusion or deceit requirement is met by the fact that the defendant duplicated the protected trademarks and sold them to the public knowing that the public would identify them as being the teams' trademarks. The certain knowledge of the buyer that the source and origin of the trademark symbols were in plaintiffs satisfies the requirement of the act. The argument that confusion must be as to the source of the manufacture of the emblem itself is unpersuasive, where the trademark, originated by the team, is the triggering mechanism for the sale of the emblem.

In *International Order of Job's Daughters v. Lindeburg & Co.*, 633 F.2d 912 (9th Cir. 1980), *cert. denied*, 452 U.S. 941 (1981), the Court of Appeals for the Ninth Circuit criticized *Boston Hockey*'s reasoning:

> Interpreted expansively, *Boston Hockey* holds that a trademark's owner has a complete monopoly over its use, including its functional use, in commercial merchandising. But our reading of the Lanham Act and its legislative history reveals no congressional design to bestow such broad property rights on trademark owners. Its scope is much narrower: to protect consumers against deceptive designations of the origin of goods and, conversely, to enable producers to differentiate their products from those of others.... The *Boston Hockey* decision transmogrifies this narrow protection into a broad monopoly. It does so by injecting its evaluation of the equities between the parties and of the desirability of bestowing broad property rights on trademark owners. A trademark is, of course, a form of business property. But the "property right" or protection accorded a trademark owner can only be understood in the context of trademark law and its purposes. A trademark owner has a property right only insofar as is necessary to prevent consumer confusion as to who produced the goods and to facilitate differentiation of the trademark owner's goods. The *Boston Hockey* court decided that broader protection was desirable. In our view, this extends the protection beyond that intended by Congress and beyond that accorded by any other court.

In *Job's Daughters*, the Plaintiff, an international federation of Masonic girls clubs, sued a jewelry manufacturer for unlicensed reproduction and sale of the organization's emblem on jewelry. The Ninth Circuit held that, in the context of jewelry, the emblem was functional because it signified the wearer's affiliation with the organization, rather than the producer of the jewelry:

> We conclude from our examination of the trial judge's findings and of the underlying evidence that Lindeburg was not using the Job's Daughters name and emblem as trademarks. The insignia were a prominent feature of each item so as to be visible to others when worn, allowing the wearer to publicly express her allegiance to the organization. Lindeburg never designated the merchandise as "official" Job's Daughters' merchandise or otherwise affirmatively indicated sponsorship. Job's Daughters did not show a single instance in which a customer was misled about the origin, sponsorship, or endorsement of Lindeburg's jewelry, nor that it received any complaints about Lindeburg's wares. Finally, there was evidence that many other jewelers sold unlicensed Job's Daughters jewelry, implying that consumers did not ordinarily purchase their fraternal jewelry from only "official" sources. We conclude that Job's Daughters did not meet its burden of proving that a typical buyer of Lindeburg's merchandise would think that the jewelry was produced, sponsored, or endorsed by the organization. The name and emblem were functional aesthetic components of the product, not trademarks. There could be, therefore, no infringement.

Neither analysis seems satisfying. Should the result turn on whether the public believes that promotional products bearing a trademark require the trademark owners' permission? Should it matter whether consumers care about the source of the promotional good? If Dallas Cap and Emblem may not sell embroidered hockey team emblems without a license from the National Hockey League, may a motion picture studio make a film about an NHL hockey player without a license? Does it matter if the player in the film wears a recognizable team uniform? Does ESPN require a license to show pictures of hockey players in their uniforms in its coverage of hockey games? Should the same analysis apply to hats or tee shirts bearing the trademarks of perfume or cigarette manufacturers?

Page 860. Renumber the question following the excerpt from *Trademarks Unplugged* Question 1, and add the following Question 2:

2. The Apple Computer Corporation advertises its iPod MP3 player with an ad campaign that features black silhouettes of happy iPod customers wearing white iPods against a brightly colored background. Apple has used this theme for print ads, web ads, billboards and television commercials. The ad campaign has been very well received.

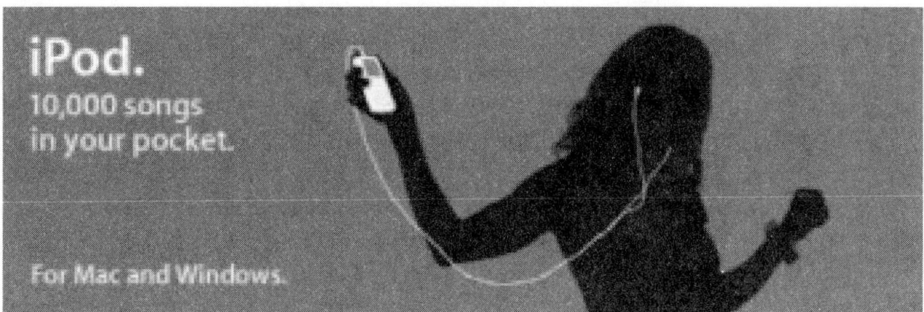

Recently, three Apple iPod fans launched a small business in which they will take any digital photograph and turn it into a silhouette styled to resemble an iPod advertisement. They charge $20 for each photo, and offer their service from a website at www.ipodmyphoto.com. Customers can upload digital photos using the website, pay with a credit card, and download the "iPod-ized" versions a week later. Editing the image to add an iPod, complete with earbud wires, is optional, and carries no additional charge. Business has been brisk. The majority of the orders involve pictures of babies and children, pets, and recently married couples. The website includes several sample photographs:

The service has neither sought nor received permission from Apple for any of its activities. Small print at the bottom of the ipodmyphoto.com web page explains: "*iPod is the property of Apple Computer. iPod My Photo is not affiliated with Apple Computer in any way except that we love iPods.*" Can Apple secure an injunction against the service? If not, why not?

Page 874. Replace the Problem with the following Question:

QUESTION

Detroit Free Press

R·E·S·P·E·C·T!

Pistons earn it with Game 5 blowout

On June 15 2004, the Detroit Pistons stunned basketball fans by winning the NBA Basketball championship against the heavily favored Los Angeles Lakers. The Detroit Free Press celebrated the victory with a story splashed across its front page, headlined "R–E–S–P–E–C–T." The story featured a large image of members of the team, in their uniforms, at the end the game. To commemorate the event, the Free Press created souvenir posters and tee-shirts bearing a reproduction of the front page of its June 16 paper. The Free Press offers the posters and tee shirts for sale at its website and, on the day of the Pistons victory parade, dispatched 20 teenagers to sell tee-shirts to fans in the crowd. The Pistons have objected to the sale of tee-shirts and posters bearing Pistons and NBA logos, insisting that the Free Press is not entitled to reproduce Pistons and NBA marks outside of the newspaper. The Free Press claims it has a right to sell images of its front page whether the images are presented on newsprint, on cotton, or in any other medium. What are the best arguments to be made on the Pistons' behalf? How should the Free Press respond to them?

C. PARODY

Page 893. Replace *Mattel v. MCA* with the following opinion:

Mattel, Inc. v. Universal Music International

296 F.3d 894 (9th Cir. 2002), *cert. denied*, 537 U.S. 1171, 123 S.Ct. 993 (2003).

■ KOZINSKI, CIRCUIT JUDGE:

If this were a sci-fi melodrama, it might be called Speech–Zilla meets Trademark Kong.

I

Barbie was born in Germany in the 1950s as an adult collector's item. Over the years, Mattel transformed her from a doll that resembled a

"German street walker," as she originally appeared, into a glamorous, long-legged blonde. Barbie has been labeled both the ideal American woman and a bimbo. She has survived attacks both psychic (from feminists critical of her fictitious figure) and physical (more than 500 professional makeovers). She remains a symbol of American girlhood, a public figure who graces the aisles of toy stores throughout the country and beyond. With Barbie, Mattel created not just a toy but a cultural icon.

With fame often comes unwanted attention. Aqua is a Danish band that has, as yet, only dreamed of attaining Barbie-like status. In 1997, Aqua produced the song Barbie Girl on the album Aquarium. In the song, one bandmember impersonates Barbie, singing in a high-pitched, doll-like voice; another bandmember, calling himself Ken, entices Barbie to "go party." ... Barbie Girl singles sold well and, to Mattel's dismay, the song made it onto Top 40 music charts.

Mattel brought this lawsuit against the music companies who produced, marketed and sold Barbie Girl ... (collectively, "MCA"). MCA in turn ... brought a defamation claim against Mattel for statements Mattel made about MCA while this lawsuit was pending. The district court concluded it had jurisdiction over the foreign defendants and under the Lanham Act, and granted MCA's motion for summary judgment on Mattel's federal and state-law claims for trademark infringement and dilution. The district court also granted Mattel's motion for summary judgment on MCA's defamation claim.

Mattel appeals the district court's ruling that Barbie Girl is a parody of Barbie and a nominative fair use; that MCA's use of the term Barbie is not likely to confuse consumers as to Mattel's affiliation with Barbie Girl or dilute the Barbie mark; and that Mattel cannot assert an unfair competition claim under the Paris Convention for the Protection of Industrial Property. MCA cross-appeals the grant of summary judgment on its defamation claim as well as the district court's jurisdictional holdings.

. . .

III

A. A trademark is a word, phrase or symbol that is used to identify a manufacturer or sponsor of a good or the provider of a service. *See New Kids on the Block v. News Am. Publ'g, Inc.*, 971 F.2d 302, 305 (9th Cir. 1992). It's the owner's way of preventing others from duping consumers into buying a product they mistakenly believe is sponsored by the trademark owner. A trademark "informs people that trademarked products come from the same source." *Id.* at 305 n.2. Limited to this core purpose—avoiding confusion in the marketplace—a trademark owner's property rights play well with the First Amendment. "Whatever first amendment rights you may have in calling the brew you make in your bathtub 'Pepsi' are easily outweighed by the buyer's interest in not being fooled into buying it." *Trademarks Unplugged*, 68 N.Y.U.L. Rev. 960, 973 (1993).

The problem arises when trademarks transcend their identifying purpose. Some trademarks enter our public discourse and become an integral part of our vocabulary. How else do you say that something's "the Rolls Royce of its class?" What else is a quick fix, but a Band–Aid? Does the average consumer know to ask for aspirin as "acetyl salicylic acid?" *See Bayer Co. v. United Drug Co.*, 272 F. 505, 510 (S.D.N.Y. 1921). Trademarks often fill in gaps in our vocabulary and add a contemporary flavor to our expressions. Once imbued with such expressive value, the trademark becomes a word in our language and assumes a role outside the bounds of trademark law.

Our likelihood-of-confusion test, *see AMF Inc. v. Sleekcraft Boats*, 599 F.2d 341, 348–49 (9th Cir. 1979), generally strikes a comfortable balance between the trademark owner's property rights and the public's expressive interests. But when a trademark owner asserts a right to control how we express ourselves—when we'd find it difficult to describe the product any other way (as in the case of aspirin), or when the mark (like Rolls Royce) has taken on an expressive meaning apart from its source-identifying function—applying the traditional test fails to account for the full weight of the public's interest in free expression.

The First Amendment may offer little protection for a competitor who labels its commercial good with a confusingly similar mark, but "trademark rights do not entitle the owner to quash an unauthorized use of the mark by another who is communicating ideas or expressing points of view." *L.L. Bean, Inc. v. Drake Publishers, Inc.*, 811 F.2d 26, 29 (1st Cir. 1987). Were we to ignore the expressive value that some marks assume, trademark rights would grow to encroach upon the zone protected by the First Amendment. *See Yankee Publ'g, Inc. v. News Am. Publ'g, Inc.*, 809 F. Supp. 267, 276 (S.D.N.Y. 1992) ("When unauthorized use of another's mark is part of a communicative message and not a source identifier, the First Amendment is implicated in opposition to the trademark right."). Simply put, the trademark owner does not have the right to control public discourse whenever the public imbues his mark with a meaning beyond its source-identifying function. *See Anti–Monopoly, Inc. v. Gen. Mills Fun Group*, 611 F.2d 296, 301 (9th Cir. 1979) ("It is the source-denoting function which trademark laws protect, and nothing more.").

B. There is no doubt that MCA uses Mattel's mark: Barbie is one half of Barbie Girl. But Barbie Girl is the title of a song about Barbie and Ken, a reference that—at least today—can only be to Mattel's famous couple. We expect a title to describe the underlying work, not to identify the producer, and Barbie Girl does just that.

The Barbie Girl title presages a song about Barbie, or at least a girl like Barbie. The title conveys a message to consumers about what they can expect to discover in the song itself; it's a quick glimpse of Aqua's take on their own song. The lyrics confirm this: The female singer, who calls herself Barbie, is "a Barbie girl, in [her] Barbie world." She tells her male counterpart (named Ken), "Life in plastic, it's fantastic. You can brush my hair, undress me everywhere/Imagination, life is your creation." And off they go to "party." The song pokes fun at Barbie and the values that Aqua contends she represents. *See Cliffs Notes, Inc. v. Bantam Doubleday Dell Publ'g Group*, 886 F.2d 490, 495–96 (2d Cir. 1989). The female singer explains, "I'm a blond bimbo girl, in a fantasy world/Dress me up, make it tight, I'm your dolly."

The song does not rely on the Barbie mark to poke fun at another subject but targets Barbie herself. *See Campbell v. Acuff–Rose Music, Inc.*, 510 U.S. 569, 580, 127 L. Ed. 2d 500, 114 S. Ct. 1164 (1994); *see also Dr. Seuss Ents., L.P. v. Penguin Books USA, Inc.*, 109 F.3d 1394, 1400 (9th Cir. 1997). This case is therefore distinguishable from *Dr. Seuss*, where we held that the book *The Cat NOT in the Hat!* borrowed Dr. Seuss's trademarks and lyrics to get attention rather than to mock *The Cat in the Hat!* The defendant's use of the Dr. Seuss trademarks and copyrighted works had "no critical bearing on the substance or style of" *The Cat in the Hat!*, and therefore could not claim First Amendment protection. *Id.* at 1401. *Dr. Seuss* recognized that, where an artistic work targets the original and does not merely borrow another's property to get attention, First Amendment interests weigh more heavily in the balance. *See id.* at 1400–02; *see also Harley–Davidson, Inc. v. Grottanelli*, 164 F.3d 806, 812–13 (2d Cir. 1999) (a parodist whose expressive work aims its parodic commentary at a trademark is given considerable leeway, but a claimed parodic use that makes no comment on the mark is not a permitted trademark parody use).

The Second Circuit has held that "in general the [Lanham] Act should be construed to apply to artistic works only where the public interest in avoiding consumer confusion outweighs the public interest in free expression." *Rogers v. Grimaldi*, 875 F.2d 994, 999 (2d Cir. 1989); *see also Cliffs Notes*, 886 F.2d at 494 (quoting *Rogers*, 875 F.2d at 999). *Rogers* considered a challenge by the actress Ginger Rogers to the film *Ginger and Fred.* The movie told the story of two Italian cabaret performers who made a living by imitating Ginger Rogers and Fred Astaire. Rogers argued that the film's title created the false impression that she was associated with it.

At first glance, Rogers certainly had a point. Ginger was her name, and Fred was her dancing partner. If a pair of dancing shoes had been labeled Ginger and Fred, a dancer might have suspected that Rogers was associated with the shoes (or at least one of them), just as Michael Jordan has endorsed Nike sneakers that claim to make you fly through the air. But Ginger and Fred was not a brand of shoe; it was the title of a movie and, for the reasons explained by the Second Circuit, deserved to be treated differently.

A title is designed to catch the eye and to promote the value of the underlying work. Consumers expect a title to communicate a message about the book or movie, but they do not expect it to identify the publisher or producer. *See Application of Cooper*, 45 C.C.P.A. 923, 254 F.2d 611, 615–16 (C.C.P.A. 1958) (A "title ... identifies a specific literary work, ... and is not associated in the public mind with the ... manufacturer." (internal quotation marks omitted)). If we see a painting titled "Campbell's Chicken Noodle Soup," we're unlikely to believe that Campbell's has branched into the art business. Nor, upon hearing Janis Joplin croon "Oh Lord, won't you buy me a Mercedes–Benz?," would we suspect that she and the carmaker had entered into a joint venture. A title tells us something about the underlying work but seldom speaks to its origin?.

Rogers concluded that literary titles do not violate the Lanham Act "unless the title has no artistic relevance to the underlying work whatsoever, or, if it has some artistic relevance, unless the title explicitly misleads as to the source or the content of the work." *Id.* at 999 (footnote omitted). We agree with the Second Circuit's analysis and adopt the *Rogers* standard as our own.

Applying *Rogers* to our case, we conclude that MCA's use of Barbie is not an infringement of Mattel's trademark. Under the first prong of *Rogers*, the use of Barbie in the song title clearly is relevant to the underlying work, namely, the song itself. As noted, the song is about Barbie and the values Aqua claims she represents. The song title does not explicitly mislead as to the source of the work; it does not, explicitly or otherwise, suggest that it was produced by Mattel. The *only* indication that Mattel might be associated with the song is the use of Barbie in the title; if this were enough to satisfy this prong of the *Rogers* test, it would render *Rogers* a nullity. We therefore agree with the district court that MCA was entitled to summary judgment on this ground. We need not consider whether the district court was correct in holding that MCA was also entitled to summary judgment because its use of Barbie was a nominative fair use.[1]

IV

Mattel separately argues that, under the Federal Trademark Dilution Act ("FTDA"), MCA's song dilutes the Barbie mark in two ways: It diminishes the mark's capacity to identify and distinguish Mattel products, and tarnishes the mark because the song is inappropriate for young girls. *See* 15 U.S.C. § 1125(c); *see also Panavision Int'l, L.P. v. Toeppen*, 141 F.3d 1316, 1324 (9th Cir. 1998).

"Dilution" refers to the "whittling away of the value of a trademark" when it's used to identify different products. 4 J. Thomas McCarthy, *McCarthy on Trademarks and Unfair Competition* § 24.67 at 24–120; § 24.70 at 24–122 (2001). For example, Tylenol snowboards, Netscape sex shops and Harry Potter dry cleaners would all weaken the "commercial magnetism" of these marks and diminish their ability to evoke their original associations. Ralph S. Brown, Jr., *Advertising and the Public Interest: Legal Protection of Trade Symbols*, 57 Yale L.J. 1165, 1187 (1948), *reprinted* in 108 Yale L.J. 1619 (1999). These uses dilute the selling power of these trademarks by blurring their "uniqueness and singularity," Frank

1. The likelihood-of-confusion test also governs Mattel's state law claims of unfair competition. *Cleary* v. *News Corporation*, 30 F.3d 1255, 1262–63 (9th Cir. 1994) (citing *Academy of Motion Picture Arts & Sciences* v. *Creative House Promotions, Inc.*, 944 F.2d 1446, 1457 (9th Cir. 1991)). Therefore, the district court properly granted summary judgment on these claims as well.

I. Schechter, *The Rational Basis of Trademark Protection*, 40 Harv. L. Rev. 813, 831 (1927), and/or by tarnishing them with negative associations.

By contrast to trademark infringement, the injury from dilution usually occurs when consumers aren't confused about the source of a product: Even if no one suspects that the maker of analgesics has entered into the snowboard business, the Tylenol mark will now bring to mind two products, not one. Whereas trademark law targets "interference with the source signaling function" of trademarks, dilution protects owners "from an appropriation of or free riding on" the substantial investment that they have made in their marks. *I.P. Lund Trading ApS v. Kohler Co.*, 163 F.3d 27, 50 (1st Cir. 1998).

Originally a creature of state law, dilution received nationwide recognition in 1996 when Congress amended the Lanham Act by enacting the FTDA.[2] The statute protects "the owner of a famous mark ... against another person's commercial use in commerce of a mark or trade name, if such use begins after the mark has become famous and causes dilution of the distinctive quality of the mark." 15 U.S.C. § 1125(c). Dilutive uses are prohibited unless they fall within one of the three statutory exemptions discussed below. *See* pp. 10495–96 *infra*. For a lucid and scholarly discussion of the statutory terms, as well as the purposes of the federal dilution statute, we refer the reader to Judge Leval's opinion in *Nabisco, Inc. v. PF Brands, Inc.*, 191 F.3d 208, 214–17 (2d Cir. 1999). Barbie easily qualifies under the FTDA as a famous and distinctive mark, and reached this status long before MCA began to market the Barbie Girl song. The commercial success of Barbie Girl establishes beyond dispute that the Barbie mark satisfies each of these elements.

We are also satisfied that the song amounts to a "commercial use in commerce." Although this statutory language is ungainly, its meaning seems clear: It refers to a use of a famous and distinctive mark to sell goods other than those produced or authorized by the mark's owner. *Panavision*, 141 F.3d at 1324–25. That is precisely what MCA did with the Barbie mark: It created and sold to consumers in the marketplace commercial products (the Barbie Girl single and the Aquarium album) that bear the Barbie mark.

MCA's use of the mark is dilutive. MCA does not dispute that, while a reference to Barbie would previously have brought to mind only Mattel's doll, after the song's popular success, some consumers hearing Barbie's name will think of both the doll and the song, or perhaps of the song only. This is a classic blurring injury and is in no way diminished by the fact that the song itself refers back to Barbie the doll. To be dilutive, use of the mark need not bring to mind the junior user alone. The distinctiveness of the

2. Even at the state level, dilution is of relatively recent vintage. The first anti-dilution statute was enacted in Massachusetts in 1947, *see* Mass. Gen. Laws Ann. Ch. 110B, § 12 (West 1992). By the time the FTDA was enacted in 1996, only twenty-six states had anti-dilution statutes on the books. *See* 4 *McCarthy* § 24:80 at 24–136.2 n.2; H.R. Rep. No. 104–374, at 3–4 (1995), *reprinted in* 1995 U.S.C.C.A.N. 1029, 1030–31.

mark is diminished if the mark no longer brings to mind the senior user alone.

We consider next the applicability of the FTDA's three statutory exemptions. These are uses that, though potentially dilutive, are nevertheless permitted: comparative advertising; news reporting and commentary; and noncommercial use. 15 U.S.C. § 1125(c)(4)(B). The first two exemptions clearly do not apply; only the exemption for noncommercial use need detain us.

A "noncommercial use" exemption, on its face, presents a bit of a conundrum because it seems at odds with the earlier requirement that the junior use be a "commercial use in commerce." If a use has to be commercial in order to be dilutive, how then can it also be noncommercial so as to satisfy the exception of section 1125(c)(4)(B)? If the term "commercial use" had the same meaning in both provisions, this would eliminate one of the three statutory exemptions defined by this subsection, because any use found to be dilutive would, of necessity, not be noncommercial.

Such a reading of the statute would also create a constitutional problem, because it would leave the FTDA with no First Amendment protection for dilutive speech other than comparative advertising and news reporting. This would be a serious problem because the primary (usually exclusive) remedy for dilution is an injunction.[5] As noted above, tension with the First Amendment also exists in the trademark context, especially where the mark has assumed an expressive function beyond mere identification of a product or service. *See* pp. 10487–89 *supra*; *New Kids on the Block v. News Am. Publ'g, Inc.*, 971 F.2d 302, 306–08 (9th Cir. 1992). These concerns apply with greater force in the dilution context because dilution lacks two very significant limitations that reduce the tension between trademark law and the First Amendment.

First, depending on the strength and distinctiveness of the mark, trademark law grants relief only against uses that are likely to confuse. *See* 5 *McCarthy* § 30:3 at 30–8 to 30–11; *Restatement* § 35 cmt. c at 370. A trademark injunction is usually limited to uses within one industry or several related industries. Dilution law is the antithesis of trademark law in this respect, because it seeks to protect the mark from association in the public's mind with wholly unrelated goods and services. The more remote the good or service associated with the junior use, the more likely it is to cause dilution rather than trademark infringement. A dilution injunction, by contrast to a trademark injunction, will generally sweep across broad vistas of the economy.

Second, a trademark injunction, even a very broad one, is premised on the need to prevent consumer confusion. This consumer protection rationale—averting what is essentially a fraud on the consuming public—is wholly consistent with the theory of the First Amendment, which does not protect commercial fraud. *Cent. Hudson Gas & Elec. v. Pub. Serv. Comm'n*,

5. The FTDA provides for both injunctive relief and damages, but the latter is only available if plaintiff can prove a willful intent to dilute. 15 U.S.C. § 1125(c)(2).

447 U.S. 557, 566, 65 L. Ed. 2d 341, 100 S. Ct. 2343 (1980); *see Thompson v. W. States Med. Ctr.*, 152 L. Ed. 2d 563, 122 S. Ct. 1497 (2002) (applying *Central Hudson*). Moreover, avoiding harm to consumers is an important interest that is independent of the senior user's interest in protecting its business.

Dilution, by contrast, does not require a showing of consumer confusion, 15 U.S.C. § 1127, and dilution injunctions therefore lack the built-in First Amendment compass of trademark injunctions. In addition, dilution law protects only the distinctiveness of the mark, which is inherently less weighty than the dual interest of protecting trademark owners and avoiding harm to consumers that is at the heart of every trademark claim.

Fortunately, the legislative history of the FTDA suggests an interpretation of the "noncommercial use" exemption that both solves our interpretive dilemma and diminishes some First Amendment concerns: "Noncommercial use" refers to a use that consists entirely of noncommercial, or fully constitutionally protected, speech. *See* 2 Jerome Gilson *et al.*, *Trademark Protection and Practice* § 5.12[1][c][vi] at 5–240 (this exemption "is intended to prevent the courts from enjoining speech that has been recognized to be [fully] constitutionally protected," "such as parodies"). Where, as here, a statute's plain meaning "produces an absurd, and perhaps unconstitutional, result[, it is] entirely appropriate to consult all public materials, including the background of [the statute] and the legislative history of its adoption." *Green v. Bock Laundry Mach. Co.*, 490 U.S. 504, 527, 104 L. Ed. 2d 557, 109 S. Ct. 1981 (1989) (Scalia, J., concurring).

The legislative history bearing on this issue is particularly persuasive. First, the FTDA's sponsors in both the House and the Senate were aware of the potential collision with the First Amendment if the statute authorized injunctions against protected speech. Upon introducing the counterpart bills, sponsors in each house explained that the proposed law "will not prohibit or threaten noncommercial expression, such as parody, satire, editorial and other forms of expression that are not a part of a commercial transaction." 141 Cong. Rec. S19306–10, S19310 (daily ed. Dec. 29, 1995) (statement of Sen. Hatch); 141 Cong. Rec. H14317–01, H14318 (daily ed. Dec. 12, 1995) (statement of Rep. Moorhead). The House Judiciary Committee agreed in its report on the FTDA. H.R. Rep. No. 104–374, at 4 (1995), *reprinted* in 1995 U.S.C.C.A.N. 1029, 1031 ("The bill will not prohibit or threaten 'noncommercial' expression, as that term has been defined by the courts.").[6]

6. Our interpretation of the noncommercial use exemption does not eliminate all tension between the FTDA and the First Amendment because the exemption does not apply to commercial speech, which enjoys "qualified but nonetheless substantial protection." *Bolger [v, Youngs Drugs Prods Corp.]*, 463 U.S. at 68 (applying *Central Hudson Gas & Electric Corp.* v. *Pub. Serv. Comm'n*, 447 U.S. 557, 65 L. Ed. 2d 341, 100 S. Ct. 2343 (1980)). *See also Thompson* v. *W. States Med. Ctr.*, 152 L. Ed. 2d 563, 122 S. Ct. 1497, 1503–04 (2002) (same). It is entirely possible that a dilution injunction against purely commercial speech would run afoul of the First Amendment. Because that question is not presented here, we do not address it.

The FTDA's section-by-section analysis presented in the House and Senate suggests that the bill's sponsors relied on the "noncommercial use" exemption to allay First Amendment concerns. H.R. Rep. No. 104–374, at 8, *reprinted* in 1995 U.S.C.C.A.N. 1029, 1035 (the exemption "expressly incorporates the concept of 'commercial' speech from the 'commercial speech' doctrine, and proscribes dilution actions that seek to enjoin use of famous marks in 'non-commercial' uses (such as consumer product reviews)"); 141 Cong. Rec. S19306–10, S19311 (daily ed. Dec. 29, 1995) (the exemption "is consistent with existing case law[, which] recognizes that the use of marks in certain forms of artistic and expressive speech is protected by the First Amendment"). At the request of one of the bill's sponsors, the section-by-section analysis was printed in the Congressional Record. 141 Cong. Rec. S19306–10, S19311 (daily ed. Dec. 29, 1995). Thus, we know that this interpretation of the exemption was before the Senate when the FTDA was passed, and that no senator rose to dispute it.

To determine whether Barbie Girl falls within this exemption, we look to our definition of commercial speech under our First Amendment caselaw. See H.R. Rep. No. 104–374, at 8, *reprinted* in 1995 U.S.C.C.A.N. 1029, 1035 (the exemption "expressly incorporates the concept of 'commercial' speech from the 'commercial speech' doctrine"); 141 Cong. Rec. S19306–10, S19311 (daily ed. Dec. 29, 1995) (the exemption "is consistent with existing [First Amendment] case law"). "Although the boundary between commercial and noncommercial speech has yet to be clearly delineated, the 'core notion of commercial speech' is that it 'does no more than propose a commercial transaction.'" *Hoffman v. Capital Cities/ABC, Inc.*, 255 F.3d 1180, 1184 (9th Cir. 2001) (quoting *Bolger v. Youngs Drug Prods Corp.*, 463 U.S. 60, 66, 77 L. Ed. 2d 469, 103 S. Ct. 2875 (1983)). If speech is not "purely commercial"—that is, if it does more than propose a commercial transaction—then it is entitled to full First Amendment protection. *Id.* at 1185–86 (internal quotation marks omitted).

In *Hoffman*, a magazine published an article featuring digitally altered images from famous films. Computer artists modified shots of Dustin Hoffman, Cary Grant, Marilyn Monroe and others to put the actors in famous designers' spring fashions; a still of Hoffman from the movie "Tootsie" was altered so that he appeared to be wearing a Richard Tyler evening gown and Ralph Lauren heels. Hoffman, who had not given permission, sued under the Lanham Act and for violation of his right to publicity. *Id.* at 1183.

The article featuring the altered image clearly served a commercial purpose: "to draw attention to the for-profit magazine in which it appeared" and to sell more copies. *Id.* at 1186. Nevertheless, we held that the article was fully protected under the First Amendment because it included protected expression: "humor" and "visual and verbal editorial comment on classic films and famous actors." *Id.* at 1185 (internal quotation marks omitted). Because its commercial purpose was "inextricably entwined with [these] expressive elements," the article and accompanying photographs enjoyed full First Amendment protection. *Id.*

Hoffman controls: Barbie Girl is not purely commercial speech, and is therefore fully protected. To be sure, MCA used Barbie's name to sell copies of the song. However, as we've already observed, *see* pp. 10489–90 *supra*, the song also lampoons the Barbie image and comments humorously on the cultural values Aqua claims she represents. Use of the Barbie mark in the song Barbie Girl therefore falls within the noncommercial use exemption to the FTDA. For precisely the same reasons, use of the mark in the song's title is also exempted.

. . .

VI

After Mattel filed suit, Mattel and MCA employees traded barbs in the press. When an MCA spokeswoman noted that each album included a disclaimer saying that Barbie Girl was a "social commentary [that was] not created or approved by the makers of the doll," a Mattel representative responded by saying, "That's unacceptable. . . . It's akin to a bank robber handing a note of apology to a teller during a heist. [It] neither diminishes the severity of the crime, nor does it make it legal." He later characterized the song as a "theft" of "another company's property."

MCA filed a counterclaim for defamation based on the Mattel representative's use of the words "bank robber," "heist," "crime" and "theft." But all of these are variants of the invective most often hurled at accused infringers, namely "piracy." No one hearing this accusation understands intellectual property owners to be saying that infringers are nautical cutthroats with eyepatches and peg legs who board galleons to plunder cargo. In context, all these terms are nonactionable "rhetorical hyperbole," *Gilbrook v. City of Westminster*, 177 F.3d 839, 863 (9th Cir. 1999). The parties are advised to chill.

AFFIRMED.

Page 900. Replace *Morrison & Foerster LLP v. Wick* with the following case:

Mattel Inc. v. Walking Mountain Productions, 353 F.3d 792 (9th Cir. 2003).

Thomas Forsythe, aka "Walking Mountain Productions," is a self-taught photographer who resides in Kanab, Utah. He produces photographs with social and political overtones. In 1997, Forsythe developed a series of 78 photographs entitled "Food Chain Barbie," in which he depicted Barbie in various absurd and often sexualized positions. Forsythe uses the word "Barbie" in some of the titles of his works. While his works vary, Forsythe generally depicts one or more nude Barbie dolls juxtaposed with vintage kitchen appliances. For example, "Malted Barbie" features a nude Barbie placed on a vintage Hamilton Beach malt machine. "Fondue a la Barbie" depicts Barbie heads in a fondue pot. "Barbie Enchiladas" depicts four Barbie dolls wrapped in tortillas and covered with salsa in a casserole dish in a lit oven.

. . .

Forsythe's market success was limited. He displayed his works at two art festivals—the Park City Art Festival in Park City, Utah, and the Plaza Art Fair in Kansas City, Missouri.[2] He promoted his works through a postcard, a business card, and a website. Forsythe printed 2000 promotional postcards depicting his work, "Barbie Enchiladas," only 500 of which were ever circulated. Of those that were circulated, some were distributed throughout his hometown of Kanab and some to a feminist scholar who used slides of Forsythe's works in her academic presentations. He also sold 180 of his postcards to a friend who owned a book store in Kanab so she could resell them in her bookstore and sold an additional 22 postcards to two other friends. Prior to this lawsuit, Forsythe received only four or five unsolicited calls inquiring about his work. The "Food Chain Barbie" series earned Forsythe total gross income of $3,659.[3]

. . .

On August 23, 1999, Mattel filed this action in the United States District Court for the Central District of California (the "Los Angeles federal district court") against Forsythe, alleging that Forsythe's "Food Chain Barbie" series infringed Mattel's copyrights, trademarks, and trade dress.

. . .

The limited purpose of trademark protections set forth in the Lanham Trade–Mark Act, 15 U.S.C. § 1051 *et. seq.*, is to "avoid confusion in the marketplace" by allowing a trademark owner to "prevent[ ] others from duping consumers into buying a product they mistakenly believe is sponsored by the trademark owner." [*Mattel, Inc. v.*] *MCA* [*Records*, 296 F.3d 894 (9th Cir. 2002)] at 900. Trademark law aims to protect trademark owners from a false perception that they are associated with or endorse a product. . . .

As we recently recognized in *MCA*, however, when marks "transcend their identifying purpose" and "enter public discourse and become an integral part of our vocabulary," they "assume[ ] a role outside the bounds of trademark law." 296 F.3d at 900. Where a mark assumes such cultural significance, First Amendment protections come into play. *Id.* In these situations, "the trademark owner does not have the right to control public discourse whenever the public imbues his mark with a meaning beyond its source-identifying function." *Id. See also New Kids on the Block v. News Am. Publ'g Inc.*, 971 F.2d 302, 307 (9th Cir. 1992).

As we determined in *MCA*, Mattel's "Barbie" mark has taken on such a role in our culture. 296 F.3d at 898–99. In *MCA*, Mattel brought

2. Additionally, Forsythe's works were chosen for display in various exhibitions, including the Dishman Competition at Lamar University in Texas, and the Through the Looking Glass Art Show in Los Alamos, New Mexico. Some of his "Food Chain Barbie" photographs were also selected for exhibition by the Deputy Director and Chief Curator of the Guggenheim Museum of Modern Art in New York.

3. Purchases by Mattel investigators comprised at least half of Forsythe's total sales.

an identical claim against MCA Records, producers of a song entitled "Barbie Girl" that contained lyrics that parodied and mocked Barbie. *296 F.3d* at 894. Recognizing that First Amendment concerns in free expression are particularly present in the realm of artistic works, we rejected Mattel's claim. In doing so, we adopted the Second Circuit's First Amendment balancing test for applying the Lanham Act to titles of artistic works as set forth in *Rogers v. Grimaldi*, 875 F.2d 994, 999 (2d Cir. 1989). *MCA*, 296 F.3d at 902.

. . .

Application of the *Rogers* test here leads to the same result as it did in *MCA*. Forsythe's use of the Barbie mark is clearly relevant to his work. . . . The Barbie mark in the titles of Forsythe's works and on his website accurately describe the subject of the photographs, which in turn, depict Barbie and target the doll with Forsythe's parodic message. . . . The photograph titles do not explicitly mislead as to Mattel's sponsorship of the works. . . .

Accordingly, the public interest in free and artistic expression greatly outweighs its interest in potential consumer confusion about Mattel's sponsorship of Forsythe's works.

B. *Trade dress*

Mattel also claims that Forsythe misappropriated its trade dress in Barbie's appearance, in violation of the Lanham Act, 15 U.S.C. § 1125. Mattel claims that it possesses a trade dress in the Superstar Barbie head and the doll's overall appearance. The district court concluded that there was no likelihood that the public would be misled into believing that Mattel endorsed Forsythe's photographs despite Forsythe's use of the Barbie figure.

Arguably, the Barbie trade dress also plays a role in our culture similar to the role played by the Barbie trademark—namely, symbolization of an unattainable ideal of femininity for some women. Forsythe's use of the Barbie trade dress, therefore, presumably would present First Amendment concerns similar to those that made us reluctant to apply the Lanham Act as a bar to the artistic uses of Mattel's Barbie trademark in both *MCA* and this case. But we need not decide how the *MCA/Rogers* First Amendment balancing might apply to Forsythe's use of the Barbie trade dress because we find, on a narrower ground, that it qualifies as nominative fair use.

. . .

In the trademark context, we recently held that a defendant's use is *classic* fair use where "a defendant has used the plaintiff's mark *only* to describe his own product, *and not at all to describe the plaintiff's product*." *Cairns*[*v. Franklin Mint*], 292 F.3d at 1151 (emphasis in original). In contrast, a defendant's use of a plaintiff's mark is *nominative* where he or she "used the plaintiff's mark to describe the plaintiff's product, *even if the defendant's ultimate goal is to describe his own product*." *Id.* (emphasis in original). The goal of a nominative use is generally for the "purposes of comparison, criticism [or] point of reference." *New Kids on the Block*, 971 F.2d at 306. These two mutually exclusive forms of fair use are equally applicable here in the trade dress context.

Applying these fair use standards to the trade dress context, we hold that a defendant's use is *classic* fair use where the defendant has used the plaintiff's dress to describe or identify the defendant's own product and not at all to describe or identify the plaintiff's product. Likewise, a defendant's use is *nominative* where he or she used the plaintiff's dress to describe or identify the plaintiff's product, even if the defendant's ultimate goal is to describe or identify his or her own product.

Forsythe's use of the Barbie trade dress is nominative. Forsythe used Mattel's Barbie figure and head in his works to conjure up associations of Mattel, while at the same time to identify his own work, which is a criticism and parody of Barbie. *See Cairns*, 292 F.3d at 1151. Where use of the trade dress or mark is grounded in the defendant's desire to refer to the plaintiff's product as a point of reference for defendant's own work, a use is nominative.

Fair use may be either nominative or classic. *Id.* at 1150. We recognize a fair use defense in claims brought under § 1125 where the use of the trademark "does not imply sponsorship or endorsement of the product because the mark is used only to describe the thing, rather than to identify its source." *New Kids on the Block*, 971 F.2d at 306. Thus, we recently reiterated that, in the trademark context, nominative use becomes nominative *fair use* when a defendant proves three elements:

> First, the plaintiff's product or service in question must be one not readily identifiable without use of the trademark; second, only so much of the mark or marks may be used as is reasonably necessary to identify the plaintiff's product or service; and third, the user must do nothing that would, in conjunction with the mark, suggest sponsorship or endorsement by the trademark holder.

Cairns, 292 F.3d at 1151 (quoting *New Kids on the Block*, 971 F.2d at 308).

. . .

We hold that Forsythe's use of Mattel's Barbie qualifies as nominative fair use. All three elements weigh in favor of Forsythe. Barbie would not be readily identifiable in a photographic work without use of the Barbie likeness and figure. Forsythe used only so much as was necessary to make his parodic use of Barbie readily identifiable, and it is highly unlikely that any reasonable consumer would have believed that Mattel sponsored or was affiliated with his work. The district court's grant of summary judgment to Forsythe on Mattel's trade dress infringement claim was, therefore, proper.

C. *Dilution*

Mattel also appeals the district court's grant of summary judgment on its trademark and dress dilution claims. The district court found that Forsythe was entitled to summary judgment because his use of the Barbie mark and trade dress was parody and thus "his expression is a non-commercial use."

Dilution may occur where use of a trademark "whittles away ... the value of a trademark" by "blurring their uniqueness and singularity" or by "tarnishing them with negative associations." *MCA*, 296 F.3d at 903 (internal citations omitted). However, "tarnishment caused merely by an editorial or artistic parody which satirizes plaintiff's product or its image is not actionable under an anti-dilution statute because of the free speech protections of the First Amendment...." 4 McCarthy, *supra*, § 24:105, at 24–225. A dilution action only applies to purely commercial speech. *MCA*, 296 F.3d at 904. Parody is a form of noncommercial expression if it does more than propose a commercial transaction. *See id.* at 906. Under *MCA*, Forsythe's artistic and parodic work is considered noncommercial speech and, therefore, not subject to a trademark dilution claim.

We reject Mattel's Lanham Act claims and affirm the district court's grant of summary judgment in favor of Forsythe. Mattel cannot use "trademark laws to ... censor all parodies or satires which use [its] name" or dress. *New Kids on the Block*, 971 F.2d at 309.

D. TRADEMARKS AS SPEECH

Page 925. Insert case following *Lucasfilm v. High Frontier:*

MasterCard International Inc. v. Nader 2000 Primary Committee, Inc.

70 U.S.P.Q.2D (BNA) 1046 (S.D.N.Y. 2004).

■ GEORGE B. DANIELS, DISTRICT JUDGE:

. . .

MasterCard, a Delaware corporation with its principal place of business in New York, is a large financial institution that engages in the interchange of funds by credit and debit payment cards through over 23,000 banks and other foreign and domestic member financial institutions. Since Fall of 1997, MasterCard has commissioned the authorship of a series of advertisements that have come to be known as the "Priceless Advertisements." These advertisements feature the names and images of several goods and services purchased by individuals which, with voice overs and visual displays, convey to the viewer the price of each of these items. At the end of each of the Priceless Advertisements a phrase identifying some priceless intangible that cannot be purchased (such as "a day where all you have to do is breathe") is followed by the words or voice over: "Priceless. There are some things money can't buy, for everything else there's MasterCard."

In August 2000, MasterCard became aware that Ralph Nader and his presidential committee were broadcasting an allegedly similar advertisement on television that promoted the presidential candidacy of Ralph Nader in the 2000 presidential election. That political ad included a sequential display of a series of items showing the price of each ("grilled tenderloin for fund-raiser; $1,000 a plate;" "campaign ads filled with half-truths: $10 million;" "promises to special interest groups: over $100 billion"). The advertisement ends with a phrase identifying a priceless intangible that cannot be purchased ("finding out the truth: priceless. There are some things that money can't buy"). The resulting ad (the "Nader ad") was shown on television during a two week period from August 6–17, during the 2000 presidential campaign, and also appeared on the defendants' web site throughout that campaign. Plaintiff sent defendants a letter explaining its concern over the similarity of the commercials, and suggested that defendants broadcast a more "original" advertisement. When plaintiff contacted representatives of defendants a few days later, plaintiff MasterCard advised defendants to cease broadcasting their political advertisement due to its similarity with MasterCard's own commercial advertisement and resulting infringement liability.

When the parties could not come to an agreement, on August 16, 2000, MasterCard filed a complaint alleging the following counts against Ralph Nader and his presidential committee; trademark infringement and false designation of origin in violation of Section 43(a) of the Lanham Act; infringement of a registered trademark in violation of Section 32(1) of the Lanham Act; dilution in violation of Section 43(c) of the Lanham Act; copyright infringement in violation of the Copyright Act; unfair competition; misappropriation; infringement of New York Common Law Trademark Rights; dilution under New York law; and deceptive trade practices. Plaintiff sought a preliminary injunction during the 2000 presidential campaign which was denied by this Court. Thereafter, defendants moved for summary judgment on all nine of plaintiff's counts.

DISCUSSION

. . .

1. Trademark Infringement

MasterCard's first count is based on Section 43(a) of the Trademark Act, 15 U.S.C. Section 1125(a). Plaintiff claims that defendants have used two of MasterCard's service marks—"THERE ARE SOME THINGS MONEY CAN'T BUY. FOR EVERYTHING ELSE THERE'S MASTERCARD," and "PRICELESS" to misrepresent that the 2000 presidential candidacy of Ralph Nader for the office of President of the United States was endorsed by MasterCard. . . .

In trademark infringement cases, the Court must apply the undisputed facts to the balancing test outlined in *Polaroid Corp. v. Polarad Elecs., Corp.*, 287 F.2d 492, 495 (2d Cir. 1961), and may grant summary judgment where it finds, as a matter of law, that there is no likelihood of confusion to the public. . . .

[The court analyzed the *Polaroid* factors. Nader conceded that Mastercard's marks were strong, and that the Nader commercials used "there are some things money can't buy" and "priceless" in a way that created the same look, sound, and impression. The court concluded that there was little similarity between Mastercard's credit card business and Nader's political campaign, and little likelihood of Mastercard's bridging the gap. There was no evidence of actual confusion. The court found no evidence that Ralph Nader intended to pass himself off as associated with Mastercard:]

There is no basis to argue that the Ralph Nader political ad which has the clear intent to criticize other political candidates who accept money from wealthy contributors, at the same time, attempts or intends to imply that he is a political candidate endorsed by MasterCard. There is uncontradicted testimony that neither Ralph Nader, nor his committees, had any such intent

The seventh factor, the quality of defendants' products or services, is of insignificant weight in this case. There is no reasonable comparison to be made between the quality of the products and services provided by MasterCard and the value of defendants' politics. . . .

The eighth and final factor to be weighed is the level of consumer sophistication in either of the relevant markets for credit card services or for political candidates. Unless otherwise demonstrated, it is reasonable to conclude that the general American public is sophisticated enough to distinguish a Political Ad from a commercial advertisement. Rarely, if ever, is there a realistic opportunity to confuse the two. . . .

. . . Thus, after balancing the Polaroid factors, this Court finds that there is no genuine issue of material fact with regard to any likelihood of confusion between MasterCard's Priceless Advertisements and Ralph Nader's Political Ad which could constitute a violation of the Trademark Act.

. . .

3. Dilution

Counts Three and Eight of plaintiff's complaint allege against defendants federal and state dilution of plaintiff's trademarks. The Federal Trademark Dilution Act, 15 U.S.C. § 1125(c) and the New York anti-dilution law, New York Gen. Bus. Law § 360–1, protect against the unauthorized use of marks that impairs the goodwill and value of plaintiff's mark. . . . Under both federal and New York law, dilution can involve either blurring or tarnishment. [Citations]

. . .

The Federal Trademark Dilution Act specifically exempts noncommercial uses of a mark from its coverage. Section 1125(c)(4) provides that "the following shall not be actionable under this section: . . . (B) Noncommercial use of a mark." Therefore, prior to even addressing whether defendants have actually diluted plaintiff's marks under the federal law, the Court must first determine whether defendants' use of the marks is "commercial," and thereby, whether that use is even covered by the statute.

Plaintiff argues that Ralph Nader's Political Ad is commercial in nature even though it neither sells products or services, is not designed to entice consumers to buy products or services, and does not propose any kind of commercial transaction. MasterCard asserts that contributions to the Nader 2000 General Committee "increased from $5125 before the Ad ran to $818,000 in August 2000, after the Ad ran through the 'DONATE ON-LINE' icon or otherwise." ... Although the Nader Ad ran before a large sum of contributions were made to his campaign, plaintiff offers no evidence of a causal connection between the Ad and the contributions. There is nothing in the record other than the inference to be drawn from the proximity in time that advances the notion that the contributions Ralph Nader and his political committee received were a direct result of the Ad.

Even assuming the Nader Ad caused greater contributions to be made to his political campaign, this would not be enough to deem Ralph Nader's Ad "commercial." If so, then presumably, as suggested by defendants, all political campaign speech would also be "commercial speech" since all political candidates collect contributions. Ralph Nader's Political Ad attempts to communicate that other presidential candidates can be bought, but that the "truth," represented by himself, cannot. The Nader Ad is a strong political message which expresses his personal opinion on presidential campaigning. The legislative history of the Lanham Act clearly indicates that Congress did not intend for the Act to chill political speech. In speaking about the amendments to Section 43(a) that expanded what was actionable as deceptive advertisements, one of the new law's sponsors, United States Representative Robert Kastenmeier, pointed out that political advertising and promotion are not meant to be covered by the term "commercial." He stated that the statute

> uses the word "commercial" to describe advertising or promotion for business purposes, whether conducted by for-profit or non-profit organizations or individuals. *Political advertising and promotion is political speech, and therefore not encompassed by the term "commercial."* This is true whether what is being promoted is an individual candidacy for public office, or a particular political issue or point of view ...

134 Cong. Rec. H. 1297 (daily ed. April 13, 1989) (statement of Wisconsin Rep. Kastenmeier) (emphasis added).

Plaintiff MasterCard urges the Court to rely on *United We Stand America, Inc. v. United We Stand, America New York, Inc.*, 128 F.3d 86 (2d Cir. 1997) to conclude that Ralph Nader's activities are "commercial" in nature. That case is not instructive in determining whether or not MasterCard has a basis to bring a claim against defendants under the Federal Trademark Dilution Act. In *United We Stand*, the Court was determining whether a certain political activity fell under the scope and the meaning of the word "services" and "use in commerce" of the Lanham Trademark

Act, § 32(1)(a), 15 U.S.C.A. § 1114(1)(a). That particular section of the Lanham Act does not have a commercial activity requirement, nor does it exempt from liability noncommercial use of a mark. *See Planned Parenthood Federation of America Inc. v. U.S. District Court Southern District of New York*, 42 U.S.P.Q.2d 1430, 1434 (S.D.N.Y. 1997). However, the Federal Trademark Dilution Act, 15 U.S.C.A. § 1125 (c), specifically exempts from the scope of all provisions of Section 1125 the "noncommercial use of a mark." See Id., at 1433.

Though not binding, this Court finds the analysis in *American Family Life Insurance Company v. Hagan, et al.*, 266 F. Supp.2d 682 (N.D.Ohio 2002), to be relevant and persuasive. In that case, similar to the case at hand, the plaintiff, American Family Life Insurance Company, or AFLAC, ran well-known "AFLAC Duck" commercials which featured a white duck quacking the company's name "AFLAC." *Id.*, at 684. One of the defendants was a candidate for Governor of the State of Ohio running against the incumbent Governor Robert Taft. The candidate and his Campaign, developed internet commercials that " 'borrow[ed]' from AFLAC's commercials. Specifically, the internet commercials included a crudely animated character made up of the incumbent Governor's head sitting on the body of a white cartoon duck; the duck quacks 'TaftQuack' several times during each commercial," which defendants ran on their website, www.taftquack.com. *Id.* Defendants' website also contained a link which visitors could use to make campaign contributions. Id. at 686–87. Among other claims, plaintiff sued defendants for federal trademark dilution and moved for a preliminary injunction.

In denying the plaintiff's motion for a preliminary injunction, and finding that the plaintiff was not likely to prevail on its dilution claim, the court also found that defendants' speech was political, rather than commercial. Specifically, the court stated that the candidate was "using a quacking cartoon character, which admittedly brings to mind AFLAC's marks, *as part of his communicative message,* in the context of expressing political speech." *Id.*, at 700 (emphasis in original). The court added that though "the consuming public may associate the AFLAC Duck and the TaftQuack character-a proposition the Court accepts-[this] is an insufficient predicate to support injunctive relief of political speech." *Id.*, at 701. The court further noted that though defendants included in their website a mechanism for visitors to make campaign contributions, "it is arguable whether [the candidate's] speech proposes a commercial transaction at all." *Id.*, at 697. The court stated that defendants' solicitation of contributions, and the resulting making of contributions, "is much more than merely a commercial transaction. Indeed, this exchange is properly classified not as a commercial transaction at all, but completely noncommercial, political speech." *Id.*

This Court finds that Ralph Nader's use of plaintiff's trademarks is not commercial, but instead political in nature and that therefore, it is exempted from coverage by the Federal Trademark Dilution Act. However, even if Ralph Nader's use of plaintiff's trademarks could be deemed commercial in nature, such use did not dilute plaintiff's marks. Defendants do not dispute that plaintiff's marks are famous, distinctive, or that they used plaintiff's marks after such marks became famous. However, there is no evidence in the record that defendants' use of plaintiff's marks actually caused dilution of the distinctiveness of plaintiff's marks. Plaintiff does not offer evidence that defendants' limited use of the Priceless marks lessened its value or the capacity of these marks to identify and distinguish plaintiff's goods or services. Further, plaintiff does not claim, nor is there any evidence in the record, that due to defendant's use of plaintiff's marks, plaintiff altered or lessened its use of the marks to identify MasterCard's products or services.

Count Three of plaintiff's complaint alleging dilution of plaintiff's trademarks is dismissed on defendants' motion for summary judgment. Ralph Nader's use of plaintiff's trademarks is political in nature, not within a commercial context, and is therefore exempted from coverage by the Federal Trademark Dilution Act. Furthermore, there is no evidence on the record that Ralph Nader's use of plaintiff's trademarks diluted plaintiff's trademarks.

Page 932. Substitute the following opinion for the District Court decision in *People for the Ethical Treatment of Animals v. Doughney*:

People for the Ethical Treatment of Animals v. Doughney

263 F.3d 359 (4th Cir. 2001).

■ GREGORY, CIRCUIT JUDGE:

People for the Ethical Treatment of Animals ("PETA") sued Michael Doughney ("Doughney") after he registered the domain name peta.org and created a website called "People Eating Tasty Animals." PETA alleged claims of service mark infringement under 15 U.S.C. § 1114 and Virginia common law, unfair competition under 15 U.S.C. § 1125(a) and Virginia common law, and service mark dilution and cybersquatting under 15 U.S.C. § 1123(c). Doughney appeals the district court's decision granting PETA's motion for summary judgment. . . . Finding no error, we affirm.

I.

PETA is an animal rights organization with more than 600,000 members worldwide. PETA "is dedicated to promoting and heightening public awareness of animal protection issues and it opposes the exploitation of animals for food, clothing, entertainment and vivisection."

Doughney is a former internet executive who has registered many domain names since 1995. For example, Doughney registered domain names such as dubyadot.com, dubyadot.net, deathbush.com, RandallTerry.org (Not Randall Terry for Congress), bwtel.com (BaltimoreWashington Telephone Company), pmrc.org ("People's Manic Repressive Church"), and ex-cult.org (Ex–Cult Archive). At the time the district court issued its summary judgment ruling, Doughney owned 50–60 domain names.

Doughney registered the domain name peta.org in 1995 with Network Solutions, Inc. ("NSI"). When registering the domain name, Doughney represented to NSI that the registration did "not interfere with or infringe upon the rights of any third party," and that a "nonprofit educational organization" called "People Eating Tasty Animals" was registering the domain name. Doughney made these representations to NSI despite knowing that no corporation, partnership, organization or entity of any kind existed or traded under that name. Moreover, Doughney was familiar with PETA and its beliefs and had been for at least 15 years before registering the domain name.

After registering the peta.org domain name, Doughney used it to create a website purportedly on behalf of "People Eating Tasty Animals." Doughney claims he created the website as a parody of PETA. A viewer accessing the website would see the title "People Eating Tasty Animals" in large, bold type. Under the title, the viewer would see a statement that the website was a "resource for those who enjoy eating meat, wearing fur and leather, hunting, and the fruits of scientific research." The website contained links to various meat, fur, leather, hunting, animal research, and other organizations, all of which held views generally antithetical to PETA's views. Another statement on the website asked the viewer whether he/she was "Feeling lost? Offended? Perhaps you should, like, exit immediately." The phrase "exit immediately" contained a hyperlink to PETA's official website.

Doughney's website appeared at "www.peta.org" for only six months in 1995–96. In 1996, PETA asked Doughney to voluntarily transfer the peta.org domain name to PETA because PETA owned the "PETA" mark ("the Mark"), which it registered in 1992. See U.S. Trademark Registration No. 1705,510. When Doughney refused to transfer the domain name to PETA, PETA complained to NSI, whose rules then required it to place the domain name on "hold" pending resolution of Doughney's dispute with PETA.[1] Consequently, Doughney moved the website to www.mtd.com/tasty and added a disclaimer stating that "People Eating Tasty Animals is in no way connected with, or endorsed by, People for the Ethical Treatment of Animals."

In response to Doughney's domain name dispute with PETA, The Chronicle of Philanthropy quoted Doughney as stating that, "if they [PETA] want one of my domains, they should make me an offer." Non–Profit Groups Upset by Unauthorized Use of Their Names on the Internet, THE CHRONICLE OF PHILANTHROPY, Nov. 14, 1996. Doughney does not dispute making this statement. Additionally, Doughney posted the following message on his website on May 12, 1996:

1. When Doughney registered peta.org, he agreed to abide by NSI's Dispute Resolution Policy, which specified that a domain name using a third party's registered trademark was subject to placement on "hold" status.

> "PeTa" has no legal grounds whatsoever to make even the slightest demands of me regarding this domain name registration. If they disagree, they can sue me. And if they don't, well, perhaps they can behave like the polite ladies and gentlemen that they evidently aren't and negotiate a settlement with me.... Otherwise, "PeTa" can wait until the significance and value of a domain name drops to nearly nothing, which is inevitable as each new web search engine comes on-line, because that's how long it's going to take for this dispute to play out.

PETA sued Doughney in 1999, asserting claims for service mark infringement, unfair competition, dilution and cybersquatting. PETA did not seek damages, but sought only to enjoin Doughney's use of the "PETA" Mark and an order requiring Doughney to transfer the peta.org domain name to PETA.

Doughney responded to the suit by arguing that the website was a constitutionally-protected parody of PETA. Nonetheless, the district court granted PETA's motion for summary judgment on June 12, 2000. *People for the Ethical Treatment of Animals, Inc. v. Doughney, 113 F.Supp.2d 915 (E.D. Va. 2000).* The district court rejected Doughney's parody defense, explaining that

> [o]nly after arriving at the "PETA.ORG" web site could the web site browser determine that this was not a web site owned, controlled or sponsored by PETA. Therefore, the two images: (1) the famous PETA name and (2) the "People Eating Tasty Animals" website was not a parody because [they were not] simultaneous.

Id. at 921.

. . .

I.

. . .

A. Trademark Infringement/Unfair Competition

. . .

There is no dispute here that PETA owns the "PETA" Mark, that Doughney used it, and that Doughney used the Mark "in commerce." Doughney disputes the district court's findings that he used the Mark in connection with goods or services and that he used it in a manner engendering a likelihood of confusion.

1.

To use PETA's Mark "in connection with" goods or services, Doughney need not have actually sold or advertised goods or services on the www.peta.org website. Rather, Doughney need only have prevented users from obtaining or using PETA's goods or services, or need only have connected the website to other's goods or services.

While sparse, existing caselaw on infringement and unfair competition in the Internet context clearly weighs in favor of this conclusion. For example, in *OBH, Inc. v. Spotlight Magazine, Inc.*, the plaintiffs owned the "*The Buffalo News*" registered trademark used by the newspaper of the same name. 86 F.Supp.2d 176 (W.D.N.Y. 2000). The defendants registered the domain name thebuffalonews.com and created a website parodying *The Buffalo News* and providing a public forum for criticism of the newspaper. *Id.* at 182. The site contained hyperlinks to other local news sources and a site owned by the defendants that advertised Buffalo-area apartments for rent. *Id.* at 183.

The court held that the defendants used the mark "in connection with" goods or services because the defendants' website was "likely to prevent or hinder Internet users from accessing plaintiffs' services on plaintiffs' own web site." *Id.*

> Prospective users of plaintiffs' services who mistakenly access defendants' web site may fail to continue to search for plaintiffs' web site due to confusion or frustration. Such users, who are presumably looking for the news services provided by the plaintiffs on their web site, may instead opt to select one of the several other news-related hyperlinks contained in defendants' web site. These news-related hyperlinks will directly link the user to other news-related web sites that are in direct competition with plaintiffs in providing news-related services over the Internet. Thus, defendants' action in appropriating plaintiff's mark has a connection to plaintiffs' distribution of its services.

Id. Moreover, the court explained that defendants' use of the plaintiffs' mark was in connection with goods or services because it contained a link to the defendants' apartment-guide website. *Id.*

Similarly, in *Planned Parenthood Federation of America, Inc. v. Bucci*, the plaintiff owned the "Planned Parenthood" mark, but the defendant registered the domain name plannedparenthood.com. 1997 U.S. Dist. LEXIS 3338, 42 U.S.P.Q.2D (BNA) 1430 (S.D.N.Y. 1997). Using the domain name, the defendant created a website containing information antithetical to the plaintiff's views. 42 U.S.P.Q.2D (BNA) at 1435. The court ruled that the defendant used the plaintiff's mark "in connection with" the distribution of services.

> because it is likely to prevent some Internet users from reaching plaintiff's own Internet web site. Prospective users of plaintiff's services who mistakenly access defendant's web site may fail to continue to search for plaintiff's own home page, due to anger, frustration, or the belief that plain tiff's home page does not exist.

Id.

> The same reasoning applies here. As the district court explained, Doughney's use of PETA's Mark in the domain name of his website is likely to prevent Internet users from reaching[PETA's] own Internet web site. The prospective users of[PETA's] services who mistakenly

> access Defendant's web site may fail to continue to search for [PETA's] own home page, due to anger, frustration, or the belief that [PETA's] home page does not exist.

Doughney, 113 F.Supp.2d at 919 (quoting *Bucci,* 1997 U.S. Dist. LEXIS 3338, 42 U.S.P.Q.2D (BNA) at 1435). Moreover, Doughney's web site provides links to more than 30 commercial operations offering goods and services. By providing links to these commercial operations, Doughney's use of PETA's Mark is "in connection with" the sale of goods or services.

2.

The unauthorized use of a trademark infringes the trademark holder's rights if it is likely to confuse an "ordinary consumer" as to the source or sponsorship of the goods. *Anheuser–Busch, Inc. v. L & L Wings, Inc.,* 962 F.2d 316, 318 (4th Cir. 1992) (citing 2 J. McCarthy, *Trademarks and Unfair Competition* § 23:28 (2d ed. 1984)). To determine whether a likelihood of confusion exists, a court should not consider "how closely a fragment of a given use duplicates the trademark," but must instead consider "whether the use in its entirety creates a likelihood of confusion." *Id.* at 319.

Doughney does not dispute that the peta.org domain name engenders a likelihood of confusion between his web site and PETA. Doughney claims, though, that the inquiry should not end with his domain name. Rather, he urges the Court to consider his website in conjunction with the domain name because, together, they purportedly parody PETA and, thus, do not cause a likelihood of confusion.

A "parody" is defined as a "simple form of entertainment conveyed by juxtaposing the irreverent representation of the trademark with the idealized image created by the mark's owner." *L.L. Bean, Inc. v. Drake Publishers, Inc.,* 811 F.2d 26, 34 (1st Cir. 1987). A parody must "convey two simultaneous—and contradictory—messages: that it is the original, but also that it is not the original and is instead a parody." *Cliffs Notes, Inc. v. Bantam Doubleday Dell Publ. Group, Inc.,* 886 F.2d 490, 494 (2d Cir. 1989) (emphasis in original). To the extent that an alleged parody conveys only the first message, "it is not only a poor parody but also vulnerable under trademark law, since the customer will be confused." *Id.* While a parody necessarily must engender some initial confusion, an effective parody will diminish the risk of consumer confusion "by conveying [only] just enough of the original design to allow the consumer to appreciate the point of parody." *Jordache Enterprises, Inc. v. Hogg Wyld, Ltd.,* 828 F.2d 1482, 1486 (10th Cir. 1987).

Looking at Doughney's domain name alone, there is no suggestion of a parody. The domain name peta.org simply copies PETA's Mark, conveying the message that it is related to PETA. The domain name does not convey the second, contradictory message needed to establish a parody—a message that the domain name is not related to PETA, but that it is a parody of PETA.

Doughney claims that this second message can be found in the content of his website. Indeed, the website's content makes it clear that it is not related to PETA. However, this second message is not conveyed simultaneously with the first message, as required to be considered a parody. The domain name conveys the first message; the second message is conveyed only when the viewer reads the content of the website. As the district court explained, "an internet user would not realize that they were not on an official PETA web site until after they had used PETA's Mark to access the web page 'www.peta.org.'" *Doughney*, 113 F.Supp.2d at 921. Thus, the messages are not conveyed simultaneously and do not constitute a parody. *See also Morrison & Foerster LLP v. Wick*, 94 F.Supp.2d 1125 (D. Co. 2000) (defendant's use of plaintiffs' mark in domain name "does not convey two simultaneous and contradictory messages" because "only by reading through the content of the sites could the user discover that the domain names are an attempt at parody"); *Bucci*, 1997 U.S. Dist. LEXIS 3338, 42 U.S.P.Q.2D (BNA) at 1435 (rejecting parody defense because "seeing or typing the 'planned parenthood' mark and accessing the web site are two separate and nonsimultaneous activities"). The district court properly rejected Doughney's parody defense and found that Doughney's use of the peta.org domain name engenders a likelihood of confusion. Accordingly, Doughney failed to raise a genuine issue of material fact regarding PETA's infringement and unfair competition claims.

B. Anticybersquatting Consumer Protection Act

The district court found Doughney liable under the Anticybersquatting Consumer Protection Act ("ACPA"), 15 U.S.C. § 1125(d)(1)(A). To establish an ACPA violation, PETA was required to (1) prove that Doughney had a bad faith intent to profit from using the peta.org domain name, and (2) that the peta.org domain name is identical or confusingly similar to, or dilutive of, the distinctive and famous PETA Mark. 15 U.S.C. § 1125(d)(1)(A).

Doughney makes several arguments relating to the district court's ACPA holding: (1) that PETA did not plead an ACPA claim, but raised it for the first time in its motion for summary judgment; (2) that the ACPA, which became effective in 1999, cannot be applied retroactively to events that occurred in 1995 and 1996; (3) that Doughney did not seek to financially profit from his use of PETA's Mark; and (4) that Doughney acted in good faith.

None of Doughney's arguments are availing.

. . .

Doughney's third argument—that he did not seek to financially profit from registering a domain name using PETA's Mark—also offers him no relief. It is undisputed that Doughney made statements to the press and on his website recommending that PETA attempt to "settle" with him and "make him an offer." The undisputed evidence belies Doughney's argument.

Doughney's fourth argument—that he did not act in bad faith—also is unavailing. Under 15 U.S.C. § 1125(d)(1)(B)(i), a court may consider several factors to determine whether a defendant acted in bad faith,.... In addition to listing ... nine factors, the ACPA contains a safe harbor provision stating that bad faith intent "shall not be found in any case in which the court determines that the person believed and had reasonable grounds to believe that the use of the domain name was fair use or otherwise lawful." 15 U.S.C. § 1225(d)(1)(B)(ii).

The district court reviewed the factors listed in the statute and properly concluded that Doughney (I) had no intellectual property right in peta.org; (II) peta.org is not Doughney's name or a name otherwise used to identify Doughney; (III) Doughney had no prior use of peta.org in connection with the bona fide offering of any goods or services; (IV) Doughney used the PETA Mark in a commercial manner; (V) Doughney "clearly intended to confuse, mislead and divert internet users into accessing his web site which contained information antithetical and therefore harmful to the goodwill represented by the PETA Mark"; (VI) Doughney made statements on his web site and in the press recommending that PETA attempt to "settle" with him and "make him an offer"; (VII) Doughney made false statements when registering the domain name; and (VIII) Doughney registered other domain names that are identical or similar to the marks or names of other famous people and organizations. *People for the Ethical Treatment of Animals,* 113 F.Supp.2d at 920.

Doughney claims that the district court's later ruling denying PETA's motion for attorney fees triggers application of the ACPA's safe harbor provision. In that ruling, the district court stated that

> Doughney registered the domain name because he thought that he had a legitimate First Amendment right to express himself this way. The Court must consider Doughney's state of mind at the time he took the actions in question. Doughney thought he was within his First Amendment rights to create a parody of the plaintiff's organization.

People for the Ethical Treatment of Animals, Inc. v. Doughney, 2000 U.S. Dist. LEXIS 13421, *5, Civil Action No. 99–1336–A, Order at 4 (E.D. Va. Aug. 31, 2000). With its attorney's fee ruling, the district court did not find that Doughney "had reasonable grounds to believe" that his use of PETA's Mark was lawful. It held only that Doughney thought it to be lawful.

Moreover, a defendant "who acts even partially in bad faith in registering a domain name is not, as a matter of law, entitled to benefit from [the ACPA's] safe harbor provision." *Virtual Works, Inc.,* 238 F.3d at 270. Doughney knowingly provided false information to NSI upon registering the domain name, knew he was registering a domain name identical to PETA's Mark, and clearly intended to confuse Internet users into accessing his website, instead of PETA's official website. Considering the evidence of Doughney's bad faith, the safe harbor provision can provide him no relief....

Page 937. Insert the following case after the Questions:

Lamparello v. Falwell

420 F.3d 309 (4th Cir. 2005).

■ DIANA GRIBBON MOTZ, CIRCUIT JUDGE:

Christopher Lamparello appeals the district court's order enjoining him from maintaining a gripe website critical of Reverend Jerry Falwell. For the reasons stated below, we reverse.

I.

Reverend Falwell is "a nationally known minister who has been active as a commentator on politics and public affairs." *Hustler Magazine, Inc. v. Falwell*, 485 U.S. 46, 47, 99 L. Ed. 2d 41, 108 S. Ct. 876 (1988). He holds the common law trademarks "Jerry Falwell" and "Falwell," and the registered trademark "Listen America with Jerry Falwell." Jerry Falwell Ministries can be found online at "www.falwell.com," a website which receives 9,000 hits (or visits) per day.

Lamparello registered the domain name "www.fallwell.com" on February 11, 1999, after hearing Reverend Falwell give an interview "in which he expressed opinions about gay people and homosexuality that [Lamparello] considered ... offensive." Lamparello created a website at that domain name to respond to what he believed were "untruths about gay people." Lamparello's website included headlines such as "Bible verses that Dr. Falwell chooses to ignore" and "Jerry Falwell has been bearing false witness (Exodus 20:16) against his gay and lesbian neighbors for a long time." The site also contained in-depth criticism of Reverend Falwell's views. For example, the website stated:

> Dr. Falwell says that he is on the side of truth. He says that he will preach that homosexuality is a sin until the day he dies. But we believe that if the reverend were to take another thoughtful look at the scriptures, he would discover that they have been twisted around to support an anti-gay political agenda ... at the expense of the gospel.

Although the interior pages of Lamparello's website did not contain a disclaimer, the homepage prominently stated, "This website is NOT affiliated with Jerry Falwell or his ministry"; advised, "If you would like to visit Rev. Falwell's website, you may click here"; and provided a hyperlink to Reverend Falwell's website.

At one point, Lamparello's website included a link to the Amazon.com webpage for a book that offered interpretations of the Bible that Lamparello favored, but the parties agree that Lamparello has never sold goods or services on his website. The parties also agree that "Lamparello's domain name and web site at www.fallwell.com," which received only 200 hits per day, "had no measurable impact on the quantity of visits to [Reverend Falwell's] web site at www.falwell.com."

Nonetheless, Reverend Falwell sent Lamparello letters in October 2001 and June 2003 demanding that he cease and desist from using www.fallwell.com or any variation of Reverend Falwell's name as a domain name. Ultimately, Lamparello filed this action against Reverend Falwell and his ministries (collectively referred to hereinafter as "Reverend Falwell"), seeking a declaratory judgment of noninfringement. Reverend Falwell counter-claimed, alleging trademark infringement under 15 U.S.C. § 1114 (2000), false designation of origin under 15 U.S.C. § 1125(a), unfair competition under 15 U.S.C. § 1126 and the common law of Virginia, and cybersquatting under 15 U.S.C. § 1125(d).

The parties stipulated to all relevant facts and filed cross-motions for summary judgment. The district court granted summary judgment to Reverend Falwell, enjoined Lamparello from using Reverend Falwell's mark at www.fallwell.com, and required Lamparello to transfer the domain name to Reverend Falwell. However, the court denied Reverend Falwell's request for statutory damages or attorney fees, reasoning that the "primary motive" of Lamparello's website was "to put forth opinions on issues that were contrary to those of [Reverend Falwell]" and "not to take away monies or to profit.".

Lamparello appeals the district court's order; Reverend Falwell cross-appeals the denial of statutory damages and attorney fees. We review de novo a district court's ruling on cross-motions for summary judgment. *See People for the Ethical Treatment of Animals v. Doughney*, 263 F.3d 359, 364 (4th Cir. 2001) [hereinafter "PETA"].

II.

We first consider Reverend Falwell's claims of trademark infringement and false designation of origin.

A.

. . .

Trademark law serves the important functions of protecting product identification, providing consumer information, and encouraging the production of quality goods and services. *See Qualitex Co. v. Jacobson Prods. Co.*, 514 U.S. 159, 164, 131 L. Ed. 2d 248, 115 S. Ct. 1300 (1995). But protections " 'against unfair competition' " cannot be transformed into " 'rights to control language.' " *CPC Int'l, Inc. v. Skippy Inc.*, 214 F.3d 456, 462 (4th Cir. 2000) (*quoting* Mark A. Lemley, The Modern Lanham Act and the Death of Common Sense, 108 Yale L.J. 1687, 1710–11 (1999)). "Such a transformation" would raise serious First Amendment concerns because it would limit the

> ability to discuss the products or criticize the conduct of companies that may be of widespread public concern and importance. Much useful social and commercial discourse would be all but impossible if speakers were under threat of an infringement lawsuit every time they made reference to a person, company or product by using its trademark.

Id. (internal quotation marks and citations omitted).

Lamparello and his amici argue at length that application of the Lanham Act must be restricted to "commercial speech" to assure that trademark law does not become a tool for unconstitutional censorship. The Sixth Circuit has endorsed this view, *see Taubman Co. v. Webfeats*, 319 F.3d 770, 774 (6th Cir. 2003), and the Ninth Circuit recently has done so as well, *see Bosley Med. Inst., Inc. v. Kremer*, 403 F.3d 672, 674 (9th Cir. 2005).

In its two most significant recent amendments to the Lanham Act, the Federal Trademark Dilution Act of 1995 ("FTDA") and the Anti-cybersquatting Consumer Protection Act of 1999 ("ACPA"), Congress left little doubt that it did not intend for trademark laws to impinge the First Amendment rights of critics and commentators. The dilution statute applies to only a "commercial use in commerce of a mark," 15 U.S.C. § 1125(c)(1), and explicitly states that the "noncommercial use of a mark" is not actionable. Id. § 1125(c)(4). Congress explained that this language was added to "adequately address[] legitimate First Amendment concerns," H.R. Rep. No. 104–374, at 4 (1995), *reprinted in* 1995 U.S.C.C.A.N. 1029, 1031, and "incorporated the concept of 'commercial' speech from the 'commercial speech' doctrine." *Id.* at 8, *reprinted in* 1995 U.S.C.C.A.N. at 1035.... Similarly, Congress directed that in determining whether an individual has engaged in cybersquatting, the courts may consider whether the person's use of the mark is a "bona fide noncommercial or fair use." 15 U.S.C. § 1125(d)(1)(B)(i)(IV). The legislature believed this provision necessary to "protect[] the rights of Internet users and the interests of all Americans in free speech and protected uses of trademarked names for such things as parody, comment, criticism, comparative advertising, news reporting, etc." S. Rep. No. 106–140 (1999), 1999 WL 594571, at *8.

In contrast, the trademark infringement and false designation of origin provisions of the Lanham Act (Sections 32 and 43(a), respectively) do not employ the term "noncommercial." They do state, however, that they pertain only to the use of a mark "in connection with the sale, offering for sale, distribution, or advertising of any goods or services," 15 U.S.C. § 1114(1)(a), or "in connection with any goods or services," *Id.* § 1125(a)(1). But courts have been reluctant to define those terms narrowly. Rather, as the Second Circuit has explained, "the term 'services' has been interpreted broadly" and so "the Lanham Act has ... been applied to defendants furnishing a wide variety of non-commercial public and civic benefits." *United We Stand Am., Inc. v. United We Stand, Am. N.Y., Inc.*, 128 F.3d 86, 89–90 (2d Cir. 1997). Similarly, in *PETA* we noted that a website need not actually sell goods or services for the use of a mark in that site's domain name to constitute a use " 'in connection with' goods or services." *PETA*, 263 F.3d at 365; *see also Taubman Co.*, 319 F.3d at 775 (concluding that website with two links to websites of for-profit entities violated the Lanham Act).

Thus, even if we accepted Lamparello's contention that Sections 32 and 43(a) of the Lanham Act apply only to commercial speech, we would still face the difficult question of what constitutes such speech under those provisions. In the case at hand, we need not resolve that question or determine whether Sections 32 and 43(a) apply exclusively to commercial speech because Reverend Falwell's claims of trademark infringement and false designation fail for a more obvious reason. The hallmark of such claims is a likelihood of confusion—and there is no likelihood of confusion here.

B.

1.

"The use of a competitor's mark that does not cause confusion as to source is permissible." *Dorr–Oliver, Inc. v. Fluid–Quip, Inc.*, 94 F.3d 376, 380 (7th Cir. 1996). Accordingly, Lamparello can only be liable for infringement and false designation if his use of Reverend Falwell's mark would be likely to cause confusion as to the source of the website found at www.fallwell.com. This likelihood-of-confusion test "generally strikes a comfortable balance" between the First Amendment and the rights of markholders. *Mattel, Inc. v. MCA Records, Inc.*, 296 F.3d 894, 900 (9th Cir. 2002).

We have identified seven factors helpful in determining whether a likelihood of confusion exists as to the source of a work, but "not all these factors are always relevant or equally emphasized in each case." *Pizzeria Uno Corp. v. Temple*, 747 F.2d 1522, 1527 (4th Cir. 1984)....

Reverend Falwell's mark is distinctive, and the domain name of Lamparello's website, www.fallwell.com, closely resembles it. But, although Lamparello and Reverend Falwell employ similar marks online, Lamparello's website looks nothing like Reverend Falwell's; indeed, Lamparello has made no attempt to imitate Reverend Falwell's website. Moreover, Reverend Falwell does not even argue that Lamparello's website constitutes advertising or a facility for business, let alone a facility or advertising similar to that of Reverend Falwell. Furthermore, Lamparello clearly created his website intending only to provide a forum to criticize ideas, not to steal customers.

Most importantly, Reverend Falwell and Lamparello do not offer similar goods or services. Rather they offer opposing ideas and commentary. Reverend Falwell's mark identifies his spiritual and political views; the website at www.fallwell.com criticizes those very views. After even a quick glance at the content of the website at www.fallwell.com, no one seeking Reverend Falwell's guidance would be misled by the domain name—www.fallwell.com—into believing Reverend Falwell authorized the content of that website. No one would believe that Reverend Falwell sponsored a site criticizing himself, his positions, and his interpretations of the Bible. *See New Kids on the Block v. News Am. Publ'g, Inc.*, 971 F.2d 302, 308–09 (9th Cir. 1992) (stating that use of a mark to solicit criticism of the markholder implies the markholder is not the sponsor of the use).

Finally, the fact that people contacted Reverend Falwell's ministry to report that they found the content at www.fallwell.com antithetical to Reverend Falwell's views does not illustrate, as Reverend Falwell claims, that the website engendered actual confusion. To the contrary, the anecdotal evidence Reverend Falwell submitted shows that those searching for Reverend Falwell's site and arriving instead at Lamparello's site quickly realized that Reverend Falwell was not the source of the content therein.

For all of these reasons, it is clear that the undisputed record evidences no likelihood of confusion. In fact, Reverend Falwell even conceded at oral argument that those viewing the content of Lamparello's website probably were unlikely to confuse Reverend Falwell with the source of that material.

2.

Nevertheless, Reverend Falwell argues that he is entitled to prevail under the "initial interest confusion" doctrine. This relatively new and sporadically applied doctrine holds that "the Lanham Act forbids a competitor from luring potential customers away from a producer by initially passing off its goods as those of the producer's, even if confusion as to the source of the goods is dispelled by the time any sales are consummated." *Dorr-Oliver*, 94 F.3d at 382. According to Reverend Falwell, this doctrine requires us to compare his mark with Lamparello's website domain name, www.fallwell.com, without considering the content of Lamparello's website. Reverend Falwell argues that some people who misspell his name may go to www.fallwell.com assuming it is his site, thus giving Lamparello an unearned audience—albeit one that quickly disappears when it realizes it has not reached Reverend Falwell's site. This argument fails for two reasons.

First, we have never adopted the initial interest confusion theory; rather, we have followed a very different mode of analysis, requiring courts to determine whether a likelihood of confusion exists by "examining the allegedly infringing use *in the context in which it is seen by the ordinary consumer.*" *Anheuser–Busch, Inc. v. L & L Wings, Inc.*, 962 F.2d 316, 319 (4th Cir. 1992) (emphasis added) (citing cases); *see also What–A–Burger of Va., Inc. v. WHATABURGER, Inc.*, 357 F.3d 441, 450 (4th Cir. 2004).

Contrary to Reverend Falwell's arguments, we did not abandon this approach in *PETA*. Our inquiry in *PETA* was limited to whether Doughney's use of the domain name "www.peta.org" constituted a successful enough parody of People for the Ethical Treatment of Animals that no one was likely to believe www.peta.org was sponsored or endorsed by that organization. For a parody to be successful, it "must convey two simultaneous—and contradictory—messages: that it is the original, but also that it is not the original and is instead a parody." *PETA*, 263 F.3d at 366 (internal quotation marks and citation omitted). Doughney argued that his domain name conveyed the first message (that it was PETA's website) and that the content of his website conveyed the requisite second message (that it was not PETA's site). Id. Although "the website's content made it clear that it was not related to PETA," *id.*, we concluded that the website's content could not convey the requisite second message because the site's content "was not conveyed *simultaneously* with the first message, [i.e., the domain name itself,] as required to be considered a parody." *Id.* at 366. Accordingly, we found the "district court properly rejected Doughney's parody defense." *Id.* at 367.

PETA simply outlines the parameters of the parody defense; it does not adopt the initial interest confusion theory or otherwise diminish the necessity of examining context when determining whether a likelihood of confusion exists. Indeed, in *PETA* itself, rather than embracing a new approach, we reiterated that "to determine whether a likelihood of confusion exists, a court should not consider how closely a *fragment* of a given use duplicates the trademark, but must instead consider *whether the use in its entirety creates a likelihood of confusion.*" *Id.* at 366 (internal quotation marks and citation omitted) (emphasis added). When dealing with domain names, this means a court must evaluate an allegedly infringing domain name in conjunction with the content of the website identified by the domain name.[4]

Moreover, even if we did endorse the initial interest confusion theory, that theory would not assist Reverend Falwell here because it provides no basis for liability in circumstances such as these. The few appellate courts that have followed the Ninth Circuit and imposed liability under this theory for using marks on the Internet have done so only in cases involving a factor utterly absent here—one business's use of another's mark for its own financial gain. [Citations]

Profiting financially from initial interest confusion is thus a key element for imposition of liability under this theory.[5] When an alleged infringer does not compete with the markholder for sales, "some initial confusion will not likely facilitate free riding on the goodwill of another mark, or otherwise harm the user claiming infringement. Where confusion has little or no meaningful effect in the marketplace, it is of little or no consequence in our analysis." *Checkpoint Sys. v. Check Point Software Techs., Inc.*, 269 F.3d 270, 296–97 (3d. Cir. 2001). For this reason, even the Ninth Circuit has stated that a firm is not liable for using another's mark in its domain name if it "could not financially capitalize on [a] misdirected consumer [looking for the markholder's site] even if it so desired." *Interstellar Starship Servs., Ltd. v. Epix, Inc.*, 304 F.3d 936, 946 (9th Cir. 2002).

4. Contrary to Reverend Falwell's suggestions, this rule does not change depending on how similar the domain name or title is to the mark. Hence, Reverend Falwell's assertion that he objects only to Lamparello using the domain name www.fallwell.com and has no objection to Lamparello posting his criticisms at "www.falwelliswrong.com," or a similar domain name, does not entitle him to a different evaluation rule. Rather it has long been established that even when alleged infringers use the *very marks at issue* in titles, courts look to the underlying *content* to determine whether the titles create a likelihood of confusion as to source. *See, e.g., Parks v. LaFace Records*, 329 F.3d 437, 452–54 (6th Cir. 2003); *Mattel*, 296 F.3d at 901–02; *Westchester Media v. PRL USA Holdings, Inc.*, 214 F.3d 658, 667–68 (5th Cir. 2000); *Rogers v. Grimaldi*, 875 F.2d 994, 1000–01 (2d Cir. 1989).

5. Offline uses of marks found to cause actionable initial interest confusion also have involved financial gain. *See Elvis Presley Enters., Inc. v. Capece*, 141 F.3d 188, 204 (5th Cir. 1998); *Mobil Oil Corp. v. Pegasus Petroleum Corp.*, 818 F.2d 254, 260 (2d Cir. 1987). And even those courts recognizing the initial interest confusion theory of liability but finding no actionable initial confusion involved one business's use of another's mark for profit. *See, e.g., Savin Corp. v. The Savin Group*, 391 F.3d 439, 462 n. 13 (2d Cir. 2004); *AM Gen. Corp. v. DaimlerChrysler Corp.*, 311 F.3d 796, 827–28 (7th Cir. 2002); *Checkpoint Sys., Inc. v. Check Point Software Techs., Inc.*, 269 F.3d 270, 298 (3d Cir. 2001); *Hasbro, Inc. v. Clue Computing, Inc.*, 232 F.3d 1, 2 (1st Cir. 2000); *Syndicate Sales, Inc. v. Hampshire Paper Corp.*, 192 F.3d 633, 638 (7th Cir. 1999); *Rust Env't & Infrastructure, Inc. v. Teunissen*, 131 F.3d 1210, 1217 (7th Cir. 1997); *Dorr-Oliver*, 94 F.3d at 383.

This critical element—use of another firm's mark to capture the markholder's customers and profits—simply does not exist when the alleged infringer establishes a gripe site that criticizes the markholder. See Hannibal Travis, The Battle For Mindshare: The Emerging Consensus that the First Amendment Protects Corporate Criticism and Parody on the Internet, 10 Va. J.L. & Tech. 3, 85 (Winter 2005)....[6] Applying the initial interest confusion theory to gripe sites like Lamparello's would enable the markholder to insulate himself from criticism—or at least to minimize access to it. We have already condemned such uses of the Lanham Act, stating that a markholder cannot " 'shield itself from criticism by forbidding the use of its name in commentaries critical of its conduct.' " *CPC Int'l*, 214 F.3d at 462 (*quoting L.L. Bean, Inc. v. Drake Publishers, Inc.*, 811 F.2d 26, 33 (1st Cir. 1987)). "Just because speech is critical of a corporation and its business practices is not a sufficient reason to enjoin the speech." *Id.*

In sum, even if we were to accept the initial interest confusion theory, that theory would not apply in the case at hand. Rather, to determine whether a likelihood of confusion exists as to the source of a gripe site like that at issue in this case, a court must look not only to the allegedly infringing domain name, but also to the underlying content of the website. When we do so here, it is clear, as explained above, that no likelihood of confusion exists. Therefore, the district court erred in granting Reverend Falwell summary judgment on his infringement, false designation, and unfair competition claims.

...

IV.

For the foregoing reasons, Lamparello, rather than Reverend Falwell, is entitled to summary judgment on all counts. Accordingly, the judgment of the district court is reversed and the case is remanded for entry of judgment for Lamparello.

QUESTION

Is the court's basis for distinguishing its decision in *PETA* persuasive?

6. Although the appellate courts that have adopted the initial interest confusion theory have only applied it to profit-seeking uses of another's mark, the district courts have not so limited the application of the theory. Without expressly referring to this theory, two frequently-discussed district court cases have held that using another's domain name to post content antithetical to the markholder constitutes infringement. *See Planned Parenthood Fed'n of Am., Inc. v. Bucci*, 1997 U.S. Dist. LEXIS 3338, No. 97 Civ. 0629, 1997 WL 133313 (S.D.N.Y. March 24, 1997), *aff'd*, 152 F.3d 920 (2d Cir. 1998) (table) (finding use of domain name "www.plannedparenthood.com" to provide links to passages of anti-abortion book constituted infringement); *Jews for Jesus v. Brodsky*, 993 F. Supp. 282 (D.N.J. 1998), *aff'd*, 159 F.3d 1351 (3d Cir. 1998) (table) (finding use of "www.jewsforjesus.org" to criticize religious group constituted infringement). We think both cases were wrongly decided to the extent that in determining whether the domain names were confusing, the courts did not consider whether the websites' content would dispel any confusion. In expanding the initial interest confusion theory of liability, these cases cut it off from its moorings to the detriment of the First Amendment.

CHAPTER 13

REMEDIES

A. INJUNCTIVE RELIEF

1. INJUNCTIONS

Page 942. Insert Question 4 below after Question 3:

4. Once an injunction is granted, are there any circumstances that would justify a modification of this relief? Consider the situation in which a registrant for a mark for Mexican cheese products was enjoined in 1988 in 4 states on the basis of the other party's prior common law rights in those states to a similar mark for Mexican cheese products. Do the facts that the Latino population has become more dispersed in the United States and that Spanish networks offering national advertising have emerged since the injunction issued justify a modification to the injunction allowing the defendant to advertise nationally in Spanish media? *See V & V Food Products, Inc. v. Cacique Cheese Co., infra* this Supplement, Chapter 3.C.2.

B. MONETARY RELIEF

1. ASSESSING PROFITS AND/OR DAMAGES

Page 963. Insert the following at the end of Question 2:

See Western Diversified Services, Inc. v. Hyundai Motor America, Inc., 77 U.S.P.Q.2d 1132 (10th Cir. 2005).

Page 963. Insert Question 5 below after Question 4:

5. Section 1117(a) provides that actual damages may be enhanced up to three times the amount and that profits may be adjusted up or down if the court finds that recovery is inadequate or excessive. Can a court add profits and damages together and apply a multiplier up to three times? *See Thompson v. Haynes*, 305 F.3d 1369 (Fed. Cir. 2002).

3. ATTORNEY'S FEES

Page 978. Add Questions 3 and 4:

3. The Lanham Act provides that attorney's fees should be awarded only in "exceptional circumstances" in non-counterfeiting cases. Are there ever any circumstances where attorney's fees can be awarded as part of damages? What if a plaintiff files an opposition in the TTAB as well as a lawsuit, can its opposition expenses be considered part of damages? *See Attrezzi LLC v. Maytag Corp.*, 436 F.3d 32 (1st Cir. 2006).

4. Where both federal and state infringement claims are brought and the state law provides for the award of attorney's fees to a prevailing plaintiff without any showing of the "exceptional circumstances" required by the Lanham Act is the state statute preempted? *See Attrezzi LLC v. Maytag Corp.*, *supra*.

C. Trademark Counterfeiting

1. Procedural Issues

Page 982. Add the following at the end of the Question:

See Waco Int'l, Inc. v. KHK Scaffolding Houston Inc., 278 F.3d 523 (5th Cir. 2002) (affirming judgment on wrongful seizure claim).

2. Substantive Issues

Page 982. Delete Section 2320 and substitute the following, which is Section 2320 as amended in November 2005:

§ 2320. Trafficking in counterfeit goods or services

(a) Whoever intentionally traffics or attempts to traffic in goods or services and knowingly uses a counterfeit mark on or in connection with such goods or services, or intentionally traffics or attempts to traffic in labels, patches, stickers, wrappers, badges, emblems, medallions, charms, boxes, containers, cans, cases, hangtags, documentation, or packaging of any type or nature, knowing that a counterfeit mark has been applied thereto, the use of which is likely to cause confusion, to cause mistake, or to deceive, shall, if an individual, be fined not more than $2,000,000 or imprisoned not more than 10 years, or both, and, if a person other than an individual, be fined not more than $5,000,000. In the case of an offense by a person under this section that occurs after that person is convicted of another offense under this section, the person convicted, if an individual, shall be fined not more than $5,000,000 or imprisoned not more than 20 years, or both, and if other than an individual, shall be fined not more than $15,000,000.

(b)(1) The following property shall be subject to forfeiture to the United States and no property right shall exist in such property:

(A) Any article bearing or consisting of a counterfeit mark used in committing a violation of subsection (a).

(B) Any property used, in any manner or part, to commit or to facilitate the commission of a violation of subsection (a).

. . .

(c) All defenses, affirmative defenses, and limitations on remedies that would be applicable in an action under the Lanham Act shall be applicable in a prosecution under this section. In a prosecution under this section, the defendant shall have the burden of proof, by a preponderance of the evidence, of any such affirmative defense.

. . .

(e) For the purposes of this section—

(1) the term "counterfeit mark" means—

(A) a spurious mark—

(i) that is used in connection with trafficking in any goods, services, labels, patches, stickers, wrappers, badges, emblems, medallions, charms, boxes, containers, cans, cases, hangtags, documentation, or packaging of any type or nature;

(ii) that is identical with, or substantially indistinguishable from, a mark registered on the principal register in the United States Patent and Trademark Office and in use, whether or not the defendant knew such mark was so registered;

(iii) that is applied to or used in connection with the goods or services for which the mark is registered with the United States Patent and Trademark Office, or is applied to or consists of a label, patch, sticker, wrapper, badge, emblem, medallion, charm, box, container, can, case, hangtag, documentation, or packaging of any type or nature that is designed, marketed, or otherwise intended to be used on or in connection with the goods or services for which the mark is registered in the United States Patent and Trademark Office; and

(iv) the use of which is likely to cause confusion, to cause mistake, or to deceive; or

(B) a spurious designation that is identical with, or substantially indistinguishable from, a designation as to which the remedies of the Lanham Act are made available by reason of section 220506 of title 36;

but such term does not include any mark or designation used in connection with goods or services, or a mark or designation applied to labels, patches, stickers, wrappers, badges, emblems, medallions, charms, boxes, containers, cans, cases, hangtags, documentation, or packaging of any type or nature used in connection with such goods or services, of which the manufacturer or producer was, at the time of the manufacture or production in question, authorized to use the mark or designation for the type of goods or services so manufactured or produced, by the holder of the right to use such mark or designation.

(2) the term "traffic" means to transport, transfer, or otherwise dispose of, to another, for purposes of commercial advantage or private financial gain, or to make, import, export, obtain control of, or possess, with intent to so transport, transfer, or otherwise dispose of;

(3) the term "financial gain" includes the receipt, or expected receipt, of anything of value; and

(4) the term "Lanham Act" means the Act entitled "An Act to provide for the registration and protection of trademarks used in commerce, to carry out the provisions of certain international conventions, and for other purposes", approved July 5, 1946 (*15 U.S.C. 1051* et seq.).

(f) Nothing in this section shall entitle the United States to bring a criminal cause of action under this section for the repackaging of genuine goods or services not intended to deceive or confuse.

CHAPTER 14

INTERNATIONAL ASPECTS OF TRADEMARK PROTECTION

A. INTERNATIONAL AGREEMENTS CONCERNING TRADEMARKS

1. THE PARIS CONVENTION FOR THE PROTECTION OF INDUSTRIAL PROPERTY

Page 999, first paragraph. The Paris Convention now has 169 members.

Page 999. Add the following citation at the end of the first paragraph:

See, e.g., In re Rath, 74 U.S.P.Q.2d 1174 (Fed. Cir. 2005)(Paris Convention is not self-executing; accordingly, applications for RATH and DR. RATH based on German registrations under section 44(e) are subject to scrutiny under Lanham Act's primarily merely a surname bar to registration).

2. THE MADRID SYSTEM

Page 1001, second full paragraph, second line. The U.S. ratified the Madrid Protocol in 2003.

Page 1001, second full paragraph, six lines from bottom. Delete from here through the first paragraph on page 102. Substitute the following:

The Madrid Protocol Implementation Act, Pub. L. No. 107–273, 116 Stat. 1758, became effective Nov. 2, 2003.

Pages 1004–07. Replace note on 3. Trademark Law Treaty Implementation Act with the following:

Singapore Treaty on the Law of Trademarks

On March 27, 2006, WIPO member States adopted a new international treaty modernizing procedural aspects of trademark registration and licensing, for example to encourage electronic filing. See http://www.wipo.int/treaties/en/ip/singapore/index.html The treaty's annexes include model registration forms. The treaty has not yet entered into force, having just been opened to ratification.

3. Trademark Law Treaty Implementation Act

Page 1007. Delete first full paragraph and Editors' Note.

4. The EU Community Trademark System

Page 1007. First paragraph under 4. The EU Commmunity Trademark System. Delete first eight lines (through "But").

5. Trademarks and International Trade: GATT/TRIPs and NAFTA

Page 1010. Delete first full paragraph. Substitute the following:

The U.S. has successfully defended two TRIPs dispute resolution proceedings concerning geographic indications. *See* "European Communities—Protection of Trademarks and Geographical Indications for Agricultural Products and Foodstuffs Complaint by the United States", WT/DS174/R (05–0955), 2005 WTO DS LEXIS 15 (Mar. 15, 2005); Section 211 Omnibus Appropriation Act of 1998, WT/DS176/R (01–3806), 2001 WTO DS LEXIS 22 (Aug. 6, 2001). *See generally* Donald R Dinan, "An Analysis of the United States–Cuba 'HAVANA CLUB' Rum Case Before the World Trade Organization", 26 FORDHAM INT'L. L. J. 337 (2003) (Havana Club for rum not produced in Cuba); Eva Gutierrez, Geographical Indicators: A Unique European Perspective on Intellectual Property, 29 HASTINGS INT'L & COMP. L. REV. 29 (2005).

B. United States Registration

Page 1012, first paragraph, first line. With ratification of the Madrid Protocol, there are now four ways in which a foreign applicant may register a trademark in the U.S.

Page 1012, insert new fourth paragraph:

Fourth, the applicant may avail itself of the Madrid Protocol's centralized filing mechanism, by filing in their countries of origin, obtaining an international registration through WIPO, and having WIPO forward the applications to the U.S. (and any other designated countries) for an "extension of protection." The USPTO would then examine the application's conformity with domestic U.S. trademark law.

C. BORDER CONTROL MEASURES

2. THE GRAY MARKET/PARALLEL IMPORTS

Pages 1025–33. Replace Note on Genuine Goods, *Lever Bros.* and Questions 1–3 with the following:

Bourdeau Bros. v. ITC

444 F.3d 1317.
(Ct. Intl. Trade 2006).

■ CLEVENGER, SENIOR CIRCUIT HUDGE.

Appellants Bourdeau Bros., Inc. (Bourdeau), Sunova Implement Co. (Sunova), and OK Enterprises (OK), (collectively, appellants) appeal the decision of the United States International Trade Commission (ITC) affirming the Initial Determination and Recommended Remedy Determination (Initial Determination) of Administrative Law Judge Luckern (ALJ) that the importation of certain Deere European version forage harvesters infringed one or more of Deere's federally registered trademarks, Certain Agric. Vehicles & Components Thereof, Inv. No. 337–TA–487 (Jan. 13, 2004) (Initial Determination), and granting a general exclusion order covering those forage harvesters as well as cease and desist orders against Bourdeau, OK, and other respondents, Certain Agric. Vehicles & Components Thereof, Inv. No. 337–TA–487 (Int'l Trade Comm'n Sept. 24, 2004) (ITC Remedy Determination). We vacate and remand.

I

On January 8, 2003, Intervenor Deere & Co. (Deere) filed a complaint with the ITC alleging violations of 19 U.S.C. § 1337 (section 1337) by the importation into the United States, and sale in the United States, of certain used agricultural vehicles that infringed United States Registered Trademark Nos. 1,503,576, 1,502,103, 1,254,339, and 91,860 (the Deere trademarks). In particular, Deere alleged that Deere forage harvesters that had been manufactured solely for sale in Europe (the European version forage harvesters) were being imported into the United States. Deere argued that the European version forage harvesters were materially different from the forage harvesters manufactured and authorized for sale in the United States (the North American version forage harvesters). Thus, Deere claimed that the European version forage harvesters constituted "gray market goods" such that they infringed Deere's trademarks. The ITC commenced an investigation on February 7, 2003. On January 13, 2004, the ALJ issued his Initial Determination in which he found that appellants' importation of used Deere European version forage harvesters violated section 1337. The ALJ recommended that the ITC issue a general exclusion order covering the infringing Deere forage harvesters and cease and desist orders against Bourdeau, OK, and other non-appellant respondents. Appellants filed a Petition for Review on January 23, 2004, and on March 30, 2004, the ITC issued a notice indicating that it had decided not to review the Initial Determination. On May 14, 2004, after analyzing the proposed remedy and the effect of any remedial orders on the public interest, the ITC followed the ALJ's recommendation and issued both the general exclusion order and the cease and desist orders. Appellants timely filed a notice of appeal. We have jurisdiction pursuant to 28 U.S.C. § 1295(a)(6).

* * *

III

Section 1337(a)(1)(c) forbids "[t]he importation into the United States, the sale for importation, or the sale within the United States after importation by the owner, importer, or consignee, of articles that infringe a valid and enforceable United States trademark registered under the Trademark Act of 1946." Thus, section 1337 grants the ITC the power to prevent the importation of goods that, if sold in the United States, would violate one of the provisions of the federal trademark statute, the Lanham Act.

Many of the goods that are forbidden from importation under section 1337 are what are referred to as "gray market goods": products that were "produced by the owner of the United States trademark or with its consent, but not authorized for sale in the United States." *Gamut Trading Co. v. Int'l Trade Comm'n*, 200 F.3d 775, 777 (Fed. Cir. 1999). The rationale behind preventing importation of these goods is that the public associates a trademark with goods having certain characteristics. *Id.* at 778–79. To the extent that foreign goods bearing a trademark have different characteristics than those trademarked goods authorized for sale in the United States, the public is likely to become confused or deceived as to which characteristics are properly associated with the trademark, thereby possibly eroding the goodwill of the trademark holder in the United States. *Id.* at 779.

Thus, gray market theory recognizes both the territorial boundaries of trademarks and a trademark owner's right to control the qualities or characteristics associated with a trademark in a certain territorial region. As such, the basic question in gray market cases "is not whether the mark was validly affixed" to the goods, "but whether there are differences between the foreign and domestic product and if so whether the differences are material." *Id.* We have applied "a low threshold of materiality, requiring no more than showing that consumers would be likely to consider the differences between the foreign and domestic products to be significant when purchasing the product." *Id.*

However, even though the threshold of materiality is low, "a plaintiff in a gray market trademark infringement case must establish that all or substantially all of its sales are accompanied by the asserted material difference in order to show that its goods are materially different." *SKF*, 423 F.3d at 1315 (emphasis added). As we noted in *SKF*, the sale by a trademark owner of the very same goods that he claims are gray market goods is inconsistent with a claim that consumers will be confused by those alleged gray market goods. *Id.* "To permit recovery by a trademark owner when less than 'substantially all' of its goods bear the material difference ... would allow the owner itself to contribute to the confusion by consumers that it accuses gray market importers of creating." *Id.* That is, a trademark owner has the right to determine the set of characteristics that are associated with his trademark in the United States; however, a trademark owner cannot authorize the sale of trademarked goods with a set of characteristics and at the same time claim that the set of characteristics should not be associated with the trademark.

This case involves the importation and sale of used forage harvesters manufactured by Deere. Deere sells 5000 and 6000 series forage harvesters in both the United States and Europe through a network of authorized dealers and distributors. The 5000 series is manufactured exclusively in the United States, regardless of the market for which it is destined, while the 6000 series is manufactured exclusively in Germany. Both the 5000 and 6000 series forage harvesters fit generally into two categories: the North American version forage harvesters, which are manufactured for sale in the United States and North America, and the European version forage harvesters, which are manufactured for sale in Europe. Although the North American and European version forage harvesters are sold under the same series numbers, they have certain differences, including labeling differences and differences in certain safety features, discussed at greater length below.

Appellants are involved in the importation into the United States and the resale of used European version forage harvesters of both the 5000 and 6000 series. The ITC determined that the European versions of these forage harvesters are materially different from their North American counterparts and that the importation and sale of these forage harvesters violates section 1337.

IV

As a threshold matter, appellants argue that, because the 5000 series forage harvesters are manufactured in the United States, they are not "gray market goods" and thus that importation and sale of these forage harvesters cannot violate section 1337. Appellants point to the Supreme Court's decision *K Mart Corp. v. Cartier, Inc.*, 486 U.S. 281, 108 S.Ct. 1811, 100 L.Ed.2d 313 (1987), in which the Court, while addressing whether certain Customs regulations were consistent with 19 U.S.C. § 1526, discussed the meaning of the term "gray market goods." The Court noted that a gray market good is "a foreign-manufactured good, bearing a valid United States trademark, that is imported without the consent of the United States trademark holder." *K Mart*, 486 U.S. at 285.... Appellants argue that the Court did not include ... a case in which a domestic firm manufactures a product in the United States for sale abroad and that good is re-imported to the United States for later sale without the trademark owner's permission. Thus, appellants argue that a good manufactured domestically for export cannot be a "gray market good" and hence cannot violate section 1337.

However, *K Mart* did not address violations of either section 1337 or of the Lanham Act. Rather, the case discussed gray market theory as the background to an analysis of whether certain Customs regulations were consistent with section 526 of the Tariff Act of 1930, 19 U.S.C. § 1526, which attempted to regulate, for the first time, the importation of "gray market goods." See *K Mart*, 486 U.S. at 285–87. Both the regulation at issue, 19 C.F.R. § 133.21, and 19 U.S.C. § 1526 specifically refer to "[f]oreign-made articles" or "merchandise of foreign manufacture." Id. at 287–88 (quoting 19 C.F.R. § 133.21 (1987) and 19 U.S.C. § 1526). Thus, it is not surprising that the Court's description of gray market theory focused on goods of foreign manufacture. Further, the Court noted that "[t]he regulations implementing § 526 . . . have not applied the prohibition to all gray-market goods." *Id.* at 288. Thus, *K Mart* should not be read to limit gray market theory, as it is applied in the context of section 1337, to goods of foreign manufacture.

In addition, the ITC has already determined that trademarked goods manufactured in the United States exclusively for sale in foreign countries may violate section 1337 if they are imported into the United States without the trademark owner's permission and if they are materially different from the trademarked goods authorized for sale in the United States. See Certain Cigarettes & Packaging, Thereof, Inv. No. 337–TA–424, USITC Pub. 3366, Commission Opinion at 2, n. 2 (Int'l Trade Comm'n, Oct. 16, 2000) (Cigarettes) (finding that cigarettes manufactured in the United States but intended for sale exclusively abroad violated section 1337). Although the ITC expressly declined to refer to the goods in Cigarettes as "gray market goods," using instead the terms "for-export" or "re-imported," the ITC analyzed whether the goods violated section 1337 using the "material difference" standard we applied in *Gamut*.

Indeed, section 1337(a)(1)(c) makes no reference to the term "gray market." In addition, unlike the statute at issue in *K Mart*, it does not distinguish between goods of domestic manufacture and goods of foreign manufacture. Rather, the statute simply declares unlawful "[t]he importation into the United States, the sale for importation, or the sale within the United States after importation by the owner, importer, or consignee, of articles that infringe a valid and enforceable United States trademark registered under the Trademark Act of 1946." 19 U.S.C. § 1337(a)(1)(c).

Finally, although this court noted in *Gamut* that "[t]he term 'gray market goods' refers to genuine goods that in this case are of foreign manufacture," we did not expressly limit the term "gray market goods"-nor yet the reach of section 1337–to foreign-manufactured goods. 200 F.3d at 778 (emphasis added). Rather, we noted that "[t]he principle of gray market law is that the importation of a product that was produced by the owner of the United States trademark or with its consent, but not authorized for sale in the United States, may, in appropriate cases infringe the United States trademark." *Id.* at 777. Thus, gray market law is not concerned with where the good was manufactured, nor is it concerned with whether the trademark owner controlled the manufacture of the product or authorized the use of the trademark on that product in another country. Instead, gray market law is concerned with whether the trademark owner has authorized use of the trademark on that particular product in the United States and thus whether the trademark owner has control over the specific characteristics associated with the trademark in the United States.

As such, we agree with the ITC, and we hold that the importation and sale of a trademarked good of domestic manufacture, produced solely for sale abroad and not authorized by the owner of the trademark for sale in the United States, may violate section 1337 if the imported good is materially different from all or substantially all of those goods bearing the same trademark that are authorized for sale in the United States.

V

In order to find a violation of section 1337, the imported goods must be materially different from all or substantially all of those trademarked goods authorized for sale in the United States. The materiality threshold is low, "requiring no more than showing that consumers would be likely to consider the differences between the foreign and domestic products to be significant when purchasing the product, for such differences would suffice to erode the goodwill of the domestic source." *Gamut*, 200 F.3d at 779. Indeed, there need only be one material difference between a domestic and a foreign product in order to determine that the latter is a gray market good eligible for exclusion. *See, e.g., id.* at 780–82 (affirming ITC finding of material difference based solely on the absence of English-language warning and instructional labels on foreign goods). However, the "plaintiff . . . must establish that all or substantially all of its sales are accompanied by the asserted material difference in order to show that its goods are materially different." *SKF*, 423 F.3d at 1315.

In this case, the ALJ found that there were numerous differences between the European and North American versions of both the 5000 and 6000 series forage harvesters that a customer in the United States would be likely to consider significant when purchasing the product. Initial Determination, slip op. at 19. While, for the most part, the appellants do not contest the existence of differences between the North American and European version forage harvesters, they argue that substantial evidence does not support the ALJ's findings that these differences are material.

However, substantial evidence supports the ALJ's determination that there are several differences between the North American and European version forage harvesters of both the 5000 and 6000 series that a customer would be likely to consider significant when purchasing the product. Both the 5000 and 6000 series harvesters contain differences in safety features that a customer would be likely to consider significant when purchasing the product. First of all, there are material differences between the lighting configuration and lighting functions of the North American and European forage harvesters, including the type of lights used during transport, the manner in which hazard lights and turn signals function, and whether safety warning lamps exist. There are also material differences between the warning labels and safety decals on the North American forage harvesters, which carry pictures and English writing, and European forage harvesters, which carry only pictures. *See In Re Certain Agric. Tractors Under 50 Power Takeoff Horsepower Investigation*, 44 U.S.P.Q.2d 1385, 1402 (Int'l Trade Comm'n 1997) ("Tractors") (finding that the absence of English-language warning and instructional labels on foreign goods constituted a material difference), *aff'd*, *Gamut*, 200 F.3d 775.

There are several other material differences between the North American and European versions of both the 5000 and 6000 series forage harvesters. There is a material difference in the hitch mechanism of the North American and European forage harvesters, as the mechanism in the European forage harvesters is not compatible with wagons used in North America. In addition, the operator's manuals of the European version forage harvesters are in the language of the target country, while the American forage harvesters' manuals are in English. Although appellants claim that North American manuals are often provided to purchasers of European version forage harvesters, this only serves to heighten confusion, as the North American and European manuals contain different information due to other differences in the products.

Finally, there are differences in the services provided along with the machines, including the Deere Product Improvement Programs (PIPs) and Service Information System (SIS). Although all three types of Deere's PIPs—mechanical, fix-it fail, and safety—are free to customers who have purchased American forage harvesters, the owners of European forage harvesters only qualify for safety PIPs. Further, the SIS, which records details about past PIPs, differs depending on the PIPs for which a machine is available, such that more information is available for North American forage harvesters than European forage harvesters.

* * *

Page 1033. Add to Question 4:

See also Abercrombie & Fitch v. Fashion Shops of Ky., 363 F.Supp.2d 952 (S.D. Ohio 2005) (licensed Abercrombie & Fitch clothing that failed U.S. quality standards, but whose sale abroad was permitted, was resold by unlicensed third party in the U.S.); *American Circuit Breaker Corp. v. Oregon Breakers Inc.*, 406 F.3d 577 (9th Cir. 2005) (resale in U.S. of circuit breakers made under license for the Canadian market; only difference between U.S.-destined and Canada-destined goods is the nonfunctional color of the plastic housing).

D. INFRINGEMENT AND UNFAIR COMPETITION

1. PROTECTION OF FOREIGN MARKS IN THE UNITED STATES

Pages 1033–39. Delete *Davidoff Extension SA v. Davidoff Int'l.*

Page 1045. Add to the end of Question 1: See *Int'l Bancorp LLC v. Société des Bains de Mer et du Cercle des Etrangers a Monaco*, 329 F.3d 359 (4th Cir. 2003).

2. PROTECTION IN U.S. COURTS AGAINST USE OF U.S. MARKS ABROAD

Pages 1053–64. Delete *Vanity Fair* and *American Rice*. Substitute before Questions:

McBee v. Delica

417 F.3d 107. (1st Cir. 2005).

■ LYNCH, CIRCUIT JUDGE.

It has long been settled that the Lanham Act can, in appropriate cases, be applied extraterritorially. *See Steele v. Bulova Watch Co.*, 344 U.S. 280, 73 S.Ct. 252, 97 L.Ed. 319 (1952). This case, dismissed for lack of subject matter jurisdiction, requires us, as a matter of first impression for this circuit, to lay out a framework for determining when such extraterritorial use of the Lanham Act is proper.

In doing so, we choose not to adopt the formulations used by various other circuits. *See, e.g., Reebok Int'l, Ltd. v. Marnatech Enters.*, 970 F.2d 552, 554–57 (9th Cir.1992); *Vanity Fair Mills v. T. Eaton Co.*, 234 F.2d 633, 642–43 (2d Cir.1956). The best-known test, the *Vanity Fair* test, asks (1) whether the defendant is an American citizen, (2) whether the defendant's actions have a substantial effect on United States commerce, and (3) whether relief would create a conflict with foreign law. 234 F.2d at 642–43. These three prongs are given an uncertain weight. Based on *Steele* and subsequent Supreme Court case law, we disaggregate the three prongs of the *Vanity Fair* test, identify the different types of "extraterritorial" application questions, and isolate the factors pertinent to subject matter jurisdiction.

Our framework asks first whether the defendant is an American citizen; that inquiry is different because a separate constitutional basis for jurisdiction exists for control of activities, even foreign activities, of an American citizen. Further, when the Lanham Act plaintiff seeks to enjoin sales in the United States, there is no question of extraterritorial application; the court has subject matter jurisdiction.

In order for a plaintiff to reach foreign activities of foreign defendants in American courts, however, we adopt a separate test. We hold that subject matter jurisdiction under the Lanham Act is proper only if the complained-of activities have a substantial effect on United States commerce, viewed in light of the purposes of the Lanham Act. If this "substantial effects" question is answered in the negative, then the court lacks jurisdiction over the defendant's extraterritorial acts; if it is answered in the affirmative, then the court possesses subject matter jurisdiction.

. . .

The plaintiff, Cecil McBee, an American citizen and resident, seeks to hold the defendant, Delica Co., Ltd. (Delica), responsible for its activities in Japan said to harm McBee's reputation in both Japan and the United States and for Delica's purported activities in the United States. McBee is a well-known American jazz musician; Delica is a Japanese corporation that adopted the name "Cecil McBee" for its adolescent female clothing line. McBee sued for false endorsement and dilution under the Lanham Act. The district court dismissed all of McBee's Lanham Act claims, concluding that it lacked subject matter jurisdiction.

We affirm, albeit on different reasoning. We conclude that the court lacked jurisdiction over McBee's claims seeking (1) an injunction in the United States barring access to Delica's Internet website, which is written in Japanese, and (2) damages for harm to McBee due to Delica's sales in Japan. McBee has made no showing that Delica's activities had a substantial effect on United States commerce. As to McBee's claim for (3) an injunction barring Delica from selling its goods in the United States, we hold that the district court had jurisdiction but conclude that this claim is without merit because the only sales Delica has made into the United States were induced by McBee for purposes of this litigation, and there is no showing that Delica plans on selling into the United States again.

I.

The relevant facts are basically undisputed. McBee, who lives in both Maine and New York, is a jazz bassist with a distinguished career spanning over forty-five years. He has performed in the United States and worldwide, has performed on over 200 albums, and has released six albums under his own name (including in Japan). He won a Grammy Award in 1989, was inducted into the Oklahoma Jazz Hall of Fame in 1991, and teaches at the New England Conservatory of Music in Boston. McBee has toured Japan several times, beginning in the early 1980s, and has performed in many major Japanese cities, including Tokyo. He continues to tour in Japan. McBee has never licensed or authorized the use of his name to anyone, except of course in direct connection with his musical performances, as for example on an album. In his own words, he has sought to "have [his] name associated only with musical excellence."

Delica is a Japanese clothing retailer. In 1984, Delica adopted the trade name "Cecil McBee" for a line of clothing and accessories primarily marketed to teen-aged girls. Delica holds a Japanese trademark for "Cecil

McBee," in both Japanese and Roman or English characters, for a variety of product types. Delica owns and operates retail shops throughout Japan under the brand name "Cecil McBee"; these are the only stores where "Cecil McBee" products are sold. There are no "Cecil McBee" retail shops outside of Japan. Delica sold approximately $23 million worth of "Cecil McBee" goods in 1996 and experienced steady growth in sales in subsequent years; in 2002, Delica sold $112 million worth of "Cecil McBee" goods.... It is undisputed that [Delica] has never shipped any "Cecil McBee" goods outside of Japan. As described later, Delica's policy generally is to decline orders from the United States.

Delica operates a website, http://www.cecilmcbee.net, which contains pictures and descriptions of "Cecil McBee" products, as well as locations and telephone numbers of retail stores selling those products. The website is created and hosted in Japan, and is written almost entirely in Japanese, using Japanese characters (although, like the style book, it contains some English words). The website contains news about the "Cecil McBee" line, including promotions. Customers can log onto the site to access their balance of bonus "points" earned for making past "Cecil McBee" purchases, as well as information about how to redeem those points for additional merchandise. However, the site does not allow purchases of "Cecil McBee" products to be made online. The website can be viewed from anywhere in the Internet-accessible world.

McBee produced evidence that, when searches on Internet search engines (such as Google) are performed for the phrase "Cecil McBee," Delica's website (www.cecilmcbee.net) generally comes up as one of the first few results, and occasionally comes up first, ahead of any of the various websites that describe the musical accomplishments of the plaintiff. Certain other websites associated with Delica's "Cecil McBee" product line also come up when such searches are performed; like www.cecilmcbee.net, it is evident from the search results page that these websites are written primarily in Japanese characters.

In 1995, plaintiff McBee became aware that Delica was using his name, without his authorization, for a line of clothing in Japan. He contacted an American lawyer, who advised him that Delica was unlikely to be subject to personal jurisdiction in the United States. McBee retained a Japanese attorney, who sent a letter to Delica asking it to cease using the "Cecil McBee" name. When Delica declined, McBee petitioned the Japanese Patent Office to invalidate Delica's English-language trademark on "Cecil McBee."

On February 28, 2002, the Japanese Patent Office ruled Delica's trademark in Japan invalid. However, Delica appealed to the Tokyo High Court, which on December 26, 2002, vacated the decision of the Japanese Patent Office. On remand, the Japanese Patent Office found for Delica and reinstated Delica's registration of the "Cecil McBee" trademark. McBee appealed that ruling to the Tokyo High Court and lost; the trademark reinstatement has become final.

In early 2002, Delica formulated a policy not to sell or ship "Cecil McBee" brand products to the United States and informed its managers throughout the company. Delica's admitted reason for this policy was to prevent McBee from being able to sue Delica in the United States.

. . .

[T]here is virtually no evidence of "Cecil McBee" brand goods entering the United States after being sold by Delica in Japan. McBee stated in affidavit that "[f]riends, fellow musicians, fans, students, and others ... have reported seeing [his] name on clothing, shopping bags [and] merchandise (whether worn or carried by a young girl walking on the street in Boston or New York or elsewhere)...." But no further evidence or detail of these sightings in the United States was provided. McBee also provided evidence that Cecil McBee goods have occasionally been sold on eBay, an auction website that allows bids to be placed and items sold anywhere in the world. Most of the sellers were not located in the United States, and there is no evidence that any of the items were purchased by American buyers.

. . .

McBee has seen his own name on "Cecil McBee" merchandise in Japan while touring and has become angry. His Japanese touring partner during his recent tours of Japan (from 2002 onwards) has made announcements before concerts that McBee had no relationship with the Delica clothing line. In McBee's view, his audience of Japanese fans at his concerts has become younger through time and therefore more in line with the core age group of consumers for Delica's brand. McBee also notes that a fan once came up to him while he was performing in Taiwan to speak with him about Delica's line; the fan apparently presumed a connection between McBee and the line. As of 2003, McBee only had one regular tour in Japan each year, lasting three weeks or so each time; in McBee's view "[i]t is speculating, but it is ... possible" that Delica's "Cecil McBee" brand had led to his failure to receive additional Japanese touring opportunities.

II.

McBee's complaint, filed October 1, 2002, alleged trademark dilution and unfair competition claims under the Lanham Act, 15 U.S.C. § 1051 et seq., as well as various pendent Maine state law claims. McBee requested injunctive relief, damages, and attorney's fees. The core of McBee's Lanham Act claims is false endorsement: that the unlicensed use of his name has "made a misleading and false inference" that McBee endorses, approves, or sponsors Delica's product, and that inference has caused McBee harm.

On appeal, McBee renews his argument that his claims for a domestic injunction, both against Delica's sales into the United States and against its broadcasting of its website in the United States, do not constitute extraterritorial applications of the Lanham Act at all. Further, while McBee concedes that United States courts lack jurisdiction over his Lanham Act claim for an injunction against Delica's sales in Japan, he argues that the district court had extraterritorial jurisdiction over damages claims against those same sales....

III.

A. Framework for Assessing Extraterritorial Use of the Lanham Act

By extraterritorial application of the Lanham Act, we mean application of the Act to activity (such as sales) of a defendant outside of the territorial boundaries of the United States. In addressing extraterritorial application of the Lanham Act, we face issues of Congressional intent to legislate extraterritorially, undergirded by issues of Congressional power to legislate extraterritorially. Usually in addressing questions of extraterritoriality, the Supreme Court has discussed Congressional intent, doing so by employing various presumptions designed to avoid unnecessary international conflict. [citations omitted] ...

The *Steele* Court did not define the outer limits of Congressional power because it was clear that the facts presented a case within those limits. The *Steele* Court explicitly and implicitly relied on two different aspects of Congressional power to reach this conclusion. First, it explicitly relied on the power of Congress to regulate "the conduct of its own citizens," even extraterritorial conduct. *Steele*, 344 U.S. at 285–86, 73 S.Ct. 252. This doctrine is based on an idea that Congressional power over American citizens is a matter of domestic law that raises no serious international concerns, even when the citizen is located abroad....

Second, *Steele* also implicitly appears to rely on Congressional power over foreign commerce, although the Foreign Commerce clause is not cited-the Court noted that the defendant's actions had an impact on the plaintiff's reputation, and thus on commerce within the United States....

For purposes of determining subject matter jurisdiction, we think certain distinctions are important at the outset. The reach of the Lanham Act depends on context; the nature of the analysis of the jurisdictional question may vary with that context. *Steele* addressed the pertinent Lanham Act jurisdictional analysis when an American citizen is the defendant. In such cases, the domestic effect of the international activities may be of lesser importance and a lesser showing of domestic effects may be all that is needed. We do not explore this further because our case does not involve an American citizen as the alleged infringer.

When the purported infringer is not an American citizen, and the alleged illegal activities occur outside the United States, then the analysis is different, and appears to rest solely on the foreign commerce power. Yet it is beyond much doubt that the Lanham Act can be applied against foreign corporations or individuals in appropriate cases; no court has ever suggested that the foreign citizenship of a defendant is always fatal....

The decisions of the Supreme Court in the antitrust context seem useful to us as a guide. The Court has written in this area, on the issue of extraterritorial application, far more recently than it has written on the

Lanham Act, and thus the decisions reflect more recent evolutions in terms of legal analysis of extraterritorial activity. As the Court noted in *Steele*, Lanham Act violations abroad often radiate unlawful consequences into the United States, see 344 U.S. at 288, 73 S.Ct. 252.... One can easily imagine a variety of harms to American commerce arising from wholly foreign activities by foreign defendants. There could be harm caused by false endorsements, passing off, or product disparagement, or confusion over sponsorship affecting American commerce and causing loss of American sales. Further, global piracy of American goods is a major problem for American companies: annual losses from unauthorized use of United States trademarks, according to one commentator, now amount to $200 billion annually. In both the antitrust and the Lanham Act areas, there is a risk that absent a certain degree of extraterritorial enforcement, violators will either take advantage of international coordination problems or hide in countries without efficacious antitrust or trademark laws, thereby avoiding legal authority.

In *Hartford Fire Ins. Co. v. California*, 509 U.S. 764, 113 S.Ct. 2891, 125 L.Ed.2d 612 (1993), the Supreme Court addressed the issue of when a United States court could assert jurisdiction over Sherman Act claims brought against foreign defendants for a conspiracy that occurred abroad to raise reinsurance prices. It held that jurisdiction over foreign conduct existed under the antitrust laws if that conduct "was meant to produce and did in fact produce some substantial effect in the United States." *Id.* at 796, 113 S.Ct. 2891 ... The *Hartford Fire* Court also held that comity considerations, such as whether relief ordered by an American court would conflict with foreign law, were properly understood not as questions of whether a United States court possessed subject matter jurisdiction, but instead as issues of whether such a court should decline to exercise the jurisdiction that it possessed.

The framework stated in *Hartford Fire* guides our analysis of the Lanham Act jurisdictional question for foreign activities of foreign defendants. We hold that the Lanham Act grants subject matter jurisdiction over extraterritorial conduct by foreign defendants only where the conduct has a substantial effect on United States commerce. Absent a showing of such a substantial effect, at least as to foreign defendants, the court lacks jurisdiction over the Lanham Act claim. Congress has little reason to assert jurisdiction over foreign defendants who are engaging in activities that have no substantial effect on the United States, and courts, absent an express statement from Congress, have no good reason to go further in such situations.

The substantial effects test requires that there be evidence of impacts within the United States, and these impacts must be of a sufficient character and magnitude to give the United States a reasonably strong interest in the litigation. The "substantial effects" test must be applied in light of the core purposes of the Lanham Act, which are both to protect the ability of American consumers to avoid confusion and to help assure a trademark's owner that it will reap the financial and reputational rewards associated with having a desirable name or product. The goal of the jurisdictional test is to ensure that the United States has a sufficient interest in the litigation, as measured by the interests protected by the Lanham Act, to assert jurisdiction.

. . .

If the substantial effects test is met, then the court should proceed, in appropriate cases, to consider comity. We also transplant for Lanham Act purposes *Hartford Fire's* holding that comity considerations are properly analyzed not as questions of whether there is subject matter jurisdiction, but as prudential questions of whether that jurisdiction should be exercised. See *Hartford Fire*, 509 U.S. at 798 n. 24, 113 S.Ct. 2891. Our analysis differs again from *Vanity Fair* on this point. *See Vanity Fair*, 234 F.2d at 642. *Vanity Fair* and other cases have considered as part of the basic jurisdictional analysis whether the defendant acted under color of protection of the trademark laws of his own country. We disagree and do not see why the scope of Congressional intent and power to create jurisdiction under the Lanham Act should turn on the existence and meaning of foreign law.

. . .

B. Application of the Framework

We apply the framework we have established to the facts of this case. Although district court fact-finding is permissible in a subject matter jurisdiction inquiry, and we defer to such fact-finding, here all the relevant facts are undisputed and the district court did not find any facts. Our review is de novo, and the burden is on McBee to establish jurisdiction . . .

1. Claim for Injunction Barring Delica's United States Sales

McBee contends that his claim for an injunction against Delica's sales to consumers inside the United States does not constitute an extraterritorial application of the Lanham Act, and therefore the district court should have taken jurisdiction over this claim without pausing to consider whether there was a substantial effect on United States commerce. The factual predicate for this argument is the $2,500 of "Cecil McBee" brand goods that Delica sold to McBee's investigators in Maine; there is no evidence of any other sales made by Delica to United States consumers. McBee is correct that the court had subject matter jurisdiction over this claim.

There can be no doubt of Congress's power to enjoin sales of infringing goods into the United States, and as a matter of Congressional intent there can be no doubt that Congress intended to reach such sales via the Lanham Act. Courts have repeatedly distinguished between domestic acts of a foreign infringer and foreign acts of that foreign infringer; the extraterritoriality analysis to determine jurisdiction attaches only to the latter. Since sales in the United States are domestic acts, McBee need not satisfy the "substantial effect on United States commerce" test for this claim; jurisdiction exists because, under the ordinary domestic test, the $2,500 worth of goods sold by Delica to McBee's investigators in the United States were in

United States commerce, at least insofar as some of those goods were shipped directly by Delica to the buyers in the United States.

. . .

The district court thus had subject matter jurisdiction over McBee's claim for an injunction against Delica's sales of "Cecil McBee" goods in the United States. Nonetheless, dismissal of the claim was appropriate [because the only sales were to McBee's investigators].

2. Claim for Injunction Barring Access to Internet Website

McBee next argues that his claim for an injunction against Delica's posting of its Internet website in a way that is visible to United States consumers also does not call for an extraterritorial application of the Lanham Act. Here McBee is incorrect: granting this relief would constitute an extraterritorial application of the Act, and thus subject matter jurisdiction would only be appropriate if McBee could show a substantial effect on United States commerce. McBee has not shown such a substantial effect from Delica's website.

We begin with McBee's argument that his website claim, like his claim for Delica's sales into the United States, is not an extraterritorial application of the Lanham Act. McBee does not seek to reach the website because it is a method, by Delica, for selling "Cecil McBee" goods into the United States. In such a case, if a court had jurisdiction to enjoin sales of goods within the United States, it might have jurisdiction to enjoin the website as well, or at least those parts of the website that are necessary to allow the sales to occur. Rather, the injury McBee complains about from the website is that its mere existence has caused him harm, because United States citizens can view the website and become confused about McBee's relationship with the Japanese clothing company. In particular, McBee argues that he has suffered harm from the fact that Delica's website often comes up on search engines ahead of fan sites about McBee's jazz career.

Delica's website, although hosted from Japan and written in Japanese, happens to be reachable from the United States just as it is reachable from other countries. That is the nature of the Internet. The website is hosted and managed overseas; its visibility within the United States is more in the nature of an effect, which occurs only when someone in the United States decides to visit the website. To hold that any website in a foreign language, wherever hosted, is automatically reachable under the Lanham Act so long as it is visible in the United States would be senseless. The United States often will have no real interest in hearing trademark lawsuits about websites that are written in a foreign language and hosted in other countries.

McBee attempts to analogize the existence of Delica's website, which happens to be visible in any country, to the direct mail advertising that the *Vanity Fair* court considered to be domestic conduct and so held outside the scope of the extraterritoriality analysis. *See Vanity Fair*, 234 F.2d at 638–39. The analogy is poor for three reasons: first, the advertising in Vanity

Fair was closely connected with mail-order sales; second, direct mail advertising is a far more targeted act than is the hosting of a website; and third, Delica's website, unlike the advertising in *Vanity Fair*, is in a foreign language.

Our conclusion that McBee's website claim calls for extraterritorial application of the Lanham Act is bolstered by a consideration of the now extensive case law relating to treatment of Internet websites with respect to personal jurisdiction. We recognize that the contexts are distinct, but the extraterritorial application of jurisdiction under the Lanham Act evokes concerns about territorial restraints on sovereigns that are similar to concerns driving personal jurisdiction. To put the principle broadly, the mere existence of a website that is visible in a forum and that gives information about a company and its products is not enough, by itself, to subject a defendant to personal jurisdiction in that forum. *See, e.g., Jennings v. AC Hydraulic A/S*, 383 F.3d 546, 549–50 (7th Cir.2004); *ALS Scan, Inc. v. Digital Serv. Consultants, Inc.*, 293 F.3d 707, 713–15 (4th Cir.2002).

Something more is necessary, such as interactive features which allow the successful online ordering of the defendant's products. The mere existence of a website does not show that a defendant is directing its business activities towards every forum where the website is visible; as well, given the omnipresence of Internet websites today, allowing personal jurisdiction to be premised on such a contact alone would "eviscerate" the limits on a state's jurisdiction over out-of-state or foreign defendants.

Similarly, allowing subject matter jurisdiction under the Lanham Act to automatically attach whenever a website is visible in the United States would eviscerate the territorial curbs on judicial authority that Congress is, quite sensibly, presumed to have imposed in this area.

Our conclusion does not make it impossible for McBee to use the Lanham Act to attack a Japan-based website; it merely requires that McBee first establish that the website has a substantial effect on commerce in the United States before there is subject matter jurisdiction under the Lanham Act. We can imagine many situations in which the presence of a website would ensure (or, at least, help to ensure) that the United States has a sufficient interest. The substantial effects test, however, is not met here.

Delica's website is written almost entirely in Japanese characters; this makes it very unlikely that any real confusion of American consumers, or diminishing of McBee's reputation, would result from the website's existence. In fact, most American consumers are unlikely to be able to understand Delica's website at all. Further, McBee's claim that Americans looking for information about him will be unable to find it is unpersuasive: the Internet searches reproduced in the record all turned up both sites about McBee and sites about Delica's clothing line on their first page of results. The two sets of results are easily distinguishable to any consumer, given that the Delica sites are clearly shown, by the search engines, as being written in Japanese characters. Finally, we stress that McBee has produced no evidence of any American consumers going to the website and then becoming confused about whether McBee had a relationship with Delica.

3. Claim for Damages for Delica's Japanese Sales

McBee's claim for damages due to Delica's sales in Japan fares no better, because these sales as well have no substantial effect on commerce in the United States. McBee seeks damages for Delica's sales in Japan to Japanese consumers based on (a) tarnishing of McBee's image in the United States, and (b) loss of income in the United States due to loss of commercial opportunity as a jazz musician in Japan, stemming from the tarnishing of McBee's reputation there. The alleged tarnishing—both in the United States and Japan—is purportedly caused by the confusion of McBee's name with a brand selling (sometimes provocative) clothing to young teenage girls in Japan. McBee presents essentially no evidence that either type of tarnishing has occurred, much less that it has any substantial effect on United States commerce.

McBee's first argument, that American consumers are being confused and/or led to think less of McBee's name because of Delica's Japanese sales, cuts very close to the core purposes of the Lanham Act. Such confusion and reputational harm in the eyes of American consumers can often-although not always-be inferred from the fact that American consumers have been exposed to the infringing mark. But no inference of dilution or other harm can be made in situations where American citizens are not exposed at all to the infringing product. The trouble with McBee's argument is that there is virtually no evidence that American consumers are actually seeing Delica's products.

Quite commonly, plaintiffs in these sorts of cases can meet their burden by presenting evidence that while the initial sales of infringing goods may occur in foreign countries, the goods subsequently tend to enter the United States in some way and in substantial quantities. McBee has presented essentially no evidence that Delica's products have been brought into the United States after their initial sale in Japan. McBee's own statement, without more, that people have seen women wearing Delica clothing in the United States does not show very much; likewise, McBee's evidence that Delica's goods are occasionally sold on eBay shows little, given particularly that such goods need not have been auctioned to buyers in the United States. The evidence indicates only one incident in which an American citizen saw McBee advertisements while traveling in Japan and demonstrated confusion upon returning to the United States.

Beyond that, there is also nothing that indicates any harm to McBee's career in the United States due to Delica's product sales. McBee's argument that there has potentially been harm to McBee's career as a product endorser is most unlikely, especially given his own disinterest in performing such endorsements. Further, McBee's statement that his teaching career may have been hindered by Delica is speculation.

McBee's second argument is that Delica's sales have confused Japanese consumers, hindering McBee's record sales and touring career in Japan.

Evidence of economic harm to McBee in Japan due to confusion of Japanese consumers is less tightly tied to the interests that the Lanham Act intends to

protect, since there is no United States interest in protecting Japanese consumers. American courts do, however, arguably have an interest in protecting American commerce by protecting McBee from lost income due to the tarnishing of his trademark in Japan. Courts have considered sales diverted from American companies in foreign countries in their analyses.

Assuming arguendo that evidence of harm to an American plaintiff's economic interests abroad, due to the tarnishing of his reputation there, might sometimes meet the substantial effects test, McBee has presented no evidence of such harm in this case. McBee has presented no evidence of economic harm due to losses in record sales or touring opportunities in Japan. McBee's statement that he might have expected more Japanese touring opportunities by now, and may have had such opportunities absent Delica's sales, is wholly speculative. There is no probative evidence of any decline in McBee's touring revenue as compared to past patterns, nor is there any evidence of any decline in McBee's Japanese record sales.

McBee has not shown that Delica's Japanese sales have a substantial effect on United States commerce, and thus McBee's claim for damages based on those sales, as well as McBee's claim for an injunction against Delica's website, must be dismissed for lack of subject matter jurisdiction. . . .

Page 1079. Delete Editor's note; replace with the following. The WIPO Standing Committee's joint recommendation was adopted at the 36th series of meetings of the Assemblies of the WIPO Member States, Sept. 24–Oct. 3, 2001.

APPENDIX A

Trademark Act of 1946, As Amended

PUBLIC LAW 79–489, CHAPTER 540, APPROVED JULY 5, 1946; 60 STAT. 427

NOTE: The headings used for sections and subsections or paragraphs in the following reprint of the Act are not part of the Act but have been added for convenience in using this reprint. Prior trademark statutes may be found in Title 15, Chapter 3, of the U.S. Code and in the Statutes at Large. The present Act forms Chapter 22 of Title 15 of the U.S. Code and the U.S. Code citations have been placed at the beginning of each section and subsection.

TITLE I—THE PRINCIPAL REGISTER

§ 1 (15 U.S.C. § 1051). Registration; application; payment of fees; designation of agent for service of process

(a)(1) The owner of a trademark used in commerce may request registration of its trademark on the principal register hereby established by paying the prescribed fee and filing in the Patent and Trademark Office an application and a verified statement, in such form as may be prescribed by the Director, and such number of specimens or facsimiles of the mark as used as may be required by the Director.

(2) The application shall include specification of the applicant's domicile and citizenship, the date of the applicant's first use of the mark, the date of the applicant's first use of the mark in commerce, the goods in connection with which the mark is used, and a drawing of the mark.

(3) The statement shall be verified by the applicant and specify that—

(A) the person making the verification believes that he or she, or the juristic person in whose behalf he or she makes the verification, to be the owner of the mark sought to be registered;

(B) to the best of the verifier's knowledge and belief, the facts recited in the application are accurate;

(C) the mark is in use in commerce; and

(D) to the best of the verifier's knowledge and belief, no other person has the right to use such mark in commerce either in the identical form thereof or in such near resemblance thereto as to be likely, when used on or in connection with the goods of such other person, to cause confusion, or to cause mistake, or to deceive, except that, in the case of every application claiming concurrent use, the applicant shall—

(i) state exceptions to the claim of exclusive use; and

(ii) shall specify, to the extent of the verifier's knowledge—

(I) any concurrent use by others;

(II) the goods on or in connection with which and the areas in which each concurrent use exists;

(III) the periods of each use; and

(IV) the goods and area for which the applicant desires registration.

(4) The applicant shall comply with such rules or regulations as may be prescribed by the Director. The Director shall promulgate rules prescribing the requirements for the application and for obtaining a filing date herein.

(b) (1) A person who has a bona fide intention, under circumstances showing the good faith of such person, to use a trademark in commerce may request registration of its trademark on the principal register hereby established by paying the prescribed fee and filing in the Patent and Trademark Office an application and a verified statement, in such form as may be prescribed by the Director.

(2) The application shall include specification of the applicant's domicile and citizenship, the goods in connection with which the applicant has a bona fide intention to use the mark, and a drawing of the mark.

(3) The statement shall be verified by the applicant and specify—

(A) that the person making the verification believes that he or she, or the juristic person in whose behalf he or she makes the verification, to be entitled to use the mark in commerce;

(B) the applicant's bona fide intention to use the mark in commerce;

(C) that, to the best of the verifier's knowledge and belief, the facts recited in the application are accurate; and

(D) that, to the best of the verifier's knowledge and belief, no other person has the right to use such mark in commerce either in the identical form thereof or in such near resemblance thereto as to be likely, when used on or in connection with the goods of such other person, to cause confusion, or to cause mistake, or to deceive.

Except for applications filed pursuant to section 44, no mark shall be registered until the applicant has met the requirements of subsections (c) and (d) of this section.

(4) The applicant shall comply with such rules or regulations as may be prescribed by the Director. The Director shall promulgate rules

prescribing the requirements for the application and for obtaining a filing date herein.

(c) At any time during examination of an application filed under subsection (b), an applicant who has made use of the mark in commerce may claim the benefits of such use for purposes of this Act, by amending his or her application to bring it into conformity with the requirements of subsection (a).

(d) (1) Within six months after the date on which the notice of allowance with respect to a mark is issued under section 13(b)(2) to an applicant under subsection (b) of this section, the applicant shall file in the Patent and Trademark Office, together with such number of specimens or facsimiles of the mark as used in commerce as may be required by the Director and payment of the prescribed fee, a verified statement that the mark is in use in commerce and specifying the date of the applicant's first use of the mark in commerce and those goods or services specified in the notice of allowance on or in connection with which the mark is used in commerce. Subject to examination and acceptance of the statement of use, the mark shall be registered in the Patent and Trademark Office, a certificate of registration shall be issued for those goods or services recited in the statement of use for which the mark is entitled to registration, and notice of registration shall be published in the Official Gazette of the Patent and Trademark Office. Such examination may include an examination of the factors set forth in subsections (a) through (e) of section 2. The notice of registration shall specify the goods or services for which the mark is registered.

(2) The Director shall extend, for one additional 6–month period, the time for filing the statement of use under paragraph (1), upon written request of the applicant before the expiration of the 6–month period provided in paragraph (1). In addition to an extension under the preceding sentence, the Director may, upon a showing of good cause by the applicant, further extend the time for filing the statement of use under paragraph (1) for periods aggregating not more than 24 months, pursuant to written request of the applicant made before the expiration of the last extension granted under this paragraph. Any request for an extension under this paragraph shall be accompanied by a verified statement that the applicant has a continued bona fide intention to use the mark in commerce and specifying those goods or services identified in the notice of allowance on or in connection with which the applicant has a continued bona fide intention to use the mark in commerce. Any request for an extension under this paragraph shall be accompanied by payment of the prescribed fee. The Director shall issue regulations setting forth guidelines for determining what constitutes good cause for purposes of this paragraph.

(3) The Director shall notify any applicant who files a statement of use of the acceptance or refusal thereof and, if the statement of use is refused, the reasons for the refusal. An applicant may amend the statement of use.

(4) The failure to timely file a verified statement of use under paragraph (1) or an extension request under paragraph (2) shall result in abandonment of the application, unless it can be shown to the satisfaction of the Director that the delay in responding was unintentional, in which case the time for filing may be extended, but for a period not to exceed the period specified in paragraphs (1) and (2) for filing a statement of use.

(e) If the applicant is not domiciled in the United States the applicant may designate, by a document filed in the United States Patent and Trademark Office, the name and address of a person resident in the United States on whom may be served notices or process in proceedings affecting the mark. Such notices or process may be served upon the person so designated by leaving with that person or mailing to that person a copy thereof at the address specified in the last designation so filed. If the person so designated cannot be found at the address given in the last designation, or if the registrant does not designate by a document filed in the United States Patent and Trademark Office the name and address of a person resident in the United States on whom may be served notices or process in proceedings affecting the mark, such notices or process may be served on the Director.

§ 2 (15 U.S.C. § 1052). Trademarks registrable on the principal register; concurrent registration

No trademark by which the goods of the applicant may be distinguished from the goods of others shall be refused registration on the principal register on account of its nature unless it—

(a) Consists of or comprises immoral, deceptive, or scandalous matter; or matter which may disparage or falsely suggest a connection with persons, living or dead, institutions, beliefs, or national symbols, or bring them into contempt, or disrepute; or a geographical indication which, when used on or in connection with wines or spirits, identifies a place other than the origin of the goods and is first used on or in connection with wines or spirits by the applicant on or after one year after the date on which the WTO Agreement (as defined in section 2(9) of the Uruguay Round Agreements Act) enters into force with respect to the United States.

(b) Consists of or comprises the flag or coat of arms or other insignia of the United States, or of any State or municipality, or of any foreign nation, or any simulation thereof.

(c) Consists of or comprises a name, portrait, or signature identifying a particular living individual except by his written consent, or the name, signature, or portrait of a deceased President of the United States during the life of his widow, if any, except by the written consent of the widow.

(d) Consists of or comprises a mark which so resembles a mark registered in the Patent and Trademark Office, or a mark or trade name previously used in the United States by another and not abandoned, as to be likely, when used on or in connection with the goods of the applicant, to cause confusion, or to cause mistake, or to deceive: Provided, That if the Director determines that confusion, mistake, or deception is not likely to result from the continued use by more than one person of the same or similar marks under conditions and limitations as to the mode or place of use of the marks or the goods on or in connection with which such marks are used, concurrent registrations may be issued to such persons when they have become entitled to use such marks as a result of their concurrent lawful use in commerce prior to (1) the earliest of the filing dates of the applications pending or of any registration issued under this Act; (2) July 5, 1947, in the case of registrations previously issued under the Act of March 3, 1881, or February 20, 1905, and continuing in full force and effect on that date; or (3) July 5, 1947, in the case of applications filed under the Act of February 20, 1905, and registered after July 5, 1947. Use prior to the filing date of any pending application or a registration shall not be required when the owner of such application or registration consents to the grant of a concurrent registration to the applicant. Concurrent registrations may also be issued by the Director when a court of competent jurisdiction has finally determined that more than one person is entitled to use the same or similar marks in commerce. In issuing concurrent registrations, the Director shall prescribe conditions and limitations as to the mode or place of use of the mark or the goods on or in connection with which such mark is registered to the respective persons.

(e) Consists of a mark which, (1) when used on or in connection with the goods of the applicant is merely descriptive or deceptively misdescriptive of them, (2) when used on or in connection with the goods of the applicant is primarily geographically descriptive of them, except as indications of regional origin may be registrable under section 4, (3) when used on or in connection with the goods of the applicant is primarily geographically deceptively misdescriptive of them, (4) is primarily merely a surname, or (5) comprises any matter that, as a whole, is functional.

(f) Except as expressly excluded in subsections (a), (b), (c), (d), (e)(3), and (e)(5) of this section, nothing herein shall prevent the registration of a mark used by the applicant which has become distinctive of the applicant's goods in commerce. The Director may accept as prima facie evidence that the mark has become distinctive, as used on or in connection with the applicant's goods in commerce, proof of substantially exclusive and continuous use thereof as a mark by the applicant in commerce for the five years before the date on which the claim of distinctiveness is made. Nothing in this section shall prevent the registration of a mark which, when used on or in connection with the goods of the applicant, is primarily geographically deceptively misdescriptive of them, and which became distinctive of the applicant's goods in commerce before the date of the enactment of the North American Free Trade Agreement Implementation Act.

A mark which when used would cause dilution under section 43(c) may be refused registration only pursuant to a proceeding brought under section 13. A registration for a mark which when used would cause dilution under section 43(c) may be canceled pursuant to a proceeding brought under either section 14 or section 24.

§ 3 (15 U.S.C. § 1053). Service marks registrable

Subject to the provisions relating to the registration of trademarks, so far as they are applicable, service marks shall be registrable, in the same manner and with the same effect as are trademarks, and when registered they shall be entitled to the protection provided herein in the case of trademarks. Applications and procedure under this section shall conform as nearly as practicable to those prescribed for the registration of trademarks.

§ 4 (15 U.S.C. § 1054). Collective marks and certification marks registrable

Subject to the provisions relating to the registration of trademarks, so far as they are applicable, collective and certification marks, including indications of regional origin, shall be registrable under this Act, in the same manner and with the same effect as are trademarks, by persons, and nations, States, municipalities, and the like, exercising legitimate control over the use of the marks sought to be registered, even though not possessing an industrial or commercial establishment, and when registered they shall be entitled to the protection provided herein in the case of trademarks, except in the case of certification marks when used so as to represent falsely that the owner or a user thereof makes or sells the goods or performs the services on or in connection with which such mark is used. Applications and procedure under this section shall conform as nearly as practicable to those prescribed for the registration of trademarks.

§ 5 (15 U.S.C. § 1055). Use by related companies

Where a registered mark or a mark sought to be registered is or may be used legitimately by related companies, such use shall inure to the benefit of the registrant or applicant for registration, and such use shall not affect the validity of such mark or of its registration, provided such mark is not used in such manner as to deceive the public. If first use of a mark by a person is controlled by the registrant or applicant for registration of the mark with respect to the nature and quality of the goods or services, such first use shall inure to the benefit of the registrant or applicant, as the case may be.

§ 6 (15 U.S.C. § 1056). Disclaimers

(a) The Director may require the applicant to disclaim an unregistrable component of a mark otherwise registrable. An applicant may voluntarily disclaim a component of a mark sought to be registered.

(b) No disclaimer, including those made under subsection (e) of section 7 of this Act, shall prejudice or affect the applicant's or registrant's rights then existing or thereafter arising in the disclaimed matter, or his right of registration on another application if the disclaimed matter be or shall have become distinctive of his goods or services.

§ 7 (15 U.S.C. § 1057). Certificates of registration

(a) Certificates of registration of marks registered upon the principal register shall be issued in the name of the United States of America, under the seal of the Patent and Trademark Office, and shall be signed by the Director or have his signature placed thereon, and a record thereof shall be kept in the Patent and Trademark Office. The registration shall reproduce the mark, and state that the mark is registered on the principal register under this Act, the date of the first use of the mark, the date of the first use of the mark in commerce, the particular goods or services for which it is registered, the number and date of the registration, the term thereof, the date on which the application for registration was received in the Patent and Trademark Office, and any conditions and limitations that may be imposed in the registration.

(b) A certificate of registration of a mark upon the principal register provided by this Act shall be prima facie evidence of the validity of the registered mark and of the registration of the mark, of the registrant's ownership of the mark, and of the registrant's exclusive right to use the registered mark in commerce on or in connection with the goods or services specified in the certificate, subject to any conditions or limitations stated in the certificate.

(c) Contingent on the registration of a mark on the principal register provided by this Act, the filing of the application to register such mark shall constitute constructive use of the mark, conferring a right of priority, nationwide in effect, on or in connection with the goods or services specified in the registration against any other person except for a person whose mark has not been abandoned and who, prior to such filing—

(1) has used the mark;

(2) has filed an application to register the mark which is pending or has resulted in registration of the mark; or

(3) has filed a foreign application to register the mark on the basis of which he or she has acquired a right of priority, and timely files an application under section 44(d) to register the mark which is pending or has resulted in registration of the mark.

(d) A certificate of registration of a mark may be issued to the assignee of the applicant, but the assignment must first be recorded in the Patent and Trademark Office. In case of change of ownership the Director shall, at the request of the owner and upon a proper showing and the payment of the prescribed fee, issue to such assignee a new certificate of registration of the said mark in the name of such assignee, and for the unexpired part of the original period.

(e) Upon application of the registrant the Director may permit any registration to be surrendered for cancellation, and upon cancellation appropriate entry shall be made in the records of the Patent and Trademark Office. Upon application of the registrant and payment of the prescribed fee, the Director for good cause may permit any registration to be amended or to be disclaimed in part: Provided, That the amendment or disclaimer does not alter materially the character of the mark. Appropriate entry shall be made in the records of the Patent and Trademark Office and upon the certificate of registration or, if said certificate is lost or destroyed, upon a certified copy thereof.

(f) Copies of any records, books, papers, or drawings belonging to the Patent and Trademark Office relating to marks, and copies of registrations, when authenticated by the seal of the Patent and Trademark Office and certified by the Director, or in his name by an employee of the Office duly designated by the Director, shall be evidence in all cases wherein the originals would be evidence; and any person making application therefor and paying the prescribed fee shall have such copies.

(g) Whenever a material mistake in a registration, incurred through the fault of the Patent and Trademark Office, is clearly disclosed by the records of the Office a certificate stating the fact and nature of such mistake shall be issued without charge and recorded and a printed copy thereof shall be attached to each printed copy of the registration and such corrected registration shall thereafter have the same effect as if the same had been originally issued in such corrected form, or in the discretion of the Director a new certificate of registration may be issued without charge. All certificates of correction heretofore issued in accordance with the rules of the Patent and Trademark Office and the registrations to which they are attached shall have the same force and effect as if such certificates and their issue had been specifically authorized by statute.

(h) Whenever a mistake has been made in a registration and a showing has been made that such mistake occurred in good faith through the fault of the applicant, the Director is authorized to issue a certificate of correction or, in his discretion, a new certificate upon the payment of the prescribed fee: Provided, That the correction does not involve such changes in the registration as to require republication of the mark.

§ 8 (15 U.S.C. § 1058). Duration

(a) Each registration shall remain in force for 10 years, except that the registration of any mark shall be canceled by the Director for failure to comply with the provisions of subsection (b) of this section, upon the expiration of the following time periods, as applicable:

(1) For registrations issued pursuant to the provisions of this Act, at the end of 6 years following the date of registration.

(2) For registrations published under the provisions of section 12(c), at the end of 6 years following the date of publication under such section.

(3) For all registrations, at the end of each successive 10–year period following the date of registration.

(b) During the 1–year period immediately preceding the end of the applicable time period set forth in subsection (a), the owner of the registration shall pay the prescribed fee and file in the Patent and Trademark Office—

(1) an affidavit setting forth those goods or services recited in the registration on or in connection with which the mark is in use in commerce and such number of specimens or facsimiles showing current use of the mark as may be required by the Director; or

(2) an affidavit setting forth those goods or services recited in the registration on or in connection with which the mark is not in use in commerce and showing that any such nonuse is due to special circumstances which excuse such nonuse and is not due to any intention to abandon the mark.

(c) (1) The owner of the registration may make the submissions required under this section within a grace period of 6 months after the end of the applicable time period set forth in subsection (a). Such submission is required to be accompanied by a surcharge prescribed by the Director.

(2) If any submission filed under this section is deficient, the deficiency may be corrected after the statutory time period and within the time prescribed after notification of the deficiency. Such submission is required to be accompanied by a surcharge prescribed by the Director.

(d) Special notice of the requirement for affidavits under this section shall be attached to each certificate of registration and notice of publication under section 12(c).

(e) The Director shall notify any owner who files 1 of the affidavits required by this section of the Director's acceptance or refusal thereof and, in the case of a refusal, the reasons therefor.

(f) If the registrant is not domiciled in the United States, the registrant may designate, by a document filed in the United States Patent and Trademark Office, the name and address of a person resident in the United States on whom may be served notices or process in proceedings affecting the mark. Such notices or process may be served upon the person so designated by leaving with that person or mailing to that person a copy thereof at the address specified in the last designation so filed. If the person so designated cannot be found at the address given in the last designation, or if the registrant does not designate by a document filed in the United States Patent and Trademark Office the name and address of a person resident in the United States on whom may be served notices or process in proceedings affecting the mark, such notices or process may be served on the Director.

§ 9 (15 U.S.C. § 1059). Renewal

(a) Subject to the provisions of section 8, each registration may be renewed for periods of 10 years at the end of each successive 10–year period following the date of registration upon payment of the prescribed fee and the filing of a written application, in such form as may be prescribed by the Director. Such application may be made at any time within 1 year before the end of each successive 10–year period for which the registration was issued or renewed, or it may be made within a grace period of 6 months after the end of each successive 10–year period, upon payment of a fee and surcharge prescribed therefor. If any application filed under this section is deficient, the deficiency may be corrected within the time prescribed after notification of the deficiency, upon payment of a surcharge prescribed therefor.

(b) If the Director refuses to renew the registration, the Director shall notify the registrant of the Director's refusal and the reasons therefor.

(c) If the registrant is not domiciled in the United States the registrant may designate, by a document filed in the United States Patent and Trademark Office, the name and address of a person resident in the United States on whom may be served notices or process in proceedings affecting the mark. Such notices or process may be served upon the person so designated by leaving with that person or mailing to that person a copy thereof at the address specified in the last designation so filed. If the person so designated cannot be found at the address given in the last designation, or if the registrant does not designate by a document filed in the United States Patent and Trademark Office the name and address of a person resident in the United States on whom may be served notices or process in proceedings affecting the mark, such notices or process may be served on the Director.

§ 10 (15 U.S.C. § 1060). Assignment

(a) (1) A registered mark or a mark for which an application to register has been filed shall be assignable with the good will of the business in which the mark is used, or with that part of the good will of the business connected with the use of and symbolized by the mark. Notwithstanding the preceding sentence, no application to register a mark under section 1(b) shall be assignable prior to the filing of an amendment under section 1(c) to bring the application into conformity with section 1(a) or the filing of the verified statement of use under section 1(d), except for an assignment to a successor to the business of the applicant, or portion thereof, to which the mark pertains, if that business is ongoing and existing.

(2) In any assignment authorized by this section, it shall not be necessary to include the good will of the business connected with the use of and symbolized by any other mark used in the business or by the name or style under which the business is conducted.

(3) Assignments shall be by instruments in writing duly executed. Acknowledgment shall be prima facie evidence of the execution of an assignment, and when the prescribed information reporting the assignment is recorded in the United States Patent and Trademark Office, the record shall be prima facie evidence of execution.

(4) An assignment shall be void against any subsequent purchaser for valuable consideration without notice, unless the prescribed information reporting the assignment is recorded in the United States Patent and Trademark Office within 3 months after the date of the assignment or prior to the subsequent purchase.

(5) The United States Patent and Trademark Office shall maintain a record of information on assignments, in such form as may be prescribed by the Director.

(b) An assignee not domiciled in the United States may designate by a document filed in the United States Patent and Trademark Office the name and address of a person resident in the United States on whom may be served notices or process in proceedings affecting the mark. Such notices or process may be served upon the person so designated by leaving with that person or mailing to that person a copy thereof at the address specified in the last designation so filed. If the person so designated cannot be found at the address given in the last designation, or if the assignee does not designate by a document filed in the United States Patent and Trademark Office the name and address of a person resident in the United States on whom may be served notices or process in proceedings affecting the mark, such notices or process may be served upon the Director.

§ 11 (15 U.S.C. § 1061). Acknowledgments and verifications

Acknowledgments and verifications required hereunder may be made before any person within the United States authorized by law to administer oaths, or, when made in a foreign country, before any diplomatic or consular officer of the United States or before any official authorized to administer oaths in the foreign country concerned whose authority shall be proved by a certificate of a diplomatic or consular officer of the United States, or apostille of an official designated by a foreign country which, by treaty or convention, accords like effect to apostilles of designated officials in the United States, and shall be valid if they comply with the laws of the state or country where made.

§ 12 (15 U.S.C. § 1062). Publication

(a) Upon the filing of an application for registration and payment of the prescribed fee, the Director shall refer the application to the examiner in charge of the registration of marks, who shall cause an examination to be made and, if on such examination it shall appear that the applicant is entitled to registration, or would be entitled to registration upon the acceptance of the statement of use required by section 1(d) of this Act, the Director shall cause the mark to be published in the Official Gazette of the Patent and Trademark Office: Provided, That in the case of an applicant claiming concurrent use, or in the case of an application to be placed in an interference as provided for in section 16 of this Act, the mark, if otherwise registrable, may be published subject to the determination of the rights of the parties to such proceedings.

(b) If the applicant is found not entitled to registration, the examiner shall advise the applicant thereof and of the reason therefor. The applicant shall have a period of six months in which to reply or amend his application, which shall then be reexamined. This procedure may be repeated until (1) the examiner finally refuses registration of the mark or (2) the applicant fails for a period of six months to reply or amend or appeal, whereupon the application shall be deemed to have been abandoned, unless it can be shown to the satisfaction of the Director that the delay in responding was unintentional, whereupon such time may be extended.

(c) A registrant of a mark registered under the provision of the Act of March 3, 1881, or the Act of February 20, 1905, may, at any time prior to the expiration of the registration thereof, upon the payment of the prescribed fee file with the Director an affidavit setting forth those goods stated in the registration on which said mark is in use in commerce and that the registrant claims the benefits of this Act for said mark. The Director shall publish notice thereof with a reproduction of said mark in the Official Gazette, and notify the registrant of such publication and of the requirement for the affidavit of use or nonuse as provided for in subsection (b) of section 8 of this Act. Marks published under this subsection shall not be subject to the provisions of section 13 of this Act.

§ 13 (15 U.S.C. § 1063). Opposition

(a) Any person who believes that he would be damaged by the registration of a mark upon the principal register, including as a result of dilution under section 43(c), may, upon payment of the prescribed fee, file an opposition in the Patent and Trademark Office, stating the grounds therefor, within thirty days after the publication under subsection (a) of section 12 of this Act of the mark sought to be registered. Upon written request prior to the expiration of the thirty-day period, the time for filing opposition shall be extended for an additional thirty days, and further extensions of time for filing opposition may be granted by the Director for good cause when requested prior to the expiration of an extension. The Director shall notify the applicant of each extension of the time for filing opposition. An opposition may be amended under such conditions as may be prescribed by the Director.

(b) Unless registration is successfully opposed—

(1) a mark entitled to registration on the principal register based on an application filed under section 1(a) or pursuant to section 44 shall be registered in the Patent and Trademark Office, a certificate of registration shall be issued, and notice of the registration shall be published in the Official Gazette of the Patent and Trademark Office; or

(2) a notice of allowance shall be issued to the applicant if the applicant applied for registration under section 1(b).

§ 14 (15 U.S.C. § 1064). Cancellation

A petition to cancel a registration of a mark, stating the grounds relied upon, may, upon payment of the prescribed fee, be filed as follows by any person who believes that he is or will be damaged, including as a result of dilution under section 43(c), by the registration of a mark on the principal register established by this Act, or under the Act of March 3, 1881, or the Act of February 20, 1905:

(1) Within five years from the date of the registration of the mark under this Act.

(2) Within five years from the date of publication under section 12(c) hereof of a mark registered under the Act of March 3, 1881, or the Act of February 20, 1905.

(3) At any time if the registered mark becomes the generic name for the goods or services, or a portion thereof, for which it is registered, or is functional, or has been abandoned, or its registration was obtained fraudulently or contrary to the provisions of section 4 or of subsection (a), (b), or (c) of section 2 for a registration under this Act, or contrary to similar prohibitory provisions of such said prior Acts for a registration under such Acts, or if the registered mark is being used by, or with the permission of, the registrant so as to misrepresent the source of the goods or services on or in connection with which the mark is used. If the registered mark becomes the generic name for less than all of the goods or services for which it is registered, a petition to cancel the registration for only those goods or services may be filed. A registered mark shall not be deemed to be the generic name of goods or services solely because such mark is also used as a name of or to identify a unique product or service. The primary significance of the registered mark to the relevant public rather than purchaser motivation shall be the test for determining whether the registered mark has become the generic name of goods or services on or in connection with which it has been used.

(4) At any time if the mark is registered under the Act of March 3, 1881, or the Act of February 20, 1905, and has not been published under the provisions of subsection (c) of section 12 of this Act.

(5) At any time in the case of a certification mark on the ground that the registrant (A) does not control, or is not able legitimately to exercise control over, the use of such mark, or (B) engages in the production or marketing of any goods or services to which the certification mark is applied, or (C) permits the use of the certification mark for purposes other than to certify, or (D) discriminately refuses to certify or to continue to certify the goods or services of any person who maintains the standards or conditions which such mark certifies:

Provided, That the Federal Trade Commission may apply to cancel on the grounds specified in paragraphs (3) and (5) of this section any mark registered on the principal register established by this Act, and the prescribed fee shall not be required.

Nothing in paragraph (5) shall be deemed to prohibit the registrant from using its certification mark in advertising or promoting recognition of the certification program or of the goods or services meeting the certification standards of the registrant. Such uses of the certification mark shall not be grounds for cancellation under paragraph (5), so long as the registrant does not itself produce, manufacture, or sell any of the certified goods or services to which its identical certification mark is applied.

§ 15 (15 U.S.C. § 1065). Incontestability of right to use mark

Except on a ground for which application to cancel may be filed at anytime under paragraphs (3) and (5) of section 14 of this Act, and except to the extent, if any, to which the use of a mark registered on the principal register infringes a valid right acquired under the law of any State or Territory by use of a mark or trade name continuing from a date prior to the date of registration under this Act of such registered mark, the right of the registrant to use such registered mark in commerce for the goods or services on or in connection with which such registered mark has been in continuous use for five consecutive years subsequent to the date of such registration and is still in use in commerce, shall be incontestable: Provided, That—

(1) there has been no final decision adverse to registrant's claim of ownership of such mark for such goods or services, or to registrant's right to register the same or to keep the same on the register; and

(2) there is no proceeding involving said rights pending in the Patent and Trademark Office or in a court and not finally disposed of; and

(3) an affidavit is filed with the Director within one year after the expiration of any such five-year period setting forth those goods or services stated in the registration on or in connection with which such mark has been in continuous use for such five consecutive years and is still in use in commerce, and the other matters specified in paragraphs (1) and (2) of this section; and

(4) no incontestable right shall be acquired in a mark which is the generic name for the goods or services or a portion thereof, for which it is registered.

Subject to the conditions above specified in this section, the incontestable right with reference to a mark registered under this Act shall apply to a mark registered under the Act of March 3, 1881, or the Act of February 20, 1905, upon the filing of the required affidavit with the Director within one year after the expiration of any period of five consecutive years after the date of publication of a mark under the provisions of subsection (c) of section 12 of this Act.

The Director shall notify any registrant who files the above-prescribed affidavit of the filing thereof.

§ 16 (15 U.S.C. § 1066). Interference

Upon petition showing extraordinary circumstances, the Director may declare that an interference exists when application is made for the registration of a mark which so resembles a mark previously registered by another, or for the registration of which another has previously made application, as to be likely when used on or in connection with the goods or services of the applicant to cause confusion or mistake or to deceive. No interference shall be declared between an application and the registration of a mark the right to the use of which has become incontestable.

§ 17 (15 U.S.C. § 1067). Notice of inter partes proceedings; hearing by Trademark Trial and Appeal Board

(a) In every case of interference, opposition to registration, application to register as a lawful concurrent user, or application to cancel the registration of a mark, the Director shall give notice to all parties and shall direct a Trademark Trial and Appeal Board to determine and decide the respective rights of registration.

(b) The Trademark Trial and Appeal Board shall include the Director, the Commissioner for Patents, the Commissioner for Trademarks, and administrative trademark judges who are appointed by the Director.

§ 18 (15 U.S.C. § 1068). Refusal, cancellation, or restriction of registration; concurrent use

In such proceedings the Director may refuse to register the opposed mark, may cancel the registration, in whole or in part, may modify the application or registration by limiting the goods or services specified therein, may otherwise restrict or rectify with respect to the register the registration of a registered mark, may refuse to register any or all of several interfering marks, or may register the mark or marks for the person or persons entitled thereto, as the rights of the parties hereunder may be established in the proceedings: Provided, That in the case of the registration of any mark based on concurrent use, the or shall determine and fix the conditions and limitations provided for in subsection (d) of section 2 of this Act. However, no final judgment shall be entered in favor of an applicant under section 1(b) before the mark is registered, if such applicant cannot prevail without establishing constructive use pursuant to section 7(c).

§ 19 (15 U.S.C. § 1069). Applicability, in inter partes proceeding, of equitable principles of laches, estoppel and acquiescence

In all inter partes proceedings equitable principles of laches, estoppel, and acquiescence, where applicable, may be considered and applied.

§ 20 (15 U.S.C. § 1070). Appeal from examiner to Trademark Trial and Appeal Board

An appeal may be taken to the Trademark Trial and Appeal Board from any final decision of the examiner in charge of the registration of marks upon the payment of the prescribed fee.

§ 21 (15 U.S.C. § 1071). Review of Director's or Trademark Trial and Appeal Board's decision

(a) (1) An applicant for registration of a mark, party to an interference proceeding, party to an opposition proceeding, party to an application to register as a lawful concurrent user, party to a cancellation proceeding, a registrant who has filed an affidavit as provided in section 8, or an applicant for renewal, who is dissatisfied with the decision of the Director or Trademark Trial and Appeal Board, may appeal to the United States Court of Appeals for the Federal Circuit thereby waiving his right to proceed under subsection (b) of this section: Provided, That such appeal shall be dismissed if any adverse party to the proceeding, other than the Director, shall, within twenty days after the appellant has filed notice of appeal according to paragraph (2) of this subsection, files notice with the Director that he elects to have all further proceedings conducted as provided in subsection (b) of this section. Thereupon the appellant shall have thirty days thereafter within which to file a civil action under subsection (b) of this section in default of which the decision appealed from shall govern the further proceedings in the case.

(2) When an appeal is taken to the United States Court of Appeals for the Federal Circuit, the appellant shall file in the Patent and Trademark Office a written notice of appeal directed to the Director, within such time after the date of the decision from which the appeal is taken as the Director prescribes, but in no case less than 60 days after that date.

(3) The Director shall transmit to the United States Court of Appeals for the Federal Circuit a certified list of the documents comprising the record in the Patent and Trademark Office. The court may request that the Director forward the original or certified copies of such documents during pendency of the appeal. In an ex parte case, the Director shall submit to that court a brief explaining the grounds for the decision of the Patent and Trademark Office, addressing all the issues involved in the appeal. The court shall, before hearing an appeal, give notice of the time and place of the hearing to the Director and parties in the appeal.

(4) The United States Court of Appeals for the Federal Circuit shall review the decision from which the appeal is taken on the record before the Patent and Trademark Office. Upon its determination the court shall issue its mandate and opinion to the Director, which shall be entered of record in the Patent and Trademark Office and shall govern the further proceedings in the case. However, no final judgment shall be entered in favor of an applicant under section 1(b) before the mark is registered, if such applicant cannot prevail without establishing constructive use pursuant to section 7(c).

(b) (1) Whenever a person authorized by subsection (a) of this section to appeal to the United States Court of Appeals for the Federal Circuit is dissatisfied with the decision of the Director or Trademark Trial and

Appeal Board, said person may, unless appeal has been taken to said United States Court of Appeals for the Federal Circuit, have remedy by a civil action if commenced within such time after such decision, not less than sixty days, as the Director appoints or as provided in subsection (a) of this section. The court may adjudge that an applicant is entitled to a registration upon the application involved, that a registration involved should be canceled, or such other matter as the issues in the proceeding require, as the facts in the case may appear. Such adjudication shall authorize the Director to take any necessary action, upon compliance with the requirements of law. However, no final judgment shall be entered in favor of an applicant under section 1(b) before the mark is registered, if such applicant cannot prevail without establishing constructive use pursuant to section 7(c).

(2) The Director shall not be made a party to an inter partes proceeding under this subsection, but he shall be notified of the filing of the complaint by the clerk of the court in which it is filed and shall have the right to intervene in the action.

(3) In any case where there is no adverse party, a copy of the complaint shall be served on the Director, and, unless the court finds the expenses to be unreasonable, all the expenses of the proceeding shall be paid by the party bringing the case, whether the final decision is in favor of such party or not. In suits brought hereunder, the record in the Patent and Trademark Office shall be admitted on motion of any party, upon such terms and conditions as to costs, expenses, and the further cross-examination of the witnesses as the court imposes, without prejudice to the right of any party to take further testimony. The testimony and exhibits of the record in the Patent and Trademark Office, when admitted, shall have the same effect as if originally taken and produced in the suit.

(4) Where there is an adverse party, such suit may be instituted against the party in interest as shown by the records of the Patent and Trademark Office at the time of the decision complained of, but any party in interest may become a party to the action. If there be adverse parties residing in a plurality of districts not embraced within the same State, or an adverse party residing in a foreign country, the United States District Court for the District of Columbia shall have jurisdiction and may issue summons against the adverse parties directed to the marshal of any district in which any adverse party resides. Summons against adverse parties residing in foreign countries may be served by publication or otherwise as the court directs.

§ 22 (15 U.S.C. § 1072). Registration as notice

Registration of a mark on the principal register provided by this Act or under the Act of March 3, 1881, or the Act of February 20, 1905, shall be constructive notice of the registrant's claim of ownership thereof.

TITLE II—THE SUPPLEMENTAL REGISTER

§ 23 (15 U.S.C. § 1091). Filing and registration for foreign use

(a) In addition to the principal register, the Director shall keep a continuation of the register provided in paragraph (b) of section 1 of the Act of March 19, 1920, entitled "An Act to give effect to certain provisions of the convention for the protection of trademarks and commercial names, made and signed in the city of Buenos Aires, in the Argentine Republic, August 20, 1910, and for other purposes," to be called the supplemental register. All marks capable of distinguishing applicant's goods or services and not registrable on the principal register herein provided, except those declared to be unregistrable under subsections (a), (b), (c), (d), and (e)(3) of section 2 of this Act, which are in lawful use in commerce by the owner thereof, on or in connection with any goods or services may be registered on the supplemental register upon the payment of the prescribed fee and compliance with the provisions of subsections (a) and (e) of section 1 so far as they are applicable. Nothing in this section shall prevent the registration on the supplemental register of a mark, capable of distinguishing the applicant's goods or services and not registrable on the principal register under this Act, that is declared to be unregistrable under section 2(e)(3), if such mark has been in lawful use in commerce by the owner thereof, on or in connection with any goods or services, since before the date of the enactment of the North American Free Trade Agreement Implementation Act.

(b) Upon the filing of an application for registration on the supplemental register and payment of the prescribed fee the Director shall refer the application to the examiner in charge of the registration of marks, who shall cause an examination to be made and if on such examination it shall appear that the applicant is entitled to registration, the registration shall be granted. If the applicant is found not entitled to registration the provisions of subsection (b) of section 12 of this Act shall apply.

(c) For the purposes of registration on the supplemental register, a mark may consist of any trademark, symbol, label, package, configuration of goods, name, word, slogan, phrase, surname, geographical name, numeral, device, any matter that as a whole is not functional, or any combination of any of the foregoing, but such mark must be capable of distinguishing the applicant's goods or services.

§ 24 (15 U.S.C. § 1092). Cancellation

Marks for the supplemental register shall not be published for or be subject to opposition, but shall be published on registration in the Official Gazette of the Patent and Trademark Office. Whenever any person believes that he is or will be damaged by the registration of a mark on this register, including as a result of dilution under section 43(c), he may at any time, upon payment of the prescribed fee and the filing of a petition stating the ground therefor, apply to the Director to cancel such registration. The Director shall refer such application to the Trademark Trial and Appeal

Board, which shall give notice thereof to the registrant. If it is found after a hearing before the Board that the registrant is not entitled to registration, or that the mark has been abandoned, the registration shall be canceled by the Director. However, no final judgment shall be entered in favor of an applicant under section 1(b) before the mark is registered, if such applicant cannot prevail without establishing constructive use pursuant to section 7(c).

§ 25 (15 U.S.C. § 1093). Supplemental registration certificate

The certificates of registration for marks registered on the supplemental register shall be conspicuously different from certificates issued for marks registered on the principal register.

§ 26 (15 U.S.C. § 1094). General provisions

The provisions of this Act shall govern so far as applicable applications for registration and registrations on the supplemental register as well as those on the principal register, but applications for and registrations on the supplemental register shall not be subject to or receive the advantages of sections 1(b), 2(e), 2(f), 7(b), 7(c), 12(a), 13 to 18, inclusive, 22, 33, and 42 of this Act.

§ 27 (15 U.S.C. § 1095). Principal registration not precluded by supplemental registration

Registration of a mark on the supplemental register, or under the Act of March 19, 1920, shall not preclude registration by the registrant on the principal register established by this Act. Registration of a mark on the supplemental register shall not constitute an admission that the mark has not acquired distinctiveness.

§ 28 (15 U.S.C. § 1096). Department of Treasury; supplemental registration not filed

Registration on the supplemental register or under the Act of March 19, 1920, shall not be filed in the Department of the Treasury or be used to stop importations.

TITLE III—NOTICE OF REGISTRATION

§ 29 (15 U.S.C. § 1111). Notice of registration; display with mark; actual notice

Notwithstanding the provisions of section 22 hereof, a registrant of a mark registered in the Patent and Trademark Office, may give notice that his mark is registered by displaying with the mark the words "Registered in U.S. Patent and Trademark Office"* or "Reg. U.S. Pat. & Tm. Off."* or the letter R enclosed within a circle, thus ®; and in any suit for infringement under this Act by such a registrant failing to give such notice of registration, no profits and no damages shall be recovered under the provisions of this Act unless the defendant had actual notice of the registration.

**Note: The amendment of the wording of this term by Public Law 93–596 became effective on January 2, 1975. However, the amendment provides that any registrant may continue to give notice of his registration in accordance with § 29 of the Trademark Act of 1946, as amended Oct. 9, 1962, as an alternative to notice in accordance with § 29 of the Trademark Act as amended by Public Law 93–596, regardless of whether his mark was registered before or after January 2, 1975.*

TITLE IV—CLASSIFICATION

§ 30 (15 U.S.C. § 1112). Classification of goods and services; registration in plurality of classes

The Director may establish a classification of goods and services, for convenience of Patent and Trademark Office administration, but not to limit or extend the applicant's or registrant's rights. The applicant may apply to register a mark for any or all of the goods or services on or in connection with which he or she is using or has a bona fide intention to use the mark in commerce: Provided, That if the Director by regulation permits the filing of an application for the registration of a mark for goods or services which fall within a plurality of classes, a fee equaling the sum of the fees for filing an application in each class shall be paid, and the Director may issue a single certificate of registration for such mark.

TITLE V—FEES AND CHARGES

§ 31 (15 U.S.C. § 1113). Fees

(a) The Director shall establish fees for the filing and processing of an application for the registration of a trademark or other mark and for all other services performed by and materials furnished by the Patent and Trademark Office related to trademarks and other marks. Fees established under this subsection may be adjusted by the Director once each year to reflect, in the aggregate, any fluctuations during the preceding 12 months in the Consumer Price Index, as determined by the Secretary of Labor. Changes of less than 1 percent may be ignored. No fee established under this section shall take effect until at least 30 days after notice of the fee has been published in the Federal Register and in the Official Gazette of the Patent and Trademark Office.

(b) The Director may waive the payment of any fee for any service or material related to trademarks or other marks in connection with an occasional request made by a department or agency of the Government, or any officer thereof. The Indian Arts and Crafts Board will not be charged any fee to register Government trademarks of genuineness and quality for Indian products or for products of particular Indian tribes and groups.

TITLE VI—REMEDIES

§ 32 (15 U.S.C. § 1114). Remedies; infringement; innocent infringers

(1) Any person who shall, without the consent of the registrant—

(a) use in commerce any reproduction, counterfeit, copy, or colorable imitation of a registered mark in connection with the sale, offering for sale, distribution, or advertising of any goods or services on or in connection with which such use is likely to cause confusion, or to cause mistake, or to deceive; or

(b) reproduce, counterfeit, copy or colorably imitate a registered mark and apply such reproduction, counterfeit, copy or colorable imitation to labels, signs, prints, packages, wrappers, receptacles or advertisements intended to be used in commerce upon or in connection with the sale, offering for sale, distribution, or advertising of goods or services on or in connection with which such use is likely to cause confusion, or to cause mistake, or to deceive,

shall be liable in a civil action by the registrant for the remedies hereinafter provided. Under subsection (b) hereof, the registrant shall not be entitled to recover profits or damages unless the acts have been committed with knowledge that such imitation is intended to be used to cause confusion, or to cause mistake, or to deceive.

As used in this paragraph, the term "any person" includes the United States, all agencies and instrumentalities thereof, and all individuals, firms, corporations, or other persons acting for the United States and with the authorization and consent of the United States, and any State, any instrumentality of a State, and any officer or employee of a State or instrumentality of a State acting in his or her official capacity. The United States, all agencies and instrumentalities thereof, and all individuals, firms, corporations, other persons acting for the United States and with the authorization and consent of the United States, and any State, and any such instrumentality, officer, or employee, shall be subject to the provisions of this Act in the same manner and to the same extent as any nongovernmental entity.

(2) Notwithstanding any other provision of this Act, the remedies given to the owner of a right infringed under this Act or to a person bringing an action under section 43(a) or (d) shall be limited as follows:

(A) Where an infringer or violator is engaged solely in the business of printing the mark or violating matter for others and establishes that he or she was an innocent infringer or innocent violator, the owner of the right infringed or person bringing the action under section 43(a) shall be entitled as against such infringer or violator only to an injunction against future printing.

(B) Where the infringement or violation complained of is contained in or is part of paid advertising matter in a newspaper, magazine, or other similar periodical or in an electronic communication as defined in section 2510(12) of Title 18, United States Code, the remedies of the owner of the right infringed or person bringing the action under section 43(a) as against the publisher or distributor of such newspaper, magazine, or other similar periodical or electronic communication shall be limited to an injunction against the presentation of such advertising matter in future issues of such newspapers, magazines, or other similar periodicals or in future transmissions of such electronic communications. The limitations of this subparagraph shall apply only to innocent infringers and innocent violators.

(C) Injunctive relief shall not be available to the owner of the right infringed or person bringing the action under section 43(a) with respect to an issue of a newspaper, magazine, or other similar periodical or an electronic communication containing infringing matter or violating matter where restraining the dissemination of such infringing matter or violating matter in any particular issue of such periodical or in an electronic communication would delay the delivery of such issue or transmission of such electronic communication after the regular time for such delivery or transmission, and such delay would be due to the method by which publication and distribution of such periodical or transmission of such electronic communication is customarily conducted in accordance with sound business practice, and not due to any method or device adopted to evade this section or to prevent or delay the issuance of an injunction or restraining order with respect to such infringing matter or violating matter.

(D) (i) (I) A domain name registrar, a domain name registry, or other domain name registration authority that takes any action described under clause (ii) affecting a domain name shall not be liable for monetary relief or, except as provided in subclause (II), for injunctive relief, to any person for such action, regardless of whether the domain name is finally determined to infringe or dilute the mark.

(II) A domain name registrar, domain name registry, or other domain name registration authority described in subclause (I) may be subject to injunctive relief only if such registrar, registry, or other registration authority has—

(aa) not expeditiously deposited with a court, in which an action has been filed regarding the disposition of the domain name, documents sufficient for the court to establish the court's control and authority regarding the disposition of the registration and use of the domain name;

(bb) transferred, suspended, or otherwise modified the domain name during the pendency of the action, except upon order of the court; or

(cc) willfully failed to comply with any such court order.

(ii) An action referred to under clause (i)(I) is any action of refusing to register, removing from registration, transferring, temporarily disabling, or permanently canceling a domain name—

(I) in compliance with a court order under section 43(d); or

(II) in the implementation of a reasonable policy by such registrar, registry, or authority prohibiting the registration of a domain name that is identical to, confusingly similar to, or dilutive of another's mark.

(iii) A domain name registrar, a domain name registry, or other domain name registration authority shall not be liable for damages under this section for the registration or maintenance of a domain name for another absent a showing of bad faith intent to profit from such registration or maintenance of the domain name.

(iv) If a registrar, registry, or other registration authority takes an action described under clause (ii) based on a knowing and material misrepresentation by any other person that a domain name is identical to, confusingly similar to, or dilutive of a mark, the person making the knowing and material misrepresentation shall be liable for any damages, including costs and attorney's fees, incurred by the domain name registrant as a result of such action. The court may also grant injunctive relief to the domain name registrant, including the reactivation of the domain name or the transfer of the domain name to the domain name registrant.

(v) A domain name registrant whose domain name has been suspended, disabled, or transferred under a policy described under clause (ii)(II) may, upon notice to the mark owner, file a civil action to establish that the registration or use of the domain name by such registrant is not unlawful under this Act. The court may grant injunctive relief to the domain name registrant, including the reactivation of the domain name or transfer of the domain name to the domain name registrant.

(E) As used in this paragraph—

(i) the term "violator" means a person who violates section 43(a); and

(ii) the term "violating matter" means matter that is the subject of a violation under section 43(a).

§ 33 (15 U.S.C. § 1115). Registration as evidence of right to exclusive use; defenses

(a) Any registration issued under the Act of March 3, 1881, or the Act of February 20, 1905, or of a mark registered on the principal register provided by this Act and owned by a party to an action shall be admissible in evidence and shall be prima facie evidence of the validity of the registered mark and of the registration of the mark, of the registrant's ownership of the mark, and of the registrant's exclusive right to use the registered mark in commerce on or in connection with the goods or services specified in the registration subject to any conditions or limitations stated therein, but shall not preclude another person from proving any legal or equitable defense or defect, including those set forth in subsection (b), which might have been asserted if such mark had not been registered.

(b) To the extent that the right to use the registered mark has become incontestable under section 15, the registration shall be conclusive evidence of the validity of the registered mark and of the registration of the mark, of the registrant's ownership of the mark, and of the registrant's exclusive right to use the registered mark in commerce. Such conclusive evidence shall relate to the exclusive right to use the mark on or in connection with the goods or services specified in the affidavit filed under the provisions of section 15, or in the renewal application filed under the provisions of section 9 if the goods or services specified in the renewal are fewer in number, subject to any conditions or limitations in the registration or in such affidavit or renewal application. Such conclusive evidence of the right to use the registered mark shall be subject to proof of infringement as defined in section 32, and shall be subject to the following defenses or defects:

(1) That the registration or the incontestable right to use the mark was obtained fraudulently; or

(2) That the mark has been abandoned by the registrant; or

(3) That the registered mark is being used, by or with the permission of the registrant or a person in privity with the registrant, so as to misrepresent the source of the goods or services on or in connection with which the mark is used; or

(4) That the use of the name, term, or device charged to be an infringement is a use, otherwise than as a mark, of the party's individual name in his own business, or of the individual name of anyone in privity with such party, or of a term or device which is descriptive of and used fairly and in good faith only to describe the goods or services of such party, or their geographic origin; or

(5) That the mark whose use by a party is charged as an infringement was adopted without knowledge of the registrant's prior use and has been continuously used by such party or those in privity with him from a date prior to (A) the date of constructive use of the mark established pursuant to section 7(c), (B) the registration of the mark under this Act if the application for registration is filed before the effective date of the Trademark Law Revision Act of 1988, or (C) publication of the registered mark under subsection (c) of section 12 of this Act: Provided, however, That this defense or defect shall apply only for the area in which such continuous prior use is proved; or

(6) That the mark whose use is charged as an infringement was registered and used prior to the registration under this Act or publication under subsection (c) of section 12 of this Act of the registered mark of the registrant, and not abandoned: Provided, however, That this defense or defect shall apply only for the area in which the mark was used prior to such registration or such publication of the registrant's mark; or

(7) That the mark has been or is being used to violate the antitrust laws of the United States; or

(8) That the mark is functional; or

(9) That equitable principles, including laches, estoppel, and acquiescence, are applicable.

§ 34 (15 U.S.C. § 1116). Injunctions; enforcement; notice of filing suit given Director

(a) The several courts vested with jurisdiction of civil actions arising under this Act shall have power to grant injunctions, according to the principles of equity and upon such terms as the court may deem reasonable, to prevent the violation of any right of the registrant of a mark registered in the Patent and Trademark Office or to prevent a violation under subsection (a), (c), or (d) of section 43. Any such injunction may include a provision directing the defendant to file with the court and serve on the plaintiff within thirty days after the service on the defendant of such injunction, or such extended period as the court may direct, a report in writing under oath setting forth in detail the manner and form in which the defendant has complied with the injunction. Any such injunction granted upon hearing, after notice to the defendant, by any district court of the United States, may be served on the parties against whom such injunction is granted anywhere in the United States where they may be found, and shall be operative and may be enforced by proceedings to punish for contempt, or otherwise, by the court by which such injunction was granted, or by any other United States district court in whose jurisdiction the defendant may be found.

(b) The said courts shall have jurisdiction to enforce said injunction, as herein provided, as fully as if the injunction had been granted by the district court in which it is sought to be enforced. The clerk of the court or judge granting the injunction shall, when required to do so by the court before which application to enforce said injunction is made, transfer without delay to said court a certified copy of all papers on file in his office upon which said injunction was granted.

(c) It shall be the duty of the clerks of such courts within one month after the filing of any action, suit, or proceeding involving a mark registered under the provisions of this Act to give notice thereof in writing to the Director setting forth in order so far as known the names and addresses of the litigants and the designating number or numbers of the registration or registrations upon which the action, suit, or proceeding has been brought, and in the event any other registration be subsequently included in the action, suit, or proceeding by amendment, answer, or other pleading, the clerk shall give like notice thereof to the Director, and within one month after the judgment is entered or an appeal is taken, the clerk of the court shall give notice thereof to the Director, and it shall be the duty of the Director on receipt of such notice forthwith to endorse the same upon the file wrapper of the said registration or registrations and to incorporate the same as a part of the contents of said file wrapper.

(d) (1) (A) In the case of a civil action arising under section 32(1)(a) of this Act or section 220506 of title 36, United States Code with respect to a violation that consists of using a counterfeit mark in connection with the sale, offering for sale, or distribution of goods or services, the court may, upon ex parte application, grant an order under subsection (a) of this section pursuant to this subsection providing for the seizure of goods and counterfeit marks involved in such violation and the means of making such marks, and records documenting the manufacture, sale, or receipt of things involved in such violation.

(B) As used in this subsection the term "counterfeit mark" means—

(i) a counterfeit of a mark that is registered on the principal register in the United States Patent and Trademark Office for such goods or services sold, offered for sale, or distributed and that is in use, whether or not the person against whom relief is sought knew such mark was so registered; or

(ii) a spurious designation that is identical with, or substantially indistinguishable from, a designation as to which the remedies of this Act are made available by reason of section 220506 of title 36, United States Code;

but such term does not include any mark or designation used on or in connection with goods or services of which the manufacturer or producer was, at the time of the manufacture or production in question authorized to use the mark or designation for the type of goods or services so manufactured or produced, by the holder of the right to use such mark or designation.

(2) The court shall not receive an application under this subsection unless the applicant has given such notice of the application as is reasonable under the circumstances to the United States attorney for the judicial district in which such order is sought. Such attorney may participate in the proceedings arising under such application if such proceedings may affect evidence of an offense against the United States. The court may deny such application if the court determines that the public interest in a potential prosecution so requires.

(3) The application for an order under this subsection shall—

(A) be based on an affidavit or the verified complaint establishing facts sufficient to support the findings of fact and conclusions of law required for such order; and

(B) contain the additional information required by paragraph (5) of this subsection to be set forth in such order.

(4) The court shall not grant such an application unless—

(A) the person obtaining an order under this subsection provides the security determined adequate by the court for the payment of such damages as any person may be entitled to recover as a result of a wrongful seizure or wrongful attempted seizure under this subsection; and

(B) the court finds that it clearly appears from specific facts that—

(i) an order other than an ex parte seizure order is not adequate to achieve the purposes of section 32 of this Act;

(ii) the applicant has not publicized the requested seizure;

(iii) the applicant is likely to succeed in showing that the person against whom seizure would be ordered used a counterfeit mark in connection with the sale, offering for sale, or distribution of goods or services;

(iv) an immediate and irreparable injury will occur if such seizure is not ordered;

(v) the matter to be seized will be located at the place identified in the application;

(vi) the harm to the applicant of denying the application outweighs the harm to the legitimate interests of the person against whom seizure would be ordered of granting the application; and

(vii) the person against whom seizure would be ordered, or persons acting in concert with such person, would destroy, move, hide, or otherwise make such matter inaccessible to the court, if the applicant were to proceed on notice to such person.

(5) An order under this subsection shall set forth—

(A) the findings of fact and conclusions of law required for the order;

(B) a particular description of the matter to be seized, and a description of each place at which such matter is to be seized;

(C) the time period, which shall end not later than seven days after the date on which such order is issued, during which the seizure is to be made;

(D) the amount of security required to be provided under this subsection; and

(E) a date for the hearing required under paragraph (10) of this subsection.

(6) The court shall take appropriate action to protect the person against whom an order under this subsection is directed from publicity, by or at the behest of the plaintiff, about such order and any seizure under such order.

(7) Any materials seized under this subsection shall be taken into the custody of the court. The court shall enter an appropriate protective order with respect to discovery by the applicant of any records that have been seized. The protective order shall provide for appropriate

procedures to assure that confidential information contained in such records is not improperly disclosed to the applicant.

(8) An order under this subsection, together with the supporting documents, shall be sealed until the person against whom the order is directed has an opportunity to contest such order, except that any person against whom such order is issued shall have access to such order and supporting documents after the seizure has been carried out.

(9) The court shall order that service of a copy of the order under this subsection shall be made by a Federal law enforcement officer (such as a United States marshal or an officer or agent of the United States Customs Service, Secret Service, Federal Bureau of Investigation, or Post Office) or may be made by a State or local law enforcement officer, who, upon making service, shall carry out the seizure under the order. The court shall issue orders, when appropriate, to protect the defendant from undue damage from the disclosure of trade secrets or other confidential information during the course of the seizure, including, when appropriate, orders restricting the access of the applicant (or any agent or employee of the applicant) to such secrets or information.

(10) (A) The court shall hold a hearing, unless waived by all the parties, on the date set by the court in the order of seizure. That date shall be not sooner than ten days after the order is issued and not later than fifteen days after the order is issued, unless the applicant for the order shows good cause for another date or unless the party against whom such order is directed consents to another date for such hearing. At such hearing the party obtaining the order shall have the burden to prove that the facts supporting findings of fact and conclusions of law necessary to support such order are still in effect. If that party fails to meet that burden, the seizure order shall be dissolved or modified appropriately.

(B) In connection with a hearing under this paragraph, the court may make such orders modifying the time limits for discovery under the Rules of Civil Procedure as may be necessary to prevent the frustration of the purposes of such hearing.

(11) A person who suffers damage by reason of wrongful seizure under this subsection has a cause of action against the applicant for the order under which such seizure was made, and shall be entitled to recover such relief as may be appropriate, including damages for lost profits, cost of materials, loss of goodwill, and punitive damages in instances where the seizure was sought in bad faith, and, unless the court finds extenuating circumstances, to recover a reasonable attorney's fee. The court in its discretion may award prejudgment interest on relief recovered under this paragraph, at an annual interest rate established under section 6621(a)(2) of the Internal Revenue Code of 1986, commencing on the date of service of the claimant's pleading setting forth the claim under this paragraph and ending on the date such recovery is granted, or for such shorter time as the court deems appropriate.

§ 35 (15 U.S.C. § 1117). Recovery of profits, damages, and costs

(a) When a violation of any right of the registrant of a mark registered in the Patent and Trademark Office, a violation under section 43(a) or (d) or a willful violation under section 43(c), shall have been established in any civil action arising under this Act, the plaintiff shall be entitled, subject to the provisions of sections 29 and 32 and subject to the principles of equity, to recover (1) defendant's profits, (2) any damages sustained by the plaintiff, and (3) the costs of the action. The court shall assess such profits and damages or cause the same to be assessed under its direction. In assessing profits the plaintiff shall be required to prove defendant's sale only; defendant must prove all elements of cost or deduction claimed. In assessing damages the court may enter judgment, according to the circumstances of the case, for any sum above the amount found as actual damages, not exceeding three times such amount. If the court shall find that the amount of the recovery based on profits is either inadequate or excessive the court may in its discretion enter judgment for such sum as the court shall find to be just, according to the circumstances of the case. Such sum in either of the above circumstances shall constitute compensation and not a penalty. The court in exceptional cases may award reasonable attorney fees to the prevailing party.

(b) In assessing damages under subsection (a), the court shall, unless the court finds extenuating circumstances, enter judgment for three times such profits or damages, whichever is greater, together with a reasonable attorney's fee, in the case of any violation of section 32(1)(a) of this Act (15 U.S.C. § 1114(1)(a)) or section 220506 of title 36, United States Code, that consists of intentionally using a mark or designation, knowing such mark or designation is a counterfeit mark (as defined in section 34(d)) of this Act (15 U.S.C. § 1116(d)), in connection with the sale, offering for sale, or distribution of goods or services. In such cases, the court may in its discretion award prejudgment interest on such amount at an annual interest rate established under section 6621(a)(2) of the Internal Revenue Code of 1986, commencing on the date of the service of the claimant's pleadings setting forth the claim for such entry and ending on the date such entry is made, or for such shorter time as the court deems appropriate.

(c) In a case involving the use of a counterfeit mark (as defined in section 1116(d) of this title) in connection with the sale, offering for sale, or distribution of goods or services, the plaintiff may elect, at any time before final judgment is rendered by the trial court, to recover, instead of actual damages and profits under subsection (a) of this section, an award of statutory damages for any such use in connection with the sale, offering for sale, or distribution of goods or services in the amount of—

(1) not less than $500 or more than $100,000 per counterfeit mark per type of goods or services sold, offered for sale, or distributed, as the court considers just; or

(2) if the court finds that the use of the counterfeit mark was willful, not more than $1,000,000 per counterfeit mark per type of goods or services sold, offered for sale, or distributed, as the court considers just.

(d) In a case involving a violation of section 43(d)(1), the plaintiff may elect, at any time before final judgment is rendered by the trial court, to recover, instead of actual damages and profits, an award of statutory damages in the amount of not less than $1,000 and not more than $100,000 per domain name, as the court considers just.

§ 36 (15 U.S.C. § 1118). Destruction of infringing articles

In any action arising under this Act, in which a violation of any right of the registrant of a mark registered in the Patent and Trademark Office, a violation under section 43(a), or a willful violation under section 43(c), shall have been established, the court may order that all labels, signs, prints, packages, wrappers, receptacles, and advertisements in the possession of the defendant, bearing the registered mark or, in the case of a violation of section 43(a) or a willful violation under section 43(c), the word, term, name, symbol, device, combination thereof, designation, description, or representation that is the subject of the violation, or any reproduction, counterfeit, copy, or colorable imitation thereof, and all plates, molds, matrices, and other means of making the same, shall be delivered up and destroyed. The party seeking an order under this section for destruction of articles seized under section 34(d) (15 U.S.C. § 1116(d)) shall give ten days' notice to the United States attorney for the judicial district in which such order is sought (unless good cause is shown for lesser notice) and such United States attorney may, if such destruction may affect evidence of an offense against the United States, seek a hearing on such destruction or participate in any hearing otherwise to be held with respect to such destruction.

§ 37 (15 U.S.C. § 1119). Power of court over registration; certification of decrees and orders

In any action involving a registered mark the court may determine the right to registration, order the cancellation of registrations, in whole or in part, restore cancelled registrations, and otherwise rectify the register with respect to the registrations of any party to the action. Decrees and orders shall be certified by the court to the Director, who shall make appropriate entry upon the records of the Patent and Trademark Office, and shall be controlled thereby.

§ 38 (15 U.S.C. § 1120). Fraud; civil liability

Any person who shall procure registration in the Patent and Trademark Office of a mark by a false or fraudulent declaration or representation, oral or in writing, or by any false means, shall be liable in a civil action by any person injured thereby for any damages sustained in consequence thereof.

§ 39 (15 U.S.C. § 1121). Jurisdiction of Federal courts; State, local, and other agency requirements

(a) The district and territorial courts of the United States shall have original jurisdiction, the courts of appeal of the United States (other than the United States Court of Appeals for the Federal Circuit) and the United States Court of Appeals for the District of Columbia shall have appellate jurisdiction, of all actions arising under this Act, without regard to the amount in controversy or to diversity or lack of diversity of the citizenship of the parties.

(b) No State or other jurisdiction of the United States or any political subdivision or any agency thereof may require alteration of a registered mark, or require that additional trademarks, service marks, trade names, or corporate names that may be associated with or incorporated into the registered mark be displayed in the mark in a manner differing from the display of such additional trademarks, service marks, trade names, or corporate names contemplated by the registered mark as exhibited in the certificate of registration issued by the United States Patent and Trademark Office.

§ 40 (15 U.S.C. § 1122). Liability of States, instrumentalities of States and State officials

(a) WAIVER OF SOVEREIGN IMMUNITY BY THE UNITED STATES— The United States, all agencies and instrumentalities thereof, and all individuals, firms, corporations, other persons acting for the United States and with the authorization and consent of the United States, shall not be immune from suit in Federal or State court by any person, including any governmental or nongovernmental entity, for any violation under this Act.

(b) WAIVER OF SOVEREIGN IMMUNITY BY STATES—Any State, instrumentality of a State or any officer or employee of a State or instrumentality of a State acting in his or her official capacity, shall not be immune, under the eleventh amendment of the Constitution of the United States or under any other doctrine of sovereign immunity, from suit in Federal court by any person, including any governmental or nongovernmental entity for any violation under this Act.

(c) In a suit described in subsection (a) or (b) for a violation described therein, remedies (including remedies both at law and in equity) are available for the violation to the same extent as such remedies are available for such a violation in a suit against any person other than the United States or any agency or instrumentality thereof, or any individual, firm, corporation, or other person acting for the United States and with authorization and consent of the United States, or a State, instrumentality of a State, or officer or employee of a State or instrumentality of a State acting in his or her official capacity. Such remedies include injunctive relief under section 34, actual damages, profits, costs and attorney's fees under section 35, destruction of infringing articles under section 36, the remedies provided for under sections 32, 37, 38, 42, and 43, and for any other remedies provided under this Act.

(Added Oct. 27, 1992, 106 Stat. 3567; Aug. 5, 1999, 113 Stat. 218.)

§ 41 (15 U.S.C. § 1123). Rules and regulations

The Director shall make rules and regulations, not inconsistent with law, for the conduct of proceedings in the Patent and Trademark Office under this Act.

TITLE VII—IMPORTATION FORBIDDEN OF GOODS BEARING INFRINGING MARKS OR NAMES

§ 42 (15 U.S.C. § 1124). Importation of goods bearing infringing marks or names forbidden

Except as provided in subsection (d) of section 526 of the Tariff Act of 1930, no article of imported merchandise which shall copy or simulate the name of any domestic manufacture, or manufacturer, or trader, or of any manufacturer or trader located in any foreign country which, by treaty, convention, or law affords similar privileges to citizens of the United States, or which shall copy or simulate a trademark registered in accordance with the provisions of this Act or shall bear a name or mark calculated to induce the public to believe that the article is manufactured in the United States, or that it is manufactured in any foreign country or locality other than the country or locality in which it is in fact manufactured, shall be admitted to entry at any customhouse of the United States; and, in order to aid the officers of the customs in enforcing this prohibition, any domestic manufacturer or trader, and any foreign manufacturer or trader, who is entitled under the provisions of a treaty, convention, declaration, or agreement between the United States and any foreign country to the advantages afforded by law to citizens of the United States in respect to trademarks and commercial names, may require his name and residence, and the name of the locality in which his goods are manufactured, and a copy of the certificate of registration of his trademark, issued in accordance with the provisions of this Act, to be recorded in books which shall be kept for this purpose in the Department of the Treasury, under such regulations as the Secretary of the Treasury shall prescribe, and may furnish to the Department facsimiles of his name, the name of the locality in which his goods are manufactured, or of his registered trademark, and thereupon the Secretary of the Treasury shall cause one or more copies of the same to be transmitted to each collector or other proper officer of customs.

TITLE VIII—FALSE DESIGNATIONS OF ORIGIN, FALSE DESCRIPTIONS. AND DILUTION FORBIDDEN

§ 43 (15 U.S.C. § 1125). False designations of origin; false description or representation

(a) (1) Any person who, on or in connection with any goods or services, or any container for goods, uses in commerce any word, term, name, symbol, or device, or any combination thereof, or any false designation of origin, false or misleading description of fact, or false or misleading representation of fact, which—

(A) is likely to cause confusion, or to cause mistake, or to deceive as to the affiliation, connection, or association of such person with another person, or as to the origin, sponsorship, or approval of his or her goods, services, or commercial activities by another person, or

(B) in commercial advertising or promotion, misrepresents the nature, characteristics, qualities, or geographic origin of his or her or another person's goods, services, or commercial activities, shall be liable in a civil action by any person who believes that he or she is or is likely to be damaged by such act.

(2) As used in this subsection, the term "any person" includes any State, instrumentality of a State or employee of a State or instrumentality of a State acting in his or her official capacity. Any State, and any such instrumentality, officer, or employee, shall be subject to the provisions of this Act in the same manner and to the same extent as any nongovernmental entity.

(3) In a civil action for trade dress infringement under this Act for trade dress not registered on the principal register, the person who asserts trade dress protection has the burden of proving that the matter sought to be protected is not functional.

(b) Any goods marked or labeled in contravention of the provisions of this section shall not be imported into the United States or admitted to entry at any customhouse of the United States. The owner, importer, or consignee of goods refused entry at any customhouse under this section may have any recourse by protest or appeal that is given under the customs revenue laws or may have the remedy given by this Act in cases involving goods refused entry or seized.

(c) (1) The owner of a famous mark shall be entitled, subject to the principles of equity and upon such terms as the court deems reasonable, to an injunction against another person's commercial use in commerce of a mark or trade name, if such use begins after the mark has become famous and causes dilution of the distinctive quality of the mark, and to obtain such other relief as is provided in this subsection. In determining whether a mark is distinctive and famous, a court may consider factors such as, but not limited to—

(A) the degree of inherent or acquired distinctiveness of the mark;

(B) the duration and extent of use of the mark in connection with the goods or services with which the mark is used;

(C) the duration and extent of advertising and publicity of the mark;

(D) the geographical extent of the trading area in which the mark is used;

(E) the channels of trade for the goods or services with which the mark is used;

(F) the degree of recognition of the mark in the trading areas and channels of trade used by the mark's owner and the person against whom the injunction is sought;

(G) the nature and extent of use of the same or similar marks by third parties; and

(H) whether the mark was registered under the Act of March 3, 1881, or the Act of February 20, 1905, or on the principal register.

(2) In an action brought under this subsection, the owner of the famous mark shall be entitled only to injunctive relief as set forth in section 34 unless the person against whom the injunction is sought willfully intended to trade on the owner's reputation or to cause dilution of the famous mark. If such willful intent is proven, the owner of the famous mark shall also be entitled to the remedies set forth in sections 35(a) and 36, subject to the discretion of the court and the principles of equity.

(3) The ownership by a person of a valid registration under the Act of March 3, 1881, or the Act of February 20, 1905, or on the principal register shall be a complete bar to an action against that person, with respect to the mark, that is brought by another person under the common law or a statute of a State and that seeks to prevent dilution of the distinctiveness of a mark, label or form or advertisement.

(4) The following shall not be actionable under this section:

(A) Fair use of a famous mark by another person in comparative commercial advertising or promotion to identify the competing goods or services of the owner of the famous mark.

(B) Noncommercial use of a mark.

(C) All forms of news reporting and news commentary.

(d) (1) (A) A person shall be liable in a civil action by the owner of a mark, including a personal name which is protected as a mark under this section, if, without regard to the goods or services of the parties, that person—

(i) has a bad faith intent to profit from that mark, including a personal name which is protected as a mark under this section; and

(ii) registers, traffics in, or uses a domain name that—

(I) in the case of a mark that is distinctive at the time of registration of the domain name, is identical or confusingly similar to that mark;

(II) in the case of a famous mark that is famous at the time of registration of the domain name, is identical or confusingly similar to or dilutive of that mark; or

(III) is a trademark, word, or name protected by reason of section 706 of Title 18, United States Code, or section 220506 of Title 36, United States Code.

(B) (i) In determining whether a person has a bad faith intent described under subparagraph (A), a court may consider factors such as, but not limited to—

(I) the trademark or other intellectual property rights of the person, if any, in the domain name;

(II) the extent to which the domain name consists of the legal name of the person or a name that is otherwise commonly used to identify that person;

(III) the person's prior use, if any, of the domain name in connection with the bona fide offering of any goods or services;

(IV) the person's bona fide noncommercial or fair use of the mark in a site accessible under the domain name;

(V) the person's intent to divert consumers from the mark owner's online location to a site accessible under the domain name that could harm the goodwill represented by the mark, either for commercial gain or with the intent to tarnish or disparage the mark, by creating a likelihood of confusion as to the source, sponsorship, affiliation, or endorsement of the site;

(VI) the person's offer to transfer, sell, or otherwise assign the domain name to the mark owner or any third party for financial gain without having used, or having an intent to use, the domain name in the bona fide offering of any goods or services, or the person's prior conduct indicating a pattern of such conduct;

(VII) the person's provision of material and misleading false contact information when applying for the registration of the domain name, the person's intentional failure to maintain accurate contact information, or the person's prior conduct indicating a pattern of such conduct;

(VIII) the person's registration or acquisition of multiple domain names which the person knows are identical or confusingly similar to marks of others that are distinctive at the time of registration of such domain names, or dilutive of famous marks of others that are famous at the time of registration of such domain names, without regard to the goods or services of the parties; and

(IX) the extent to which the mark incorporated in the person's domain name registration is or is not distinctive and famous within the meaning of subsection (c)(1) of section 43.

(ii) Bad faith intent described under subparagraph (A) shall not be found in any case in which the court determines that the person believed and had reasonable grounds to believe that the use of the domain name was a fair use or otherwise lawful.

(C) In any civil action involving the registration, trafficking, or use of a domain name under this paragraph, a court may order the forfeiture or cancellation of the domain name or the transfer of the domain name to the owner of the mark.

(D) A person shall be liable for using a domain name under subparagraph (A) only if that person is the domain name registrant or that registrant's authorized licensee.

(E) As used in this paragraph, the term "traffics in" refers to transactions that include, but are not limited to, sales, purchases, loans, pledges, licenses, exchanges of currency, and any other transfer for consideration or receipt in exchange for consideration.

(2) (A) The owner of a mark may file an in rem civil action against a domain name in the judicial district in which the domain name registrar, domain name registry, or other domain name authority that registered or assigned the domain name is located if—

(i) the domain name violates any right of the owner of a mark registered in the Patent and Trademark Office, or protected under subsection (a) or (c); and

(ii) the court finds that the owner—

(I) is not able to obtain in personam jurisdiction over a person who would have been a defendant in a civil action under paragraph (1); or

(II) through due diligence was not able to find a person who would have been a defendant in a civil action under paragraph (1) by—

(aa) sending a notice of the alleged violation and intent to proceed under this paragraph to the registrant of the domain name at the postal and e-mail address provided by the registrant to the registrar; and

(bb) publishing notice of the action as the court may direct promptly after filing the action.

(B) The actions under subparagraph (A)(ii) shall constitute service of process.

(C) In an in rem action under this paragraph, a domain name shall be deemed to have its situs in the judicial district in which—

(i) the domain name registrar, registry, or other domain name authority that registered or assigned the domain name is located; or

(ii) documents sufficient to establish control and authority regarding the disposition of the registration and use of the domain name are deposited with the court.

(D) (i) The remedies in an in rem action under this paragraph shall be limited to a court order for the forfeiture or cancellation of the domain name or the transfer of the domain name to the owner of the mark. Upon receipt of written notification of a filed, stamped copy of a complaint filed by the owner of a mark in a United States district court under this paragraph, the domain name registrar, domain name registry, or other domain name authority shall—

(I) expeditiously deposit with the court documents sufficient to establish the court's control and authority regarding the disposition of the registration and use of the domain name to the court; and

(II) not transfer, suspend, or otherwise modify the domain name during the pendency of the action, except upon order of the court.

(ii) The domain name registrar or registry or other domain name authority shall not be liable for injunctive or monetary relief under this paragraph except in the case of bad faith or reckless disregard, which includes a willful failure to comply with any such court order.

(3) The civil action established under paragraph (1) and the in rem action established under paragraph (2), and any remedy available under either such action, shall be in addition to any other civil action or remedy otherwise applicable.

(4) The in rem jurisdiction established under paragraph (2) shall be in addition to any other jurisdiction that otherwise exists, whether in rem or in personam.

TITLE IX—INTERNATIONAL CONVENTIONS

§ 44 (15 U.S.C. § 1126). International conventions; register of marks

(a) The Director shall keep a register of all marks communicated to him by the international bureaus provided for by the conventions for the protection of industrial property, trademarks, trade and commercial names, and the repression of unfair competition to which the United States is or may become a party, and upon the payment of the fees required by such conventions and the fees required in this Act may place the marks so communicated upon such register. This register shall show a facsimile of the mark or trade or commercial name; the name, citizenship, and address of the registrant; the number, date, and place of the first registration of the mark, including the dates on which application for such registration was filed and granted and the term of such registration; a list of goods or services to which the mark is applied as shown by the registration in the country of origin, and such other data as may be useful concerning the mark. This register shall be a continuation of the register provided in section 1(a) of the Act of March 19, 1920.

Note: The United States is not at present a party to the parts of the international conventions providing for international bureaus for the registration or communication of trademarks.

(b) Any person whose country of origin is a party to any convention or treaty relating to trademarks, trade or commercial names, or the repression of unfair competition, to which the United States is also a party, or extends reciprocal rights to nationals of the United States by law, shall be entitled to the benefits of this section under the conditions expressed herein to the extent necessary to give effect to any provision of such convention, treaty or reciprocal law, in addition to the rights to which any owner of a mark is otherwise entitled by this Act.

Notes: International Convention for the Protection of Industrial Property of 1883 (Paris); revised at Washington in 1911, 204 O.G. 1011, July 21, 1914 (37 Stat. 1645; Treaty Series 579); at the Hague in 1925, 407 O.G. 298, June 9, 1931 (47 Stat. 1789; Treaty Series 834; 2 Bevans 524); at London in 1934, 613 O.G. 23, August 3, 1948 (53 Stat. 1748; Treaty Series 941; 3 Bevans 223); at Lisbon in 1958, 775 O.G. 321, February 13, 1962 (53 Stat. 1748; 13 U.S.T. 1; TIAS 9431); and at Stockholm July 14, 1967, 852 O.G. 511, July 16, 1968 (21 U.S.T. 1583; TIAS 6923). A list of the member countries together with an indication of the latest Act by which each country is bound and the date from which each is considered to be bound appears annually (January issue) in "Industrial Property," a monthly review of the World Intellectual Property Organization (WIPO), Geneva, Switzerland.

General Inter–American Convention for Trade–Mark and Commercial Protection (Pan–American Trade–Mark Convention) of 1929, 46 Stat. 2907; Pan–American Trade–Mark Convention of 1923, 44 Stat. 2494; Pan–American Trade–Mark Convention of 1910, 39 Stat. 1675.

List of the States which are parties to the above conventions may be found in "Treaties in Force," a list of treaties and other international agreements in force on the first day of January of each year, compiled annually by the Office of the Legal Adviser, U.S. Department of State.

(c) No registration of a mark in the United States by a person described in subsection (b) of this section shall be granted until such mark has been registered in the country of origin of the applicant, unless the applicant alleges use in commerce. For the purposes of this section, the country of origin of the applicant is the country in which he has a bona fide and effective industrial or commercial establishment, or if he has not such an establishment the country in which he is domiciled, or if he has not a domicile in any of the countries described in subsection (b) of this section, the country of which he is a national.

(d) An application for registration of a mark under sections 1, 3, 4, or 23 of this Act or under subsection (e) of this section filed by a person described in subsection (b) of this section who has previously duly filed an application for registration of the same mark in one of the countries described in subsection (b) shall be accorded the same force and effect as would be accorded to the same application if filed in the United States on the same date on which the application was first filed in such foreign country: Provided, That—

(1) the application in the United States is filed within 6 months from the date on which the application was first filed in the foreign country;

(2) the application conforms as nearly as practicable to the requirements of this Act, including a statement that the applicant has a bona fide intention to use the mark in commerce;

(3) the rights acquired by third parties before the date of the filing of the first application in the foreign country shall in no way be affected by a registration obtained on an application filed under this subsection;

(4) nothing in this subsection shall entitle the owner of a registration granted under this section to sue for acts committed prior to the date on which his mark was registered in this country unless the registration is based on use in commerce.

In like manner and subject to the same conditions and requirements, the right provided in this section may be based upon a subsequent regularly filed application in the same foreign country, instead of the first filed foreign application: Provided, That any foreign application filed prior to such subsequent application has been withdrawn, abandoned, or otherwise disposed of, without having been laid open to public inspection and without leaving any rights outstanding, and has not served, nor thereafter shall serve, as a basis for claiming a right of priority.

Note: Section 3 of Public Law 333, 87th Cong., approved October 3, 1961, 75 Stat. 748, the provision which added the last paragraph above provided that "This Act shall take effect on the date when the Convention of Paris for the Protection of Industrial Property of March 20, 1883, as revised at Lisbon October 31, 1958, comes into force with respect to the United States and is applied only to applications thereafter filed in the United States by persons entitled to the benefit of said convention, as revised at the time of such filing." This provision became effective Jan. 4, 1962.

(e) A mark duly registered in the country of origin of the foreign applicant may be registered on the principal register if eligible, otherwise on the supplemental register herein provided. Such applicant shall submit, within such time period as may be prescribed by the Director, a true copy, a photocopy, a certification or a certified copy of the registration in the country of origin of the applicant. The application must state the applicant's bona fide intention to use the mark in commerce, but use in commerce shall not be required prior to registration.

(f) The registration of a mark under the provisions of subsections (c), (d), and (e) of this section by a person described in subsection (b) shall be independent of the registration in the country of origin and the duration, validity, or transfer in the United States of such registration shall be governed by the provisions of this Act.

(g) Trade names or commercial names of persons described in subsection (b) of this section shall be protected without the obligation of filing or registration whether or not they form parts of marks.

(h) Any person designated in subsection (b) of this section as entitled to the benefits and subject to the provisions of this Act shall be entitled to effective protection against unfair competition, and the remedies provided herein for infringement of marks shall be available so far as they may be appropriate in repressing acts of unfair competition.

(i) Citizens or residents of the United States shall have the same benefits as are granted by this section to persons described in subsection (b) of this section.

TITLE X—CONSTRUCTION AND DEFINITIONS

§ 45 (15 U.S.C. § 1127).

In the construction of this Act, unless the contrary is plainly apparent from the context—

United States. The United States includes and embraces all territory which is under its jurisdiction and control.

Commerce. The word "commerce" means all commerce which may lawfully be regulated by Congress.

Principal Register, Supplemental Register. The term "principal register" refers to the register provided for by sections 1 through 22 hereof, and the term "supplemental register" refers to the register provided for by sections 23 through 28 thereof.

Person, juristic person. The term "person" and any other word or term used to designate the applicant or other entitled to a benefit or privilege or rendered liable under the provisions of this Act includes a juristic person as well as a natural person. The term "juristic person" includes a firm, corporation, union, association, or other organization capable of suing and being sued in a court of law.

The term "person" also includes the United States, any agency or instrumentality thereof, or any individual, firm, or corporation acting for the United States and with the authorization and consent of the United States. The United States, any agency or instrumentality thereof, and any individual, firm, or corporation acting for the United States and with the authorization and consent of the United States, shall be subject to the provisions of this Act in the same manner and to the same extent as any nongovernmental entity.

The term "person" also includes any State, any instrumentality of a State, and any officer or employee of a State or instrumentality of a State acting in his or her official capacity. Any State, and any such instrumentality, officer, or employee, shall be subject to the provisions of this Act in the same manner and to the same extent as any non-governmental entity.

Applicant, registrant. The terms "applicant" and "registrant" embrace the legal representatives, predecessors, successors and assigns of such applicant or registrant.

Director. The term "Director" means the Under Secretary of Commerce for Intellectual Property and Director of the United States Patent and Trademark Office.

Related company. The term "related company" means any person whose use of a mark is controlled by the owner of the mark with respect to the nature and quality of the goods or services on or in connection with which the mark is used.

Trade name, commercial name. The terms "trade name" and "commercial name" mean any name used by a person to identify his or her business or vocation.

Trademark. The term "trademark" includes any word, name, symbol, or device, or any combination thereof—

(1) used by a person, or

(2) which a person has a bona fide intention to use in commerce and applies to register on the principal register established by this Act,

to identify and distinguish his or her goods, including a unique product, from those manufactured or sold by others and to indicate the source of the goods, even if that source is unknown.

Service mark. The term "service mark" means any word, name, symbol, or device, or any combination thereof—

(1) used by a person, or

(2) which a person has a bona fide intention to use in commerce and applies to register on the principal register established by this Act,

to identify and distinguish the services of one person, including a unique service, from the services of others and to indicate the source of the services, even if that source is unknown. Titles, character names, and other distinctive features of radio or television programs may be registered as service marks notwithstanding that they, or the programs, may advertise the goods of the sponsor.

Certification mark. The term "certification mark" means any word, name, symbol, or device, or any combination thereof—

(1) used by a person other than its owner, or

(2) which its owner has a bona fide intention to permit a person other than the owner to use in commerce and files an application to register on the principal register established by this Act,

to certify regional or other origin, material, mode of manufacture, quality, accuracy, or other characteristics of such person's goods or services or that the work or labor on the goods or services was performed by members of a union or other organization.

Collective mark. The term "collective mark" means a trademark or service mark—

(1) used by the members of a cooperative, an association, or other collective group or organization, or

(2) which such cooperative, association, or other collective group or organization has a bona fide intention to use in commerce and applies to register on the principal register established by this Act, and includes marks indicating membership in a union, an association, or other organization.

Mark. The term "mark" includes any trademark, service mark, collective mark, or certification mark.

Use in commerce. The term "use in commerce" means the bona fide use of a mark in the ordinary course of trade, and not made merely to reserve a right in a mark. For purposes of this Act, a mark shall be deemed to be in use in commerce—

(1) on goods when—

(A) it is placed in any manner on the goods or their containers or the displays associated therewith or on the tags or labels affixed thereto, or if the nature of the goods makes such placement impracticable, then on documents associated with the goods or their sale, and

(B) the goods are sold or transported in commerce, and

(2) on services when it is used or displayed in the sale or advertising of services and the services are rendered in commerce, or the services are rendered in more than one State or in the United States and a foreign country and the person rendering the services is engaged in commerce in connection with the services.

Abandonment of mark. A mark shall be deemed to be "abandoned" when either of the following occurs:

(1) When its use has been discontinued with intent not to resume such use. Intent not to resume may be inferred from circumstances. Nonuse for three consecutive years shall be prima facie evidence of abandonment. "Use" of a mark means the bona fide use of that mark made in the ordinary course of trade, and not made merely to reserve a right in a mark.

(2) When any course of conduct of the owner, including acts of omission as well as commission, causes the mark to become the generic name for the goods or services on or in connection with which it is used or otherwise to lose its significance as a mark. Purchaser motivation shall not be a test for determining abandonment under this paragraph.

Colorable imitation. The term "colorable imitation" includes any mark which so resembles a registered mark as to be likely to cause confusion or mistake or to deceive.

Dilution. The term "dilution" means the lessening of the capacity of a famous mark to identify and distinguish goods or services, regardless of the presence or absence of—

(1) competition between the owner of the famous mark and other parties, or

(2) likelihood of confusion, mistake or deception.

Registered mark. The term "registered mark" means a mark registered in the United States Patent and Trademark Office under this Act or under the Act of March 3, 1881, or the Act of February 20, 1905, or the Act of March 19, 1920. The phrase "marks registered in the Patent and Trademark Office" means registered marks.

Prior acts. The term "Act of March 3, 1881," "Act of February 20, 1905," or "Act of March 19, 1920," means the respective Act as amended.

Counterfeit. A "counterfeit" is a spurious mark which is identical with, or substantially indistinguishable from, a registered mark.

Domain name. The term "domain name" means any alphanumeric designation which is registered with or assigned by any domain name registrar, domain name registry, or other domain name registration authority as part of an electronic address on the Internet.

Internet. The term "Internet" has the meaning given that term in section 230(f)(1) of the Communications Act of 1934 (47 U.S.C. § 230(f)(1)).

Singular and plural. Words used in the singular include the plural and vice versa.

Intent of Act. The intent of this Act is to regulate commerce within the control of Congress by making actionable the deceptive and misleading use of marks in such commerce; to protect registered marks; and to provide rights and remedies stipulated by treaties and conventions respecting trademarks, tradenames, and unfair competition entered into between the United States and foreign nations.

TITLE XI—REPEAL OF PREVIOUS ACTS

§ 46(a) (15 U.S.C. § 1051 note). Time of taking effect—Repeal of prior acts

This Act shall be in force and take effect one year from its enactment, but except as otherwise herein specifically provided shall not affect any suit, proceeding, or appeal then pending. All Acts and parts of Acts inconsistent herewith are hereby repealed effective one year from the enactment hereof, including the following Acts insofar as they are inconsistent herewith: The Act of Congress approved March 3, 1881, entitled "An Act to authorize the registration of trademarks and protect the same"; the Act approved August 5, 1882, entitled "An Act relating to the registration of trademarks"; the Act of February 20, 1905 (U.S.C., Title 15, secs. 81 to 109, inclusive), entitled "An Act to authorize the registration of trademarks used in commerce with foreign nations or among the several States or with Indian tribes, and to protect the same", and the amendments thereto by the Acts of May 4, 1906 (U.S.C., Title 15, secs. 131 and 132; 34 Stat. 169), March 2, 1907 (34 Stat. 1251, 1252), February 18, 1909 (35 Stat. 627, 628), February 18, 1911 (36 Stat. 918), January 8, 1913 (37 Stat. 649), June 7, 1924 (43 Stat. 647), March 4, 1925 (43 Stat. 1268, 1269), April 11, 1930 (46 Stat. 155), June 10, 1938 (Public, Numbered 586, Seventy-fifth Congress, ch. 332, third session); the Act of March 19, 1920 (U.S.C., Title 15, secs. 121 to 128, inclusive), entitled "an Act to give effect to certain provisions of the convention for the protection of trademarks and commercial names made and signed in the city of Buenos Aires, in the Argentine Republic, August 20, 1910, and for other purposes", and the amendments thereto, including the Act of June 10, 1938 (Public, Numbered 586, Seventy-fifth Congress, ch. 332, third session): Provided, That this repeal shall not affect the validity of registrations granted or applied for under any of said Acts prior to the effective date of this Act, or rights or remedies thereunder except as provided in sections 8, 12, 14, 15, and 47 of this Act; but nothing contained in this Act shall be construed as limiting, restricting, modifying, or repealing any statute in force on the effective date of this Act which does not relate to trademarks, or as restricting or increasing the authority of any Federal departments or regulatory agency except as may be specifically provided in this Act.

§ 46(b) (15 U.S.C. § 1051 note). Existing registrations under prior acts

Acts of 1881 and 1905. Registrations now existing under the Act of March 3, 1881, or the Act of February 20, 1905, shall continue in full force and effect for the unexpired terms thereof and may be renewed under the provisions of section 9 of this Act. Such registrations and the renewals thereof shall be subject to and shall be entitled to the benefits of the provisions of this Act to the same extent and with the same force and effect as though registered on the principal register established by this Act except as limited in sections 8, 12, 14, and 15 of this Act. Marks registered under the "10-year proviso" of section 5 of the Act of February 20, 1905, as amended, shall be deemed to have become distinctive of the registrant's goods in commerce under paragraph (f) of section 2 of this Act and may be renewed under section 9 hereof as marks coming within said paragraph.

Act of 1920. Registrations now existing under the Act of March 19, 1920, shall expire 6 months after the effective date of this Act, or twenty years from the dates of their registrations, whichever date is later. Such registrations shall be subject to and entitled to the benefits of the provisions of this Act relating to marks registered on the supplemental register established by this Act, and may not be renewed unless renewal is required to support foreign registrations. In that event renewal may be effected on the supplemental register under the provisions of section 9 of this Act.

Subject to registration under this Act. Marks registered under previous Acts may, if eligible, also be registered under this Act.

§ 47(a) (15 U.S.C. § 1051 note). Applications pending on effective date of Act

All applications for registration pending in the Patent and Trademark Office at the effective date of this Act may be amended, if practicable, to bring them under the provisions of this Act. The prosecution of such applications so amended and the grant of registrations thereon shall be proceeded with in accordance with the provisions of this Act. If such amendments are not made, the prosecution of said applications shall be proceeded with and registrations thereon granted in accordance with the Acts under which said applications were filed, and said Acts are hereby continued in force to this extent for this purpose only, notwithstanding the foregoing general repeal thereof.

§ 47(b) (15 U.S.C. § 1051 note). Appeals pending on effective date of Act

In any case in which an appeal is pending before the United States Court of Customs and Patent Appeals or any United States Circuit Court of Appeals or the United States Court of Appeals for the District of Columbia or the United States Supreme Court at the effective date of this Act, the court, if it be of the opinion that the provisions of this Act are applicable to the subject matter of the appeal, may apply such provision or may remand the case to the Director or to the district court for the taking of additional evidence or a new trial or for reconsideration of the decision on the record as made, as the appellate court may deem proper.

§ 48 (15 U.S.C. § 1051 note). Prior acts not repealed

Section 4 of the Act of January 5, 1905 (U.S.C., Title 36, section 4), as amended, entitled "An Act to incorporate the National Red Cross," and section 7 of the Act of June 15, 1916 (U.S.C., Title 36, section 27), entitled "An Act to incorporate the Boy Scouts of America, and for other purposes," and the Act of June 20, 1936 (U.S.C., Title 22, section 248), entitled "An Act to prohibit the commercial use of the coat of arms of the Swiss Confederation," are not repealed or affected by this Act.

Note: The first and third of the laws referred to in this section have been repealed and replaced by § § 706 and 708, respectively, of U.S.C., Title 18,

Crimes and Criminal Procedure, enacted June 25, 1948, effective September 1, 1948.

§ 49 (15 U.S.C. § 1051 note). Preservation of existing rights

Nothing herein shall adversely affect the rights or the enforcement of rights in marks acquired in good faith prior to the effective date of this Act.

§ 50 (15 U.S.C. § 1051 note). Severability

If any provision of this Act or the application of such provision to any person or circumstance is held invalid, the remainder of the Act shall not be affected thereby.

§ 51 (15 U.S.C. § 1058 note). Applications pending on effective date of the Trademark Law Revision Act of 1988

All certificates of registration based upon applications for registration pending in the Patent and Trademark Office on the effective date of the Trademark Law Revision Act of 1988 shall remain in force for a period of 10 years.

TITLE XII—THE MADRID PROTOCOL

§ 60 (15 U.S.C. § 1141). Definitions

In this title:

(1) Basic application.—The term "basic application" means the application for the registration of a mark that has been filed with an Office of a Contracting Party and that constitutes the basis for an application for the international registration of that mark.

(2) Basic registration.—The term "basic registration" means the registration of a mark that has been granted by an Office of a Contracting Party and that constitutes the basis for an application for the international registration of that mark.

(3) Contracting party.—The term "Contracting Party" means any country or inter-governmental organization that is a party to the Madrid Protocol.

(4) Date of recordal.—The term "date of recordal" means the date on which a request for extension of protection, filed after an international registration is granted, is recorded on the International Register.

(5) Declaration of bona fide intention to use the mark in commerce.—The term "declaration of bona fide intention to use the mark in commerce" means a declaration that is signed by the applicant for, or holder of, an international registration who is seeking extension of protection of a mark to the United States and that contains a statement that—

(A) the applicant or holder has a bona fide intention to use the mark in commerce;

(B) the person making the declaration believes himself or herself, or the firm, corporation, or association in whose behalf he or she makes the declaration, to be entitled to use the mark in commerce; and

(C) no other person, firm, corporation, or association, to the best of his or her knowledge and belief, has the right to use such mark in commerce either in the identical form of the mark or in such near resemblance to the mark as to be likely, when used on or in connection with the goods of such other person, firm, corporation, or association, to cause confusion, mistake, or deception.

(6) Extension of protection.—The term "extension of protection" means the protection resulting from an international registration that extends to the United States at the request of the holder of the international registration, in accordance with the Madrid Protocol.

(7) Holder of an international registration.—A "holder" of an international registration is the natural or juristic person in whose name the international registration is recorded on the International Register.

(8) International application.—The term "international application" means an application for international registration that is filed under the Madrid Protocol.

(9) International bureau.—The term "International Bureau" means the International Bureau of the World Intellectual Property Organization.

(10) International register.—The term "International Register" means the official collection of data concerning international registrations maintained by the International Bureau that the Madrid Protocol or its implementing regulations require or permit to be recorded.

(11) International registration.—The term "international registration" means the registration of a mark granted under the Madrid Protocol.

(12) International registration date.—The term "international registration date" means the date assigned to the international registration by the International Bureau.

(13) Madrid protocol.—The term "Madrid Protocol" means the Protocol Relating to the Madrid Agreement Concerning the International Registration of Marks, adopted at Madrid, Spain, on June 27, 1989.

(14) Notification of refusal.—The term "notification of refusal" means the notice sent by the United States Patent and Trademark Office to the International Bureau declaring that an extension of protection cannot be granted.

(15) Office of a contracting party.—The term "Office of a Contracting Party" means—

(A) the office, or governmental entity, of a Contracting Party that is responsible for the registration of marks; or

(B) the common office, or governmental entity, of more than 1 Contracting Party that is responsible for the registration of marks and is so recognized by the International Bureau.

(16) Office of origin.—The term "office of origin" means the Office of a Contracting Party with which a basic application was filed or by which a basic registration was granted.

(17) Opposition period.—The term "opposition period" means the time allowed for filing an opposition in the United States Patent and Trademark Office, including any extension of time granted under section 13.

§ 61 (15 U.S.C. § 1141a). International applications based on United States applications or registrations

(a) In General.—The owner of a basic application pending before the United States Patent and Trademark Office, or the owner of a basic registration granted by the United States Patent and Trademark Office may file an international application by submitting to the United States Patent and Trademark Office a written application in such form, together with such fees, as may be prescribed by the Director.

(b) Qualified Owners.—A qualified owner, under subsection (a), shall—

(1) be a national of the United States;

(2) be domiciled in the United States; or

(3) have a real and effective industrial or commercial establishment in the United States.

§ 62 (15 U.S.C. § 1141b). Certification of the international application

(a) Certification Procedure.—Upon the filing of an application for international registration and payment of the prescribed fees, the Director shall examine the international application for the purpose of certifying that the information contained in the international application corresponds to the information contained in the basic application or basic registration at the time of the certification.

(b) Transmittal.—Upon examination and certification of the international application, the Director shall transmit the international application to the International Bureau.

§ 63 (15 U.S.C. § 1141c). Restriction, abandonment, cancellation, or expiration of a basic application or basic registration

With respect to an international application transmitted to the International Bureau under section 62, the Director shall notify the International Bureau whenever the basic application or basic registration which is the basis for the international application has been restricted, abandoned, or canceled, or has expired, with respect to some or all of the goods and services listed in the international registration—

(1) within 5 years after the international registration date; or

(2) more than 5 years after the international registration date if the restriction, abandonment, or cancellation of the basic application or basic registration resulted from an action that began before the end of that 5–year period.

§ 64 (15 U.S.C. § 1141d). Request for extension of protection subsequent to international registration

The holder of an international registration that is based upon a basic application filed with the United States Patent and Trademark Office or a basic registration granted by the Patent and Trademark Office may request an extension of protection of its international registration by filing such a request—

(1) directly with the International Bureau; or

(2) with the United States Patent and Trademark Office for transmittal to the International Bureau, if the request is in such form, and contains such transmittal fee, as may be prescribed by the Director.

§ 65 (15 U.S.C. § 1141e). Extension of protection of an international registration to the United States under the Madrid Protocol

(a) In General.—Subject to the provisions of section 68, the holder of an international registration shall be entitled to the benefits of extension of protection of that international registration to the United States to the extent necessary to give effect to any provision of the Madrid Protocol.

(b) If the United States Is Office of Origin.—Where the United States Patent and Trademark Office is the office of origin for a trademark application or registration, any international registration based on such application or registration cannot be used to obtain the benefits of the Madrid Protocol in the United States.

§ 66 (15 U.S.C. § 1141f). Effect of filing a request for extension of protection of an international registration to the United States

(a) Requirement for Request for Extension of Protection.—A request for extension of protection of an international registration to the United States that the International Bureau transmits to the United States Patent and Trademark Office shall be deemed to be properly filed in the United States if such request, when received by the International Bureau, has attached to it a declaration of bona fide intention to use the mark in commerce that is verified by the applicant for, or holder of, the international registration.

(b) Effect of Proper Filing.—Unless extension of protection is refused under section 68, the proper filing of the request for extension of protection under subsection (a) shall constitute constructive use of the mark, conferring the same rights as those specified in section 7(c), as of the earliest of the following:

(1) The international registration date, if the request for extension of protection was filed in the international application.

(2) The date of recordal of the request for extension of protection, if the request for extension of protection was made after the international registration date.

(3) The date of priority claimed pursuant to section 67.

§ 67 (15 U.S.C. § 1141g). Right of priority for request for extension of protection to the United States

The holder of an international registration with a request for an extension of protection to the United States shall be entitled to claim a date of priority based on a right of priority within the meaning of Article 4 of the Paris Convention for the Protection of Industrial Property if—

(1) the request for extension of protection contains a claim of priority; and

(2) the date of international registration or the date of the recordal of the request for extension of protection to the United States is not later than 6 months after the date of the first regular national filing (within the meaning of Article 4(A)(3) of the Paris Convention for the Protection of Industrial Property) or a subsequent application (within the meaning of Article 4(C)(4) of the Paris Convention for the Protection of Industrial Property).

§ 68 (15 U.S.C. § 1141h). Examination of and opposition to request for extension of protection; notification of refusal

(a) Examination and Opposition.—

(1) A request for extension of protection described in section 66(a) shall be examined as an application for registration on the Principal Register under this Act, and if on such examination it appears that the applicant is entitled to extension of protection under this title, the Director shall cause the mark to be published in the Official Gazette of the United States Patent and Trademark Office.

(2) Subject to the provisions of subsection (c), a request for extension of protection under this Title shall be subject to opposition under section 13.

(3) Extension of protection shall not be refused on the ground that the mark has not been used in commerce.

(4) Extension of protection shall be refused to any mark not registrable on the Principal Register.

(b) Notification of Refusal.—If, a request for extension of protection is refused under subsection (a), the Director shall declare in a notification of refusal (as provided in subsection (c)) that the extension of protection cannot be granted, together with a statement of all grounds on which the refusal was based.

(c) Notice to International Bureau.—

(1) Within 18 months after the date on which the International Bureau transmits to the Patent and Trademark Office a notification of a request for extension of protection, the Director shall transmit to the International Bureau any of the following that applies to such request:

(A) A notification of refusal based on an examination of the request for extension of protection.

(B) A notification of refusal based on the filing of an opposition to the request.

(C) A notification of the possibility that an opposition to the request may be filed after the end of that 18–month period.

(2) If the Director has sent a notification of the possibility of opposition under paragraph (1)(C), the Director shall, if applicable, transmit to the International Bureau a notification of refusal on the basis of the opposition, together with a statement of all the grounds for the opposition, within 7 months after the beginning of the opposition period or within 1 month after the end of the opposition period, whichever is earlier.

(3) If a notification of refusal of a request for extension of protection is transmitted under paragraph (1) or (2), no grounds for refusal of such request other than those set forth in such notification may be transmitted to the International Bureau by the Director after the expiration of the time periods set forth in paragraph (1) or (2), as the case may be.

(4) If a notification specified in paragraph (1) or (2) is not sent to the International Bureau within the time period set forth in such paragraph, with respect to a request for extension of protection, the request for extension of protection shall not be refused and the Director shall issue a certificate of extension of protection pursuant to the request.

(d) Designation of Agent for Service of Process.—In responding to a notification of refusal with respect to a mark, the holder of the international registration of the mark may designate, by a document filed in the United States Patent and Trademark Office, the name and address of a person residing in the United States on whom notices or process in proceedings affecting the mark may be served. Such notices or process may be served upon the person designated by leaving with that person, or mailing to that person, a copy thereof at the address specified in the last designation filed. If the person designated cannot be found at the address given in the last designation, or if the holder does not designate by a document filed in the United States Patent and Trademark Office the name and address of a person residing in the United States for service of notices or process in proceedings affecting the mark, the notice or process may be served on the Director.

§ 69 (15 U.S.C. § 1141i). Effect of extension of protection

(a) Issuance of Extension of Protection.—Unless a request for extension of protection is refused under section 68, the Director shall issue a certificate of extension of protection pursuant to the request and shall cause notice of such certificate of extension of protection to be published in the Official Gazette of the United States Patent and Trademark Office.

(b) Effect of Extension of Protection.—From the date on which a certificate of extension of protection is issued under subsection (a)—

(1) such extension of protection shall have the same effect and validity as a registration on the Principal Register; and

(2) the holder of the international registration shall have the same rights and remedies as the owner of a registration on the Principal Register.

§ 70 (15 U.S.C. § 1141j). Dependence of extension of protection to the United States on the underlying international registration

(a) Effect of Cancellation of International Registration.—If the International Bureau notifies the United States Patent and Trademark Office of the cancellation of an international registration with respect to some or all of the goods and services listed in the international registration, the Director shall cancel any extension of protection to the United States with respect to such goods and services as of the date on which the international registration was canceled.

(b) Effect of Failure To Renew International Registration.—If the International Bureau does not renew an international registration, the corresponding extension of protection to the United States shall cease to be valid as of the date of the expiration of the international registration.

(c) Transformation of an Extension of Protection Into a United States Application.—The holder of an international registration canceled in whole or in part by the International Bureau at the request of the office of origin, under article 6(4) of the Madrid Protocol, may file an application, under section 1 or 44 of this Act, for the registration of the same mark for any of the goods and services to which the cancellation applies that were covered by an extension of protection to the United States based on that international registration. Such an application shall be treated as if it had been filed on the international registration date or the date of recordal of the request for extension of protection with the International Bureau, whichever date applies, and, if the extension of protection enjoyed priority under section 67 of this title, shall enjoy the same priority. Such an application shall be entitled to the benefits conferred by this subsection only if the application is filed not later than 3 months after the date on which the international registration was canceled, in whole or in part, and only if the application complies with all the requirements of this Act which apply to any application filed pursuant to section 1 or 44.

§ 71 (15 U.S.C. § 1141k). Affidavits and fees

(a) Required Affidavits and Fees.—An extension of protection for which a certificate of extension of protection has been issued under section 69 shall remain in force for the term of the international registration upon which it is based, except that the extension of protection of any mark shall be canceled by the Director—

(1) at the end of the 6–year period beginning on the date on which the certificate of extension of protection was issued by the Director, unless within the 1–year period preceding the expiration of that 6–year period the holder of the international registration files in the Patent and Trademark Office an affidavit under subsection (b) together with a fee prescribed by the Director; and

(2) at the end of the 10–year period beginning on the date on which the certificate of extension of protection was issued by the Director, and at the end of each 10–year period thereafter, unless—

(A) within the 6–month period preceding the expiration of such 10–year period the holder of the international registration files in the United States Patent and Trademark Office an affidavit under subsection (b) together with a fee prescribed by the Director; or

(B) within 3 months after the expiration of such 10–year period, the holder of the international registration files in the Patent and Trademark Office an affidavit under subsection (b) together with the fee described in subparagraph (A) and the surcharge prescribed by the Director.

(b) Contents of Affidavit.—The affidavit referred to in subsection (a) shall set forth those goods or services recited in the extension of protection on or in connection with which the mark is in use in commerce and the holder of the international registration shall attach to the affidavit a specimen or facsimile showing the current use of the mark in commerce, or shall set forth that any nonuse is due to special circumstances which excuse such nonuse and is not due to any intention to abandon the mark. Special notice of the requirement for such affidavit shall be attached to each certificate of extension of protection.

(c) Notification.—The Director shall notify the holder of the international registration who files 1 of the affidavits of the Director's acceptance or refusal thereof and, in case of a refusal, the reasons therefor.

(d) Service of Notice or Process.—The holder of the international registration of the mark may designate, by a document filed in the United States Patent and Trademark Office, the name and address of a person residing in the United States on whom notices or process in proceedings affecting the mark may be served. Such notices or process may be served upon the person so designated by leaving with that person, or mailing to that person, a copy thereof at the address specified in the last designation so filed. If the person designated cannot be found at the address given in the last designation, or if the holder does not designate by a document filed in the United States Patent and Trademark Office the name and address of a person residing in the United States for service of notices or process in proceedings affecting the mark, the notice or process may be served on the Director.

§ 72 (15 U.S.C. § 1141l). Assignment of an extension of protection

An extension of protection may be assigned, together with the goodwill associated with the mark, only to a person who is a national of, is domiciled in, or has a bona fide and effective industrial or commercial establishment either in a country that is a Contracting Party or in a country that is a member of an intergovernmental organization that is a Contracting Party.

§ 73 (15 U.S.C. § 1141m). Incontestability

The period of continuous use prescribed under section 15 for a mark covered by an extension of protection issued under this Title may begin no earlier than the date on which the Director issues the certificate of the extension of protection under section 69, except as provided in section 74.

§ 74 (15 U.S.C. § 1141n). Rights of extension of protection

When a United States registration and a subsequently issued certificate of extension of protection to the United States are owned by the same person, identify the same mark, and list the same goods or services, the extension of protection shall have the same rights that accrued to the registration prior to issuance of the certificate of extension of protection.

APPENDIX B

RESTATEMENT OF THE LAW (THIRD) OF UNFAIR COMPETITION, §§ 1, 9, 13, 16–17, 20–27

Topic 3. Infringement of Rights

Section

§ 1. General Principles

One who causes harm to the commercial relations of another by engaging in a business or trade is not subject to liability to the other for such harm unless:

(a) the harm results from acts or practices of the actor actionable by the other under the rules of this Restatement relating to:

(1) deceptive marketing, as specified in Chapter Two;

(2) infringement of trademarks and other indicia of identification, as specified in Chapter Three;

(3) appropriation of intangible trade values including trade secrets and the right of publicity, as specified in Chapter Four;

or from other acts or practices of the actor determined to be actionable as an unfair method of competition, taking into account the nature of the conduct and its likely effect on both the person seeking relief and the public; or

(b) the acts or practices of the actor are actionable by the other under federal or state statutes, international agreements, or general principles of common law apart from those considered in this Restatement.

§ 9. Definitions of Trademark and Service Mark

A trademark is a word, name, symbol, device, or other designation, or a combination of such designations, that is distinctive of a person's goods or services and that is used in a manner that identifies those goods or services and distinguishes them from the goods or services of others. A service mark is a trademark that is used in connection with services.

§ 13. Distinctiveness; Secondary Meaning

A word name, symbol, device, or other designation, or a combination of such designations, is "distinctive" under the rules stated in §§ 9–12 if:

(a) the designation is "inherently distinctive," in that, because of the nature of the designation and the context in which it is used, prospective purchasers are likely to perceive it as a designation that, in the case of a trademark, identifies goods or services produced or sponsored by a particular person, whether known or anonymous, or in the case of a trade name, identifies the business or other enterprise of a particular person, whether known or anonymous, or in the case of a collective mark, identifies members of the collective group or goods or services produced or sponsored by members, or in the case of a certification mark, identifies the certified goods or services; or

(b) the designation, although not "inherently distinctive," has become distinctive, in that, as a result of its use, prospective purchasers have come to perceive it as a designation that identifies goods, services, businesses, or members in the manner described in Subsection (a). Such acquired distinctiveness is commonly referred to as "secondary meaning."

§ 16. Configurations of Packaging and Products: Trade Dress and Product Designs

The design of elements that constitute the appearance or image of goods or services as presented to prospective purchasers, including the design of packaging, labels, containers, displays, decor, or the design of a product, a product feature, or a combination of product features, is eligible for protection as a mark under the rules stated in this Chapter if:

(a) the design is distinctive under the rule stated in § 13; and

(b) the design is not functional under the rule stated in § 17.

§ 17. Functional Designs

A design is "functional" for purposes of the rule stated in § 16 if the design affords benefits in the manufacturing, marketing, or use of the goods or services with which the design is used, apart from any benefits attributable to the design's significance as an indication of source, that are important to effective competition by others and that are not practically available through the use of alternative designs.

§ 20. Standard of Infringement

(1) One is subject to liability for infringement of another's trademark, trade name, collective mark, or certification mark if the other's use has priority under the rules stated in § 19 and in identifying the actor's business or marketing the actor's goods or services the actor uses a designation that causes a likelihood of confusion

(a) that the actor's business is the business of the other or is associated or otherwise connected with the other; or

(b) that the goods or services marketed by the actor are produced, sponsored, certified, or approved by the other; or

(c) that the goods or services marketed by the other are produced, sponsored, certified, or approved by the actor.

(2) One is also subject to liability for infringement of another's collective membership mark if the other's use has priority under the rules stated in § 19 and the actor uses a designation that causes a likelihood of confusion that the actor is a member of or otherwise associated with the collective group.

§ 21. Proof of Likelihood of Confusion—Market Factors

Whether an actor's use of a designation causes a likelihood of confusion with the use of a trademark, trade name, collective mark, or certification mark by another under the rule stated in § 20 is determined by a consideration of all the circumstances involved in the marketing of the respective goods or services or the operation of the respective businesses. In making that determination the following market factors, among others, may be important:

(a) the degree of similarity between the respective designations, including a comparison of

(i) the overall impression created by the designations as they are used in marketing the respective goods or services or in identifying the respective businesses;

(ii) the pronunciation of the designations;

(iii) the translation of foreign words contained in the designations;

(iv) the verbal translation of pictures, illustrations, or designs contained in the designations;

(v) the suggestions, connotations, or meanings of the designations;

(b) the degree of similarity in the marketing methods and channels of distribution used for the respective goods or services;

(c) the characteristics of the prospective purchasers of the goods or services and the degree of care they are likely to exercise in making purchasing decisions;

(d) the degree of distinctiveness of the other's designation;

(e) when the goods, services, or business of the actor differ in kind from those of the other, the likelihood that the actor's prospective purchasers would expect a person in the position of the other to expand its marketing or sponsorship into the product, service, or business market of the actor;

(f) when the actor and the other sell their goods or services or carry on their businesses in different geographic markets, the extent to which the other's designation is identified with the other in the geographic market of the actor.

§ 22. Proof of Likelihood of Confusion—Intent of the Actor

(1) A likelihood of confusion may be inferred from proof that the actor used a designation resembling another's trademark, trade name, collective mark, or certification mark with the intent to cause confusion or to deceive.

(2) A likelihood of confusion should not be inferred from proof that the actor intentionally copied the other's designation if the actor acted in good faith under circumstances that do not otherwise indicate an intent to cause confusion or to deceive.

§ 23. Proof of Likelihood of Confusion— Evidence of Actual Confusion

(1) A likelihood of confusion may be inferred from proof of actual confusion.

(2) An absence of likelihood of confusion may be inferred from the absence of proof of actual confusion if the actor and the other have made significant use of their respective designations in the same geographic market for a substantial period of time, and any resulting confusion would ordinarily be manifested by provable facts.

§ 24. Use of Another's Trademark on Genuine Goods

One is not subject to liability under the rule stated in § 20 for using another's trademark, trade name, collective mark, or certification mark in marketing genuine goods or services the source, sponsorship, or certification of which is accurately identified by the mark unless:

(a) the other uses a different mark for different types or grades of goods or services and the actor markets one of the types or grades under a mark used for another type or grade; or

(b) the actor markets under the mark the genuine goods of the other that have been repaired, reconditioned, altered, or used, or genuine services that do not conform to the standards imposed by the other, and the actor's use of the mark causes a likelihood of confusion that the goods are new or unaltered or that the repair, reconditioning, or alteration was performed, authorized, or certified by the other, or that the services as performed conform to the other's standards.

§ 25. Liability Without Proof of Confusion—Dilution and Tarnishment

(1) One may be subject to liability under the law of trademarks for the use of a designation that resembles the trademark, trade name, collective mark, or certification mark of another without proof of a likelihood of confusion only under an applicable antidilution statute. An actor is subject to liability under an antidilution statute if the actor uses such a designation in a manner that is likely to associate the other's mark with the goods, services, or business of the actor and:

(a) the other's mark is highly distinctive and the association of the mark with the actor's goods, services, or business is likely to cause a reduction in that distinctiveness; or

(b) the association of the other's mark with the actor's goods, services, or business, or the nature of the actor's use, is likely to cause prospective purchasers to associate the actor's and the other's goods, services, businesses, or marks in a manner that disparages the other's goods, services, or business or tarnishes the images associated with the other's mark.

(2) One who uses a designation that resembles the trademark, trade name, collective mark, or certification mark of another, not in a manner that is likely to associate the other's mark with the goods, services, or business of the actor, but rather to comment on, criticize, ridicule, parody, or disparage the other or the other's goods, services, business, or mark, is subject to liability without proof of a likelihood of confusion only if the actor's conduct meets the requirements of a cause of action for defamation, invasion of privacy, or injurious falsehood.

§ 26. Contributory Infringement by Printers, Publishers, and Other Suppliers

(1) One who, on behalf of a third person, reproduces or imitates the trademark, trade name, collective mark, or certification mark of another on goods, labels, packaging, advertisements, or other materials that are used by the third person in a manner that subjects the third person to liability to the other for infringement under the rule stated in § 20 is subject to liability to that other for contributory infringement.

(2) If an actor subject to contributory liability under the rule stated in Subsection (1) acted without knowledge that the reproduction or imitation

was intended by the third person to confuse or deceive, the actor is subject only to appropriate injunctive relief.

§ 27. Contributory Infringement by Manufacturers and Distributors

One who markets goods or services to a third person who further markets the goods or services in a manner that subjects the third person to liability to another for infringement under the rule stated in § 20 is subject to liability to that other for contributory infringement if:

(a) the actor intentionally induces the third person to engage in the infringing conduct; or

(b) the actor fails to take reasonable precautions against the occurrence of the third person's infringing conduct in circumstances in which the infringing conduct can be reasonably anticipated.

APPENDIX C

Trademark Manual of Examining Procedure Second Edition, Revision 1.1 (Excerpts)

PROCEDURAL EXAMINATION OF APPLICATIONS AND RELATED DOCUMENTS

1114 Supplemental Register, Application Filed on

See TMEP § 202.02(b) regarding application to register a mark on the Supplemental Register.

1114.01 Marks Eligible

A mark which is clearly eligible for the Principal Register may not be registered on the Supplemental Register. An application requesting registration of such a mark on the Supplemental Register must be amended to the Principal Register, or refused registration. *Daggett & Ramsdell, Inc. v. I. Posner, Inc.*, 115 USPQ 96 (Comm'r Pats. 1957); *In re United States Catheter & Instrument Corp.*, 158 USPQ 54 (TTAB 1968). (Regarding amendment, *see* 37 C.F.R. § 2.75; TMEP § 1115 *et seq.*)

1114.02 Elements Required

The application should state that the applicant requests registration on the Supplemental Register. If the application does not so state, the Office will assume a request to register on the Principal Register.

Before an application requesting registration on the Supplemental Register may be filed, the mark must be in lawful use in commerce by the owner of the mark, on or in connection with the goods and services. 15 U.S.C. § 1091(a); 37 C.F.R. § 2.47.

Moreover, an intent-to-use applicant may not seek registration on the Supplemental Register until the applicant has timely filed either an acceptable amendment to allege use or statement of use. 37 C.F.R. §§ 2.47(c) and 2.75(b). Regarding the effective filing date of a § 1(b) application which is amended to request registration on the Supplemental Register, after the filing of an acceptable allegation of use, *see* TMEP § 1115.02.

If an applicant submits an application for the Supplemental Register based on intent to use, under § 1(b) of the Act, 15 U.S.C. § 1051(b), the Office will reject the application because it was void as filed and will return all papers to the applicant with any fees submitted. If any such application reaches an examining attorney in error, the examining attorney should return the papers to the Pre–Examination Section for appropriate action.

The only exception from the use requirement in seeking registration on the Supplemental Register is for applications based solely on § 44 of the Trademark Act, 15 U.S.C. § 1126. In an application under § 44, the applicant may seek registration on the Supplemental Register without alleging lawful use in commerce and without alleging use anywhere in the world. 15 U.S.C. § 1126(e); 37 C.F.R. § 2.47(b). *See also* TMEP § 1003.

1114.03 Lawful Use

In requesting registration on the Supplemental Register in either the original application or in an amendment to the Supplemental Register, the applicant need not include an additional statement as to lawful use. While § 23(a) of the Trademark Act, 15 U.S.C. § 1091(a), includes an explicit reference to lawful use, any use which is the basis for an application on either the Principal or the Supplemental Register must be lawful. It need not be stated explicitly.

1114.04 Examining Attorney Signs File for Issue

Upon approval of registration, the examining attorney will sign the face of the file in the space marked "Approved for Supplemental Registration" rather than the space for approval for publication. Marks on the Supplemental Register are not published for opposition, but are issued as registered marks on the date on which they are printed in the *Official Gazette*.

1114.05 Supplemental Registration Not an Admission that the Mark Has Not Acquired Distinctiveness

Section 27 of the Trademark Act, 15 U.S.C. § 1095, provides, in part, "Registration of a mark on the Supplemental Register shall not constitute an admission that the mark has not acquired distinctiveness." Examining attorneys should note this provision in presenting any refusals or requirements related to the nondistinctive character of a mark previously registered on the Supplemental Register.

1115 Supplemental Register, Amending Application to 1115.01 How to Amend

Provided an application meets the requirements noted in TMEP § 1114.02, it may be amended by requesting that the words "Principal Register" be changed to "Supplemental Register," which in effect changes the application from one requesting registration on the Principal Register to one requesting registration on the Supplemental Register.

1115.02 Effective Filing Date

As of November 16, 1989, the effective date of the Trademark Law Revision Act of 1988, Public Law 100–667, 102 Stat. 3935, the one-year-lawful-use requirement for eligibility for the Supplemental Register was eliminated.

Therefore, as of that date, an applicant may apply for registration on the Supplemental Register at any time after commencing use of the mark in commerce.

Likewise, as of November 16, 1989, an applicant may amend a pending application to seek registration on the Supplemental Register at any time after use of the mark has commenced, even if the original application for the Principal Register was filed before November 16, 1989. However, if the application was filed before November 16, 1989 and the applicant had not used the mark in commerce for one year before the filing date, and the applicant amends to the Supplemental Register on or after November 16, 1989, the date of the amendment to the Supplemental Register becomes the effective filing date of the application.

As noted in TMEP § 1114.02, an intent-to-use applicant may file an amendment to the Supplemental Register only after use has commenced and after the filing of an acceptable amendment to allege use or statement of use. In such a case, the effective filing date of the application is the date on which the applicant filed the amendment to allege use under § 1(c) or the statement of use under § 1(d) of the Act.

If an intent-to-use applicant files an acceptable amendment to allege use or statement of use and an acceptable amendment to the Supplemental Register, the date of the filing of the amendment to allege use or the statement of use is the effective filing date of the application. 37 C.F.R. § 2.75(b). The amendment to allege use or statement of use should be examined before any action is taken on an amendment to the Supplemental Register.

See TMEP § 708 *et seq.* regarding effective filing date. *See* TMEP § 1208.03(a) regarding effective filing date in relation to conflicting applications.

1115.03 Amendment to Different Register

There is no restriction on the number of times amendments may be made changing the request in an application from one register to another register. Normally, however, one amendment is sufficient, and subsequent amendments should be avoided except for unusual circumstances. *See* 37 C.F.R. § 2.75.

1115.04 Amendment After Refusal

Amendment requesting registration on the Supplemental Register may be made after a refusal to register on the Principal Register, including final refusal. If the final refusal was under § 2(e) of the Trademark Act, or on grounds pertaining to other non-inherently distinctive subject matter, amendment to the Supplemental Register is procedurally an acceptable response. *See* 37 C.F.R. § 2.75.

1115.05 Amendment After Decision on Appeal

Amendment to the Supplemental Register may not be made after appeal has been taken from a refusal to register on the Principal Register and the decision has been adverse to the applicant. After having elected one of the remedies available for contesting the basis for the refusal, namely, appeal rather than amendment to the Supplemental Register, and having pursued such remedy to a conclusion, the applicant may not return to its previous position and pursue another remedy for the same refusal anew. The applicant may file a new application, if the applicant wishes to do so. See the following cases wherein the Commissioner refused to grant petitions to reopen prosecution and return jurisdiction to the examining attorney for the purpose of considering an amendment to the Supplemental Register after decision on appeal: *Ex parte Simoniz Co.,* 161 USPQ 365 (Comm'r Pats. 1969); *Ex parte Helene Curtis Industries, Inc.*, 134 USPQ 73 (Comm'r Pats. 1962); *In re Application Filed July 24, 1948*, 663 O.G. 267 (Comm'r Pats. 1951); *Ex parte Sightmaster Corp.*, 95 USPQ 43 (Comm'r Pats. 1951).

See also TMEP § 1501.05 and *In re Vesper Corp.*, 8 USPQ2d 1788, 1789 n.3 (Comm'r Pats. 1988).

SUBSTANTIVE EXAMINATION OF APPLICATIONS

1203.03 Matter which May Disparage, Falsely Suggest a Connection, or Bring into Contempt or Disrepute

Section 2(a) of the Trademark Act, 15 U.S.C. § 1052(a), bars the registration of any mark that consists of or comprises matter which, with regard to persons, institutions, beliefs, or national symbols, does any of the following: (1) disparages them, (2) falsely suggests a connection with them, (3) brings them into contempt, or (4) brings them into disrepute.

This provision bars the registration of such marks on both the Principal Register and, pursuant to § 23(a), 15 U.S.C. § 1091(a), the Supplemental Register.

Section 2(a) is distinctly different from § 2(d), 15 U.S.C. § 1052(d), for which the relevant test is likelihood of confusion. In *University of Notre Dame du Lac v. J.C. Gourmet Food Imports Co., Inc.,* 703 F.2d 1372, 1375–76, 217 USPQ 505, 508–09 (Fed. Cir. 1983), the Court of Appeals for the Federal Circuit noted as follows:

> A reading of the legislative history with respect to what became § 2(a) shows that the drafters were concerned with protecting the name of an individual or institution which was not a technical "trademark" or "trade name" upon which an objection could be made under § 2(d)....
>
> . . .

Although not articulated as such, it appears that the drafters sought by § 2(a) to embrace concepts of the right to privacy, an area of the law then in an embryonic state (footnote omitted). Our review of case law discloses that the elements of a claim of invasion of one's privacy have emerged as distinctly different from those of trademark or trade name infringement. There may be no likelihood of such confusion as to the source of goods even under a theory of "sponsorship" or "endorsement," and, nevertheless, one's right of privacy, or the related right of publicity, may be violated.

The right to privacy protects a party's control over the use of its identity or "persona." A party acquires a protectible interest in a name or equivalent designation under § 2(a) where the name or designation is unmistakably associated with, and points uniquely to, that party's personality or "persona." A party's interest in a name or designation does not depend upon adoption and use as a technical trademark or trade name. *University of Notre Dame du Lac v. J.C. Gourmet Food Imports Co., Inc.*, 703 F.2d 1372, 1376–77, 217 USPQ 505, 509 (Fed. Cir. 1983); *Buffett v. Chi-Chi's, Inc.*, 226 USPQ 428, 429 (TTAB 1985).

Regarding disparagement, bringing into contempt and bringing into disrepute, *see* TMEP §§ 1203.03(c) and 1203.03(d). Regarding false suggestion of a connection, *see* TMEP §§ 1203.03(e) and 1203.03(f).

See Carson v. Here's Johnny Portable Toilets, Inc., 698 F.2d 831, 218 USPQ 1 (6th Cir. 1983), concerning the various forms of identity which have been protected under the rights of privacy and publicity.

1203.03(a) "Persons" Defined

Section 2(a) of the Trademark Act, 15 U.S.C. § 1052(a), protects, *inter alia*, "persons, living or dead."

Section 45 of the Act, 15 U.S.C. § 1127, defines "person" and "juristic person" as follows:

The term "person" and any other word or term used to designate the applicant or other entitled to a benefit or privilege or rendered liable under the provisions of this Act includes a juristic person as well as a natural person. The term "juristic person" includes a firm, corporation, union, association, or other organization capable of suing and being sued in a court of law. The term "person" also includes any State, any instrumentality of a State, and any officer or employee of a State or instrumentality of a State acting in his or her official capacity. Any State, and any such instrumentality, officer, or employee, shall be subject to the provisions of this Act in the same manner and to the same extent as any non-governmental entity.

The term "persons" in § 2(a) refers to real persons, not fictitious characters. In addition to natural persons, it includes juristic persons, *i.e.*, legally-created entities such as firms, corporations, unions, associations or any other organizations capable of suing and being sued in a court of law. *See Morehouse Mfg. Corp. v. J. Strickland & Co.*, 407 F.2d 881, 160 USPQ 715 (C.C.P.A. 1969); *Popular Merchandise Co. v. "21" Club, Inc.*, 343 F.2d 1011, 145 USPQ 203 (C.C.P.A. 1965); *John Walker & Sons, Ltd. v.*

American Tobacco Co., 110 USPQ 249 (Comm'r Pats. 1956); *Copacabana, Inc. v. Breslauer,* 101 USPQ 467 (Comm'r Pats. 1954).

With respect to natural persons, they may be living or dead. However, § 2(a) may not be applicable with regard to a deceased person for whom there is no longer anyone entitled to assert a propriety right or right of privacy. *Lucien Piccard Watch Corp. v. Since 1868 Crescent Corp.,* 314 F.Supp. 329, 165 USPQ 459 (S.D.N.Y. 1970).

Juristic persons or institutions need not be well known to be protected from the registration of a mark which falsely suggests a connection with or disparages them, or brings them into contempt or disrepute. *Gavel Club v. Toastmasters International,* 127 USPQ 88, 94 (TTAB 1960) ("[T]here is nothing in Section 2(a) of the Act which would indicate that it is intended to afford protection only to large or nationally known institutions.").

It is well settled that the United States Government is a juristic person. *See NASA v. Record Chemical Co. Inc.*, 185 USPQ 563, 566 (TTAB 1975), and cases cited therein.

A mark need not comprise a person's full or correct name to be unregistrable; a nickname or other designation by which a person is known by the public may be unregistrable under this provision of the Act. *Buffett v. Chi–Chi's, Inc.*, 226 USPQ 428, 430 (TTAB 1985) (evidence of record "sufficient to raise a genuine issue of material fact as to whether the term 'MARGARITAVILLE' is so uniquely and unmistakably associated with opposer as to constitute opposer's name or identity such that when applicant's mark is used in connection with its [restaurant] services, a connection with opposer would be assumed").

1203.03(b) "National Symbols" Defined

A "national symbol" is subject matter of unique and special significance which, because of its meaning, appearance and/or sound, immediately suggests or refers to the country for which it stands. *In re Consolidated Foods Corp.*, 187 USPQ 63 (TTAB 1975). National symbols include the symbols of foreign countries as well as those of the United States. *In re Anti–Communist World Freedom Congress, Inc.*, 161 USPQ 304 (TTAB 1969).

The Trademark Act does not prohibit registration of marks comprising national symbols; the pertinent provision merely prohibits registration of matter which may disparage national symbols, falsely suggest a connection with them, or hold them up to contempt or disrepute. *Liberty Mutual Insurance Co. v. Liberty Insurance Co. of Texas,* 185 F.Supp. 895, 908, 127 USPQ 312, 323 (E.D. Ark. 1960) (marks comprising portion of the Statue of Liberty found not to disparage, bring into contempt or disrepute, or falsely suggest a connection with the Statue of Liberty or the United States government, the Court "[a]ssuming without deciding" that the statue is a national symbol).

Designations have been held to be national symbols within the meaning of § 2(a) in the following cases: *In re Anti–Communist World Freedom Congress, Inc.,* 161 USPQ 304 (TTAB 1969) (representation of a hammer and sickle held to be a national symbol of the Union of Soviet Socialist Republics (U.S.S.R.)); *In re National Collection & Credit Control, Inc.,* 152 USPQ 200, 201 n.2 (TTAB 1966) ("The American or bald eagle with wings extended is a well-known national symbol or emblem of the United States."); *In re Teasdale Packing Co., Inc.*, 137 USPQ 482 (TTAB 1963) (U. S. AQUA and design held unregistrable under § 2(a) on the ground that purchasers of applicant's canned drinking water would be misled into assuming approval or sponsorship by the United States government in view of the nature of the mark, including a red, white and blue shield design, and the nature of the goods, the Board noting a program for stocking emergency supplies of water in fallout shelters and the setting of standards for drinking water by United States government agencies).

Specific terms have been held not to be national symbols in the following cases: *W. H. Snyder and Sons, Inc. v. Ladd*, 140 USPQ 647 (D.D.C. 1964) (HOUSE OF WINDSOR held not to be a national symbol of England, but merely the name of its present reigning family); *NASA v. Bully Hill Vineyards, Inc.*, 3 USPQ2d 1671 (TTAB 1987) (SPACE SHUTTLE found not to constitute a national symbol on the evidence of record, the Board also finding "shuttle" to be a generic term for a space vehicle or system); *Jacobs v. International Multifoods Corp.*, 211 USPQ 165, 170–71 (TTAB 1981), *aff'd on other grounds*, 212 USPQ 641 (C.C.P.A. 1982) ("[H]istorical events such as the 'BOSTON TEA PARTY' . . ., although undoubtedly associated with the American heritage, do not take on that unique and special significance of a 'national symbol' designed to be equated with and associated with a particular country."); *In re Mohawk Air Services Inc.*, 196 USPQ 851, 854 (TTAB 1977) ("[T]he term 'MOHAWK' does not immediately suggest the United States; hence it is not a national symbol."); *In re General Mills, Inc.*, 169 USPQ 244 (TTAB 1971) (UNION JACK, which applicant was using on packages of frozen fish marked "English cut cod" and, in its restaurant, near representations of the British national flag, found not to suggest a particular country, the Board noting that it could consider only the matter for which registration was sought); *In re Horwitt*, 125 USPQ 145, 146 (TTAB 1960) (U. S. HEALTH CLUB found registrable for vitamin tablets. "Considering both the nature of the mark and the goods, it is concluded that the purchasing public would not be likely to mistakenly assume that the United States Government is operating a health club, that it is distributing vitamins, or that it has approved applicant's goods.").

The name of a country is not a national symbol within the meaning of § 2(a) of the Trademark Act. *In re Sweden Freezer Mfg. Co.*, 159 USPQ 246, 248–249 (TTAB 1968). Nor does use of the name of a country as a mark, by itself, amount to deception, disparagement, or a "false connection" under § 2(a). *In re Fortune Star Products Corp.*, 217 USPQ 277 (TTAB 1982).

The acronyms for, and names of, government agencies and bureaus are not considered to be national symbols. *In re Consolidated Foods Corp.*, 187 USPQ 63, 64 (TTAB 1975) (OSS, acronym for the Office of Strategic Services, held not to be a national symbol, but merely to designate a particular (and long defunct) government agency, the Board contrasting national symbols with names and acronyms of government agencies. " 'National symbols' ... are more enduring in time, ... and immediately conjure up the image of the country as a whole. Symbols of a country take on a special significance and are not so numerous as to dilute the special significance that each has.").

"National symbols" cannot be equated with the "insignia" of nations. As noted in *Liberty Mutual Insurance Co. v. Liberty Insurance Co. of Texas,* 185 F.Supp. 895, 908, 127 USPQ 312, 323 (E.D. Ark. 1960):

The Act ... does not put national symbols on a par with the flag, coat of arms, or other insignia of the United States, which may not in any event be made the subject matter of a trade or service mark. With regard to national symbols the statute provides merely that they shall not be disparaged or held up to contempt or disrepute, and shall not be used as falsely to suggest a connection between the holder of the mark and the symbol.

Regarding insignia, *see* § 2(b) of the Trademark Act, 15 U.S.C. § 1052(b); TMEP § 1204.

While the prohibition of § 2(a) against the registration of matter which may disparage or falsely suggest a connection with national symbols, or bring them into contempt or disrepute, may not be applicable to a particular designation, many names, acronyms, titles, terms, and symbols are protected by other statutes or rules. *See* TMEP § 1205.01 and the listing of special protection sections in Chapter 1900.

1203.03(c) Disparagement, Bringing into Contempt and Bringing into Disrepute

Section 2(a) prohibits the registration of a mark that consists of or comprises matter which may disparage, or bring into contempt or disrepute, persons, institutions, beliefs or national symbols. Regarding persons, *see* 15 U.S.C. § 1127; TMEP § 1203.03(a). Regarding national symbols, *see* TMEP § 1203.03(b).

In sustaining an opposition on this ground, the Trademark Trial and Appeal Board stated as follows:

> Disparagement is essentially a violation of one's right of privacy—the right to be "let alone" from contempt or ridicule. See, *Carson v. Here's Johnny Portable Toilets, Inc.*, 698 F.2d 831, 218 USPQ 1 (6th Cir. 1983). It has been defined as the publication of a statement which the publisher intends to be understood, or which the recipient reasonably should understand, as tending "to cast doubt upon the quality of another's land, chattels, or intangible things." Restatement (Second) of

> Torts § 629 (1977). The two elements of such a claim are (1) that the communication reasonably would be understood as referring to the plaintiff; and (2) that the communication is disparaging, that is, would be considered offensive or objectionable by a reasonable person of ordinary sensibilities. Id.

Greyhound Corp. v. Both Worlds Inc., 6 USPQ2d 1635, 1639 (TTAB 1988).

With regard to the first element set forth, the Board found that the design of a dog defecating, for which the applicant sought registration, strongly resembled the opposer's running dog symbol and that the evidence of record established that the symbol "points uniquely and unmistakably to opposer's persona."

With regard to the second element, the Board noted the negative nature of the design and stated as follows:

> As it relates to opposer, ... the offensiveness of the design becomes even more objectionable because it makes a statement about opposer itself, and holds opposer up to ridicule and contempt.

Id. at 1640.

1203.03(d) Disparagement, Bringing into Contempt and Bringing into Disrepute: Case References

See In re In Over Our Heads Inc., 16 USPQ2d 1653, 1654 (TTAB 1990) (MOONIES and design incorporating a "buttocks caricature," for dolls whose pants can be dropped, held not to be disparaging matter which would be unregistrable under § 2(a), the Board finding that the mark "would, when used on a doll, most likely be perceived as indicating that the doll 'moons,' and would not be perceived as referencing members of The Unification Church."); *Greyhound Corp. v. Both Worlds Inc.*, 6 USPQ2d 1635, 1639–40 (TTAB 1988) (design of dog defecating, for clothing, held to disparage, and bring into contempt or disrepute, opposer's running dog symbol, the Board finding the evidence of record "sufficient to show prima facie that this design [the running dog symbol] is, in effect, an alter ego of opposer which points uniquely and unmistakably to opposer's persona."); *In re Anti–Communist World Freedom Congress, Inc.*, 161 USPQ 304 (TTAB 1969) (design of an "X" superimposed over a hammer and sickle held to disparage, and hold in contempt and disrepute, a national symbol of the U.S.S.R.).

1203.03(e) False Suggestion of a Connection

Section 2(a) prohibits the registration of a mark that consists of or comprises matter which may falsely suggest a connection with persons, institutions, beliefs or national symbols. Regarding persons, *see* 15 U.S.C. § 1127; TMEP § 1203.03(a). Regarding national symbols, *see* TMEP § 1203.03(b). Regarding the underlying intent of Congress in drafting this section of the Trademark Act, *see* TMEP § 1203.03.

The following are necessary to support a refusal to register a mark on the ground that it consists of or comprises matter which may falsely suggest a connection with a person or an institution: (1) The examining attorney must show that the mark is the same as, or a close approximation of, the name or identity of a person or an institution, and that it would be recognized as such. (2) It must also be clear that such person or institution is not connected with the goods sold or services performed by the applicant under the mark. The examining attorney should make an explicit inquiry to ensure that the relevant facts are of record with respect to the second criterion (*see* 37 C.F.R. § 2.61(b)). (3) Finally, it must be shown that the fame or reputation of the person or institution is such that, when the mark is used with the applicant's goods or services, a connection with the person or institution would be presumed. *In re Nuclear Research Corp.*, 16 USPQ2d 1316, 1317 (TTAB 1990); *In re Cotter & Co.*, 228 USPQ 202, 204 (TTAB 1985).

A refusal on this basis requires, by implication, that the person or institution with which a connection is falsely suggested must be the prior user. *In re Nuclear Research Corp.,* 16 USPQ2d 1316, 1317 (TTAB 1990); *In re Mohawk Air Services Inc.,* 196 USPQ 851, 854–55 (TTAB 1977).

Similarly, the Trademark Trial and Appeal Board has indicated that a plaintiff asserting a claim that a mark falsely suggests a connection with persons or institutions must demonstrate: (1) that the defendant's mark is the same as, or a close approximation of, the plaintiff's previously used name or identity; (2) that the mark would be recognized as such; (3) that the plaintiff is not connected with the activities performed by the defendant under the mark; and (4) that the plaintiff's name or identity is of sufficient fame or reputation that the defendant's use will presumably result in an association with the plaintiff. *Buffett v. Chi–Chi's, Inc.*, 226 USPQ 428, 429 (TTAB 1985).

Regarding pleading in this type of case, *see Ritz Hotel Ltd. v. Ritz Closet Seat Corp.*, 17 USPQ2d 1466, 1471 (TTAB 1990) ("[O]pposer has failed to plead or prove that applicant's use of its mark points uniquely to opposer, a necessary element of a claim that a mark falsely suggests a connection with one's identity or persona."); *S & L Acquisition Co. v. Helene Arpels Inc.*, 9 USPQ2d 1221, 1224 (TTAB 1987) ("[S]ince the Board is not persuaded that the grounds for pleading a 2(a) counterclaim were not available to applicant at the time it filed its answer, applicant's motion for leave to amend its answer is denied."); *Squirrel Brand Co. v. Green Gables Investment Co.*, 223 USPQ 154, 156 (TTAB 1984) ("[I]t is essential that the record show a connection with opposer as an organization and not merely the use of confusingly similar marks."); *Canovas v. Venezia 80 S.R.L.*, 220 USPQ 660 (TTAB 1983) (failure of foreign opposer to plead that fame of party extends to the United States).

Intent to identify a party or trade upon its goodwill is not a required element of a § 2(a) claim of false suggestion of an association with such party. *S & L Acquisition Co. v. Helene Arpels, Inc.*, 9 USPQ2d 1221, 1224

(TTAB 1987); *Consolidated Natural Gas Co. v. CNG Fuel Systems, Ltd.*, 228 USPQ 752, 754 (TTAB 1985). However, evidence of such an intent could be highly persuasive that the public would make the intended false association. *University of Notre Dame du Lac v. J.C. Gourmet Food Imports Co., Inc.*, 703 F.2d 1372, 1377, 217 USPQ 505, 509 (Fed. Cir. 1983).

1203.03(f) False Suggestion of a Connection: Case References

See University of Notre Dame du Lac v. J.C. Gourmet Food Imports Co., Inc., 703 F.2d 1372, 1377, 217 USPQ 505, 509 (Fed. Cir. 1983), *aff'g* 213 USPQ 594 (TTAB 1982) (NOTRE DAME and design, for cheese, held not to falsely suggest a connection with the University of Notre Dame. "As the board noted, 'Notre Dame' is not a name solely associated with the University. It serves to identify a famous and sacred religious figure and is used in the names of churches dedicated to Notre Dame, such as the Cathedral of Notre Dame in Paris, France. Thus it cannot be said that the only 'person' which the name possibly identifies is the University and that the mere use of NOTRE DAME by another appropriates its identity."); *In re Sauer,* 27 USPQ2d 1073 (TTAB 1993) (registration of BO BALL for oblong shaped leather ball with white stitching properly refused under § 2(a), since use of "Bo" would be recognized by purchasers as reference to football and baseball player Bo Jackson, and there was no connection between Jackson and applicant); *Ritz Hotel Ltd. v. Ritz Closet Seat Corp.*, 17 USPQ2d 1466, 1471 (TTAB 1990) (RIT–Z in stylized form, for toilet seats, held not to falsely suggest a connection with opposer, the Board observing that there was "no evidence of record directed to showing a connection of applicant's mark with opposer corporation, The Ritz Hotel Limited"); *In re Nuclear Research Corp.*, 16 USPQ2d 1316 (TTAB 1990) (NRC and design, for radiation and chemical agent monitors, electronic testers and nuclear gauges, held not to falsely suggest a connection with the U.S. Nuclear Regulatory Commission in view of applicant's use of NRC long prior to the inception of that agency); *NASA v. Bully Hill Vineyards, Inc.,* 3 USPQ2d 1671, 1676 (TTAB 1987) (opposition to the registration of SPACE SHUTTLE for wines dismissed, the Board finding "shuttle" to be a generic term for a space vehicle or system. "Where a name claimed to be appropriated does not point uniquely and unmistakably to that party's personality or 'persona,' there can be no false suggestion."); *Board of Trustees of University of Alabama v. BAMA–Werke Curt Baumann,* 231 USPQ 408 (TTAB 1986) (petition to cancel registration of BAMA, for shoes, slippers, stockings, socks and insoles, granted, the Board finding that the evidence of record indicated that BAMA points uniquely to the University of Alabama and thus falsely suggests a connection with the University); *In re Cotter & Co.*, 228 USPQ 202 (TTAB 1985) (WESTPOINT, for shotguns and rifles, held to falsely suggest a connection with an institution, the United States Military Academy). For examples of findings of false suggestion of a connection prior to the decision of the Court of Appeals for the Federal Circuit in *Notre Dame, supra, see In re U.S. Bicentennial Society,* 197 USPQ 905 (TTAB 1978) (U.S. BICENTENNIAL SOCIETY, for ceremonial swords, held to falsely suggest a connection with the American Revolution Bicentennial Commission and the United States government); *In re National Intelligence Academy*, 190 USPQ2d 570 (TTAB 1976) (NATIONAL INTELLIGENCE ACADEMY, for educational and instructional services in intelligence gathering for law enforcement officers, held to falsely suggest a connection with the United States government).

1203.04 Geographical Indication Which, When Used on or in Connection with Wines or Spirits, Identifies a Place Other than the Origin of the Goods

Section 2(a) of the Trademark Act prohibits the registration of a designation which consists of or comprises "a geographical indication which, when used on or in connection with wines or spirits, identifies a place other than the origin of the goods and is first used on or in connection with wines or spirits by the applicant on or after [January 1, 1996]." This provision was added by the Uruguay Round Agreements Act, implementing the Trade Related Intellectual Property (TRIPs) portions of the General Agreement on Tariffs and Trade (GATT). It applies only to geographic indications that were first used in commerce on or after January 1, 1996, one year after the effective date of the legislation implementing GATT.

The examining attorney must refuse registration under § 2(a) of any geographical designation that was first used in commerce on or in connection with wines or spirits on or after January 1, 1996, if it identifies a place other than the origin of the goods. Section 2(a) is an absolute bar to the registration of such geographical designations on both the Principal Register and the Supplemental Register. Neither a disclaimer of the geographical designation nor a claim that it has acquired distinctiveness under § 2(f) can obviate a § 2(a) refusal if the mark consists of or comprises a geographical indication which identifies a place other than the origin of wines or spirits.

See TMEP §§ 1203.02 and 1203.02(a) as to geographical designations that are deceptive under § 2(a) of the Trademark Act, and TMEP §§ 1210.06 and 1210.07 as to geographically deceptively misdescriptive marks, under § 2(e)(3) of the Act.

1204 Refusal on Basis of Flag, Coat of Arms or Other Insignia of United States, State or Municipality, or Foreign Nation

Extract from 15 U.S.C. § 1052. No trademark by which the goods of the applicant may be distinguished from the goods of others shall be refused registration on the principal register on account of its nature unless it ... (b) Consists of or comprises the flag or coat of arms or other insignia of the United States, or of any State or municipality, or of any foreign nation, or any simulation thereof.

Section 2(b) of the Trademark Act, 15 U.S.C. § 1052(b), bars the registration of marks which consist of or comprise (whether consisting solely of, or having incorporated in them) the flag, coat of arms, or other insignia of the United States, of any state or municipality, or of any foreign nation.

Section 2(b) also bars the registration of marks which consist of or comprise any simulation of such symbols.

This section is an absolute bar to the registration of such marks on both the Principal Register and, pursuant to § 23(a), 15 U.S.C. § 1091(a), the Supplemental Register. Section 2(b) differs from the provision of § 2(a) regarding national symbols in that § 2(b) requires no additional element, such as disparagement or a false suggestion of a connection, to preclude registration. (Regarding national symbols, *see* TMEP § 1203.03(b).)

Flags and coats of arms are specific designs formally adopted to serve as emblems of governmental authority. The wording "other insignia" should not be interpreted broadly, but should be considered to include only those emblems and devices which also represent such authority and which are of the same general class and character as flags and coats of arms. The Trademark Trial and Appeal Board has construed the statutory language as follows:

[T]he wording "or other insignia of the United States" must be restricted in its application to insignia of the same general class as "the flag or coats of arms" of the United States. Since both the flag and coat of arms are emblems of national authority it seems evident that other insignia of national authority such as the Great Seal of the United States, the Presidential Seal, and seals of government departments would be equally prohibited registration under Section 2(b). On the other hand, it appears equally evident that department insignia which are merely used to identify a service or facility of the Government are not insignia of national authority and that they therefore do not fall within the general prohibitions of this section of the Statute.

In re United States Department of the Interior, 142 USPQ 506, 507 (TTAB 1964) (logo comprising the words "NATIONAL PARK SERVICE" and "Department of the Interior," with depiction of trees, mountains and a buffalo, surrounded by an arrowhead design held not to be an insignia of the United States).

Letters which merely identify people and things associated with a particular agency or department of the United States government, instead of representing the authority of the government or the nation as a whole, are generally not considered to be "insignia of the United States" as contemplated by § 2(b). The Board, in dismissing an opposition to the registration of "USMC" in a stylized presentation, for prostheses, fracture braces and orthopedic components, discussed what is meant by "insignia" under § 2(b), as follows:

> The letters "USMC" are nothing like a flag or coat of arms. These types of insignia are pictorial in nature, they can be described, but cannot be pronounced. Even if the letters could be construed to be an insignia, opposer has not shown that they would be seen as an insignia of the United States.

U.S. Navy v. United States Mfg. Co., 2 USPQ2d 1254, 1256 (TTAB 1987). As a result of the enactment of Public Law 98–525 on October 19, 1984, the initials, seal and emblem of the United States Marine Corps are "deemed to be insignia of the United States," under 10 U.S.C. § 7881, pertaining to unauthorized use of Marine Corps insignia. However, "USMC" was not so protected when the applicant began using its stylized version of those letters as a mark. In view of the provision in Public Law 98–525 that the amendments adding Chapter 663 (10 U.S.C. § 7881) shall not affect rights that vested before the date of its enactment, the majority of the Board found that enactment of the law did not adversely affect the mark's registrability, stating that "opposer has not shown that applicant's mark was an insignia of the United States prior to the law making it one, or that the law effectively bars registration to applicant." *Id.* at 1260. (Regarding subject matter which is protected by statute, *see* TMEP § 1205.01 and the listing of citations for special protection sections in TMEP Chapter 1900.)

See also Liberty Mutual Insurance Co. v. Liberty Insurance Co. of Texas, 185 F.Supp. 895, 908, 127 USPQ 312, 323 (E.D. Ark. 1960) ("That the Statue of Liberty is not a part of the 'insignia of the United States' is too clear to require discussion.")

As stated above, marks which consist of or comprise any simulation of the flag, coat of arms, or other insignia of the United States, of any state or municipality, or of any foreign nation are also unregistrable under § 2(b). "Simulation," as contemplated by § 2(b), refers to "something that gives the appearance or effect or has the characteristics of an original item." Whether a mark comprises such a simulation must be gathered from a visual comparison of the mark vis-à-vis replicas of the flag, coat of arms or other insignia in question. *In re Waltham Watch Co.*, 179 USPQ 59, 60 (TTAB 1973) (mark consisting of wording and the design of a globe and six flags, for watches, found registrable, the Board stating, "[A]lthough the flags depicted in applicant's mark incorporate common elements of flag designs such as horizontal or vertical lines, crosses or stars, they are readily distinguishable from any of the flags of the nations alluded to by the examiner. In fact, applicant's mark would be regarded as nothing more than a conglomeration of nondescript flags utilized to symbolize the significance of the globe design and the slogan 'TIMING THE WORLD' appearing thereon.").

The view of the mark in relation to replicas of the pertinent flag, coat of arms or other insignia must be "without a careful analysis and side-by-side comparison." The public should be considered to retain only a general or overall, rather than specific, recollection of the various elements or characteristics of design marks. *In re Advance Industrial Security, Inc.*, 194 USPQ 344, 346–47 (TTAB 1977) (ADVANCE SECURITY and design consisting of an eagle on a triangular shield, in gold and brown, for detective and investigative services and providing security systems and services, found registrable, the Board stating, "When the mark of the applicant and the Coat of Arms or Great Seal of the United States are compared in their entireties, it is adjudged that applicant's mark does not consist of or comprise the Coat of Arms of the United States or any simulation thereof. . . .").

The incorporation in a mark of individual or distorted features which are merely suggestive of flags, coats of arms or other insignia does not bar registration under § 2(b). *See Knorr-Nahrmittel A.G. v. Havland International, Inc.*, 206 USPQ 827, 833 (TTAB 1980) (While applicant originally may have intended to include the flags of the Scandinavian countries in the mark, NOR-KING and design, "[a]ll that the record reflects is that the mark contains a representation of certain flags, but not the flag or flags of any particular nation." Opposer's cause of action under § 2(b) deemed to be without merit; opposition sustained on other grounds); *In re National Van Lines, Inc.,* 123 USPQ 510 (TTAB 1959) (mark comprising words and the design of a shield with vertical stripes held registrable, the Board finding the design to be readily distinguishable from the shield of the Great Seal of the United States and, thus, not a simulation of the seal or any portion thereof); *In re American Box Board Co.,* 123 USPQ 508 (TTAB 1959) (design mark comprising an eagle and shield held registrable, the Board finding that it did not involve a simulation of the Great Seal of the United States because the eagle and shield of applicant's mark differed substantially from those on the seal in both appearance and manner of display).

See TMEP § 1205 *et seq.* regarding matter which is protected by statute or by Article 6*ter* of the Paris Convention.

1205 Refusal on Basis of Matter Protected by Statute or Convention

1205.01 Statutory Protection

Various federal statutes and regulations prohibit or restrict the use of certain words, names, symbols, terms, initials, marks, emblems, seals, insignia, badges, decorations, medals and characters adopted by the United States government or particular national and international organizations. These designations are reserved for the specific purposes prescribed in the relevant statute and must be free for use in the prescribed manner. (In addition, there are other statutes which affect marks. *See* the listings, in TMEP Chapter 1900, of citations to sections of the United States Code and the Code of Federal Regulations.)

For example, Congress has created about 70 statutes through which exclusive rights to use certain designations are granted to federally created private corporations and organizations. Violation of some of these statutes may be a criminal offense, *e.g.*, 18 U.S.C. §§ 705 (regarding badges, medals, emblems or other insignia of veterans' organizations); 706 (Red Cross); 707 (4-H Club); 708 (coat of arms of the Swiss Confederation); 711 ("Smokey Bear"); and 711a ("Woodsy Owl" and slogan, "Give a Hoot, Don't Pollute"). Other statutes provide for civil enforcement, *e.g.*, 36 U.S.C. §§ 18c (Daughters of the American Revolution); 27 (Boy Scouts); 36 (Girl Scouts);

1086 (Little League); and 3305 (The American National Theater and Academy).

The following are examples of the protection of words and symbols by statute.

(1) The Copyright Act of 1976 includes provisions regarding the use of appropriate notices of copyright. These include provisions concerning the use of the letter "C" in a circle, the word "Copyright" and the abbreviation "Copr." to identify visually perceptible copies (17 U.S.C. § 401); the use of the letter "P" in a circle to indicate phonorecords of sound recordings (17 U.S.C. § 402); and the use of the words "mask force," the symbol *M* and the letter "M" in a circle to designate mask works (17 U.S.C. § 909). The Act designates these symbols to perform the function of indicating that the user of the symbol is asserting specific statutory rights.

(2) Use of the Greek red cross other than by the American National Red Cross is proscribed by statute. 18 U.S.C. § 706. Use of the coat of arms of the Swiss Confederation for trade or commercial purposes is proscribed by statute. 18 U.S.C. § 708. *See In re Health Maintenance Organizations, Inc.*, 188 USPQ 473 (TTAB 1975) (mark comprising a dark cross with legs of equal length on which a caduceus is symmetrically imposed (representation of caduceus disclaimed) held registrable, the Board finding the mark readily distinguishable from the Greek red cross (on white background) and the Swiss confederation coat of arms (white cross on red background)).

(3) False advertising or misuse of names to indicate a federal agency is proscribed by 18 U.S.C. § 709. For example, this provision prohibits knowing use, without written permission of the Director of the Federal Bureau of Investigation, of the words "Federal Bureau of Investigation," the initials "F.B.I." or any colorable imitation, in various formats "in a manner reasonably calculated to convey the impression that such advertisement, ... publication, ... broadcast, telecast, or other production, is approved, endorsed, or authorized by the Federal Bureau of Investigation." Thus, an examining attorney must refuse to register such matter, pursuant to 18 U.S.C. § 709, if its use is reasonably calculated to convey an approval, endorsement or authorization by the Federal Bureau of Investigation.

(4) Section 110 of the Amateur Sports Act of 1978, codified at 36 U.S.C. § 380, protects various designations associated with the Olympics. Under 36 U.S.C. § 380(c), the United States Olympic Committee has the exclusive right to use the name "United States Olympic Committee," its symbol and emblem, and the words "Olympic," "Olympiad," "Citius Altius Fortius" or any combination thereof. The United States Supreme Court has held that the grant by Congress to the United States Olympic Committee of the exclusive right to use the word "Olympic" does not violate the First Amendment. *San Francisco Arts & Athletics, Inc. v. U.S. Olympic Committee*, 483 U.S. 522, 3 USPQ2d 1145 (1987) (concerning petitioner's use of "Gay Olympic Games"). Under 36 U.S.C. § 380(a), a person is subject to suit in a civil action by the Committee if such person, without the Committee's consent, uses for the purpose of trade, to induce the sale

of goods or services, or to promote any theatrical exhibition, athletic performance, or competition, a designation noted above (listed in § 380(c)) or "any trademark, trade name, sign, symbol, or insignia falsely representing association with, or authorization by, the International Olympic Committee or ... [the United States Olympic Committee]" or any simulation of the words "Olympic," "Olympiad" or "Citius Altius Fortius" "tending to cause confusion, to cause mistake, to deceive, or to falsely suggest a connection with ... [the United States Olympic Committee] or any Olympic activity." Regarding action by the United States Olympic Committee to enforce its rights under the statute, *see U.S. Olympic Committee v. Union Sport Apparel*, 220 USPQ 526 (E.D. Va. 1983); *U.S. Olympic Committee v. International Federation of Body Builders*, 219 USPQ 353 (D.D.C. 1982); *Stop the Olympic Prison v. U.S. Olympic Committee*, 489 F.Supp. 1112, 207 USPQ 237 (S.D.N.Y. 1980).

(5) In chartering the Blinded Veterans Association, Congress granted it the sole right to use its name and such seals, emblems and badges as it may lawfully adopt. 36 U.S.C. § 867. This protection of its exclusive right to use "Blinded Veterans Association" does not extend to the term "blinded veterans," which has been found generic. *Blinded Veterans Association v. Blinded American Veterans Foundation*, 872 F.2d 1035, 10 USPQ2d 1432 (D.C. App. 1989).

Usually the statute will define the appropriate use of a designation and will prescribe criminal penalties or civil remedies for improper use. However, the statutes themselves do not provide the basis for refusal of trademark registration. In determining whether registration should be refused in a particular application, the examining attorney should consult the relevant statute to determine the function of the designation and its appropriate use. If a statute provides that a specific party or government agency has the exclusive right to use a designation, and a party other than that specified in the statute has applied to register such designation, the examining attorney must refuse registration under all appropriate sections of the Trademark Act and reference all relevant statutory provisions.

If the applicant's use of the mark is or would be unlawful under the referenced provision, the examining attorney should refuse registration on that ground, citing §§ 1 and 45 of the Trademark Act, 15 U.S.C. §§ 1051 and 1127. For marks to which the above statutes pertain, this will usually be the basis for refusal.

Depending upon the nature and use of the mark, other sections of the Trademark Act may also bar registration and must be cited where appropriate in order that a complete refusal is issued. For example, it may be appropriate for the examining attorney to refuse registration under § 2(a) of the Trademark Act, 15 U.S.C. § 1052(a), on the ground that the mark comprises matter which may falsely suggest a connection with a national symbol, institution or person specified in the statute (*e.g.*, the United States Olympic Committee). *See* TMEP § 1203.03(e). Other § 2(a) bases for refusal could also apply. *See* TMEP § 1203 *et seq*. It may be appropriate to refuse registration under § 2(b), 15 U.S.C. § 1052(b), for matter which comprises a flag, coat of arms or other similar insignia. *See* TMEP § 1204. It may be appropriate to refuse registration under § 2(d), 15 U.S.C. § 1052(d), if the party specified in the statute owns a registration for a mark which is the same or similar. *Cf. U.S. Olympic Committee v. Olymp-Herren-waschefabriken Bezner GmbH & Co.*, 224 USPQ 497 (TTAB 1984) (opposition to the registration of OLYMP sustained on ground of likelihood of confusion with opposer's registered mark OLYMPIC, under § 2(d), the Board finding that the evidence of record did not show that OLYMP falsely suggests a connection with opposer, under § 2(a), and that the remedies provided in 36 U.S.C. § 380(a) for misuse of Olympic designations are not pertinent to opposition proceedings).

In some instances, it may be appropriate for the examining attorney to refuse registration pursuant to §§ 1, 2 (preamble) and 45 of the Trademark Act, 15 U.S.C. §§ 1051, 1052 and 1127, on the ground that the subject matter would not be perceived as a trademark. (For service mark applications, § 3 of the Act, 15 U.S.C. 1053, should also be cited in this type of refusal).

To determine what action is appropriate, the examining attorney should look to the particular use of a symbol or term by the applicant. For example, where it is evident that the applicant has merely included a copyright symbol in the drawing of the mark inadvertently, and the symbol is not a material portion of the mark, the examining attorney should indicate that the symbol is not part of the mark and require that the applicant amend the drawing to remove the symbol, instead of issuing statutory refusals of the types noted above.

Examining attorneys should also consider whether registration of matter as a trademark by the applicant may be prohibited by Article 6*ter* of the Paris Convention. *See* TMEP § 1205.02.

1205.02 Article 6*ter* of the Paris Convention

The United States is a member of the Paris Convention for the Protection of Industrial Property, as revised at Stockholm on July 14, 1967, the members of which constitute a Union for the protection of industrial property. As a treaty made under the authority of the United States, the Paris Convention is the law of the United States pursuant to Article 6 of the United States Constitution.

Under Article 6*ter* of the Paris Convention, the contracting countries have agreed to refuse or to invalidate the registration, and to prohibit the unauthorized use, as trademarks or as elements of trademarks, of armorial bearings, flags, and other State emblems of the member countries, official signs and hallmarks indicating control and warranty adopted by member countries, and any imitation from a heraldic point of view. The provision applies equally to armorial bearings, flags, other emblems, abbreviations and names of international intergovernmental organizations of which one or more countries of the Union are members, except for those that are already the subject of international agreements in force, intended to ensure their protection (*e.g.*, "Red Cross" and emblems protected by the Geneva Convention of August 12, 1949).

Article 6*ter* of the Paris Convention provides for each member country to communicate the list of emblems, official signs and hallmarks which it wishes to protect, and all subsequent modifications of its list, to the International Bureau of Intellectual Property (the International Bureau), which will transmit the communications to the member countries. Within twelve months from receipt of such notification, a member country may transmit its objections, through the International Bureau.

The Paris Convention thus obligates the United States to refuse to register, as trademarks or as elements of trademarks, designations which have been deposited pursuant to Article 6*ter* and to which the United States has transmitted no objections. (In the United States Patent and Trademark Office, such designations are assigned serial numbers in the "89" series code, *i.e.*, serial numbers beginning with the digits "89." Copies are filed in the paper records of the Trademark Search Library, and pertinent information is entered in the automated search records of the Office and should be discovered in an examining attorney's search for conflicting marks. However, since many of the images associated with these entries are not currently available by computer, they must be found in the Search Library.)

Depending upon the nature and use of the mark, the sections of the Trademark Act which may bar registration include §§ 2(a) and 2(b), 15 U.S.C. §§ 1052(a) and 1052(b). For example, it may be appropriate for the examining attorney to refuse registration under § 2(a) of the Trademark Act, 15 U.S.C. § 1052(a), on the ground that the mark comprises matter which may falsely suggest a connection with a national symbol of a member country or an international intergovernmental organization. *See* TMEP § 1203.03(e). Other § 2(a) bases for refusal could also apply. *See* TMEP § 1203 *et seq*. It may be appropriate to refuse registration under § 2(b), 15 U.S.C. § 1052(b), for matter which comprises a flag, coat of arms or other similar insignia. *See* TMEP § 1204. In some instances, it may be appropriate for the examining attorney to refuse registration pursuant to §§ 1, 2 (preamble) and 45 of the Trademark Act, 15 U.S.C. §§ 1051, 1052 and 1127, on the ground that the subject matter would not be perceived as a trademark. (For service mark applications, § 3 of the Act, 15 U.S.C. § 1053, should also be cited in this type of refusal.)

1206 Refusal on Basis of Name, Portrait or Signature of Particular Living Individual or Deceased U.S. President Without Consent

Extract from 15 U.S.C. § 1052. No trademark by which the goods of the applicant may be distinguished from the goods of others shall be refused registration on the principal register on account of its nature unless it . . . (c) Consists of or comprises a name, portrait, or signature identifying a particular living individual except by his written consent, or the name, signature, or portrait of a deceased President of the United States during the life of his widow, if any, except by the written consent of the widow.

Section 2(c) of the Trademark Act, 15 U.S.C. § 1052(c), bars the registration of a mark that consists of or comprises (whether consisting solely of, or having incorporated in the mark) a name, portrait or signature which identifies a particular living individual, or a deceased United States president during the life of his widow, except by the written consent of such individual or such president's widow.

Section 2(c) bars the registration of such marks on the Principal Register and, pursuant to § 23(a), 15 U.S.C. § 1091(a), the Supplemental Register.

The purpose of requiring the consent of a living individual to the registration of his or her name, signature or portrait is to protect rights of privacy and publicity which living persons have in the designations which identify them. *University of Notre Dame du Lac v. J.C. Gourmet Food Imports Co., Inc.*, 703 F.2d 1372, 1376, 217 USPQ 505, 509 (Fed. Cir. 1983); *Canovas v. Venezia 80 S.R.L.*, 220 USPQ 660, 661 (TTAB 1983). *See* TMEP § 1203.03 for a discussion of the right to control the use of one's identity, which underlies part of § 2(a) as well as § 2(c).

See TMEP § 813 regarding when it is necessary for an examining attorney to inquire of the applicant as to whether a name, signature or depiction in a mark identifies a particular living individual, and regarding the entry of pertinent statements in the record for printing in the *Official Gazette* and on a registration certificate.

1206.01 Name, Portrait or Signature

Section 2(c) explicitly pertains to any name, portrait or signature which identifies a particular living individual, or a deceased president of the United States during the life of the president's widow.

In order to identify a particular living individual, a name need not be the person's full name. *See In re Steak and Ale Restaurants of America, Inc.*, 185 USPQ 447 (TTAB 1975) (PRINCE CHARLES, for which registration was sought for meat, found to identify a particular living individual whose consent was not of record); *Laub v. Industrial Development Laboratories, Inc.*, 121 USPQ 595 (TTAB 1959) (LAUB, for flowmeters, found to identify the holder of a patent for flowmeters, whose written consent was not of record); *Reed v. Bakers Engineering & Equipment Co.*, 100 USPQ 196, 199 (PO Ex. Ch. 1954) (registration of REED REEL OVEN, for ovens, held to be barred by § 2(c) without written consent of the designer and builder of the ovens, Paul N. Reed. " 'Name' in section 2(c) is not restricted to the full name of an individual but refers to any name regardless of whether it is a full name, or a surname or given name, or even a nickname, which identifies a particular living individual. . . ."). *Cf. Societe Civile Des Domaines Dourthe Freres v. S.A. Consortium Vinicole De Bordeaux Et De La Gironde*, 6 USPQ2d 1205, 1209 (TTAB 1988) ("Section 2(c) does not apply to surnames except in those cases where a particular individual is known by a surname alone.").

Cases involving portraits include *In re McKee Baking Co.*, 218 USPQ 287 (TTAB 1983) (mark comprising a sign on which the portrait of a young girl appears below the words LITTLE DEBBIE); *In re Masucci*, 179 USPQ 829 (TTAB 1973) (mark comprising name and portrait of a deceased president of the United States, President Eisenhower); *Garden v. Parfumerie Rigaud, Inc.*, 34 USPQ 30 (Comm'r Pats. 1937) (marks comprising name and portrait of Mary Garden).

1206.02 Particular Living Individual or Deceased U.S. President

Section 2(c) applies to marks that comprise matter which identifies living individuals; it does not apply to marks that comprise matter which identifies deceased persons, except for a deceased president of the United States during the life of the president's widow. *See McGraw–Edison Co. v. Thomas Edison Life Insurance Co.*, 160 USPQ 685 (TTAB 1969), *vacated on other grounds*, 162 USPQ 372 (N.D. Ill. 1969) (opposition to the registration of THOMAS EDISON dismissed, the Board finding § 2(c) inapplicable, as the particular individual whom the name identifies is deceased); *In re Masucci*, 179 USPQ 829 (TTAB 1973) (affirming refusal to register mark consisting of the name EISENHOWER, a portrait of President Dwight D. Eisenhower and the words PRESIDENT EISENHOWER REGISTERED PLATINUM MEDALLION #13, for greeting cards, on the ground that the mark comprises the name, signature or portrait of a deceased United States president without the written consent of his widow, under § 2(c)).

The fact that a name appearing in a mark may actually be the name of more than one person does not negate the requirement for a written consent to registration, so long as the mark identifies, to the relevant public, a particular living individual or deceased United States president whose spouse is living. *In re Steak and Ale Restaurants of America, Inc.*, 185 USPQ 447, 447 (TTAB 1975) (affirming refusal to register PRINCE CHARLES, for meat, in the absence of consent to register by Prince Charles, a member of the English royal family. "Even accepting the existence of more than one living 'Prince Charles,' it does not follow that each is not a particular living individual.").

If it appears that a name, portrait or signature in a mark may identify a particular living individual but in fact the applicant devised such matter as fanciful, or believes it to be fanciful, a statement to that effect should be placed in the record. If appropriate, the statement that a name, portrait or signature does not identify a particular living individual will be printed in the *Official Gazette* and on the registration certificate. *See* TMEP § 813. Additional relevant circumstances should also be explained. For example, if the matter identifies a certain character in literature, or a deceased historical person, then a statement of such facts in the record may be helpful. Such information should not be printed, however, in the *Official Gazette* or on a registration certificate.

Although a mark may have been devised to be fanciful or arbitrary and not to identify a particular living individual, it nevertheless may name or otherwise identify one or more living individuals. Whether consent to register is required depends upon whether the public would recognize and understand the mark as identifying the person. Thus, if the person is not generally known, nor well known in the field relating to the relevant goods or services, it may be that the mark would not constitute the identification of a particular person under § 2(c), and consent would not be required. The Trademark Trial and Appeal Board noted as follows in *Martin v. Carter Hawley Hale Stores, Inc.*, 206 USPQ 931, 933 (TTAB 1979):

[Section] 2(c) was not designed to protect every person from having a name which is similar or identical to his or her name registered as a trademark. Such a scope of protection would practically preclude the registration of a trademark consisting of a name since in most cases there would be someone somewhere who is known by the name and who might be expected to protest its registration. Rather, the Statute was intended to protect one who, for valid reasons, could expect to suffer damage from another's trademark use of his name. That is, it is more than likely that any trademark which is comprised of a given name and surname will, in fact, be the name of a real person. But that coincidence, in and of itself, does not give rise to damage to that individual in the absence of other factors from which it may be determined that the particular individual bearing the name in question will be associated with the mark as used on the goods, either because that person is so well known that the public would reasonably assume the connection or because the individual is publicly connected with the business in which the mark is used.

See also Fanta v. Coca–Cola Co., 140 USPQ 674 (TTAB 1964) (dismissing a petition to cancel registrations of FANTA, for soft drinks and syrup concentrate, the Board noting no use by the petitioner, Robert D. Fanta, of his name in connection with the sale of soft drinks, nor any indication that petitioner had attained recognition in that field); *DeCecco v. Wright*, 120 USPQ 20, 20 (TTAB 1958) ("The question whether the name 'DECECCO' as used by applicant in connection with his goods serves to identify opposer is a matter for proof."); *Brand v. Fairchester Packing Co.*, 84 USPQ 97 (Comm'r Pats. 1950) (dismissing a petition to cancel the registration of ARNOLD BRAND, for fresh tomatoes, the Commissioner finding nothing in the record to indicate that the mark identified the petitioner, Arnold Brand, an attorney specializing in patent and trademark matters, with the tomato business, or that use of the mark would lead the public to make such a connection).

1211 Refusal on Basis of Surname

Extract from 15 U.S.C. § 1052. No trademark by which the goods of the applicant may be distinguished from the goods of others shall be refused registration on the principal register on account of its nature unless it ... (e) Consists of a mark which ... (4) is primarily merely a surname.

Under § 2(e)(4) of the Trademark Act, 15 U.S.C. § 1052(e)(4), a mark which is primarily merely a surname is not registrable on the Principal Register, absent a showing of acquired distinctiveness under § 2(f), 15 U.S.C. § 1052(f). Formerly § 2(e)(3) of the Act, 15 U.S.C. § 1052(e)(3), this section was designated § 2(e)(4), 15 U.S.C. § 1052(e)(4), by the North American Free Trade Agreement Implementation Act, Public Law 103–182, which took effect January 1, 1994. Amendments to the Trademark Act by the North American Free Trade Agreement Implementation Act apply to trademark applications filed on or after December 8, 1993. (*See* TMEP § 1212 *et seq.* regarding registration of marks which have acquired distinctiveness.) A mark that is primarily merely a surname may be registrable on the Supplemental Register.

The Trademark Act, in § 2(e)(4), reflects the common law that exclusive rights in a surname *per se* cannot be established without evidence of long and exclusive use which changes its significance to the public from that of a surname of an individual to that of a mark for particular goods or services. The common law also recognizes that surnames are shared by more than one individual, each of whom may have an interest in using his surname in business and, by the requirement for evidence of distinctiveness, in effect, delays appropriation of exclusive rights in the name. *In re Etablissements Darty et Fils,* 759 F.2d 15, 16, 225 USPQ 652, 653 (Fed. Cir. 1985), *aff'g* 222 USPQ 260 (TTAB 1984).

It is settled that the test to be applied in determining whether or not a mark is primarily merely a surname is its primary significance to the purchasing public. *See, e.g., Ex parte Rivera Watch Corp.*, 106 USPQ 145, 149 (Comm'r Pats. 1955).

1211.01 "Primarily Merely a Surname"

The legislative history of the Trademark Act of 1946 indicates that the word "primarily" was added to the existing statutory language "merely" with the intent, while excluding registration of names such as "Johnson" or "Jones," not to exclude registration of names such as "Cotton" or "King" which, while surnames, have a primary significance other than as a surname. *See Ex parte Rivera Watch Corp.*, 106 USPQ 145, 149 (Comm'r Pats. 1955); *Sears, Roebuck & Co. v. Watson*, 204 F.2d 32, 33–34, 96 USPQ 360, 362 (D.C. Cir. 1953).

1211.01(a) Non–Surname Significance

Often a word will have a meaning or significance in addition to its significance as a surname. A determination must be made as to which is the primary meaning to the public. The following are considerations which commonly arise in determining whether a mark is primarily merely a surname:

The term has an ordinary language meaning. If there is a readily recognized meaning of a term, apart from its surname significance, such that the primary significance of the term is not that of a surname, registration should be granted on the Principal Register without evidence of acquired distinctiveness. *See Fisher Radio Corp. v. Bird Electronic Corp.*, 162 USPQ 265 (TTAB 1969) (BIRD held not primarily merely a surname despite surname significance); *In re Hunt Electronics Co.*, 155 USPQ 606 (TTAB 1967) (HUNT held not primarily merely a surname despite surname significance). However, this does not mean that one need only uncover a non-surname meaning of the term in question in order to obviate a refusal under § 2(e)(4). *See In re Piquet*, 5 USPQ2d 1367, 1368 (TTAB 1987) (N. PIQUET (stylized) held primarily merely a surname despite significance of the term "piquet" as "the name of a relatively obscure card game").

The term is the phonetic equivalent of a term which has an ordinary language meaning. The mere fact that a term which has surname significance is also the phonetic equivalent of a word having ordinary language meaning does not preclude a finding that the term is primarily merely a surname (*e.g.*, Byrne/burn; Knott/not or knot; Chappell/chapel). *See In re Pickett Hotel Co.*, 229 USPQ 760 (TTAB 1986) (PICKETT SUITE HOTEL held primarily merely a surname despite applicant's argument that PICKETT is the phonetic equivalent of the word "picket"). *Cf. In re Monotype Corp. PLC*, 14 USPQ2d 1070, 1071 (TTAB 1989) (CALISTO) held not primarily merely a surname, the Board characterizing the telephone directory evidence of surname significance as "minimal" and noting the mythological significance of the name "Callisto" and stating that it is common knowledge that there are variations in the rendering of mythological names transliterated from the Greek alphabet (distinguishing *In re Pickett Hotel Co., supra*). Similarly, the fact that a word which has surname significance is also a hybrid or derivative of another word having ordinary language meaning is insufficient to overcome the surname significance unless the perception of non-surname significance would displace the primary surname import of the word. *See In re Petrin Corp.*, 231 USPQ 902 (TTAB 1986) (PETRIN held primarily merely a surname despite applicant's argument that the mark represents an abbreviation of "petroleum" and "insulation"); *In re Etablissements Darty et Fils*, 759 F.2d 15, 225 USPQ 652 (Fed. Cir. 1985), *aff'g* 222 USPQ 260 (TTAB 1984) (DARTY held primarily merely a surname despite applicant's argument that the mark is a play on the word "dart").

The term has geographical significance. A well-known geographical meaning could be more significant than the surname significance of a term. *In re Colt Industries Operating Corp.*, 195 USPQ 75 (TTAB 1977) (FAIRBANKS held not primarily merely a surname because the geographical significance of the mark was determined to be just as dominant as its surname significance). However, the fact that a term is shown to have some minor significance as a geographical term will not dissipate its primary significance as a surname. *In re Hamilton Pharmaceuticals Ltd.*, 27 USPQ2d 1939, 1943 (TTAB 1993) (HAMILTON held primarily merely a surname).

The term identifies a historical place or person. The significance of identifying a historical place or person could outweigh the surname meaning of a term. *See Lucien Piccard Watch Corp. v. Since 1868 Crescent Corp.*, 314 F.Supp. 329, 165 USPQ 459 (S.D.N.Y. 1970) (DA VINCI found not primarily merely a surname because it primarily connotes Leonardo Da Vinci). *Cf. In re Champion International Corp.*, 229 USPQ 550 (TTAB 1985) (McKINLEY held primarily merely a surname despite being the name of a deceased president).

The term is a rare surname. The rarity of a surname does not *per se* preclude a finding that a term is primarily merely a surname. Even a rare surname may be held primarily merely a surname if its primary significance to purchasers is that of a surname. *See In re Rebo High Definition Studio Inc.*, 15 USPQ2d 1314 (TTAB 1990) (REBO held primarily merely a surname); *In re Pohang Iron & Steel Co., Ltd.*, 230 USPQ 79 (TTAB 1986) (POSTEN held primarily merely a surname). Regardless of the rarity of the surname, the test to be applied in the administration of § 2(e)(4) is whether the primary significance of the term to the purchasing public is that of a surname. There is a category of surnames that are so rare that they do not even have the appearance of surnames. Where these are involved, even in the absence of non-surname significance, a reasonable application of the test of "primary significance to the purchasing public" could result in a finding that such a surname, when used as a mark, would be perceived as arbitrary or fanciful. *In re Etablissements Darty et Fils*, 222 USPQ 260, 262 (TTAB 1984), *aff'd*, 759 F.2d 15, 225 USPQ 652 (Fed. Cir. 1985) (DARTY held primarily merely a surname, the Trademark Trial and Appeal Board being unwilling to find that DARTY fell within this category of rare names that do not look like and would not be perceived as a surname); *In re Garan Inc.*, 3 USPQ2d 1537 (TTAB 1987) (GARAN held not primarily merely a surname). Conversely, as noted in *Ex parte Rivera Watch Corp.*, 106 USPQ 145, 149 (Comm'r Pats. 1955), "[t]here are some names which by their very nature have only a surname significance even though they are rare surnames. 'Seidenberg,' if rare, would be in this class." *See In re Industrie Pirelli*, 9 USPQ2d 1564, 1566 (TTAB 1988) (PIRELLI held primarily merely a surname, the Board stating that "certain rare surnames look like surnames and certain rare surnames do not and ... 'PIRELLI' falls into the former category...."); *In re Petrin Corp.*, 231 USPQ 902 (TTAB 1986) (PETRIN held primarily merely a surname).

1211.01(b) Surname Combined with Additional Matter

Often a mark will be comprised of a word which, standing by itself, would be primarily merely a surname, coupled with additional matter (*e.g.*, letters, words, designs). The question remains whether the mark sought to be registered would be perceived by the public primarily merely as a surname. The following are considerations which commonly arise in determining whether such a mark is primarily merely a surname.

Double Surnames. *See In re Standard Elektrik Lorenz A.G.*, 371 F.2d 870, 152 USPQ 563 (C.C.P.A. 1967) (SCHAUB–LORENZ held not primarily merely a surname, the Court noting that there was no evidence submitted that the mark sought to be registered was primarily merely a surname; that the only evidence of surname significance related to "SCHAUB" and "LORENZ," portions of the mark; and that the mark must be considered in its entirety rather than dissected).

Surname Combined with Design Element. A mark comprised of a word which, standing by itself, would be considered primarily merely a surname, coupled with a distinctive design element is not considered primarily merely a surname. *In re Benthin Management GmbH*, 37 USPQ2d 1332 (TTAB 1995). However, the addition of a nondistinctive design element or stylization to a term which, standing by itself, is primarily merely a surname does not remove the term from that category. The primary significance of such a mark, in its entirety, would be merely that of a surname. *See In re Pickett Hotel Co.*, 229 USPQ 760, 763 (TTAB 1986) (PICKETT SUITE HOTEL held primarily merely a surname despite the stylization of the lettering which was considered "insignificant, in that it is clearly not so distinctive as to create any separate commercial impression in the minds of purchasers of appellant's services").

Surname Combined with Initials. The addition of initials to a term which, standing by itself, is primarily merely a surname does not remove the term from that category. In fact, the use of the first name initial followed by a surname has been held to reinforce, rather than diminish, the surname significance of a term. *See In re I. Lewis Cigar Mfg. Co.*, 205 F.2d 204, 98 USPQ 265 (C.C.P.A. 1953) (S. SEIDENBERG & CO'S. held primarily merely a surname); *In re Piquet*, 5 USPQ2d 1367 (TTAB 1987) (N. PIQUET held primarily merely a surname); *In re Taverniti*, SARL, 225 USPQ 1263 (TTAB 1985), *recon. denied,* 228 USPQ 975 (TTAB 1985) (J. TAVERNITI held primarily merely a surname); *Ex parte Sears, Roebuck & Co.*, 87 USPQ 400 (PO Ex. Ch. 1950) (J.C. HIGGINS held primarily merely a surname).

Surname Combined with Title. A title, such as "Mr.," "Mrs." or "Mlle.," does not diminish the surname significance of a term; rather, it may enhance the surname significance of a term. *In re Revillon*, 154 USPQ 494, 495 (TTAB 1967) (MLLE. REVILLON held primarily merely a surname). *Cf. In re Hilton Hotels Corp.*, 166 USPQ 216 (TTAB 1970)(LADY HILTON held not primarily merely a surname because it suggests a person or lady of nobility).

Surname in Plural or Possessive Form. The surname significance of a term is not diminished by the fact that the term is presented in its plural or possessive form. *See In re Woolley's Petite Suites*, 18 USPQ2d 1810 (TTAB 1991) (WOOLLEY'S PETITE SUITES for hotel and motel services held primarily merely a surname); *In re Directional Marketing Corp.*, 204 USPQ 675 (TTAB 1979) (DRUMMONDS held primarily merely a surname based on a showing of surname significance of "Drummond"). *See also In re McDonald's Corp.*, 230 USPQ 304, 306 (TTAB 1986) (MCDONALD'S held primarily merely a surname based on a showing of surname significance of

"McDonald," the Board noting that "it is clear that people use their surnames in possessive and plural forms to identify their businesses or trades"); *In re Luis Caballero, S.A.*, 223 USPQ 355 (TTAB 1984) (BURDONS held primarily merely a surname based in part on telephone listings showing surname significance of "Burdon").

Surname Combined with Wording. The treatment of marks which include wording in addition to a term which, standing by itself, is primarily merely a surname, depends upon the significance of the non-surname wording.

If the wording combined with the surname is incapable of functioning as a mark (*i.e.*, a generic name for the goods or services), registration is refused on the ground that the entire mark is primarily merely a surname within the meaning of § 2(e)(4). If the policy were otherwise, one could evade § 2(e)(4) by the easy expedient of adding the generic name of the goods or services to a word which is primarily merely a surname. *In re Hamilton Pharmaceuticals Ltd.*, 27 USPQ2d 1939 (TTAB 1993) (HAMILTON PHARMACEUTICALS for pharmaceutical products held primarily merely a surname); *In re E. Martinoni Co.*, 189 USPQ 589, 591 (TTAB 1975) (LIQUORE MARTINONI (stylized) held primarily merely a surname where the goods are liqueur, "liquore" being the Italian word for "liqueur"). *See also In re Cazes*, 21 USPQ2d 1796, 1797 (TTAB 1991) (BRASSERIE LIPP held primarily merely a surname where " 'brasserie' is a generic term for applicant's restaurant services"); *In re Possis Medical, Inc.*, 230 USPQ 72, 73 (TTAB 1986) (POSSIS PERFUSION CUP held primarily merely a surname, the Board finding that "[a]pplicant's argument that PERFUSION CUP is not a generic name for its goods . . . is contradicted by the evidence the Examining Attorney has pointed to.").

If the wording combined with the surname is capable of functioning as a mark (*i.e.*, matter which is arbitrary, suggestive or merely descriptive of the goods or services), the mark is not considered to be primarily merely a surname under § 2(e)(4). However, if the additional wording is merely descriptive or the equivalent, and a disclaimer is otherwise proper, the examining attorney should require a disclaimer of the additional wording. *See In re Hutchinson Technology, Inc.*, 852 F.2d 552, 7 USPQ2d 1490 (Fed. Cir. 1988) (HUTCHINSON TECHNOLOGY for computer products held not primarily merely a surname when the mark is considered as a whole, the Court remanding the case for entry of a disclaimer of "technology" before publication).

1211.02 Evidence Relating to Surname Refusal

1211.02(a) Evidentiary Burden—Generally

The burden is on the examining attorney to establish a *prima facie* case that a mark is primarily merely a surname. Only then does the burden shift to the applicant to rebut this showing. The evidence submitted by the examining attorney was found insufficient to establish a *prima facie* case in the following decisions: *In re Kahan & Weisz Jewelry Mfg. Corp.*, 508 F.2d

831, 184 USPQ 421 (C.C.P.A. 1975); *In re Raivico*, 9 USPQ2d 2006 (TTAB 1988); *In re Garan Inc.*, 3 USPQ2d 1537 (TTAB 1987).

There is no rule as to the kind or amount of evidence necessary to make out a *prima facie* showing that a term is primarily merely a surname. This question must be resolved on a case-by-case basis. *See, e.g., In re Monotype Corp. PLC*, 14 USPQ2d 1070 (TTAB 1989); *In re Pohang Iron & Steel Co., Ltd.*, 230 USPQ 79 (TTAB 1986). The entire record is examined to determine the surname significance of a term. The following are examples of relevant considerations in determining whether or not a term is primarily merely a surname: telephone directory listings; excerpted articles from computerized research data bases; evidence in the record that the term is in fact a surname; the manner of use on specimens; dictionary definitions of the term and evidence from dictionaries showing no definition of the term. The quantum of evidence which is persuasive in finding surname significance in one case may be insufficient in another because of the differences in the names themselves. *See In re Etablissements Darty et Fils*, 759 F.2d 15, 17, 225 USPQ 652, 653 (Fed. Cir. 1985), *aff'g* 222 USPQ 260 (TTAB 1984).

1211.02(b) Evidentiary Considerations

In appropriate cases, the examining attorney may present evidence which may appear contrary to the Office position with an appropriate explanation as to why this evidence was not considered controlling. In some cases, this may foreclose objections from an applicant and present a more complete picture in the event of an appeal.

The following are examples of evidentiary considerations which arise in determining whether a mark is primarily merely a surname:

Telephone Directory Listings. Telephone directory listings are one type of credible evidence of the surname significance of a term. The Trademark Trial and Appeal Board has declined to hold that a minimum number of listings in telephone directories must be found in order to establish a *prima facie* showing that the mark is primarily merely a surname. *See, e.g., In re Petrin Corp.*, 231 USPQ 902 (TTAB 1986); *In re Wickuler–Kupper–Brauerei KGaA*, 221 USPQ 469 (TTAB 1983). It is the American public's perception of a term which is determinative. Therefore, foreign telephone directory listings are not probative of the significance of a term to the purchasing public in the United States, regardless of whether the applicant is of foreign origin. *See, e.g., Societe Civile Des Domaines Dourthe Freres v. S.A. Consortium Vinicole De Bordeaux Et De La Gironde,* 6 USPQ2d 1205 (TTAB 1988); *In re Stromsholmens Mekaniska Verkstad AB*, 228 USPQ 968 (TTAB 1986); *In re Wickuler–Kupper–Brauerei KGaA,* 221 USPQ 469 (TTAB 1983).

LEXIS/NEXIS Research Data Base Evidence. Excerpted articles from the LEXIS/NEXIS research data base are one type of credible evidence of the surname significance of a term. There is no requirement that the examining attorney make of record every story found in a LEXIS/NEXIS search. However, the examining attorney is presumed to provide the best support of the refusal to register available from the source. *See In re Federated Department Stores Inc.*, 3 USPQ2d 1541, 1542 n.2 (TTAB 1987). *See also In re Monotype Corp. PLC*, 14 USPQ2d 1070, 1071 (TTAB 1989) ("We must conclude that, because the Examining Attorney is presumed to have made the best case possible, the 46 stories not made of record [the search yielded 48 stories] do not support the position that CALISTO is a surname and, indeed, show that CALISTO has non-surname meanings."). An Office Action which includes any evidence obtained from a research data base should include a citation to the research service and a clear record of the specific search that was conducted, indicating the libraries or files that were searched and the date of the search (*e.g.*, LEXIS®, NEXIS® library, CURRNT file as of April 28, 1992). The printout summarizing the search should be made a part of the record. Relevant information not included on the printout, such as the number of documents viewed, should be stated in narrative in the Office Action.

Surname of Person Associated with Applicant. The fact that a term is the surname of an individual associated with the applicant (*e.g.*, an officer or founder) is evidence of the surname significance of the term. *See In re Etablissements Darty et Fils,* 759 F.2d 15, 225 USPQ 652 (Fed. Cir. 1985), *aff'g* 222 USPQ 260 (TTAB 1984); *In re Rebo High Definition Studio Inc.,* 15 USPQ2d 1314 (TTAB 1990); *In re Industrie Pirelli,* 9 USPQ2d 1564 (TTAB 1988); *In re Taverniti, SARL,* 225 USPQ 1263 (TTAB 1985), *recon. denied*, 228 USPQ 975 (TTAB 1985).

Specimens Confirming Surname Significance of Term. The fact that a term appears on the specimens of record in a manner that confirms its surname significance is evidence of the surname significance of a term. *See Societe Civile Des Domaines Dourthe Freres v. S.A. Consortium Vinicole De Bordeaux Et De La Gironde,* 6 USPQ2d 1205, 1208 (TTAB 1988) (DOURTHE found primarily merely a surname, the Board noting applicant's references to "Dourthe" as the name of a particular family and finding the surname significance of the term to be reinforced by the appearance on applicant's wine labels of the name and/or signature of an individual named Pierre Dourthe); *In re Taverniti, SARL,* 225 USPQ 1263 (TTAB 1985), *recon. denied*, 228 USPQ 975 (TTAB 1985) (J. TAVERNITI held primarily merely a surname, the Board considering, among other factors, the presentation of the mark on the specimens in signature form); *In re Luis Caballero, S.A.*, 223 USPQ 355 (TTAB 1984) (BURDONS held primarily merely a surname, the Board weighting heavily the applicant's use of "Burdon" on the specimens as a surname, albeit of a fictitious character ("John William Burdon")).

Negative Dictionary Evidence. Negative dictionary evidence, that is, dictionary evidence which indicates an absence of lexicographic or geographic meanings for a term, is one type of evidence of the lack of non-surname significance of a term.

Evidence of Fame of a Mark. Evidence of the fame of a mark (*e.g.*, regarding consumer recognition of a mark, expenditures made in promoting or advertising a mark) does not enter into the determination as to registrability of a surname unless registration is sought under § 2(f). *In re McDonald's Corp.*, 230 USPQ 304, 307 (TTAB 1986) (McDonald's held primarily merely a surname in spite of strong secondary meaning. "[T]he word 'primarily' refers to the primary significance of the term, that is, the ordinary meaning of the word, and not to the term's strength as a trademark due to widespread advertising and promotion of the term as a mark to identify goods and/or services."). *See also In re Industrie Pirelli*, 9 USPQ2d 1564 (TTAB 1988); *In re Piquet*, 5 USPQ2d 1367 (TTAB 1987); *In re Garan Inc.*, 3 USPQ2d 1537 (TTAB 1987).

EXAMINATION OF DIFFERENT TYPES OF MARKS

1301 Service Marks

Section 45 of the Trademark Act, 15 U.S.C. § 1127, defines "service mark" as follows:

> The term "service mark" means any word, name, symbol, or device, or any combination thereof—
>
> used by a person, or
>
> which a person has a bona fide intention to use in commerce and applies to register on the principal register established by this Act, to identify and distinguish the services of one person, including a unique service, from the services of others and to indicate the source of the services, even if that source is unknown. Titles, character names, and other distinctive features of radio or television programs may be registered as service marks notwithstanding that they, or the programs, may advertise the goods of the sponsor.

To be registrable as a service mark, therefore, the asserted mark must function both to *identify and distinguish* the services recited in the application from the services of others and to *indicate the source of* the recited services, even if that source is unknown. The activities recited in the identification must constitute services as contemplated by the Trademark Act. *See* TMEP § 1301.01.

A refusal to register, either because the proposed mark does not function as a service mark for the services recited or because the activities identified are not services, is generally predicated on §§ 1, 2 (preamble), 3 and 45 of the Trademark Act, 15 U.S.C. §§ 1051, 1052, 1053 and 1127.

See TMEP § 1303 concerning collective service marks.

1301.01 What Is a Service

The activities for which a service mark can be registered must constitute services as contemplated by the Trademark Act. 15 U.S.C. §§ 1051, 1053 and 1127. The Trademark Act defines the term "service mark," but it does not define what constitutes a service. It has been suggested that no attempt was made to define the latter term simply because of the plethora of services which the human mind is capable of conceiving. Many activities are obviously services (*e.g.*, dry cleaning, banking, shoe repairing, transportation, and house painting). Other activities, whose nature is not so obvious, became accepted as services in connection with which a service mark may be registered only after examination of many applications, under a variety of circumstances. For a discussion of the development of the law in relation to service marks, *see Springfield Fire & Marine Ins. Co. v. Founders' Fire & Marine Ins. Co.,* 115 F.Supp. 787, 99 USPQ 38 (N.D. Cal. 1953).

1301.01(a) Criteria for Determining What Constitutes a Service

The following criteria have evolved for determining what constitutes a service in connection with which a mark may be registered: (1) a service must be a real activity; (2) a service must be performed to the order of, or for the benefit of, someone other than the applicant; and (3) a service cannot be merely an ancillary activity or one which is necessary to the applicant's larger business (*i.e.,* the activity performed must be qualitatively different from anything necessarily done in connection with the sale of the applicant's goods or the performance of another service). *In re Canadian Pacific Limited*, 754 F.2d 992, 224 USPQ 971 (Fed. Cir. 1985); *In re Betz Paperchem, Inc.,* 222 USPQ 89 (TTAB 1984); *In re Integrated Resources, Inc.,* 218 USPQ 829 (TTAB 1983); *In re Landmark Communications, Inc.,* 204 USPQ 692 (TTAB 1979). These criteria are explained more fully below.

1301.01(a)(i) Performance of a Real Activity

For a service to be real, there must be performance of some activity, involving either physical or mental action. For example, a mere idea or concept, *e.g.*, an idea for an accounting organizational format or a recipe for a baked item, is not a service. *See In re Scientific Methods, Inc.,* 201 USPQ 917 (TTAB 1979) (registration denied to design that specimens showed to be used merely as a graphic representation of an educational concept, rather than as a mark identifying applicant's consulting services). In addition, a process is not itself a service and terms which merely designate processes or techniques are not marks for services. For a discussion of processes, *see* TMEP § 1301.01(b)(iii). Additionally, there is a distinction between terminology which merely identifies a device or instrument used in the performance of a service or collaterally related to the service and a mark which identifies the service itself. *See In re Compagnie Nationale Air France,* 265 F.2d 938, 121 USPQ 460 (C.C.P.A. 1959) (registration denied to SKY-ROOM for air transportation services where specimens showed use to identify a particular type of small room or enclosed compartment on an airplane "regardless of who provides it" rather than to distinguish applicant's air transport services); *In re British Caledonia Airways Ltd.,* 218 USPQ 737 (TTAB 1983) (registration denied to SKY-LOUNGER as mark for air transportation services where specimens showed use primarily to signify a particular kind of reclining aircraft seat). *But see In re Holiday Inns, Inc.,* 223 USPQ 149 (TTAB 1984) (KING LEISURE used as a registrable service mark, in relation to the primary service of renting rooms, to identify a particular class of service offered).

The determination of whether a real service is being performed must be considered in the commercial context. For example, at one time the activities of grocery stores, department stores, and similar retail stores were not considered to be services. However, it has now come to be recognized that gathering together various products, making available a place for purchasers to select goods, and providing any other necessary means for consummating purchases constitutes the performance of a service. Marks which identify such services are registrable as service marks.

The licensing of intangible property has been recognized as a service because the licensor confers a real benefit on the recipient of the license. *In re Universal Press Syndicate,* 229 USPQ 638 (TTAB 1986).

1301.01(a)(ii) For the Benefit of Others

To be a service, an activity must be for the benefit of someone other than the applicant. For example, while an advertising agency provides a service when it promotes the goods or services of its clients, a company which promotes the sale of its own goods or services is doing so for its own benefit and is not rendering a service for others. *In re Reichhold Chemicals, Inc.,* 167 USPQ 376 (TTAB 1970). Similarly, a company which sets up a personnel department to employ workers for itself is merely facilitating the conduct of its own business, while a company whose business is to recruit and place workers for other companies is performing employment agency services. In *In re Integrated Resources, Inc.,* 218 USPQ 829 (TTAB 1983), it was held that the claimed activity of syndicating investment partnerships did not constitute a service within the meaning of the Trademark Act, there being no evidence that the applicant was in the business of syndicating the investment partnerships of others; rather, the applicant partnership was engaged only in syndication of interests in its own organization following which the partnership intended to perform certain services. *But see In re Venture Lending Associates,* 226 USPQ 285, 286 (TTAB 1985) (applicant's investment of funds of institutional investors and providing capital for management found to be "clearly an activity which benefits others within the meaning of the statute").

Sponsoring and operating a contest to promote one's own goods has been held not to constitute a distinct service because deemed an ordinary and routine activity associated with the sale of goods. *In re Dr. Pepper Co.,* 836 F.2d 508, 5 USPQ2d 1207 (Fed. Cir. 1987). *But see In re Congoleum Corp.,* 222 USPQ 452 (TTAB 1984) (finding that applicant's activity of awarding prizes to its retailer customers, while having as one of its goals an increase in sales of its own flooring products, nevertheless conferred a benefit beyond that normally expected of distributors of products like the applicant's and therefore constituted services).

In *In re Canadian Pacific Ltd.*, 754 F.2d 992, 224 USPQ 971 (Fed. Cir. 1985), the Court determined that the offering of a stock purchasing plan to existing shareholders of the applicant did not constitute a service because the activity was not sufficiently separate from the routine corporate activity of offering shares of stock to the public. The Trademark Act does not preclude registration, however, simply because the services are offered only to a limited segment of the public. *American International Reinsurance Co., Inc. v. Airco, Inc.*, 570 F.2d 941, 197 USPQ 69 (C.C.P.A. 1978) (offering to employees and ex-employees of a retirement income plan, by the applicant, whose principal business was the manufacture of sundry products, found to constitute a service within the meaning of the Act).

1301.01(a)(iii) Sufficiently Distinct from Activities Involved in Sale of Goods or Performance of Other Services

In determining whether an activity is sufficiently separate from an applicant's principal activity to constitute a service in connection with which the applicant may obtain a service mark registration, the examining attorney should:

> first ascertain what is an applicant's principal activity under the mark in question, i.e., the sale of a service or the sale of a tangible product, and then determine whether the activity embraced by the description of services ... is in any material way a different kind of economic activity than what any purveyor of the principal service or tangible product necessarily provides. In order to determine when an activity is necessarily related to an applicant's principal business, consideration should be given to the customs and practices of the industry or business, the history of the applicant, any Federal or state laws or regulations which control the principal business activity, and possibly other factors. These are factual inquiries about which an applicant, when called upon, should furnish as much information as is available.

In re Landmark Communications, Inc., 204 USPQ 692, 695 (TTAB 1979).

For example, the operation of a grocery store is clearly a service. The bagging of groceries for customers is not considered a separate service for purposes of the Trademark Act since such an activity is a necessary and customary accommodation to grocery store customers and, therefore, is ancillary to the primary service. Similarly, while the repair of the goods of others is a recognized service, an applicant's guarantee of performance of its goods, although perhaps serving as an inducement in the sale of those goods, does not normally constitute a separate service. That activity is, rather, what would normally be expected in the trade. *In re Orion Research Inc.*, 523 F.2d 1398, 187 USPQ 485 (C.C.P.A. 1975); *In re Lenox, Inc.*, 228 USPQ 966 (TTAB 1986). However, a warranty which is considerably more extensive than that offered by others may constitute a service. *See In re Mitsubishi Motor Sales of America, Inc.*, 11 USPQ2d 1312 (TTAB 1989); *In re Sun Valley Waterbeds Inc.*, 7 USPQ2d 1825 (TTAB 1988).

See also In re Billfish International Corporation, 229 USPQ 152 (TTAB 1986); *In re Alaska Northwest Publishing Co.,* 212 USPQ 316 (TTAB 1981) (publishing of one's own periodical magazine does not constitute a service); *In re SCM Corp.,* 209 USPQ 278 (TTAB 1980) (the supplying by a wholesaler of merchandising aids to retailers and, by means of store displays, decorating assistance to retail customers as part of a program to increase paint sales does not constitute a separate service); *In re Television Digest, Inc.,* 169 USPQ 505 (TTAB 1971) (TAILORED RATE found to identify a method of calculating advertising rates for applicant's trade publication which, as an inherent part of the production of any publication, is not a service). However, the fact that the activities are limited to the applicant's own goods is not, per se, determinative of registrability. *In re Otis Engineering Corp.,* 217 USPQ 278 (TTAB 1982) (applicant's certification service in relation to its oil and gas industry products, which is neither provided nor requested in connection with most of its product sales, constitutes a service over and above that normally provided in such sales).

The following cases identify relevant points to be considered in determining whether a separate service exists: *American International Reinsurance Co., Inc. v. Airco, Inc.,* 570 F.2d 941, 197 USPQ 69 (C.C.P.A. 1978) (providing a voluntary contributory pension annuity plan for employees is different from applicant's principal activity involving manufacture of products); *In re C.I.T. Financial Corp.,* 201 USPQ 124 (TTAB 1978) (providing customers with use of computerized communication system is separate and distinct from primary service of making consumer loans; significant factors included the fact that the recited services were not previously available to applicant's customers, and the services benefited those who used them; furthermore, the mark for these services differed from the mark used to identify the primary services); *In re Heavenly Creations, Inc.,* 168 USPQ 317 (TTAB 1971) (applicant's free hairstyling instructional "parties" are a service separate from the applicant's sale of wigs); *In re John Breuner Co.,* 136 USPQ 94 (TTAB 1963) (credit services provided by a retail home furnishing store constitute a separate service, extension of credit being neither mandatory nor required in the operation of a retail establishment and the benefits resulting therefrom accruing to both customers and applicant; another important factor was that the mark for the credit services was different from the mark used for the home furnishing store services). However, the mark identifying the ancillary services need not be different from the mark identifying, for example, the applicant's goods. *See Ex parte Handmacher–Vogel, Inc.,* 98 USPQ 413 (Comm'r Pats. 1953) (the conducting of women's golf tournaments constituted a bona fide service over and above activities normally expected in promoting the sale of applicant's wearing apparel for women, where the goods were neither sold nor promoted at the tournament).

Where a mark was used by the provider of a racing car on the hood of the car, a distinct service was found because it (1) represented an activity beyond the ordinary promotion of the applicant's products, (2) did not involve the mere rental of advertising space on someone else's racer, and

(3) provided a separate benefit, namely, entertainment. The services would appropriately be identified as "entertainment services, namely, participating in professional auto races." *In re United States Tobacco Co.,* 1 USPQ2d 1502 (TTAB 1986).

1301.01(b) Whether Particular Activities Constitute "Services"

1301.01(b)(i) Titles of Programs and Names of Artists

Titles of continuing radio or television programs may constitute marks for either entertainment services or educational services. However, the title of a single program, that is, the title of one episode or event presented as one program, does not function as a service mark. A continuing series of presentations (*e.g.,* a television "series"), each having content different from the other, can be designated by a title which identifies and distinguishes the entire continuing program as a service. *See In re Cooper,* 254 F.2d 611, 117 USPQ 396 (C.C.P.A. 1958), *cert. denied,* 358 U.S. 840, 119 USPQ 501 (1958), and *In re Scholastic Inc.,* 223 USPQ 431 (TTAB 1984), wherein analogous situations concerning book titles are discussed. The evidence in the application must show that the matter sought to be registered is more than the title of one presentation, story, book or recording.

Names of performing individuals or groups may constitute marks for entertainment services when the names are used to identify and distinguish the performance or the entertainment rather than to identify the individual or group. *See* TMEP § 1301.02(b).

Specimens evidencing use of a service mark in relation to television programs or a movie series may be in the nature of a photograph of the video or film frame wherein the mark is used in the program. For live entertainment, acceptable specimens would include a photograph of the group or individual in performance with the name displayed, *e.g.,* the name printed on the drum of a band. For any entertainment service, advertisements or radio or television listings showing the mark may be submitted, but the specimens must show that, rather than merely identifying the performer, the matter sought to be registered identifies the stated service.

Service marks in the nature of titles of entertainment programs may be owned by the producer of the show, by the broadcasting system or station, or by the author or creator of the show, depending upon the circumstances. Normally, an applicant's statement that the applicant owns the mark is sufficient; the examining attorney should not inquire regarding ownership unless information in the record clearly contradicts the applicant's verified statement that it is the owner of the mark.

1301.01(b)(ii) Contests and Promotional Services

Where a service mark is used to identify the conducting of a contest or other promotional service, the examining attorney should ascertain the specific nature of the service offered.

There are many promotional schemes in the nature of contests which a promotional company creates, and may or may not conduct, for other businesses to promote the sale of the goods or services of such businesses. In general, these contests consist of the distribution of printed material in the form of trading stamps, lottery tickets, entry blanks, registration cards, coupons, etc., to customers or users of the participating businesses. In some instances, the promotional company completely operates the contest, in which case the service may be identified as "promoting the goods and services of others through the conducting of a contest." In other instances, the participating business gives the material to customers and, in effect, conducts the contest, in which case the promotional company's services may be identified as "promoting the sale of goods and services of others through the distribution of printed materials designed for promotional contests." *See In re Goodwill Advertising Co.,* 135 USPQ 331 (TTAB 1962). In both situations, the services are classified in International Class 35.

The conducting of a contest to promote the sale of one's own goods or services is usually not a service as contemplated by the Trademark Act and a designation or name for such a contest is not registrable. Such a contest is usually ancillary to the sale of goods or services and is nothing more than a device to advertise and foster their sale. *In re Dr. Pepper Co.,* 836 F.2d 508, 5 USPQ2d 1207 (Fed. Cir. 1987); *In re Loew's Theaters, Inc.,* 179 USPQ 126 (TTAB 1973); *In re Sea & Ski Corp.,* 169 USPQ 749 (TTAB 1971); *In re Johnson Publishing Co., Inc.,* 130 USPQ 185 (TTAB 1961). *But see In re United States Tobacco Co.,* 1 USPQ2d 1502 (TTAB 1986); *In re Congoleum Corp.,* 222 USPQ 452 (TTAB 1984), wherein a mark, other than the one used to identify the principal goods, was considered registrable for use in relation to the manufacturer's promotional services, which were considered to be clearly over and above what was normally expected of a manufacturer in that field.

A mark identifying a beauty contest is registrable either as a promotional service, rendered by the organizer of the contest to the businesses or groups which sponsor the contest, or as an entertainment service. *In re Miss American Teen-Ager, Inc.,* 137 USPQ 82 (TTAB 1963). Where the record shows the primary purpose of conducting such a pageant is to promote the sale of goods or services of the sponsors, the service should be recited as, "promoting the goods or services of others by means of a beauty contest," and should be classified in International Class 35. Where the beauty contest is presented primarily as entertainment for the general public (such as those offered in theaters or amusement parks), the service should be identified as, "entertainment services in the nature of beauty contests," and should be classified in International Class 41.

1301.01(b)(iii) Process, System or Method

Registration of a designation for a process, method, system, or the like, is sometimes sought on the assumption that a process, or the like, is a service and the name applied to it is registrable as a service mark. A process, however, is only a way of doing something. It is not, in itself, an activity for the benefit of others. A term which merely designates a process, or is used only as the name of a process, is not registrable as a service mark. *In re Universal Oil Products Co.,* 167 USPQ 245 (TTAB 1970), *aff'd,* 177 USPQ 456 (C.C.P.A. 1973) (PENEX and PACOL used only in the context of a process and not in association with provision of the services, even though applicant is in the business of rendering services generally and the services are advertised in the same specimen brochure in which the name of the process is used).

See also In re Griffin Pollution Control Corp., 517 F.2d 1356, 186 USPQ 166 (C.C.P.A. 1975) (OXINITE not used as a mark, rather, to identify a water treatment process); *In re Hughes Aircraft Co.,* 222 USPQ 263 (TTAB 1984) (specimens and other material offered by the applicant showed proposed mark used only in connection with a photochemical process or method, and there was no association between the applicant's offer of services and the proposed mark); *In re J.F. Pritchard & Co.,* 201 USPQ 951 (TTAB 1979) (proposed mark used only to identify liquefaction process, and not used in association with design and construction services); *Ex parte Phillips Petroleum Co.,* 100 USPQ 25 (Comm'r Pats. 1953) (although used in advertising of applicant's engineering services, CYCLOVERSION was only used in the advertisements to identify a catalytic treating and conversion process).

Refusal to register a term which merely designates a process is also illustrated in *In re Vsesoyuzny Ordena Trudovogo Krasnogo Znameni Nauchoissledovatelsky Gorno–Metallurgichesky Institut Tsvetnykh Mettalov "Vnitsvetmet",* 219 USPQ 69 (TTAB 1983) (KIVCET identifies only a process and plant configuration, not an offer of engineering services); *In re Big Stone Canning Co.,* 169 USPQ 815 (TTAB 1971) (FLASH COOK merely indicates a process of cooking rather than identifying applicant's canned vegetables, which are identified by another mark on the label); *Ex parte General Dyestuff Corp.,* 110 USPQ 319 (Comm'r Pats. 1956) (GEN-RAY is used by manufacturer of dyestuffs to identify its dying process, not as a mark for printed trade publications concerning dyeing processes).

However, if the name of the process is used to identify *both* the process *and* the services rendered by means of the process by the proprietor thereof, the designation may be registrable as a service mark. *See In re J.F. Pritchard & Co.,* 201 USPQ 951 (TTAB 1979); *In re Produits Chimiques Ugine Kuhlmann Societe Anonyme,* 190 USPQ 305 (TTAB 1976).

Before determining that a process designation is eligible for registration as a service mark, the examining attorney must find, first, that the applicant is performing a service and, second, that the designation identifies, and indicates the source of, the service offered. In making these findings, the examining attorney should refer to specimens of use to discover how the applicant uses the designation. The mere advertising of recited services in a brochure that separately refers to the applicant's process is not evidence that a designation functions as a mark to identify the applicant's services; there must be some association between the offer of services and the matter sought to be registered. *In re J.F. Pritchard & Co.,* 201 USPQ 951 (TTAB 1979). Other pertinent material in the application may be considered to determine whether a term apparently identifying a process is also being used as a service mark. *See Liquacon Corp. v. Browning–Ferris Industries, Inc.,* 203 USPQ 305 (TTAB 1979) (evidence submitted during opposition proceeding established that, in addition to identifying a process, term was used as a service mark).

1301.02 What Is a Service Mark

To be registrable as a service mark, the asserted mark must identify and distinguish, and indicate the source of, the services recited in the application, even if that source is unknown. Even if it is clear that the activities recited are services in connection with which a mark may be registered (*see* TMEP § 1301.01) and that the applicant provides the recited service, the record must indicate that the asserted mark actually identifies and distinguishes the recited service and indicates its source. For a mark to fulfill the service mark functions of identifying and distinguishing a service, there must be an association between the mark and the service. *See In re Universal Oil Products Co.,* 476 F.2d 653, 177 USPQ 456 (C.C.P.A. 1973), *aff'g* 167 USPQ 245 (TTAB 1970).

Whether a mark has been used in association with a particular service is a question of fact to be determined primarily on the basis of the specimens. *In re Advertising and Marketing Development Inc.,* 821 F.2d 614, 2 USPQ2d 2010 (Fed. Cir. 1987); *In re Duratech Industries Inc.,* 13 USPQ2d 2052 (TTAB 1989); *In re Moody's Investors Service Inc.,* 13 USPQ2d 2043 (TTAB 1989); *In re Brown & Portillo Inc.,* 5 USPQ2d 1381 (TTAB 1987); *In re Signal Companies, Inc.,* 228 USPQ 956 (TTAB 1986); *Peopleware Systems, Inc. v. Peopleware, Inc.,* 226 USPQ 320, 323 (TTAB 1985); *In re Hughes Aircraft Co.,* 222 USPQ 263 (TTAB 1984); *In re J.F. Pritchard & Co.,* 201 USPQ 951 (TTAB 1979).

In determining whether the asserted mark functions as a mark for the recited services, the examining attorney should rely on specimens and other evidence submitted in support of such usage, as appropriate. *See In re Admark, Inc.,* 214 USPQ 302 (TTAB 1982); *In re Republic of Austria Spanische Reitschule,* 197 USPQ 494 (TTAB 1977). *See* TMEP § 1301.04 regarding specimens evidencing service mark use. It is the perception of the ordinary customer which determines whether the asserted mark functions as a service mark, not the applicant's intent, hope or expectation that it do so. *See In re Standard Oil Co.,* 275 F.2d 945, 125 USPQ 227 (C.C.P.A. 1960).

A service mark need not be displayed in any particular size or degree of prominence. The important question is not how readily a mark will be noticed but whether, when noticed, it will be understood as identifying, and indicating the origin of, the services. *See In re Singer Mfg. Co.,* 255 F.2d 939, 118 USPQ 310 (C.C.P.A. 1958). However, this does not mean that the public will be expected to browse through a group of words, or scan an entire page, in order to determine whether a particular term, apart from its context, may be intended to serve as a mark. *Ex parte National Geographic Society,* 83 USPQ 260 (Comm'r Pats. 1949). *See also In re C.R. Anthony Co.,* 3 USPQ2d 1894 (TTAB 1987); *In re Royal Viking Line A/S,* 216 USPQ 795 (TTAB 1982).

Factors which the examining attorney should consider in determining whether the asserted mark is used as a service mark include, but are not limited to, whether wording is physically separate from textual matter, whether a term is displayed in capital letters or enclosed in quotation marks, and the manner in which a term is used in relation to other material on the specimens. *See Smith International, Inc. v. Olin Corp.,* 209 USPQ 1033 (TTAB 1981); *In re Morganroth,* 208 USPQ 284 (TTAB 1980). The presence of the letters "SM" or "TM" is not dispositive of the issue of whether matter sought to be registered is used as a mark. *In re B.C. Switzer & Co.,* 211 USPQ 644 (TTAB 1981).

Use of a designation or slogan to convey advertising or promotional information, rather than to identify and indicate the source of the services, is not service mark use. *See In re Gilbert Eiseman, P.C.,* 220 USPQ 89 (TTAB 1983) (the wording "IN ONE DAY," as utilized on specimens, held not a service mark but, rather, a component of advertising matter which conveyed a characteristic of applicant's plastic surgery services). *Cf. In re Post Properties, Inc.,* 227 USPQ 334 (TTAB 1985) (the slogan "QUALITY SHOWS," set off from text of ad copy in extremely large typeface and reiterated at conclusion of the narrative portion, held to be a registrable service mark for applicant's real estate management and leasing services).

See TMEP § 1301.01 regarding what constitutes a service.

1301.02(a) Matter which Does Not Function as a Service Mark

Subject matter presented for registration as a service mark may be unregistrable because it does not in fact function as a service mark. For example, the matter may be merely ornamental in nature. *See In re Tad's Wholesale, Inc.,* 132 USPQ 648 (TTAB 1962) (wallpaper design not registrable as a service mark for restaurant services). (*But see In re Eagle Fence Rentals, Inc.,* 231 USPQ 228 (TTAB 1986) (alternately colored strands of wire arranged vertically held a valid service mark for rental of chain-link fences).) The matter may not be registrable because it is merely a trade name. *See Ex parte Walker Process Equipment Inc.,* 233 F.2d 329, 110 USPQ 41 (C.C.P.A. 1956), *aff'g* 102 USPQ 443 (Comm'r Pats. 1954). Or it may identify only a device or instrument used in the performance of a service rather than identifying the service itself. *See In re Oscar Mayer & Co.,* 171 USPQ 571 (TTAB 1971) (WEINERMOBILE identifies a unique vehicle rather than advertising services).

See TMEP Chapter 1200 for further discussion of substantive grounds for refusal of registration.

1301.02(b) Marks Consisting of Names of Characters or Personal Names

While the definition of "service mark" in § 45 of the Trademark Act, 15 U.S.C. § 1127, includes a reference to character names, such names must be used to identify and indicate the source of a service before they are registrable. If a name serves merely as the name of a character who is a participant in a story or program, the name is not used as a service mark. *In re Burger King Corp.,* 183 USPQ 698 (TTAB 1974); *Ex parte Carter Publications, Inc.,* 92 USPQ 251 (Comm'r Pats. 1952). *But see In re Folk,* 160 USPQ 213 (TTAB 1968), where "THE LOLLIPOP PRINCESS" was held to function as a service mark for entertainment services in the form of radio programs and personal appearances.

Personal names (actual names and pseudonyms) are also subject to the requirement that they identify the services recited and not merely the individuals so named. *See In re Mancino,* 219 USPQ 1047 (TTAB 1983) (BOOM BOOM viewed by public solely as applicant's professional boxing nickname and not as an identifier of services.) *See also In re Lee Trevino Enterprises, Inc.,* 182 USPQ 253 (TTAB 1974) (LEE TREVINO used merely to identify a famous professional golfer of that name rather than as a mark to identify and distinguish any services rendered by him); and *In re Generation Gap Products, Inc.,* 170 USPQ 423 (TTAB 1971) (GORDON ROSE used only to identify a particular individual and not as a service mark to identify the services of a singing group). However, *see In re Florida Cypress Gardens Inc.,* 208 USPQ 288 (TTAB 1980) and *In re Carson,* 197 USPQ 554 (TTAB 1977), where the names CORKY THE CLOWN and JOHNNY CARSON, respectively, were held to be used as service marks and not merely as the names of characters in a program or show. It is clear from these cases that an individual's name may be registered as a trademark or service mark only if the record demonstrates that the name functions in that manner, *i.e.,* the name identifies the goods or services and indicates their origin. (Regarding consent by an individual to the registration of his or her name, *see* 15 U.S.C. § 1052(c); TMEP § 1206 *et seq.*)

1301.02(c) Three–Dimensional Marks

Three-dimensional marks are those which, when in use, have depth as well as height and breadth, for example, a three-dimensional display or structure at or near the place, such as a restaurant, where the service is performed.

The three-dimensional configuration of a building is registrable only if it is used in such a way that it is or could be perceived as a mark. Evidence of such use might include menus, letterhead stationery, and the like, which show promotion of the building's design, or configuration, as a mark. *See In re Lean–To Barbecue, Inc.,* 172 USPQ 151 (TTAB 1971); *In re Master Kleens of America, Inc.,* 171 USPQ 438 (TTAB 1971); and *In re Griffs of America, Inc.,* 157 USPQ 592 (TTAB 1968). *Cf. In re Wendy's International, Inc.,* 227 USPQ 884 (TTAB 1985); *Fotomat Corp. v. Cochran,* 437 F.Supp.

1231, 194 USPQ 128 (D. Kan. 1977); *Fotomat Corp. v. Photo Drive–Thru, Inc.,* 425 F.Supp. 693, 193 USPQ 342 (D.N.J. 1977); and *In re City of Anaheim,* 185 USPQ 244 (TTAB 1974).

A three-dimensional costume design may function as a mark. This may be so even though it is also an integral part of the services being rendered. *See In re Red Robin Enterprises, Inc.,* 222 USPQ 911 (TTAB 1984).

Generally, photographs are proper specimens of use for a three-dimensional mark. *See* TMEP § 905.06. However, photographs of a building would not be sufficient to demonstrate use of the building design as a mark for services performed in the building if they showed no more than the building in which the services are performed.

A mark with three-dimensional features must be shown on the drawing in perspective in a single rendition. 37 C.F.R. § 2.51(d). If the drawing of the mark does not immediately convey the fact that the mark is three-dimensional, the examining attorney may require a written description. The description should specify exactly what the features of the mark are. To provide sufficient notice to third parties, it is strongly encouraged that a description be included in the drawing heading. *See* 37 C.F.R. § 2.52(d); TMEP § 807.02.

1301.02(d) Sound Marks

A sound mark identifies and distinguishes services through audio rather than visual means. Examples of sound marks include: (1) a series of tones or musical notes, with or without words, and (2) a word or words accompanied by music. For a discussion of the criteria for registration of sound marks, *see In re General Electric Broadcasting Co., Inc.,* 199 USPQ 560 (TTAB 1978).

The requirement for a drawing does not apply to sound marks. Trademark Rule 2.51(c), 37 C.F.R. § 2.51(c), provides, "The drawing of a mark may be dispensed with in the case of a mark not capable of representation by a drawing, but in any such case the application must contain an adequate description of the mark." It is customary to write on the drawing sheet, "No drawing; the mark consists of (describing precisely what the sound is)." TMEP § 807.03(b). If the mark comprises music or words set to music, the applicant may also submit the musical score.

Audio cassettes may be accepted as specimens for sound marks. 37 C.F.R. § 2.58(b). To demonstrate that the sound mark actually identifies and distinguishes the services and indicates their source, the cassette should contain a sufficient portion of the audio content to indicate the nature of the services.

REGISTRATION AND POST–REGISTRATION PROCEDURES

1605 Renewal of Registration

15 U.S.C. § 1059. Renewal.

Each registration may be renewed for periods of ten years from the end of the expiring period upon payment of the prescribed fee and the filing of a verified application therefor, setting forth those goods or services recited in the registration on or in connection with which the mark is still in use in commerce and having attached thereto a specimen or facsimile showing current use of the mark, or showing that any nonuse is due to special circumstances which excuse such nonuse and it is not due to any intention to abandon the mark. Such application may be made at any time within six months before the expiration of the period for which the registration was issued or renewed, or it may be made within three months after such expiration on payment of the additional fee herein prescribed.

If the Commissioner refuses to renew the registration, he shall notify the registrant of his refusal and the reasons therefor.

An applicant for renewal not domiciled in the United States shall be subject to and comply with the provisions of section 1(e) of this Act.

1605.01 Time for Filing Application for Renewal

The application for renewal should be filed within the six-month period preceding the expiration of the registration. It may not be filed prior to the six months, but there is a "grace period" of three months following the expiration of a registration during which an application for renewal may be filed on payment of the required additional fee. *See* 37 C.F.R. § 2.182. An application filed during the three months following expiration is commonly called a late or delayed application to renew.

The application for renewal must be executed within the times specified for filing.

An application for renewal filed during the three-month grace period is subject to payment of an additional fee, regardless of whether it was executed before or after the expiration of the registration. If deficiencies in an application to renew are cured during the three-month grace period, the additional fee must be paid. If a substitute application (replacing an earlier-filed unacceptable application) is filed during the three-month period, the additional fee must be paid. *See* 37 C.F.R. § 2.183(b).

It is acceptable to file an application for renewal on the anniversary date at the end of the statutory period.

Effective December 2, 1996, an application for renewal of a registration will be considered timely if it is mailed or transmitted by the due date with a certificate of mailing or facsimile transmission in accordance with 37 C.F.R. § 1.8(a)(1). *See* notices at 61 FR 56439 (Nov. 1, 1996) and 1192 TMOG 95 (Nov. 26, 1996). *See* TMEP §§ 702.02, 702.03 and 702.04 for certificate of mailing, certificate of facsimile transmission, and "Express Mail" procedures to avoid lateness.

1605.01(a) Premature Filing of Application for Renewal

An application for renewal may be filed at any time within the six months preceding the expiration of the registration or, on payment of the additional fee, within the three months after the expiration. 15 U.S.C. § 1059(a); 37 C.F.R. § 2.182. The application must be executed not more than six months before the expiration of the registration. *See* 37 C.F.R. § 2.183(a).

If an application for renewal is filed prior to the six-month period preceding its expiration, the Office will advise the registrant of that fact; of the appropriate time period for filing a renewal application; that the fees submitted will be held; and that the registrant may file a new application at the appropriate time or may request a refund at any time. The premature application for renewal is placed in the file. If a newly executed renewal application is not filed within the statutory period, the registration is deemed expired and the fees are refunded.

If an application for renewal, although filed within the time period set forth in § 9 of the Act, is executed prior to the six-month period preceding its expiration, the Office will refuse to renew the registration on that basis. It will be necessary for the registrant to submit a newly executed application for renewal, which is both executed and filed within the appropriate period.

1605.03 Ownership, and Who May File Application for Renewal

The application for renewal must be executed and filed by the person who is the owner of the registration. Section 9 (the renewal section of the Act) speaks in terms of the registrant renewing the registration. The term "registrant" includes both the original registrant and a person who has acquired ownership through proper transfer of title. *See* Trademark Act § 45, 15 U.S.C. § 1127.

A change in the state of incorporation is a change of legal entity, creating a new party.

Unless the partnership agreement provides for continuation of the partnership and the relevant state law permits this, the death of a partner, or other change in the membership of a partnership, creates a change in legal entity.

A merger of companies into a new company normally constitutes a change of legal entity.

Applications may be accepted from trustees, executors, administrators, and the like, when supported by court order or other evidence of such person's authority to act on behalf of the present owner.

Trademark Rule 2.183, 37 C.F.R. § 2.183, requires that a statement verified "by the registrant" be filed within the period prescribed by the Trademark Act for applying for renewal. The standards for determining whether a renewal application has been verified by the registrant are the same standards used to determine whether a § 8 affidavit has been properly executed. In limited circumstances, an application for renewal may be considered as being filed by the registrant even though executed by someone other than an officer of a corporate registrant. In such a case, the registrant is responsible for establishing circumstances warranting a broad construction of "registrant." That is, the registrant must set forth facts establishing an appropriate relationship between the signer and the registrant, the signer's personal knowledge of the facts as to use or nonuse of the mark and the registrant's ratification of the signer's action. *See* TMEP § 1603.05.

Whenever possible, an application to renew the registration of a mark which is owned by joint owners should be executed by each of the joint owners. However, the relationship between joint owners is such that a document signed by one of the owners can be considered as being properly executed and filed "by the registrant" if the signer's action is subsequently ratified by each of the other owners. Such a ratification can be accepted after expiration of the period for applying for renewal because it is not a statutory requirement. *In re Murray*, 21 USPQ2d 1937 (Comm'r Pats. 1991).

1605.03(a) Change of Owner

If the owner, as set forth in the application for renewal, is not the same person or the same legal entity as the registrant shown in the registration, continuity of title from the registrant to the present owner must be shown. Trademark Rule 3.73, 37 C.F.R. § 3.73, states, in part:

When the assignee of the entire right, title and interest seeks to take action in a matter before the Office with respect to a ... registration, ... the assignee must establish its ownership of the property to the satisfaction of the Commissioner. Ownership is established by submitting to the Office documentary evidence of a chain of title from the original owner to the assignee or by specifying (e.g. reel and frame number, etc.) where such evidence is recorded in the Office.

If, therefore, the present owner is a different person or entity from the registrant of record, the owner must establish its ownership of the registration by (1) recording papers evidencing each change of ownership in the Assignment Division of the Patent and Trademark Office and specifying where such evidence is recorded in the Office (*e.g.*, the reel and frame numbers) or (2) submitting other proof of the change or changes of ownership, (*i.e.*, material showing the transfer of title), so that the record will show that title is in the entity which has filed the application for renewal.

"Documentary evidence of a chain of title from the original owner to the assignee," as referred to in 37 C.F.R. § 3.73, would normally consist of the same type of documents which would be recorded in the Assignment Division, *i.e.*, assignment documents, certificates of merger, certificates of change of name. In the alternative, an affidavit signed by the registrant or similar document containing sufficient facts to support the transfer of title may be accepted as proof.

1605.03(b) Change of Name

A mere change of the name of a party is not a change of entity. However, to support the taking of action on a registration by a party whose name differs from the name of the registrant of record, evidence of the change of name must either be recorded in the Assignment Division or be submitted as proof. For a corporation, this is done by recording or submitting a certificate of change of name issued by the Secretary of State (or other authorized body) of the state of incorporation.

A mere mistake in setting out the registrant's name can be corrected. *See In re Atlanta Blue Print Co.,* 19 USPQ2d 1078 (Comm'r Pats. 1990).

1605.03(c) Registration Renewed in Name of Registrant of Record

Registrations are renewed by the Office in the name of the registrant of record. Thus, for purposes of filing an application for renewal, a party who is not the original registrant may establish ownership of a registration by submitting documentary evidence of the chain of title; however, the registration will not be renewed in the name of the present owner unless all relevant documents have been recorded in the Assignment Division.

Similarly, in response to requests for copies of registrations, the Office provides copies which reflect ownership according to the records of the Office. The copy of a registration provided by the Office will not indicate any transfer of ownership which has not been recorded in the Assignment Division.

1605.04 Goods and/or Services Set Forth in Application for Renewal

Section 9(a) of the Trademark Act, 15 U.S.C. § 1059(a), and Trademark Rule 2.183, 37 C.F.R. § 2.183, require that the application for renewal set forth those goods or services which are recited in the registration on or in connection with which the mark is still in use in commerce or show that any nonuse is excusable. The goods or services should be set forth in the body of the application for renewal.

Goods or services which are not recited in the registration being renewed should not be included in the application for renewal. If wording is not precisely the same as in the registration, it may be regarded as representing different goods or services.

If goods or services not recited in the registration are set forth in the application to renew, the Post Registration Section will notify the registrant that the registration cannot be renewed for such items. Changed circumstances (*e.g.*, a change in the focus of a registrant's business) will not render acceptable a statement of goods or services which is not otherwise permissible.

In certain limited situations, the identification of goods or services in an application for renewal can be clarified after expiration of the period within which the application may be filed. Such clarification is permitted where the identification in the registration contains very broad language limited by other qualifying language, but the renewal application contains only the broad language without the qualifying language.

If the goods or services set forth in the application for renewal are fewer than those recited in the registration being renewed, the goods or services for which there is neither an averment that the mark is still in use in commerce or a showing that nonuse is excusable will be deleted from the registration.

1605.05 Character of Use of Mark

The use on the basis of which a registration is renewed must be use *in commerce*, *i.e.*, use in a type of commerce which Congress may lawfully regulate. *See* TMEP § 901 for a discussion of what constitutes "use in commerce." The application for renewal must specify the nature of such commerce. 37 C.F.R. § 2.183(a).

While the registrant may provide information regarding the type of commerce after the period for applying for renewal has passed, the averment that the mark is in use "in commerce" is a statutory requirement which must be met within the six months prior to expiration of the registration or, with payment of the applicable fee, during the three-month grace period. 15 U.S.C. § 1059(a).

1605.06 Specimen Showing Current Use of Mark in Commerce

Section 9(a) of the Trademark Act, 15 U.S.C. § 1059(a), states that the application for renewal must have attached to it a specimen or facsimile showing current use of the mark. Regarding material that is appropriate as trademark or service mark specimens, *see* TMEP §§ 905.04 and 1301.04.

There must be a specimen or facsimile showing current use of the mark for each class of goods or services in the registration for which renewal is sought. 37 C.F.R. § 2.183(a)(1). Normally, one specimen must be submitted per class. However, a single specimen is acceptable to show use of the mark for goods or services in more than one class in certain situations, *e.g.*, under the following circumstances:

> the specimen submitted, on its face, clearly evidences continuing use of the mark for goods or services in each of the relevant classes; or
>
> the registrant or attorney indicates in the record that the specimen submitted is used for goods or services in each of the relevant classes.

See In re Home Fashions Inc., 21 USPQ2d 1947 (Comm'r Pats. 1991).

The requirement for the specimen or facsimile must be completed, for each class, within the six months prior to expiration of the registration or, with payment of the applicable fee, during the three-month grace period. *In re Holland American Wafer Co.*, 737 F.2d 1015, 222 USPQ 273 (Fed. Cir. 1984); *Ex parte Firmenich & Co.*, 137 USPQ 476 (Comm'r Pats. 1963). If specimens are defective or insufficient the requirement cannot be completed after the period for applying for renewal has passed; if completed during the grace period, the application can be considered only as a late application for renewal. *See* 37 C.F.R. § 2.183(b).

1605.07 Showing Regarding Nonuse of Mark

37 CFR § 2.183(c). If the mark is not in use in commerce at the time of filing of the declaration or verified statement as to any class for which renewal is sought, facts must be recited to show that nonuse is due to special circumstances which excuse such nonuse and is not due to any intention to abandon the mark. There must be a recitation of facts as to nonuse for each class for which renewal is sought or it must be clear that the facts recited apply to each class sought to be renewed. If the facts recited require amplification, or explanation, in order to show excusable nonuse, further evidence may be submitted and considered even though filed after the period for applying for renewal has passed.

If the mark is not in use in commerce at the time of filing the application for renewal, the registration may still be renewed if facts presented in the application show (1) that the nonuse is due to special circumstances which excuse such nonuse, and (2) that nonuse is not due to any intention to abandon the mark. The registrant must recite such facts for each class for which renewal is sought, or it must be clear that the facts recited apply to each such class. The specific goods or services for which nonuse is due to special circumstances must be clear from the renewal application.

For evaluating whether or not nonuse is excusable, the same criteria are used on renewal as are used in connection with § 8 affidavits. For discussion of these criteria, *see* TMEP § 1603.09.

1605.08 Change from Mark as Registered

The mark in connection with which the application for renewal is filed must be essentially the same as the mark which appears in the registration. Where the mark has been changed since the original registration, acceptance of the application for renewal will depend on the degree of change. A *material* alteration of the mark will result in refusal of the application on the ground that the mark currently in use is a new mark and that the registered mark is no longer in use. *See Torres v. Cantine Torresella S.r.l.*, 808 F.2d 46, 1 USPQ2d 1483 (Fed. Cir. 1986) (TORRES used on renewal specimen held materially different from registered mark LAS TORRES); *In re Holland American Wafer Co.*, 737 F.2d 1015, 222 USPQ 273 (Fed. Cir. 1984) (use of "DUTCH TWIN" mark with a different background and different associated design elements than in registered version held inadequate to support renewal or amendment).

The standard used to determine whether a difference is material on renewal is the same as the standard used to determine whether the mark in a § 8 affidavit is materially different from the registered mark and the same as the standard used to determine whether a registered mark may be amended under § 7(e) of the Trademark Act, 15 U.S.C. § 1057(e). For discussion of such standard, *see* TMEP §§ 1603.10 and 1607.02(a). In determining whether a change constitutes a material alteration, the Office will always compare the mark in the specimens to the mark as originally registered. Where the registered mark is currently used as one of several elements in a composite mark, the decision as to the sufficiency of the renewal specimen requires consideration of whether the registered mark makes an impression apart from the other elements of the composite mark. If the display of the composite is such that the essence of the registered mark does make a separate impression, then the specimen may be sufficient to support the renewal application. In many cases, word elements are severable from design elements, since words tend to dominate in forming a commercial impression. *In re DeWitt International Corp.*, 21 USPQ2d 1620 (Comm'r Pats. 1991).

If the Office concludes that the mark, as used on the specimen, creates a separate impression apart from any other material on the specimen and that any difference between the mark as used and the mark as registered is not material, the specimen (if otherwise acceptable) will be accepted as evidence of current use of the registered mark. The Office will not require amendment of the mark in the registration.

Regarding possible amendment of the mark in the registration, *see* TMEP §§ 1603.10(a) and 1607.02.

1605.09 Foreign Applicant for Renewal

Section 9(c) of the Trademark Act, 15 U.S.C. § 1059(c), and Trademark Rule 2.183(d), 37 C.F.R. § 2.183(d), require that if an applicant for renewal is not domiciled in the United States, the application for renewal must include the designation of a domestic representative. *See* TMEP § 604 for further details.

If accurate, the application for renewal must specify that the mark is in use in commerce between the United States and some foreign country. (A statement that the mark is in use in "foreign commerce" is not sufficient because that term might include commerce which may not lawfully be regulated by Congress.)

1605.10 Office Action upon Examination of Application for Renewal

The Office notifies each registrant who files an application to renew of the acceptance or refusal of the application. Upon receipt of a paper filed pursuant to § 9 of the Act, the prosecution history for the relevant registration is updated by reporting, in the automated TRAM (Trademark Reporting and Monitoring) System, that a § 9 paper has been filed.

If, upon examination, the application for renewal is found acceptable, the Office sends to the registrant a notification which acknowledges receipt of the request for renewal and indicates that renewal has been granted. No acknowledgment of receipt of the renewal application is sent before the application has been examined.

If, upon examination, the application for renewal is found unacceptable, the Office sends a letter refusing renewal and giving the reasons for refusal. 15 U.S.C. § 1059(b).

The propriety of the original registration is not re-examined on renewal. *Ex parte Quaker Rubber Corp.*, 92 USPQ 392 (PO Ex. Ch. 1952).

1605.11 Registrant's Recourse

Within six months from the mailing date of an action in which the examiner refuses to accept the application for renewal, the registrant may take appropriate action to overcome the refusal; however, the requirement for the verified statement or declaration setting forth the items with which the mark is still in use in commerce, the specimen or facsimile specimen and the prescribed fee or fees must be completed within the period for applying for renewal as required by the Act. *See* 37 C.F.R. §§ 2.183(a) and (b) and 2.184(a).

If no response to a refusal of renewal is filed within six months from the date of mailing of the action, the application for renewal will be considered abandoned, and the registration treated as expired. *See* 37 C.F.R. § 2.184(a).

1605.11(a) Petition to Commissioner

In general, a request for reconsideration of the refusal of renewal is a condition precedent to a petition to the Commissioner seeking review of the refusal. *See* 37 C.F.R. § 2.184(a). However, a request for reconsideration need not be pursued if the action refusing renewal indicates that the registrant's only recourse is to petition the Commissioner.

An indication that the registrant's only recourse is to petition the Commissioner may be explicit or may be implicit, as when the action indicates that the registration is expired. Also, the requirement that a request for reconsideration be pursued prior to a petition is often waived if the registrant has been informed during a telephone conference that a request for reconsideration would be fruitless. *See* TMEP § 1603.13(a).

If, upon reconsideration, the examiner adheres to the refusal of renewal, the registrant may petition the Commissioner to review the action pursuant to 37 C.F.R. § 2.146(a)(2). A petition to the Commissioner requesting review of the action adhering to the refusal of the renewal must be filed within six months from the date of mailing of the action which adhered to the refusal. If a timely petition to the Commissioner is not filed, the application for renewal will be considered abandoned. 37 C.F.R. § 2.184(b).

The decision of the Commissioner on a petition under 37 C.F.R. § 2.146 constitutes the final action of the Patent and Trademark Office. 37 C.F.R. § 2.184(c).

1605.11(b) Appeal

Actions of examiners on applications to renew are not appealable to the Trademark Trial and Appeal Board.

Appeal may be taken to a federal court from the decision of the Commissioner. 15 U.S.C. § 1071; 37 C.F.R. § 2.145. A petition to the Commissioner for review of the action is a condition precedent to an appeal to or action for review by any court. 37 C.F.R. § 2.184(d).

1605.11(c) Petition or Appeal Does Not Stay Time for Filing of Acceptable Renewal Application

Proceedings in which the sufficiency of an application to renew is considered do not change the time during which an acceptable application must be filed. If such proceedings hold a renewal application to be acceptable, the application is acceptable as of the date it was originally filed. If, as a result of reconsideration, petition or appeal, an application for renewal is found to be unacceptable after the time for filing has passed, it is not then possible for the registrant to file a new application for renewal.

APPENDIX D

UNIFORM DOMAIN NAME DISPUTE RESOLUTION POLICY

(As Approved by ICANN on October 24, 1999)

1. Purpose. This Uniform Domain Name Dispute Resolution Policy (the "Policy") has been adopted by the Internet Corporation for Assigned Names and Numbers ("ICANN"), is incorporated by reference into your Registration Agreement, and sets forth the terms and conditions in connection with a dispute between you and any party other than us (the registrar) over the registration and use of an Internet domain name registered by you. Proceedings under Paragraph 4 of this Policy will be conducted according to the Rules for Uniform Domain Name Dispute Resolution Policy (the "Rules of Procedure"), which are available at www.icann.org/udrp/udrp-rules–24oct99.htm, and the selected administrative-dispute-resolution service provider's supplemental rules.

2. Your Representations. By applying to register a domain name, or by asking us to maintain or renew a domain name registration, you hereby represent and warrant to us that (a) the statements that you made in your Registration Agreement are complete and accurate; (b) to your knowledge, the registration of the domain name will not infringe upon or otherwise violate the rights of any third party; (c) you are not registering the domain name for an unlawful purpose; and (d) you will not knowingly use the domain name in violation of any applicable laws or regulations. It is your responsibility to determine whether your domain name registration infringes or violates someone else's rights.

3. Cancellations, Transfers, and Changes. We will cancel, transfer or otherwise make changes to domain name registrations under the following circumstances:

(a) subject to the provisions of Paragraph 8, our receipt of written or appropriate electronic instructions from you or your authorized agent to take such action;

(b) our receipt of an order from a court or arbitral tribunal, in each case of competent jurisdiction, requiring such action; and/or

(c) our receipt of a decision of an Administrative Panel requiring such action in any administrative proceeding to which you were a party and which was conducted under this Policy or a later version of this Policy adopted by ICANN. (See Paragraph 4(i) and (k) below.)

We may also cancel, transfer or otherwise make changes to a domain name registration in accordance with the terms of your Registration Agreement or other legal requirements.

4. Mandatory Administrative Proceeding. This Paragraph sets forth the type of disputes for which you are required to submit to a mandatory administrative proceeding. These proceedings will be conducted before one of the administrative-dispute-resolution service providers listed at www.icann.org/udrp/approved-providers.htm. (each, a "Provider").

(a) Applicable Disputes. You are required to submit to a mandatory administrative proceeding in the event that a third party (a "complainant") asserts to the applicable Provider, in compliance with the Rules of Procedure, that

(i) your domain name is identical or confusingly similar to a trademark or service mark in which the complainant has rights; and

(ii) you have no rights or legitimate interests in respect of the domain name; and

(iii) your domain name has been registered and is being used in bad faith.

In the administrative proceeding, the complainant must prove that each of these three elements are present.

(b) Evidence of Registration and Use in Bad Faith. For the purposes of Paragraph 4 (a) (iii), the following circumstances, in particular but without limitation, if found by the Panel to be present, shall be evidence of the registration and use of a domain name in bad faith:

(i) circumstances indicating that you have registered or you have acquired the domain name primarily for the purpose of selling, renting, or otherwise transferring the domain name registration to the complainant who is the owner of the trademark or service mark or to a competitor of that complainant, for valuable consideration in excess of your documented out-of-pocket costs directly related to the domain name; or

(ii) you have registered the domain name in order to prevent the owner of the trademark or service mark from reflecting the mark in a corresponding domain name, provided that you have engaged in a pattern of such conduct; or

(iii) you have registered the domain name primarily for the purpose of disrupting the business of a competitor; or

(iv) by using the domain name, you have intentionally attempted to attract, for commercial gain, Internet users to your web site or other on-line location, by creating a likelihood of confusion with the complainant's mark as to the source, sponsorship, affiliation, or endorsement of your web site or location or of a product or service on your web site or location.

(c) How to Demonstrate Your Rights to and Legitimate Interests in the Domain Name in Responding to a Complaint. When you receive a complaint, you should refer to Paragraph 5 of the Rules of Procedure in determining how your response should be prepared. Any of the following circumstances, in particular but without limitation, if found by the Panel to be proved based on its evaluation of all evidence presented, shall demonstrate your rights or legitimate interests to the domain name for purposes of Paragraph 4(a)(ii):

(i) before any notice to you of the dispute, your use of, or demonstrable preparations to use, the domain name or a name corresponding to the domain name in connection with a bona fide offering of goods or services; or

(ii) you (as an individual, business, or other organization) have been commonly known by the domain name, even if you have acquired no trademark or service mark rights; or

(iii) you are making a legitimate noncommercial or fair use of the domain name, without intent for commercial gain to misleadingly divert consumers or to tarnish the trademark or service mark at issue.

(d) Selection of Provider. The complainant shall select the Provider from among those approved by ICANN by submitting the complaint to that Provider. The selected Provider will administer the proceeding, except in cases of consolidation as described in Paragraph 4(f).

(e) Initiation of Proceeding and Process and Appointment of Administrative Panel. The Rules of Procedure state the process for initiating and conducting a proceeding and for appointing the panel that will decide the dispute (the "Administrative Panel").

(f) Consolidation. In the event of multiple disputes between you and a complainant, either you or the complainant may petition to consolidate the disputes before a single Administrative Panel. This petition shall be made to the first Administrative Panel appointed to hear a pending dispute between the parties. This Administrative Panel may consolidate before it any or all such disputes in its sole discretion, provided that the disputes being consolidated are governed by this Policy or a later version of this Policy adopted by ICANN.

(g) Fees. All fees charged by a Provider in connection with any dispute before an Administrative Panel pursuant to this Policy shall be paid by the complainant, except in cases where you elect to expand the Administrative Panel from one to three panelists as provided in Paragraph 5(b)(iv) of the Rules of Procedure, in which case all fees will be split evenly by you and the complainant.

(h) Our Involvement in Administrative Proceedings. We do not, and will not, participate in the administration or conduct of any proceeding before an Administrative Panel. In addition, we will not be liable as a result of any decisions rendered by the Administrative Panel.

(i) Remedies. The remedies available to a complainant pursuant to any proceeding before an Administrative Panel shall be limited to requiring the cancellation of your domain name or the transfer of your domain name registration to the complainant.

(j) Notification and Publication. The Provider shall notify us of any decision made by an Administrative Panel with respect to a domain name you have registered with us. All decisions under this Policy will be published in full over the Internet, except when an Administrative Panel determines in an exceptional case to redact portions of its decision.

(k) Availability of Court Proceedings. The mandatory administrative proceeding requirements set forth in Paragraph 4 shall not prevent either you or the complainant from submitting the dispute to a court of competent jurisdiction for independent resolution before such mandatory administrative proceeding is commenced or after such proceeding is concluded. If an Administrative Panel decides that your domain name registration should be canceled or transferred, we will wait ten (10) business days (as observed in the location of our principal office) after we are informed by the applicable Provider of the Administrative Panel's decision before implementing that decision. We will then implement the decision unless we have received from you during that ten (10) business day period official documentation (such as a copy of a complaint, file-stamped by the clerk of the court) that you have commenced a lawsuit against the complainant in a jurisdiction to which the complainant has submitted under Paragraph 3(b)(xiii) of the Rules of Procedure. (In general, that jurisdiction is either the location of our principal office or of your address as shown in our Whois database. See Paragraphs 1 and 3(b)(xiii) of the Rules of Procedure for details.) If we receive such documentation within the ten (10) business day period, we will not implement the Administrative Panel's decision, and we will take no further action, until we receive (i) evidence satisfactory to us of a resolution between the parties; (ii) evidence satisfactory to us that your lawsuit has been dismissed or withdrawn; or (iii) a copy of an order from such court dismissing your lawsuit or ordering that you do not have the right to continue to use your domain name.

5. All Other Disputes and Litigation. All other disputes between you and any party other than us regarding your domain name registration that are not brought pursuant to the mandatory administrative proceeding provisions of Paragraph 4 shall be resolved between you and such other party through any court, arbitration or other proceeding that may be available.

6. Our Involvement in Disputes. We will not participate in any way in any dispute between you and any party other than us regarding the registration and use of your domain name. You shall not name us as a party or otherwise include us in any such proceeding. In the event that we are named as a party in any such proceeding, we reserve the right to raise any and all defenses deemed appropriate, and to take any other action necessary to defend ourselves.

7. Maintaining the Status Quo. We will not cancel, transfer, activate, deactivate, or otherwise change the status of any domain name registration under this Policy except as provided in Paragraph 3 above.

8. Transfers During a Dispute.

(a) Transfers of a Domain Name to a New Holder. You may not transfer your domain name registration to another holder (i) during a pending administrative proceeding brought pursuant to Paragraph 4 or for a period of fifteen (15) business days (as observed in the location of our principal place of business) after such proceeding is concluded; or (ii) during a pending court proceeding or arbitration commenced regarding your domain name unless the party to whom the domain name registration is being transferred agrees, in writing, to be bound by the decision of the court or arbitrator. We reserve the right to cancel any transfer of a domain name registration to another holder that is made in violation of this subparagraph.

(b) Changing Registrars. You may not transfer your domain name registration to another registrar during a pending administrative proceeding brought pursuant to Paragraph 4 or for a period of fifteen (15) business days (as observed in the location of our principal place of business) after such proceeding is concluded. You may transfer administration of your domain name registration to another registrar during a pending court action or arbitration, provided that the domain name you have registered with us shall continue to be subject to the proceedings commenced against you in accordance with the terms of this Policy. In the event that you transfer a domain name registration to us during the pendency of a court action or arbitration, such dispute shall remain subject to the domain name dispute policy of the registrar from which the domain name registration was transferred.

9. Policy Modifications. We reserve the right to modify this Policy at any time with the permission of ICANN. We will post our revised Policy. . . at least thirty (30) calendar days before it becomes effective. Unless this Policy has already been invoked by the submission of a complaint to a Provider, in which event the version of the Policy in effect at the time it was invoked will apply to you until the dispute is over, all such changes will be binding upon you with respect to any domain name registration dispute, whether the dispute arose before, on or after the effective date of our change. In the event that you object to a change in this Policy, your sole remedy is to cancel your domain name registration with us, provided that you will not be entitled to a refund of any fees you paid to us. The revised Policy will apply to you until you cancel your domain name registration.

APPENDIX E

Paris Convention for the Protection of Industrial Property (excerpts)

of March 20, 1883,
as revised

At BRUSSELS on December 14, 1900, at WASHINGTON on June 2, 1911, at THE HAGUE on November 6, 1925, at LONDON on June 2, 1934, at LISBON on October 31, 1958, and at STOCKHOLM on July 14, 1967

Note: Headings enclosed in brackets are supplied by the World Intellectual Property Organization.

Article 1

[Establishment of the Union; Scope of Industrial Property]

(1) The countries to which this Convention applies constitute a Union for the protection of industrial property.

(2) The protection of industrial property has as its object patents, utility models, industrial designs, trademarks, service marks, trade names, indications of source or appellations of origin, and the repression of unfair competition.

(3) Industrial property shall be understood in the broadest sense and shall apply not only to industry and commerce proper, but likewise to agricultural and extractive industries and to all manufactured or natural products, for example, wines, grain, tobacco leaf, fruit, cattle, minerals, mineral waters, beer, flowers, and flour.

(4) Patents shall include the various kinds of industrial patents recognized by the laws of the countries of the Union, such as patents of importation, patents of improvement, patents and certificates of addition, etc.

Article 2

[National Treatment for Nationals of Countries of the Union]

(1) Nationals of any country of the Union shall, as regards the protection of industrial property, enjoy in all the other countries of the Union the advantages that their respective laws now grant, or may hereafter grant, to nationals; all without prejudice to the rights specially provided for by this Convention. Consequently, they shall have the same protection as the latter, and the same legal remedy against any infringement of their rights, provided that the conditions and formalities imposed upon nationals are complied with.

(2) However, no requirement as to domicile or establishment in the country where protection is claimed may be imposed upon nationals of countries of the Union for the enjoyment of any industrial property rights.

(3) The provisions of the laws of each of the countries of the Union relating to judicial and administrative procedure and to jurisdiction, and to the designation of an address for service or the appointment of an agent, which may be required by the laws on industrial property are expressly reserved.

Article 3

[Same Treatment for Certain Categories of Persons as for Nationals of Countries of the Union]

Nationals of countries outside the Union who are domiciled or who have real and effective industrial or commercial establishments in the territory of one of the countries of the Union shall be treated in the same manner as nationals of the countries of the Union.

Article 4

[A to D, F. Patents, Utility Models, Industrial Designs, Marks: Right of Priority]

A.—(1) Any person who has duly filed an application for a patent, or for the registration of a utility model, or of an industrial design, or of a trademark, in one of the countries of the Union, or his successor in title, shall enjoy, for the purpose of filing in the other countries, a right of priority during the periods hereinafter fixed.

(2) Any filing that is equivalent to a regular national filing under the domestic legislation of any country of the Union or under bilateral or multilateral treaties concluded between countries of the Union shall be recognized as giving rise to the right of priority.

(3) By a regular national filing is meant any filing that is adequate to establish the date on which the application was filed in the country concerned, whatever may be the subsequent fate of the application.

B.—Consequently, any subsequent filing in any of the other countries of the Union before the expiration of the periods referred to above shall not be invalidated by reason of any acts accomplished in the interval, in particular, another filing, the publication or exploitation of the invention, the putting on sale of copies of the design, or the use of the mark, and such acts cannot give rise to any third-party right or any right of personal possession. Rights acquired by third parties before the date of the first application that serves as the basis for the right of priority are reserved in accordance with the domestic legislation of each country of the Union.

C.—(1) The periods of priority referred to above shall be twelve months for patents and utility models, and six months for industrial designs and trademarks.

(2) These periods shall start from the date of filing of the first application; the day of filing shall not be included in the period.

(3) If the last day of the period is an official holiday, or a day when the Office is not open for the filing of applications in the country where protection is claimed, the period shall be extended until the first following working day.

(4) A subsequent application concerning the same subject as a previous first application within the meaning of paragraph (2), above, filed in the same country of the Union, shall be considered as the first application, of which the filing date shall be the starting point of the period of priority, if, at the time of filing the subsequent application, the said previous application has been withdrawn, abandoned, or refused, without having been laid open to public inspection and without leaving any rights outstanding, and if it has not yet served as a basis for claiming a right of priority. The previous application may not thereafter serve as a basis for claiming a right of priority.

D.—(1) Any person desiring to take advantage of the priority of a previous filing shall be required to make a declaration indicating the date of such filing and the country in which it was made. Each country shall determine the latest date on which such declaration must be made.

(2) These particulars shall be mentioned in the publications issued by the competent authority, and in particular in the patents and the specifications relating thereto.

(3) The countries of the Union may require any person making a declaration of priority to produce a copy of the application (description, drawings, etc.) previously filed. The copy, certified as correct by the authority which received such application, shall not require any authentication, and may in any case be filed, without fee, at any time within three months of the filing of the subsequent application. They may require it to be accompanied by a certificate from the same authority showing the date of filing, and by a translation.

(4) No other formalities may be required for the declaration of priority at the time of filing the application. Each country of the Union shall deter-

mine the consequences of failure to comply with the formalities prescribed by this Article, but such consequences shall in no case go beyond the loss of the right of priority.

(5) Subsequently, further proof may be required.

Any person who avails himself of the priority of a previous application shall be required to specify the number of that application; this number shall be published as provided for by paragraph (2), above.

. . .

Article 5

[C. *Marks:* Failure to Use; Different Forms; Use by Co-proprietors.— D. *Patents, Utility Models, Marks, Industrial Designs.* Marking]

C.—(1) If, in any country, use of the registered mark is compulsory, the registration may be cancelled only after a reasonable period, and then only if the person concerned does not justify his inaction.

(2) Use of a trademark by the proprietor in a form differing in elements which do not alter the distinctive character of the mark in the form in which it was registered in one of the countries of the Union shall not entail invalidation of the registration and shall not diminish the protection granted to the mark.

(3) Concurrent use of the same mark on identical or similar goods by industrial or commercial establishments considered as co-proprietors of the mark according to the provisions of the domestic law of the country where protection is claimed shall not prevent registration or diminish in any way the protection granted to the said mark in any country of the Union, provided that such use does not result in misleading the public and is not contrary to the public interest.

D.—No indication or mention of the patent, of the utility model, of the registration of the trademark, or of the deposit of the industrial design, shall be required upon the goods as a condition of recognition of the right to protection.

Article 5bis

[All Industrial Property Rights: Period of Grace for the Payment of Fees for the Maintenance of Rights]

(1) A period of grace of not less than six months shall be allowed for the payment of the fees prescribed for the maintenance of industrial property rights, subject, if the domestic legislation so provides, to the payment of a surcharge.

Article 6

[*Marks*: Conditions of Registration; Independence of Protection of Same Mark in Different Countries]

(1) The conditions for the filing and registration of trademarks shall be determined in each country of the Union by its domestic legislation.

(2) However, an application for the registration of a mark filed by a national of a country of the Union in any country of the Union may not be refused, nor may a registration be invalidated, on the ground that filing, registration, or renewal, has not been effected in the country of origin.

(3) A mark duly registered in a country of the Union shall be regarded as independent of marks registered in the other countries of the Union, including the country of origin.

Article 6bis

[*Marks:* Well–Known Marks]

(1) The countries of the Union undertake, ex officio if their legislation so permits, or at the request of an interested party, to refuse or to cancel the registration, and to prohibit the use, of a trademark which constitutes a reproduction, an imitation, or a translation, liable to create confusion, of a mark considered by the competent authority of the country of registration or use to be well known in that country as being already the mark of a person entitled to the benefits of this Convention and used for identical or similar goods. These provisions shall also apply when the essential part of the mark constitutes a reproduction of any such well-known mark or an imitation liable to create confusion therewith.

(2) A period of at least five years from the date of registration shall be allowed for requesting the cancellation of such a mark. The countries of the Union may provide for a period within which the prohibition of use must be requested.

(3) No time limit shall be fixed for requesting the cancellation or the prohibition of the use of marks registered or used in bad faith.

Article 6ter

[*Marks:* Prohibitions Concerning State Emblems, Official Hallmarks, and Emblems of Intergovernmental Organizations]

(1)(a) The countries of the Union agree to refuse or to invalidate the registration, and to prohibit by appropriate measures the use, without authorization by the competent authorities, either as trademarks or as elements of trademarks, of armorial bearings, flags, and other State emblems, of the countries of the Union, official signs and hallmarks indicating control and warranty adopted by them, and any imitation from a heraldic point of view.

(b) The provisions of subparagraph (a), above, shall apply equally to armorial bearings, flags, other emblems, abbreviations, and names, of international intergovernmental organizations of which one or more countries of the Union are members, with the exception of armorial bearings, flags, other emblems, abbreviations, and names, that are already the subject of international agreements in force, intended to ensure their protection.

(c) No country of the Union shall be required to apply the provisions of subparagraph (b), above, to the prejudice of the owners of rights acquired in good faith before the entry into force, in that country, of this Convention. The countries of the Union shall not be required to apply the said provisions when the use or registration referred to in subparagraph (a), above, is not of such a nature as to suggest to the public that a connection exists between the organization concerned and the armorial bearings, flags, emblems, abbreviations, and names, or if such use or registration is probably not of such a nature as to mislead the public as to the existence of a connection between the user and the organization.

(2) Prohibition of the use of official signs and hallmarks indicating control and warranty shall apply solely in cases where the marks in which they are incorporated are intended to be used on goods of the same or a similar kind.

(3)(a) For the application of these provisions, the countries of the Union agree to communicate reciprocally, through the intermediary of the International Bureau, the list of State emblems, and official signs and hallmarks indicating control and warranty, which they desire, or may hereafter desire, to place wholly or within certain limits under the protection of this Article, and all subsequent modifications of such list. Each country of the Union shall in due course make available to the public the lists so communicated.

Nevertheless such communication is not obligatory in respect of flags of States.

(b) The provisions of subparagraph (b) of paragraph (1) of this Article shall apply only to such armorial bearings, flags, other emblems, abbreviations, and names, of international intergovernmental organizations as the latter have communicated to the countries of the Union through the intermediary of the International Bureau.

(4) Any country of the Union may, within a period of twelve months from the receipt of the notification, transmit its objections, if any, through the intermediary of the International Bureau, to the country or international intergovernmental organization concerned.

(5) In the case of State flags, the measures prescribed by paragraph (1), above, shall apply solely to marks registered after November 6, 1925.

(6) In the case of State emblems other than flags, and of official signs and hallmarks of the countries of the Union, and in the case of armorial bearings, flags, other emblems, abbreviations, and names, of international intergovernmental organizations, these provisions shall apply only to marks registered more than two months after receipt of the communication provided for in paragraph (3), above.

(7) In cases of bad faith, the countries shall have the right to cancel even those marks incorporating State emblems, signs, and hallmarks, which were registered before November 6, 1925.

(8) Nationals of any country who are authorized to make use of the State emblems, signs, and hallmarks, of their country may use them even if they are similar to those of another country.

(9) The countries of the Union undertake to prohibit the unauthorized use in trade of the State armorial bearings of the other countries of the Union, when the use is of such a nature as to be misleading as to the origin of the goods.

(10) The above provisions shall not prevent the countries from exercising the right given in paragraph (3) of Article 6^{quinquies}, Section B, to refuse or to invalidate the registration of marks incorporating, without authorization, armorial bearings, flags, other State emblems, or official signs and hallmarks adopted by a country of the Union, as well as the distinctive signs of international intergovernmental organizations referred to in paragraph (1), above.

Article 6^{quater}

[*Marks:* Assignment of Marks]

(1) When, in accordance with the law of a country of the Union, the assignment of a mark is valid only if it takes place at the same time as the transfer of the business or goodwill to which the mark belongs, it shall suffice for the recognition of such validity that the portion of the business or goodwill located in that country be transferred to the assignee, together with the exclusive right to manufacture in the said country, or to sell therein, the goods bearing the mark assigned.

(2) The foregoing provision does not impose upon the countries of the Union any obligation to regard as valid the assignment of any mark the use of which by the assignee would, in fact, be of such a nature as to mislead the public, particularly as regards the origin, nature, or essential qualities, of the goods to which the mark is applied.

Article 6^{quinquies}

[*Marks:* Protection of Marks Registered in One Country of the Union in the Other Countries of the Union]

A.—(1) Every trademark duly registered in the country of origin shall be accepted for filing and protected as is in the other countries of the Union, subject to the reservations indicated in this Article. Such countries may, before proceeding to final registration, require the production of a certificate of registration in the country of origin, issued by the competent authority. No authentication shall be required for this certificate.

(2) Shall be considered the country of origin the country of the Union where the applicant has a real and effective industrial or commercial establishment, or, if he has no such establishment within the Union, the country of the Union where he has his domicile, or, if he has no domicile

within the Union but is a national of a country of the Union, the country of which he is a national.

B.—Trademarks covered by this Article may be neither denied registration nor invalidated except in the following cases:

1. when they are of such a nature as to infringe rights acquired by third parties in the country where protection is claimed;

2. when they are devoid of any distinctive character, or consist exclusively of signs or indications which may serve, in trade, to designate the kind, quality, quantity, intended purpose, value, place of origin, of the goods, or the time of production, or have become customary in the current language or in the bona fide and established practices of the trade of the country where protection is claimed;

3. when they are contrary to morality or public order and, in particular, of such a nature as to deceive the public. It is understood that a mark may not be considered contrary to public order for the sole reason that it does not conform to a provision of the legislation on marks, except if such provision itself relates to public order.

This provision is subject, however, to the application of Article 10bis.

C.—(1) In determining whether a mark is eligible for protection, all the factual circumstances must be taken into consideration, particularly the length of time the mark has been in use.

(2) No trademark shall be refused in the other countries of the Union for the sole reason that it differs from the mark protected in the country of origin only in respect of elements that do not alter its distinctive character and do not affect its identity in the form in which it has been registered in the said country of origin.

D.—No person may benefit from the provisions of this Article if the mark for which he claims protection is not registered in the country of origin.

E.—However, in no case shall the renewal of the registration of the mark in the country of origin involve an obligation to renew the registration in the other countries of the Union in which the mark has been registered.

F.—The benefit of priority shall remain unaffected for applications for the registration of marks filed within the period fixed by Article 4, even if registration in the country of origin is effected after the expiration of such period.

Article 6^{sexies}

[*Marks:* Service Marks]

The countries of the Union undertake to protect service marks. They shall not be required to provide for the registration of such marks.

Article 6septies

[*Marks:* Registration in the Name of the Agent or Representative of the Proprietor Without the Latter's Authorization]

(1) If the agent or representative of the person who is the proprietor of a mark in one of the countries of the Union applies, without such proprietor's authorization, for the registration of the mark in his own name, in one or more countries of the Union, the proprietor shall be entitled to oppose the registration applied for or demand its cancellation or, if the law of the country so allows, the assignment in his favor of the said registration, unless such agent or representative justifies his action.

(2) The proprietor of the mark shall, subject to the provisions of paragraph (1), above, be entitled to oppose the use of his mark by his agent or representative if he has not authorized such use.

(3) Domestic legislation may provide an equitable time limit within which the proprietor of a mark must exercise the rights provided for in this Article.

Article 7

[*Marks:* Nature of the Goods to Which the Mark Is Applied]

The nature of the goods to which a trademark is to be applied shall in no case form an obstacle to the registration of the mark.

Article 7bis

[*Marks:* Collective Marks]

(1) The countries of the Union undertake to accept for filing and to protect collective marks belonging to associations the existence of which is not contrary to the law of the country of origin, even if such associations do not possess an industrial or commercial establishment.

(2) Each country shall be the judge of the particular conditions under which a collective mark shall be protected and may refuse protection if the mark is contrary to the public interest.

(3) Nevertheless, the protection of these marks shall not be refused to any association the existence of which is not contrary to the law of the country of origin, on the ground that such association is not established in the country where protection is sought or is not constituted according to the law of the latter country.

Article 8

[*Trade Names*]

A trade name shall be protected in all the countries of the Union without the obligation of filing or registration, whether or not it forms part of a trademark.

Article 9

[*Marks, Trade Names:* Seizure, on Importation, etc., of Goods Unlawfully Bearing a Mark or Trade Name]

(1) All goods unlawfully bearing a trademark or trade name shall be seized on importation into those countries of the Union where such mark or trade name is entitled to legal protection.

(2) Seizure shall likewise be effected in the country where the unlawful affixation occurred or in the country into which the goods were imported.

(3) Seizure shall take place at the request of the public prosecutor, or any other competent authority, or any interested party, whether a natural person or a legal entity, in conformity with the domestic legislation of each country.

(4) The authorities shall not be bound to effect seizure of goods in transit.

(5) If the legislation of a country does not permit seizure on importation, seizure shall be replaced by prohibition of importation or by seizure inside the country.

(6) If the legislation of a country permits neither seizure on importation nor prohibition of importation nor seizure inside the country, then, until such time as the legislation is modified accordingly, these measures shall be replaced by the actions and remedies available in such cases to nationals under the law of such country.

Article 10

[*False Indications:* Seizure, on Importation, etc., of Goods Bearing False Indications as to Their Source or the Identity of the Producer]

(1) The provisions of the preceding Article shall apply in cases of direct or indirect use of a false indication of the source of the goods or the identity of the producer, manufacturer, or merchant.

(2) Any producer, manufacturer, or merchant, whether a natural person or a legal entity, engaged in the production or manufacture of or trade in such goods and established either in the locality falsely indicated as the source, or in the region where such locality is situated, or in the country falsely indicated, or in the country where the false indication of source is used, shall in any case be deemed an interested party.

Article 10bis

[*Unfair Competition*]

(1) The countries of the Union are bound to assure to nationals of such countries effective protection against unfair competition.

(2) Any act of competition contrary to honest practices in industrial or commercial matters constitutes an act of unfair competition.

(3) The following in particular shall be prohibited:

1. all acts of such a nature as to create confusion by any means whatever with the establishment, the goods, or the industrial or commercial activities, of a competitor;

2. false allegations in the course of trade of such a nature as to discredit the establishment, the goods, or the industrial or commercial activities, of a competitor;

3. indications or allegations the use of which in the course of trade is liable to mislead the public as to the nature, the manufacturing process, the characteristics, the suitability for their purpose, or the quantity, of the goods.

Article 10ter

[Marks, Trade Names, False Indications, Unfair Competition: Remedies, Right to Sue]

(1) The countries of the Union undertake to assure to nationals of the other countries of the Union appropriate legal remedies effectively to repress all the acts referred to in Articles 9, 10, and 10bis.

(2) They undertake, further, to provide measures to permit federations and associations representing interested industrialists, producers, or merchants, provided that existence of such federations and associations is not contrary to the laws of their countries, to take action in the courts or before the administrative authorities, with a view to the repression of the acts referred to in Articles 9, 10, and 10bis, in so far as the law of the country in which protection is claimed allows such action by federations and associations of that country.

Article 11

[*Inventions, Utility Models, Industrial Designs, Marks:* Temporary Protection at Certain International Exhibitions]

(1) The countries of the Union shall, in conformity with their domestic legislation, grant temporary protection to patentable inventions, utility models, industrial designs, and trademarks, in respect of goods exhibited at official or officially recognized international exhibitions held in the territory of any of them.

(2) Such temporary protection shall not extend the periods provided by Article 4. If, later, the right of priority is invoked, the authorities of any country may provide that the period shall start from the date of introduction of the goods into the exhibition.

(3) Each country may require, as proof of the identity of the article exhibited and of the date of its introduction, such documentary evidence as it considers necessary.

Article 12

[Special National Industrial Property Services]

(1) Each country of the Union undertakes to establish a special industrial property service and a central office for the communication to the public of patents, utility models, industrial designs, and trademarks.

(2) This service shall publish an official periodical journal. It shall publish regularly:

. . .

(b) the reproductions of registered trademarks.

APPENDIX F

Agreement on Trade–Related Aspects of Intellectual Property Rights (TRIPs) (excerpts)

PART I

GENERAL PROVISIONS AND BASIC PRINCIPLES

Article 1

Nature and Scope of Obligations

1. Members shall give effect to the provisions of this Agreement. Members may, but shall not be obliged to, implement in their law more extensive protection than is required by this Agreement, provided that such protection does not contravene the provisions of this Agreement. Members shall be free to determine the appropriate method of implementing the provisions of this Agreement within their own legal system and practice.

2. For the purposes of this Agreement, the term "intellectual property" refers to all categories of intellectual property that are the subject of Sections 1 through 7 of Part II.

3. Members shall accord the treatment provided for in this Agreement to the nationals of other Members.[1] In respect of the relevant intellectual property right, the nationals of other Members shall be understood as those natural or legal persons that would meet the criteria for eligibility for protection provided for in the Paris Convention (1967), the Berne Convention (1971), the Rome Convention and the Treaty on Intellectual Property in Respect of Integrated Circuits, were all Members of the WTO members of those conventions.[2] Any Member availing itself of the possibilities

1. When "nationals" are referred to in this Agreement, they shall be deemed, in the case of a separate customs territory Member of the WTO, to mean persons, natural or legal, who are domiciled or who have a real and effective industrial or commercial establishment in that customs territory.

2. In this Agreement, "Paris Convention" refers to the Paris Convention for the Protection of Industrial Property; "Paris Convention (1967)" refers to the Stockholm Act of this Convention of 14 July 1967. "Berne Convention" refers to the Berne Convention for the Protection of Literary and Artistic Works; "Berne Convention (1971)" refers to the Paris Act of this Convention of 24 July 1971. "Rome Convention" refers to the International Convention for the Protec-

provided in paragraph 3 of Article 5 or paragraph 2 of Article 6 of the Rome Convention shall make a notification as foreseen in those provisions to the Council for Trade–Related Aspects of Intellectual Property Rights (the "Council for TRIPS").

Article 2

Intellectual Property Conventions

1. In respect of Parts II, III and IV of this Agreement, Members shall comply with Articles 1 through 12, and Article 19, of the Paris Convention (1967).

2. Nothing in Parts I to IV of this Agreement shall derogate from existing obligations that Members may have to each other under the Paris Convention, the Berne Convention, the Rome Convention and the Treaty on Intellectual Property in Respect of Integrated Circuits.

Article 3

National Treatment

1. Each Member shall accord to the nationals of other Members treatment no less favourable than that it accords to its own nationals with regard to the protection[3] of intellectual property, subject to the exceptions already provided in, respectively, the Paris Convention (1967), the Berne Convention (1971), the Rome Convention or the Treaty on Intellectual Property in Respect of Integrated Circuits. In respect of performers, producers of phonograms and broadcasting organizations, this obligation only applies in respect of the rights provided under this Agreement. Any Member availing itself of the possibilities provided in Article 6 of the Berne Convention (1971) or paragraph 1 (b) of Article 16 of the Rome Convention shall make a notification as foreseen in those provisions to the Council for TRIPS.

2. Members may avail themselves of the exceptions permitted under paragraph 1 in relation to judicial and administrative procedures, including the designation of an address for service or the appointment of an agent within the jurisdiction of a Member, only where such exceptions are necessary to secure compliance with laws and regulations which are not inconsistent with the provisions of this Agreement and where such practices are not applied in a manner which would constitute a disguised restriction on trade.

tion of Performers, Producers of Phonograms and Broadcasting Organizations, adopted at Rome on 26 October 1961. "Treaty on Intellectual Property in Respect of Integrated Circuits" (IPIC Treaty) refers to the Treaty on Intellectual Property in Respect of Integrated Circuits, adopted at Washington on 26 May 1989. "WTO Agreement" refers to the Agreement Establishing the WTO.

3. For the purposes of Articles 3 and 4, "protection" shall include matters affecting the availability, acquisition, scope, maintenance and enforcement of intellectual property rights as well as those matters affecting the use of intellectual property rights specifically addressed in this Agreement.

Article 4

Most–Favoured–Nation Treatment

With regard to the protection of intellectual property, any advantage, favour, privilege or immunity granted by a Member to the nationals of any other country shall be accorded immediately and unconditionally to the nationals of all other Members. Exempted from this obligation are any advantage, favour, privilege or immunity accorded by a Member:

(a) deriving from international agreements on judicial assistance or law enforcement of a general nature and not particularly confined to the protection of intellectual property;

(b) granted in accordance with the provisions of the Berne Convention (1971) or the Rome Convention authorizing that the treatment accorded be a function not of national treatment but of the treatment accorded in another country;

(c) in respect of the rights of performers, producers of phonograms and broadcasting organizations not provided under this Agreement;

(d) deriving from international agreements related to the protection of intellectual property which entered into force prior to the entry into force of the WTO Agreement, provided that such agreements are notified to the Council for TRIPS and do not constitute an arbitrary or unjustifiable discrimination against nationals of other Members.

Article 5

Multilateral Agreements on Acquisition or Maintenance of Protection

The obligations under Articles 3 and 4 do not apply to procedures provided in multilateral agreements concluded under the auspices of WIPO relating to the acquisition or maintenance of intellectual property rights.

Article 6

Exhaustion

For the purposes of dispute settlement under this Agreement, subject to the provisions of Articles 3 and 4 nothing in this Agreement shall be used to address the issue of the exhaustion of intellectual property rights.

Article 7

Objectives

The protection and enforcement of intellectual property rights should contribute to the promotion of technological innovation and to the transfer and dissemination of technology, to the mutual advantage of producers and users of technological knowledge and in a manner conducive to social and economic welfare, and to a balance of rights and obligations.

Article 8

Principles

1. Members may, in formulating or amending their laws and regulations, adopt measures necessary to protect public health and nutrition, and to promote the public interest in sectors of vital importance to their socio-economic and technological development, provided that such measures are consistent with the provisions of this Agreement.

2. Appropriate measures, provided that they are consistent with the provisions of this Agreement, may be needed to prevent the abuse of intellectual property rights by right holders or the resort to practices which unreasonably restrain trade or adversely affect the international transfer of technology.

PART II

STANDARDS CONCERNING THE AVAILABILITY, SCOPE AND USE OF INTELLECTUAL PROPERTY RIGHTS

. . .

SECTION 2: TRADEMARKS

Article 15

Protectable Subject Matter

1. Any sign, or any combination of signs, capable of distinguishing the goods or services of one undertaking from those of other undertakings, shall be capable of constituting a trademark. Such signs, in particular words including personal names, letters, numerals, figurative elements and combinations of colors as well as any combination of such signs, shall be eligible for registration as trademarks. Where signs are not inherently capable of distinguishing the relevant goods or services, Members may make registrability depend on distinctiveness acquired through use. Members may require, as a condition of registration that signs be visually perceptible.

2. Paragraph 1 above shall not be understood to prevent a Member from denying registration of a trademark on other grounds, provided that they do not derogate from the provisions of the Paris Convention (1967).

3. Members may make registrability depend on use. However, actual use of a trademark shall not be a condition for filing an application for registration. An application shall not be refused solely on the ground that intended use has not taken place before the expiry of a period of three years from the date of application.

4. The nature of the goods or services to which a trademark is to be applied shall in no case form an obstacle to registration of the trademark.

5. Members shall publish each trademark either before it is registered or promptly after it is registered and shall afford a reasonable opportunity for petitions to cancel the registration. In addition, Members may afford an opportunity for the registration of a trademark to be opposed.

Article 16

Rights Conferred

1. The owner of a registered trademark shall have the exclusive right to prevent all third parties not having his consent from using in the course of trade identical or similar signs for goods or services which are identical or similar to those in respect of which the trademark is registered where such use would result in a likelihood of confusion. In case of the use of an identical sign for identical goods or services, a likelihood of confusion shall be presumed. The rights described above shall not prejudice any existing prior rights, nor shall they affect the possibility of Members making rights available on the basis of use.

2. Article 6bis of the Paris Convention (1967) shall apply, mutatis mutandis, to services. In determining whether a trademark is well-known, account shall be taken of the knowledge of the trademark in the relevant sector of the public, including knowledge in that Member obtained as a result of the promotion of the trademark.

3. Article 6bis of the Paris Convention (1967) shall apply, mutatis mutandis, to goods or services which are not similar to those in respect of which a trademark is registered, provided that use of that trademark in relation to those goods or services would indicate a connection between those goods or services and the owner of the registered trademark and provided that the interests of the owner of the registered trademark are likely to be damaged by such use.

Article 17

Exceptions

Members may provide limited exceptions to the rights conferred by a trademark, such as fair use of descriptive terms, provided that such exceptions take account of the legitimate interests of the owner of the trademark and of third parties.

Article 18

Term of Protection

Initial registration, and each renewal of registration, of a trademark shall be for a term of no less than seven years. The registration of a trademark shall be renewable indefinitely.

Article 19

Requirement of Use

1. If use is required to maintain a registration, the registration may be cancelled only after an uninterrupted period of at least three years of non-

use, unless valid reasons based on the existence of obstacles to such use are shown by the trademark owner. Circumstances arising independently of the will of the owner of the trademark which constitute an obstacle to the use of the trademark, such as import restrictions on or other government requirements for goods or services protected by the trademark, shall be recognized as valid reasons for non-use.

2. When subject to the control of its owner, use of a trademark by another person shall be recognized as use of the trademark for the purpose of maintaining the registration.

Article 20

Other Requirements

The use of a trademark in the course of trade shall not be unjustifiably encumbered by special requirements, such as use with another trademark, use in a special form or use in a manner detrimental to its capability to distinguish the goods or services of one undertaking from those of other undertakings. This will not preclude a requirement prescribing the use of the trademark identifying the undertaking producing the goods or services along with, but without linking it to, the trademark distinguishing the specific goods or services in question of that undertaking.

Article 21

Licensing and Assignment

Members may determine conditions on the licensing and assignment of trademarks, it being understood that the compulsory licensing of trademarks shall not be permitted and that the owner of a registered trademark shall have the right to assign his trademark with or without the transfer of the business to which the trademark belongs.

SECTION 3: GEOGRAPHICAL INDICATIONS

Article 22

Protection of Geographical Indications

1. Geographical indications are, for the purposes of this Agreement, indications which identify a good as originating in the territory of a Member, or a region or locality in that territory, where a given quality, reputation or other characteristic of the good is essentially attributable to its geographical origin.

2. In respect of geographical indications, Members shall provide the legal means for interested parties to prevent:

(a) the use of any means in the designation or presentation of a good that indicates or suggests that the good in question originates in a geographical area other than the true place of origin in a manner which misleads the public as to the geographical origin of the good;

(b) any use which constitutes an act of unfair competition within the meaning of Article 10bis of the Paris Convention (1967).

3. A Member shall, ex officio if its legislation so permits or at the request of an interested party, refuse or invalidate the registration of a trademark which contains or consists of a geographical indication with respect to goods not originating in the territory indicated, if use of the indication in the trademark for such goods in that Member is of such a nature as to mislead the public as to the true place of origin.

4. The provisions of the preceding paragraphs of this Article shall apply to a geographical indication which, although literally true as to the territory, region or locality in which the goods originate, falsely represents to the public that the goods originate in another territory.

Article 23

Additional Protection for Geographical Indications for Wines and Spirits

1. Each Member shall provide the legal means for interested parties to prevent use of a geographical indication identifying wines for wines not originating in the place indicated by the geographical indication in question or identifying spirits for spirits not originating in the place indicated by the geographical indication in question, even where the true origin of the goods is indicated or the geographical indication is used in translation or accompanied by expressions such as "kind," "type," "style," "imitation" or the like.[4]

2. The registration of a trademark for wines which contains or consists of a geographical indication identifying wines or for spirits which contains or consists of a geographical indication identifying spirits shall be refused or invalidated, ex officio if domestic legislation so permits or at the request of an interested party, with respect to such wines or spirits not having this origin.

3. In the case of homonymous geographical indications for wines, protection shall be accorded to each indication, subject to the provisions of paragraph 4 of Article 22 above. Each Member shall determine the practical conditions under which the homonymous indications in question will be differentiated from each other, taking into account the need to ensure equitable treatment of the producers concerned and that consumers are not misled.

4. In order to facilitate the protection of geographical indications for wines, negotiations shall be undertaken in the Council for Trade-Related Aspects of Intellectual Property Rights concerning the establishment of a multilateral system of notification and registration of geographical indica-

4. Notwithstanding the first sentence of Article 42, Members may, with respect to these obligations, instead provide for enforcement by administrative action.

tions for wines eligible for protection in those Members participating in the system.

Article 24

International Negotiations; Exceptions

1. Members agree to enter into negotiations aimed at increasing the protection of individual geographical indications under Article 23. The provisions of paragraphs 4–8 below shall not be used by a Member to refuse to conduct negotiations or to conclude bilateral or multilateral agreements. In the context of such negotiations, Members shall be willing to consider the continued applicability of these provisions to individual geographical indications whose use was the subject of such negotiations.

2. The Council for Trade–Related Aspects of Intellectual Property Rights shall keep under review the application of the provisions of this Section; the first such review shall take place within two years of the entry into force of the Agreement Establishing the MTO. Any matter affecting the compliance with the obligations under these provisions may be drawn to the attention of the Council, which, at the request of a Member, shall consult with any Member or Members in respect of such matter in respect of which it has not been possible to find a satisfactory solution through bilateral or pluralateral consultations between the Members concerned. The Council shall take such action as may be agreed to facilitate the operation and further the objectives of this Section.

3. In implementing this Section, a Member shall not diminish the protection of geographical indications that existed in that Member immediately prior to the date of entry into force of the Agreement Establishing the MTO.

4. Nothing in this Section shall require a Member to prevent continued and similar use of a particular geographical indication of another Member identifying wines or spirits in connection with goods or services by any of its nationals or domiciliaries who have used that geographical indication in a continuous manner with regard to the same or related goods or services in the territory of that Member either (a) for at least ten years preceding the date of the Ministerial Meeting concluding the Uruguay Round of Multilateral Trade Negotiations or (b) in good faith preceding that date.

5. Where a trademark has been applied for or registered in good faith, or where rights to a trademark have been acquired through use in good faith either:

(a) before the date of application of these provisions in that Member as defined in Part VI below; or

(b) before the geographical indication is protected in its county of origin; measures adopted to implement this Section shall not prejudice eligibility for or the validity of the registration of a trademark, or the right to use a trademark, on the basis that such a trademark is identical with, or similar to, a geographical indication.

6. Nothing in this Section shall require a Member to apply its provisions in respect of a geographical indication of any other Member with respect to goods or services for which the relevant indication is identical with the term customary in common language as the common name for such goods or services in the territory of that Member. Nothing in this Section shall require a Member to apply its provisions in respect of a geographical indication of any other Member with respect to products of the vine for which the relevant indication is identical with the customary name of a grape variety existing in the territory of that Member as of the date of entry into force of the Agreement Establishing the MTO.

7. A Member may provide that any request made under this Section in connection with the use or registration of a trademark must be presented within five years after the adverse use of the protected indication has become generally known in that Member or after the date of registration of the trademark in that Member provided that the trademark has been published by that date, if such date is earlier than the date on which the adverse use became generally known in that Member, provided that the geographical indication is not used or registered in bad faith.

8. The provisions of this Section shall in no way prejudice the right of any person to use, in the course of trade, his name or the name of his predecessor in business, except where such name is used in such a manner as to mislead the public.

9. There shall be no obligation under this Agreement to protect geographical indications which are not or cease to be protected in their country of origin, or which have fallen into disuse in that country.

APPENDIX G

North American Free Trade Agreement (excerpts)

Article 1708: Trademarks

1. For purposes of this Agreement, a trademark consists of any sign, or any combination of signs, capable of distinguishing the goods or services of one person from those of another, including personal names, designs, letters, numerals, colors, figurative elements, or the shape of goods or of their packaging. Trademarks shall include service marks and collective marks, and may include certification marks. A Party may require, as a condition for registration that a sign be visually perceptible.

2. Each Party shall provide to the owner of a registered trademark the right to prevent all persons not having the owner's consent from using in commerce identical or similar signs for goods or services that are identical or similar to those goods or services in respect of which the owner's trademark is registered, where such use would result in a likelihood of confusion. In the case of the use of an identical sign for identical goods or services, a likelihood of confusion shall be presumed. The rights described above shall not prejudice any prior rights, nor shall they affect the possibility of a Party making rights available on the basis of use.

3. A Party may make registrability depend on use. However, actual use of a trademark shall not be a condition for filing an application for registration. No Party may refuse an application solely on the ground that intended use has not taken place before the expiry of a period of three years from the date of application for registration.

4. Each Party shall provide a system for the registration of trademarks, which shall include:

(a) examination of applications;

(b) notice to be given to an applicant of the reasons for the refusal to register a trademark;

(c) a reasonable opportunity for the applicant to respond to the notice;

(d) publication of each trademark either before or promptly after it is registered; and

(e) a reasonable opportunity for interested persons to petition to cancel the registration of a trademark.

A Party may provide for a reasonable opportunity for interested persons to oppose the registration of a trademark.

5. The nature of the goods or services to which a trademark is to be applied shall in no case form an obstacle to the registration of the trademark.

6. Article 6<bis> of the Paris Convention shall apply, with such modifications as may be necessary, to services. In determining whether a trademark is well-known, account shall be taken of the knowledge of the trademark in the relevant sector of the public, including knowledge in the Party's territory obtained as a result of the promotion of the trademark. No Party may require that the reputation of the trademark extend beyond the sector of the public that normally deals with the relevant goods or services.

7. Each Party shall provide that the initial registration of a trademark be for a term of at least 10 years and that the registration be indefinitely renewable for terms of not less than 10 years when conditions for renewal have been met.

8. Each Party shall require the use of a trademark to maintain a registration. The registration may be cancelled for the reason of non-use only after an uninterrupted period of at least two years of non-use, unless valid reasons based on the existence of obstacles to such use are shown by the trademark owner. Each Party shall recognize, as valid reasons for non-use, circumstances arising independently of the will of the trademark owner that constitute an obstacle to the use of the trademark, such as import restrictions on, or other government requirements for, goods or services identified by the trademark.

9. Each Party shall recognize use of a trademark by a person other than the trademark owner, where such use is subject to the owner's control, as use of the trademark for purposes of maintaining the registration.

10. No Party may encumber the use of a trademark in commerce by special requirements, such as a use that reduces the trademark's function as an indication of source or a use with another trademark.

11. A Party may determine conditions on the licensing and assignment of trademarks, it being understood that the compulsory licensing of trademarks shall not be permitted and that the owner of a registered trademark shall have the right to assign its trademark with or without the transfer of the business to which the trademark belongs.

12. A Party may provide limited exceptions to the rights conferred by a trademark, such as fair use of descriptive terms, provided that such exceptions take into account the legitimate interests of the trademark owner and of other persons.

13. Each Party shall prohibit the registration as a trademark of words, at least in English, French or Spanish, that generically designate goods or services or types of goods or services to which the trademark applies.

14. Each Party shall refuse to register trademarks that consist of or comprise immoral, deceptive or scandalous matter, or matter that may disparage or falsely suggest a connection with persons, living or dead, institutions, beliefs or any Party's national symbols, or bring them into contempt or disrepute.

†